IMMIGRATION
OF THE
IRISH QUAKERS
INTO
PENNSYLVANIA

1682-1750

Albert Cook Myers

HERITAGE BOOKS
2006

To

My Father and Mother

John T. and Sarah A. Myers

This Book is

Gratefully Inscribed

PREFACE

THIS volume is the outgrowth of an investigation begun in the year 1897, and carried on at intervals to the present time. While the movement of the English and Welsh Quakers to Pennsylvania has been treated to some extent by historians, that of the Irish Quakers has been overlooked, and it was with the hope of filling, in a measure, this deficiency that the present work was undertaken.

It has been my endeavor to give a plain, orderly presentation of the facts, without embellishment; and I have deemed it of greater interest to let the contemporary records, as much as possible, tell their own story. The inequality of treatment in portions of the book is due partly to variation in the materials; at one point they are abundant and at another scanty. In Part I., I have attempted only an outline of the early history of the Quakers in Ireland; the full history is yet to be written. An abundance of material for such a study lies buried in the manuscript records of the Society in Ireland, and it is to be hoped that some one will be sufficiently interested to prepare a thorough and systematic treatise upon the subject. The propriety of introducing so much genealogical matter in the Appendix may be open to question, but I find justification in the belief that this ma-

terial will have a special interest for many of Irish
Quaker ancestry.

While I have endeavored to be careful and
painstaking, yet by the very nature of this work,
drawn as it is from many sources, errors and
omissions are likely to occur ; and I shall be very
glad to receive corrections, so that they may be
noted in a standard copy of the book to be placed
in the collection of the Historical Society of Pennsylvania, or incorporated in a possible future
edition of the work.

I desire to express my grateful appreciation of
the kindness of the many persons who have assisted me in various ways in connection with this
work ; especially would I mention Professors William I. Hull and John Russell Hayes, of Swarthmore
College, to whom I have been indebted throughout for helpful criticism and kind encouragement.
In no less degree am I under obligation to Gilbert
Cope, of West Chester, Pa., for valuable suggestions and for material from his unrivaled private
collection of manuscripts relating to the early
history of Chester County.

My thanks are also due to Howard M. Jenkins,
of Philadelphia ; to Professor Arthur Beardsley,
Librarian of Friends' Historical Library of Swarthmore College; to John W. Jordan, A.M., and the
other courteous officials of the Historical Society
of Pennsylvania ; to Professor John Bach Mc-
Master, of the University of Pennsylvania ; to

Hon. Samuel W. Pennypacker, of Philadelphia ; to Dr. Henry C. McCook, of Philadelphia ; to President Isaac Sharpless, of Haverford College ; to Dr. Joseph S. Walton, of George School, Pa.; to Dr. John A. M. Passmore, of Philadelphia ; to the late Charles Roberts, of Philadelphia ; to Thomas Hamilton Murray, of Woonsocket, R. I., Secretary-General of the American-Irish Historical Society (for a copy of his paper "Early Irish Friends in Rhode Island"); to Warren S. Ely, of Doylestown, Pa.; to Ellwood Roberts, of Norristown, Pa.; to Edward H. Ogden, of Philadelphia ; to Thomas Maxwell Potts, of Canonsburg, Pa.; and to custodians of Friends' records, in particular, George J. Scattergood, John H. Dillingham, Alfred Moore, Benjamin Walton and the late Joseph M. Truman, Jr., of Philadelphia, the late Ellwood Michener, of Toughkenamon, Pa., Truman C. Moore and wife, of West Grove, Pa., Lewis Palmer, of Concordville, Pa., Charles Palmer, of Chester, Pa., Henry Mendenhall, of Media, Pa., Morgan Bunting, of Darby, Pa., William Woodman, of Buckmanville, Pa., and Kirk Brown, of Baltimore, Md.

Nor must I neglect to make acknowledgment of the many courtesies extended to me in the course of my researches in England and Ireland during the summer of 1900. At the British Museum and at the Bodleian Library I received kind attention. To Isaac Sharp, Secretary of the Society of Friends, I owe thanks for his kindness in giving me access to the great collection of Friends' books at Devonshire House, Bishopsgate Street, Without, London.

In an especial measure do I wish to express my appreciation of the kind interest and generous hospitality accorded me in Ireland. I am indebted to William Moore, K.C., M.P., of Moore Lodge, County Antrim, who received me most cordially at his pleasant seat, and in every way possible befriended my investigations ; to John Pim, J.P., of Belfast, who freely opened to me his rich stores of notes on the early Friends of Ireland ; to Jane M. Richardson, of Moyallon House, Gilford, County Down, author of *Six Generations of Friends in Ireland*, for kindly reception and valued criticism upon parts of my manuscript ; to William D. Braithwaite, Head Master, Joseph Radley, formerly Head Master, and Frederiç Bell, Secretary, of Ulster Provincial School, Lisburn, for much courtesy and valuable information ; to John Bewley Beale, for opportunity to examine the Friends' records in the Meeting House in Eustace Street, Dublin ; and to Henry F. Berry, M.A., of the Public Record Office, Dublin, for permission to search the records in his care. I also received kindly attention in Paris at the Bibliothèque Nationale.

ALBERT COOK MYERS

SWARTHMORE COLLEGE, March 17, 1902

CONTENTS

PART I.

	PAGE
THE PLANTING OF QUAKERISM IN IRELAND........	3-37

CHAPTER I.

THE RISE OF QUAKERISM IN ENGLAND	3-6
State of England in the Middle of the Seventeenth Century	3
Beginnings of Quakerism...............................	3-6
George Fox...	3-5
His Work and Followers...............................	5-6

CHAPTER II.

THE CROMWELLIAN SETTLEMENT OF IRELAND.........	7-12
The Plantations	7-8
The Great Rebellion of 1641...........................	8-9
Cromwell in Ireland...................................	9-10
The Settlement..	10-12

CHAPTER III.

THE BEGINNINGS OF QUAKERISM IN IRELAND..........	13-31
William Edmundson...................................	13-16
In England...	13-14
Settles in Ireland	15
Becomes a Quaker....................................	15-16
The First Meeting in Ireland, 1654....................	16
The Travelling Ministers and their Work............	16-25
The First Ministers Arrive	16
Ulster in 1655..	16-19
Richard Clayton's Visit..............................	17-18
Anne Gould and Juliann Wastwood..............	18-19
Edmundson Bears a Testimony Against Tithes	19

                                                                    PAGE
Leinster and Munster in 1655 19–25
Elizabeth Fletcher and Elizabeth Smith......... 19–20
Francis Howgill....................................... 20–24
Edward Burrough, " A Son of Thunder ".... .. 21–24
Cromwell's Cornet of Horse Becomes a Quaker   21
Howgill and Burrough Banished.................. 24
Barbara Blaugden Arrives 24
The Restoration of Charles II. and the Organiza-
   tion of Quakerism 25–28
    The Restoration.................................... 25
    Persecutions 26
    Edmundson Secures Release of Friends from
     Prison 26–27
    Thomas Loe Converts William Penn, 1666..... 27
    Organization... 27–28
Troubles Under James II. and William III.......... 28–31
    Tyrconnel 28
    Terror of Protestants.............................. 28
    The Friends 28
    The Revolution of 1689.......................... 29–30
    After Battle of the Boyne........................ 30
    William Edmundson's Sufferings 30–31
    Edmundson's Death................................. 31

CHAPTER IV.

RACIAL ORIGIN OF THE FRIENDS OF IRELAND......... 32–37
   The Celtic-Irish.. 32–35
   The Scotch-Irish.. 35–36
   The Anglo-Irish.. 36–37

PART II.

THE MIGRATION OF IRISH FRIENDS TO PENNSYL-
VANIA... 41–102

CHAPTER I.

CAUSES OF EMIGRATION..................................... 41–49
   Introductory.. 41–42

Contents

PAGE

Religious Causes... 43–46
  Acts of Uniformity..................................... 43
  Tithes and Other Ecclesiastical Dues............ 43
  Oaths.. 44–45
  Lawlessness of the Irish Catholics................. 45–46
Economic Causes.. 46–49
  Restriction on Manufacture and Commerce..... 46–47
  High Rents... 47–48
  Failure of Crops and Famine........................ 48–49

CHAPTER II.

INDUCEMENTS THAT LED THE IRISH FRIENDS TO IMMI-
GRATE INTO PENNSYLVANIA.............................. 50–80
  William Penn and his Colony......................... 50–52
    His Charter... 50–51
    His Scheme of Colonization........................ 51
    Constitution and Laws............................... 51
    Growth of the Colony................................. 52
  Penn's Invitation.. 52–55
    His Personal Influence............................... 53–54
    Descriptive Pamphlets............................... 54
    Activity of the Free Society of Traders.......... 54–55
  Favorable Reports Returned to Ireland............ 55–80
    By the Traveling Ministers and Others.......... 56
    Ann Millcum's Certificate........................... 56–57
    Nicholas Newlin's Certificate...................... 57–59
    Ministers Traveling in Ireland Tell of Penn-
      sylvania... 59
    Friends Return to Ireland for Short Visits...... 60
    Favorable Reports by Letters....................... 60–80
    George Harlan's Letter, 1696....................... 62–63
    Thomas Hutton's Letters, 1726–1734............ 64–67
    John Carpenter's Visit to Ireland, 1755......... 67–68
    Robert Parke's Letter, 1725........................ 69
    The Parke Family Emigrate......................... 69–70
  Parke's Letter... 70–79

	PAGE
False Reports...	71
A Good Country for Working Folk.......................	71
Purchase of Land......................................	71
Cultivating the Land..................................	72
Good Crops..	73
Prices for Farm Products..............................	73
Country Abounds in Fruit..............................	74
Laborers' Wages.......................................	74
Climate...	74
Dress...	74
Markets and Fairs.....................................	74
What to Bring to Pennsylvania.........................	76
How to Come...	77

CHAPTER III.

PLACES IN IRELAND WHENCE THE FRIENDS CAME	81–82
Statistical Table	82

CHAPTER IV.

WAVES OF MIGRATION.............................	83
First Wave, 1682–1710..........................	83
Second Wave, 1710–1730.........................	83
Third Wave, 1730–1750..........................	83

CHAPTER V.

WAYS AND MEANS OF MIGRATION...........................	84–102
The Certificate of Removal............................	84–89
Certificate of Joshua Marsh...........................	85–89
Places of Embarking and Landing	89
Obstructions to Emigration............................	89–92
Dangers of Voyage	92–93
Robert Parke's Diary of a Voyage from Ireland, 1728............	93–94
A Favorite Vessel.....................................	94–95
Immigrants Assisted by Meetings	95–98
Emigrants Assisted by Meetings in Ireland.....	98

PAGE

Cost of Passage.. 98–99
Redemptioners. 99–102
    Robert Turner's Redemptioners 101–102
    James Logan's Runaway Servant 102

PART III.

THE IRISH FRIENDS IN PENNSYLVANIA 105–127

CHAPTER I.

PLACES OF SETTLEMENT 105–185
    Distribution of the Irish Friends 105–106
        Statistical Table 106
    Philadelphia 107–109
        First Meeting at Shackamaxon..................... 107
        Bank Meeting House............................... 107
        Center Square Meeting House.................... 108
        Great Meeting House.............................. 108
    Bucks County.. 109
    Montgomery County 109
    Berks County 109–110
    Delaware County.. 110–118
    Chester Monthly Meeting................................. 110–116
        First Meeting in Pennsylvania at Upland, 1675 110–111
        Arrival of William Penn, 1682..................... 111–113
        Irish Friends on Board the *Welcome*.............. 111
        First Meeting House at Chester, 1693............ 113
        Monthly Meeting Established, 1681 113–115
    Concord Monthly Meeting.............................. 116–118
        Chichester Meeting 116
        Concord Meeting 116–117
        Birmingham Meeting................................. 117
        The Monthly Meeting Established, 1684 117–118
    Meetings in New Castle County on Delaware 118–124
        Newark Meeting..................................... 118–120
        New Castle Meeting................................. 120–121
        Hockessin Meeting.................................. 121

PAGE

Wilmington Meeting 121 122
Center Meeting....................................... 122–124
Chester County.. 124–159
Newark or Kennett Monthly Meeting.................. 125–130
    Kennett Meeting.. 126
Manor of Steyning or Letitia's Manor................. 127–128
Kennett Township 128–130
New Garden Township.................................... 130–136
New Garden Meeting 136–138
New Garden Monthly Meeting, Erected 1718........ 138–139
London Grove Township................................. 139–143
    London Company.................................... 139–141
London Grove Meeting................................... 143
Marlborough Township................................... 143–147
    Joseph Pennock...................................... 144–145
    Joseph Pennock's Letter, 1725.................... 145–146
Newlin Township Owned by an Irish Quaker........ 147–150
    Newlin's Difficulty with the Indians............. 147–149
Pikeland Township Granted to Joseph Pike, an Irish
    Friend, of Cork,... 150–152
The Great Valley... 152–154
    Caln Meeting.. 152–153
    East Caln Township.................................. 153–154
Coatesville Named for an Irish Quaker................ 154
Phoenixville First Settled by Irish Quakers........... 154–155
East Nantmeal Township................................. 155–156
Nottingham... 156–159
Lancaster County.. 159–162
    Sadsbury Meeting.................................... 161
    Leacock Meeting..................................... 161–162
Sadsbury Monthly Meeting.............................. 162
York and Adams Counties............................... 162–177
Newberry Meeting... 163–167
Warrington Meeting....................................... 168–172
Huntington Meeting....................................... 172–173
Menallen Meeting.. 173–176

Contents   XV

PAGE

York Meeting... 176 177
Expansion of Pennsylvania Quakerism............... 177–185
  · Southward.. 177–179
  Westward 180–185

CHAPTER II.

SOCIAL LIFE OF THE IRISH FRIENDS..................... 186–236
  Introductory
    Irish Friends Well Adapted for Pioneer Life... 186–187
    Mostly of English Stock but Modified by Irish
      Environment...................................... 187–188
  The Arrival... 188
    Hospitality of Old Settlers......................... 188
    Small Capital of Immigrants....................... 188
    Household Goods Brought from Ireland......... 188
    Temporary Home Near Landing Place.......... 188
  The Settlement.. 188–190
    Selection of Land Affected by Ties of Kin and
      Friendship 188–189
    Journey to New Home............................. 189–190
    Clearing the Land................................. 190
  House Building.. 190–193
    The Clapboard House.............................. 190–192
    The Log House 192–193
  Equipment of House and Farm...................... 193–202
    The Hearth.. 193
    Inventories 195–204
    John Lowden's Goods, 1714...................... 195–196
    John Miller's Inventory........................... 196–197
    A New Garden Dinner Table, 1714............. 197–198
    Outfit of Farm...................................... 198
    John Fred's Inventory, 1720...................... 198–199
    The Warming-pan.................................. 199
    Redemptioners...................................... 199
    James Lindley's Estate, 1726.................... 200–201
    The "Grandfather" Clock.......... 201
    George McMillan's Clock...... 201–202

PAGE

Dress 202–205
Work on the Farm....................................... 205–206
Markets and Fairs... 206–207
Wild Animals.. 207–208
    A Bear Story.. 208
Social Intercourse.. 208–222
    Weddings 209–215
    The Marriage Certificate........................... 210–211
    Courtship.. 215–216
    Funerals 216–217
    Physicians' Charges,................................. 217
    Meetings for Worship............................... 217–220
    Business Meetings..................................... 220–222
    Quarterly Meeting..................................... 220–221
    Yearly Meeting... 221
    Monthly Meeting....................................... 221–222
Meeting Discipline.. 222–233
    Card-playing and Dancing......................... 222–223
    Drinking.. 223–227
    Disorderly Conduct.,................................. 227–228
    Care of Indented Servants 228
    Case of Lowden *versus* Smith....................... 228–231
    Military Service 231–233
    Revolutionary Taxes and Fines................... 233
    George McMillan's Fines........................... 233–235
Schools and Books.. 235–236

CHAPTER III.

SOME PROMINENT IRISH FRIENDS.......................... 237–276
James Logan.. 237–247
    His Autobiography..................................... 238–240
    Ancestry 238
    Education and Apprenticeship..................... 238
    Family Flees to Scotland, 1689 238
    His Father Teaches Friends' School at Bristol.. 238–239
    His Father Returns to Ireland and Leaves Him
        in Charge of School, 1693....................... 239

PAGE

Studies Mathematics and the Languages 239
Engages in Shipping, 1697........................... 240
Becomes Penn's Secretary, 1699.................. 240
Comes to Pennsylvania............................... 240
Public Life.. 240–243
Governor of Pennsylvania........................... 241
Leader of Proprietary Party 241–242
Relations with the Indians 242–243
Literary Pursuits....................................... 243–245
Personal Appearance.................................. 245
Unsuccessful Courtship.............................. 245–247
Marriage 247
Death.. 247
Thomas Holme... 247–256
In Ireland... 248–252
Commissioned Surveyor-General of Pennsyl-
  vania 251–252
Sails for the Province................................. 252–253
Lays out Philadelphia 253–254
Holme's Map of Pennsylvania...................... 254
Work of the Surveyor-General..................... 254–255
Member of the Provincial Council................. 255
Acts as Governor of the Province................. 256
Places of Residence................................... 256
Robert Turner.. 257–262
Thomas Griffitts... 262–263
Robert Strettell.. 263–267
William Stockdale....................................... 267–271
Nicholas Newlin.. 271–273
Nathaniel Newlin... 273
Lydia Darragh.. 273–274
Contribution of the Irish Quakers................. 274–276

APPENDIX.. 277–433
BIBLIOGRAPHY 434–444
INDEX.. 445

PART I.

THE PLANTING OF QUAKERISM IN IRELAND

CHAPTER I.

THE RISE OF QUAKERISM IN ENGLAND

THE period of the Civil War and Common- State of Eng-
wealth in England was one of contro- land in the Middle of the
versy and upheaval. The introduction of Seventeenth Century
the Bible into every cottage of the land had
set the people to thinking, and they gave themselves up to the consideration of questions of
civil and religious liberty and to the solution of
the great problems of life and death. Puritanism
became a mighty power, and in the middle of the
seventeenth century it arose in all its strength
and freed the nation from the yoke of Episcopacy
and from the tyranny of Charles I. Under the
Commonwealth and Cromwell toleration existed in
some measure, and there was greater opportunity
than formerly for the development of such sects as
that of the Society of Friends or so-called Quakers.

The history of the early years Beginnings of
of the Society of Friends is the Quakerism
history of its great leader and
founder. George Fox (1624–1691)
was born at Drayton-in-the-Clay, now known as
Fenny Drayton, Leicestershire, England, in 1624.
He says, "My father's name was Christopher Fox;

George Fox he was by profession a weaver, an honest man. . . . The neighbors called him Righteous Christer.   My mother was an honest woman ; her maiden name was Mary Lago, of the family of the Lagos and of the stock of the martyrs."[1]   At an early age Fox had a " gravity and stayedness of mind not usual in children,"[1] and as he grew up, under good home influences, he came to know " pureness and righteousness ";[1] so truthful and so determined was he the that it was a saying among his associates, "If George says ' *Verily*' there's no altering him." [2]

In 1643, as a youth of nineteen, "graceful . . . in countenance," stalwart and "manly in personage,"[3] and with a bright piercing eye he left his home, and spent the next five years wandering from sect to sect, weighing and considering the religious opinions which obtained in that seething and fervid time ; but with all his seeking he seemed unable to find anything that appealed to his spiritual condition.   Finally, after much conflict of spirit, he became convinced that the true source of religious comfort and consolation is the " Inner Light," the voice of God speaking directly to each human soul without the aid of any earthly mediator. With this idea as the basis of his religious system, George Fox developed those doctrines and

[1] *Journal*, I.
[2] *Ibid.*, 2.
[3] Thomas Ellwood's testimony in Fox's *Journal*.

practices peculiar to the Society of Friends and felt himself divinely called to proclaim this message to the world.

In 1647 and 1648, amid the conflicting ideas of the time, he began to preach, and went forth with all the ardor of a youthful knight of the Crusades, *sans peur et sans reproche,* spreading his new doctrine of the "Divine Light" through the towns and shires of England. He appealed to judges and justices to give righteous judgments, and to inn-keepers to be moderate in the sale of drink. He petitioned Parliament against allowing more inns than were needful for travelers. He raised his voice against wakes, feasts, sports, and plays. He went to fairs and markets urging men to deal justly and to speak the truth. He went into the "steeple houses" and openly testified against a "hireling ministry" and formalism of worship, the churches in which he spoke being usually those belonging to the Independents, who allowed discussion after the sermon. For these and other peculiar testimonies, so foreign to the ideas of the time, he was subjected to the most severe and cruel persecution ; but not even years of confinement in dark and loathsome dungeons could restrain his dauntless spirit.

The first years of his ministry were spent chiefly in the midland counties, where he found but few assistants in his missionary work, but when he

His Work and Followers

reached the northern counties many were convinced, and by 1654 he had organized a band of
sixty traveling ministers, who had caught his
spirit and who had began to preach his doctrines.
This zealous missionary band of young spirits—
yeomen, tradesmen, gentlemen—went up and
down the land carrying the message of Quakerism
with such power and courage that thousands
flocked to their standard, and by the end of the
century, 60,000 Quakers were numbered in England.[1]

[1] Brown in Traill's *Social England*, IV., 258-9.

CHAPTER II.

D URING the reign of Queen Mary, there had been adopted, for the first time, the plan of clearing off the native tribes of Irish from whole districts of Ireland, by expulsion or extermination, to make room for English and Scotch settlers. But the natives resisted and defended their homes with desperation; and from the beginning the settlers had to fight for their newly acquired possessions, aided, however, in their work of extermination by Government forces. During the twenty years from 1556 to 1576, plantations were attempted in the present Queen's County and County Antrim; but though the planters committed frightful atrocities, both attempts in a great measure failed.[1]

By far the most successful of all the plantations was that made by James I., who confiscated six counties of the Province of Ulster, and then poured in English and Scotch colonists, giving the natives only the poorest land to live on.[2] The

The Plantations

---

[1] Joyce in *Traill*, III., 411.
[2] *Ibid.*, IV., 195; *Gardiner*, 484.

7

new settlers were an industrious class of farmers, mechanics, weavers, and laborers;[1] and soon farms, homesteads, churches, and mills rose amidst the desolate wilds. "The foundations of the economic prosperity which has raised Ulster high above the rest of Ireland in wealth and in intelligence were undoubtedly laid in the confiscations of 1610."[2] This confiscation met with no opposition at the time from the evicted Irish, who sullenly withdrew to the lands which had been left to them.[2] The "earth tillers," the lowest class, however, in this, as in the other plantations, were spared and allowed to live in peace, scattered among the colonists.[3] Further confiscations were made in the Province of Leinster, under James; and Charles I. and his agent, Strafford, continued the work.[4] These confiscations and plantations were carried on for about a century and a half, and were the chief cause of the great rebellion of 1641.[5]

The Great Rebellion of 1641   After the departure of Strafford from Ireland in 1640, the natives all over the county were in a state of dangerous exasperation, due partly to the spread of the plantation system and partly to the measures taken to suppress the Catholic religion.[6]

[1] *Froude*, I., 76.
[2] *Green*, 458.
[3] *Froude*, I., 76.
[4] Joyce in *Traill*, IV., 196–7.
[5] *Ibid.*, III., 411.
[6] *Ibid.*, IV., 339.

The disbanded soldiers of the army that Strafford had raised, spread over the country, and blew the smouldering disaffection into a flame. A conspiracy, organized with wonderful power and secrecy by the Irish, broke forth in Ulster, and spread like wildfire over the center and west of the Island. Dublin was saved by a mere chance; but in the open country the work of murder went on unchecked. Great numbers of the settlers were butchered by the Irish, and the most dreadful outrages were perpetrated.[1] The estimates of those who were slain vary all the way from 50,000 to 200,000. The real number was probably less than 5,000.[2] In England a cry for bitter vengeance arose, but, the Civil War breaking out, the troops were detained for home service, and eight stirring years, which witnessed the fall of the Monarchy and the rise of the Commonwealth, had passed before active measures could be taken for the subjugation of Ireland.[3]

Meanwhile, the turn of events in Ireland had brought the Irish Catholics and the Royalists into power, and to subdue them the Parliament of the Commonwealth sent over Cromwell as Lord Lieutenant, in 1649, to reduce the country to obedience. "We are come," said Cromwell on landing

Cromwell in Ireland

---

[1] *Green*, 541.
[2] *Church*, 139.
[3] *Froude*, I., 126-7.

at Dublin with his "New Model," "to ask an account of the innocent blood that hath been shed, and to endeavour to bring to an account all who by appearing in arms shall justify the same."[1] From Dublin he marched to Drogheda, and the storming and taking of that stronghold was the first of a series of awful massacres. This was followed by the terrible slaughter of Wexford. The fate of these two towns produced such terror that town after town surrendered. Finally, in the spring of 1650, seeing the island almost subdued, Cromwell sailed for England, leaving Ireton, his son-in-law, to finish the war. Ireton and his successor, Ludlow, followed up the work with savage effectiveness, and by 1652 the conquest of the country was complete.[2]

The Settlement   In 1642, just after the rebellion, the English Parliament confiscated between two and three million acres of Irish soil. Debenture bonds were issued, payable in land when the country should be re-conquered. Bonds for a million acres had been taken up, and money had been raised on them for the payment of troops sent to Ireland previous to Cromwell's arrival. Similar debentures were issued afterwards for Cromwell's own army, though not thrown on the market like the first, but given to the soldiers in lieu of their pay ; and

[1] *Green*, 575.
[2] *Ibid.*, 574–6; *Gardiner*, 562–3; Joyce in *Traill*, IV., 341–2.

now that the Island was subdued, the time had come when all these engagements were to be redeemed.[1] To accomplish this end, to prevent the intermixture of the Teutonic and Celtic races, which had been a result of the previous plantations, and to remove all cause for future Irish rebellions, Parliament, in 1652, passed an act to dispossess the Irish landholders. The whole of the population of the three provinces of Ulster, Leinster, and Munster, except the poorer sort—small farmers, tradesmen laborers, etc.—were ordered to transport themselves across the River Shannon into the Province of Connaught, where they were to be given small allotments of ground that had been left waste. The exodus, for the most part of the middle and upper class, across the Shannon, went on from 1652 to 1654. Later, however, many of the exiles returned to their old homes, forming bands of outlaws or " Rapparees,"[2] and from their lurking places in bogs, mountains, and forests, made the most cruel depredations on the colonists whenever opportunity offered. The lands vacated by the Irish gentry were given to Cromwell's officers and soldiers, and to other bondholders.

Under the direction of the Lord Lieutenant, Henry Cromwell, son of Oliver, the great Cromwellian plantation was begun. The soldiers were

[1] *Froude*, I., 146.
[2] An Irish word meaning an armed plunderer.

settled down regiment by regiment, troop by troop, company by company, almost on the lands they had conquered. Many of them, however, sold their lands to the incoming Protestant pioneers from England and Scotland. The Irish poor classes remained in their natural homes, as under-tenants, or farm servants to the settlers. The order and industry of the new owners soon changed the face of Ireland, and it began to wear a look of quiet and prosperity. [1]

The Cromwellian Settlement, and the other plantations which preceded it, bear the closest relation to our subject, for they virtually prepared the ground for the planting of Quakerism in the Island ; and it was from these Protestant planters and soldiers, almost entirely, that the first Quaker missionaries to Ireland drew their recuits.

[1] *Prendergast;* Joyce in *Traill,* IV., 242–3; *Froude* I., 146–150 ; *Green,* 589–90.

CHAPTER III.

THE BEGINNINGS OF QUAKERISM IN IRELAND

THE founder and leader of Quakerism in Ireland was William Edmundson (1627–1712), one of Cromwell's soldiers. He was born at Little Musgrave, in Westmoreland, England, in 1627, the son of John and Grace Edmundson. " My father," he says, "was well accounted among men who knew him and religious in what he knew." His parents died while he was quite young, and he was bound an apprentice in York to learn the carpenter's trade. Then, he relates, "I went into the Parliaments' Army, and there continued part of the War betwixt the King and Parliament; and when that was over, I went into Scotland under Oliver Cromwell in the year 1650." He was greatly influenced by the Puritan movement of the time, and during his apprenticeship and army life his mind was often exercised over religious questions. "Sometimes when I had been on Service most of the Day, and was lying down in my Tent at Night, then would arise in my Mind the eminent Dangers I had passed that Day, and the

William Edmundson

In England

13

narrow Escape my Life had, and what would become of my Soul, if I had fallen.

In the Year 1651, the Scotch Army marched for England, we followed and engaged them at Worcester, and overthrew their Army." He was at the taking of the Isle of Man, then returned to England, and was quartered in Derbyshire, where at this time "the common Discourse of all Sorts of People was of the Quakers," but he did not have an opportunity of hearing any of them preach at this time. "After some Time spent in divers Exercises, we marched again for Scotland, at which Time I had a Charge of some Men for recruiting other Companies in Scotland, then left the Army, came back to England, and visited my Relations in the North; from thence rode into Derbyshire, and married a young woman, to whom I was contracted before.[1] After some time I was about to settle in Derbyshire in the way of Shop-keeping, at which Time my Brother, [John] who was a soldier in Ireland, came into England to see his Relations and highly commending Ireland, pursuaded me to go and live there, which I, with my wife, concluded to do."[2]

---

[1] William Edmundson was first married to Margaret Stanford, of Bramley, Derbyshire, daughter of Thomas Stanford. She died in 1691, at the house of her son-in-law, William Fayle, near Dublin, and William Edmundson was married a second time, 10 Mo. 1, 1697, to Mary Strangman, of Mountmellick Meeting.—*Records in possession of a descendant, Joshua William Edmunsdon, of Dublin.*

[2] *Journal,* 1–6.

Taking with him a stock of goods to commence *Settles in Ireland* a "Trade in Merchandise," William Edmundson, his wife, and servant took shipping at Whitehaven and landed at Dublin in 1652. On learning of his brother's arrival, John Edmundson came down from the north of the island, where his troop was then stationed, and transported William and his household to the town of Antrim. Here William rented a house and opened a shop, his brother living with him. Trade being then very brisk, the goods were soon disposed of, and in 1653, William returned to England to renew his stock.

On coming into the north of England, he says, "George Fox and James Naylor were in that country, James Naylor having a Meeting about three Miles from where I was, I went to it with my eldest brother, Thomas, and another Kinsman, having an earnest Desire to have Converse with some of that People, retaining a Love for and believing well of them from the first hearing the Report of them, and I was glad of this Opportunity, *Becomes a Quaker* and we were all three convinced of the Lord's blessed Truth." Having accomplished his business in England, he returned to Ireland, and in the spring of 1654 removed with his family from Antrim to Lurgan, in the County of Armagh, where he kept a shop and took some land for grazing cattle. In his new home the use of the plain language, the keeping on of his hat, and the other peculiar Quaker customs which he had adopted since his convincement, were the cause of much wonder and offence to his neighbors, and socially and in his business relations he was subjected to much vexation and discomfort.

The First Meeting in Ireland, 1654   His wife and brother had been convinced of the principles of Friends shortly after his journey to England and they all now met together in a meeting twice a week at his house. He says, "In a while after four more were convinced; then we were seven that met together to wait upon God, and to worship Him in Spirit and Truth." Thus in the year 1654, at Lurgan was established the first meeting of Friends in Ireland.[1]

The Traveling Ministers and Their Work

The First Ministers Arrive   Now came a period of earnest and zealous proselyting on the part of missionaries from England. The first of the ministers to arrive were Miles Halhead, James Lancaster, and Miles Bateman, who came over from England in the early part of 1654, and made a short tour from town to town through the Island, preaching to the people, to magistrates, and to officers of the army. Having convinced many of the truth of their principles, they went into the north and took shipping at Belfast for England.[2]

Ulster in 1655   The next year was an important one in the history of the Society of Friends in Ireland. Ten

---

[1] *Journal of William Edmundson*, 1-15; *Janney*, I., 261-4.
[2] *Besse*, II., 457; *Rutty*, 87.

earnest preachers came over and laid the foundations of the most important Quaker strongholds
in the island. John Tiffin was the first to arrive.
He came to William Edmundson's at Lurgan, and
during his sojourn of five or six weeks many members were added to that meeting. He and William Edmundson went to neighboring fairs and
other public gatherings, explaining their principles
and carrying on discussion with those of other beliefs. "Truth began to spread, tho' thro' great
opposition ; for now the Priests and People began
to be alarmed in a rage, and Friends were exposed
to great Sufferings upon several accounts, particularly, as the testimony of Truth was against all
hireling Teachers and their forced maintenance,
these made it their business to incense the Magistrates and Rulers against Friends."[1]

About this time William Edmundson went over *Richard
to England and conferred with George Fox, whom* *Clayton's
he had not yet seen, telling him of the convince-* *Visit*
ment of Friends in Ireland, "of the Openness
among People in the North of that Nation, to hear
the Truth declared, and of the Want of ministering
Friends in the Gospel there."[2] Soon after his
return to Lurgan, Richard Clayton came on a
religious visit from England, and the two spent
several days journeying on foot through the coun-

[1] *Rutty*, 88.
[2] *Edmundson's Journal*, 18.

2

ties of Antrim, Londonderry, Tyrone, and Armagh. At Coleraine they preached in the streets, but the people drove them out of the town, so that they had to lodge in a cabin on the mountain. At Londonderry and Kilmore they met with better success, and at these places many were convinced and meetings were settled.

Anne Gould and Juliann Wastwood About the year 1655 two women ministers from London, Anne Gould and Juliann Wastwood, landed at Dublin and "all on Foot in Winter Time, wading Rivers, and dirty miry Ways,"[1] traveled in religious service to Londonderry, from there to Coleraine and through the country of the "Scotch People and Presbyterians" to Clough. Here the poor women sank down exhausted and disheartened, and Anne Gould was confined to bed. But William Edmundson happening to come that way, they were so rejoiced at seeing him that they recovered sufficiently to be taken to his home, where they were well cared for until their departure for England.

William Edmundson had now gained more experience as a minister, and traveled continually, preaching in public places and in churches. Other meetings sprang up, and "People more and more were convinced, insomuch that the Priests and Professors still raged, many tender people leaving them ; and to revenge themselves they cast Wil-

---

[1] *Edmundson's Journal,* 21.

liam Edmundson into prison," at Armagh.[1] He was soon liberated, however, and came forth with even greater zeal than before. Soon after his liberation, he felt a religious calling to leave shop-keeping and to rent a farm in order that he might set the example of bearing testimony against tithes, for as yet no one had borne that testimony in Ireland. With this in view, he and several other Friends and their families, leaving Lurgan Meeting well-settled, removed into the County of Cavan in the southern part of Ulster, where they rented land and began farming. Cavan Meeting was founded and many converts were made in that neighborhood. It was not long before these Friends experienced the sufferings they had anticipated. Many of them, for non-payment of tithes and other non-conformities, had their goods taken from them and were imprisoned.[2]

Edmundson bears a Testimony against Tithes

But the Quaker movement was not confined to the north of Ireland. At the same time that William Edmundson and his co-workers were spreading Quakerism through Ulster, other missionaries were working with equal zeal in the provinces of Leinster and Munster. In the beginning of the year, Elizabeth Fletcher and Elizabeth Smith, from England, landed at Dublin and made a few prose-lytes. For preaching in the Church of St. Audeon in that city, they were imprisioned by order of the

Leinster and Munster in 1655

Elizabeth Fletcher and Elizabeth Smith

[1] *Rutty*, 91.
[2] *Ibid.*, 87–91 ; *Edmundson*, 16–29 ; *Janney*, I., 256–270.

Lord Mayor, in Newgate. After their release they had a meeting at the house of Richard Foukes, a tailor, near Polegate. This was the earliest meeting of Friends held in Dublin, although the first established meeting in that city was at George Latham's near Polegate. From Dublin these faithful women traveled south into Munster, holding meetings in the towns through which they passed. At Youghall, among numerous converts, were Captain James Sicklemore and Lieutenant Robert Sandham, two of the Cromwellian soldiers stationed in that town. Elizabeth Fletcher and Elizabeth Smith were the first Quakers to enter Cork, and in that city an equal success attended their efforts.

The summer of this year, 1655, is memorable for the landing at Dublin of two of the most determined and courageous apostles of Quakerism, Francis Howgill and Edward Burrough. Francis

Francis Howgill

Howgill had been educated for the Church at one of the English universities, and his magnetic personality and persuasive eloquence drew so many to his doctrines that he is conspicuous in the annals of Quakerism as one of the chief founders of the Society. Edward Burrough, perhaps not so polished a man as his companion, was one who performed every un-dertaking with all his might, and his power and vigor as a speaker were so marked that he was known as "A Son of Thunder."[1] They spent three months of aggres-sive work in Dublin, holding successful meetings and issuing tracts of appeal to magistrates and soldiers. Then, leaving Edward Burrough to continue the work in Dublin, Francis Howgill set out in company with a cornet of the army, and others, for the dangerous journey to the south of the island, visiting only the "great towns and cities ; for generally the country is without in-habitants, except bands of robbers, which wait for their prey and devour many."[2] At Kilkenny and the coast towns of Waterford, Youghall, and Cork he was enabled to carry on successfully the work begun by the women Friends. At Bandon, a large market town, he was hospitably entertained by one Edward Cook, a man of ability and in-fluence, " Cornet of Horse in Oliver Cromwell's own troop, and Receiver to the Lord Cork."[3]

[1] *Beck*, 84.

[2] Edward Burrough in a letter to Margaret Fell, Barclay's *Letters of Early Friends*, 265.

[3] *Rutty*, 95.

They went toge ther tothe church, where Francis preached and where Edward Cook invited the people to a meeting at his house that evening. Many attended this meeting and there embraced the principles of Friends.[1]

At Kinsale, a great port town, Major Stoding, Governor of the fort, was kindly disposed, and numbers of the soldiers became Friends. Many meetings were held in the garrison, which so enraged the "priests" that they informed against the officers and sent to Dublin for a warrant ordering the arrest of the Quakers. The Governors of Kinsale and Cork, however, having a friendly regard for Francis Howgill, did not enforce the warrant and allowed him to go on with his work unmolested. For his encouragement of the Quakers Major Stoding, shortly afterward, was dismissed from the "commission of the peace" at Kinsale. Colonel Phayre, Governor of Cork, seems to have been especially impressed with Friends, for in a letter from Cork, Francis Howgill writes to Margaret Fell at Swarthmore Hall,

---

[1] Among those convinced at Bandon at this time was Thomas Wight (1640-1724), son of Rice Wight, minister of the town of Bandon, and grandson of Thomas Wight, also minister of the same town and originally from Guilford, in Surrey, England. Thomas Wight is to be remembered as the first historian of the Irish Friends, having compiled an excellent contemporary " History of the Rise and Progress of the People called Quakers in Ireland," from 1653 to 1700. His manuscript was revised and carried down to the year 1751 by Dr. John Rutty (1699-1775), a Friend of Dublin, and a native of England, who published the work in Dublin, in 1751. (See *Rutty* in Bibliography.)

SWARTHMORE HALL
"—that old house in ancient Lancashire
Where Fox, the high-souled Founder of his sect,
Oft sought retirement from the world's loud noise
And steeled his godly heart for fresh crusades."
—John Russell Hayes.

the headquarters, as it were, of the Society in
England, that the Colonel has said, "More is
done by the Quakers, than all the priests in the
country have done [in] a hundred years." Francis then says of his work: "Now many are moved
daily to bear witness against the priests: the work
of the Lord is great,—glory to Him forever!"[1]

In the meantime Edward Burrough had left
Dublin, and following Howgill's route came

[1] *Barclay*, 268-9.

preaching through the towns to Cork, where he met Francis again after a separation of several months. In company with James Sickelmore and Edward Cook, they went to Limerick and attempted to speak in the Church, but were rudely driven out of the city. As they rode through the streets, Edward Burrough preached on horseback, and outside the city gates, he and his companions had an opportunity to speak to the great multitude that followed them. Richard Pearce, an apothecary, and others of the city, became Friends as a result of this preaching, and a flourishing meeting was established. The ministers now returned to Cork, but the "priests" *Howgill and Burrough Banished* had been so active during their absence that both Howgill and Burrough were arrested and carried to Dublin by order of Henry Cromwell. As they were conducted on the way, the guard of soldiers were kind to them and allowed them to hold meetings in the towns through which they passed. After seven months of active work they were finally banished from Ireland and compelled to embark at Dublin for England.

Barbara Blaugden Arrives One of the most intrepid of these early ministers was Barbara Blaugden, who made two effective visits through the southern part of the island. After an adventurous voyage from England, she landed at Dublin on the very day that witnessed the enforced departure of Howgill and Burrough. Nothing daunted she gained admittance to Henry Cromwell, the Lord Lieutenant, and warned him of the consequences of his cruelty to her people. Her message seems to have had some effect, for Captain Rich, at whose house she was staying, told her that the Lord Lieutenant " was so troubled and so melancholy that he could not go to Bowles, nor to any other Pastime." [1]

The stream of Quaker missionaries continued to pour into the country, so that nearly two hundred had come over before 1700. Dr. Rutty shows in his table, that during the first century of the history of the Society some five hundred and fifty men and women ministers visited Ireland. [2]

With the Restoration of Charles II., in 1660, Friends everywhere looked for a respite from their persecutions, but the rising of the Fifth Monarchy men under Venner gave the clergy a pretext for checking the growing power of Quakerism, and an act was passed forbidding the Quakers to meet in public worship. [3] As a result, persecutions among the Friends in Ireland were carried on with greater rigor than under the Commonwealth. William Edmundson says : " Now was King Charles coming in, and these Nations were in Heaps of Confusion, and ran upon us as if they

Restoration of Charles II. and the Organization of Quakerism

The Restoration

Persecutions

[1] *Besse*, II., 459.
[2] *Rutty*, 92–109, 351–363; *Besse*, II., 458–9 ; *Backhouse*, 51–3 ; *Barclay*, 260–273 ; *Janney*, I., 273–9.
[3] *Janney*, II., 13–14, 25–6.

would have destroyed us at once, or swallow'd us up ; breaking up our Meetings, taking us up in Highways, and haling us to Prison ; so that it was a general Imprisonment of Friends in this Nation." [1]

At this time Edmundson was a prisoner at Marysborough, but obtained a short leave of absence from the sheriff, went to Dublin and petitioned the Earls of Orrery and Mountrath and *Edmundson Secures the Release of Friends from Prison* Sir Morris Eustace, Chancellor, that Friends in the nation might be set at liberty. He says : "I was close exercised in that Service, but the Lord's Power gave me Courage, opened my Way to proceed and gave Success to it ; so that I got an Order for Friends' Liberty throughout the Nation, though they were full of Business ; and Abundance of People of all Sorts attending." On this as on many similar occasions, he seems to have exerted a strong and subtle influence over those in power, and we may well believe that men were drawn to him by his attractive qualities of mind and person, as well as by his strong and noble character.

The persecutions, however, did not end here. The Church of England being now thoroughly established, the clergy bent all their efforts upon making the dissenters conform,[2] and Friends con-

---

[1] *Journal*, 45.
[2] *Froude*, I., 171-2.

tinued to suffer for their non-conformity until the Act of Toleration for Protestant Dissenters was passed in 1689, in the reign of William and Mary. During the reign of Charles II., 1660–1685, according to Rutty's table, seven hundred and eighty Friends suffered imprisonment.[1]

It was during this time of persecution that Thomas Loe, a gifted minister of Oxford, and at one time of Oxford University, made one of his frequent visits to Ireland, and at Cork converted to the principles of Quakerism the young cavalier, William Penn, the great founder of the Commonwealth on the Delaware.[2]

Thomas Loe Converts William Penn, 1666

By 1668, the number of Friends had so greatly increased that it became necessary to adopt some form of church government, and William Edmundson, as one of the chief instruments in gathering and preserving the Society in Ireland, was a prime mover in the work of carrying out George Fox's scheme of organization in Ireland. Provincial meetings were established to be held once in six weeks, the chief business being to take care of the poor, the fatherless and the widows ; to see that marriages were properly solemnized ; and to watch over the moral conduct of the members. In the following year George Fox himself came over, and he and William Edmundson traveled all over

Organization

---

[1] *Rutty*, 367.
[2] *Ibid.*, 123, 130.

the Island, establishing national half-year meetings and monthly meetings.[1]

Troubles Under James II. and William III.   Great alarm was created among the English and Scotch Protestants in Ireland, by the accession of James II. and by his measures taken for the restoration of the Catholic religion.   The

Tyrconnel   Earl of Tyrconnel, a strict Catholic, was sent over as commander of the forces, and immediately proceeded to disarm the Protestant militia and to place Irish Catholics in the Army.   This innovation, and later Tyrconnel's appointment as Lord Lieutenant, together with the efforts of the Irish

Terror of Protestants   to recover their confiscated estates, and the raids of the Rapparees, caused the wildest alarm among the Protestants, and they trembled both for their estates and for their lives.   Rumors of a general massacre, like that of the Rebellion of 1641, flew through the land, and many of the terrified people left the country or hastened to the fortified towns, such as Enniskillen and Londonderry, where at the latter place they bravely withstood the siege of James in 1689.[2]

The Friends   In the war that followed, the Friends generally kept their places and maintained their meetings.[3] In some districts, however, the danger was so great that members moved into the towns until the conflict was over.[4]   Those who remained were

[1] *Rutty*, 127 ; *Janney*, II., 170.
[2] Joyce in *Traill*, IV., 616 ; *Lawless*, 280–1 ; *Janney*, II., 320–1.
[3] *Rutty*, 156.
[4] See account of John Barcroft and other Friends in *Leadbeater*.

continually being robbed by the Irish soldiers and Rapparees. In this, as in many other trials which came upon him, William Edmundson stood forth as the sturdy champion of his sect, and on many occasions went to Dublin to solicit the government in behalf of Friends. Tyrconnel heard him with attention, and measures were taken with a view of protecting the Quakers from robbery ; but such was the state of anarchy prevailing that no effectual remedy could be applied. As the Friends were known to be an inoffensive people, opposed to war, the Catholics in authority were disposed to shield them from the severities inflicted upon other Protestants. But, notwithstanding all the endeavors made, the Friends were exposed to great perils. Many of the lostm all of their personal property, and some were even stripped of their clothing and had their homes burned to the ground.[1] In 1692, after the war was over, it was estimated that the material loss of Friends throughout the nation amounted to £100,000.

After the landing of William and Mary in England, James had fled to France, and now, with the hope of recovering his lost kingdom, he was come again with an army into Ireland. During the fierce struggle that ensued, the Provinces of Leinster and Munster were ravaged by advancing or retreating armies, and many Friends who contin-

The Revolution of 1689

---

[1] *Janney*, II., 322.

ued in their homes were plundered and subjected
to gross maltreatment ; but not being classed as
belligerents, their lives were generally spared.
They were sometimes enabled, indeed, to per-
form kind offices for both sides, at one time pleading for their Irish neighbors, when the English
had obtained the ascendency, and at another shel-
tering the Protestant English when the Irish had
gained a temporary advantage.

After Battle of the Boyne   After the defeat of James at the Boyne, in 1690,
his Irish troops disbanded, and roamed through
the country, carrying terror and devastation into
the Protestant districts.[1]   William Edmundson,
now living at Rosinallis, was one of the greatest
sufferers in this war.   In reading his quaint and
graphic account of his sufferings and experiences
in these unhappy times one is filled with admira-
tion for his courage and heroism.   At one time he
is at Dublin telling James of the calamities which
have fallen upon the Protestants, and at another
he risks his life in pleading with infuriated English
soldiers for his Irish neighbors.   He relates that
after the Battle of Boyne, the Rapparees burst
into his house one night, abused his wife with such
violence and cruelty that she died soon after, and
ruthlessly seized him and his two sons and carried
them away with intent to hang them.   This crime,
undoubtedly, would have been committed if an
Irish officer had not opportunely interfered.

*William Ed-
mundson's
Sufferings*

[1] *Janney*, II., 323-4.

In spite of all the trials and hardships so nobly endured in his foster land, and in spite of long and wearisome journeys in Europe and America, *Edmundson's Death* William Edmundson lived to the ripe old age of eighty-five, and on the Thirty-first day of the Sixth Month (O. S.), 1712, departed this life, well deserving the name, Father of Irish Quakerism.[1]

After William III. had brought the nation into a peaceful condition, the Friends continued to increase in numbers, and during the next half century many new meetings were formed. At the present day, although the Society has greatly decreased, there still remains a considerable number of meetings, many of which are well attended.

[1] *Journal.*

CHAPTER IV.

RACIAL ORIGIN OF THE FRIENDS OF IRELAND

THE converts to Quakerism in Ireland were drawn almost exclusively from the English and Scotch Protestants. Most of them had previously been in membership with other non-conforming denominations, such as the Baptists, Independents, and Presbyterians, although some few had been members of the Church of England.

The principles of Friends in early days found little acceptance with the Celtic-Irish, nor has the Society acquired much increase in after years from that source. For, aside from race differences and antipathies, arising from the English plantation system, the Irish almost to a man were Catholics, and as Beck says : " It seems to need the passing through the various stages of non-conformity, before a Catholic can appreciate the doctrinal views of Friends."[1] During the early period, at least prior to 1700, I have been unable to find in Stockdale, Rutty, Besse, Sewell, Leadbeater, or in the journals of ministers, any instance of a Celtic-Irishman becoming a Quaker. Of Besse's two hundred and ninety-one names of representative

The Celtic-Irish

---

[1] *The Friends*, 88.

Quaker sufferers in Ireland, from the rise of the Society to 1689, there is not one *Mc* or other Celtic prefix ; all are old English names.[1]

Although the statement of Joyce [2] and Prendergast, that the Cromwellian settlers were absorbed by the Irish in two generations, may be true to a large extent of the other Protestants, it is, I believe, by reason of the strict church discipline which obtained, but slightly true of those who remained in the Society of Friends.[3] Apropos of this, John Grubb Richardson (1813-1890), a prominent and representative Irish Friend, says of his family : "We were members of the Society of Friends, our forefathers having been convinced by the preaching of William Edmundson in 1660. All our ancestors came from the north of England in Cromwell's army, and received grants of land from him to settle in Ireland."[4]

In the migration of the Irish Quakers to Pennsylvania, there were represented only five surnames with the Celtic prefix *Mc* — McCool,

[1] *Besse*, II., 457-493.

[2] *Traill*, IV., 343.

[3] Rutty states in his table of meetings in Ireland (*Rise and Progress*, page 350) that between 1714 and 1739 a small meeting was established at Connaught, the province to which the Irish were expelled in the Cromwellian Settlement, and it is possible that the members of this meeting were of Celtic-Irish stock, but unfortunately I have been unable to find any data bearing on the point. I am able to state, however, from my examination of Friends' records of Pennsylvania, that no members from this meeting came over during the emigration period, 1682-1750.

[4] *Richardson*, 217-218.

McMollin, or McMillan, McClum, McNabb, and McNice; but, as this prefix is common to both Irish and Scotch surnames, it is unsafe to use it as a means of distinction.   The McCool and McMollin families were from Ballinacree Meeting, near Ballymoney, County Antrim, in the midst of the "Scotch country," hence if any distinction can be made, it lies in favor of the Scotch or Scotch-Irish descent.   The McClums were from County West Meath; the McNabbs from County Meath, and the NcNices from County Cavan, localities in which the Scotch had also settled, although not in such great numbers as in the more northern counties. The only Quaker family with a distinctively Irish name, that came over to Pennsylvania, was that of the O'Mooneys, who came from Ballinacree Meeting, and settled at Sadsbury, Lancaster County.

In a letter of 1898,[1] John Bewley Beale, an Irish Friend, writes: "There were additions from the pure Irish stock to the Society, but much fewer in number than from the Protestant settlers and their descendants. We have some Irish names amongst us still, such as Murphy, Macquillan, etc."   This view is confirmed still further by Joseph Radley, until recently Headmaster of Ulster Provincial School, the Friends' School, at Prospect Hill, Lisburn, Ireland.   He writes (May

[1] From Dublin, dated 3 mo. 5, 1898. For many years J. Bewley Beale has had charge of the Friends' records collected at Friends' Meeting House, 6 Eustace Street, Dublin.

7, 1898) : " The Quaker character found little on which it could be grafted in the Celtic population. This was almost entirely Roman Catholic. Consequently, but few names of the old Celtic families occur now amongst Friends. A few O'Heils, McQuillans, etc., still are to found." During my travels in Ireland, in the summer of 1900, I heard similar views expressed by many other Irish Friends, notable among whom were John Pim, J.P., of Belfast, for many years a student of the history of Irish Friends, and Jane M. Richardson, of Moyallon House, Gilford, County Down, the author of *Six Generation of Friends in Ireland.* My own conclusion is, that the increase from the Celtic or Hibernian stock was very slight indeed, and that such converts as were made were obtained after the great migration to Pennsylvania.

The Scotch Presbyterians had come over in great numbers to the north of Ireland during the spread of the plantation system, and at the time of the Cromwellian Settlement constituted the largest part of the Protestant population of Antrim, Down, and some other counties of Ulster. The early traveling preachers of the Friends report in their journals that the meetings in the " Scotch country" were well attended by the Presbyterians. There is no evidence, however, that any considerable number became Friends. J. Bewley Beale says in his letter : " There were also some Ulster

The Scotch-Irish

Scotch amongst the early Friends, but I think the proportion was also small."

Quite early, meetings were established at Coleraine, Ballynacree, Lisburn and other places in Antrim, but they were not as large as other meetings without the pale of the Scotch. Thomas Story,[1] in his account of a religious visit to Ireland in 1716, relates that at Grange in Antrim great numbers of the Presbyterians came to hear him, and that one of their ministers, Moses Cleck, educated at Glasgow, Scotland, had been convinced of the Quaker principles. Prominent among Scotch-Irish Quakers were John Chambers, a minister of Dublin; Alexander Seaton, of Hillsborough, County Down; Archibald Bell, of Shankill, County Armagh; Patrick Logan, of Lurgan, County Armagh, and his son, James Logan, later one of the most distinguished statesmen of colonial Pennsylvania.

The Anglo-Irish We may safely say that the great majority of the Quakers in Ireland were English, or of English descent. Long after the Cromwellian Settlement, and well into the first half of the eighteenth century, Quaker colonists continued to come from England. Some of these were members when they arrived, and others became members after their settlement.[2] The certificates of removal

[1] *Journal,* 537.

[2] See Mary Leadbeater's " Biographical Notices " of the most prominent Irish Friends, from the rise of the Society to 1828. This excellent work was carefully compiled from printed and manuscript sources.

which the Irish Friends brought to Pennsylvania show that many of the emigrants were natives of England and had lived but a few years in Ireland. It is especially interesting to note that so many of these early Irish Friends had been officers and soldiers in Cromwell's "New Model," and that the same splendid zeal and courage shown at Naseby and Worcester, but now directed in a peaceful cause, contributed so largely to the up-building of Quakerism in the nation.

PART II.

THE MIGRATION OF IRISH FRIENDS TO PENNSYLVANIA

CHAPTER I.

CAUSES OF EMIGRATION

THERE was but little foreign immigration of Quakers into the colonies of New England, New York, and the South during any period. The Society in these provinces was composed, for the most part, of converts and the descendants of converts made during the period from 1656 to the end of the seventeenth century by that zealous band of Old World missionaries under the stirring and effective leadership of such men as George Fox, John Burnyeat, and William Edmundson. In the distinctively Quaker colonies of Pennsylvania and New Jersey, however, the Society was made up almost entirely of immigrant Friends from Europe attracted by the superior opportunities for settlement.

While it is true that the majority of the Quaker settlers of Pennsylvania came from England and Wales, it is also true that a considerable body of them were immigrants from Ireland, who took a prominent and useful place in the affairs of the Province and rendered an important contribution to the making of the State. Historians hitherto have overlooked this feature of the early immigration, but it is one that deserves in the fullest measure their close attention and study.

The Irish Friends removed to several of the American colonies. At an early date they were on the eastern shore of Maryland. In 1682 a shipload of them came to West Jersey.[1] They are also known to have gone to the Quaker settlements in the Carolinas,[2] and Virginia.[3] But by far the greatest and most important migration was that to Pennsylvania during the period 1682 to 1750, and it is this movement that we are now to consider.

Causes   Although the causes which led to the migration are well known, it seems fitting, if only for the sake of completeness, to enumerate and briefly discuss them. The religious persecutions were powerful factors in the movement, and during its first stages gave to it its greatest impetus. Later, however,

[1] These Friends were from in and near Dublin, and having purchased an interest in West Jersey, they chartered the ship of the adventurous Quaker captain, Thomas Lurting, and sailed from Dublin the latter part of September, 1682. In about eight weeks they arrived at Elsinburg, near Salem, New Jersey, and made a settlement in what later was called the Irish Tenth, in Camden County. Here was established Newton Meeting, first held at the house of Mark Newby, one of this company. A full history of the Irish Friends of the Newton settlement is given in Judge John Clement's *Sketches of the First Emigrant Settlers in Newton Township, Old Gloucester County, West New Jersey*. Also, see *Clement Papers*, Vol. A, Hist. Soc. of Penna.; Mickle's *Reminiscences of Old Gloucester*, 47; *Michener*, 118; *Smith* in *Hazard's Register*, VI., 184; *Bowden*, II., 16; *New Jersey Hist. Soc. Collections*, VII., 45; *Comly's Friends' Miscellany*, Vol. 3, p. 134 (Phila., 1832).

[2] *MS. Friends' Records; Weeks*, 115–116.

[3] *William Edmundson's Journal*, 114.

especially after the passing of the Act of Toleration of 1689, by which the persecutions were somewhat relaxed, it would appear that the economic
restrictions had a greater influence. Then, too,
along with these causes went that old Teutonic
love for adventure, that same historic force which,
to a great extent, inspired the *Völkerwanderung*—
the Wandering of the Peoples—of the Early Middle Ages, which led the Angles and Saxons to
Britain, which took the Franks and later the Nor-
mans into Gaul, and which led to the discovery and
exploration of the New World.

The causes are given herewith under the two
main heads : I. Religious Causes ; II. Economic
Causes.

I. Religious Causes

The Acts of Uniformity passed at the time of
the Restoration of Charles II. continued to be enforced with varying severity far into the eighteenth
century. All the non-conformists suffered more or
less by them, but especially the Friends and Scotch-
Irish Presbyterians. These sufferings were re-
lieved in a large degree, in 1719, by the passing
of an act which allowed greater freedom of worship.[1]

The Friends were continually persecuted for
maintaining their testimony against tithes. Says
Rutty (p. 364), " The Priests were commonly the

Religious Causes

Acts of Uniformity

Tithes and Other Ec- clesiastical Dues

[1] *Rutty*, 282–3.

Instruments of stirring up the Magistrates, and
even the Rabble against them; and . . . they
very frequently had their goods spoiled and taken
away; sometimes to three, six, ten, or twenty
times the value, and were kept Prisoners several
years, and sometimes unto Death." During the
four years of King James II. (1685–1689) the
Friends were deprived of £1,583 worth of goods,
and twelve suffered imprisonment. In the thirteen years of William and Mary (1689–1702), their
"sufferings" included £13,724 and thirty-three
prisoners; in the twelve years of Queen Anne
(1702–1714) £16,199 and thirteen prisoners; in
the thirteen years of George I. (1714–1727) £22,-
513 and twenty-seven prisoners; and in the first
twenty-seven years of George II. (1727–1760) until
1750, about £38,726 and six prisoners. During the
whole period from 1685 to 1750 the "sufferings"
amounted to £92,745 and ninety-one prisoners.[1]

Oaths   The Friends were constantly inconvenienced and
defrauded in business on account of their refusal
to take the oath in a court of justice; "For instance," says Rutty, "in the county of Wexford,
Thomas Holme [who afterward became Surveyor-
General of Pennsylva-
nia] having about £200
due to him from one
Captain Thornhill, for
which judgment was obtained against him in com-

[1] *Rutty*, 367–8.

mon Law, was subpœna'd into Chancery by the said
Thornhill, where he well knew Thomas could not
answer Oath, and so this Friend lost his Debt. And
in Dublin, James Fade having about £40 due to
him from one Ezekiel Webb, was by the said Webb,
subpœna'd into Chancery and because the Friend
could not give in his answer upon Oath, he not
only lost the said debt, but was constrained to give
about £70 to get clear of the Debtor."[1] This form
of persecution continued until 1719, when Parliament passed an Act which allowed Friends to sub-
stitute affirmation for the oath.[2]

The Friends often endured the greatest cruel-
ties and depredations at the hands of the rebel-
lious Irish. In 1719 one of the Irish gentry, *Lawlessness*
James Cotter, was hanged for an outrage com- *of the Irish*
mitted against a Quaker family of Cork. Upon *Catholics*
this, "All Cork and all the South of Ireland burst
into a wail of rage, and the Friends were marked
for retribution. Placards covered the walls. . . .
No quaker could show in the streets. . . . The
passion spread to Limerick, to Tipperary and at
last over all Catholic Ireland. Quakers' meeting-
houses were sacked and burnt. Quakers travelling about the country were waylaid and beaten."[3]
The rage against the Friends continued, until in
1725 it culminated in the most inhuman and bar-

[1] *Rutty*, 137-8.
[2] *Ibid.*, 282-3.
[3] *Froude*, I., 481-82.

barous murder of Edward Johnston, a Friend of
Carroe. [1]

II. ECONOMIC CAUSES

*Economic
Causes*

Cromwell had placed English and Irish commerce on an equal footing ; but early in the reign
of Charles II. an Act was passed, with the result
that all export trade from Ireland to the colonies
was forbidden, as was also the import of Irish

*Restriction
on Manufac-
ture and
Commerce*

cattle into England.   Dreadful distress all over
Ireland followed immediately, for the people could
find no market for their produce.   When the cattle
trade ceased, much of the land had been turned
into sheep walks.   A large and increasing woolen
trade and manufacture now sprang up, so that it
became one of the chief industries of Ireland ;
whereupon the English merchants, fearful for
their own trade, in 1699, succeeded in having
passed an Act which forbade the export of woolen
goods from Ireland, and thus ruined the wool
trade of the Island.   About 40,000 industrious
Protestant workmen were thus thrown out of employment and reduced to poverty ; 20,000 of these
emigrated to America.   Many of those that remained suffered all the misery of famine.   Subsequently, almost all branches of Irish industry
were interfered with and suppressed by England. [2]

As an example of this distress, may be cited

[1] *Ibid.*, I., 479–483.
[2] Joyce in *Traill*, IV., 620–1 ; *Gardiner*, 686–7 ; *Lawless*, 308–9.

the instance of Samuel Combe, of Cork, one of the Irish Friends who came over with his family to Philadelphia about 1709. In his certificate of removal, signed 5 Mo. 26, 1709, the Friends of Cork say, "yᵉ sayd Samuel being a bristall [England] man came over into this Country with his wife som time after yᵉ Wars ended to settle in Corke and follow yᵉ Cooping trade and although he was observed to be a Laborious painful man ye world favoured him not with success. We hope and Desire it may be better in that Countrey where we suppose workmen of that Calling are no so plenty as in this nor materials to worke on so hard to be obtained as here."[2]   Again, the Friends of Waterford, in a certificate, dated 2 Mo. 13, 1712, sent to Philadelphia, for William Moore, say, "A great Reson of his Removeall is for want of a good Imploy his trade being bad here."[1]

At times the landlords became very oppressive, *High Rents* raising the rents all they possibly could, regardless of what the tenants had done to make the land valuable. Much land was held on long leases, and when these expired the rates of renewal were made almost prohibitive, many tracts of land being secured by the Celtic-Irish, who were ready to give almost any price to recover possession of the soil.[2]   The Friends of Cork, in a cer-

[1] *MS. Records, Philadelphia Monthly Meeting.*
[2] *Bolles*, II., 129.

tificate, dated 5 Mo. 17, 1710, sent to Philadelphia
for Samuel Massey, tallow chandler and soap
boiler, say : "The cheife motive Represented to
us for his Remove is ye want of trade to answer
ye great Rents here and charges of his family w^{ch}
he hopes will be easier to him in that Country he
is Industrious and Carefull, and his Conversation
orderly having a wife and five children besides servants."[1]

The majority of the Friends of Munster and
many of those of Leinster lived in the cities and
Failure of towns ; but those of Ulster were largely farmers
crops, and or yeomen, and were directly affected by the
Famine memorable failure of crops in the year 1729.
Famine and sickness prevailed in that year
throughout the whole of Ulster. In spite of aid
from their brethren in England and in other provinces of Ireland, the Friends of Ulster suffered
severely,[2] and it was evidently this calamity that
caused the Pennsylvania migration to reach its
highest point in this year. Crop failures seem to
have been frequent in those times, as they are
to-day, for in a letter that has come down to us,
Mungo Bewley, a Friend of Edenderry, King's
County, Ireland, writes to Israel Pemberton, merchant of Philadelphia, under date of 1 Mo. 16,
1742–3, "Some time Since there hath been a

---

[1] *MS. Records, Philadelphia Monthly Meeting.*
[2] *Rutty*, 316.

heavy affliction over this Nation, which hath taken a Number of People off, Some for want of Bread, and many with Sore Distemper, among wch were Several worthy Friends, . . . but at present is a time of Peace, health, and great Plenty." [3]

[3] *Pemberton Papers* (MSS.), III., 61, in Library of Historical Society of Pennsylvania, Philadelphia.

CHAPTER II.

*William
Penn and
His Colony*

THE severe persecutions to which the Friends were subjected in both the Old and the New Worlds, but especially in New England, led George Fox as early as 1660, to suggest the purchase of land in America for a Quaker colony, where Friends' views and principles might be fully exemplified.[1] Fox's proposition was carried out with considerable success in the Quaker settlement of West Jersey, but it remained for the broad and liberal mind of William Penn to bring the idea to its fullest realization in the Province of Pennsylvania.

William Penn (1644–1718), as we have seen in a preceding chapter, had been convinced of the

*His
Charter*

principles of Quakerism in Ireland, and was now one of the most prominent and influential members of the sect. As one of the owners of West Jersey he had become directly interested in American colonization. His father, Sir William Penn, an admiral in the English navy, bequeathed to

---

[1] Frederick W. Stone, in *Winsor*, III., 473; *Penna. Mag.*, Vol. XXI., page xxx; *Ibid.*, VI., 174.

him a claim against the crown for sixteen thousand pounds. In payment of this he induced Charles II. (1681) to give him a proprietary charter for forty thousand square miles in America.

Penn immediately began the work of settling his colony of Pennsylvania. He offered to sell land at very low rates. "He proposed to establish a popular government, based on the principle of exact justice to all, red and white, regardless of religious beliefs ; there was to be trial by jury ; murder and treason were to be the only capital crimes ; and punishment for other offences was to have reformation, not retaliation, in view. By the terms of the Charter Penn was, in conjunction with and by the consent of the free-men, to make all necessary laws."[2] These proposals attracted widespread attention, not only among the Friends and other persecuted sects, but among many enterprising people who wanted to better their economic condition. The stream of colonists from many countries, more especially from England, Wales, and Ireland, now set in, and Pennsylvania was rapidly settled. *His Scheme of Colonizatio*

The constitution drawn up by Penn provided that the proprietor was to choose the governor, but the people were to elect the council and also the members of a representative assembly. The first assembly, called by Penn soon after his *Constitutio and Laws*

[2] Thwaites, *The Colonies*, 215.

arrival in 1682, sustained his idea of government. Among other important measures, laws were passed providing for the humane treatment of the Indians and for religious toleration.[1]

Under the wise and benificent rule of Penn, the progress of Pennsylvania was rapid. The care taken to maintain friendly relations with the *Growth of* Indians spared the colonists from the cruel Indian *the Colony* warfare of New England and left them to pursue the arts of peace uninterruptedly. The fertile soil and temperate climate made agriculture the chief industry. The soil was carefully cultivated and gave rich returns, the principal crop being wheat, although there was much variety of products. There were some small manufactories, and a good export trade in grain, flour, and furs was carried on with England and the West Indies. So prosperous was Pennsylvania that it became one of the richest and most populous of the American settlements ; and before the Revolution, Philadelphia, the great market of the province, became the largest town in the thirteen colonies.

With this brief account of the beginnings of Penn's province, let us turn our attention to those agencies that were directly influential in leading the Quakers to come to the " Promised Land " of Pennsylvania.

Penn's From his first convincement William Penn had *Invitation* been brought prominently before the Friends of

---

[1] *Thwaites*, 216.

Ireland, and was often able by the use of his power
and influence to relieve his fellow members from
their sufferings.   In 1669 he had gone to Ireland   *His Persona*
to settle some business on the Penn estates, but   *Influence*
was so affected by the general imprisonment and
persecution of Friends, that he left all private affairs and went at once to Dublin to work for their
relief.   At the General Half Year Meeting, held
at his lodgings in the city, an account of the sufferings of the Society was drawn up in an address
to the Lord Lieutenant.   Penn himself carried
the document to the Castle and presented it with
such success that Friends in prison were soon released.[1]   His general work for the good of the
Society, his own sufferings, his writings in defense
of Friends' principles, but especially his travels in
the ministry through Ireland, made him well known
to Irish Friends, and they had the greatest confidence in him.   They were among the first to
whom he opened his Pennsylvania project, for, on
March 5, 1681, the very next day after his Charter was signed, he writes to his friend, Robert
Turner, a Quaker of Dublin, stating that his
province has been confirmed, and adds : " Thou
mayest communicate my graunt to friends, and
expect shortly my proposals."[2]

The series of pamphlets descriptive of Penn-

---

[1] Janney's *William Penn*, 63-4 ; *Rutty*, 134.
[2] Stone in *Winsor*, III., 477.

sylvania, issued by Penn and others between 1681 and 1691, were widely scattered through Ireland, and the attractive accounts gave a strong impetus to the first wave of migration. The first of these pamphlets, entitled *Some Account of the Province of Pennsylvania, etc.*, a folio of eleven pages, printed in 1681, contained Penn's proposals for settlement and a general description of the country. Other pamphlets went further into details, telling of the rich natural resources of the colony, of improvements that had been made and were to be made, of the best kind of houses to build, of the ways and means of migration, and all details that intending colonists might wish to know.[1]

The Free Society of Traders was also influential in the first migration of the Irish Friends. This Society, consisting of over three hundred members, made a purchase of twenty thousand acres of land in Pennsylvania with the purpose of developing it.[2] Several of the prominent Irish Friends, as Robert Turner and Samuel Clarridge,[3] of Dublin, John White, of Carlow, and Dennis Rochford, at this time residing in England, were mem-

[1] Stone in *Winsor*, III., 495–502; reprints of pamphlets in *Penna. Mag.*, IV., 187–201, 329–342, 445–453, VI., 174–181, 312–328, IX., 62–81.

[2] Stone in *Winsor*, 497; *Penna. Mag.*, XI., 175–180.

[3] Samuel Claridge, of Dublin, became a Friend in 1655 (*Rutty*, 92). In 1660 he was imprisoned in Newgate and in 1661 in Bridwell, Dublin. He also suffered persecution in 1663 and in 1669 (*Besse*, 466, 467, 471, 473, 476, 477). In 1670 he was living near Nicholas Gate, Dublin. (Leadbeater's *Bio. Notices*, 65.)

bers. In the letter-book of James Claypoole,
secretary of the Society, we find a collection of
letters to Turner, Clarridge, and others, telling of
the activity of the Society, between 1681 and
1683, in the work of settlement.[1] Robert Turner, one of the committee of twelve at the head

of the organization, was a wealthy Quaker merchant in Dublin, and had already been actively
interested in the settlement of New Jersey.   In
1683, with his daughter and seventeen indented
servants,[2] he removed to Philadelphia, where he
took a prominent part in the affairs of the colony,
and no doubt by his personal influence did much
to forward the migration of his countrymen, "who,"
as he says in one of his many letters sent back to
Ireland, "sojourn in a Land of great distress,
wherein I have been."[3]

During the period of migration there was more
communication between Pennsylvania and Ireland
than has been generally supposed. People were
continually going back and forth, and in spite of
the difficulties and slowness of travel and the

Favorable
Reports
Returned to
Ireland

[1] *Penna. Mag.*, X., 188–202, 267–282, 401–413.
[2] *Ibid.*, VII., 334.
[3] *Ibid.*, IV., 192–3, V., 37–50.

dangers incident to those primitive times, many letters and messages were exchanged between the colonists and their friends in Ireland.

By the Traveling Ministers and Others   From the first visits of George Fox and William Edmundson to the Delaware, before Penn received his grant, to the end of the eighteenth century, a steady stream of traveling ministers came over to the Province. These preachers, and those who had come to reside in the colony, carried favorable reports of Pennsylvania to Ireland, and no doubt did much to counteract false rumors and silence objections to migration; for in the first years of the migration many Friends took a somewhat conservative attitude toward the Pennsylvania movement and carefully examined into the reasons for removal, as is instanced by the certificate given forth by Ballyhagan Meeting, County Armagh, 1 Mo. 31, 1682, and brought over to Middleton Meeting, Bucks County, by the widow Ann Millcum and her children, who arrived in the Delaware on the ship *Antelope*, 10 Mo. 10, 1682.[1] The following is quoted from the certificate:

Ann Millcum's Certificate   "The said meeting inquired of them the reason why they had a mind to such a great journey, having no man in their family except they might get a servant or servants, and having no want of things necessary for a liveli-

[1] *Penna. Mag.*, IX., 224.

hood; the said Ann Millcum replied that her daughter Jane had a great desire to go and being not willing to part with her, after such a manner, was rather willing to take her adventure with her other daughter, and so go all together, being accompanied with another daughter of hers, and her husband and children with several other neighbors also, and seeing it was her resolution to go as aforesaid," the meeting gives its consent.[1]

There were many friends also who thought that to emigrate was to fly from persecution and to desert a cause. That such views existed is shown by the certificate of removal brought over to Pennsylvania, in 1683, by Nicholas Newlin, a gentleman

Nicholas Newlin

in easy circumstances,[2] who settled in Concord, then Chester County. The certificate is as follows :

"At the request of Nicholas Newlin we do hereby certify, that the said Nicholas Newland acquainted our mens meeting with his intention of removing himself and family out of this Nation into New Jersey or Pennsylvania in America, and we have nothing to charge against him or his family as to their conversation in the

Nicholas Newlin's Certificate of Removal

[1] *Records of Middletown Monthly Meeting.*
[2] Futhey and Cope's *History of Chester County*, 668.

world since they frequented our meetings, but
hath walked honestly among men for aught we
know or can hear of by inquiry, which hath
been made, but our Friends' meeting is generally dissatisfied with his removing, he being well
settled with his family, and having sufficient
substance for food and raiment, which all that
possess godliness in Christ Jesus ought to be
contented with, for we have brought nothing
into this world, and we are sure to take nothing
out.   And he hath given us no satisfactory
reason for his removing, but our godly jealousy
is that his chief ground is fearfulness of sufferings here for the testimony of Jesus, or courting
worldly liberty—all of which we certify from our
mens' meeting at Mountmellick, 25th of 12th
Mo. 1682.   And we further certify that inquiry
hath been made concerning the clearness of
Nathaniel and John Newland, sons of said
Nicholas Newland, from all entanglements of
marriage, and that they are released for aught
we find.   Signed by the advice and in the behalf of the meeting.[1]

"TOBIAS PADWELL,
"WILLIAM EDMUNDSON,
"CHRISTOPHER ROFER."
(And others.)

[1] *Penna. Magazine*, VI., 174; Halliday Jackson's *Jackson Genealogy*,
117-118.   The above copy from the *Penna. Mag.* varies somewhat from
that printed in the *Jackson Genealogy*, where the names of two of the

The traveling ministers journeyed from meeting to meeting and from house to house among the Friends in Ireland, and in their social mingling we may well believe they did not confine their discourse to religious subjects, but when the conversation turned to Penn and his colony, an interesting topic in all Quaker households, we may be assured that these influential preachers would relate to their eager listeners accounts of their travels in America, and would give glowing accounts of that "sweet asylum" on the Delaware, where the broad and generous terms of the philanthropic founder gave opportunity for the oppressed of all nations to find a home with religious and political liberty.

Ministers traveling in Ireland tell of Pennsylvania

But aside from the work of these traveling missionaries, the later migrations were stimulated

signers are given as Tobias *Bladwell* [*Pleadweil ?*] and Christopher *Rober* [*Raper ?*].

I have tried to find the original certificate, intending to reproduce it in this work, but my search has been in vain. It is stated in a footnote of the *Jackson Genealogy*, page 118, that the copy printed in that work " was taken by J. J. Parker, of West Chester, Pa., 1 Mo. 19, 1874, from the original, which was in the possession of Nicholas Newland's granddaughter, Mary Mifflin of Hartford Co., Md., then in her 79th year" ; but Gilbert Cope, of West Chester, in a letter dated 2 Mo. 17, 1901, corrects this statement. He writes : " The *Jackson Genealogy* is in error where it says that John J. Parker copied the original Newlin certificate in 1874, as I am satisfied he never saw it. In 1888 I made an effort to locate the old document, but without success. I have two copies from different sources and have known of others, but believe no copy has been made from the original since 1820. Amongst others I wrote to Joshua Husband, Dublin, Hartford Co., Md., aged about eighty, a grandson of Mary Mifflin, and got a copy of a copy made in 1820. He obtained his copy from some one in Washington, and perhaps I should have tried to trace back on this line but did not."

Friends return to Ireland for short Visits by the return to Ireland, on short business trips, of those who had gone over to settle in Pennsylvania some years before.   In 1688, Henry Hollingsworth, of Newark or Kennett Meeting, who

had come over as a servant to Robert Turner in 1683, returned to Ireland to marry and brought back his wife.   In the latter part of 1713, Benjamin Fredd, of Concord Meeting, who had arrived in the early part of the year, made a business trip back to Ireland.   Amos Boaks, of the same meeting, came over in 1734 and made two visits to Ireland, one in 1735 and the other in 1736.   In 1738, Chester Monthly Meeting signed a certificate for Thomas Faucett, son of Thomas Faucett, to go to Lisburn Meeting in Ireland.   Many other such instances could be cited.

Favorable Reports by Letters Then, too, numerous Irish Friends made the journey merely to see the country and to visit friends and relatives.   John Parvin came over to Chester Meeting, in 1732, to make a short stay, and William Lightfoot, of Moate Meeting, County West Meath, in 1725, came to "visit his father [Thomas   Lightfoot] and relations."   After his return to Ireland,

Thomas Hutton, of Carlow, County Carlow, under date of 6 Mo. 20, 1726, writes to his sons in New Garden, that "Cousin Wm. Lightfoot tould me y' you dwelt in love."[1]

The number of favorable and urgent letters written by the first settlers back to Ireland were strong incentives for the Irish Friends to join their relatives and old neighbors in Pennsylvania. By the merest chance some of these letters have been preserved; but from hints and references to other letters in those extant we know that there must have been many others. In the meeting records, also, there are frequent references to letters sent in relation to the business of the meeting, and often these afforded opportunities for the exchange of personal messages. All these letters were read with the greatest interest in Ireland, and passed from house to house in a neighborhood, a custom also in Pennsylvania when letters came from the old home.

These letters afford us interesting glimpses of the migratory movement and of the social side of colonial life. A few of the first letters were printed in the descriptive pamphlets, but the first manuscript letter that has come under notice is one to William Porter in Ireland, from George Harlan,[2] a Friend, who had come over from

[1] *Hutton Letters* (MSS.).

[2] *Taylor Papers* (*MSS.*), *Miscellaneous*, No. 3307, Historical Society of Pennsylvania, Philadelphia.

Donnahlong, County Down, in the north of Ireland, about 1687, and who at the time of his writing, 10 Mo. 27, 1696, was living on Brandywine Creek, in Chester county, just over the famous circular line of Delaware. The communication relates particularly to the estate of Thomas Childs, an Irishman, who had died in New Castle County, at the house of Valentine Hollingsworth, another

Vallintine Hollingsworth [signature]

Irish Friend.   It is as follows :

"BRANDYWINE CREEK,
"the 27th of ye 10th month 1696.
"LOVING FRIEND
"William Porter This may acquaint thee that I have Received 4 Letters from thee all of one date and tennor being ye 20th of ye 9th m. '95 in Relation to Mary Child whose Son Thomas Died Something more than two years Since at Vallentine Hollingsworths he hapning to fall Sick there, & as to what is Reported Concerning his Bequest to his mother I have here Sent thee the Coppy of his Will on the other side. . . . I was with him in time of his Sickness and he being about to make his will I put him in mind of his Relations in Ireland and his

George Harlan's Letter, 1696

answer was thus he had never Received any
Letter Since he had been in the Countrie from
any of them Replying further he had been
troublesom to his friends in his Life time &
Questioning by Reason of the Warrs and Mor-
tallity that had been of Late in Ireland whoe
of his relations might be Living or Dead and to
Impose Soe troublesom an undertaking uppon
his friends (as the making Sale of what he had
& turning it into mony. . . .) he would not doe
it.

"Mine with my Wifes dear Love is Remembered unto thee & to the Rest of our friends &
relations Let my Bro understand that wee are
all indiffrent well & Know of no alteration Since
I wrote by Thomas Musgrave my Wifes dear
Love is Remembred in perticular to Robert
Hoop and Elenor ; having often desired to hear
from them Soe having not Else at present but
remain thy friend

George Harlan

[Endorsed.]
"Coppy of a Letter
to William Porter in
Ireland."

A series of four letters[1] written by Thomas Hutton, of Carlow, Ireland, to his sons in Pennsylvania, are interesting and full of news. The Huttons, yeomen by occupation, lived at first in New Garden, Chester County, but later some of them removed to the Friends' settlement in Berks County. Extracts from each of these letters are here inserted:

No. 1.

CARLO, 6 mo. 20, 1726. To children Joseph, Nehemiah, and John Hutton, New Garden Township, Chester Co., Pa. Letters dated 12 mo. 20, last, have been received. "Wm. Malones family y^t now is in ye small pox himself and 3 of his children but is likely to get over it except little Tom." Let James Starr and his wife hear this letter. "I cannot get your sisters with their husbands in mind to come to you & they are hard set to pay what they ow and So is Sam White his children is all got over ye small pox Samuel Wattsons wife is dead. She was an honest Concerned friend Bro: Russel & his children are all well Sam Laybourn wife & his 2 sons is well," etc. "We have a good harvest time as ever I remember, but had a great wind ye last day or 2 of last month which

---

[1] The original Hutton letters were in the possession of the late Samuel L. Smedley, of Philadelphia. These extracts were made from copies in the collection of Gilbert Cope, of West Chester, Pa.

did shake much corn & frute land is very deer
& Corn Cheap at present as also woll, but
cattle gives a good price. I desire you to remember my love to my relations and friends y^t
went hence as if I had named them one by one
for they are often with you in my mind and so
shall conclude with my deare love once more to
you my dear Children & bids you farewell farewell in y^t which Changes not."

Thomas Hutton

No. 2.

CARLO, 3 mo. 20, 1732. To "Nehemiah Hutton Living it Antilea," [Berks (?) County.]
Letter of the 14th inst. received.   ".You have
some friends near where ships harbours y^t
Comes to Ireland, & may send [letters ?] in
order to be ready at such times.   Your Mother
is not pleased that your Account is so short
about Ja: Starr and thought he might have
sent her a few lines himself for w[e] wrote to
him along with you, neither do we know where
he and his family dwells, for Nehe: writes in
his of 8 ^m 1730 y^t they were to go to one place,
& now mentions some others and to not him
nor Moses Starr, so let us know how they are
& where," etc.   "Let me know whether your
ground is Come to gras any better and if your

stock increases for we hear y^t grass doth not mend and that your ground will not bring 3 crops," etc.

"THOMAS HUTTON."

No. 3.

Hutton Letter No. 3

DUBLIN, 2 mo. 25, 1733. To Joseph and John Hutton, New Garden Township, Chester County. Letter of 7 mo. 28, 1732 received 10 mo. 28. "Tell Rob: Sharmon I writ to his father & am glad to hear y^t hes like to do well."

"THOMAS HUTTON."

No. 4.

Hutton Letter No. 4

DATED 1 mo. 22, 1733-4. To Nehemiah Hutton, "Liveing beyond Oly in Philadelphia [now Berks] County." Received a letter from Joseph, from Philadelphia, 9 mo. 22, dated 7 mo. 20, 1733; also one from Joseph and John on 19th inst., dated 10 mo. 18th last. "Lett me know if thou has got a Patent for thy Land & how thou Likes it & whether there be much flax in that part of ye Country or in any of Pensilvenia, for he I send this by intends to move thither from Belfast & he says there coms a deal of flax-seed into Ireland thence to sell very good seed it exceds dutch seed much & y^t there is a ship from thence with wheat which is well for Corn was like to be deer if it did not com from other places, y[t] wheat was sold for 16s. a barall," etc. "THOMAS HUTTON."

Benjamin Holme, of Cork, under date of 9 mo. 1, 1736, writes to Israel Pemberton, merchant, of Philadelphia, "I have wrote a Letter to William Hudson & Sam[ll] Preston & thee & some other friends to Endavor to promoate the history of the Settlement of friends & progress of truth."[1]

The following quaint letter[2] was written by John Carpenter, while traveling in Ireland, to his friend and neighbor, Michael Gregg, of Chester County. Unfortunately we have but this one letter of his; had more of his letters come down to us we should, no doubt, learn as to whether he found the girls in England more to his "fansy" and not so much like "Prispaterans," and whether he finally met the "trusty Companion" for whom he seems to have been seeking.

John Carpenter's Visit to Ireland

"DUNGANNON THE COUNTY TERONE [Tyrone]
"y[e] 19th of y[e] 2th mo: 1755
"Respected Friend: Now having an opertunity to Send thee a few Lines by way of Love and Respects to thee to let thee know that I am Safe arivd in Ireland and is now in good helth; hoping that these will find thee and all the

---

[1] *Pemberton Papers* (MSS.), III., 17, Hist. Soc. of Penna.
[2] The original MS. is in the collection of Editor William W. Polk, of the *Kennett Square* (Pa.) *Advance*.

family in like manner; I have had a very good Passage of four weeks and two Days which I was very seasick for Nine or Ten Days and I Cant say that I was Right well all the Passage for we had Very hard wether and I was a little Sick for the Most part but now I am in good helth thanks to god for the same I am very well Satesfied of my jurny but I Could be better Satesfied if I had thy Company for to Travil with me for that is all I want a trusty Companion.

"I yould have thee not marry untill thee Travils Sume the girls in this Country I believe thee wod not fansy for the are more like Prispaterans than Quakers but I Dont no what the are In England but I hope to no before two weeks for I Sales in five Days to Liverpool and from that to London by land So no more at present but Remember my love to all thy brothers and Sisters I Do Expt to Return to Pensylvania a bought harvest If I Can but I no the seas will be fowl before then We have an account that there never was such Preparation for war no more at present but Remains thy Respected friend   "JOHN CARPENTER."

            "To
    Michael Gregg
In Kennett Township
    Chester County
    Pensylvania."

By far the most important and comprehensive
of these letters is that written by Robert Parke
(1694/5–1736/7), of near Chester, to his sister Mary,
wife of Thomas Val-
entine, of Ballybrum-
hill, County Carlow,
and as it throws such
a flood of light on all phases of our subject, I venture to insert it in full. But first, a few details
about the Parke family, by way of introduction,
will give a better understanding of the migration
of a representative Irish Quaker family.

Thomas Parke (1660–1738), the father of
Robert Parke, was
a farmer and owned
several tracts of
land in Ballilean, Ballaghmore, and Coolisnacktah, County Carlow. On May 21, 1724, with all
of his family, excepting two married daughters,
he took passage at Dublin, on the ship *Sizargh*, of
Whitehaven, Jeremiah Cowman, master, and after
a rough passage of three months, on August 21st
arrived in Delaware Bay. Thomas leased a
property from an Irish Friend, Mary Head, near
Chester, as a temporary home, but on December
2d, purchased 500 acres from another Irish Friend,
Thomas Lindley, in the Great Valley of Chester
County, on the west side of what is now Downingtown, where he removed and lived the remainder

Robert Parke's Letter, 1725

The Parke Family Emigrate

of his life.   His son Robert was a clerk at Chester, and for some years acted as Recorder of Deeds. Robert died unmarried.[1]   The letter is as follows:

CHESTER TOWNSHIP the — of the 10th Mo. 1725.
DEAR SISTER MARY VALENTINE,[2]

Parke's
Letter

This goes with a Salutation of Love to thee, Brother Thomas & the children & in a word to all friends Relations & well Wishers in Generall as if named, hoping it may find you all in Good Health, as I with all our family in General are in at this present writing & has been since our arival, for we have not had a days Sickness in the family Since we came to the Country, Blessed be god for it, my father in Particular has not had his health better these ten years than since he Came here, his ancient age considered.   Our Irish Acquaintance in general are well Except Tho! Lightfoot who Departed this Life at Darby in a Good old age about 4 weeks Since.

---

[1] Parke Family, in Futhey and Cope's *History of Chester County*, 673 ; A sketch of the Parke Family, by James Pemberton Parke, of Philadelphia, in the *Chester County Journal*, issued at Downingtown, Chester County, Feb. 8, 1868.   According to J. P. Parke, Robert Parke kept a journal of the passage over in 1724, and also of a voyage made back to England and Ireland, in 1727 ; likewise of the return voyage in 1728, when the list of passengers included sixty-three servants, of whom six were brought over by Parke himself.   Unfortunately, I have been unable to locate these MS. journals, which no doubt would contain many interesting details of sea-travel during the period we have under consideration.

[2] See *Taylor Papers* (MSS.), Hist. Soc. of Penna.; letter is printed in *Penna. Mag.*, V., 349–352.

Thee writes in thy letter than there was a talk went back to Ireland that we were not Satisfied in coming here, which was Utterly false: now let this Suffice to Convince you. In *False Reports* the first place he that carried back this Story was an Idle fellow, & one of our Ship-Mates, but not thinking this country Suitable to his Idleness; went back with Cowman again, he is Sort of a Lawyer, or Rather a Lyar as I may term him, therefore I wod not have you give credit to Such false reports for the future, for there is not one of the family but what likes the country very well and wod If we were in Ireland again come here Directly it being the best country for working folk & tradesmen of *A Good Country for Working Folk* any in the world, but for Drunkards and Idlers, they cannot live well any where, it is likewise an Extradin healthy country.

We were all much troubled when we found you did not come in with Capt. Cowman as we Expected nor none of our acquaintance Except Isaac Jackson & his family, tho at his coming in one thinks it Something odd but that is soon over.

Land is of all Prices Even from ten Pounds, *Purchase of Land* to one hundred pounds a hundred, according to the goodness or else the Situation thereof, & Grows dearer every year by Reason of Vast Quantities of People that come here yearly

from Several Parts of the world, therefore thee
& thy family or any that I wish well I wod desire to make what Speed you can to come here
the Sooner the better we have traveled over a
Pretty deal of this country to seek for Land
and (tho) we met with many fine Tracts of
Land here & there in the country, yet my father
being curious & somewhat hard Please Did
not buy any Land until the Second day of 10th
mo : Last and then he bought a Tract of Land
consisting of five hundred Acres for which he
gave 350 pounds, it is Excellent good land but
none cleared, Except about 20 Acres, with a
small log house & Orchard Planted, We are
going to clear some of it Directly, for our next
Sumers fallow, we might have bought Land
much cheaper but not so much to our satisfaction.   We stayed in Chester 3 months & then
Rented a Place 1 mile from Chester, with a
good brick house & 200 Acres of Land for [?]
pounds a year where we continue till next
May.

*Cultivating
the Land*
We have sowed about 200 Acres of wheat &
7 acres of rye, this season we sowed but a
bushel· on an acre, 3 pecks is Enough on new
ground.   I am grown an Experienced Plowman
& my brother Abell is Learning.   Jonathan &
thy Son John drives for us he is grown a Lusty
fellow Since thou Saw him, we have the finest

plows here that Can be. We plowed up our
Sumers fallows in May & June, with a Yoak of
Oxen & 2 horses & they goe with as much
Ease as Double the number in Ireland. We
sow our wheat with 2 horses, a boy of 12 or 14
years old Can hold Plow here, a man Comonly
hold and Drives himself, they Plow an Acre,
nay some Plows 2 Acres a day, they sow Wheat
& Rye in August or September.

We have had a crop oats, barley & very
good flax & hemp, Indian Corn & buckwheat
all of our own Sowing & Planting this Last sum- *Good Crops*
mer, we also Planted a bushel of white potatoes
which Cost us 5 Shills & we had 10 or 12
bushels Increase, this country yields Extraordinary Increase of all sorts of Grain—Likewise
for Nicholas Hooper had of 3 Acres of Land &
at most 3 bushels of Seed above 80 bushels Increase so that it is as Plentifull a Country as
any Can be if people will be Industrious.

Wheat is 4 Shills a bushel, Rye 2s. 9d. oats
2. 3 pence, barley 3 Shills, Indian Corn 2
Shills all Strike measure, Beef is 2½ pence a *Prices for*
pound Sometimes more Sometimes less. mut- *Farm*
ton 2½, pork 2½ pr Pound Turnips 12 pence *Products*
a bushel heap'd measure & so Plenty that an
acre Produceth 200 bushells, all sorts of pro-
visions are Extraordinary Plenty in Philadelphia market, where Country people bring in

their commodities their markets are on the 4th and 7th day [Wednesdays and Saturdays crossed out] this country abounds in fruit, Scarce an house but has an Apple, Peach & Cherry orchard, as for chestnuts, Wallnuts, & hazel nuts, Strawberrys, Billberrys & Mulberrys they grow wild in the woods & fields in Vast quantities.

Country Abounds in Fruit

They also make great Preparations against harvest ; both Roast & boyled, Cakes & Tarts & Rum, stand at the Lands End, so that they may eat and Drink at Pleasure. A Reaper has 2 shills & 3 pence a day, a mower has 2 Shills & 6 pence & a pint of Rum besides meat & Drink of the best ; for no workman works without their Victuals in the bargain throughout the Country. A Laboring man has 18 or 20 pence a day in Winter.

Laborers' Wages

The Winters are not so Cold as we Expected nor the Sumers so Extreme hot as formerly, for both Summer & Winter are moderater than they ever were known, in Summer time they wear nothing but a Shirt & Linnen drawers Trousers, which are breeches and stockings all in one made of Linnen, they are fine Cool wear in Summer.

Climate

Dress

As to what thee writt about the Governours Opening Letters it is Utterly false & nothing but a Lye & any one Except bound Servants

may go out of the Country when they will &
Servants when they Serve their time may Come
away If they please but it is Rare any are such
fools to leave the Country Except mens business require it, they pay 9 Pounds for their
Passage (of this money) to go to Ireland.

There is 2 fairs yearly & 2 markets weekly *Fairs*
in Philadelphia also 2 fairs yearly in Chester &
Likewise in New Castle, but they Sell no Cattle
nor horses no Living Creatures but altogether
Merchants Goods, as hatts, Linnen & woolen
Cloth, handkerchiefs, knives, Scizars, tapes &
treds buckels, Ribonds & all Sorts of necessarys
fit for our wooden Country & here all young
men and women that wants wives or husbands
may be Supplyed. Lett this suffice for our
fairs.

As to meetings they are so plenty one may
ride to their choice. I desire thee to bring or
Send me a bottle of good Oyle fit for guns, thee
may buy it in Dublin. Martha Weanhouse Lives
very well about 4 miles from James Lindseys
[Lindley's] ; we live all together since we
Came into the Country Except hugh Hoaker
[or Stoaker] & his family who live 6 or 7 miles
from us, & follows his trade. Sister Rebecka
was Delivered of a Daughter y^e —— day the
11 month Last past its name is Mary. Abel's
wife had a young Son 12 months Since his

name is Thomas.   Dear Sister I wod not have thee Doubt the truth of what I write, for I know it to be true Tho I have not been Long here.

I wod have you Cloath yourselves well with Woolen & Linnen, Shoes & Stockings & hats for such things are dear here, & yet a man will Sooner Earn a Suit of Cloths here than in Ireland, by Reason workmans Labour is so Dear. A wool hat costs 7 Shills, a pair of mens Shoes 7 Shills, womens Shoes Cost 5 Shills 6 pence, a pair of mens stockings yarn costs 4 Shills, feather beds are very dear here and not to be had for money.   Gunpowder is 2 Shills & 6 pence a pound.   Shott & Lead 5 pence a pound.   I wod have you bring for your own use 2 or 3 good falling Axes, a pair of beetle rings & 3 Iron wedges, for they are of good ... ce here. your Plow Irons will not answer here, therefore you had better bring 1 or 2 hundred Iron, you may bring your Plow Chains as they are also a good —— Iron.

Letters going to you these you Accompt what to bring into the Country & also for your Sea Store or else I should not omitt it but besure you come with Capt. Cowman & you will be well Used for he is an honest man & has as Civell Saylors as any that Cross the Seas, which I know by Experience, the Ship has been weather bound Since before Christmas by rea-

son of frost & Ice that floats about in the River &
the Saylors being at a Loose End came down to
Chester to See us & we have given them ———.

Dear Sister I desire thee may tell my old
friend Samuel Thornton that he could give so
much Credit to my words & find no Iffs nor
ands in my Letter that in Plain terms he could
not do better than to Come here, for both his
& his wife's trade are very good here, the best
way for him to do is to pay what money he Can
Conveniently Spare at that Side & Engage *How to come*
himself to Pay the rest at this Side & when he
Comes here if he Can get no friend to lay down
the money for him, when it Comes to the worst,
he may hire out 2 or 3 Children & I wod have
him Cloath his family as well as his Small Ability will allow, thee may tell him what things are
proper to bring with him both for his Sea Store
& for his Use in this Country. I wod have him
Procure, 3 or 4 Lusty Servants & Agree to pay
their passage at this Side he might sell 2 & pay
the others passage with the money. I fear my
good will to him will be of Little Effect by reason
he is So hard of beleif, but thou mayest Assure
him from me that if I had not a particular Respect for him & his family I Should not have
writ so much for his Encouragement, his brother
Joseph & Moses Coats Came to See us Since
we came here, they live about 6 or 7 miles
apart & above 20 miles from where we live.

Unkle James Lindly & family is well & Thrives exceedingly, he has 11 children & Reaped last harvest about 800 bushels of wheat, he is a thriving man anywhere he lives, he has a thousand acres of Land, A fine Estate. Unkle Nicholas hooper lives very well he rents a Plantation & teaches School & his man dos his Plantation work.   Martha Hobson.

Dear Sister I think I have writ the most needful to thee, but considering that when I was in Ireland I never thought a Letter to Long that Came from this Country, I wod willingly give thee as full an Account as Possible, tho I could have given thee a fuller Account of what things are fit to bring here, but only I knew other Letters might Suffice in that point. I desire thee may Send or bring me 2 hundred Choice Quills for my own Use for they are very Scarce here & Sister Raichell Desires thee wod bring hir some bits of Silk for trashbags thee may bring [buy] them in Johns Zane [or Lane] also —— yards of white Mode or Silk for 2 hoods & She will Pay thee when thee comes here. I wod have brother Thomas to bring a good Saddle (& bridle) with Crooper & Housen to it by reason the horses sweat in hot weather, for they are very dear here, a Saddle that will cost 18 or 20 Shills in Ireland will cost here 50 Shills or 3 pounds & not so good neither, he had bet-

ter get Charles Howell to make it, Lett the tree
be well Plated & Indifferent Narrow for the
horses here are So Large as in Ireland, but the
best racers & finest Pacers in the World. I have
known Several that could Pace 14 or 15 miles
in an hour, I write within Compass, as for
women Saddles, they will not Suit so well here.

I wod not have thee think much at my Irregu-
lar way of writing by reason I write as it offer'd
to me, for they that write to you should have
more wits than I can Pretend to.[1]

Parke's influence seems finally to have had the
desired effect, for in the spring of 1728 we find
Thomas and Mary Valentine presenting a certificate of removal to New Garden Monthly Meeting, in Chester County.

Hundreds of just such favorable letters and
descriptions found their way to the Old World,
urgently setting forth the desirability of removal
to America and presenting the special inducements offered to immigrants in the Quaker Colony. These pleasant pictures of the happy conditions existing in Pennsylvania—the great and
good character of the Founder, his wise and liberal

---

[1] The letter ends abruptly and is not signed, but it is endorsed on the
back, "Letter to Mary Valentine from Robert Park, 10 mo., 1725." It
seems to be a rough copy kept by the writer. At the end of the letter is
written in a different hand, " And several Letters with Long full of accompt of al things George Tooke or Rooke," and on the back of the letter the name of Round is scribbled several times and the name of R. D.
Rownd.

laws, his cheap and fertile lands, the mild and healthful climate, the successful peace policy with the Indians which Penn adopted, and above all his religious toleration—filled the minds of the poor and persecuted of Europe with ardent longings, and made them leave behind forever kinsfolk and fatherland and risk all that was near and dear to them for the long and perilous journey to the strange land beyond the sea.

CHAPTER III.

TO make some attempt at an accurate determination of the places in Ireland whence
the Friends emigrated, an examination of
records of all the monthly meetings in Pennsylvania
has been made for all certificates of removal
brought over by Irish Friends between the years
1682 and 1750. With these data as a basis,
supplemented by additional facts from authentic
manuscripts, county histories, genealogies, and
other works, I have compiled the following statistical table showing as nearly as possible, the number of adult Friends that came over from each meeting, county, and province of Ireland, during the
above-mentioned period. The meetings were not
as careful to record all certificates of removal
brought over during the first two decades of the
colony, as they should have been; but later a
faithful account was kept.

The table shows that from Ulster came 172
adult members; from Leinster 183; from Munster
42; and from places which are not specified
43. This makes a total of 440 adult persons
from twenty-nine or more meetings. If, however,

we count the children and the women whose names evidently have not been recorded, and likewise those persons of whose emigration we have no record, we may safely estimate that at least between 1,500 and 2,000 Irish Friends came to Pennsylvania between 1682 and 1750.

County Armagh in the Province of Ulster sent ninety-five colonists, more than any other county. Dublin Meeting sent fifty-four, more than any other meeting. Grange Meeting, in a country district near Charlemount, County Armagh, comes next with forty-one ; then follows Ballynacree, an obscure county meeting near Ballymoney, County Antrim, with thirty-five. | The Friends from Ulster and those from Leinster, with the exception of Dublin, were almost wholly from the country districts. Some few were tradespeople, but the majority were yeomen or farmers, and when they came to Pennsylvania, they bought farms and engaged in agriculture. The Quaker colonists from Munster, on the other hand, were nearly all tradesmen from the cities and towns. They, with the emigrants from Dublin, settled for the most part in Philadelphia.

showing, as nearly as possible, the number of adult Friends that migrated to Pennsylv
inclusive.   Compiled from MS. records of all the monthly meetings of Pennsylvania, ar
(See Bibliography.)

		1682	1685	1687	1688	1689	1699-1701	1702	1705	1707	1708	1709	1710	1711	1712	1713	1714
ULSTER PROVINCE.	172																
Co. Antrim	63																
Antrim Mtg	11																
Ballinderry Mtg	12													1			
Ballinacree Mtg	35																
Lisburn Mtg.	5																
Co. Armagh	95																
Ballyhagen Mtg	28	7					1			2						2	
Grange (Upper) Mtg.	41												3				
Lurgan Mtg	26	6	1	1		1			1						1		
Co. Cavan	5																
Ballyhays Mtg	2																
Cootehill Mtg	3																
Co. Meath	9																
Old Castle Mtg	9																
LEINSTER PROVINCE	183																
Co. Carlow.	38																
New Garden Mtg.	4															2	
Carlow Mtg	34														8	7	1
Dublin	54																
Dublin Mtg	54		4					1	1	1					1	1	2
Co. Kildare	1																
Ballytore Mtg	1																1
King's Co.	8																
Edenderry Mtg	8						1										
Queen's Co.	25																
Mountmellick Mtg	22		6										3		3		
Mountrath Mtg	3																
Co. West Meath	30																
Moate Mtg	30														1	2	
Co. Wexford	13																
Cooladine Mtg	10																
Wexford Mtg	3								2					1			
Co. Wicklow.	14																
Ballycane Mtg	12								1								1
Kilcommon Mtg	2																
MUNSTER PROVINCE	42																
Co. Cork	22																
Cork Mtg	22							1		4	3	1	3				
Co. Limerick	3																
Limerick Mtg	3																
Co. Tipperary	12																
Cashell Mtg	7	4															3
Kilcommonbegg Mtg	2																2
Clonmel Mtg	3																
Co. Waterford.	5																
Waterford Mtg	5	1														2	
MEETINGS NOT SPECIFIED	43	3		3	2		1	2					2	4	1	3	3
Total	440	21	11	4	2	1	3	3	4	2	7	5	5	12	16	20	1

from each province, county, and meeting of Ireland, between the years 1682 and 1750,
plemented by county histories, genealogies, Friends' records in Ireland, and other MSS.

1717	1718	1719	1721	1722	1723	1724	1725	1727	1728	1729	1730	1731	1732	1733	1734	1735	1736	1737	1738	1739	1740	1741	1742	1743	1746	1747	1748	1749	1750
										2						1		4			1		2			1			
									2	3							5							1					
			4	4			2			9							8	5	3										
										1				1	1		1												1
										1			2			1	6	1								2	1	2	
								2	1	5		1					8		3	1	2	11		1			2		1
	1						1			8							1										2		2
																	2				1		1						
5										4																			
5						7	4		2																				
1	1		1		1	3				1	17	3	2	2			2		2	2	1		1						3
										1	2		1											3					
4	1	1																1						3					
															3														
							1		4	7					3			1											2
									2	2		1																	5
3						2	2			3																			
				2						2					1								1						
															3														
2																													
																							1						1
				2			1	1		4	4		1		1		2	1					2						
21	2	2	1	6	7	12	9	7	12	64	13	3	7	5	3	7	33	12	10	4	4	16	6	4	1	3	5	3	14

CHAPTER IV.

WAVES OF MIGRATION

THE migration may be considered in three waves. The first wave, beginning in 1682 and continuing to 1710, was caused largely by the severe religious persecutions carried on against the Friends before the Act of Toleration of 1683 was passed. The wave was the heaviest in 1682 and 1683, thirty-two adult colonists coming over in these two years. After this, the wars of James and William coming on, there was little migration until 1708. From 1710 the stream continued to flow steadily, reaching the highest point of the whole migration in the great famine year of 1729, when sixty-four adults came over. After 1710, the economic causes of migration were probably more potent than the religious.

The third wave reached its highest point in 1736, when thirty-three adult settlers arrived. From 1741, the movement declined, and after 1750 very few Friends came over to settle.

First Wave
1682-1710

Second Wave
1710-1730

Third Wave
1730-1750

CHAPTER V.

WAYS AND MEANS OF MIGRATION

The Certificate of Removal IN preparing to emigrate the Friends usually gave at least a month's notice to the meeting to which they belonged, of their intended departure, requesting that a certificate of removal, certifying to their membership in the Society, be given them to take into the new land. If, after due inquiry by a committee appointed for the purpose, the applicants were found to be in good standing in the Society and in the neighborhood in which they lived, the document was drawn up and signed by members of meeting in due time for the day of departure. In many cases, however the emigrants waited until after their arrival in Pennsylvania before writing to Ireland for the certificate. The following extract from the minutes of the Preparative Meeting at Grange, near Charlemount, Ireland, shows the mode of procedure in the preparation of the certificates :

"Att a men's meeting held y⁰ 2ᵈ of y⁰ 4ᵗʰ month [1736] Joshua March [Marsh] having an Intention to transport himself & family to America & desires from us a certificate therefore Jacob Marshill James Pillar is desired to

84

draw Suitable ones for him and his Son John allso one for Thos Willson according to his Behavour yᵗ they may be signed next meeting. William Pigion Samuel Douglas & Benjᵃ. Marshill is desired to attend next Quarterly meeting & Jacob Marshill & James Pillar is desired to draw Suitable papers to Said Meeting."

The common form of the certificate may be seen in two of those drawn up at this meeting:[1]

"From our Monthly Meeting of men & women friends held at Grange Near Charlimount in the North of Ireland yᵉ 2 of 4 mo. 1736 To friends & Brethren of pensylvania or elsewhere in America Greeting. *Certificate of Joshua Marsh*

Dear Friends whereas our friend Joshua March [Marsh] & his Wife Did Acquaint us Some Time Ago that they had a mind to transport themselves & family to pensylvania or Some place in America and Desires of us a Certificate we therefore Do Certify that He the Sᵈ Joshua & his wife was of an orderly Life & good Conversation Both amongst us their Brethren as amongst their Neighbours where they Dwelt & now Leaveth us in Unity they had also the privilege of Sitting in our Meeting of Disapline likewise their three children Viz Jonathan peter & Abigail were of Orderly Lives

[1] *Book of Certificates of Removal Received by Goshen Monthly Meeting,* Penna., p. 39.

& Conversation whilst here & is free from marriage or any Entanglement that way & all the
Above friends have left this place free from
Debts or Defraud to any man & we have Cause
to hope & believe that they will So behave
themselves for y⁰ future y' they may Deserve
y⁰ Religious notice & Care of friends for their
good.
    Signed by order & on behalf of our Sd Meet-
ing by

Mary Greer	Thos. Nichalson	William Gray
Eliz. Greer	Joseph Kerr	Jacob Marshall
Abigail King	Benjᵃ Marshill	Jno. Whitsitt
Mary Pow	James pillar	Thomas Greer
Ann Sloan	James Dawson	Tho. Griffith
Mary Pillar	francis Robson	Israel Thompson
Eliz. Dawson	Samˡ Gray	Wm. Vance
Abigail Gray	Jonaᵗ Richardson	
Ruth Delapp		

Certificate of John Marsh

[1]From our Men & Womens Meeting held at
Grange Near Charles Mount in Ireland y⁰ 2 of
y⁰ 4th mo 1736 to friends of pensylvania or
Elsewhere In America Greeting Whereas our
friends John March [Marsh] & his wife Did
sometime ago Acquaint us that they had to
transport themselves to pensylvania or Some
place In America & Desires of a Certificate we

[1]*Book of Certificates of Removal received by Goshen Monthly Meeting,*
p. 52.

therefore do Certifie y^t the Said John h &Marc his wife hath behaved themselves Orderly amongst us their Brethren & Sisters Also was of a peaceable Life & Conversation amongst their Neighbours having Left us & our Neighbours Clear of Debt They had Also privilege to Set in our Meetings for Decipline & we hope they will So behave as will deserve the Religious Notice & Care of our friends & Brethren whose it may Please Divine providence So to order their Lot to Settle & Remain.

Signed by order & on behalf of our Said Meeting by

Mary Greer	Thos. Nichalson	Jacob Marshill
Eliz. Greer	Jos. Kerr	John Whitsitt
Abigail King	Benj^a Marshil	Thos. Greer
Mary Pow	James Dawson	Thos Griffith
Ann Sloan	James Pillar	Israel Thompson
Mary pillar		Wm Vance
Eliz. Dawson		

The Marshes, father and son, purchased land and settled with their families in East Nantmeal, Chester County, and soon after their arrival presented their certificates of removal to Goshen Monthly Meeting. Whereupon the following action was taken by the meeting :

Minutes of Men's Meeting, 8 Mo. 18, 1736.—

"John Marsh Produced a Certificate to this Monthly Meeting from the Monthly Meeting of friends held at Grange near Charlemount in ye North of Ireland dated ye 2^d of ye 4 mo : 1736 in behalf of himself & wife [Elizabeth] which [is] to friends Satisfaction & ordered to be recorded."

Minutes of Women's Meeting.—

"At our Monthly Meeting held at Goshen the Eighteenth Day of the Eighth Month [1736] Elizabeth Marsh Produced to this Meeting a Certificate from Friends in Ireland jointly with her Husband which we accept on her Behalf."

Minutes Men's Meeting.—

"At our Monthly Meeting held at Goshen ye 15th day of ye 9th mo 1736 Joshua March [Marsh] Produced a Certificate to this Monthly Meeting from the Monthly Meeting of friends at Grange in Charlemount in the North of Ireland dated ye 2^d of ye 4th month last in behalf of himself & wife [Elizabeth] & 3 of his children viz. Jonathan, Peter & Abigail which is to the Satisfaction of friends here & ordered to be Recorded."

Minutes of Women's Meeting.—

"At our Monthly Meeting held at Goshen

the Fifteenth Day of the Ninth Month [1736]
. . . Elizabeth Marsh Produced to this Meeting a Certificate fron the Monthly Meeting of Grange in Ireland which this Meeting Accepts on her behalf."

The principal ports whence the Irish emigrants embarked for Pennsylvania were Belfast, Dublin, Cork, and Waterford. Frequently vessels were sailing directly from the Irish ports, but more often passage was taken in vessels which had sailed from Whitehaven, Liverpool, or Bristol, in England, and which touched at the Irish ports for passengers and cargo.[1] Philadelphia was the principal port of entry, but many settlers landed at New Castle, on the Delaware, and some few at points in Maryland and Virginia.

Places of Embarking and Landing

At times obstructions were placed in the way of Irish emigrants, as appears from the following letter written to Proprietor Penn, in 1763, by a sea captain at Dublin :[2]

Obstructions to Emigration

[1] Sometimes vessels sailing from English ports, bound for America, were driven into Irish ports by contrary winds, as stated in certificate of removal dated 6 Mo. 6, 1709, brought over from Cork to Philadelphia by Martha Griffitts, " whose Husband of Late being settled at kingstown in Jaimaca and hath wrote to his wife to com over to him and shee being willing to goe by An opertunity of Shiping that put into this Harbour by Contrary winds bound to Jaimaca."

[2] The original, which is in the Penn MSS. of the Historical Society of Pennsylvania, and which is printed in the *Penna. Mag.*, XXI., 485–7, is addressed : " To Sr Penn, Knight Proprietor of Pensilvania now in London," and is endorsed, " Letter from an Irish Captn. about Ships being stopd going to Pensilva ".

Dublin, May 3, 1736.

"Hon.ᵈ Sr.

"As you are the proprietor of pensylvania .
. . I would beg Liberty to inform your Worship
of some of the Deficulty wᶜʰ poor people that
are flying from the oppresion of Landlords &
tyeths . . . to severall parts of America Viz:
When Last our Irish parlement was sitting
there was a Bill brought in respecting the
Transportation to America which made it next
to a prohibition said Bill greatly allarmed the
people perticularly in the north of Ireland and
least a second should suckceed greater numʳˢ
than usual made ready but when said Landlords found it so the fell on with other means by
destressing the Owners & Masters of the Ships
there being now ten in the harbour of Belfast.

The methoud they fell in with first was that
when anny of said ships Advertised that they
were Bound for such a Port & when they would
be in redeness to seal & thire willingness to
agree with the passengers for which & no
other Reasons they Esued out thire Warrants
and had severall of said Owners & Masters
apprehended & likewise the printers of said
Advertisements & Bound in bonds of a thousand pounds to appear att Carrickfergus assizes
or be thrown into a Lowthsome Geoal and for
no other reason than Encuraging his Majesty's

subjects as they were pleased to call thire In-
dectment from on plantation to another. . . .
But the Judge was pleased to Discharge them.

But yett a more Hellish contrivance has been
thought of & is put in practice by Coll^r. Geo.
Maartney of Belfast he will not now when said
ships and passengers was redy to seal so
much as allow the poor people to carry thire
old Bed Cloathes with them allthow ever so old
under pretence of An Act of the British
parlement made the tenth & Eleventh Years
of the Rean of King William & Repealed in ye
year 1732 and said Ships . . . [are] obliged
to lay this affair before the Com^rs· of Dublin . .
I & likewise most of the mert^s. in this Town are
affraid of success even with the Com^rs· will be
obliged to lay it before the Lord Lieut. of this
Kingdom & if that should feal than nothing less
than his Majesty's Gratious Interpotion can effect
. . . but a loss what does that in the meantime
when no less then ten ships has been these 18
or 20 days and no aperance of getting away
and advanst charge the seson passing and which
is yet much moveing 17 or 18 hun^d. many of
which are in most deplorable circumstances not
being so much as able to pay thire passage and
all of them destitute of howses to put thire
heads into or of means wherewith to support
themselves maney of which has depended on

their Friends in America from home they yearly
have Accts and one [torn] they only depend
for thire information.   But our Landlords here
affirms that these Accts are all of them
Forgerys & Lyes the Contrivances of the proprietors Trustees & Masters of the American
Ships. . . .

"Your Hon^{rs} Most Hum^{bl} & Most obt Ser

"John Stewart."

.   .   .   .

"N. B.   I did not think proper in the body of
the Letter to acquaint Your Honr y^t of those
ten Ships there is eight bound for Dalour
[Delaware] & verry connciderable with them.
I am &c.

"John Stewart."

Dangers of Voyage   The voyage was a long and trying one, especially so when attended by rough weather.   The
length of the passage varied all the way from six
weeks to three months.   Vessels were often
driven far out of the course by contrary winds and
carried as far south as the West Indies.   Dangerous diseases, such as small-pox, were of frequent
occurrence, and many passengers died at sea.
During the French Wars, vessels were often attacked and the passengers imprisoned or subjected to loss of property and to harsh treatment.
As an instance of this, may be cited the case of

Samuel Massey and family who sailed from Cork in 1710, intending for Philadelphia, but the vessel was seized by the French and they were carried off to the Island of Antigua in the West Indies.[1] Finally, after much suffering and hardship, they reached Philadelphia, but so impoverished that they were unable to pay for their passage from Antigua, and Philadelphia Monthly Meeting had to assist them to the extent of thirty pounds. The French had taken even their certificate of removal, and Massey had to request the meeting in Cork to send a duplicate certificate. [2]

In 1728, Robert Parke, while on the return voyage from a business journey to England and Ireland, notes in his diary[3] that there were a number of cases of small-pox aboard, several persons dying with it. Under date of June 11, 1728, he says: "This day one Margaret Darlington took the small pox and three of her children being

Robert Parke's Diary of a Voyage from Ireland, 1728

[1] In a certificate of removal, dated 7 Mo. 12, 1752, received at Wilmington Monthly Meeting, Delaware, Ballycane Meeting, County Wicklow, states that Elizabeth Robinson removed with her husband, Francis Robinson, from Ballycane some years before and has now requested the said certificate. "We also some years ago Gave he[r] a certificate to the same purpose which with her Daughter was taken by the french and miscarried."

[2] See *MS. Records of Philadelphia Monthly Meeting: Book of Certificates Received* and *Men's Minutes, 1682–1714*, Vol. I., 288–289 ; *Penna. Mag.*, VII., 473, note ; Philadelphia *Friend*, LII., 101–2, 106–7. Sarah, wife of Samuel Massey, was a daughter of Thomas Wight, of Cork, the original author of Rutty's *Rise and Progress of the Quakers in Ireland*, printed in 1751.

[3] Cited by J. P. Parke. See footnote, page 71.

down in it. Our true course is judged to be south."
It seems that even in those days the sailors were
ready to exact tribute from the unwary landsman.
On June 14th, Parke writes : "This day Samuel Ask
and I paid our observing muggs on the fore staff."
It is inferred from this that the sailors demanded
a mug of grog from any one who took an ob-
servation of the sun by means of the "fore staff"
or "cross-staff," the predecessor of the sextant.
Another curious incident of the voyage is thus
quaintly recorded in the diary, as of July 3 :

"At 12 last night we seen a light right a starn
which some caled the half way house and said,
'There lived one Peg Trotter.' Then all hands
were called upon deck to se the said house and
if possible to purchase some buttermilk for the
passengers. It caused great rejoicing among all
hands fore and aft. It contained a light upwards
of one hour and half. The above light we put out
on purpose to encourage the passengers, it being
the imitation of yᵉ half way house. It was a
pitched barrel fixed in a large tub."

A Favorite
Vessel
One of the favorite vessels with the emigrants
was the *Sizargh* of Whitehaven, Jeremiah Cowman, master. The Parkes, Jacksons, and many
other Irish Friends, settlers in Chester County,
came over on her. Robert Parke says in his letter of 1725 : "Be sure you come with Capt. Cowman & you will be well used for he is an honest

man and has Civell Saylors as any that Cross the
Seas, which I know by Experience, the Ship has
been weather bound Since before Christmas by
reason of frost & Ice that floats about in the River
& the Saylors being at a Loose End Came down
to Chester to See us."

The following advertisement of this vessel appeared in the *American Weekly Mercury*[1] a
newspaper printed at Philadelphia, September 2,
1731:

"For BRISTOL directly.

THE SHIP *Sizargh, Nathan Cowman* Master
she being almost Loaded, and intends to Sail in
Ten Days for the above Port, if any Persons
have a mind to take Passage on Board the said
Ship they may apply to said Master on Board
where they may agree on reasonable Terms
and be kindly used."

The meetings in Pennsylvania, and particularly   Immigrants
Philadelphia Monthly Meeting, extended a pater-   Assisted by
nal care over immigrant Friends, advising them   Meetings
as to settlement and frequently rendering needed
financial assistance, especially in the payment of
passage money, as in the case of Samuel Massey,
just referred to. As early as 1685, Philadelphia
Monthly Meeting took action in the matter, as appears by the following extracts from the Minutes:

[1] Files of this newspaper are in the collection of the Historical Society
of Pennsylvania.

9 Mo. 2, 1685.—"It being taken notice of by several friends of this meeting, that this meeting is greatly burthened and oppressed by the increase of the poor, more than any other place in the province by reason of people's general landing here, the meeting appoints Edward Luffe to mention the same at the Quarterly meeting for their conversation & advise for assistance."

11 Mo. 4, 1685.—"The testimony of advice to friends from Frances Taylor before she deceased, was read and ordered to be Recorded, and as to that part of her advise for counselling such as come over from England, at their first arrival, what course to take, to manage what they bring and also relating to their settlement," a committee of thirteen is appointed "to Enquire as Ships come in, and as occasion presents Give account to the monthly and Quarterly meeting."

At Philadelphia Monthly Meeting, 8 Mo. 25, 1711, "The widow of Mark Carlton applies herself to this meeting for advice in relation to her affairs, being lately come from Ireland. In order, therefore, Anthony Morris and Richard Hill are desired to assist her with the best advice they are capable of." And, 7 Mo. 24, 1736, "A Certificate from the Mens Meeting at Coote Hill in Ireland dated the 21st Second Month 1736 on behalf of Isaac [Isaiah] McNiece who intends to settle in this City was read and well received, the Meeting being apprised that he labours under some Difficulty to raise Money to pay his passage Consent to lend four Pounds which Sum John Jones is directed to let him have and take his Obligation payable in twelve Months."

Many of the Irish Friends who came to Pennsylvania were young men just starting out in the world, and it was quite common for them to bring with them letters of introduction from well-known Friends in Ireland to prominent Friends in Pennsylvania, requesting assistance for the young immigrants in securing business positions. A letter of this character is preserved among the Pemberton Papers of the Historical Society of Pennsylvania. John Barclay writes from Dublin, June 17, 1743, to Israel Pemberton, of Philadelphia:

"I send this by Thos: Henderson 3d Son to our late Friend Patt^k Henderson[1] who left a great Family of Children behind & this Young Man inclined to go to your Country, he has

[1] Patrick Henderson, the author of a work called *Truth and Innocence, The Armour and Defense of the People called Quakers,* was a prominent minister among the Friends in the North of Ireland. In 1707, accompanied by Samuel Wilkinson, he travelled on a gospel mission throughout the limits of Philadelphia Yearly Meeting. " Patrick Henderson," writes James Logan to William Penn, " is I think Scotch by birth, and is a most extraordinary young man as ever visited these parts."—*Bowden,* II., 227.

7

been of a Sober Conversation so far as I know of, the Ship going away Sooner than his Mother & he expected, they did not ask for a Certificate from Mountmelick Meeting in time, but I believe there will be one Sent after him ℔ next Ship. He has no great stock I believe to trade with therefore I should think it would be advisable to get him into Some Friends Counting house."

Emigrants Assisted by Meetings in Ireland   The meetings in Ireland also gave assistance to their needy emigrant members. An instance of this is found in the Minutes of the Preparative Meeting of Grange, near Charlemount. At the meeting 2 Mo. 3, 1741, " Patrick Holm & his wife also Hugh Kenedy & his family having Laid before our meeting their Intention of Removing to America, they being poor friends & in want of help therefore this meeting agrees that William Delap doe Lay out ye Sum of fifteen pounds Ster : to help to pay their fraughts and other necessaries for ye Jurnay untill he be paid ye Same out of ye Interest Left to poor friends of this meeting also John Whitsit James Pillar William delap Thos Greer & Benjn Marshill are Desired to Draw Suitable Certificates for ye S^d Hugh Kenedy and for Jacob Hinshaw & his wife who Intends ye Same Journy."

The Cost of Passage   The cost of passage varied somewhat according to the time, but was, as Robert Parke states

in his letter, about £9. Some of the ways of paying the expense of the sea voyage are suggested
by Parke. He says : " I desire thee may tell my
old friend Samuel Thornton . . . to Come here
for both his & his wife's trade are Very good
here, the best way for him to do is to pay what
money he Can Conveniently Spare at that Side &
Engage himself to Pay the rest at this Side &
when he Comes here if he Can get no friend to
lay down the money for him when it Comes to
the worst, he may hire out 2 or 3 Children & wod
have him Cloath his family as well as his Small
Ability will allow, thee may tell him what things
are proper to bring with him both for his Sea
Store & for his use in this Country. I wod have
him Procure 3 or 4 Lusty Servants & Agree to
pay their passage at this Side he might sell 2 &
pay the others passage with the money."

It was a frequent occurrence for poor emigrants
to sell themselves into temporary servitude,
usually for a term of four years, in order to de-
fray the cost of their transportation to Pennsylvania. On engaging passage the emigrants made
an agreement or indenture with the shipmaster
that they were to be sold after their arrival, and
were known on this account as indented servants
or redemptioners. It is evident from certificates of **Redemptioners**
removal and other manuscripts that many Friends,
particularly those from Ireland, arrived in this

manner.[1] The redemptioners could not be sold
out of the Province without their consent freely
given in open court or before a justice of the
peace. At the end of their service, if their behavior merited it, they received a suit of clothes,
a set of tools of the occupation in which they were
engaged,[2] and frequently a sum of money, and those
who had come over with first purchasers were
allowed by Penn to take up fifty acres of land at
a rent of one half-penny an acre per annum.[3]

Many of the Irish Friends brought over indented
servants and disposed of them to advantage in
the colony, where there was a great demand for
laborers. William Pim writes in 1732, from Chester County, Pennsylvania, to his uncles in Ireland,
that he had lost a servant, "Jo: Gavin, by the
small-pox," and adds, "I am in expectation of Ja:
Nicholson in a little time, ℔ whom I expect an
acct from Ireland & if he dont bring me a servant
or servants I shall be in great want, for I am soe
now. I hired an Indifferent hand lately at Husbandry & it cost me 36[s] for 4 weeks (and diet)."[4]

1 Mungo Bewley, a minister, who made a religious visit to Pennsylvania
in 1732, in writing from Edenderry, Ireland, to Israel Pemberton, of
Philadelphia, under date 1 Mo. 16, 1742–3, says : "I now Send these
lines by the Hands of Samuel & Joshua Fayle the sons of a Poor Friend
belonging to our Meeting who is for transporting themselves into your Country as Servants as also a Certificate from our mens meeting recommending
of them." The Fayles were probably grandsons of William Edmundson.
2 John Fiske's *Dutch and Quaker Colonies in America*, II., 325–6.
3 Futhey and Cope's *History of Chester County*, 154, 430.
4 See Pim Family in Appendix.

When Robert Parke returned from his business trip to Ireland, in 1728, he brought with him six servants, there being sixty-seven others on board the vessel.

Among the earliest and most prominent of the Irish Friends to bring in servants was Robert Turner, who arrived at Philadelphia in 1683, with his family and a cargo of seventeen redemptioners. Fortunately, a list of these, with their time of service and other interesting particulars, has been preserved and is given herewith :[1]

Robert Turner Redemptioners.

" In the Lion of Leverpoole,—

Robert Turner late of Dublin in Ireland, merch^t came in y^e Lion of Leverpoole, John Crumpton M^r. arrived here [Philadelphia] the 14th $\frac{mo.}{8}$ 1683 [Child] Martha Turner.

Servants.	Time of Service.	Payment in Money.	Acres of Land.	Time of Freedom.
Robt. Threwecks...	4 yrs.	£8	50	
Henry Furnace......	4 "	3	50	
Robt. Selford	4 "	6.10	50	
Ben: Acton..........	4 "	3	50	
John Reeves.........	4 "	6.10	50	14 $\frac{mo.}{8}$ 1687
Row: Hambridge...	4 "	....	50	
Richard Curlis......	4 "	3	50	
John Furnace........	4 "	3	50	
Daniel Furnace	9 "	....	50	14 $\frac{mo}{8}$ 1692
Robert Threewecks	13 "	....	50	14 $\frac{mo}{8}$ 1695
Lemuel Bradshaw..	4 "	2.10	50	
Robt. Lloyd	4 "	4	50	14 $\frac{mo}{8}$ 1687
Wm. Louge	4 "	3	50	
Hen. Hollingsworth	2 "	....	50	14 $\frac{mo}{8}$ 1685
Aiolce Cales.........	4 "	3	50	14 $\frac{mo}{8}$ 1687
Kath: Furnace......	6 "	....	50	14 $\frac{mo}{8}$ 1689
Jos. Furnace.........	4 "	3	50	14 $\frac{mo}{8}$ 1687

[1] "Families who arrived at Philadelphia, 1682–1687," in *Penna. Mag.*, VIII., 334.

Owing to harsh treatment and to dissatisfaction with their condition of servitude, the redemptioners were continually running away, and much of the business of the provincial courts consisted in hearing the complaints of masters and servants. The colonial newspapers are filled with advertisements of rewards offered for the return of bond servants, such as the following[1] by James Logan, the most eminent of the Irish Quakers in Pennsylvania :

James Logan's Runaway Servant
"RUN away from James Logan's Plantation near German Town the 28th Instant, an Irish Servant Lad, named Patrick Boyd, aged about 17 or 18 years, with streight dark Hair, a freckled Face and a smooth Tongue, cloathed with a double-Breasted Pee-Jacket, a brownish Kersey Coat, a Pair of Leather Briches, and a good Felt Hat; but he had other Cloaths with him. Also a fine short Fowling Piece of a Carbine Length, or less. He went in Company with one Miles MacWard. Whoever takes and secures him shall be well rewarded for their Trouble."

[1] From the *American Weekly Mercury*, issued at Philadelphia, Thursday, March 3, 1721. A facsimile of this early newspaper (Hist. Soc. of Penna.) was published by the Colonial Society of Pennsylvania, 1900.

PART III.

THE IRISH FRIENDS IN PENNSYLVANIA

CHAPTER I.

A S the population of the Province increased
by birth and immigration, the richest lands
of the old settlements along the Delaware
were purchased and placed under cultivation, with
a resultant rise in value ; and the later comers, if
unable to purchase the best lands, or if not satisfied with the less desirable lands, had to seek out
fertile plantations in the forest wilds beyond the
pale of the settlements. The latter course was
usually pursued by the greater part of the later
immigrants, excepting those who settled in the
towns ; for to a large extent these people had but
small means with which to establish themselves
in the new country,

Although some few Irish Friends came over
during the first decade of the Colony and secured
good lands in the old settlements, the greater part
of them arrived later, after the best lands had been
seated, and having little other capital than strong
arms and brave hearts, the farming element in
particular were obliged to leave behind the cultivated districts and push into the wilderness to fell
the forests and clear the land for the upbuilding
of the frontier homes.

The table given herewith shows that fully ninety per cent. of the Irish Friends presented their certificates of removal to Philadelphia Monthly Meeting and to the monthly meetings of Chester County, then including Delaware County. Chester County heads the list with nearly sixty-five per cent. of the total number, or two hundred and eighty-three adults, eighty-two of these being received at monthly meetings in what is now Delaware County. Philadelphia follows with twenty-six per cent. of the whole, or one hundred and seventeen adults. After Philadelphia Monthly Meeting comes New Garden, with one hundred adults ; then Kennett, formerly Newark, with eighty-two ; and Chester, with sixty-three.

A large number of the Irish Friends remained within the limits of the monthly meetings to which they brought their certificates, but many of them made only a temporary home until a more suitable location could be found. The tradespeople, who were chiefly from Dublin, Cork, Waterford, Limerick, and Wexford, naturally settled in Philadelphia, where conditions seemed most favorable for their occupations and for their former mode of life. On the other hand, the farmers, or yeomen, who came largely from the country districts of Ulster and Leinster, and who constituted the greatest part of the migration, mostly sought out farms away from the towns.

A Statistical Table, showing, as nearly as possible, the number of adult Friends who migra
1682–1

	1682	1683	1687	1688	1689	1699-1701	1702	1705	1707	1708	1709	1710	1711	1712	1713	1714	1715
BUCKS COUNTY...... 12																	
Falls Mo. Mtg...... 1													1				
Buckingham Mo. Mtg...... 2																	
Wrightstown Mo. Mtg...... 4																	
Middletown Mo. Mtg...... 5	4														1		
MONTGOMERY COUNTY [1]...... 14																	
Abington Mo. Mtg......10										1							
Gwynedd Mo. Mtg...... 4																	
PHILADELPHIA COUNTY......117																	
Philadelphia Mo. Mtg......117	6	3	1	1		3	1	4	2	6	3		7		1	3	1
DELAWARE COUNTY [2]...... 82																	
Radnor Mo. Mtg...... 3																	
Chester Mo. Mtg......63	11	8										1		3	3	4	2
Concord Mo. Mtg......16														2	4	1	
CHESTER COUNTY......201																	
Kennett Mo. Mtg...... 82			3	1	1		2				2	4	4	11	11	2	
New Garden Mo. Mtg......100																	
Bradford Mo. Mtg......... 7																	
Goshen Mo. Mtg......12																	
LANCASTER COUNTY [3]...... 6																	
Sadsbury Mo. Mtg...... 6																	
YORK COUNTY [4]...... 8																	
Warrington Mo. Mtg...... 8																	
Total......440	21	11	4	2	1	3	3	4	2	7	5	5	12	16	20	10	3

[1] Formed from Philadelphia County in 1784.
[2] Formed from Chester County in 1789.

ited from Ireland to each monthly meeting and county in Pennsylvania, during the period 750.

1716	1717	1718	1719	1721	1722	1723	1724	1725	1727	1728	1729	1730	1731	1732	1733	1734	1735	1736	1737	1738	1739	1740	1741	1742	1743	1746	1747	1748	1749	1750
											1													1						
																							1	2		1				
	1										1			4			1						2							
						2									1					1										
1	7		1		2		1	1	2	4	18	2	2	1		1	1	6		2	2	2	4	1	2		1			11
	2																						1							
7	6						10		1	1						1		5												
		1			2		1							1		1		1				2								
7	6		1	1				1	2		7	1	1	3				3		1	1	1			2				2	1
					2	5		7	2	7	37	5		1	5		3	14	4	2			4		1	1				1
																		3	2	1					1					1
																	7		2				2							1
																3	1						2							
																											2	3	2	1
15	21	2	2	1	6	7	12	9	7	12	64	13	3	7	5	3	7	33	12	10	4	4	16	6	4	1	3	5	3	14

[3] Formed from Chester County in 1729.

[4] Formed from Lancaster County in 1749.

Philadelphia, as the metropolis of the new Prov- *Philadelphia*
ince, became better known in the Old World than
any other part of Pennsylvania, and a large proportion of the steady stream of Quaker colonists
which poured into the country made this city its
objective point; and of the nineteen monthly
meetings established in Pennsylvania prior to
1750, as the writer's investigations have shown,
Philadelphia Monthly Meeting easily ranked first
as to the number of certificates of removal received.

The first Quaker settlers on the west side of
the Delaware, within the present limits of Philadelphia, attended business meetings of the Society at Burlington, in New Jersey, but as their
numbers increased they established a meeting of
their own early in the year 1682, at Thomas Fair- *First Meeting*
man's house at Shackamaxon, now Kensington, *at Shacka-*
where in the autumn of the same year William *maxon*
Penn is reputed to have made his Great Treaty
with the Indians. Later in this memorable year a
meeting was founded in the city proper, and a
temporary house of worship called "the boarded
meeting-house" was erected. This structure, it is
supposed, was located on Front above Arch Street,
where afterwards the Bank Meeting House was
built, in 1685.

The Bank Meeting House was intended for *Bank Meet-*
First-day afternoon meetings, and the Center *ing House*

Square Meeting House, built in 1685–86, where the City Hall now stands, for the more important *Center* First-day morning and business meetings ; but as *Square Meet-* the Center Square was in the midst of the forest, *ing House* far from the center of the town's population along the Delaware, the meeting was not well attended, the Friends preferring to wait for the afternoon meeting at the Bank Meeting rather than take the long walk to the morning meeting at Center Square, so that in a few years the meeting here was abandoned.

In 1695 the Great Meeting House was built at *Great Meet-* the southwest corner of Second Street and High *ing House* (now Market) Street, opposite the spot, where several years later the historic Old Court House was placed. This meeting house with some additions was used until 1754, when it gave way to a more commodious building. Here for more than a century were held the most important business and religious meetings of the Society in the City.[1]

The Irish Friends of Philadelphia, with the notable exceptions of James Logan, Thomas Holme, Robert Turner, and some others, seem to have taken but a small part in meeting and civil affairs, and in associating with other nationalities appar-

[1] Proud's *Pennsylvania*, I., 229 ; Watson's *Annals of Philadelphia*, 299–300, 335–338 ; Michener's *Retrospect*, 50–52 ; Jacob R. Elfreth's "Philadelphia Meeting Houses," in *The American Friend* (Philadelphia) Vol. VII. (1900); *Minutes of Philadelphia Monthly Meeting*.

ently soon lost those characteristics which had been acquired in their Irish environment. For this reason little will be said of them collectively, but attention will be given to those Irish Friends who removed to the country districts, usually to settle, clanlike, near each other, and who intermarried and for generations preserved much of their racial identity.

Several families of Irish Friends produced certificates of removal to the Monthly Meetings of Falls, Middletown, Buckingham, and Wrightstown, in Bucks County, but they were too few in number to deserve further mention than is given in the Appendix.

Bucks County

A few Irish Friends came to the Monthly Meetings of Gwynedd and Abington, in what is now Montgomery County, but their number was also small.

Montgomery County

Although no certificates from Ireland were received at Exeter[1] Monthly Meeting in Berks County, yet many Irish Friends, who had first settled in New Garden and other places in Chester County, removed there and settled within the limits of the meetings of Exeter and Maiden Creek. Conspicuous among these Friends were: Moses

Berks County

[1] The Particular Meeting of Oley, later called Exeter, was established by Gwynedd Monthly Meeting, in 1721, and the Monthly Meeting in 1737. Among the first Friends to settle here was George Boone, originally from Bradwinck, near Exeter, Devonshire, England, grandfather of Daniel Boone, the celebrated Kentucky pioneer.—Howard M. Jenkins' *Gwynedd*, 80, 325 *et seq.*

Starr, from County Meath, justice of the peace
and first representative from Berks County into the
Provincial Assembly; Benjamin Lightfoot, justice
of the peace and sheriff of Berks County, 1752–
1754; Francis Parvin, from County West Meath,
justice of the peace and representative to the Provincial Assembly; and Nehemiah Hutton (son of
Thomas), from County Carlow.

Delaware County   As the table shows, eighty-two adult Irish
Friends arrived at the three monthly meetings in
what is now Delaware County, sixty-three being
received at Chester Monthly Meeting, sixteen at
Concord Monthly Meeting, and but few at the
Welsh Monthly Meeting at Radnor, or Haver-
ford, with its subordinate or particular meetings of
Haverford, Radnor and Merion (Montgomery
County).

Chester Monthly Meeting   Robert Wade, an English Friend, the first member of the Society to locate on the west side of the
Delaware, settled among the Swedes and Dutch on
the west bank of Chester Creek at Upland, later

First Meeting in Pennsylvania at Upland, 1675 called Chester, in 1675, and in that year William
Edmundson,[1] then on a religious visit to the
American colonies, held a meeting at his house.[2]
This was the first Friends' meeting held in the
Province of Pennsylvania.[2] A meeting was prob-
ably held regularly after 1677, by which time

[1] *Journal*, 108.
[2] Ashmead's *Delaware County*, 334; Dr. Smith's *Delaware County*,
103–4.

several other Friends had arrived in the neighborhood.[1] No doubt the First-day and mid-week meetings continued to be held at Robert Wade's house, known as Essex House, until 7 Mo. (September) 11, 1682, shortly before the coming of William Penn, when the Monthly Meeting "agreed y^t a meeting shall be held for ye service & worship of god every first day at ye court house[2] at Vpland."[3]

It was at the landing place opposite the famous Essex House that the Proprietor first touched the soil of the Province which bears his name. Penn sailed from[4] Deal, in England, 6 Mo. (August) 30, 1682, on board of the ship *Welcome*, of three hundred tons burden, Robert Greenaway, commander, in company with about one hundred passengers, mostly Friends from Sussex, among whom was at least one party of Irish Friends, Dennis Rochford, with his family and two servants, originally from Enniscorthy, County Wexford.[5] Great distress was experienced during the passage in consequence of the breaking out of small-pox,

Arrival of William Penn, 1682

Irish Friends on Board the " Welcome"

[1] Futhey and Cope, *History of Chester County*, 230.

[2] This court house was doubtless "ye house of defence att upland" ordered to be completed and fitted up for the use of the Upland Court, in 1677.—Dr. Smith's *Delaware County*, 114, 137.

[3] Futhey and Cope, *Chester County*, 231.

[4] The *London Gazette* of September 4, 1682, announced that on August 31, "sailed out of the Downs three ships bound for Pennsylvania on board of which was Mr. Pen, with a great many who go to settle there."—Stone in *Winsor*, III., 480.

[5] Futhey and Cope, *Chester County*, 23.

of which thirty of the emigrants died, among them being two of Rochford's daughters. In this trying situation, writes Richard Townsend, one of the passengers, Penn's "care was manifested in contributing to the necessities of many, who were sick of

MEMORIAL STONE AT CHESTER, MARKING LANDING PLACE
OF WILLIAM PENN, 1682.

the Small-pox." [1] Otherwise the voyage was prosperous, the vessel arriving, 8 Mo. (October) 27, at New Castle, where Penn landed and with much ceremony received from the inhabitants "turf and twig and water," the feudal signs of his possession of the Three Lower Counties. [2] The next

[1] *Proud*, I., 228.
[2] Hazard's *Annals of Pennsylvania*, 597.

day the *Welcome* stood up the Delaware and casting anchor off the mouth of Chester Creek Penn
landed, and was hospitably received and entertained by Robert Wade at Essex House.[1]

As early as 1687, steps were taken for the
building of a meeting-house at Chester, but this
was not finally accomplished until in 1693, when
a stone structure was erected on the east bank
of Chester Creek.

*First Meet-
ing House at
Chester, 1693*

The first "monthly meeting of friends belonging to marcus hooke & vpland held then at Robert
Wad's house," occurred "the 19 day of y⁰ 11
month, 1681," and was the first monthly meeting
established in Pennsylvania. The Monthly Meeting was sometimes held at Chester, possibly at
Robert Wade's house or perhaps at the old Court
House, where the Particular Meeting of Chester
was held; but at a Monthly Meeting held 12 Mo.
7, 1686, it was "order'd yᵗ yᵉ monthly meeting
from hence forthe be kept at Walter fossett's[2]
house [in Ridley Township] untell farther order."

*Monthly
Meeting Es-
tablished, 1681*

---

[1] *Proud*, I., 204–206; Dr. Smith's *Delaware County*, 138–139; Ashmead's *Delaware County*, 20.

[2] Walter Faucett, with his wife Grace, arrived at Chester as early as
1684. For a time I thought it probable that he had come from Ireland,
whence came the other Faucetts of Chester Monthly Meeting, but Gilbert
Cope, of West Chester, Pa., informs me that Walter Fawcet, of Haverah
Park, in the West Riding of Yorkshire, England, was married, 3 Mo. 23,
1675, in a Friends' Meeting, at Henry Settle's house, Harefield, in Nether-
dale, Yorkshire, to Grace Atkinson. Besse notes in *Sufferings of the
Quakers* (II., 156) that in 1683 one "Walter Fawcett, for being at a

8

FIRST MEETING HOUSE OF FRIENDS AT CHESTER, BUILT 1693.

Thus it continued until 1693, when it began to
"circulate" at the houses of John Simcock, in
Ridley; Robert Vernon, Thomas and Randall
Vernon, and John Edge, in Nether Providence;
George Maris, Joseph Stedman and Bartholo-
mew Coppock, Jr., in Springfield; and Caleb
Pusey,[1] at Chester Mills, near Chester. After 1700,
meeting-houses having been erected for the par-
ticular meetings constituting Chester Monthly
Meeting — especially for Chester, Springfield,
Providence and Middletown—the Monthly Meet-
ing circulated more at the meeting-houses, finally

meeting at Askwith [four miles southwest of Haverah Park], had taken from
him two Oxen worth £9," and that in 1684 " For Meetings at Skipworth,
were taken from Walter Fawcett, two Oxen worth £9 " (II., 159). Besse
also notes (II., 122) : " May 27d, 1670. At a Meeting of Quakers at the
House of Thomas Fawcett, at Hawes in Wenslydale ['Wenslydale North-
Riding, in the County of York'] : His Fine £20 " ; and June, 12, 1670,
at a meeting at Bainbrigg Pastures, Yorkshire, Thomas Fawcett had a fine
taken from him (II., 123). Walter Faucett settled on the north-east
side of Ridley Creek, his land extending to Crum Creek, and took a
prominent and active part in civil affairs and in meeting work, being a minister among Friends. In 1685 he was appointed one of the *Peace Makers*
for Chester County—then an office of considerable responsibility—and also
served one year as a member of the Assembly. For many years Chester
Monthly Meeting was held at his house, notwithstanding that it was kept as
a tavern or inn for at least part of the time. His wife Grace having died
in 1686, he was married to Rebecca Fearne, of Darby, in 1694. He died
in 1704, leaving two sons—John (who married Grace Crook) and Nathan,
by his first wife ; and three daughters, Rebecca, Mary and Sarah, by his
second wife. In 1698 he paid a religious visit to England (Dr. Smith's
Delaware County, 462).

[1] Caleb Pusey's house, built in 1682, is still standing at Upland, near
Chester, in a good state of preservation, and is the oldest building in
Pennsylvania.

becoming settled at Providence[1] (near the present Borough of Media).

Concord
Monthly
Meeting   A particular meeting was established by Chester Monthly Meeting at Chichester, in the latter part of 1682, and a meeting-house was built in 1688 on

Chichester   a tract of two acres of land given to the meeting
Meeting   by James Brown. This building was destroyed by fire in 1768, and the present house erected the following year.[2]

Concord
Meeting   Concord Particular Meeting was regularly established in 1685; for at Chester (now Concord) Quarterly Meeting, 9 Mo. 1, 1685, "It is agreed y[t] y[e] meeting formerly held at John Gibbons house should from this time forward be held one first day & one fourth day at John Gibbons' & another first day & fourth day at Nicholas Newland's, until further order." At the meeting 6 Mo. 2, 1686, it was "Agreed y[t] y[e] meeting formerly ordered to be one first day at Nicolas Newland's[3] and y[e] other first day at John Gibbon's be from this time removed & kept at Nicholas Newlands only, till further order (viz.) y[e] first & fourth days meeting." 9 Mo. 4, 1695, "it was agreed that Concord meeting which was moveable be now fixed at the *new meeting house*."[4] It would seem

[1] Futhey and Cope, *Chester County*, 230–231.
[2] *Ibid.*, 232–233; Ashmead, 450–1.
[3] Nicholas Newlin and his son Nathaniel who were from Mountmellick Meeting, Queen's County, Ireland, settled in Concord in 1683, and were the most prominent Friends of Concord Meeting.
[4] Futhey and Cope, *Chester County*, 232.

from the latter extract that the meeting-house was erected as early as 1695. In 1728 the old wooden meeting-house was replaced by a brick building. In 1788 this structure was consumed by fire and the present meeting-house erected.[1]

Birmingham Meeting, in Birmingham Township, Chester County, was subordinate to Concord Monthly Meeting until its erection into a monthly meeting in 1815. The meeting was first held " att John Bennet's house," in 1704. The first meeting-house was built about 1721 on an acre of ground " near the Great Road," conveyed to the Meeting by Elizabeth, widow of Richard Webb, for a consideration of £3. The present meeting-house was built in 1763, Benjamin Hawley noting in his diary of that year that he "went to the Raising of ye meeting-house." *Birmingham Meeting*

Three of the prominent Irish members of this meeting were John Fred, from County Carlow; his son Nicholas Fred; and Samuel Hollingsworth (son of Valentine Hollingsworth), justice of the peace and representative to the Provincial Assembly.[2]

In its earliest days the Monthly Meeting was known as Chichester, then as Chichester and Concord, and finally as Concord Monthly Meeting. At the Quarterly Meeting at Chester, 12 Mo. 4, *The Monthly Meeting Established, 1684*

[1] Ashmead's *Delaware County*, 484.
[2] *Futhey and Cope*, 162, 233-4.

1683-4, it was ordered that " Chechester Monethly Meateing be yᵉ second second day of eavery moneth," and according to the records of the Monthly Meeting, " The fearst monthly meeting held by friends in Chichester [was] on yᵉ 17ᵗʰ of the first month, in yᵉ year 1684." At the Quarterly Meeting, 6 Mo. 2, 1686, it was " Ordered that yᵉ monthly meeting formerly held at Chechester be from henceforth kept one month at Chechester and one month kept at Concord & yᵉ next monthly meeting to begin at Concord, until farther order." After 1729 it was held altogether at Concord.[1]

Meetings in New Castle County on Delaware   The meetings in New Castle County " on Delaware " received an important migration of Irish Friends, and although now within the State of Delaware, in those early days were in that part of Penn's possessions known as " The Territories " or " Lower Counties " of Pennsylvania[2]; therefore they come properly within the range of our study.

Newark Meeting   About 1682, several Friends with their families arrived and settled near each other on the east side of Brandywine Creek, in New Castle County. Among these were: Valentine Hollingsworth, from Parish of Segoe, County Armagh, justice of the peace and for many years a representative to

[1] *Futhey and Cope*, 232.
[2] Thwaites, *Colonies*, 210.

the Provincial Assembly; his son-in-law, Thomas
Conway, or Connaway, from Lisburn, County
Antrim; William Stockdale,[1] justice of the peace,
probably from County Tyrone, Ireland; Adam
Sharply,[2] possibly related to Ralph Sharply, of
Belfast; John Musgrave, from north of Ireland,
later a settler in Lancaster County and a rep-
resentative to the Provincial Assembly; Morgan
Drewett, who came from London to Burlington,

[1] He may have been nearly related to William Stockdale, a minister, of
County Tyrone, who came over to Philadelphia on the ship *Friendship*, in
1684, and served as a member of the Provincial Council.

[2] Adam Sharply and wife Mary were active in the affairs of Newark or
Kennett Monthly Meeting. Their children, Benjamin and Charity, were
born 11 Mo. 10, 1686-7. Adam died 9 Mo. 27, 1694, and was buried in
Friends' burial ground at Newark. Rachel Sharpley, probably a daughter,
was married about 8 Mo., 1686, under the auspices of Newark Monthly
Meeting, to Thomas Pierson, Deputy Surveyor, of New Castle County, and
died 7 Mo. 2, 1687; burial at Newark. (*Records of Newark Monthly
Meeting.*) A daughter, Abagail, was married, 12 Mo. 23, 1692-3 to
Alphonsus Kirk, and died in 1748. There was also a William Sharply,
probably a son (authority of Gilbert Cope).

Possibly Adam Sharply was related to one Ralph Sharply mentioned,
by *Rutty* (343), who states that a meeting was settled at Belfast about
1671 or 1672, "and Ralph Sharpley came from England and resided there;
but apostatizing into evil Practices, lost his condition and corrupted others,
which with the removal of some to America proved a means of that meeting being lost." No doubt this was Ralph Sharply, the Friend, of Derbyshire, of whom the following account is found in *Besse* (I., 137): "On
the 21st of the Month called August [1659] Ralph Sharpley" and
others, "going toward the Meeting at Ashburn, were, by Order of two
Justices, set in the Stocks above an Hour. After they were released thence,
Ralph Sharpley was concerned to preach to the People, for which he was
sent to the House of Correction," for two days, and finally committed to
"Derby Goal, where he was kept ten Days." In 1661 for attending a
meeting at Eyam in the High-Peak he was imprisoned and subjected to
cruel treatment (*Besse*, I., 138-139).

New Jersey, in 1677;[1] and Cornelius Empson.[2] They held meetings for worship at the houses of Valentine Hollingsworth and Cornelius Empson.[3] Valentine Hollingsworth lived on a large plantation of nearly a thousand acres on Shelpot Creek, in Brandywine Hundred, about five miles north-east of the present City of Wilmington, Delaware, and in 1687, he gave " unto ffriends for A burying place half an Acre of [his] land for y^t purpose there being Some already buried in ye Spot. ffriends have referred fencing of it." [4]   A meeting-house was afterward built on this plot and the meeting known as Newark, from the name of the plantation, which in the original survey of 1684 was called " New Worke," doubtless a corruption of Newark. A meeting was continued here until 1754, when the Friends "being suited with a better conveniency, it was laid down." [5]

New Castle Meeting

In 1684, "John Hussey, John Richardson, Edward Blake, Benjamin Swett and other Friends, being settled in and near New Castle, held meetings at each other's houses. . . . In 1705 a lot of ground was purchased, and a meeting-house built." [6]   Very few Irish Friends settled here.

---

[1] Dr. Smith's *Delaware County*, 456.
[2] From Yorkshire.—Gilbert Cope.
[3] Samuel Smith in *Hazard's Register*, VII., cited by *Michener*, 95.
[4] *Minutes of Newark Monthly Meeting*.
[5] Futhey and Cope, *Chester County*, 233 ; *Michener*, 95.
[6] Samuel Smith in *Hazard's Register*, VII., cited by *Michener*, 95.

The meeting was discontinued in 1758, its members attending Wilmington Meeting.[1]

A meeting was held at the house of William *Hockessin* Cox, at Hockessin, in Mill Creek Hundred, in *Meeting* New Castle County, as early as 1730, but was not regularly established until 1737. The meeting received its name of Hockessin from an Indian village formerly near the place. Among the first settlers were John Baldwin, William Cox, and the Irish Friends, Henry and John Dixon. In 1738, a meeting-house was built, and enlarged in 1745.[2]

A meeting for worship was established in *Wilmington* the newly founded town of Wilmington in the *Meeting* early part of 1738, and held for a few months at the house of William Shipley, one of the founders of the town, until later in the year a small brick meeting-house—now a part of Friends' School at Fourth and West Streets—was erected. In 1748 a larger house was built. This in turn was succeeded by the present structure, erected in 1816. The monthly meeting was formed in 1750 by a division of Newark Monthly Meeting.[3] Quite early in its history, Wilmington received Irish

---

[1] *Michener*, 95.

[2] *Ibid.*, 103; *Futhey and Cope*, 239.

[3] *Michener*, 73; *Futhey and Cope*, 240; *A Sketch of the Early History of Wilmington*, by Margaret Tatnall Canby, in *Literary Era* (Philadelphia), VIII. (1901), 242–45; *Friends' Intelligencer* (Philadelphia), LIV. (1897), 569; Scharfe's *History of Delaware*, II., 711.

Friends as settlers, and at the present day as a great center of commerce and industry no small part of its large population springs from Irish Quaker stock.

About 1687, the brothers George and Michael Harlan, from Parish of Donnahlong, County Down ; Thomas Hollingsworth, son of Valentine Hollingsworth ; Alphonsus Kirk, from Lurgan,

County Armagh ; William Gregg, probably from the north of Ireland; William Dixon or Dixson, from Parish of Segoe, County Armagh; and other Friends settled on the west side of Brandywine Creek, in Christiana Hundred, New Castle County, near the present village of Centerville, and became the founders of what later was known as Centre Meeting.

For several years during the summer months they attended Newark Meeting at Valentine Hollingsworth's, but in the winter season were allowed to hold a meeting of their own at the homes of some of their number, doubtless most of the time at the house of George Harlan. At Newark Monthly Meeting, 10 Mo. 7, 1687, was granted "ye request of friends beyond Brandywine to have a meeting there this winter Season"; and 10 Mo. 2, 1689, " George Harlan Desireing ye Concurrance of ffriends on behalf of ye familys on ye other side of Brandywine for ye holding of a Meeting this winter Season amongst themselves by reason of the dangerousness of ye ford to which ye Meeting agrees & Consents."[1]   9 Mo. 7, 1702, " ffriends on ye south side of Brandywine haveing requested y^t they may have Every other first day a meeting on their side ye Creek this meeting having taken it into Consideration allows thereof and for ye more certain knowledge and settlement of our meeting it is thought Expedient and necessary y^t our meetings be kept only at two places vizt at Newark, at Valentine Hollingsworth's, one first day, and on ye other side of Brandywine ye other first day."

The records indicate that a meeting-house was not built until about 1711. At the Monthly Meeting, 5 Mo. 1, 1710, "Its agreed upon y^t Alphonsus Kirk is to be allowed 7s. 6d. ℔ acre for what Land ye meeting have occation for not Exceeding six Acres."   9 Mo. 3, 1711, " This meeting appoints George Harlan, Thos. Hollingsworth Alphonsus Kirk and Sam^ll Graves to take ye oversight of ye building of ye Center meeting house requesting y^m wth all Convenient speed to let out ye work to some workmen in order y^t it

---

[1] *Minutes Newark Monthly Meeting.*

may be ye more speedily done and return an acc^{tt} to ye next meeting how they proceed." [1]   About 1795, the wooden structure erected at this time was replaced by the present brick building.[2]   One of the most prominent of the early ministers of this meeting was Christopher Wilson, who came over from Ireland in 1712, and settled in New Castle County.

Christopher Willson

Chester County   Chester County,[3] one of the three original Counties of the Province established by Penn in 1682, received the larger part of the Irish Quaker migration and deserves a full measure of our attention.   Early in the eighteenth century the tide of migration began to move into the backwoods, and we find Friends from the old settlements in New Castle County and what is now Delaware County pushing their way through the forests and developing new locations in the wild but fat and fertile uplands of Chester County.   For a time these

---

[1] *Futhey and Cope,* 233.

[2] Ellwood Michener's sketch of Centre Meeting in an issue of the *Kennett Square* (Pa.) *Advance,* about 1890.

[3] With the kind permission of Gilbert Cope, the surviving author, the writer has obtained the main facts of this section on Chester County from Futhey and Cope's excellent History of the County, and that work is the authority used unless otherwise indicated.

Quaker pioneers made the long and often dangerous journey to attend the meetings of the old
settlements, but as other members settled near
them, meetings of their own were erected, held
at first in private houses, later in rude log meeting-houses, and ultimately, keeping pace with the
development of the country, in more substantial
buildings of brick or stone.

Four monthly meetings, Newark, New Garden,
Bradford, and Goshen, were held within the present
limits of Chester County previous to 1750. Newark Monthly Meeting, the parent of New Garden
and Bradford, was established in New Castle
County, in 1686, and included not only the meetings of New Castle County, but all those of southern
Chester County, until the erection of the Monthly
Meetings of New Garden in 1718, and Bradford
in 1737. Goshen Monthly Meeting, formed from
Chester Monthly Meeting in 1722, included within
its bounds nearly all the northern meetings of the
County.

Newark Monthly Meeting, since 1760 known
as Kennett Monthly Meeting, held its first sessions, according to the minutes, in 1686, at the
house of the widow Welsh in New Castle, and
continued there until 6 Mo. 28, 1687, when it was
decided "y^t it may be more Convenient| for y^e
present, that it be kept twice over ye other Side
of Brandywine ye third . . . to be kept at New-

Newark or
Kennett
Monthly Meet-
ing

castle."[1]   The Monthly Meeting was held mostly
at Valentine Hollingsworth's after 1689, but circulated to various houses up to 3 Mo. 6, 1704,
when "This meeting Orders that our next
Monthly Meeting be held at ye Center wch is supposed to be George Harlans ould house." It
was held last at Newark in 1707, but after Center
Meeting House was built it was usually held at
the latter place for some years. At length it became settled at Kennett, and on that account
dropped the old name of Newark [2]

Kennett   Samuel Smith, in his history of the Pennsylvania
Meeting meetings,[3] says that in 1707, "Vincent Caldwell,
Thomas Wickersham, Joel Baily, Thomas Hope,
Guyan Miller [an Irish Friend], and others, being
settled in Kennet and the east end of Marlborough, had liberty to keep a meeting for worship sometimes in private houses. In the year
1710 a piece of land was purchased and a meeting-house built, which was enlarged in 1719; in

Thomas Carleton

1731 it was further enlarged." One of the most
eminent ministers of this meeting was Thomas
Carleton, a native of King's County, Ireland.

1 *Minutes Newark Monthly Meeting.*
2 *Futhey and Cope*, 232-3.
3 *Hazard's Register*, VII.

In 1699, William Penn directed Henry Hollings- Manor of Steyning or Letitia's Manor worth, deputy-surveyor of Chester County, to lay out a tract of 30,000 acres of land for his two children, William and Letitia Penn. This survey included all of the present Township of New Garden and the greater part of Kennett, with several thousand acres in the northern part of New Castle County.

The large survey was divided, the eastern part, consisting of 15,500 acres, being conveyed to Letitia Penn, and the western part, of 14,500 acres, to her brother William Penn, Jr. Letitia's tract was confirmed to her by her father's patent, dated October 23, 1701, in consideration of one "Bever skinn" yearly and "the fatherly love and natural affection I bear to her my said daughter." This tract received the name of the Manor of Steyning, also called Letitia's Manor, with the privilege "To have and to hold a Court Baron with all things whatsoever to a Court Baron belonging, and to have and to hold view of ffranck pledge for the conservation of the peace and the better Government of ye tenants holding or hereafter to hold of the said Mannor."

Letitia Penn, who had come over to Pennsylvania with her father on his second visit in 1699, returned with him to England in 1701, before her departure by power of attorney authorizing James Logan and Edward Pennington to dispose of land

and to have the management of her property here.
Pennington soon died and Logan was her sole at-
torney, until in 1711, having married William
Aubrey, a London merchant, Letitia and her hus-
band executed another power of attorney to
Logan and Samuel Carpenter.

Kennett The land described in Letitia Penn's patent in-
Township cluded nearly all of the Township of Kennett,
excepting a few small tracts already conveyed to
settlers, and although for some years known by
its manorial name, it soon came to be called Kennett.[1] Kennett is first mentioned on the court
records in February, 1705, when Henry Peirce
appeared in court as constable for that township.
In 1706, he was appointed supervisor of the highways, and Ezekiel Harlan (son of George Harlan), the heaviest tax payer in the Township, succeeded him as constable. George Harlan and
Gayen Miller were probably the first of the Irish

Gayen Miller

Friends to secure land in Kennett. In 1702,
Miller purchased 200 acres on the east branch of
Red Clay Creek, including the eastern part of the

[1] The name Kennett, it is thought, was suggested by Francis Smith, who
in 1686 had taken up 200 acres of land at the mouth of Pocopson Creek,
within the original limits of the township, and who had come from Devizes,
in Wiltshire, England, in which county there is a creek and a village
called Kennett.

present Borough of Kennett Square.[1] He was elected to the Provincial Assembly in 1714.[2] Harlan, as we have previously stated, settled at first at Centre in New Castle County, but soon moved up the Brandywine and purchased 470 acres in Kennett, now Pennsbury, Township. While living here he had for his neighbors, over the creek in a great bend, a settlement of Indians. After they had gone away he obtained, in 1701, a warrant for 200 acres in this bend of the creek, the land being granted "in regard of the great trouble and charge he has bore in fencing and maintaining the same for the said Indians while living thereon." George Harlan was elected to the Provincial Assembly from New Castle County in 1695, and from Chester County in 1712.[3]

Of the forty-three persons taxed in Kennett, in 1715, there were nine Irish Friends, as follows: Gayen Miller, 8s. 6d.; Michael Harlan, 5s. 6d.; Ezekiel Harlan, 12s. 6d.; Aaron Harlan, 5s. 6d.; Moses Harlan, 4s. 2d.; Valentine Hollingsworth, 2s. 9d.; James Harlan, 2s. 6d.; Joshua Harlan,

---

[1] Kennett Square was laid out and named about 1768 or 1769; for in a deed of 9 Mo. 29, 1768, William Dixson conveyed to Joseph Musgrave a tract of 3 acres in Kennett Township, "in a place intended to be laid out for an inland town called —— town," the blank indicating that a name had not yet been chosen; and the next year Dixson conveyed to Musgrave another tract "near a place called Kennett Square." Both grantor and grantee in this transaction were of Irish Quaker stock.

[2] *Penna. Archives*, 2nd Series, IX., 686.

[3] *Ibid.*, 652, 686.

9

2s. 6d. ; John Gregg, 3s. 4d.   In 1716, Benjamin
Fred, originally from Carlow Meeting, Ireland,
purchased 200 acres in the Township.

New Garden Township   As we have stated, William Penn, Jr., received
the western part of the 30,000 acres surveyed
by Hollingsworth, in 1699, and his sister Letitia
the eastern part.   The western tract of 14,500
acres was granted by patent to Penn, by the commissioners of property, May 24, 1706, and like his
sister's land received the name of the Manor of
Steyning.   Before obtaining the patent young
Penn had already appointed Griffith Owen, James
Logan, and Robert Ashton as his attorneys, he
being about to return to England.   The land was
not immediately taken up by settlers, but about
1711, several families of Friends from Ireland,
principally from the Province of Leinster, with a
few from the Province of Ulster, arrived and, presenting their certificates of removal to Newark
Monthly Meeting, settled in that part of the Manor
which lay north of the circular line, giving to their
new home the name of New Garden in remem-
brance of New Garden Meeting, in County Carlow, Ireland, whence came John Lowden and
others of the company.   Some time after, the part
of the Manor north of the circular line was erected
into a township and called New Garden.

These Irish Friends in most cases had been
settled on the land some years before obtaining

their titles. In 1712, Gayen Miller, of Kennett, purchased 700 acres, while the next year grants were made to John Lowden, James Lindley, Michael Lightfoot, Joseph Hutton, from County Carlow ; James Starr, from County Meath ; William Halliday, from County West Meath ; Thomas Jackson, from Queen's County; and John Miller, from Grange near Charlemont; and in 1714, to Thomas Garnett, from Grange near Charlemont, and to Joseph Sharp, possibly from Dublin or near by. The whole amount of land purchased by these Friends, including two grants to Mary Rowland, in 1708, and to Abram Marshall in 1713, Friends not from Ireland, was 5413 acres, at the rate of £ 20 per hundred, or according to modern computation, one dollar per acre.

A draft[1] of the Manor, made not long after the above grants, probably by John Taylor, surveyor, is reproduced on the next page in the form of a map, and shows that nearly the whole of what is now New Garden Township was seated by Irish Friends.[2] The following is a list of the first settlers of the Manor, as shown on this map, the numbers indicating the location of the land and the asterisk showing who were Irish Friends:

[1] The original draft is in possession of Thompson Richards, of Toughkenamon, who is a descendant of several families of Irish Friends, and who owns and resides upon a large part of the 700 acres granted to his ancestor, Mary Rowland, in 1708.

[2] With the kind permission of Ellwood Michener, I have made use of his *History of New Garden*, a valuable series of sketches tracing the his-

Marlborough.

E 923. Perches.

4

3

6

5

a

1

2

7   8   9

28   25   10   24

26   23

27   11

12   22

13

B   14

32   21

15

20

C

31   30   16   19

29   17   18

W.

W. S. W. 930. Perches.

Newcastle Co. Del.

London Land Co - London Grove Twp.

N. 2674 Perches.

S. 23¼ Perches.

Letitia. Aubrees Manor - Kennett Twp.

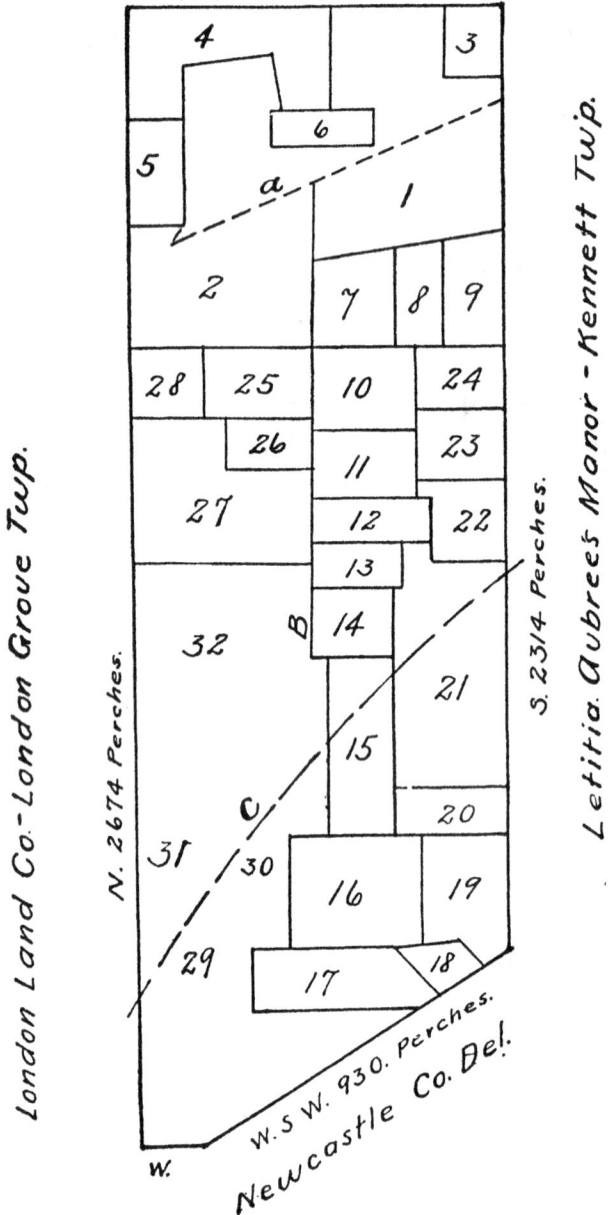

MAP OF THE MANOR OF STENNING, LATER NEW GARDEN TOWNSHIP

A. Toughkenamon Hill line.
B. Middle division line.
C. Pennsylvania and Delaware State line.
  1. Mary Rowland.
*2. John Miller.
*3. Robert Johnson.
  4. Evan Evans.
*5. Joseph Sharp.
*6. James Lindley.
*7. Thomas Garnett.
*8. Joseph Sharp.
*9. John Sharp.
*10. Michael Lightfoot.
*11. John Wily.
*12. Thomas Jackson.
*13. William Halliday.
  14. Abram Marshall.
*15. John Miller.

16. Thos. Edmunds and Thos John.
17. Reece Meredith.
18. Anthony Houston.
19. Vacant.
20. William Rutledge.
*21. Simon Hadly.
*22. Benjamin Fred.
*23. John Lowden.
*24. Thomas Milhous.
*25. James Starr.
*26. Francis Hobson.
*27. Gayen Miller.
*28. Joseph Hutton.
29. William Huse.
30. John Thomas.
31. John Evans.
32. Vacant.

The tracts, as may be seen, were mostly rectangular. In the north-east corner we find Robert Johnson, from County Carlow, with 200 acres, confirmed to him in 1715; Evan Evans, probably a Welshman, with 500 acres in the north-west corner, which he sold some time prior to 1716 to Thomas Garnett; Joseph Sharp below him on White Clay Creek, 200 acres,

tory of the land, as laid out in this draft, from the first to the present owners, which appeared in the weekly issues of the *Kennett Square* (Pa.) *Advance*, during the years 1898 and 1899. Ellwood Michener, who is a prominent member of New Garden Monthly Meeting and a son of the late Dr. Ezra Michener, author of *A Retrospect of Quakerism*, so frequently cited in this work, is the custodian of a large collection of Friends' records kept in a safe at his residence in New Garden, and as a surveyor and conveyancer for many years in the Township, he has had exceptional opportunities for the compilation of these sketches. What makes the sketches of special value is the fact that he has made use of the original title deeds, many of which have not been recorded.

granted in 1717; James Lindley, 200 acres, lying north of the Toughkenamon[1] Hill. The remaining land north of the hill, about 1,050 acres, was vacant. From the hill a line ran south through the middle of the Manor, following the course of the present road from Toughkenamon to New Garden Meeting House, almost to the circular line. Taking the east side we have first, Mary Rowland, 700 acres, including the beautiful valley which extends from the present village of Toughkenamon to Kennett Square. Next south of this tract 800 acres were divided among John Sharp, doubtless a brother of Joseph Sharp, on the east side 300 acres; Joseph Sharp, 200 acres, confirmed to him in 1714, but sold by him the next year; and Thomas Garnett, with 300 acres. South of these on the Kennett line were William Tanner, probably an Irish Friend, with 200 acres, which passed finally into the hands of Thomas Milhous,

Thos Milhous

an arrival from Dublin, in 1729; John Lowden, from County Carlow, with 300 acres; and Benjamin Fred, with 300 acres, the latter almost touching on the circular line. Below Benjamin Fred came Simon Hadly, from County West Meath,

[1] "Dochcanamon Hill" is mentioned in the original survey of the Manor, in 1700. The name is of Indian origin and is said to mean "Fire-brand hill."

with a large tract, the greater part of which extended into New Castle County. He was appointed a justice of the peace in New Castle County, in 1726.[1] Between these and the middle line were Michael Lightfoot, (300 acres), who arrived in 1712, became an eminent minister of the Society, and some years later removed to Philadelphia, at the time of his death being Treasurer of the Province ; John Wily, from County West Meath, with 200 acres ; Thomas Jackson, with 200 acres ; and continuing southward, William Halliday, with 200 acres. John Miller owned 1,013 acres which extended from the middle line to London Grove Township on the west, and from Toughkenamon Hill to New Garden Meeting House. He lived on White Clay Creek, on or near the site of Avondale, and built a grist mill—the first in that region —which did the grinding for the inhabitants many miles around, even, it is said, as far as Lancaster. New Garden Meeting was held at his house as early as 1712. He also owned a smaller tract of land, No. 15, the greater part of which extended into New Castle County. He was appointed a representative to the Provincial As-

---

[1] *Penna. Archives*, 2d Series, IX., 649.

sembly in 1714, but died the same year.[1] Next south of Miller's large tract, Joseph Hutton held 250 acres on the west line, and James Starr 350 acres on the middle line. Of 900 acres south of these, Francis Hobson, from Grange near Charlemont, held 200 acres in the north-east corner and the remainder was purchased by Gayen Miller. From this southward there was a vacant tract of several thousand acres.

Of the twenty-two persons taxed in New Garden in 1715, fifteen were Irish Friends, as follows : Mary Miller, 9s.; Michael Lightfoot, 2s.; William Halliday, 2s. 7d.; Margaret Lowden, 2s.; James Lindley, 4s. 6d.; Thomas Jackson, 3s.; James Starr, 3s.; Francis Hobson, 2s.; Joseph Garnett, 2s.; Robert Johnson, 2s.; John Sharp, 3s. 6d.; Joseph Sharp, 2s.; John Wiley, 2s. 4d.; Thomas Garnett, 3s. 9d.; Benjamin Fred, 2s. 1d.

New Garden Meeting   At first the Friends of the New Garden settlement attended Kennett Meeting, but soon they were allowed to hold a meeting of their own, as evidenced by the following extracts from the Minutes of Chester Quarterly Meeting :

12 Mo. 2, 1712.—" Newark monthly meeting requests that there may be a first & fifth Days meeting settled at John Miller's. This meeting, considering thereof, thinks fitt to Refer the further Consideration thereof to the next Quarterly meeting."

[1] *Penna. Archives*, 2d Series, IX., 686.

3 Mo. 4, 1713.—"This meeting, Considering further of settleing a meeting at or nere John Miller's, Do allow that a first and fifth Dayes meeting be kept at John Miller's Dwelling House for this Ensuing Quarter, or until further order, and the said meeting to belong to Kennet Preparative Meeting for the Present."

6 Mo. 3, 1713.—"Also the said Meeting Requests that the ffriends of the meeting kept at John Miller's may have Liberty to Build a meeting house near Michel Lightfoot's, which this meeting, takeing into Consideration, do allow the same ffriends of that meeting so to do, and not to Exceed half a mile from the said Michel's."

A meeting-house was built probably later in this year, on a rectangular tract of six acres, in the south-east corner of John Miller's original plantation. James Miller, of New Garden, yeoman, son and heir of John Miller, for a consideration of £1, 16s., granted the six acres, by deed of 10 Mo. 26, 1717, to Simon Hadly, James Starr, Thomas Jackson, and Michael Lightfoot, evidently in trust for New Garden Meeting, for by deed of December 12, 1723, the latter Friends formally transferred the land to the Meeting.[1]

At Newark Monthly Meeting 10 Mo. 3, 1715 " ffriends belonging to Newgardin first day's meeting, having requested of this meeting the Liberty

[1] Original deeds in possession of the Meeting.

of houlding a prepiritive meeting at the meeting
house of Newgarden, this meeting aproves their
Request and grants them the Liberty of houlding
such a preparative meeting."

NEW GARDEN MEETING HOUSE
From a drawing by Ellwood Michener, 1850

In 1743 the south end of the present brick
house was erected in the room of the former log
one. The north end was added about the year
1790.

New Garden
Monthly Meet-
ing Erected,
1718

New Garden Monthly meeting, formed from
Newark Monthly Meeting, in 1718, included the
meetings of New Garden, Nottingham, London

Grove, and others subsequently formed to the westward, and was first convened 5 Mo. 12, 1718. It was held sometimes at Nottingham, now in Cecil County, Maryland, until the establishment of Nottingham Monthly meeting, in 1730; and afterward alternated to London Grove, until the erection of London Grove Monthly Meeting, in 1792. The first clerk of the Monthly Meeting was James Starr, who served until 1726, when he was succeeded by Benjamin Fred.[1]

Adjoining New Garden on the west is London Grove Township to which also came many Irish Friends. This township was organized in 1723. On August 12, 1699, William Penn sold to Tobias Collet, Daniel Quare, Henry Goldney, and Michael Russell, Friends of London, among other lands, 60,000 acres, not then located, and granted a warrant, dated 6 Mo. (August) 17, 1699, for the survey thereof. These persons admitted others into partnership with them, and formed a company, generally known as the London Company, for the improvement of their property, the number of shares eventually reaching 8,800, and the shareholders several hundred. As a part of the 60,000

London Grove Township

London Company

[1] At the Monthly Meeting, 2 Mo. 11, 1719, " Caleb Pusey is Appointed to procure a Book to Enter ye records of ye Monthly Meeting in, & one to records births & Burials, & also one To Record Marriage Certificates & Certificates of Settlements In." 9 Mo. 12, 1720, " Caleb Pusey According to Appointment hath Procured Three Books for ye Use of this Meeting, which are brought heere & att present to be Lodged att Thomas Lightfoots."

acres, a survey in Chester County, was made of 16,500 acres, which included nearly all of the present Township of London Grove and the greater part of the Townships of Franklin (formerly a part of New London) and London Britain. This tract was rectangular, being over three miles wide, and about eight and six-tenths miles long. That part of London Grove which lies directly north of New Garden, containing 718 acres, was subsequently added to the former survey, so that the London Company owned, altogether, 17,218 acres in Chester County, for which a patent was granted June 25, 1718. Much of the land was originally leased for a term of years, with stipulations that a certain number of acres should be cleared and plowed yearly, orchards planted, etc.

The following advertisement was probably circulated soon after the land was taken up :

"The Proprietors Of The Pensilvania Land Company In London Do Hereby Give Notice

"To all persons that are willing to settle upon lands in Pensilvania, and the territories thereunto belonging,

"That they will Give to Every such Person or Persons Fifty Acres of Land to them and their Heirs for ever, Free and Clear of all manner of Quit-Rents : Ten Families to Settle together for the Conveniency of Good Neighbourhood in every

Five Thousand Acres. This Encouragement we promise to Give to a Hundred Families ; and so soon as each Family have Built them a Cottage, and cleared Ten Acres of Land, every Family so settling shall have Deeds executed by the trustees, and sent them over upon Certificate for that purpose first obtained under the Hands of this Company's Agent or Agents Residing in Pensilvania.

"*Samuel Carpenter & Tho. ffairman* are the Comp's Agents."

Under the direction of the Company's agent, John Estaugh, of Haddonfield, in New Jersey, Isaac Taylor, Deputy-Surveyor of Chester County, surveyed many tracts for settlers on the Company's lands. Like those of New Garden the subdivisions in London Grove were mostly rectangular, and a large number of them seem to have been laid out in 1718 and 1719. Many of the settlers obtained deeds for their lands, dated March 14, 1722–3, from Collet, Quare, and Goldney.

John Cane, a Friend, who with his wife Ann came over from County Armagh about 1713, was one of the first settlers of London Grove, but he did not long survive to enjoy his new home. John Allen, who was an Irish Friend, arrived as early as 1714 and lo-

cated in the Township on the north-west line of New Garden. Here he built and operated one of the earliest mills of that section. In 1719 he purchased from Thomas Garnett an adjoining tract of 200 acres over the line in New Garden, being part of the 500 acres granted to Garnett by Evan Evans, as previously stated. Below Allen we find Joseph Sharp with a tract of 100 acres, which joined his plantation in New Garden. Joseph Sharp, a tanner by trade, was appointed one of the overseers of the poor in the newly-organized Township of London Grove in 1723. His son, Samuel Sharp, a resident in London Grove, served as a member of the Continental Congress. In 1722, James Lindley, of New Garden, purchased 400 acres and in the next year became the first constable of the Township. Jeremiah Starr, of Oldcastle, County Meath, brother of James Starr, of New Garden, arrived with his family in the year 1717, and took up a tract of land in London Grove, a little north-west of Avondale. He represented Chester County in the Assembly from 1738 until 1743, when he became Collector of Excise, a position he held until 1756.[1]

Of the forty-two taxable persons in London Grove in 1724 there were ten Irish Friends : John Allen, 8s.; Joseph Sharp, 13s.; Jeremiah Starr, 4s.

---

[1] *Penn'a Archives*, 2nd Series, IX., 690-1,674.

6d.; James Lindley, 19s.; Robert Cane, 4s.; John Cane, 7s.; Moses Harlan, 4s.; Michael Harlan, Sr., 13s. 4d.; Michael Harlan, Jr., 2s. 4d.; Joseph Garnett, 1s. 8d.

London Grove Meeting was established by au- London Grove
thority of Chester Quarterly Meeting in 1714, and Meeting
was held at the house of John Smith, son-in-law of
Caleb Pusey, in what is now East Marlborough,
until 1724, when a meeting-house was erected in
the north-east corner of London Grove. In 1743
this was replaced by a larger house. An addition
was made to this building in 1775, for Richard
Barnard, a member of the meeting, notes in his
diary under date of 10 Mo. 19, 1775, that he was
" At London Grove, raising adition to meeting
house."[1] This structure was removed in 1818,
and the present meeting-house built.[2]

North of Kennett, New Garden, and London Marlborough
Grove was Marlborough Township, named from Township
Marlborough, in Wiltshire, England, and organized
in 1704. The eastern part was laid out about
1700, in right of purchases made in England, as
was also some of the western part. The Township was divided into East and West Marlborough
in 1729.

[1] MS. Diary of Richard Barnard, in possession of a descendant, Milton
Barnard, Northbrook, Chester County.

[2] "Historical Sketch of the Friends' Meeting-house at London Grove,"
by Thompson Frame, in Philadelphia *Friend*, 7 Mo. 27, 1901. (Vol.
LXXV., p. 11.)

Joseph Pennock

The only resident Irish Friend mentioned in the list of twenty-eight persons taxed in the Township in 1715, was Joseph Pennock, a native of Clonmel, County Tipperary. He removed to what is now West Marlborough Township as early as 1714 and settled on a large tract of 1250 acres, of which he became proprietor by virtue of a grant from William Penn to his grandfather, George Collett, of Clonmel. In 1738 he built a mansion called "Primitive Hall," which is still standing in a good state of preservation. Pennock took a prominent and active part in meeting and civil affairs, serving as a member of the Provincial Assembly almost continuously from 1716 to 1744.[1] For many years he was a justice of the peace,[2] and in 1736, during the Cresap War, rising from the dispute over the boundary between Pennsylvania and Maryland, he was one of the five men appointed by Governor Thomas Penn to investigate a conspiracy hatched by agents of Maryland among the settlers of New Garden and London Grove.

By the Minutes of the Board of Property, 1 Mo. 6, 1724–5, we find that "Joseph Pennock requests the Grant of —— acres of the tract called S'r John Fagg's [Fagg's Manor], if to be disposed of."[3] This land was probably in that part of Fagg's

[1] *Penn'a Archives*, 2nd Series, IX., 686–691.
[2] *Ibid.*, 678–9.
[3] *Ibid.*, XIX., 726.

Manor which later was erected into Londonderry
Township and which adjoined London Grove on
the west. At this period the Manor was exposed
to the encroachments of the Scotch-Irish squatters,
who caused the authorities much annoyance by
the irregularities of their settlements. John Taylor, the surveyor, notes in his memorandum-book
that on April 3rd, 1730 he " went and warned the
Irish off Fagg's Manor." In the following letter
to James Steel, manager of the land-office, in
Philadelphia, Pennock evidently is writing of the
tract requested of the Board of Property, and, not
having a patent, doubtless has been having trouble
to hold his land against the squatters. The letter[1]
is given with the quaintness and phonetic spelling
of the original.

malborah ye 9th of ye 7^br 1725
" ffrend James Steel

I am ondar Som consarn *Joseph Pen-*
of minde relating to Simkoks affair, when I was at *nock's Letter* *1725*
Chester I met with James Logan whoo tould mee
to ye best of my rememborens) y^t ye Proprietors
amily was at present so distrackted or unsettled
r^t ye Commishonars nu not how to form a pattin
[patent] or make titols to Land y^t thay had Set
Som days & had Com to no Conclution about
t. it has Cost mee som pounds olredy to de-

<hr>

[1] The original MS. is in the collection of a descendant, Mrs. William
I. Miller, of Media, Pa.

10

fend the Land bot if I cannot hefe a patten whic
would be my Gost foundetion I will quit it for it
more adviseble to drop it with those skars olred
resefd then bee obliged heer after to Retret
with wounds.   I met J. L. yᵉ next day on yᵉ rod
hee tould mee yᵗ hee would doo what hee Coul
in my affair which is incorriging.   Now whot
Request of yᵉ is ℘resent my kind Respekts to]
Logan & Let him no my resolutions yᵗ if I Ca
hefe a patten am redy to defend yᵉ Land if nc
most Quit it for it would be vanity in mee to ha$
sord my Estete at blind mans bof undar ℘tens c
defending a skrip of yᵉ Proprietors.   I intrete y
when yᵉᵉ knows yᵉ resolt favor mee with a lin
which will delvar mee from yᵉ payn & greatl
oblige thy asureed ffrend   J. Pennock "

Joseph Pennock's son Nathaniel Pennock als
served many years in the Assembly, until in th
memorable year of 1756, with the beginning of th
war against the Indians, he and other Friend
resigned their seats declaring that they could nc
be a part of a government openly at war.

In the moving and drifting about which wa
continually occurring among the settlers, othe
Irish Friends made their way to the Mar
boroughs, among the earliest of whom wer
Ezekiel and William Harlan of the numerous prc
geny of the Harlans, Thomas Jackson, who cam

over from New Garden Township as early as 1718, and Samuel Beverly, from Ballinacree Meeting, County Antrim.

Crossing the northern boundary of Marlborough we come to a township the whole of which was owned by an Irish Friend, Nathaniel Newlin, of Concord, and named in his honor Newlin Township. This tract, consisting of seven thousand seven hundred acres, through the center of which flows Brandywine Creek, was purchased by Newlin, evidently as a land speculation, from the trustees of the Free Society of Traders, by deed of June 10, 1724, for a consideration of £800, and at once negotiations were entered into for the sale of portions of it.

Newlin Township Owned by an Irish Quaker

Soon a difficulty arose with the Indians, who had a village on the north side of the Brandywine in the east end of the tract, and laid claim to the land one mile wide on each side of the Creek; but Newlin and the purchasers from him paid no attention to their demands. Thereupon, in the summer of 1725, several of the tribe led by the chief Checochinican proceeded to Philadelphia and appeared before the Provincial Assembly, through their interpreters, one of whom was Ezekiel Harlan, making complaint of the encroachments upon their lands. The Assembly carefully considered the case, but made no satisfactory adjustment before adjourning.

Newlin's Difficulty with the Indians

At the beginning of the next session in the following year, the Indians again appeared and urged their claims. The subject was again taken up and James Logan on behalf of the Commissioners of Property reported that they had "used such means as they thought most likely to satisfy" the Indians, "and continues them in the quiet possession of their claims, and for that end . . . had agreed and accommodated the matter with Nathaniel Newlin." Newlin was then summoned before the Assembly, and declared in writing that "neither he nor his heirs will, by any means, disturb or molest the Indians in their possessions or claims." With these assurances the Indians expressed themselves as satisfied, and after shaking hands with Newlin in a friendly manner, quietly returned to their homes.

The work of settlement, however, seems not to have been retarded, and in 1729 the chief Checochinican, on behalf of his people, appealed once more to the government, writing that notwithstanding Newlin's promise that they should not be disturbed in the free and peaceable enjoyment of their lands on the Brandywine, some of their lands had been sold, and they had been forbidden even to make use of timber growing thereon for the building of cabins. What action, if any, was taken upon this complaint has not been learned, but not long after, the greater part of the Indians

removed from the County, and all trouble growing out of their claims ceased.

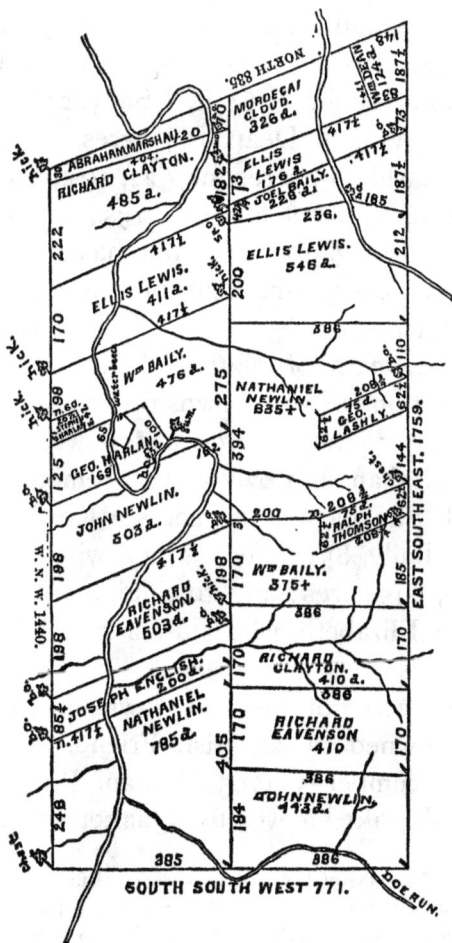

NEWLIN TOWNSHIP, CHESTER COUNTY, IN 1730

The following is a list of the first purchasers

from Newlin: George Harlan, 169 acres for £50,
14s.; Stephen Harlan, 20½ acres for £20, 10s.;
Joseph England, 200 acres for £30; Mordecai
Cloud, 326 acres for £97, 16s.; Abraham Marshall, 120 acres for £36; Joel Baily, 228 acres for
£68, 8s.; William Dean, 124 acres for £37, 4s.;
George Lashly, 75 acres for £22, 10s.; and Ralph
Thompson, 75 acres for £19, 19s., 9d., a total of
1337 acres for £383.   The purchasers were also
to pay a yearly quit rent of one shilling per
hundred acres.

On the death of Nathaniel Newlin in 1729,
those portions of the Township yet unsold were
divided among his children as follows: John, 946
acres; Nathaniel, 1,620 acres; Jemima, wife of
Richard Eavenson, 913 acres; Kesia, wife of
William Baily, 851 acres; Mary, wife of Richard
Clayton, 895 acres; and to children of deceased
daughter Elizabeth, who had married Ellis Lewis,
1,133 acres.

Pikeland Township Granted to Joseph Pike, an Irish Friend, of Cork   Newlin was not the only township in Chester
County owned by an Irish Friend. By patent
dated December 3, 1705, William Penn granted
to Joseph Pike,[1] a wealthy Quaker merchant, of

[1] Joseph Pike, the author of several works relating to Friends (see
Joseph Smith's *Catalogue of Friends' Books*, II., 414), son of Richard
and Elizabeth Pike, was born 11 Mo. 15, 1657, on a farm called Kilcreagh, seven miles west of Cork. The father, Richard Pike, was born
about 1627, in the town of Newberry, Berkshire, England, of parents of
good reputation " and having some estate in houses there " ; and about

Cork, a tract of over 10,000 acres of land, lying
north of the Great Valley, which was organized
under the name of Pikeland Township, and in
1838 divided into East and West Pikeland.
Joseph Pike died in 1729, and by his will, dated
1727, and proved in the Prerogative Court of the
Archbishop of Armagh, devised Pikeland and a
tract of over 1,500 acres in Caln, on the southern part of which is now Caln Meeting House,

1648, he "came over to Ireland a Corporal in a Troop of Horse in Cromwell's Army." He married Elizabeth Jackson, born in London about
1636, of parents of good repute, "some of her connexions having been
chief magistrates of that city," and settled near Cork. Richard and
Elizabeth Pike were among the Friends convinced by the ministry of Edward Burrough at Cork in 1655. In 1664, they removed from the farm of
Kilcreagh to Cork and kept a shop. Richard died 4 Mo. 1668, while a
prisoner for his Quaker principles, and was the first Friend interred in the
burial ground of the Society outside the south gate of Cork. Elizabeth
died in 1688. Their children were : Elizabeth, married Henry Wheddon,
merchant, and died in 1693; Joseph; Ebenezer; Richard; Sarah; and
Benjamin, who died the same day as his father.

Joseph Pike was married in 1682, to Elizabeth Rogers, eldest daughter
of Francis Rogers, a minister of the Society. After his marriage he joined
his brother Richard in opening a linen-draper's shop in Cork, the first of
the kind in the city. His business affairs frequently took him to England,
Holland, and Flanders. On one of these journeys he accompanied William
Penn to Holland and attended the yearly meeting at Amsterdam. Thomas
Story notes in his journal (p. 533) that in 1716, while on a religious journey
to Ireland, he visited Joseph Pike, of Cork, among whose guests one day
at dinner were the young Countess of Kildare, her maiden sister, and three
others of the gentry. Joseph and Elizabeth Pike had fourteen children,
of whom seven survived : Richard; Mary, married Thomas Beale, son of
Joshua, of Mountmellick; Elizabeth, married to Joshua Beale, brother of
Thomas; Rachel; Samuel; Benjamin; and Anne.—Autobiography of
Joseph Pike, *Friends' Library*, II., 351–414; *Leadbeater*, 169–184;
Rutty, 316–318.

to his wife Elizabeth. The widow Pike held the lands until her death in 1733, when they came into possession of her son, Richard Pike. He died about 1752, and by his will[1] bequeathed all his estate in Pennsylvania to his kinsmen, Samuel Hoare and Nathaniel Newberry, merchants of London. In 1756, Hoare purchased Newberry's interest and became the sole owner. The land was then offered for sale in small tracts. Among the first settlers were Samuel Lightfoot (son of Thomas), a surveyor, and builder of the first mill in that neighborhood; Michael Lightfoot; Thomas Milhous, who removed there from New Garden Township about 1744; and Timothy Kirk, of the Kirks of Lurgan, County Armagh.

The Great Valley   A number of Irish Friends removed to the rich limestone lands of the Great Valley, which extends from east to west across the center of Chester County, and most of them became members of Bradford Monthly Meeting and of Caln Particular Meeting. Bradford Monthly Meeting, consisting of the Particular Meetings of Bradford and Caln, was formed from Newark Monthly Meeting in 1737.

Caln Meeting   A meeting "at Calne in yᵉ Valey" was held as early as 1716, and a meeting-house was probably

---

[1] Richard Pike, of Stoke Newington, Middlesex, England, made his will September 2, 1752 (proved April 5, 1755), and mentions his nephews, Joshua and Joseph Beale, sons of Joshua, of Cork, and Samuel Beale, son of sister, Rachel Beale, and niece, Sarah Beale, daughter of Joshua.

erected the same year on John Mendenhall's land. In 1726, it was decided to build another meeting-house " upon the further side of yᵉ mounten." Some years later Richard Pike, a Friend, of Cork, who owned over 1,500 acres in Caln Township, conveyed to Thomas Parke and Robert Miller, of East Caln, for the use of Friends, a lot of ground on which a meeting-house had been built with his consent ; whether this was the second or a third location has not been determined. In 1801 the meeting-house was enlarged to accommodate the new Quarterly Meeting of Caln.

Caln Township, originally including the territory now embraced in Caln, East Caln, West Caln, East Brandywine, West Brandywine, and a part of Valley Township, and the Borough of Downingtown, and that part of Coatesville lying east of the west branch of Brandywine Creek, was named from the town of Calne, in Wiltshire, England, and was organized as a township about 1714. In 1728 it was divided into the Townships of East and West Caln.

East Caln Township

In East Caln settled William Pim, from Queen's County, for many years clerk of Bradford Monthly Meeting, overseer and elder of Caln Meeting, and justice of the peace ; his sons Thomas and Richard Pim ; Thomas Parke, from County Carlow, an elder of Caln Meeting, purchaser of 500 acres of land at the site of Downingtown or near by, where

some of his descendants of the name yet reside;
Robert Valentine (son of Thomas Valentine and
grandson of Thomas Parke), from County Carlow, an eminent minister of the Society of Friends,
who made a religious visit to Great Britain at the
close of the Revolution ; Thomas Coates, son of
Moses Coates, from County Carlow ; Thomas
Pain, from Queen's County ; Joseph Wilkinson,
son of Francis Wilkinson, from Ballinacree,
County Antrim ; and Evan Wilkinson, probably
the latter's brother, from Ballinacree, a settler in
West Caln.

Coatesville Named for an Irish Quaker   Moses Coates, grandson of Moses Coates, the
emigrant from County Carlow, was married in
1770 to Hannah Musgrave, daughter of Thomas
Musgrave, an Irish Quaker, of Sadsbury, Lancaster County, and became the owner of a tract
of land now occupied by the Borough of Coatesville, which was laid out and named in his honor
by his son Dr. Jesse Coates.

Phoenixville First Settled by Irish Quakers   In 1731, Moses Coates, a Friend, originally from
County Carlow, purchased 600 acres, and James
Starr, one of the first settlers of New Garden, 350
acres, in Charlestown, now Schuylkill, Township,
on the north side of French Creek at its junction
with Schuylkill River, and became the first settlers
at the site of Phoenixville. Judge Pennypacker,
who has written an interesting history of the beginnings of this town, relates that previous to his

purchase Moses Coates "had lived for about a year upon the other side of the Schuylkill, where stands the present village of Mont Clare, a locality he selected because the Indians were there less numerous. At night he slept with a loaded gun at his side, and a servant lay at the door of his hut with a pitch fork. Upon longer acquaintance, however, he found the Indians disposed to be friendly, and his fear of their hostility being dissipated he changed his place of residence"[1] to the other side of the River. Here he "blazed paths through the wilderness about his home, by cutting chips from the sides of the trees, so that his children should not be lost."[2]

In 1732, James Starr erected a mill which was placed under control of his two sons, James and Moses; and this was the first use of the water power of French Creek.[3] A near neighbor of the Starrs and Coates was Thomas Valentine, originally from Ballybrumhill, County Carlow, who settled across the Schuylkill in New Providence Township, now Montgomery County.

In the summer of 1736, Joshua Marsh and his son John Marsh, with their families, from Grange near Charlemont, arrived and settled among the Welsh in East Nantmeal Township. Two years later they were joined by Joshua's son-in-law,

East Nantmeal Township

---

[1] *Annals of Phoenixville*, 20.
[2] *Ibid.*, 71.
[3] *Ibid.*, 21.

Thomas McMillan, and family from Ballinacree, County Antrim. The only other Irish Friends known to be in the locality were their nearest neighbors, William and Timothy Kirk, sons of Alphonsus Kirk, of New Castle County, William Kirk for many years serving as overseer of Nantmeal Meeting.

These Friends brought their certificates to Goshen Monthly Meeting, thereby becoming members thereof, and attended Uwchlan Particular and Preparative meetings until the establishment of Nantmeal Particular Meeting and the erection of a meeting house there in 1741, when Nantmeal became their place of worship, although they still attended preparative meetings at Uwchlan.

A meeting-house was built at Nantmeal in 1777. This was burned about 1795, and another house was built. For many years the meeting has been extinct. Uwchlan Particular Meeting was established in 1712, and the Preparative Meeting two years later. The present meeting-house was built in 1756.

About 1750, the Marshes and McMillans joined the early westward movement and migrated to Warrington Township, York County, becoming members of Warrington Meeting.

Nottingham   Among the Irish Friends who made their way to the Nottingham settlements, now in Maryland,

were: Roger Kirk, son of Alphonsus Kirk, of
New Castle County; his kinsman, Roger Kirk,

UWCHLAN MEETING HOUSE, CHESTER COUNTY, BUILT 1756

son of Timothy Kirk, of Lurgan, County Armagh ;
Benjamin Chandlee, originally from County Kil-
dare; and Eli Crockett, from Ballinacree, County
Antrim, a settler at Bush River Meeting.

The Friends of Nottingham were residents of Chester County, until about 1765, when the running of the famous Mason and Dixon line brought them within the limits of Cecil County, Maryland. In 1701, a company of friends, prominent among whom were John Churchman, Andrew Job, William and James Brown, and Henry Reynolds, removed from the old settlements in the vicinity of Chester and settled on a tract of some 18,000 acres of land called Nottingham on Octorara Creek.

In 1705, they had a meeting settled among them, held at the home of William Brown, until the erection of a meeting-house in 1708–9. This building was replaced by one of brick in 1724. John Churchman notes in his journal that in 1748 the latter was destroyed by fire, and until a new meeting-house could be built the meetings were held in a private house. When rebuilt, a stone addition was made to the original brick-work. The wood-work was again destroyed by fire in 1810. In 1811 the present structure was erected, and although one-half stone, has always been known as the "Brick Meeting."

Nottingham Meeting constituted a part of Concord Monthly Meeting until in 1715 it was transferred to Newark Monthly Meeting. On the erection of New Garden in 1718 it became a part of that Monthly Meeting, thus continuing until

1730, when Nottingham Monthly Meeting, consisting of the meetings of East Nottingham, West Nottingham, and Bush River, was established.

The first of the Irish Friends to settle in what is now Lancaster County were John Musgrave and his son, Moses Musgrave, who as early as 1713 had taken up land in the almost uninhabited region on Octoraro Creek within the present limits of Sadsbury Meeting, the father purchasing 600 acres and the son 300 acres.[1] John Musgrave, as we have stated before, came over from the north of Ireland in 1682, as an indented servant to Valentine Hollingsworth, and served his time with his master in New Castle County.[2] He was an active participant in the local affairs of his neighborhood, and in 1730 and 1731 represented Lancaster County in the Provincial Assembly.[3]

For a decade the Musgraves were probably the only Irish Friends in Sadsbury, or indeed in all the County, there being no others mentioned in the tax lists of 1718 for either Sadsbury or Conestoga;[4] but about 1723 an advance-guard of a larger migration, conspicuous among whom were Andrew Moore and Samuel Jackson, from Ballinacree, County Antrim, arrived and located near

[1] *Penn'a Archives*, 2d Series, XIX., 561, 569, 637, 708.
[2] Deposition of John Musgrave in Pennsylvania-Maryland boundary dispute, cited in *McFarlan-Stern Genealogy*, 59.
[3] *Penn'a Archives*, 2d Series, IX., 775.
[4] *Futhey and Cope*, 203, 171.

the Gap at the end of the Great Chester Valley. Soon these pioneers were joined by other members of the Society, many of them remaining in Sadsbury, and others, under the leadership of Hattill Varman, from County Wexford, pushing farther to the westward and forming a settlement in Leacock. Such a large proportion of these Friends were from Ireland that the meetings, which were soon established, were frequently known as the Irish meetings. Edmund Peckover, a Friend of the ministry, from England, who visited these "back-settlers" in 1742, speaks of them as "Friends from Ireland" who have "three or four meetings ; though Friends are but thin to what they are in other parts of the province."[1]

In addition to those just mentioned, the following were some of the immigrants to this region : Thomas McClun or McClung, from County West Meath; William McNabb, from Oldcastle, County Meath ; Neal O'Moony, John Boyd and sons William and Samuel, James Hunter, Samuel Wilkinson, and William Courtney, from Ballinacree, County Antrim ; William Evans, from County Wicklow ; John Griffith and son Christopher, from Grange near Charlemont ; Jonas Chamberlin, from King's County ; James Love and Thomas Nevitt, from County Cavan ; Isaac Steer and sons John

[1] Minutes of London Yearly Meeting, IX., 322, cited by *Bowden*, II., 243.

and Nicholas, from County Antrim ; James Smith, from County Armagh ; Thomas Bulla and Lawrence Richardson, from Grange, probably near Charlemont; and Thomas Lindley (son of James Lindly), a representative to the Provincial Assembly.

Meetings of an informal character were held in Sadsbury in 1723,[1] but a regular meeting was not established until the following year, when "Samuel Miller and Andrew Moore made application, on behalf of themselves and their friends settled about Sadsbury, for liberty to build a meeting, which being granted by the Quarterly Meeting, they built one in 1725, which goes by the name of Sadsbury Meeting."[2] The stone-work of the present meeting-house was built about 1760, but the wood-work was burned during the period of the Revolution.[3] *Sadsbury Meeting*

In 1729, "Sadsbury Preparative Meeting requested on behalf of Friends who live beyond Pequea, to have a meeting at the house of Hattell Varman [in Leacock Township] every sixth-day of the week ; which this meeting allows."[4] The regular First-day meeting at Leacock was established in 1732 and held at Varman's house. In 1749, the meeting was removed to Lampeter *Leacock Meeting*

[1] *Futhey and Cope*, 239.
[2] Samuel Smith in *Hazard's Register*, VII.
[3] Ellis and Evans, *History of Lancaster County*, 1036.
[4] *Minutes New Garden Monthly Meeting*, cited by *Michener*, 130.

II

Township and the name of the meeting changed
to Lampeter.

Sadsbury Monthly Meeting   In 1737, the Meetings of Sadsbury and Leacock,
which up to this date had formed a part of New
Garden Monthly Meeting, were erected into Sadsbury Monthly Meeting, sessions being held alter-
nately at the two places. The Meetings of Newberry, Warrington, Huntington, and Menallen, in
what is now York and Adams Counties, formed a
part of Sadsbury Monthly Meeting, until 1747,
when a monthly meeting of their own called Warrington was established.

York and Adams Counties   The founding of the Sadsbury settlements initiated that westward migration of Friends which
during the several succeeding decades moved
across Lancaster County to the west side of the
Susquehanna and gave rise to the meetings in
that part of the County which in 1749 became
York County. By 1727 this movement had reached
the east bank of the Susquehanna, at Hempfield,
now Columbia, where in that year settled John
Wright, Robert Barber, Samuel Blunston, and
others. Here it was delayed for a time by the
Cresap War rising from the boundary dispute between the Penns and the Lords Baltimore, but
soon it crossed to the west side of the River, and
as early as 1738 at Newberry had begun the first
of that belt of Quaker settlements extending across
the northern sections of what is now York and

Adams Counties.   The Irish Friends were not in
the vanguard of the York County migration, but
during the middle decades of the century they arrived in large numbers and figured prominently
in the affairs of the settlements.

Newberry[1] Meeting, during its first three or **Newberry**
four years called Manchester Meeting, was in- **Meeting**
cluded in Manchester Township, until in 1742 with
the organization of Newberry Township it fell
in the latter.[2]   The first settlers came from the
meetings in southern Chester County and New
Castle County and presented their certificates of
removal to Sadsbury Monthly Meeting.   The
Sadsbury minutes contain an interesting account
of the beginnings of the York County meetings
and we shall let the records tell their own tale.

3 Mo. 7, 1739.—"There being Divers families
of friends of late Settled on the West Side of Sus-
quohanno, Some of them have produced Certificates to this Meeting from Kenet Meeting, where
they formerly Dwelt, their being four Mentioned In
one Certificate bearing Date ye 10th of ye 2 ^{mo} 1738[1]
Vizt Nathan Husy [Hussey], Ann his wife, John
Garrison [Garretson] & Content his wife, John
Day and Ann his wife Christopher Husy [Hussey]
& Ann his wife & another Certificate from the

---

[1] The spelling of this name in the old records is about equally divided
between *Newberry* and *Newbury*, but the former is the accepted form at
the present day.

[2] Gibson's *History of York County.*

same place bearing date ye 4th of ye 5mo 1738,[1] Recommends Joseph Benett & Rebecka his wife All wch this Meeting receives in Membership with us.

" The Friends of that Settlement being desirous of a Toleration from this meeting to keep meetings of worship Every first day and fourth day of of ye week for six months time wch request Is Granted."

9 Mo. 5, 1739.—"The New Meeting Settled on the west Side of Suckahana haveing had Some time past a tolleration from this meeting to hould meetings of worship Every first Day and fourth day of the week and ye time being Expired att the request of several of them, being in this meeting, friends allows them twelf monts longer to be held as afore."

Until some years later, when a meeting-house was built, this meeting evidently was held at the house of John Day, for the early marriages[2] are known to have taken place there.

6 Mo. 5, 1745.—Andrew Moore, Calvin Cooper, Jonas Chamberlin, and Thomas Bulla are ap-

[1] The minutes of Newark or Kennett Monthly Meeting indicate that these certificates were dated on the first days of the months mentioned.

[2] The first Quaker wedding in what is now York County was that of Rodert Hodgin, carpenter, of Manchester, later Newberry Township, who was married 5 Mo. 29, 1740, at the house of John Day, in said township, to Theodate Seal, widow of Joseph Seal. The following list of witnesses to the marriage certificate is of interest as showing who were the settlers at that date :

pointed to visit the meetings on the west side of the Susquehanna, "to see how they fare in the Truth and report to next meeting." 8 Mo. 7, 1745,—"Friends Expressed their Satisfaction in respect of a visit to friends on the West Side of Susquehana." 9 Mo. 4, 1745.—"Friends of Newbery Requests to have a meeting settled; its sent to ye Quarterly Meeting for aprobation." 1 Mo. 3, 1745-6.—"The Request that went to Last Quarterly Meeting was Granted, *i. e.* that Newberry Meeting has Liberty to hold Meeting of Worship every first day and fourth days of the week as Warrington has on Every first day and fifth days of the week; and those two Meetings

Rebecca Bennett	James Clemson	ROBERT HODGIN
Hannah Fincher	Francis ffincher	her
Mary Cocks	Joseph Bennett	THEODATE × HODGIN
Rebecca Cocks	James Alison Junr	mark
Ester Davis	Wm Garretson	Anne Hussey
Anne Garratson	Joseph Garretson	Nathan Hussey
Martha Garratson	Wm Griffith	John Hussey
Sarah McAnabley	James Moore	Christopher Hussey
Elizabeth price	Thomas Riley	Content Garretson
Margrett Carson	Caisia Belley	Ann Day
	Jacob Youngblod	John Day
	Wm Baley	Thomas fioland
	James Baley	Petr Worall
	John Baley	Thomas Cocks
	James Aleson Senr	John Noblet
	Charles Mcanele	Ann Noblet
	Patrick Carson	Ann Hussy
		Margret Hussy
		John Garretson
		Wm Cocks
		Samuel Cocks

to make up one preparative meeting, to be held at each place turn about." 2 Mo. 7, 1746.—"Newberry preparative meeting recommends John Day and William Garretson for overseers in that meeting which is approved."

The original Newberry Meeting land, which is in the present village of Newberrytown, consisted of a hexagonal tract[1] of 42 acres and 61 perches, surveyed April 10, 1767, to John Garretson and Joseph Hutton, in trust for the Society of Friends. Our information about the early meeting-houses is very meagre, but the first building, which is said to have been of logs,[2] was probably erected on this tract. The old burial ground,[3] which at the time of the writer's visit to the place in 1897 was an almost impenetrable wilderness of briers and sumac, is all of the plot that is now owned by the Society. The remainder of the land and the meeting-house,[4] which according to the inscribed stone in the west gable was erected in 1792,[5] was

[1] The original draft of the tract is in possession of Joel V. Garretson, of Flora Dale, Adams Co., Pa.

[2] Gibson's *York County*.

[3] At Warrington Monthly Meeting, 5 Mo., 21, 1840, "Newberry Friends inform they have enclosed a graveyard at Newberry meeting-house; they propose closing the former one [in Newberrytown] it being full."

[4] This is a substantial structure of stone, similar in appearance to the old meeting-house at Warrington, and is now occupied as a dwelling, but there has been no material change in its exterior.

[5] At Warrington Quarterly Meeting, 8 Mo., 26, 1793, in answer to the second annual query, report was made that "one new Meeting house [has been] built in the room of an old one at Newberry."

sold about 1811, by authority of a special act of the State Legislature,[1] and the meeting was moved to another location about two miles from the town. Here a stone meeting-house was built on a five-acre lot sold to Jesse Wickersham and George Garretson, in trust for the Society, by Samuel Garretson and Alice his wife, by deed of 10 Mo. 4, 1811.[2] The meeting is now extinct, and at the time of my visit in 1897 the meeting-house was in a sad state of decay, but recently it has been re-covered with a slate roof and thoroughly repaired.[3] In 1897, the graveyard presented a well-kept appearance and was enclosed by an iron fence.

The Newberry community received a considerable body of the Irish Friends, but not so large as did Warrington and Menallen. Some of those who located at Newberry were: Timothy Kirk and his sons Jacob, Timothy, Caleb, Ezekiel, and Jonathan Kirk; Robert Whinery, originally from Grange, probably near Charlemont; Robert Miller and his son Samuel; George Boyd; Joshua Low; Joseph and John Hutton; William Wilson; and several members of the Hobson family.

[1] At Warrington Monthly Meeting, 12 Mo., 19, 1810, "Newberry preparative meeting informs they have agreed to sell the land where the present meeting House is built and to purchase other in a more convenient and central place."

[2] Deed in possession of Menallen Monthly Meeting, recorded in Deed Book LLL, p. 51, Recorder's Office, York, Pa.

[3] Dr. William H. Egle's historical *Notes and Queries*, 110–113, annual volume for 1900, Harrisburg, Pa., 1901.

Warrington Meeting

Warrington Meeting, in Warrington Township, about nine miles south-west of Newberry and midway between the present villages of Wellsville and Rossville, was regularly established[1] in 1745,[2] and a log meeting-house[3] erected the same year on a tract of 29 acres and 156 perches, " near the

[1] It is probable that meetings were held in the vicinity of Warrington as early as 1740, for on the 22d of 8 Mo. of that year a marriage was held "at yᵉ house of William Garretson," who resided in Warrington. This was the marriage of James Frazier to Rebecca Cox, daughter of Thomas Cox. The following is a list of the persons who signed the marriage certificate :

Eleazer Mires	Christopher Hussey	Ann Cox	JAMES FRAZIER
Joseph Garretson	John Garretson	Anne Noblett	
Joshua Kenworthy	Joseph Bennett	Content Garretson	REBECCA FRAZIER
Francis Fincher	John Earl	Theodate Hodgin	Thomas Cocks
Edward Mulleanoux	Samuel Underwood	Mary Crage	Alexander Frazier
Wm. Griffith	John Noblitt	Anne Waankin	Mary Cocks
Andrew Rogers	Charles Phillips	Ester Daviss	Alexander Frazier
	Wm. Garretson	Anne Garretson	Isaac Cox
	Daniel Early	Rebecca Rogers	John Cox
	George Alford		Rebecca Bennett
			John Fincher
			Jane Fincher
			Nathan Hussey

[2] *Minutes of Sadsbury Monthly Meeting*; Samuel Smith in *Hazard's Register*, VII., 134.

[3] The following paper drawn up at that time is of interest as showing who were the subscribers to the fund for the building of the first meeting-house :

" We the Subscribers knowing the Necessity of Publick Worship, & being Destitute of a pice of Land to Set a Meeting House on Do Each of us Promise to pay the Respective sums under written in order to get a Warrent for 25 acres of Land adjoyning Stephen Ails Land, as witness our Hands : John Earl, 5s ; Alexander Underwood, 3s ; Thomas Cox, 5s ; Joseph Garretson, 5s ; William Garretson, 5s ; Christopher Hussey, 5s ; James Frazier, 4s ; Isaac Cox, 3s ; Samuel Underwood, 3s ; Thomas Cook, 3s ; Richard Wickersham, 3s ; William Underwood, 3s ; Peter Cook 1s. 6d."—*MS. among title papers of Menallen Monthly Meeting.*

This log meeting-house stood a little south-east of the present stone building, on a part of the tract that has since been enclosed in the graveyard. The foundations were discovered in the latter 80's by persons digging in the graveyard.

Land of Stephen Eyles [Ailes] on a Branch of Conewago" Creek. A warrant, dated July 5, 1745, was issued for the land to be held in trust for the Society of Friends, but owing to an irregularity, the land was later, by proclamation, declared vacant and afterward granted by patent, dated 1 Mo. 22, 1767, from John Penn, Lieutenant-Governor, to William Garretson, William Underwood, William Penrose, and Peter Cleaver, in trust for the Society, the consideration being £9, 12s, 9d.[1]

In 1769,[2] a new stone meeting-house was built near the old one.[3] In 1782, it was found necessary to enlarge the building to almost double its original size in order to accommodate the Quarterly Meeting, and a stone addition was made to the north end.[4] The following year the old end was thoroughly repaired and given a new floor and a new

[1] Patent (Recorded page 207, Patent Book A. H., Vol. 7, Department of Internal Affairs, Harrisburg, Pa.) and other title papers in possession of trustees of Menallen Monthly Meeting.

[2] A stone bearing this date may be seen in the south gable.

[3] At Western Quarterly Meeting, held in Chester County, 8 Mo. 21, 1769, Warrington Monthly Meeting reported "One new Meeting House built at Warrington near the old one." George McMillan, an Irish Friend, of Warrington, son of Thomas McMillan, from Ballinacree Meeting, County Antrim, notes in the credit column of his Account Book (1769-1795), which is in possession of the writer, a descendant, that in March, 1769, there was "due by subscription to Wm. Garitson for bilding a New meeting house in Warnton, £3," and in January, 1770 "by ditto, £1." In the debtor column he notes : "May 5th, 1769, Pay^d to Wm. Garitson for said subscription first by haling timber with wag[on] one day, 10s; by an order from Jacob Williams £1, 0, 2; dito by Cash to Pay for Lime £1 ; dito by Cash May 5th £1, 10s."

[4] *Minutes of Warrington Monthly Meeting.*

roof.[1] With the exception of a slate roof and other
repairs effected in the latter 80's the old structure
remains substantially as it was in 1782, and is
still surrounded by a strip of the primitive forest.
On account of the westward emigration the regular meeting was discontinued about the middle of

[1] Benjamin Walker, a member of the Meeting, who resided on an adjoining farm to the south, was on the building committee, and in his Diary
(1780–1786), a copy of which is in my collection, gives a detailed account
of the work of construction. 4 Mo. 13, 1782, he is "one to provide
Nesareys and go on with Building an addishing to our Meeting house."
5 Mo. 16, they "agreed with yᵉ Carpenters to Do yᵉ work for the Meeting house ; flowring [flooring] 6s by yᵉ Square, Lining yᵉ walls 7s–6d, Galo-
reer [gallery] 12s by Square, Sash 7d pʳ Light, Sheters [shutters] 4s apeace,
Doars 10s, Window Cases 4s–6d, Doars 5s 6d." 6 Mo. 13, 5th day,
" at Meeting this Day we agreed with John & Jonah Thomas to Build a
Stone End to the Meeting house and with yᵉ Carpenters."

For several months afterward we find Walker turning aside from his
many other duties and actively engaged in pushing forward the building of
the meeting-house. One day (7 Mo. 30) he goes to York for lime ;
another he is hauling stone ; and another (8 Mo. 7), he drives "to the
pigeon hills for Lime 35 Bushels." 8 Mo. 8, "Ditto and halling Corner
Stone from Elihu Underwood." 8 Mo. 27 he is "halling the Summer
Beam." By 9 Mo. 6, 6th day, the stone work had so far progressed that
our diarist notes, "At our Meeting f[or] Suffrings Raising yᵉ New End of
yᵉ meeting house." 10 Mo. 14, he hauled "Shingles from yᵉ Meeting
house to Wm. McMullins [brother of George McMillan] to Soak." By
10 Mo. 21, no doubt the shingles were sufficiently soaked, and evidently
he is returning them, when he writes under this date, "halling Shingals
for yᵉ Meeting house."

The addition was soon completed, and, 1 Mo. 2, 1783, we find the
committee settling with "the Masons for Building yᵉ new meeting house
and ther is Due to them £44–4–0."

Repairs on the old end were begun the following summer. 5 Mo. 27,
1783, they were "Striping the old Roof of[f]," and 6 Mo. 20, "halling
Sleepers for the Meeting house." 8 Mo. 11, they were "taking up the
Meeting house floore." 9 Mo. 26, Walker went "to Manahan to Allin
Tarbuts for a Load of Boards for yᵉ Meeting." 11 Mo. 17, they settled
"with the Carpenters that Built the Meeting house ; it Came to £47–
15–7½."

the nineteenth century, and now meetings are held on only one First-day each year.

A large number of Irish Friends made their way to the Warrington settlement. Among them were Thomas Wilson, from Grange, near Charlemont, about 1748, a little later removing to Fairfax Meeting, Virginia ; Thomas Blackburn, from Ballyhagen, County Armagh, about 1749 ; the brothers George, John, and William McMillan, from Nantmeal, Chester County, about 1750 ; John Marsh and sons John, Joshua, Jonathan, and William, also from Nantmeal, about same date ; Peter Marsh, brother of John, from same place about same date ; William Nevitt, a minister in the Society, from Moate, County West Meath, about 1751 ; William Hutton, from New Garden, Chester County, about 1751 ; Samuel Hutton, from Exeter, Berks County, about 1753 ; Nicholas Steer, from Sadsbury, about 1759 ; John Boyd and son William, from Sadsbury, the former about 1765 and the latter about 1754 ; James Love, from Sadsbury, about 1761 ; Francis and Thomas Wilkinson, with their mother, Elizabeth, widow of Joseph Wilkinson, from Chester County, about 1760 ; Francis Hobson,[1] from Ballyhagen, County Armagh, about 1764 ; Aaron Coates, from Bradford, Chester County, about 1767 ; William Pillar, from Grange near Charlemont, about 1767,

[1] Ancester of Richmond P. Hobson, U. S. Navy, hero of the *Merrimac* incident off Santiago, in the Spanish War of 1898.

returning to Ireland about 1769 ; William Chandlee, from Deer Creek Meeting, Maryland, about
1773 ; and Peter Milhous, from Chester County.
Huntington About nine miles south-west of Warrington, in
Meeting Latimer, now Huntington, Township, Adams
County, is Huntington Meeting House, situated
on a wooded ridge overlooking Bermudian Creek,
some two miles south-east of the Borough of
York Springs, formerly Petersburg. Unauthor-
ized meetings were held in the neighborhood as
early as 1745, for at Sadsbury Monthly Meeting,
9 Mo. 4, 1745, William Garretson was directed to
read three papers of acknowledgment "at Huntington Meeting." These meetings evidently
convened at the house of John Cox, where nearly
all the early marriages[1] are known to have oc-

---

[1] *Minutes and Marriage Book of Sadsbury Monthly Meeting.*
  The first marriage at Huntington was that of Nicholas Wierman, son
of William Wierman, of Huntington, to Sarah Cox, daughter of John
Cox, of the same place, 8 Mo. 24, 1745. The signers were :

Alexander Underwood	Rebecca Kenworthy	NICHOLAS WIERMAN
William Underwood	Sarah Cook	SARAH WIERMAN
Joseph Cox	Martha Garretson	William Wireman
John Powell	Naomi Garretson	Gertruyed Wireman
John Wireman	Hannah Cox	John Cox
Thomas Powel	Ann Hussey	Thomas Cox
Jacob Beals	Mary Garretson	William Cox
Valintine Isickers	Naomi Cox	Samuel Cox
Benj. Underwood	Rachel Beals	Ann Cox
Richard Underwood	Hannah Wireman	Joseph Garretson
John Pope	Pricila Wireman	Henry Wireman
William Wireman	Sarah Proctor	Benjamin Cox
Joshua Kenworthy	Elizabeth Brown	
John Beals	Elizabeth Powel	
Caleb Beals	Jane Underwood	
	Olive Underwood	
	Ruth Underwood	

curred. The Meeting was not regularly established until 1750.[1]

The Meeting land, consisting of a rectangular
tract of five acres, called " Zion," was conveyed
to trustees of the Meeting by William Beals, by
deed of 12 Mo. 9, 1766, and was part of 50 acres
granted to Beals by the Proprietors' warrant of
June 24, 1763.[2] The present edifice, erected in
1790,[3] has recently been covered with a slate roof
and otherwise placed in a good state of preservation, but regular meetings have long ceased to be
held.

In the early years of the Huntington settlement, few if any Irish Friends located there, but
in the latter half of the century several families
made it their home.

The first location of Menallen[4] Meeting was
about seven miles west of Huntington, on the
east side of Opossum Creek, in Menallen, now
Butler, Township, Adams County. 6 Mo. 4, 1746,
Sadsbury Monthly Meeting " tolerates the Friends

Menallen
Meeting

[1] *Minutes of Sadsbury Monthly Meeting.*

[2] Original deeds in custody of the trustees of Menallen Monthly Meeting; recorded in Patent Book N, 34, p. 403, Department of Internal Affairs, Harrisburg, Pa., and in Deed Book KK, pp. 252, 485, Recorder's
Office, York, Pa.

[3] At Warrington Quarterly Meeting, 8 Mo. 23, 1790, report was made
that a new meeting-house had been built " at Huntington in place of an
old one."

[4] This name, doubtless of Irish origin, is spelled in all possible ways in
the old records but *Menallen* is the form used at the present day.

of Monalin to have Meetings of Worship to be kept on First Day and Fifth Day until Further Orders." 2 Mo. 16, 1748, "friends of Minallen requsts to have their meeting settled," and later in the year the meeting was regularly established.[1] The Meeting land, consisting of 20 acres and 153 perches, was not granted until May 26, 1788.[2] It is not known when the first edifice was built, but Nicholas Scull's map of the State shows that one had been erected as early as 1758.[3]

In 1838, the original site was abandoned[4]; the

---

[1] One of the first marriages at Menallen was that of Samuel Pope, of Tyrone Township, to Elizabeth Stevenson, of Menallen Township, 7 Mo. 4, 1751. The signers were as follows :

Jacob Hinshaw	Sarah Underwood	SAMUEL POPE
William Wright	Mary Wood	ELIZABETH POPE
Richard Proctor	Elizabeth McGrew	John Pope
Charles Pidgen	Elizabeth Dicks	William Shepherd
Daniel Winter	Rebeca Blackburn	Alex^r. Underwood
Walter Carson	Elizabeth Pope	Jno. Blackburn
Thomas Hamilton	Richmunday Shepherd	John Mickle
Richard Sadler	Sarah Ruddock	William Delap
William Young	Jane Shepherd	Finley McGrew
John Wilson	Sarah Shepherd	Jno. Wright
Nicholas Bishon	Eamey Cox	Thomas Blackburn
Anthony Blackburn	Agness Carson	Robert More
Edward Whitehead	Elen Carson	John Cox
Michal Willson	Jane Young	
John Shepherd	precila Wireman	
Richard Chesnon		

[2] Patent granted Feb. 8, 1813, recorded in Patent Book H, No. 8, page 533, Department of Internal Affairs, Harrisburg, Pa.

[3] *Penna Archives*, 3d Series, Appendix.

[4] By indenture (Deed Book S, page 478, Recorder's Office, Gettysburg, Pa.), dated April 24, 1852, the Friends leased 3 acres and 6 perches of

old log meeting-house was taken down, removed about three miles to the north-west, and rebuilt in a more convenient place,[1] near Flora Dale, about one mile south of what is now Bendersville.[2] In 1884, the old log house gave way to the present brick building, erected to the rear of the former one on a plot of 84 perches, purchased in 1871.[3] The Meeting is still well attended, and with the exception of Fawn Meeting, in the south-east corner of York County, is the only surviving meeting of the original York County.

In its early years Menallen Meeting was distinctively an Irish meeting, the majority of its members being from Ireland. Among them were John Blackburn,[4] Judge of the York County Court in 1764, County Treasurer in 1759 and 1766,[5] and

the tract to the Dunkers or German Baptists, at the rate of one dollar annually for a term of fifty years. Upon this plot the Dunkers erected a wooden meeting house and laid out a burial ground. The Friends continued to make their interments in the original graveyard until 1853, when a piece of land adjoining the new site was purchased and another graveyard opened (*Land Title Papers*, in possession of Menallen Meeting).

[1] The land for the new location, consisting of 142.4 perches, was conveyed to the Meeting by Nathan Wright and Elizabeth, his wife, by deed of May 15, 1839, for a consideration of $17.75 and with the condition that should it cease to be used as a place of worship it should revert to the original tract.—*Land Title Papers*.

[2] *History of Adams County*, 226, 311.

[3] Menallen Meeting land is now an L-shaped tract of 1 acre and 142 perches.

[4] In 1755, he joined the forces sent to subdue the Indians and was disowned by the Society.

[5] Gibson's *York County*, 304, 494.

member of Assembly. Daniel Winter, William Delap, Joseph Hewitt and son George, from Bally-hagen Meeting, County Armagh; John Wright, from Castleshane, County Monaghan; John Morton, from New Garden, Chester County; Thomas Nevitt, from Sadsbury; William Newlin, and Moses Harlan,[1] son of George, from Chester County; George Wilson, Solomon Shepherd, and Jacob Hinshaw, from Grange near Charlemont; Robert Mickle, from Dublin; and Francis Hobson, Jr.

York Meeting   The Friends were among the earliest settlers at York, the county-seat of York County, but a meeting seems not to have been held there until 1754. Under date of 12 Mo. 21st of that year, Warrington Monthly Meeting minutes state: "Our Friends in and about York, living remote from any of our meetings, Requests the liberty of holding a meeting among themselves for this winter season, which this meeting has good unity with." A regular meeting was established in 1764, and on October 29th of the following year a lot of ground on the north side of Philadelphia

---

[1] Moses Harlan obtained a patent for 855 acres of land on the upper fork of the Conewago Creek, in Menallen Township, Oct. 9, 1745. He and Margaret, his wife, by deed of July 21, 1747, conveyed to John Blackburn, 258 acres thereof. The will of Moses Harlan, of Menallen Township, was dated 10 Mo. 10, 1747 and proven March 29, 1749. He mentions his son-in-law John Blackburn; grandson Jacob Cox, son of daughter Mary Cox; grandsons Thomas and Moses Blackburn; and grand-daughter Dinah Cox

Street was purchased from Nathan Hussey and Edith his wife.[1] Upon this lot a brick meeting-house was erected in 1766.[2] By will, dated 1 Mo. 25, 1773, Nathan Hussey bequeathed to the Meeting a lot adjoining on the west. About 1786 the meeting-house was enlarged to its present proportions, an addition being made to the west end. The Society in the city is now almost extinct and regular meetings have been discontinued.

Among the most prominent of the Irish Friends to settle in York were the Loves and Kirks.

We see, then, that the Irish Friends first located in the original counties of Philadelphia and Chester. Thence, with the expansion of the Province, many of them joined the southward and westward migrations of Friends, which during the third and fourth decades of the eighteenth century began from the Quaker strongholds of the original settlements.

Expansion of Pennsylvania Quakerism

For three-quarters of a century one of these streams of Quaker migration injected a new and vigorous element into the Quakerism of the South.[3]

Southward

---

[1] *Deed Book CC, page 153*, Recorder's Office, York.

[2] The following Friends subscribed to a paper, dated 1 Mo. 1, 1766, contributing to the building fund : Nathan Hussey, William Willis, Joseph Updegraff, Joseph Garretson, William Matthews, Harman Updegraff, Jesse Falkner, James Love, John Collins, and Joseph Collins.

At Western Quarterly Meeting, 8 Mo. 11, 1767, report was made that "Friends in and about York have now built a Meeting-House."

[3] For the principal facts of the southward movement I am indebted to Dr. Stephen B. Weeks' *Southern Quakers and Slavery*, which is a most thorough and scholarly treatment of the subject.

12

The movement reached the Monocacy region of Maryland about 1725. Here it rested for a time, and then crossed the Potomac River and struck Hopewell, north of what is now Winchester, in Frederick County, Virginia, in 1732.[1] In that year a company of Friends from Pennsylvania, under the leadership of Alexander Ross, an Irish Friend, settled on a tract of 100,000 acres of land, called Hopewell, on Opequan Creek, in the beautiful Shenandoah Valley, obtaining a charter for the land from the government of Virginia. A meeting called Opequan, afterward Hopewell, was established two years later; and Hopewell Monthly Meeting, including the meetings of Hopewell and Monocacy, in 1735.[2] Among the Pennsylvania Friends of Irish name who made their way to Hopewell we find the Kirks, Hollingsworths, Wilsons, Greggs, Hiatts, and Steers.

About the same time with the founding of the Hopewell settlement a branch of the same migration moved from Maryland into Loudon and Fairfax Counties, Virginia; thence to the southern counties of that colony; and by 1743 it had gotten as far as Carver's Creek in Bladen County, North Carolina. During the next twenty years Friends swarmed into the central sections of the latter state and founded Cane Creek, New Garden, and

[1] *Weeks*, 70, 96.
[2] *Janney*, III., 248; *Minutes of Chester Quarterly Meeting*; sketch of Hopewell Meeting, *Friends' Intelligencer*, LIII., 461–3.

a large number of other monthly meetings. About 1760, the movement was once more on its way southward, and by the time of the Revolution had spent itself in the founding of a series of meetings in South Carolina and Georgia.

Among the Friends of the Carolinas we find the Starrs, McCools, Steers, Greggs, Musgraves, Sharps, Hobsons, Newlins, Hadlys, Harlans, Hollingsworths, Coates', Dixons, Stanfields, Jacksons, Johnsons, Lindleys, Milhous', Hiatts, Hinshaws,[1] and many other families of Irish name, formerly from Pennsylvania.

By the end of the eighteenth century the southern Friends had taken such a firm stand against the institution of slavery, that they were no longer able to come into economic competition with their neighbors who utilized slave labor. Their situation was rendered still more uncomfortable by the hostile attitude assumed by these slave-holding neighbors, and the passing of the century witnessed a great exodus of the Society to the newly opened free Northwest Territory. Thousands of Friends, including many of Irish name originally from Pennsylvania, left their old homes to escape the hated system, and following several routes through Virginia and Kentucky, poured into the new country.

[1] The Hinshaws settled at Cane Creek, in North Carolina, several of them coming directly from Grange near Charlemont, Ireland, and others from Warrington, York County, Pennsylvania.

Westward   The direct westward migration,[1] as previously
narrated, reached Sadsbury, in Lancaster County,
about 1723. By 1727 it was on the east bank of
the Susquehanna, where it halted for a decade;
then with the close of the Cresap War it moved
in full force upon York County. Here its westward course was checked for a time by the great
barriers of the South Mountain and the Allegheny
ranges, and by the French occupation of the western country, and the movement was deflected
southward into Maryland, Virginia, and the Carolinas; but with the close of the French and Indian
War, at the Peace of Paris in 1763, the rich allu-
vial lands of the Monongahela Valley or Redstone
Region in Western Pennsylvania, which with the
Mississippi Valley had now come into possession
of the English, were thrown open to settlement,
and once more the tide of migration was westward bound.

From the original York County the migration
passed to points in the Cumberland Valley, most
detachments moving through Shippensburg.
Here the migration divided. One branch, taking
the less mountainous and, for a time at least, the
more popular route, proceeded down the Cumberland Valley into Maryland and then followed
the devious course of the valley of the Potomac to

[1] This sketch of the westward movement of the Quakers from Pennsylvania is drawn from a mass of material, chiefly from the original manuscript sources, which I have collected preparatory to a more extended
study of the subject.

Fort Cumberland; thence, advancing along the line of march of the ill-fated Braddock, it crossed the great ridge of the Alleghenies, and passing again into Pennsylvania made its way over Laurel Hill through Beesontown,[1] to Redstone Old Fort, later Brownsville, on the Monongahela, where it was diffused over the valley of that river. The other branch, crossing an almost continuous series of mountain ridges, advanced directly westward along the old military road from Shippensburg by way of Fort Littleton and Bedford[2] to Redstone, where the two branches were again united.

So far as known, the first Friend to settle in the Redstone region was Henry Beeson, who removed from Berkeley County, Virginia, in 1768, and became the founder of Beesontown, now Uniontown.[3] He was soon joined by other Friends from Virginia, Maryland, and a little later by those from the eastern part of Pennsylvania;[4] and by 1773, when the ministers John Parrish and Zebulon Heston,[5] on their return from a mission to the

[1] Now Uniontown, Fayette County.

[2] At Dunnings Creek, near Bedford, settled Thomas Blackburn, of Menallen, ancestor of the numerous progeny of the name in Bedford County (See *History of Bedford County*, 282). Benjamin Walker, of Warrington, York County, notes in his diary, 12 Mo. 5, 1783: "to Bedford then Thos. Blackburns on Dennings Creek Lodged."

[3] Ellis, *History of Fayette County*, 279; *Friends' Intelligencer*, LIV., 347, footnote.

[4] Veech, *The Monongahela of Old*, 99.

[5] Heston's grand-nephew John Lacy, afterward Brigadier-General in the Continental Army, accompanied them and has left some account of the journey in his *Memoirs*. (*Penn'a Mag.*, XXV., 1 *et seq.*)

Ohio Indians, visited the region, several small
Quaker settlements had been made.[1] In 1776,
report was made to Warrington and Fairfax
Quarterly Meeting that about eighteen families
" have removed from different parts of this &
the neighboring Provinces & settled over the
Alligahania Mountains "[2]; but the War of the
Revolution having now begun in earnest the work
of settlement was greatly retarded.

In this same year of 1776, the British commander
at Detroit began to incite the Indians to attack the
frontier of Pennsylvania, and the assaults of the
red men upon Wheeling and the neighborhood of
Pittsburgh in this and the following year caused
such alarm among the settlers that large numbers,
including some Friends, returned to their former
homes.   Margaret Cook, a minister, on her way
to this county in the spring of 1778, mentions in
her *Journal* that she and her companions " met
some going back with their fleetings[3] driving as if
the Indians were just behind them, and the road
was so filled with pack horses that it was difficult
getting along."[4]   Later in this year the Quarterly
Meeting was informed "that many of the Fami-

[1] Journal of John Parrish, *Penn'a Mag.*, XVI., 446–8.
[2] MS. copy of Minutes, Library Hist. Soc. of Penn'a.
[3] Flittings,—household effects in the course of removal.
[4] *Friends' Intelligencer*, LIV., 347.   On her return journey she notes
that, 5 Mo. 20th, on the Alleghany Mountains, they " met a company going to fight the Indians."

lies of Friends settled there have removed back to the Meetings from whence they went and they were much dispersed."[1]

After the victories of George Rogers Clark in 1778–79, and the subjugation of the Indians, the Redstone settlers feared attack no longer, and many of those who had fled now returned; but the remainder of the war period was marked by few accessions of emigrants, a census of the Friends in these sections in 1780 showing only seventeen families or about one hundred and fifty persons.[2] The close of active hostilities, however, witnessed a great inpouring of immigrants along the two routes. In 1782, a meeting for worship and a preparative meeting were established at Westland, about six miles west of Redstone Fort. By 1785, the Quaker population had so increased that another meeting for worship was erected at Redstone, and these two meetings were formed into a monthly meeting called Westland. Other meetings soon followed, and in 1793 a new monthly meeting called Redstone was organized.

Among the Irish Friends in the van of the movement, as mentioned by Parrish in his *Journal* of 1773, were Joseph and Anthony Blackburn and Simon and James McGrew, living between the two Sewicklys; Solomon Shepherd and his brother

---

[1] *Minutes.*

[2] *Ibid.*

John, located near Fort Ligonier,—all from Menallen; and Barnabas McNamee and Thomas Gregg, near Redstone Fort, the former from Nottingham and the latter from Kennett. Joshua Brown, travelling in 1787, speaks of Joshua Dixon, of Fallowfield, in what is now Washington County[1]; and Peter Yarnall, who made a visit in 1789, mentions Alexander and Finly McGrew, of near the Sewicklys, and Henry Dixon on the Monongahela.[2] Other Quaker arrivals of Irish name, as shown by the records of Westland and Redstone Monthly Meetings, were the Huttons, Pennocks, Hobsons, Newlins, McMillans, Whinerys, and Kirks; in fact, few Irish names were unrepresented in this and the later great migration to the Middle West.

By the opening of the nineteenth century the Friends became infected more strongly than ever with the prevailing spirit of migration, and again we find them on the westward march. A stream of migration more powerful than any of the preceding, arising to considerable extent from new sources in eastern Pennsylvania, New Jersey, and even New York, now flowed in a steady current through the two well-worn channels to the gateway of the Redstone region, where, gathering new

[1] *MS. Journal of Joshua Brown*, Friends' Library, 142 North Sixteenth Street, Philadelphia.

[2] *Journal of Peter Yarnall*, Comly's *Friends' Miscellany*, vol. 2, pages 252-261.

strength, it moved to the River Ohio and spread out over the broad and fertile plains of the Old Northwest. Here, mingling with the great stream of Quakers from the South, it gave rise to many new meetings, almost if not equaling in number those of the Atlantic seaboard, and became an important factor in the formation and development of the great commonwealths of the Mississippi Valley.

CHAPTER II.

SOCIAL LIFE OF THE IRISH FRIENDS

Introductory

OF the social conditions among the Irish Friends in early Pennsylvania some idea will have been formed from the preceding chapters, particularly from Robert Parke's long letter[1]; now let us consider this phase of our history more in detail, dwelling especially upon some of the more important sides of country life. The diaries, wills, and inventories of the time, and the ancient records of Friends, abound in quaint and interesting items reflecting the manners and customs of the period, and it is these rich stores chiefly that have been drawn upon. On many points, however, authentic material was not at hand, and this in part accounts for the somewhat inadequate and fragmentary character of portions of the chapter.

Irish Friends Well Adapted for Pioneer Life

The Irish Friends were an active and enterprising people, particularly well adapted for pioneer life, doubtless more so than the English and Welsh Friends; for the unsettled state of Ireland through so long a period,—that of the Cromwellian Settlement, the raids of the Rapparees, the troubles

[1] Pp. 71-79.

between James II. and William III., and the religious persecutions and other causes of emigration—had inured them to privation and hardship and prepared them to contend with the difficulties of the new country.

Although the majority of these Friends were of English stock, yet those families that had been in Ireland for a generation or more had become modified by their Irish environment and by contact with their restless and aggressive Celtic- and Scotch-Irish neighbors, developing habits and characteristics that distinguished them from the English Friends of the Province. *Mostly of English Stock but Modified by Irish Environment*

These characteristics crop out in the old meeting records, which show that the younger Irish Friends especially were impulsive and full of spirit, chafing under the restraint of the strict and repressive discipline of the Society as enforced in those days and it is quite common, as we shall see, to find them " marrying out by ye priest " and otherwise breaking the rules.   In this connection it is also worthy of note that in those meetings in which the Irish element was strong there was a tendency to be more liberal in belief and less stringent in the administration of some of the rules of discipline.

In those neighborhoods where the clan spirit was strong, and where most of the marriages occurred among their own number, these Friends

preserved much of their Irish identity for generations ; but by the early years of the nineteenth century they had lost much of this peculiarity and were
becoming rapidly absorbed in the new composite
American race.

The Arrival On their first arrival from Ireland, and before
their own homes could be provided, immigrant
Friends did not want for food and shelter ; in that
Hospitality of Old Settlers era of simple kindliness and free-hearted hospitality the old settlers were ever ready with open
door to receive the newcomers and to assist and
counsel them in choosing a location.   The great
Small Capital of Immigrants body of these Friends brought only small capital
with them, but they were young and vigorous and
the favorable opportunities offered here enabled
the most of them to begin a fairly comfortable
Household Goods Brought from Ireland settlement.   Men with families usually brought
their household goods with them, purchasing in
the Colony, horses, cattle, and such other necessaries that could be bought to better advantage
on this side of the water.

It was customary for those Friends who in-
Temporary Home near Landing Place tended to establish themselves upon inland plantations, first to provide temporary homes for their
families near the place of landing, and then to go,
often several in a company, prospecting for farm
land in the interior.

The Settlement Ties of kin and of friendship had an important
bearing on the selection of lands ; those who had

been kinsmen or old friends in Ireland naturally *Selection of Land Affected by Ties of Kin and Friendship* desired to locate near each other in Pennsylvania, and in consequence we find such distinctive Irish Quaker settlements as those of Newark and Centre in New Castle County, New Garden in Chester County, Sadsbury in Lancaster County, and Menallen in the original York County.

Once the land was selected and steps taken to *Journey to New Home* secure the title thereto, usually by warrant[1] from the Proprietary, haste was made to remove the families thither so that the settlement might be well advanced before the winter season had begun.[2] Pack-horses, almost the only means of transportation, were now made ready with saddles and pillions, and the women and children and farm and household effects were loaded upon them, the men frequently travelling on foot, leading the horses and driving the flocks and herds before them. Thus equipped the little procession would set off through the dark and lonely woods, follow-

[1] The planter applied at the land office for the warrant, which was issued by the Proprietary, or the Commissioners, and addressed to the Receiver-General, authorizing that official to have a survey made on terms described in the document. The warrant then passed to the Surveyor-General, who made a copy, returning the original to the warrantee to be held as evidence of title until the patent was issued. The Surveyor-General gave the copy of the warrant with an order to the Deputy-Surveyor of the county in which the land was located, directing the survey to be made. After the Deputy-Surveyor had completed his measurements, he reported to the office of the Surveyor-General, who then issued a patent to the purchaser of the land. It usually happened that the patent was not issued until some years after the warrant.

[2] In this connection see Robert Parke's letter, pages 71-79.

ing the Indian trails and the paths marked by blazed trees to the new abode.

The site of the dwelling on the plantation was generally near a spring of water, either on low ground or on the warm southern slope of a hill, for the sake of protection from the bleak and piercing winds of winter. With an energy and enthusiasm born of the thought that they were no longer tenants but absolute owners of the soil, the whole family now worked to win a home from the unconquered wilds. The trees fell quickly under the sturdy blows of the woodman's sharp-edged axe, and soon a little clearing appeared amidst the encircling forest. The next concern was the erection of a house. This first habitation was only a rude cabin built of timber hewn and sawed by hand from the fallen trees; but before many years had elapsed, with the large increase that blessed his labors, the farmer was enabled to erect a more comfortable and commodious dwelling of brick or stone, often making it an addition to the original house.

There were several methods of constructing the first wooden house. One of those suggested by Penn in his *Directions to Such Persons as are inclined to America*,[1] issued about 1682, was doubtless
followed by many of the early settlers. He writes:[2]

[1] Reprinted in *Penna. Mag.*, IV., 329–342; see also Oldmixon's *British Empire in America* (printed in 1708), reprinted in Hazard's *Register* (Phila., 1830), V., 177.

[2] *Penna. Mag.*, IV., 334–5.

To build then, an House of thirty foot long and eighteen foot broad, with a partition neer the middle, and an other to divide one end of the House into two small Rooms, there must be eight Trees of about sixteen Inches square, and cut off, to Posts of about fifteen long, which the House must stand upon, and four pieces, two of thirty foot long, and two of eighteen foot long, for Plates, which must lie upon the top of those Posts, the whole length and breadth of the House, for the Gists to rest upon. There must be ten Gists of twenty foot long, to bear the Loft, and two false Plates of thirty foot long to lie upon the ends of the Gists for the Rafters to be fixed upon, twelve pare of Rafters of about twenty foot, to bear the Roof of the House, with several other small pieces; as Wind-beams, Braces, Studs, etc. which are made out of the Waste Timber. For Covering the House, Ends, and Sides, and for the Loft, we use Clab-board, which is Rived feather-edged, of five foot and a half long, that well Drawn, lyes close and smooth: The Lodging Room may be lined with the same, and filled up between, which is very Warm. These homes usually endure ten years without Repair. . . . The lower flour is the Ground, the upper Clabboard. This may seem a mean way of Building but 'tis sufficient and safest for ordinary beginners.

Dankers and Sluyter [1] the Dutch Labadists, on their journey from New York to the Delaware, in 1679, met with this form of house at the Falls of Delaware, now Trenton, New Jersey. and have left the following description:

Nov. 17th.—Most of the English, and many others, have their houses made of nothing but clapboards, as they call them there, in this manner: they first made a wooden frame, the same as they do in Westphalia, and at Altona, but most so strong; they then split the boards of clapboard, so that they are like cooper's pipe staves, except they are not bent. These are made very thin with a large knife, so that the thickest end is about a *pinck* (little finger) thick, and the other is made sharp, like the edge of a knife. They are about five or six feet long, and are nailed on the outside of the frame, with the ends lapped over each other. They are not usually laid so close together, as to prevent you from sticking a finger be-ween them, in consequence either of their not being well joined, or the boards being crooked. When it is cold and windy the best people plaster

---

[1] *Memoirs of the Long Island Historical Society*, I., 172.

them with clay.   Such are most all the English houses in the country, except those they have which were built by people of other nations.   Now
this house was new and airy ; and as the night was very windy from the
north, and extremey cold.

    This description is confirmed in " An Account of East Jersey, in 1684 " :[1]
" They build not only of Wood, but also of Stone and brick, yet most of
Country Houses are built of Wood only Trees split and set up on end on the
ground, and coverings to their Houses are mostly Shingles made of Oak,
Chestnut and Cedar Wood, which makes a very neat covering : "

    The most common form of the early dwell-
ing, however, was the more permanent log
The Log cabin,[2] built of squared logs, placed horizontally
House one upon the other and notched together at the
corners.   The interstices between the logs were
filled in or " chinked " with stones or wedges of
wood, and then plastered over with mortar or
clay.   The roof was covered with boards or oak
shingles, either pinned by wooden pins or pegs or
held in place by " weight timbers." [3]   Says Ash-

    [1] Hart's *American History told by Contemporaries*, I., 569.

    [2] Dankers and Sluyter (*Memoirs L. I. Hist. Soc.*, I., 175) in their
journey of 1679, give an account of the log house of Jacob Hendricks, a
Swede, of Burlington, New Jersey, stating that it was "*made according
to the Swedish mode*, and as they usually build their houses here, which
are block houses, being nothing else than entire trees, split through the
middle, or squared out of the rough, and placed in the form of a square,
upon each other, as high as they wish to have the house ; the ends of these
timbers are let into each other, about a foot from the ends, half of one into
half of the other.   The whole structure is thus made, without a nail or a
spike.   The ceiling and roof do not exhibit much finer work, except
among the most careful people, who have the ceiling planked and a glass
window.   The doors are wide enough, but very low, so that you have to
stoop in entering.   These houses are quite light and warm ; but the chimney is placed in a corner."

    [3] Isaac Weld, *Travels through the States of North America*, in 1795,
21–22 ; Peter Kalm, *Travels into America*, in 1748, p. 166 ; Lodge's

mead:[1] "Locks in ordinary use were unknown ;
the doors [were hung on wooden hinges or straps
of hide and] were opened by strings, which on being pulled from the outside raised heavy wooden
latches within, to which they were made fast, and
intrusion was prevented when the inmates pulled
the latch-strings in at the outer doors. From this
common practice originated the ancient saying
descriptive of generous hospitality, 'the latch-
string is always out.' "

A stone chimney of immense size, capable of *Equipment o*
receiving a whole cord stick on the hearth, was *House and Farm*
built into one end of the house. The great fireplace was used for cooking and heating. Here
were to be found frying-pans, chafing-dishes, and *The Hearth*
spits, and suspended over the andirons by pothooks from an iron bar or crane, were the pots
and kettles, which were so highly prized by the
settlers that they were frequently bequeathed by
will. George Harlan, of Kennett, in his will of
1714, devised to his son Aaron a "great brass
kettle," and William Halliday, of New Garden, in
1741, left "unto my Daughter Deborah Lindly
my big pott that I brought from Ireland." We
may be sure that his bequest was all the more
righly regarded because it had come over sea.

Colonies, 248; Ashmead's *Delaware County*, 179; Alice Morse Earle's
Home Life in Colonial Days ; Acrelius, *History New Sweden* in *Memoirs
Hist. Soc. Penna.*, XI., 157.

[1] *Delaware County*, 179.

13

Halliday also gave to his daughter-in-law, Mabel Halliday, "a gridle."

The great hearth fire was the center of attraction in the long winter evenings. Its dancing flames filled the room with good cheer, throwing into the shadow the bare and homely outlines and lighting up with gentle touch the prominent features,—the rude furniture, the floor bare save for a rug or two, the overhanging beams, the mantel bright with pewter and brass,[1] and the walls unadorned excepting perhaps for a map or sampler or a fowling-piece. Here by the fireside the household and perhaps a few neighbors would assemble to enjoy the evening fire and to chat of affairs of common interest and to exchange the marvelous stories current in those days ; but no one has equalled the gentle Whittier in giving the spirit of this scene of domestic peace and contentment :

> Shut in from all the world without,
> We sat the clean-winged hearth about,
> Content to let the north-wind roar
> In baffled rage at pane and door,
> While the red logs before us beat
> The frost-line back with tropic heat ;
> And ever, when a louder blast
> Shook beam and rafter as it passed,
> The merrier up its roaring draught
> The great throat of the chimney laughed ;
> The house-dog on its paws outspread
> Laid to the fire his drowsy head,

[1] Dublin Half Year Meeting, in writing to Friends on the Delaware, in 1681, advise them to avoid "flourishing needless Pewter and Brass" in their kitchens.

The cat's dark silhouette on the wall
A couchant tiger's seemed to fall ;
And, for the winter fireside meet,
Between the andirons' straddling feet,
The mug of cider simmered slow,
The apples sputtered in a row,
And, close at hand, the basket stood
With nuts from brown October's wood.

What matter how the night behaved ?
What matter how the north-wind raved ?
Blow high, blow low, not all its snow
Could quench our hearth-fire's ruddy glow.[1]

A study of the inventories of the estates of some of the deceased Irish Friends shows quite accurately the character and extent of their possessions, and enables us to form a fairly clear idea of the furnishings of the houses and of the stock and implements of the farms, and to compare the wealth of the settlers with that of their neighbors.[2] The inventory[3] of "all & Singular ye Goods & Chattels Rights & Credits of John Lowdon Late of New Garden in the County of

Inventories

John Lowden's Goods, 1714

[1] *Snow-Bound.*

[2] Extracts from the inventory of George Harlan, of Kennett, made Oct. 29, 1714 : wearing apparrell £ 5 ; 1 Bed 1 Bolster 2 pillows & pillow Cases ; 2 ℔ of Sheets ; 1 Rug and 1 blanket ; 1 Bedstead ; 1 Chest ; 1 Table ; 1 Couch ; 1 old warming pan ; two Chests ; 6 pieces of pewter ; 1 Bress Skillet ; 1 frying pan ; 3 floats 3 pails 1 Churn 1 wooden bottle ; 1 Gun ; 2 Cows 1 black 1 Red ; 1 Stone horse ; 1 Dark brown meare Called Midge & this years horse Colt ; 1 Black Ridgelin (?) ; 1 Dark Brown mare with a bay yearling ; saws, augers, planes, axes, etc ; one old Bed tick and Bolster ; one Bay mare about 15 years old in the woods ; one Brown Bay Horse Colt about 1 year old ; 1 bay horse one bay mare ; one Sorril Colt ; 1 Grey Mare and Colt [Total value of estate £ 270. 8. 2.]

[3] Made 3 Mo. 10, 1714, by James Starr and Michael Lightfoot.—*Papers No. 3, Register's Office, West Chester, Pa.*

Chester, weaver," made in 1714, after Lowden had been in this country about three years, indicates how bare and meagre were some of these homes :

> One Cow and Calf; a horse; wheat 6 acres; a ffeather Bedd and Bedding; a fflock Bedd and Bedding; Course Sheets; Table Linnen Wareing Apparell; Linnings; 2 Saddles and a pair of Boots; Iron Tools; Gunn and Gunn Barrell; Small irons; Twoo potts; Pewter & two Brass Candlesticks; two Chests; An Old Box; Some Wooden Vessels; A Spade; Three Hundred Acres of Land. [Total value of estate £ 205-2-0].

The absence of the items of furniture such as chairs, tables, and bedsteads, from this and other inventories of the time, seems due to the fact that much of the furniture was of such crude construction, that it was not considered worthy of inclusion in the list. John Miller, yeoman and miller, one of the largest land owners of the New Garden settlement, died in the same year as Lowdon, but seems to have been more well-to-do. His househood goods were : [1]

John Miller's Inventory

> Three Ruggs; two pare of Sheets; fourteen yards of Cloath; two pillows; two bed ticks; three bedd steds; twelve napkins & two table Cloaths; twelve felt hats; one Chist; 1 beef barrell; 1 brewing Ceive; one washing tub & a half bushell; two dozen of trenshers fourteen noggens and three platters; one Couch & two tables; three puter dishes; twelve plates; one tankard a Saltseler & a mustard cup; two brass and one Iron Candlestick; one beef barrell; A Copper kettle & three Iron

[1] Inventory made "ye 12th of ye 1mo 171¼ " by Simon Hadly, Thomas Garnett, Michael Lightfoot, and James Starr.—*Papers No. 9, Register's Office, West Chester, Pa.*

potts; an old Gunn barrell & a spitt; nine Sickles[1]; a spade & two Shovles; Seven bars of Lead; Some barr Iron; two Crooks & two Smoothing Irons; four old bells.

From the articles of this list we can well picture to ourselves the appointments of a New Garden dinner table in 1714. The rough home-made board with its supporting trestles was covered with snowy cloth—board-cloth—and napkins of linen, spun, woven, and bleached by the good housewife, doubtless, in her old home in Ireland. The dishes were mostly of wood with some few pieces of pewter, always kept bright and shining. The center-piece was the salt-cellar, which in many colonial homes divided the guests, seated "above the salt," from those of lesser note, placed "below the salt." Large shallow pewter platters were heaped high with meats and vegetables. Wooden trenchers served as plates, and wooden noggins as drinking cups; and mustard cup, wooden tankards for water or liquor, and pewter porringers likewise graced the board. There were no covered dishes, saucers, glass or china, although earthenware was to be found on some tables.

A New Garden Dinner Table, 1714

[1] From evidence of old diaries the sickle seems to have been used in Chester County up to the Revolution, and then the grain-cradle was introduced. Richard Barnard, of East Marlborough, on a visit to Deer Creek, Harford County, Md., notes in his manuscript diary, 6 Mo. 4, 1775, that he "observed a Creadle to Cradle wheat," and on 7 Mo. 10th we find him engaged "about Cradle to Cradle wheat." On the 24th of the same month Samuel Hunt (see *Futhey and Cope*, 338), of East Caln, records that "Leathe Ingrum began to Cradle Oats at 1s. 6 d. pr acre & 1 Pint of Rum a Day."

Knives were used, but forks did not come into general use until later, so that the hands had to be constantly employed for holding the food, and on that account napkins were a necessity.[1]

Outfit of Farm

From other items enumerated in Miller's inventory, we may judge of his general equipment for farming :

Six Cows & two Calves; two yoak of oxen; one Bull; a two-year old hefer 2 year old bulocks & 1 hefer; twenty Sheep & Eight Lambs; three Horses a mare & Coult; whate in yᵉ barn; a field of yᵉ wheat & barly; one Stack of oats ; flower & wheate in yᵉ mill ; the mill and Bolting mills and four hundred ackers of Land ; three hundred ackers of Land near yᵉ Meeting hous ; The Housing & plantation Containing three hundred ackers ; Joyners Small tools ; oagers & hand Saws ; two old whip Saws & a Cross Cut Saw ; one Cart & gears belonging to it ; two plows & three Irons ; three pitching & three Grubing axes ; two old Squaring axes & two hand axes ; one grinding Stone ; an old Mare & Colt. [Total value of estate over £938.]

John Fred's Inventory, 1720

The inventory[2] of John Fred, cooper, of Birmingham, Chester County, an arrival from County Carlow in 1713, was made 2 Mo. 21, 1720, and is of particular interest as showing the arrangement of the furniture in the various rooms of the house.

To Cash £8 ; To Wearing Apperall £13. 10 s. &

The Lower Room : bed and furniture ; Chairs Table & Chests ; Books ; a warming pan.

The first Room above Stairs : A bed and furniture ; another bed & beden ; a dressing table & desk.

The Second Room above : bed & furniture ; a Desk Chest & other things.

[1] *See* Alice Morse Earle's charming book, *Home Life in Colonial Days*, 76-107.

[2] Made by William Brinton and William Horne. *Papers 86, Office of Register of Wills, West Chester, Pa.*

The Kitchen : Pewter and brass ; Tongs & fire Shovel ; pans potts & pott hooks & Rakens ; box and heaters ; Earthen we*ar* & Lumber.

The Seller : Several things & vessels.

[*Other Articles*] *:* Sheets and pillow Cases ; Table Cloaths and Napkins ; a Sarvant Man and Maide, £21 ; a Sadle ; Cart and gears & plow and Tacklen ; falling axes & grubing axes ; Wheat in house & Mill ; green wheat ; two hores & Maire and Coult ; five oxen ; two Cows ; three heifers & three yearlings ; a grinding Stone buckett & Chaine harrow teeth and Crow Iron ; the plantation & Land Containing 146 acres, £600. [Total value, £826, 16 s.]

The warming-pan, which in this inventory was *The Warming-pan* valued at 12s., was used to make the bed comfortable on a cold night ; the pan was filled with hot coals, and, held by its long wooden handle, was thrust into the bed and rapidly moved back and forth to keep from scorching the linen sheets.

In the item "Sarvant Man and Maide," mentioned in the will as John Kitchien and Margaret Mathews), we have further evidence of the system of redemptioners or indented servants that played such an important part in the economic history of the colony.[1] Evidently by this time

Redemptioners

[1] Some wills and other inventories of Irish Quakers mentioning indented servants were those of Joseph Coebourn, of Aston Township, now Delaware County, 1723, " A Woman Sarv^t 3 years £8 " and " A nagro man called Tobitt £30," the latter no doubt held as a slave ; Thomas Jackson, of Marlborough, Chester County, 1727, " my two Sarvants Samuel Hughes and Elizabeth Driskle [£15]," Joseph Kelly [£10], and William Kean, 20£ " ; Ann Marshill, of New Garden, " late from Ireland," 1729, " a Sarvant Man wch She Sould to 'ffra : Hobson," £8, and " ye halfe of ye time of a sarvant girl," £4 ; James Miller, of New Garden, 1732, " a Sarvan man," 12£ ; Joseph Hutton, of New Garden, 1735, " 2 Servant Women," £15 ; Neal Moony, of London Grove, 1751, " a Boy," £10 ; William Pim, of East Caln, Chester, County, 1751, " a Servant Lads time, £9."

carts had come into use on the farm.   The dressing table is rather an unexpected luxury.

There is much of similarity in all these lists, but I shall give yet another including a number of articles not enumerated in the preceding lists. *James Lindley's Estate, 1726* It is the inventory[1] of James Lindley, smith, of London Grove, Chester County, who had the most considerable estate of any of those mentioned :

> Purs and apparell £22. 12s ; 7 Beds and Furniture thereto belonging ; 1 Chest of Drawers 2 Chests 2 Boxes and 1 Looking glass ; 4 Table Cloaths 13 Sheets and 1 Warming pan ; 2 Pieces of Stuff and 1 Sett of New Curtains ; fllax, 1 hackle, Chains, Salt box, Iron pots & Candle sticks ; 2 mens Saddles 2 weomans Sadles 1 Pillion & 2 Bridles ; Wool Cards, Sole Leather, Pewter, Brass Tin, & wooden ware ; to Baggs, Mault, Indian Corn, Salt, Wheels, & a half Bushell ; Irons in the Kitchen, Coopers ware & Earthen ware &c ; Dressed Skin, Books Iron, Steel 2 whip saws & 1 Cross ; Carpenters Tools, Pincers, Hows, Plows, Harrows & Ox Chains ; Grinding Stones, Coles, Bells, Shovells, and forks &c ; A Cart with the Geers and Chains, hooks, and hors Shoes ; Oak Boards, Scantling, 3 Guns & Bullet Moulds ; Grubing Axes, Well Chain, Wolf Trap, falling axes &c ; Sickles, Sythes and Doe Trough ; Corn in the Barn, and Corn in the Mill ; Corn in the Ground, and Hay in the Meadow ; 16 horses, Mares and Colts ; 27 Cows, Oxen and Young Cattle ; 10 Sheep and Swine ; Smiths Tools in the Shop ; one Servant Man ; 5 Bonds and one Bill ; Book Debts ; Plantation and Improvements. [Total value £1115.9s.8d.]

The bells mentioned, no doubt, were those attached to cattle and sheep in order to trace the animals in their wanderings through the woods. This is the only reference to a " Looking glass " that I have noted in the inventories.   The best

---

[1] Made 10 Mo. 23, 1726.—*Papers No. 229, Register's Office, West Chester, Pa.*

beds were filled with feathers, but many persons of the poorer sort had to be satisfied with ticks filled with chaff. William Pim, of East Caln, in 1751, had a "Beadstead, Curtains and Rods."

The tall "Grandfather" clock was seldom met with in the early years, but later it was not uncommon to find it in the homes of the prosperous farmers. In 1723, Joseph Coeburn's "Clock & Case" was appraised at £10, and in 1728, Thomas Jackson, of Marlborough, Chester County, had a clock and case valued at £12, and also a watch. *The "Grandfather" Clock*

The manner of purchasing one of these clocks, shown in the manuscript account book of George McMillan (a native of County Antrim, Ireland), of Warrington, York County, is an interesting example of the system of barter common in new countries where money is scarce. In 1 Mo., 1774, we find this Friend buying a clock case from Thomas Kirk, an Irish Friend, of York ; he notes on the credit side of the account under that date : *George McMillan's Clock*

George Mc Millan

	£.	s.	d.
Thomas Kirk Credit by one Clock Case and Lock	2	11	0

and on the debit side at another date :

	£.	s.	d.
Thomas Kirk, Upon Balance	0	3	0
dit by 3 yards of Thick Cloath	1	5	0
Allso by 2 bushels of Indin corn	0	6	0
dito by wooll	0	1	0
By Cash	0	16	0

This case McMillan took to Rudolph Spangler, clockmaker and silversmith, of York, later a captain in the "Flying Camp" of the Revolution, and had it fitted with clock works.   He then records in his credit column :

£. s. d.

Rudy Spangler Credit by one Clock Set agoing at 12 oclock
31ˢᵗ of 3ᵈ month 1774..12

and a little later in the same year in the debit column :

£. s. d.

Rudolph Spangler Dr by 18 bushels of Inden Corn..............2 14 0
and 1 b of dry apels & 1 of beans.....................................0 8 0
Dito By 2200 and 55 Shingels..5 1 5
Dito by 1800 Shingles..4 1 0
                                                                      12 4 5

This ancient clock,[1] measuring about seven feet in height and bearing on its face the inscription, "Rudy Spangler, York-town," is preserved as a precious heirloom in the McMillan family[1] and is still an excellent timekeeper.

Dress   The dress of the Friends in the early years of Pennsylvania differed but little from that of the other settlers of the same class.   It was not until the close of the first quarter of the eighteenth century that Friends began to make an effective protest against extravagance in apparel and to adopt a more formal costume[2] of "home-spun

[1] It is now in possession of Smith Bell McMillan, of Signal, Ohio, a descendant of the original owner.

[2] At Falls Monthly Meeting, Bucks County, in 1701 one of the members being reported " very poor and in necessity " a committee was ordered " to get [for him] a good pair of leather briches and a good warm coat and waist coat, one pair of stockings and shoes."

drab and gray." The clothing of the planters was generally simple and substantial, coarse cloth and deerskin being used for that of the men, and linsey and worsted for that of the women. The costume of a man consisted of leather breeches, long collarless coat reaching to the knees, waist-coat, neck cloth, woolen yarn stockings, low buckle shoes, and a flat felt or beaver hat. Often in summer, breeches made of a coarse linen called osenbrig were worn. Robert Parke, in his letter of 1725, writes :

In Summer time they wear nothing but a Shirt & Linnen Trousers, which are breeches and stockings all in one made of Linnen, they are fine Cool wear in Summer.

Wigs were worn by many Friends. Penn attended carefully to his wigs, and purchased several during his short stay here. In a letter from London in 1702, he writes to Logan : " Did not a fine new wig come to thy hands for me ? It cost me fifty shillings sterling."[1] In 1719, Jonathan Dickinson, a Friend, in writing to London for his clothes, says: "I want for myself and my three sons, each a wig, light good bobs."[2] The Friends to a large extent had laid aside their "Wiggs" some time before the middle of the century, but the fashion was kept up in general society until 1755 ; then, with the return of Braddock's de-

[1] *Penn and Logan Correspondence*, I., 114, *Memoirs of the Hist. Soc. of Pa.*
[2] *Bolles*, II., 320–1

feated army, who had lost their wigs in flight, the custom was abandoned.

Some of the wealthy Friends of Philadelphia had large and costly wardrobes for that time, as, for example, that of Robert Turner, one of the richest of the settlers, enumerated in his inventory,[1] made after his death, in 1700 :

Upper Room above Stairs : 2 pairs of hair Plush Breeches lined wth lether, £3. 10s; 1 Jacket & one Dublett Ditto £3. 10s; 1 ℔^{r} of Old Black Lether Breeches £1; 2 ℔ of Leather Summer Breeches £1; 1 ℔r of Shagg Breeches 10s; 1 Course Broad Cloth Coat new, £2.10s; 1 old Shagg Coat 15s; 1 Old Grey Coat, 10s; 1 Old Cloth Searge Coat Turned, 15s; 1 Old Jackett, 10s; 2 Wusted ffustian Jacketts £1.4s; 1 lining frock, 6s; 1 do. new, 10s; 2 white swan skin wast coats, £1.4s; 2 Pair loosed Stockings; 3 ℔^{r} yarn ditto 8s; 2 ℔^{r} of Stirrup Stockings & 1 ℔^{r} of Socks, 4s; 1 leather Belt, 3s; 2 Old Caster hatts, 8s; 1 ℔^{r} of New Shoos & one D° old, 10s; 1 gray Jackett & and a Neck Hood, 6s; 1 fustian Wastcoat, 10s; 5 ℔^{r} of Sturrup Stockings, 11s. 8d; 9 Shirts at 10s., £4. 10s; 7 handkerchiefs, 10s. 4d; 5 Neck Cloths & 8 Night Capps, 13s; 2 Very old Jacketts two Old Coats three pair of Breeches & three ℔^{r} old Stockings, 10s; 1 light Coulered Broad Cloth Coat not new, £2. 5s; 2 new Caster[2] hatts.

In 1726, Philadelphia Yearly Meeting took a decided position on the subject of plainness of apparel, the women in particular being advised to greater simplicity in such matters as follows :

"That immodest fashion of hooped petticoats, or the immitation of them, either by something put into their petticoats to make them set full

[1] *Office of Register of Wills, Philadelphia.*

[2] The caster hat, at the end of the seventeenth and beginning of the eighteenth century was distinguished from the "beaver" and was said to be of rabbit's fur. In 1688, "Of Hats . . . the Caster is made of Coney Wooll mixt with Polony Wooll."—R. Holme in *Armory*, III., 129 (cited in Murray's *Oxford Dictionary*).

or wearing more than is necessary, or any imitation whatsoever, which we take to be but a branch springing from the same corrupt root of pride. And also that none of our friends accustom themselves to wear gowns with superfluous folds behind but plain and decent ; nor without aprons ;[1] nor to wear superfluous gathers or plaits in their caps or pinners ; nor to wear their heads dressed high behind ; neither to cut or lay their hair on their foreheads or temples.

And that ffriends be careful to avoid striped shoes, or red or white heeled shoes or clogs ; or shoes trinmed with gaudy colors.

Likewise that all ffriends be careful to avoid all superfluity of ffurniture in their houses, and as much as may be to refrain using gaudy flowers or striped calicoes and stuffs.

And also that no ffriends use that irreverant practice of taking snuff, or hand snuff-boxes one to the other in meetings.

Also that ffriends avoid the unnecessary use of fans in meetings, lest it divert the mind from more inward and spiritual exercise which all ought to be concerned in.

And also that ffriends do not accustom themselves to go with breasts or bare necks.[2]

The high degree of interdependence and division of labor that characterizes our modern life was quite unknown in these early days. At that time every farm house was a little factory and every farmer an adept in many branches of labor, and independent to a considerable extent of the outside world. In summer the farmer and his sons were busily engaged in clearing and planting the land; in winter, if the weather were too severe for outside work, they applied themselves to indoor labors, making shoes for the family, beating out implements of iron or constructing household furniture and utensils.

Work on the Farm

[1] It was the custom of the women to wear green aprons.
[2] Scharfe and Wescott, *History of Philadelphi*., II., 861

The wife and daughters were even more fully occupied than the men. They not only attended to a score or more of domestic duties—cooking, washing, dairying, candle-making, soap-making, spinning, knitting, and weeding the garden—but also frequently assisted the men in the work of the field ; and in truth they might say with the old adage,   Man works from sun to sun,
But woman's work is never done.

The women devoted much time to the home-spun industries, picking, carding, and spinning wool, and swingling, hatcheling and spinning flax ; and from their own homespun they manufactured the clothing of the family. The large stores of linen that were produced by this industry were folded away with lavender in wooden chests, and were a source of much pride to the colonial house-wife. Beautiful specimens of the linen made by the Irish Friends are still treasured as heirlooms in the families of descendants, and attest that the ancient skill in the handicraft for which Ireland is famous was not forgotten in the foster land.

Markets
and Fairs   The produce of the farm was carried to Philadelphia, Chester, and New Castle, on horseback, and sold or exchanged for articles to be found at shops, fairs, and markets. Parke writes, in 1725 : "There is 2 fairs yearly & 2 markets weekly in Philadelphia also 2 fairs yearly in Chester & Likewise in New Castle, but they Sell

no Cattle nor horses no Living Creatures but altogether Merchants Goods, as hatts, Linen & woolen Cloth, handkerchiefs, knives, Scizars, tapes & treds, buckels, Ribonds & all Sorts of necessarys fit for our wooden Country." He humorously adds : " & here all young men and women that wants wives or husbands may be Supplyed. Lett this suffice for our fairs."

The early settlers were much annoyed by certain of the wild animals that preyed on their flocks and herds.   Foxes and wolves were the most persistently destructive, but black bears also frequently stole into the farm yard and carried off fine porkers.   In 1721, a bear was killed near Darby, now Delaware County, and yet ten or fifteen years later, when Nathaniel Newlin (son of Nathaniel), of Concord, married Esther Midkiff, of Darby, her parents were inclined to make objections because Newlin lived in the backwoods of Concord where bears abounded.   Mrs. Deborah Logan relates that one night in 1740–41, one of these animals was seen at the old Logan home in Chester.[1]   The family of Alphonsus Kirk, the early Irish Quaker settler, of New Castle County, had a thrilling experience with a bear.   A granddaughter of Alphonsus Kirk, Rachael Price, a minister of Birmingham Meeting, Chester County, tells the story in her *Recollections :*[2]

Wild Animals

---

[1] Ashmead, *History of Delaware County*, 212.
[2] *The Friend* (Philadelphia) for 1885, Vol. LVIII., 315.

A Bear Story   My father, William Kirk (son of Alphonsus and Abigail Kirk) was born 1st mo., 1708. He and his youngest brother Timothy, had many adventures together when they were young ; they used frequently to meet and talk these over, which was very entertaining to us children.   One occurrence, however, which took place in their childhood, and which I heard my father relate, struck my infant mind with horror and dismay.   It so happened that my grandmother was left at home with only these two little boys when a large bear came up near the door before she saw it.   It was a double door, and she had only time to shut the lower part before he had his feet upon it, and she could not get the upper door shut quickly, as there was something hanging on it that prevented the door from closing. She pushed it against his paws with all her strength and called to the little boys to bring her the axe which was in the house, but they could not find it ; then she told them to bring her the rolling pin, with which she beat his feet until he withdrew them, when she could get the door fastened. He then attempted to climb on a shed which was over the door, and which extended to a window in the second story.   She seeing his determination told her little sons to go to the cellar and get into a chest that was there, but not to shut down the lid so tightly they could not breathe, while she went up stairs to keep him out, if possible.   The shed was built of round saplings, which were covered with brush (wood) and a light snow.   Some of these rolled under the clumsy creature and let him fall through.   They had killed a beef that day, the smell of which had probably attracted him ; she threw some parts of it to him which he devoured with great eagerness, appearing to be very hungry, and then went off.

The next morning several men went in search of him ; his foot being wounded the blood upon the snow enabled them to track him, so that they soon came up to him.   Grandfather's stout dogs attacked him with violence, but the bear seeming likely to gain the victory, he went to their assistance with his axe.   In the meantime the eldest son and the rest of the company came up, and seeing the scuffle but not that his father was there, [the son] incautiously raised his gun in order to fire, but his companions called to him in time to prevent it.   They soon succeeded in killing the bear.

Social Intercourse   Colonial farm life was not all a monotonous round of labor and care ; time was also found for social enjoyment. The Irish Friends, as well as other members of the Society, were eminently a sociable people, and despite the hard travelling, visited each other continually. All the events of community—harvests, huskings, raisings, vendues, meetings, weddings, funerals—brought the widely scattered neighbors together in social mingling. On such occasions a spirit of sincere and hearty good-will and neighborliness generally prevailed, and in time of distress and need there was never lack of help and sympathy.

A great event among the Friends was a wed- *Weddings* ding. The first and important preliminary to the marriage was "to pass meeting," or obtain the consent of the monthly meeting. To this end the contracting parties appeared in two monthly meetings and declared their intentions. Then, after a searching inquiry by a committee, if the couple were found to be "clear of all entanglements," they were left at liberty to accomplish their marriage, according to "yᵉ good order," of Friends. As an example of a "passing" of the Irish Friends the following extracts from the minutes of New Garden Monthly Meeting, Chester County, are given:

Att our Monthly Meeting of New garden held att New garden the 8ᵗʰ of yᵉ 9ᵗʰ mo: 1718 . . . Thomas Jackson of New garden Alice [alias] Marlborough, & Mary Willy of New garden, Appeared Att this Meeting & Signified Their Intentions of Taking Each Other In Marriage it Beeing yᵉ first time, Therefore this Meeting Appoints John Smith & Robert Johnson To Make Enquiry concerning his Conversation & Clearness on yᵉ Account of Marriage, & to give an Account To yᵉ Next Monthly Meeting.

On the same date the Women's meeting appointed

14

Margaret Johnson & Sarah Worsley to Make Inquiry into her [Mary Wily's] Clearness of Marriage with any other and of her Conversation.

One month later the couple again declared their intention:

Att our Monthly Meeting held att New garden yᵉ 13ᵗʰ of yᵉ 10 ᵗʰ/mo 1718 Thomas Jackson & Mary Willy Appeared att this Meeting & Signified yᵗ they Continue their Intentions of Taking Each other In Marriage It beeing yᵉ Second time, & yᵒ friends Appointed To Make Enquiry Concerning his Conversation & Clearness, have Given an Account that they find Nothing but yᵗ he is Clear from All others [The Women's Meeting at the same time "finde nothing to hinder her Intentions of Marriage"], Therefore this Meeting Leaves them to their Liberty to Accomplish their Said Marriage According to yᵉ good order Used Amongst friends, Robert Johnson & James Lindley is Appointed [The Women's Meeting appointed Margaret Johnson and Sarah Worsley] to See yᵉ orderly Accomplishment Thereof, & give an Account To yᵉ Next Monthly Meeting.

The form of the marriage ceremony is illustrated by the following certificate[1]:

The Marriage Certificate

Wbereas[2] Thomas Jackson of yᵉ Township of Marlborough In yᵉ County of Chester & Province of Pensilvania & Mary Willy In yᵉ Township of New garden & County & Province Afforesaid Haveing Declared Their Intentions of Takeing Each other In Marriage before Severall Monthly Meetings of yᵉ People Called Quakers In yᵉ County of Chester According to yᵉ good order Used Among Them whose Proceedings Therein After a Dileberate Consideration Thereof & Consent of Parents & Relations Concerned They appearing Clear of all others were approved of by the Said Meetings.

Now This Is To Certifie whom It May Concern That for yᵉ full Accomplishing of Their Sᵈ Intentions this Twenty fifth day of yᵉ 10ᵗʰ/mo: caled December In yᵉ Year of our Lord one Thousand Seven hundred & Eighteen They yᵉ Sᵈ Thomas Jackson & Mary Wily apeared In a Publick &

---

[1] Certificate recorded page I, Vol. I of New Garden Marriage Book.

[2] At New Garden Monthly Meeting, 9 Mo. 7, 1724, "Benjanin ffred is appointed by this Meeting to write yᵉ Marriage Certificates for friends belonging to New Garden preparative meeting and James Wright for Notingham."

Solemn Assembly of yᵉ affores⁴, People & others Mett Together Att yᵉ Pub-
lick Meeting house att New garden Afforesaid & In a Solem Manner he yᵉ
S⁴ Thomas Jackson Taking her yᵉ S⁴ Mary Wily by yᵉ hand did openly
Declare as followeth friends In yᵉ fear of yᵉ Lord & before This Assembly
I Take this my friend Mary Wily To be my wife Promising wᵗ yᵉ Lords
Assistance To be Unto her a Loving & faithfull husband Until death
Separate Us & Then & There yᵉ Abovesaid Mary Wily Did declare
friends In yᵉ fear of yᵉ Lord & in yᵉ presence of this Assembly I Take
Thomas Jackson to be my Husband Promising wᵗ yᵉ Lords Assistance To
be unto him A Loving & faithful wife Untill death Separate us or words to
This Effect & for a further Confirmation thereof They yᵉ S⁴ Thomas Jack-
son & Mary Wily She according To yᵉ Custom of Marriage Assuming yᵉ
Name of her Husband did Then and There Sett their hands & we whose
Names are hereunto Written beeing Present Among others at yᵉ Solemniza-
tion of their S⁴ Marige & Subscription In manner afforesaid as witnesses
hereunto have Also to These presents Subscribed our names yᵉ day & year
Above written :

Thomas Wickersham	Thomas Lightfoot	THOMAS JACKSON
Caleb Pusey	Sarah Lightfoot	MARY JACKSON
Francis Swayne	Martha Willy	John Willy
Benjamin Holme	Abigall Willy	Joseph Willy
Abram Marshall	Ruth Martin	Arthur Jones
Simon Hadly	Mary Hutton	Benjaⁿ, Fredd
John Chambers	Margarett Johnson	Samuel Jackson
William Holiday	Rebecka Starr	Joseph Hutton
Gayen Miller	Deborah Starr	Samuˡ, Lightfoot
John Smith	Mary Head	Jacob Lightfoot
Robert Johnson	Rachel Fredd	Nehemiah Hutton
James Lindley	Alice Wickersham	Benjamⁿ Fredd
Ellinor Lindley	Ann Jackson	John Fredd
Tho : Jackson	Deborah Holyday	Jeremiah Starr
James Johnson	Sarah Worsley	Thomas Jackson
James Starr	Mary Miller	
Michael Lightfoot	Deborah Chambers	
	Martha Miller	
	Sarah Miller	
	Mary Power	
	Margaret Miller	

At the next Monthly Meeting the committee
reported on the marriage as follows:

Att our Monthly Meeting of New garden held att Notingham the 10th of y[e] 11th/[mo]: 1718–19

The friends y[t] were Appointed To See y[e] orderly Accomplishment of Thomas Jackson & Mary Willeys Marriage, Make report That it was Accomplished orderly.

It often happened that marriages were not celebrated with that high degree of good order which the committee thought necessary at such functions. There seems to have been a constant tendency, especially after the fourth decade of the century, to bring some of the ways of the "world's people" into the marriage ceremony. In 1761, at Warrington Monthly, a marriage was reported orderly, except for the couple[1] "having a man & maid to wait on them, which practice this meeting doth not approve." In 1773, at the said Monthly Meeting, a groom[2] was complained of for having "assistance in taking of his Gloves." In 1775, the nuptials of Richard Atherton and Phebe Hobson seem to have passed off to the satisfaction of the men Friends of the meeting, but the women members were scandalized at the presence of "assistants to pull off the glove and hat." In 1785, Friends had a concern as to the "practice of keeping on the Hat at the time of Solemnizing Marriage."[3]

Many young Friends, impatient of the slow and troublesome process of passing meeting, would

[1] Richard Carson and Mary Passmore.

[2] Nehemiah Hutton who married Rachel Yarnall.

[3] *Minutes of Warrington Monthly Meeting.*

hasten off to "ye priest" or to a magistrate, and be married without any delay or formality.   Ancient church registers, notably those of the Old Swedes' Churches of Philadelphia and Wilmington, record the marriages of many young runaway Quaker couples.   The monthly meeting minutes abound in the record of such infractions of discipline, and the elders of the meeting were ever busy laboring and dealing with the delinquents.   If the offenders would not confess their faults they were " disowned " or expelled from the Society.   At New Garden Monthly Meeting, in 1730, a complaint was made that " Mary Moore [1] is gone out from friends & is Marryed by a Justice of ye peace Contrary to freinds advice to her."   For this she was disowned.

At the same meeting in 1736, " John Mickle is married out by ye priest," and was disowned. Again, in 1737, " Sadsbury preparative Meeting informs y^t John Musgrove Junr is married out of ye Unity of friends (by ye priest.)' "   He was then expelled.   At Warrington Monthly Meeting, in 1767, Sarah Delap made a written acknowledgment " for keeping company with a young man not of our Society and attempting marriage with him by a priest to the great grief of my tender parents."   She was then re-instated.   Even those members who were present on the occasion of a marriage by " ye

[1] Married Thomas McCollum.

priest" were dealt with for misconduct. Such complaints as this are frequent in the minutes: New Garden Monthly Meeting, 12 Mo. 22, 1734-5, is informed "y^t Thos. Jackson Junr went a Long with Stephen Hayes when he went & gott married by ye priest."

Warrington Monthly Meeting, in 1779, had a difficult love affair to settle. John Delap made objections to the marriage proposals of Joseph Garretson and Rebecca McMillan, declaring that he had a prior claim to her "which he is not willing to give up, and it appears that she kept company with him a considerable time after she altered her mind." The meeting finally decided against poor John, and the marriage was duly consummated without any further interruption from him.

The bride would ride to meeting behind her father or next friend seated on a pillion, but after the ceremony the pillion was transferred to the husband's horse, behind his saddle, and with him she rode home.[1] After the wedding the company were invited to return to the home of the bride's father, where a bountiful repast was served. Great preparations were made for the wedding dinner, and Friends had frequently to be cau-

[1] Reminiscences of William Worrall, a centenarian, by John F. Watson, *Memoirs of the Historical Society of Pennsylvania*, Philadelphia, 1827, Vol. II.

tioned against lavish entertainment on such occasions. At Warrington, in 1767, a marriage was reported orderly, "Except some unnecessary provision."[1]

Courtship among Friends was a solemn affair, *Courtship* and must be pursued in a most decorous and circumspect manner. Before declaring his affections, the young man must first have the consent of the young woman's parents. This permission granted, he came "a courting," but he must strive by his grave and staid demeanor and "solid conversation" to make an impression on the object of his regards. If, however, he did not first obtain the paternal sanction, he was dealt with by the meeting. In 1726, George Robinson[2] had to sign the following paper before he was allowed to proceed with his marriage:

WHEREAS I have Made My Mind Known to Mary McKoy Upon yᵉ Account of Marriage before I had her parents Consent Contrary to yᵉ order of friends for which I am Sory as witnes my hand

George Robinson

[1] In 1725, Thomas Chalkley " was at a Marriage at Horsham (at which was present William Keith, our Governor) and I was concerned to speak . . . After this Meeting I return'd Home without going to the Marriage Dinner, as I generally avoided such Entertainments as much as I could, having no Life, or liking to them, being sensible that great Companies and Preparations at Weddings, were growing Inconveniences among us."— p. 147, *Journal*, London, 1751.

[2] George Robinson, of Cecil Co., Md., son of George and Catharine (Hollingsworth) Robinson, " of Newark In yᵉ County of New Castle upon Delaware" was married 2 Mo., 14, 1726, at Nottingham to Mary, daughter of Robert McKoy, of Cecil Co., Md.—*New Garden Marriage Book*, 33

Again, in 1732, when Robert Johnson, son of Robert Johnson, of New Garden, and Katharine Hadley, daughter of Simon Hadley, of New Castle County, declared their intentions of marriage for the first time, they were not permitted to proceed until Robert produced the following acknowledgment:

> WHEREAS I have Endeavored to draw out ye affections of my friend Katherine Hadley before I had ye Consent of her parents, which s^d Action of mine being Contrary to ye Rules of friends & I knowing in my Self it not to be Right Wherefore I do Condemn all Such practices & do take ye blame on my Selfe & desire y^t friends may pass it by & hopes I Shall be more Carefull for time to come of giving any just offence to friends as Witness my hand this 26 day of ye sixth mo^th 1732
>
>   Robert Johnson

Funerals   A funeral was always an occasion for a great gathering of Friends. Thomas Chalkley notes that in 1725 as many as a thousand persons were present at a funeral.[1] The body was placed in a plain coffin and borne to the meeting-house, where after a short meeting in memory of the deceased, interment was made in the adjoining graveyard. The company then repaired to the house for dinner, which was almost as elaborate a repast as that served at weddings. Friends were warned to " keep out of superfluity at maredges and bueriels." The funeral expenses of James Lindley, of London Grove, as shown by the accounts filed by his executors, were £4. 10s., and " ye Coffin," £1. 8s. The funeral charges of Thomas

[1] *Journal*, 153.

Jackson, in 1728, were £3. In the estate accounts
of John Lowden, of New Garden, is the item:
"for yᵉ funerall of William Johnson," £5. In the
accounts of Ann Marshall, deceased, of New
Garden, "late of Ireland," are recorded these
charges: "A Coffin £1; Sider at yᵉ funerall
10s; ye Grave Diging, 3s. 6d."

A few items gleaned from executors' accounts *Physicians'*
show what physicians' fees were in this early period. *Charges*
George Harlan's estate "paid Isaac Taylor for
Physic as ℔ his receipt Dated yᵉ 25: 1 ᵐᵒ 1715
£8. 18. 0." Ann Marshall was ill thirteen weeks
but her estate had to pay "to ye Doctors" only 2s.
In Thomas Jackson's account were items: "to
Doctter Curry, £3"; "to Doctter Dellwood,
£2. 4. 7"; to Doctter Taylor, 7s."

The meeting was one of the strongest forces in *Meetings for*
the social life of the Friends. Twice a week, on *Worship*
"First-day" and usually on "Fifth-day," it brought
together the members from their scattered holdings for worship, and at the close afforded opportunity for a short season of quiet and genial converse. Of the two meetings for worship, that of
the Sabbath had the better attendance. On

> Fair First-day mornings steeped in Summer calm
> Warm, tender, restful, sweet with woodland balm,

family parties, either walking or riding,[1] might be

[1] Some young Friends in going to meeting evidently did not always
carry themselves with that degree of " gravity and moderation " that was

seen wending their way to the plain little meeting-house, embowered amid the trees.   Reining up by the horse-block at the door the riders dismounted, and before entering the edifice would linger, perchance, for a few words of friendly greeting with the neighbors.   There was no

> peal of bells to call them to the house of praise,

but at the appointed time the company took their places on the hard, unpainted benches, the men on the one side and the women on the other side of the house.   After a few moments of silent and reverent worship, seeking

> The Soul's communion with the Eternal Mind,—

from the raised seats of the gallery, where sat the ministers and elders facing the body of the meeting a minister would arise to deliver his spiritual message.   Frequently the speaker was a travelling Friend, from England or Ireland or other distant parts.   Perhaps it was Thomas Chalkley,

> Gentlest of skippers, rare sea saint,[1]

or Thomas Lightfoot, who

expected of them by their elders, but took advantage of the ride to show off the paces of their fine young horses.   As early as 1681, Friends of Dublin Half Year Meeting had a concern as to this departure from "yᵉ path of truth" and sent an epistle, signed by William Edmundson, Abraham Fuller, and Amos Strettell, to Friends on the Delaware, urging that "all young Men and others in Riding to or from Meetings or other occasions refrain from Galloping and Riding after an aiery flurting manner."—Amelia Mott Gummere, *Friends in Burlington, Penna. Mag.*, VII., 354.

   [1] Whittier in *Snow-Bound.*

Did like Noah's dove,
Sweetly declare God's universal love,[1]

or John Fothervill, "an antient man tall and Well
Shap'd Very Zealous against Sin and Iniquity"[2];
or perchance it was quaint and eccentric old John
Salkeld, of Chester, of whom a contemporary
writes, in 1739:

Salkeld from silent sitting slow would rise
And seemed as with himself he did advise.
His first words would be soft, but might be heard;
He looked resolved, yet spoke as if he feared

. . . . . .

Proposed his theme, and sometimes would repeat,
Lest some should not observe, or should forget:

. . . . . .

Thus louder then he strained his cheerful voice,
The sounds grow tuneful and their hearts rejoice.[3]

It not infrequently happened that some good
Friends, wearied with the arduous duties of the
week, would drop off into restful slumber. But
woe betide these offenders of good order and the
testimony of truth, if John Salkeld chanced to be
present at the meeting! Their dreams were then
of short duration. On one occasion, it is related,
when he noted several members overcome with
drowsiness, he suddenly sprang to his feet, ex-
claiming, "Fire! Fire!" Every one was awake

---

[1] Samuel Keimer, of Philadelphia, writing in 1723.—*Scharfe and Wescott*, II., 867.

[2] *MS. Diary (1736-1752) of John Smith*, of Burlington, N. J.

[3] Lines attributed to Joseph Brientnall, a Friend, of Philadelphia.—*The Salkeld Family*.

immediately and one of the excited sleepers cried
out, " Where? Where?" "In Hell!" responded
John, "to burn up the drowsy and uncon-
cerned."[1]

The close of meeting was announced by the
shaking of hands by two gallery Friends, the
signal passing down seat by seat through the
house. After a friendly and genial chat the
Friends dispersed, many of them taking guests
home to dinner.

Business
Meetings
The business meetings of the Society, from the
point of view of social opportunity, were of greater
moment even than the meetings for worship. The
latter were usually only local in extent, but the
former, especially the quarterly and yearly meetings, brought together large numbers of Friends
from many distant points and thus enlarged and
broadened the range of social intercourse. The
business meeting was usually preceded by a meeting for worship, at the close of which wooden
shutters were drawn down from the ceiling, leaving the women to conduct their branch of the
meeting separate from that of the men.

Quarterly
Meeting
The Quarterly Meeting, which continued often
for several days, and in early times "circulated"
to various fixed places in a district, occupied a
conspicuous place in the life of the Friends. The

---

[1] *The Salkeld Family*, a rare little pamphlet of 8 pp., printed in Delaware County, in 1867.

season was looked forward to with pleasant anticipation by young and old as a time not only for religious worship but for social pleasure. Great preparations in the way of cooking and baking were made for Quarterly Meeting guests. Whole families would often come from great distances to "Quarterly" and visit around in the neighborhood during the progress of the meeting.

Philadelphia Yearly Meeting, the central authority, to which all the other meetings of Pennsylvania, Delaware, and parts of New Jersey and Maryland were subordinate, was the most important of the meetings and had the largest attendance. The meeting lasted for upwards of a week each year, oscillating for a time between Philadelphia and Burlington, but finally settling down to regular sessions in Philadelphia. Country Friends took advantage of Yearly Meeting week to bring to town farm products, to exchange for articles to be found in the shops and markets. The visitors were always received and entertained with generous hospitality by the city members. *Yearly Meeting*

The Monthly Meeting, local in its character, was the real working body of the Society, in matters relating to the individual members. It "undertook to see that justice was done between man and man, that disputes were settled, that the poor were supported, that delinquents, whether as to the Society's own rules or those of the State, were *Monthly Meeting* reformed, or if reformation seemed impossible, were 'disowned' by the Society, that applicants for membership were tested and finally, if satisfactory, received, that all the children were educated, that certificates of good standing were granted to members changing their abodes, that marriages and burials were simply and properly performed, and that records were fully and accurately kept. Under these were the Preparative Meetings."[1]

Meeting Discipline

The Friends in general maintained a high standard of conduct and morality, but among the young members, especially in the later generations, there was a falling off in this respect and a tendency to drift into the ways of the world's people. The monthly meeting was constantly engaged in laboring with offenders.

Some additional extracts from the meeting records throw light on disciplinary action and afford further interesting glimpses of the manner of life among the Irish Friends.

Card-playing and Dancing

The Friends had a strong testimony against such "wicked practices" as card-playing and dancing, their sentiments being expressed by Thomas Chalkley, who denounces cards as "engines of Satan" and declares "that as many Paces as the Person takes in the Dance, so many Paces or Steps they take towards Hell."[2]   But in spite

---

[1] *A Quaker Experiment in Government* (21–22), by Isaac Sharpless, President of Haverford College.

[2] *Journal*, 225.

of all such protests many young members were
found playing cards and engaging in such "vain
and vicecious Proseedings as Frollicking Fiddling
and Dancing."

At New Garden Monthly Meeting, 4mo. 12,
1725:

" New Garden Preparative Meeting has Acquainted this Meeting y^t
Nehemiah Hutton has been found In Company keeping & playing Cards
which has brought reproach upon truth & friends, & this Meeting has put
him upon to Draw up Something for ye Clearing of truth Against ye Next
Monthly Meeting which he Acknowledges and is willing to do

" Joseph Hadley being Also in Company w^t Nehemiah Hutton and had
ye Cards In his hand which he is Sory for y^t he did not leave ye Company.
It is ye Mind of this Meeting y^t he condemn the Same So far as he is
Guilty"

6 Mo., 6, 1725. " Nehemiah Hutton has given in a paper Condemn-
ing himself for his playing at Cards which paper this meeting receives &
orders him to read ye S^d Paper in ye place where he was playing & in y^e
Presents of Benjamin ffred & Willm Halliday & that they give an Account
to ye next Monthly Meeting & that he is desired to forbear coming to meetings of business until friends be better Satisfied with him as to his conversation and Sincerity to truth." Joseph Hadley was dealt with in the same
way.

At Warrington Monthly Meeting, in 1769,
Timothy Kirk acknowledged his error in dancing,
and in 1777, Elizabeth Blackburn expressed her
sorrow for " having Endeavored to dance."

The Friends, in common with other people of
the early part of the period under our study, seem
to have indulged freely in strong drink. The Tem-   *Drinking.*
perance movement, which was initiated by Friends,
was of later origin. So long as members kept
sober no complaint was made, but when they got

so deep in their cups as to become foolish and belligerent they were promptly taken in hand by the meeting. It was thought that no crop could be garnered, no building raised, in fact no difficult work accomplished, without the use of stimulants. On all social occasions liquor was freely passed around.

In 1725, Chester Quarterly Meeting, which included nearly all the meetings of what is now New Castle County in Delaware, and the counties of Delaware and Chester in Pennsylvania, made some attempt to correct abuses that had sprung up. "It was desired [that] ye friends take care at Burralls not to make great provision as to provide strong Liquors and hand it about ; but lett Every one take y^t is free to take it as they have ocation and not more than will doe them Good."

The next year the Yearly Meeting took up the subject and adopted strong resolutions against the practice of giving liquor at public vendues, as it excited bidders and created an incautious rivalry. The expenditure for rum was frequently the largest item in vendue accounts. At the vendue of Ann Marshall, of New Garden, as shown in her accounts of 1729, there was paid "To John Read for Rum at ye Vendue 13s. 4d.," while "ye Clerke" received only 4s. and "William Rowan Cryer at ye Vendue" only 10 s.

In 1733, a writer in the *Pennsylvania Gazette* complains that

" It is now become the practice of some otherwise discreet women, instead of a draught of beer and toast, or a chunk of bread and cheese or a wooden noggin of good porrige and bread, as our good old English custom is, or milk and bread boiled, or tea and bread and butter or milk or milk coffee &c that they must have their two or three drams in the morning."

Here are some cases of intemperance of Irish Friends brought before New Garden Monthly Meeting:

10 Mo 12, 1724.—" Whereas Joseph & Nehemiah H——— being both overtaken in Drink in y⁰ County of New Castle & have condemned y⁰ Same Under their hands which papers were read heere to y⁰ Satisfaction of this Meeting & Appoints Benjamin ffred to read y⁰ Same in y⁰ Next first dayes Meeting."

10 Mo 12, 1724.—" Thomas Jackson of Thomas Town in Marlborough has appeared at this meeting as desired & has Signified yᵗ it was not y⁰ greatness of y⁰ quantity of drink but beeing unwell for Some time before which he thinks was y⁰ cause of this Sickness but for y⁰ Clearing of truth he is willing to give in a paper, therefore he is desired to bring it y⁰ next Monthly Meeting."

2. Mo. 10, 1726.—" Dear friends whereas it Accidentally hapened yᵗ I was overtaken In Licquor and I do believe yᵗ my being before unwell & weak of body was Some occasion of it & I am Sory for it as witness my hand.   THOMAS JACKSON."

4 Mo. 24, 1732.—London Grove Preparative Meeting reports "yᵗ Joseph P——— was over taken with Strong Drink at Darby & and he being feavored with a deep Sence thereof have given this Meeting a paper" of acknowledgment.

11 Mo. 25, 1734.—New Garden Preparative Meeting reports "yᵗ James M——— Senʳ was overcome with Strong Licqor & did Strik & abuse his wife." He was disowned, 12 Mo. 22, 1734-5.

8 Mo. 30, 1736.—Mary B——ly has " been Adicted to Drunkenness for some years past & has been visited and Admonished against it Divers times yett Does not Desist from it." Disowned 9 Mo. 27, 1736.

15

In harvest time neighboring families assisted each other, the women often working in the fields with the men. Says Parke: "The[y] also make great Preparations against harvest both Roast & boyled, Cakes & Tarts & Rum stand at the Lands End, so that they may eat and drink at Pleasure." Frequently refreshments of cider and rum were too much for Friends, and exciting scenes attended the harvest. We have an instance of this in Warrington Monthly Meeting records of 1748. A Friend made the following acknowledgment:

> I was overtaken with the effects of spirituous liquor in the harvest field, reaping for John Rankin in Red Land Valley [near Lewisberry, York County] last harvest. It was a hot day, I drank more than I should have to drive out the sweat to make me in better capacity to follow my work, but it produced the contrary effect, so that I was for a time light in the head and I talked foolish.

At New Garden Monthly Meeting, 5 Mo. 29, 1729, London Grove Preparative Meeting made report:

> yt Willm Lowdon was a fighting with Michaell Harlan Junr ye Last Harvest for wch he is Sorry & has Given a paper Condemning ye Same which this meeting Takes as Sattisfaction.

In 1754, Warrington Monthly Meeting expelled Robert W———, on complaint of John Farmer who said that R. W. came " to his house full of drink and did abuse him and his family, and when he provoked some of them to strike him he took warrants for the whole family, considerably to their damage."

Again, in 1758, John W————, of Menallen
Meeting, made the following acknowledgment:

"Whereas, some time ago I went to the Burial of one of my Neighbours; from the Grave yard I went a few miles where I heard there was a Gathering of men, Expecting to see some men I had business with, and notwithstanding I have made profession of the blessed truth for many years past, thro' unwatchfulness Committed that great Evil of taking more strong drink than I ought to have done, the Effect of which brought on another Evil, for Rideing home in Company with some of my Neighbours, a difference fell out amongst us where I received, as I thought at that time, provocation Enough to do as I did, (but I am far from thinking so now,) which was the putting of my hat and Jacket in order to have satisfaction," etc.

In 1758, James McG————, of Menallen, produced an acceptable acknowledgment for being overtaken with strong drink; "the adversary having got the advantage I took the undue liberty of singing Idle songs along with a company that was Engaged in that Exercise." His paper was read on "First-day" at Menallen Meeting.

Here are some further cases of disorder in which Irish Friends were concerned:

At New Garden Monthly Meeting, 2 Mo. 26, 1729, Nottingham Preparative reports "that Roger Keirk son of Alphancius Keirk was a Rasseling for a weger which he seems to aveade." 4 Mo. 28th, it is reported "y^t he said he hoped to be more Carefull but did not appear at this meeting nor is not willing to Condemn it any further." 7 Mo. 27th, he appeared at the meeting but being of "Rather a Cavelling Contentious Spirit than otherwise this meeting thinks it of Necessity to disown him."

11 Mo. 31,1729, New Garden was informed that John C—n in Controversie with Thomas L--ly did through provecation Curse & Swear, and that ye s^d L—ly Did use Scurrilous vain & unbecoming Language to John C—n." An acknowledgment from these offenders was accepted, but the privilege to sit in business meetings was withdrawn. 2 Mo. 25, 1730, "John C—n & Thomas L—ly was a fighting." The former was then disowned, while the latter expressing his sorrow was retained in membership.

Report was made to New Garden Monthly Meeting, 11 Mo. 28, 1737–8, that certain Friends appointed to read a testimony against John St—r, of Sadsbury Meeting, for not complying with "yᵉ Award of yᵉ friends Chosen by him & his brother" in a dispute,

shewed it to sᵈ John, and that he & and his father Joyned in running out against friends & said yᵉ Testamony was a parsil of lies that they had made up amongst themselves and when a friend stood up & began to read it at yᵉ breaking up of a first day meeting according to yᵉ Direction of yᵉ monthly meeting, Isaac St——r [father of John] stood up & bid him leave of reading it for it is a parsil of lies & steped to yᵉ friend & Catched yᵉ paper & tore it to pieces, whereby yᵉ reading of it was stoped at that time."

Isaac St—r was then dealt with "for his Contempt of yᵉ Authority of yᵉ meeting" and was required to bring in a written acknowledgment of his fault.

Care of Indented Servants One of the duties of the monthly meeting was to investigate cases of alleged mistreatment of indented servants. At New Garden, 12 Mo. 25, 1726–7, Sadsbury Preparative Meeting

made a Complaint against James Musgrave Son of Jnᵒ Musgrave of Sadsbury for Strikeing a Servant man of Caleb Perces [Peirce's] the which he Seems to Justifie therefore this meeting appoints Samlᴵ Miller & Caleb Perse to Endeavour to bring him to a Sence of his Evill Action.

Case of Lowden versus Smith One of the most interesting cases concerning indented servants that Friends were called upon to settle was that of Lowden *versus* Smith, brought before New Garden Monthly Meeting. It seems that William Lowden, probably after the death of his father, John Lowden, in 1714, was bound as a servant, until the age of twenty-one, to John Smith, of Marlborough, son-in-law of Caleb Pusey. As young Lowden approached his majority a difference arose between him and his master as to the date of expiration of the term of service. Evidently there were not exact data at hand to determine the point. Thereupon, 3 Mo. 9, 1724, the matter was brought up for the Monthly Meeting to decide.

At this meeting, as a first step in the proceedings, a committee was appointed "to write to ye Monthly Meetings of ye Grange In ye County of Antrim & to New Garden In ye County of Carlow both In Ireland for ye Ages of ye Children of John Lowdon."

At the next Monthly Meeting, held 5 Mo. 11th,

Friends being Informed Att our Last Monthly Meeting of A Difference between John Smith and William Lowden about ye Age of William Lowden he being bound to John Smith Untill he come of Age & ye Last Meeting Appointed Thomas Jackson James Lindley Benjamin ffredd Simon Hadly Joseph Sharp & Michaell Lightfoot to See they could help them to Accommodate it,

And Now these friends gives this Meeting An Account that they Mett with them & they could not fully End it, but John & William Mutually have Chosen four friends whom they have left it to fully to determine.

The young man, becoming impatient of the delay of the arbitrators, probably left his master before the proper time, for on 9 Mo. 7, 1724, just three days before what later proved to be his twenty-first birthday,

A Concern coming Upon this Meeting concerning Wm : Lowdens disorder In not Leaving his Difference he had w^t his Master to ye Arbitrators as he had agreed to do, Therefore we now desire ye Visiters to speak to him to bring him to a Sence thereof that he may condemn ye Same & y^t they give an account to ye Next Monthly Meeting.

No further mention of the matter is to be found in the minutes until 7 Mo. 11, 1725, when the desired evidence from Irish registers—showing the value of such records—had arrived :

" This Meeting has received an account from ye Mens Meeting In Ireland held at James Moores Senr In ye County of Antrim Concerning ye Age of Wm. Lowden which account is Satisfaction to John Smith & William Lowden & to this Meeting Also, A Coppy whereof here followeth,

To friends of ye Monthly Meeting held at New Garden In Chester County in ye Province of pensilvania In America,

Dearly beloved friends & brethren In y^e fellowship of y^e gospell & unity of y^e Church in our Lord Jesus Christ do we brotherly Salute you w^t fervent desires for your growth prosperity and Establishment in y^e blessed truth, wherein we give you an Acco^t y^t we read y^e Letter from Eli Crokett dated y^e 6$^{th}_{mo}$: y^e 12th day 1724 Directed to James More Senr & Junr giving an Account of Strife y^t hath hapened In relation to y^e age of William Lowden desireing a Certificate Signed by our Mens Meeting In determination thereof, Therefore pursuant to y^e Said Advice we y^e After named Subscribers do hereby Certifie you y^t y^e register book of y^e Grange Meeting was brought to our Mens Meeting & Every Individuall & particular person Subscribing to this Certificate did there read & find y^e following Account upon record (viz.) William Lowdon Son of John Lowdon was born y^e 10th of y^e 9$^{th}_{mo}$: 1703 & we do further Certifie y^t we believe y^e Same to be true Signed In behalf of our Mens Meeting held at James Moores Senr this 21st of y^e 9$^{th}_{mo}$: 1724

John m^o:Ranells	Benjn Boyd	James Dean
Thomas Erwin	Allex^r Dean	William Moore
James Moore Junr	James Moore	James Istariot
Samuell Willkison	Lewis Reford	ffrancis Willkinson
William Willkinson	Wm Robinson	

1 Mo. 12, 1725–6, "The Matter of Difference y^t have been between John Smith & William Lowden is Ended to ye Satisfaction of friends The S^d William having given Satisfaction wch is as followeth

> To ye Monthly Meeting of New Garden to be held att New Garden ye 12th of ye 1st moth 1725–6 Dear friends whereas Some time Ago, there was a Difference happened between my Master John Smith & My Self about what time I was to be free from his Servitude, & I hearkening to Much to ye Affirmations & presentations of others, though Contrary to ye Credible Accounts y^t came from friends, as taken out of ye register book for births belonging to ye Grange Meeting in Ireland ye place of my birth did put my S^d Master & other friends to great Exercise & trouble as also y^t I refused to Stand to ye friends Judgment y^t was Appointed by ye Meeting to Determine y^t Difference for all which I do hereby Acknowledge my Self to blame and desire this Meeting to Accept thereof promising by ye Lord's Assistance to be So carefull for ye time to come as no More to give friends any Occasion against me for I Desire to Live ye rest of my dayes in unity w^t friends.
>
> WILLIAM LOWDEN.

The records show that during the several wars *Military Service* in which the Province was involved, not a few Friends departed from their peace principles and enlisted as soldiers. In the period of the French and Indian war, we have an instance in the Warrington minutes. 1 Mo. 17, 1756, "Menallen Meeting informs this meeting that John Blackburn [an Irish Friend, sometime Judge of York County] and John Pope, at a report of Indians doing mischief at a great distance from them went out in a warlike manner to meet them Contrary to our Peaceable principles." For this breach of discipline the offenders finally expressed their

sorrow and were continued in membership.   With
the opening of the Revolution, however, Judge
Blackburn was reported to the Monthly Meeting,
2 Mo. 10, 1776, as having " inlisted as a soldier "
and was subsequently disowned.   Other members
of the same family also joined the American ranks.
6 Mo. 7, 1777, Joseph Blackburn " hath Enlisted
to be a soldier."   7 Mo. 12, 1777, Thomas Blackburn, Jr., and Anthony Blackburn, Jr., have "as-
sociated or joined in the Military Exercises."

As President Sharpless points out in his valuable monograph,[1] the Society of Friends in the
struggle for independence took a neutral position
and stood firmly by their testimony against war.
They were "friends of liberty, but opposed to
war, desirous of maintaining their civil rights, but
by other means than illegality and revolution, and
unwilling to afford aid to the British ; divided in
their sympathies, but largely united in the stand
that they could take no part in the strife of the
day. . . . When war and revolution became in-
evitable . . . they issued a declaration of neu-
trality.[2]   They were neither Tories nor revolu-
tionists."   In considering the question of Quaker
sympathies in the conflict, the author continues : " About four hundred, perhaps, actively
espoused the American side by joining the army,

[1] *The Quakers in the Revolution.*
[2] *Ibid.*, Preface.

accepting positions under the revolutionary government, or taking an affirmation of allegiance to it, and lost their birthright among Friends as a result. Perhaps a score in a similar way openly espoused the British cause, and also were disowned by their brethren. These members very likely represented proportions of silent sympathizers." [1]

The Revolutionary government of Pennsylvania was resolved that if the Quakers and other non-combatants would not fight they should at least pay the expenses of those who did. The Friends accordingly were ordered to pay heavy war taxes. This, however, they refused to do on the ground that they could not consistently contribute to the support of war, and those members who obeyed were dealt with by the meeting. Thereupon, the tax collectors seized the property of Friends to the value of the taxes and the fines imposed for non-compliance. An example of such exactions, covering the period 1778–1790, is recorded by George McMillan, an Irish Friend, of York County, in his manuscript account book, and it is of such interest that I venture to print it in full: *Revolutionary Taxes and Fines*

On the 22nd of 1st mo 1778 btwen one and two oclock in the afternoon Came henry Lewis James Perkeson and John Witherow to my hous and Lewis told me he had an Execution for me for substotuk money telling he would teak my horses If I did not Pay him Producing an Execution bearing deat 22 of 1st mo 1778 for 100 dollers with Cost and Cost acruing for Substetut money aledged to be Laid out for me the while I refused to Pay he Saised on 2 of my horses and bore them of for Sail, which was *George Mc-Millan's Fines*

[1] Sharpless, *The Quakers in the Revolution*, 204-5.

done 26 of Instant January and one sold the other Returned worth £30 silver money

the — day 6 month 1778 Came James Pargeson and John Moody to my hous and asked me for old or Provence tax of 1-2-6. And then Sarched my drawers and took 3 Pound ten Shillings Without Giveng the Reazen how it came to be So much

on the — day of the 3 month 1779 Came John moody and opened my Desk in my absence and took for a steat tax £5 a muster fin £3-12s and an Inden Subtetut fine £4 Demanded took the Lick Sum of Congress money and again on the — day of 11 month 1779 the Saim moody Came and Searched as Before and found 37 dolers and ——— (?) of Congress and took it in my absence for a tax £9 and some other demands (6d per doller

on the 18 day of 4 mo 1780 Came John may to my house [I being in the field at work] went into my Roome Serched my desk and took £95 19s 9d of Congress money and then went to the Loft to seize on wheat, and on 27 of 5 mo he came ocompaned by d mᶜcurdy S henderson and 2 Persons more and took 12 B: of: wheat for a Demand of tax and 4 fold rent {1d Per doller

On the 28ᵗʰ of 12 mo 1780 Came thomas Shanks Searched my Drawers and took 74 dollars Demanded for the 7 mo Volenteers (worth 1 Per doller

on 24 of 1 mo 1781 Came James Gray, opened my drawers and took 76-8-3d of conantal Corancey and Leved on a Stack of hay for a demand of 224 Pound for a 4 months tax and on the 26 of the 2ⁿᵈ mo took and bore away a Stack of hay worth 6 pound

on the 14 of 3ᵈ mo Came william Potter with a Guard and in a rude manner Executed my bodey or Goods Serched my hous took and bore away £67 for a tax Demanded for the Place in manahan 48£ (1 d per doler

on the 17ᵗʰ of 3 mo Came John moodey Serched my Drawers took and bear away £81-2s-6d and on the 9 of 5 mo following Came Acompaned by J. perkinson and Seized on wheat and on the 14 Instant came Said moodey a J p with a waggen and bear of 15 of wheat Said to be for 2 taxes amounting to £336 had to be sold at 76½ dollers Per bushel

" On 20ᵗʰ of 6 mo 1782 Came John may and opned my desk drawer found my Pocket book and took twenty dollers silver a guiney and half of gold and 40 S of stat corancey and on 29 of 7 mo following in Lick maner and took 7 dallers for a demand of 3 taxees and a draft tax of 39 shillings.

On — day of 8 month 1782 Came John Cane and in a forcible and Lawless maner took 3 bushels of wheat demanded for a class tax for the Place in Managhan———

March 27-1783 Came a Son of tho Shank Serched my desk and took one Pound five Shillings and three Pence demanded for a muster fine—

Coart week—day of April 1783 Came Samuel Moodey acompaned By andrew Roos and his waggon and took 20 bushels of wheat for a demand which John Moodey maid for a 4 months tax—

On 15 of 1mo 1784 Came James Perkinson and John may Searched my hous found a pocket book and took 18 dollers and 2 Crowns for a tax demanded

on 12 of 5 mo 1784 Came James Perkinson and James fegan and maid Search for and found money in the Desk drawer 3£ and 7s. 6d for a tax demanded

1783 feb Samuel Nelson colector for manahan Sold and bear off 10 b of wheat and 15 of rye for a demand of 3£ tax

1783 About christmus Daniel williams and Caused my Grean to be thrashed in manahan with Great weast and Sold and bore away 15 bushels of rye—10 of wheat and 5 of Spels Sold all for 4ˢ-1ᵈ per bushel 6-2-6 for a tax of about 4-17-0

3 mo 1784 Came yong Shank and opened my drawer and took and bore off — 4 dollers for a muster fine demand of 1-8-0

12 mo 1784 Daniel McCurdey went to William Michels and Saized on and took Eight Dollers of my money for a tax in manachan

12 mo 1785 Came George Elly and Serched the desk and took 3-00-0
Also a ross..1-6-0
                                                                                               £ s d
Jan 1790 Came John may and took....................................2 19 7

But little data on early schools attended by *Schools and Books* Irish Friends have been gleaned, but the evidence indicates that from the earliest days of the Colony provision of some sort was made for education in nearly all Quaker neighborhoods. In 1725, Parke mentions an Irish Quaker pedagogue. " Unkle Nicholas Hooper," he writes, " lives very well he rents a Plantation & teaches School & his man dos his Plantation work."

Reading matter in the country districts was confined chiefly to the Bible and Friends' books. Among the most popular of such works was

"—painful Sewel's ancient tome
Beloved in every Quaker home."

At New Garden Monthly Meeting, 3 Mo. 6, 1721, " The following friends have Subscribed To Take The following Books beeing a history of The Rise & Progress of Truth Composed by William Sewell :

Caleb Pusey **1**		Thomas Lightfoot **1**
James Lindley **1**		Daniel Worsley **1**
Jeremiah Starr		James Miller of Kenit **1**
James Starr	} **1**	William Brown Sen**r** **1**
Michael Lightfoot		Samuel Littler **1**
Jeremiah Brown **1**		Joseph Haines **1**
Simon Hadley **1**		Thomas Jackson of Marlborough **1**
Andrew Job **1**		John Churchman **1**
Henry Reynolds **1**		William Beals **1**

For ye Monthly Meeting 4.' "

Nearly all the inventories of the period contain the item of books. In 1751 the inventory of William Pim, of East Caln, Chester County, included the following : " To a number of Books, 8 s. 3 d ; To a Large Bible, 2 s. 10 d ; To Sewels History, 16 s ; To Crisps Sermons & banks Journal, 8 s."

CHAPTER III.

SOME PROMINENT IRISH FRIENDS OF PENNSYLVANIA

THE most eminent of the Irish Friends and one of the most important personages of the Province, was James Logan, the faithful friend and efficient secretary and agent of the Proprietor, William Penn. He was born of Scotch parentage, 8 Mo. (October) 20, 1674, at Lurgan, County Armagh, Ireland.[1] His father, Patrick Logan, a native of East Lothian, Scotland, whose ancestry has not yet been satisfactorily determined, was graduated from the University of Edinburgh, with the degree of Master of Arts,[2] and became a clergyman of the Established Church, serving for a time as chaplain to Lord Belhaven[3]; but later he joined the Society of Friends and removed with his family to Lurgan, where he took charge of a Latin school.

James Logan (signature)

[1] Penn and Logan Correspondence, I., liii., *Memoirs of the Historical Society of Pennsylvania*, Vol. IX.

[2] *Proud*, I., 473.

[3] Keith, *Provincial Councillors of Pennsylvania*, 5.

About all that is known of James Logan's early
life is contained in his autobiography, which, as it
has never been published—so far as I can learn—
is here printed in its entirety:

Ancestry

My Father was born in E Lothain in Scotland: was educated for the
Clergy, & was a Chaplain for some time; but turning Quaker, he was
obliged to go to Ireland & to teach a Latin School there—He had
several children,[1] of whom none are now living, nor have been, more than
these 50 years past, saving my Br Wm who took his degree of Doctor of
Physick in Holland—and is now the chief Physician in Bristol—and myself—My Mother was Isabel Hume Daughᵗ of James Hume—a younger
Brother of the House of St Leonards (as I think) in the Shire of Mers (as I think) in
the South of Scotland. He was Manager of the Estate of the Earl of
Murray—who owed, but never paid him £1500 Sterl. tho the said Earl
lodged for some years in his House in the Shire of Fife—My Grandmother,
before she married, was Bethia Dundas,[2] Sister of the Laird of Dundas, of
Didiston, about 8 miles west of Edinburgh a fine seat, and the Earl of
Murray assisted my Grandfather in carrying off my Grandmother—She was
nearly related to the Earl of Panmat [Panmure] &c.

*Education
and Appren-
ticeship*

*The Family
Flees to Scot-
land, 1689*

*His Father
Teaches
Friends'
School at
Bristol*

Having learned Latin, Greek, and some Hebrew, before I was 13 years
of age—in my 14th I was put Apprentice to a Linnen Draper—one as considerable with his Partner as any in Dublin. But the Prince of Orange,
landing before I was bound (tho' I served my Master 6 months) in the
winter 1688, I went down to my Parents—and the wars in Ireland coming
on, In the Spring I went over to Edinburgh with my Mother—after
which my Father soon followed, who being out of employment—repair'd
to London, & was there gladly receiv'd by our friends—Deputies to the
Genl Meeting from Bristol in that City—as their schoolmaster[3]—for the

[1] Hannah Logan, daughter of Patrick Logan, of Lurgan, died 7 Mo. 15,
1678, and was interred in the burial place at Monreanerty.—*MS. Lurgan
Meeting Records.*

[2] Isabel, sister of Bethia, and daughter of William Maule of Glaster,
grandson of Lord Panmure, married James Dundas, of Dudingston in West
Lothian.—Robert Douglas, *Peerage of Scotland*, p. 544 (Edinburgh, 1764)
and *Baronage of Scotland*, p. 178 (Edinburgh, 1798).

[3] In the Bristol Meeting minutes of 4 Mo., 1690, is the following reference to Patrick, father of James Logan: "Paul Moone acquaints this meeting that Patrick Logan, a Friend, late of Ireland, and now at London—a

Latin Language, and I followed him the next year; but tho' the wages were good, and well paid, he could not brook the Mothers taking upon them to direct his treatment of their children, and thereupon soon disliking it, having ordered my Mother to return to Irel^d to take care of what they had left there.

In 1693 after above 3 years stay there, pretending to go over for my Mother,[1] but with a real design never to return He left me in his school, not full 19 years of age—ordering me on the receipt of his Letter Signifying my Mother would not come over, that I should give up the school & return to him. But our Friends would not give me up, I therefore continued in the same employment untill the peace of Reswick in 1697. *His Father Returns to Ireland and Leaves Son in Charge of School, 1693*

In which time, as I had in Edinburgh in my 16th year, happily met with a book of the Leyborns on the Mathematics, I made myself Master of that, without any manner of Instruction, and in the time in which I kept school, I further improved myself in the Greek looking a little further into the Hebrew—I also learned French & Italian with some Spanish; but went 3 mos. to French Master to learn the Pronunciation, without which I was sensible I should never be able to speak it. But otherwise I never paid one penny for Learning any thing whatsoever, and tho' I had my course of Humanity—as it is called in Ireland from my Father, I can safely say, he never gave me the least instruction whatsoever, more than he gave to the other scholars— *Studies Mathematics and the Languages*

good scholar, and an apt schoolmaster to instruct youth in Latin, &c., is a present out of employment, and, upon some discourse of it among Friends at London, is in some expectation that he may be serviceable to Friends' children at Bristol. upon consideration of which this meeting is desirous to promote it, in hopes it may be serviceable to our youth." In 9 Mo. following the treasurer was desired to hand Patrick Logan " £50, and to pay Jno. Harwood's note of carpenter's work for the said school."—William Tanner, *Three Lectures on the Early History of the Society of Friends in Bristol and Somersetshire*, London, 1858, p. 124.

[1] At Ulster Province Meeting, 2 Mo. 13, 1695, " Some Books being brought To Patt^k Loagan Sent him from George Keeth & friends being Sensiblee of ye hurt which ensued if y^o Said Books Should be received amongst any professing Truth have Therefore Concluded ye Said Books Shall be viewed and Pres^{ed} [perused] by Some Sencible friends and ye Errours noated in ye margent and Then Sent back To George Keeth To London for prevention of his Sending any more Such factious Books and That a Letter be also Sent with ye Said Books on behalfe of y^o Province Meeting To George Keeth."

Engages in Shipping, 1697

But to return; After the Peace, having first agreed in Bristol, to go over with another Factor to Jamaica, I went over to Ireland to see my Parents[1] : and having told them my intention of going over to that Island, my Mother was so averse to it, that she affirmed she would much rather see me dead— On this I was obliged to change my measures, & began with a cargo, from Dublin, to enter on a trade between that place and Bristol, which I followed for about 8 months.

Becomes Penn's Secretary, 1699

When in the spring of 1699, our old Proprietor [William Penn] sent for me, and made me his proposals to come over to Penn[a] as his Secretary, and desired me to take time & advice upon it—Some of my Friends advised me to accept, & some others as strenuously against it; but in some few days I went over to Bath—with my fr[d] E[d] Hackel, & accepted of it.

Comes to Pennsylvania

In 8[or] 1699, being then at Sea, in our voyage hither—I was 25 ys. of age—The Proprietor continued here 2 years wanting about 5 weeks, and left me in more offices that I was fit to undertake & got thro'. But had I left his whole business—at the time of his departure, I might—considering my singular good fortune—or the kind Providence that has ever attended me—for which I can never be sufficiently grateful, I might I say with great ease have doubled my present fortune—& equaled what the Prop[tr] son Tho[s] charged me with having—according to an information he had rec[d] viz:—£ 60,000 but I am fully content with what I have tho' not half so much—The old Proprietor was willing to give me what I would ask, for my ten years service, & considering his melancholy circumstances in 1711 I set it at £ 100 a year cur[cy] for all manner of services whatsoever, But told him I would stay in his service no more than 2 years—But he was seized with an apoplectic fit in less than 1 year which tied me down to his business, vastly it proved to my loss—as my Letters designed at first for our Proprietor Thos Penn fully demonstrate—[2]

Public Life

Penn brought Logan to Pennsylvania on his second coming, in the *Canterbury*, in 1699, and immediately plunged him into the affairs of the

[1] William Penn wrote to James Logan from London, 4 Mo. 21, 1702: " Of thy Family.—Thou hast heard of the death of thy father and marriage of thy mother with one not a Friend ; an exercise W. Ed [William Edmundson] &c told me so at our Yearly Meeting."—*Penn and Logan Correspondence*, I., 117.

[2] From a copy (No. 108) in the *Smith MSS.*, Vol. 1, 1678–1743 (F. 7287½), Ridgeway Branch, Philadelphia Library Company.

Colony. Young Logan soon showed such marked
capacity for business and administration that his
services became indispensable, and Penn, on his
departure for England in 1701, not only continued
him as Secretary of the Province but gave him a
general charge both of the government and
property, saying, "I have left thee in an uncommon trust with a singular dependence on thy
justice and care."[1]

The Proprietor's confidence was not misplaced; *Governor of*
for though beset by many troubles and vexations, *Province*
Logan ever remained true to his trust, and discharged his duties with fidelity and judgment.
His life becoming more and more occupied with
public affairs, for the next forty years he was
always holding some high office—Commissioner
of Property, member of Provincial Council, Judge
of Common Pleas, Mayor of Philadelphia, Chief
Justice; and, in 1736–38, as President of the
Provincial Council, acting as Governor of Pennsylvania.[2]

He became the devoted leader of the Proprie- *Leader of*
tary Party in the long and bitter political conflict *Proprietary*
that was waged after Penn's return to England, *Party*
and zealously guarded the Penn interests and
prerogatives against what were deemed the encroachments of the Popular Party of the Assem-

[1] *Penn and Logan Correspondence*, I., 59.
[2] See Wilson Armistead's *Memoirs of James Logan*, London, 1851.

16

bly, led by David Lloyd, and of the Church Party, led by Colonel Robert Quarry. It is true that in these earlier years of his life Logan did at times become heated in partisan controversy, to such an extent as to make himself unpopular; but later in life he was generally respected for his learning, character, and ability. He remained a Friend all his life, but differed from the great body of the Society in his belief in defensive war.

Relations with the Indians   Like his friend Penn, Logan knew how to win and keep the confidence of the Indians. It was largely due to him that friendship and alliance between them and the Province was so long maintained. He often had them as guests at Stenton, his beautiful county-seat, near Germantown. On some occasions, it is said, there were as many as three or four hundred, who would remain for days enjoying the hospitality of the plantation.[1] The high regard in which he was held by the Indians was expressed by Cannassetego, chief of the Onondagas, in a speech at the making of a treaty between the Six Nations and Governor Thomas and the Council, at Philadelphia, in July, 1742:

Brethren, we called at our friend James Logan's on our way to this city, and to our grief found him hid in the bushes and retired through infirmities from public business. We pressed him to leave his retirement, and prevailed with him to assist once more on our account at your council. He is a wise man and a fast friend to the Indians, and we desire when his soul goes to God you may choose in his room just such another person of the

[1] *Armistead*, 176.

same prudence and ability in counseling, and of the same tender disposition and affection for the Indians.[1]

It is not only as a statesman but also as a man of letters and science that James Logan is conspicuous in our colonial annals. The fortune which he acquired in commerce and in trade with the Indians enabled him to spend his later days in scholarly retirement at Stenton,[2] in the enjoyment of his library and in writing. He carried on an extensive correspondence with the most learned men of Europe and America, and wrote numerous

Literary Pursuits

[1] Cited in Westcott's *Historic Mansions*, 149.

[2] The picturesque and dignified old mansion of Stenton, built by Logan in 1728, is one of the most interesting examples of colonial architecture extant. Thanks to the loving zeal of the Pennsylvania Society of the Colonial Dames of America, it has recently been carefully restored, and under their trusty guardianship it has been opened to the public. The house, still surrounded by ample grounds and reached by a fine avenue of hemlocks, is a two story brick structure with two great towering chimneys and a heavy roof set with dormer windows.

Passing up the curious circular stone steps, firmly clamped together with iron, one enters the great hall, paved with brick and wainscoted to the ceiling. In one corner is an open fireplace, and in the rear the stately double staircase. On either hand are lofty rooms, also handsomely wainscoted. The large fireplace in the room to the left has in it a backplate of iron inscribed "J. L. 1728." In another room the fireplace still retains some of its original blue and white Dutch tiles, of most grotesque pattern. One of the most attractive rooms is the library, in which the book-loving master of the place spent much of his time. This is a large, finely lighted apartment, taking up half of the front of the house in the second story. Indeed, the ancient house is full of delights for the antiquary and the lover of the olden time. From garret to cellar there are all sorts of quaint nooks and corners, mysterious cupboards and closets and secret staircases; and leading from the cellar to the stables is a long underground passage, the subject of many a strange legend.

works, many of which are still unprinted. His letters and writings show that there was almost no topic in science or literature that he could not discuss with the scholars of his time. " Sometimes Hebrew or Arabic characters and algebraic formulas roughen the pages of his letter-books. Sometimes his letters convey a lively Greek ode to a learned friend ; and often they are written in the Latin tongue."[1]   His friend Linnaeus, in compliment to his botanical knowledge, named after him a natural order of herbs and shrubs, the Loganiaceæ, containing some thirty genera in three hundred and fifty species.   He published Latin essays on reproduction in plants, and on the aberration of light ; translated Cato's *Disticha* and Cicero's *De Senectute*, and issued many other works which are listed in Joseph Smith's monumental *Catalogue of Friends' Books*.[2]   His correspondence with the Penn family, from 1700–1750, which is a mine of historical information, reveals his carefulness and intellectual breadth.   Says Professor Tyler, " Occasionally one finds in it a passage of general discussion, in which the clear brain and the noble heart of the writer utter themselves in language of real beauty and force."[3]

[1] J. F. Fisher, in Spark's *Works of Franklin*, VII., 24–27, note.

[2] See also Hildeburn's *Issues of the Pennsylvania Press.*

[3] Moses Coit Tyler, *A History of American Literature* (New York, 1881), II., 234.

He bequeathed to the City of Philadelphia his private library of 3,000 volumes, comprising all the Latin classics and more than a hundred folios in Greek. These books formed the foundation of the Loganian Library which later was included in the Philadelphia Library Company.[1]

"In personal appearance," says Watson,[2] "James Logan was tall and well proportioned, with a graceful yet grave demeaner. He had a good complexion, and was quite florid even in old age, nor did his hair, which was brown, turn gray in his decline of life, nor his eyes require spectacles. According to the customs of the times, he wore a powdered wig. His whole manner was dignified, so as to abash impertinence ; yet he was kind and strictly just in all the minor duties of acquaintance and society." William Black, a Virginia gentleman, who visited Logan at Stenton, in 1744, says of his host, that he "seem'd to have some Remains of a handsome . . . Person and a Complection beyond his years, for he was turn'd off 70."[3]

Personal Appearance

From his correspondence with Penn we learn of Logan's early disappointment in love. It seems that he had formed an attachment for Ann Shippen, daughter of Edward Shippen, the first

Unsuccessful Courtship

[1] *Armistead*, 174-5.
[2] *Annals of Philadelphia*, I., 524.
[3] Journal of William Black, *Penn'a Mag.*, I., 407.

Mayor of Philadelphia, but the fair Ann was inclined to listen to the vows of another suitor, Thomas Story, the eminent minister. The progress of the love affair soon became the town-talk, and even reached the ears of Penn in England.[1] "I am anxiously grieved for thy unhappy love," writes Penn to Logan, under date, 11 Mo. 16, 1704–5, "for thy sake and my own, for T. S. and thy discord has been of no service here, any more than there ; and some say that come thence that thy amours have so altered or influenced thee that thou art grown touchy and apt to give rough and short answers, which many call haughty, &c. I make no judgment, but caution thee, as in former letters to let truth preside and bear impertinencies as patiently as thou canst."[2]   To this Logan replied, 12 Mo. 11, 1704–5, "I cannot understand that paragraph in thy letter relating to T. S. and myself ; thou says our discord has done no more good there than here, and know not who carried the account of it for I wrote to none that I know but thyself in 7ber, 1703. . . . Before that we had lived eighteen months very good friends, without any manner of provocation, only that I had about three or four months before spoke something to Edward Shippen. . . ."[3]

[1] See Thomson Wescott's *Historic Mansions of Philadelphia* (Philadelphia, 1895), 144–5.
[2] *Penn and Logan Correspondence*, I., 358.
[3] *Ibid.*, I., 367.

In the following year Ann Shippen and Thomas Story were married, and Logan seems to have become reconciled to the match. He wrote to William Penn, Jr., August 12, 1706, "Thomas Story carries very well since his marriage. He and I are very great friends, for I think the whole business is not now worth a quarrel."[1] In the course of time he recovered from his disappointment, and on the 9th of 10 Mo., 1714, was happily *Marriage* married to Sarah Read, daughter of Charles Read, a wealthy merchant of the City, sometime Mayor and Provincial Councilor.[2]

James Logan died 10 Mo. 31, 1751, in his *Death* seventy-seventh year, and was interred in Friends' burial ground at Fourth and Arch Streets, Philadelphia. Of his children, Sarah married, in 1739, Isaac Norris; William Logan, who married Hannah Emlen,[3] served as Provincial Councilor, 1747–1776[4]; and Hannah married John Smith,[3] of the scholarly Smiths of Burlington, New Jersey, ancestor of John Jay Smith, for many years at the head of the Philadelphia Library Company.[5]

Of the Irish Friends following closely after James Logan in the order of prominence, is Cap-

---

[1] *Penn and Logan Correspondence*, II., 158.

[2] Westcott, *Historic Mansions*, 146.

[3] See *The Burlington Smiths*, by R. Morris Smith.

[4] *Penna. Archives*, 2nd Series, IX., 624.

[5] For a genealogical account of the Logan family see Keith's *Provincial Councillors of Pennsylvania* and *Memoir of Dr. George Logan of Stenton*, (issued by the Historical Society of Pennsylvania, 1899).

tain Thomas Holme, Surveyor-General of Pennsylvania and Provincial Councilor.[1] He was born in
1624; although a great
part of his life was spent
in Ireland, his biogra-
pher, Oliver Hough,
thinks there is little doubt that his birthplace is in
England, possibly in Yorkshire. He is styled
" gentleman," and evidently came of good family,
probably from a younger branch of the family of
Holme of Huntington, in Yorkshire, as he used
an armorial seal on his official papers, correspond-
ing with the arms [2] of this family.

In Ireland Thomas Holme was residing in Limerick, Ireland, in 1655, for it is stated in A Compendious
VIEW Of Some Extraordinary SUFFERINGS Of
the . . . QUAKERS . . . In . . . Ireland, etc.,[3]
that in 1655, James Sicklemore, one of the early
converts made by Elizabeth Fletcher and Elizabeth Smith " being peacably in Thomas Holme's
House in Limerick, was seized on with a Guard

---

[1] For helpful suggestions and many of the facts used in this sketch of
Thomas Holme I am indebted to Mr. Oliver Hough's carefully prepared
biography of him in *Penna. Magazine*, XIX., 413–427; XX. 128–131,
248–256.

[2] The arms are described in Burke's *General Armory* as : " Argent, a
chrevon azure, between three chaplets gules." Mr. Hough says that the
shield on Thomas Holme's seal is the same, surrounded by a bordure with
ten roundels, the bordure being used to distinguish the branch of the
family.

[3] Dublin : Printed by and for SAMUEL FULLER, at the *Globe* in *Meath-
Street*, 1731.

of Soldiers, and committed to Prison and banished the City by Order of Colonel Ingoldsby."[1]

In 1657, Thomas Holme and others, " being peaceably in their Friends House in Cashel, and their Horses at an Inn, as travelling Men, were apprehended by a Guard of Soldiers, in the Year 1657, by Order of Colonel Richard Le Hunt, and being brought before him and examined, were violently (by Soldiers) turned out of the Town, and the Gates kept against them though it was near Night, and a dangerous Time for Englishmen to lie out of Garrison, because of the Tories or Robbers, and thereby exposed to the Hazard of their Lives."[2]

In 1659, he and fifty-two others published an address to Parliament reciting " the Cruel and Unjust Sufferings of the People of God in the Nation of Ireland Called Quakers." This pamphlet[3] relates that " Thomas Holme (late a Captain in the Army) . . . and several of the Lords people, being in a peaceable meeting at Wexford had their meeting forcibly broken and many of them violently haled and turned out of the Town, by order from Edward Withers Mayor then." It may reasonably be presumed from this account that Thomas Holme came into Ireland as a member of

[1] *A Compendious View*, etc., 51.

[2] *Ibid.*, 53.

[3] London, Printed for Thomas Simmons at the Bull and Mouth, near Aldersgate, 1659.

the New Model, and in the Cromwellian Settlement doubtless received his allotment of land along with his fellow officers.

He became one of the earliest converts to Quakerism in the Island, and about the time of the issue of the address of 1659 was living in Limerick, for it is stated that a guard of soldiers from Colonel Ingoldesby, Governor of the town, "rifled the houses of Richard Piercy and Thomas Holme, and took away what books and papers they pleased." At a later date he was residing in Waterford, but probably held property in Wexford. He seems to have travelled extensively over the central and southern parts of the country, attending meetings of the Society. At Cashell, as related in the pamphlet, he, Thomas Loe, and others, being "on their Journey" were brought before the officer in charge of the town, who commanded his soldiers "(violently) to turne them out of the town and to cut their pates; three of them were not suffered to go into the town again for their horses."

In 1660,[1] and also in 1661,[2] Thomas Holme and other Friends were taken from meetings in Dublin and committed to Newgate prison by order of the Mayor of the City. In 1672, he and Abraham Duller, of Ireland, published "A Brief Rela-

[1] *Besse*, II., 466.
[2] *Ibid.*, II., 471.

tion of some of the Sufferings of the True Christians, the People of God (called in scorn Quakers) in Ireland for these last 11 years, viz. from 1660 until 1671. Collected by T. H. and A. F."[1] On page 44 we have seen how in 1673, Holme lost £200 on account of his scruples against taking an oath in court. In 1676, "Thomas Holme of Kilbride Parish [County Wexford] had taken from him for Tithe, by Garret Cavenagh Tithmonger," wheat, barley, and oats, valued at £1. 5s.;[2] at another time in the same year the "Priest" of Stephen's Parish, County Waterford, seized his "Warming-pan," worth 10s., for a tithe of 5s.[3].

Thomas Holme was one of the first of the Irish Friends to take an active interest in William Penn's proposed colony of Pennsylvania; he was a First Purchaser, having acquired the title to 5,000 acres,[4] and also became a member of the Free Society of

Commissioned Surveyor-General of Pennsylvania

[1] In 1731, there was printed a work called " A Compendious VIEW of Some Extraordinary SUFFERINGS of the People call'd QUAKERS both in **Person** and **Substance** in the Kingdom of Ireland, from the year 1655 to the End of the Reign of King GEORGE the First. In Three Parts. 1. Contains the true Grounds and Reasons of their Consciencious Dissent from other Religious Denominations in Sundry Particulars,—By A. Fuller and T. Holmes, Anno 1671. 2. Contains Manifold Examples of their grievous Sufferings under *Oliver Cromwell* and the Reign of King *Charles* the IId for the aforesaid Reasons. III. Is a Brief Synopsis of the Number of Prisoners," &c.

Dublin: Printed by and for Samuel Fuller, at the Globe in Meath-street. 8 vo. 1731.

[2] William Stockdale's *A Great Cry of Oppression*, 71.

[3] *Ibid.*, 73.

[4] Hazard's *Annals of Pennsylvania*, 641.

Traders, subscribing for £50 of stock.[1] On April 18, 1682, Penn appointed him Surveyor-General of the Province. The commission reads:

> I, the said William Penn, reposing special confidence in the integrity and ability of my loving friend, Captain Thomas Holme, of the city of Waterford, in the kingdom of Ireland, do by these presents elect, empower, and establish him, the said Thomas Holme, in the office, trust, and employment of surveyor-general of the said province of Pennsylvania, for and during his natural life, he behaving himself honestly and faithfully in the said office.[2]

Sails for the Province

Captain Holme sailed for Pennsylvania in the *Amity*, which left the Downs April 23, 1682,[3] bringing with him his family and John Claypoole, an assistant surveyor. James Claypoole, the father of John, wrote from London to his brother, on the 30th, "I have been at Gravesend with My son John, who has gone per the *Amity*, Richard Dimond, Master, for Pennsylvania, to be assistant to the general surveyor, whose name is Thomas Holmes, a very honest, ingenious, worthy man."[4]

The Surveyor-General and his family arrived in Pennsylvania late in June[5] and made their residence at Shackamaxon, staying for a time at the

[1] *Penna. Mag.*, XI., 180. At the first meeting of the Society, held in London May 29, 1682, he was appointed on a committee of twelve to reside in Pennsylvania.—*Hazard*, 576.

[2] *Hazard*, 555.

[3] Hough in *Penna. Mag.*, XIX., 417–418 ; Claypoole's Letter-book (MS. in collection of Hist. Soc. of Penna.; extracts are printed in *Penna. Mag.*, X., 188–202, 267–282, 401–413), cited by *Hazard*, 558.

[4] Hough in *Penna. Mag.*, XIX , 417 ; *Hazard*, 558.

[5] Hazard's *Annals of Pennsylvaniq*, 577 ; Stone in *Winsor*, III., 481 ; H. M. Jenkins, *Philadelphia*, I., 31.

house of Thomas Fairman, who in this year sent a bill of charges to William Penn for lodging Captain Holme and his two sons and two daughters.[1] Holme brought a friendly letter from Penn to the Indians, which says of Holme himself, "The man which delivers this unto you, is my Special ffriend, Sober, wise and Loving, you may believe him." He made a memorandum on the letter, "I read this to the Indians by an Interpreter 6 mo 1682—Tho Holme."[2]

Holme at once entered upon the duties of his office, and was much occupied with the country purchasers and surveys of their land. At the same time he was also acting with the commissioners in the development of plans for the City of Philadelphia, the site of which, no doubt, had been selected before his arrival. After Penn had come to a decision as to the final plan, Holme laid out the city in much the same form as we know it to-day. "A Portraiture of the City of Philadelphia," drawn up by him and printed in a book[3] published in London in 1683, is the earliest

Lays Out Philadelphia

[1] Hough in *Penna. Mag.*, XIX., 418.

[2] See facsimile of letter, *Penna. Mag.*, XIX., 413.

[3] *A Letter from William Penn Proprietary and Governor of Pennsylvania In America, to the Committee of the Free Society of Traders of the Province, residing in London,* etc. *To which is Added, An Account of the City of Philadelphia Newly laid out Its Scituation between two Navigable Rivers, Delaware and Skulkill with a Portraiture or Plat-form thereof,* etc. "Printed and sold by Andrew Sowle, at the Crooked-Billet, in the Halloway-Lane, in Shoreditch, and at several stationers in London, 1683."

map of Pennsylvania under the dominion of Penn.[1]

Holme's Map of Pennsylvania

This was followed in 1687 or 1688,[2] by his best known work, a large "Map of the Improved Part of the Province of Pennsilvania in America Begun by Wil: Penn Proprietary & Governor thereof Anno 1681." It has a subheading, "A Map of the Province of Pennsylvania, Containing the three Countyes of Chester Philadelphia & Bucks as far as yet surveyed and laid out, the divisions or distinctions made by the coullers respect the settlements by way of townships. By Thos. Holme, Survey[r] Gen!"[3] This is the most important of all the early maps, and it is of particular interest as showing the settled portion of the Province and the lands seated, with the owner's name on each tract.[4]

Work of the Surveyor-General

The Surveyor-General had deputies in each county, whose returns were made to him; and the

A part of this work is a description of the city by Holme, under the heading, "A short advertisement upon the situation and extent of the city of Philadelphia and the Ensuing platform thereof, by the Surveyor General." This map of the city, however, did not remain in effect, for as early as 1684, a number of changes in the arrangements of streets, etc., had been made.—Hough, in *Penna. Mag.* XIX., 420-1.

[1] Stone in *Winsor*, III., 481, 516; Jenkins, *Philadelphia*, I., 33; Sharpless, *Two Centuries of Pennsylvania History*, 46-47.

[2] Hough in *Penna. Mag.*, XIX., 423-425.

[3] It was "Sold by Robert Greene at the Rose & Crown in Budgrow, and by Iohn Thornton at the Platt in the Minories London," and dedicated by them to William Penn.

[4] Hough in *Penna. Mag.*, XIX.

whole work of laying out the land of the settlers and locating towns and highways was under his supervision. With the rapid growth of the country the responsibilities of the office increased, so that it became one of the most important positions in the Province. Holme held this post the remainder of his life and discharged his duties with faithfulness and ability.

He was also appointed to many other places of trust and honor. In 1682, he served as a member of the first Assembly of the Province, which began its session at Upland, December 4th, Penn presiding. In 1683, he was elected a representative from Philadelphia County to the Provincial Council for a term of three years, and took a prominent part in its transactions, serving on several important committees. In 1 Mo., 1683, he was a member of the joint committee of the Council and Assembly that drew up the new Charter, or Frame of Government. Later in the year he was one of the commissioners appointed to treat with the Governor and Council of West Jersey in regard to certain differences between the two colonies. In the following year he and two others were on a committee to investigate the actions of Lord Baltimore in connection with the boundary dispute. In the same year, 1684, he was one of three appointed to draw up a charter for the incorporation of Philadelphia as a borough, with a Mayor and six Alderman.

Member of the Provincial Council

Acts as Governor of the Province

About the middle of Holme's term (6 Mo. 18, 1684), Penn authorized the Council to act in his place as Governor. Thomas Lloyd, as President of the Council, now became acting Governor, but in 1685 he was absent a large part of the time, and Holme was elected to act in his place, presiding at twenty-seven out of the fifty meetings held this year and also at a number of meetings the next year ; so that during Lloyd's absence Thomas Holme acted as Governor of the Province.

Places of Residence

After Philadelphia was laid out in 1682, Holme removed his family to a house he had built on his lot[1] at the northwest corner of Front and what is now Arch Street, and lived there until 1688. Then he took up his residence at his plantation of "Well-Spring," in Dublin Township, Philadelphia County, and, excepting for several extended visits to England, continued there for the rest of his life, which terminated in March or April, 1695.[2]

---

[1] It was on a part of this lot farther up Front Street, sold by Holme to the Trustees of the Meeting, that the Bank Meeting House was erected in 1685.

[2] The name of Thomas Holme's wife is not known. Oliver Hough says she probably died before 1682, as she did not come to Pennsylvania with her husband. Their children were : Sarah Holme, who married Richard Holcombe, but is not known to have come to Pennsylvania ; Michael (?) Holme, who died without issue before his father ; Tryall Holme, who also died without issue before his father ; Eleanor Holme, married (1) Joseph Moss, and (2) Joseph Smallwood, by the latter having one daughter, Sarah Smallwood ; Esther Holme, married, in 1683, Silas Crispin, son of Captain William Crispin, formerly of the English navy, and died April 17, 1696, leaving six children.—*See* Hough in *Penna. Mag.*, XX., 251-256.

Robert Turner, who has several times been referred to in previous chapters as a prominent Irish Quaker, and one of the wealthiest men in the Province, was the son of Robert and Mary Turner,[1] of Royston, Hertfordshire, and was born 8 Mo., 1635, in Cambridge, England.[2] We first hear of him as a Quaker in Ireland about 1657; Rutty[3] states that about this year he was "instrumental to the convincement of a few [Friends] who lived at Grange, near Charlemont [County Armagh], in the province of Ulster."[4] In 1658, according to Joseph Smith,[5] he issued a book in behalf of the Friends called *Truth's Defense*, etc.[6]

In the pamphlet "To the PARLIAMENT of ENGLAND . . . A NARRATIVE of the Cruel and Unjust Sufferings of the People of God of the Nation of

---

[1] She died in Dublin in 1670.

[2] *Records of Dublin Monthly Meeting*, cited in "Some Genealogical Notes Regarding Robert Turner," collected by a descendant, William Brooke Rawle, Esq., of Philadelphia, and printed in the *American Genealogist* (edited by Thomas Allen Glenn, Ardmore, Pa.) Feb., 1900.

[3] *Rise and Progress*, 119.

[4] Possibly as Robert Turner was only about twenty-two years of age at this time, this refers to his father Robert Turner.

[5] *Catalogue of Friends' Books*, II., 835.

[6] "Truth's Defence . . . Also Here is a swift and close pursuite, after severall dangerous Errors, which by *Robert Child* Preist, hath lately been sowen, & spread abroad, and sold for mony (instead of Truth) to his Hearers the People of *Bandon-Bridge* in *Ireland*, which Errors, are answered by R. T. by Scorners, Scorned, Reviled, & called a *Quaker*, So was *Moses*, who was a QUAKER : . . . —Also, a true Information of the Evil and Error of one *Humphrey Whittingh* Priest &c.; with a few words to the Heads & Rulers of the Nation of Ireland ; and of the Colledge of Dublin." Large 4to, "*Printed in the Yeare*," 1658.

17

Ireland, called Quakers," printed in London, in
1659, is this entry concerning Robert Turner:

Rob. Turner, for speaking a few words in the Steeple house at *Bandon*,
(after the Priest had done) had his Hat taken away, and was beaten :
And for speaking a few words in the Steeple-house at *Dublin*, was very
much abused, and had his coat taken from him in the said place, and not
restored to him again : And for asking a Question of a Priest in *Dublin*,
was sent to Bridewell, and after kept three months in prison, was put into
a Cell or Dungeon, a very noisome place, graves being over his head, and
under his feet : And being in a meeting at *London-Derry*, was violently
haled thereout, and drawn along the street by the Arms and Legs, (the
Mayor of that City then present, and helped with his own hands) and put
him out of the said town ; and two dayes after hailed him as before, and
one with a Knif in his hand, threatened to cut off his Members, and turned
him out again, and tyed him back and legs on a Horses bare back, with a
haire rope, and led him about as their sport, at their pleasure.

In 1660 and also in 1661, for attending Quaker
meetings in Dublin, Robert Turner was committed
to Newgate; and in 1662 for the same offense was
sent to Bridewell.[1]

In William Stockdale's rare little book[2] there is
an interesting recital of Turner's sufferings, in
Dublin, in 1672, as follows:

"Robert Turner of Brides Alley having his Shop open on the day called
Thomas day, the Mayor came and took Samuel Randall his Servant, sent him
to Goal, and the same day released him : and for the like cause on Christmas
day (called) the Mayor come with a Guard of Souldiers and abused the
said Robert, sent him to Newgate, where he was detained five days : also
the rude multitude did beset his House with stones and staves, and throwing, broke down the Windows, to the hurting of some, endangering the
Lives of others, one stone weighing nine pounds, and said they had
Orders from the said Mayor : also on the day called Newyears day, for the
said cause, the said Mayor committed the said Robert and Samuel Randall

[1] *Besse* II., 466, 471.
[2] *A Great Cry of Oppression*, 212.

to Newgate, but released them next day : and on the day called Twelfth
day the said Mayor for the like cause committed Robert Fuller Servant to
the said Robert to Prison, and released him the same day : besides other
wrongs the said Robert by breaking his Windows was damnified fourteen
shillings six pence.''

In 1675, he had taken ''by the Wardens, for Priest Gowburns Wages,
out of the Shop-box three shillings.'' [1]

He seems first to have become interested in
colonization in 1677, when he and other Irish
Friends acquired one whole share of West Jersey,
their land being laid out on Newton Creek, near
the site of Camden, in 1681, and settled by Irish
Friends.[2] In 1681, he joined with the Earl of
Perth, William Penn, Robert Barclay, the Apolo-
gist, and other eminent personages, in the purchase of East Jersey from the estate of Sir
George Carteret.[3] About the same time his
friend Penn received the grant of Pennsylvania, and Turner became actively concerned
in that project, purchasing 5,000 acres of
land in the Province[4] and subscribing £500 of
stock in the Free Society of Traders.[5] It is evident from a letter of James Claypoole that before
11 Mo. 9, 1682, Turner had a prospect of going
to Pennsylvania,[6] but he did not take his departure
until a few months later, probably in 5 Mo. 1683,

[1] *A Great Cry of Oppression*, 55.
[2] Clement's *Newton*, 13, *passim*.
[3] Whitehead in *Winsor*, III., 435.
[4] Hazard's *Annals of Pennsylvania*, 641.
[5] *Penna. Mag.*, XI., 175, 177.
[6] *Ibid.*, X., 201.

his certificate of removal being signed 5 Mo. 3rd. As previously stated[1] he arrived at Philadelphia, 8 Mo. 14, 1683, in the Lion of Liverpoole, bringing with him his daughter Martha and seventeen redemptioners. Here he took up his residence and continued his mercantile business. In the summer of 1684, he erected the first brick house[2] in the city, using brick, as he writes to Penn, "after a good manner to encourage others . . . and now (6 Mo. 3, 1685) many brave brick houses are going up."[3]

Almost from the day of his arrival until his death in 1700, Turner was closely identified with public affairs.[4] At the Province Council, 8 Mo. 26, 1683, he was impaneled as a juryman.[5] In the following year he became Justice of the Peace and Judge of the Court of Common Pleas;[6] he also served as Register of Wills and Judge of Quarter Sessions and Orphans' Court.[7] In 1686, he was appointed Deputy Surveyor of Philadelphia County[8] and Receiver-General.[9] For a time he was one of the Commissioners of Property. In

[1] Page 55.

[2] At the southwest corner of Front and what is now Arch Streets.

[3] *A Further Account of Pennsylvania*, published in 1685; cited in Wescott's *Historic Mansions*, 15–16.

[4] *Colonial Records of Penna.*, I., *passim*.

[5] *Ibid.*, 87.

[6] *Ibid.*, 119.

[7] Rawle in *American Genealogist*.

[8] *Penna. Archives*, 2d Series, IX., 699.

[9] *Ibid.*, 626.

1686, he was elected a member of the Provincial Council, being re-elected in 1693 and 1700. In 1688, he was one of the five Commissioners from the Council appointed by Penn to govern the Province.[1]

He seems to have been active in the business of Philadelphia Monthly Meeting, but in the controversy between the Friends and George Keith he took the side of the latter.[2]

Robert Turner was first married in Dublin, 1 Mo. 27, 1662, to Elizabeth Ruddock, of Dover, who survived only one year.[3]   He then was married at Rosenallis, Queen's County, 10 Mo. 7, 1665, to Martha Fisher, of Cheshire.   She died 3 Mo. 1682,[4] and at the time of his emigration, as his certificate states, he was a "Widdow man and clear from all women upon account of marriage." He was married the third time, under the care of Newark Monthly Meeting, New Castle County, about 12 Mo., 1686, to Susanna Welch,[5] of New Castle, daughter of William Welch.   Turner died in 6 Mo., 1700, and was buried on the 24th.[6]   His daughter Martha, was married, 8 Mo. 18, 1689, to

[1] *Penna. Archives*, 2d Series, IX.

[2] *Proud*, 369; Hazard's *Register*, VI., 242, 306.

[3] By her he had one child, Elizabeth, born 1 Mo. 12, 1663, died 1678.

[4] The births of their children were: Martha, 7 Mo. 24, 1668; Robert, 6 Mo. 25, 1672 (died same year); Abraham, 7 Mo. 28, 1673 (died 1675); and Mary, 12 Mo. 7, 1674.—*Records of Dublin Meeting*.

[5] By her he had one son, Robert, who was buried 10 Mo. 18, 1692.

[6] *Records of Philadelphia Monthly Meeting*.

Francis Rawle, the younger, of Philadelphia, and left numerous descendants.[1] Another daughter, Mary, married Joseph Pidgeon, and died before her father.

Thomas Griffitts   Thomas Griffitts, son of George[2] and Frances Griffitts, of Cork, was another of the Irish Friends to serve as Provincial Councillor and to hold other important positions. The Friends of Cork signed him a certificate of removal, 8 Mo. 16, 1716, stating that he was clear "in respect to marriage." At that date he was residing on the Bay of Donna Maria in Jamaica, but was about to remove to Pennsylvania.

The Meeting at Kingston, in that island, also gave him a certificate, 11 Mo. 21, 1716, and his parents wrote from Cork to Isaac Norris and Jonathan Dickinson, of Philadelphia, desiring them to assist him "in that weighty affair." He then settled in Philadelphia, became a merchant, and in 1717 married Mary, daughter of Isaac Norris.

In 1723, he was appointed Treasurer to the

---

[1] See Rawle in *American Genealogist;* Glenn, *Some Colonial Mansions and Those Who Lived in Them*, II.

[2] In 1677, George Griffits, a Friend of Shandon Parish, County Cork, for "Priests Dues," had taken from him "two pewter dishes worth nine shillings 6 pence" and "a Brass Chafing dish and Skellet," valued at 10 s. In the following year, in the City of Cork, George Griffits for a tithe of 3 s. 6 d. had taken "one large pewter dish and a Tankard," valued at 8 s. and 10 s. "taken out of a purse ,from his Servant," by the church wardens.—William Stockdale, *A Great Cry of Oppression*, 74, 93, 114.

Trustees for the Free Society of Traders ; and in 1724, he, James Logan, and three others were chosen by the Penn family to sell land and to issue land warrants and patents. In 1729–30 and in 1733, he served as Mayor of Philadelphia. He was Keeper of the Great Seal of the Province from 1732 to 1734, and in 1733, took his seat in the Provincial Council. He was Judge of the Supreme Court from 1739 to 1743. He died in 1746, leaving three children to survive him : Isaac Griffitts, sometime Sheriff of Philadelphia County, married Sarah Fitzwater, in July, 1745, and died July 1, 1755 ; Mary, born March 20, 1721, died, unmarried, in 1791 ; and Hannah, born 1727, died, unmarried, in August 24, 1817.[1]

Robert Strettell,[2] Provincial Councillor and **Robert** Mayor of Philadelphia, was born of Quaker par- **Strettell** entage, 10 Mo. 25, 1693, in Back Lane, Dublin. His father, Amos Strettell,[3] descended from a

[1] See Keith's *Provincial Councillors,* 184.

[2] See Keith's *Provincial Councillors of Pennsylvania,* 196–208 ; also entries from Strettell family Bible in *Miscellanea Genealogica et Heraldica,* III., 212, 2d Series, London, 1890, and *Penn'a Mag.,* I., 241, II., 114–115.

[3] His father, Hugh Strettell, son of Thomas Strettell (of Blakley, born 1598, died Aug., 1657) and his wife, Margaret Graffitt (of Alderley, married 1619), was born 1622, and was married to Mary Hulme, daughter of Francis Hulme. Hugh and Mary Strettell became members of the Society of Friends and resided at Saltersley, Cheshire ; he died 7 Mo. 5, 1671, and she died 7 Mo. 11, 1662 ; buried in Friends' ground at Mobberly.

Children of Amos and Experience Strettell : Robert, b. 10 Mo. 25,

respectable Cheshire family, was born 12 Mo.
(Feb.) 24, 1657, at Saltersley, in Mobberly, Cheshire, and removed to Dublin in 1 Mo. (March)
1678–9, where he was married to Anne, daughter
of Roger and Mary Roberts, of Dublin. She died
11 Mo. 8, 1685–6, and he then was married, 1 Mo.
(March) 23, 1692–3, by Friends' ceremony, to
Experience Cuppage, daughter of Major Robert
Cuppage[1] and Elizabeth his wife, prominent
Friends of Lambstown, County Wexford. Amos
Strettel made a purchase of 5,000 acres of land
in Pennsylvania,[2] but there is no evidence to show
that he ever came to this country; he also held
large tracts of land in New Jersey. In 1688, he

1693; Anne, b. 12 Mo. 23, 1694–5; Amos, b. 4 Mo. 1, 1696, d. 11 Mo.
30, 1712; Elizabeth, b. 7 Mo. 25, 1697; Thomas, b. 7 Mo. 13, 1699;
Ebenezer, b. 12 Mo. 27, 1700, d. 3 Mo., 1703; Jacob, b. 3 Mo. 5, 1702,
d. 11 Mo., 1703–4; Experience, b. 5 Mo. 23, 1704, d. 4 Mo. 26, 1705;
Lydia, b. 6 Mo. 28, 1706; Benjamin, b. 9 Mo. 1, 1707, d. 10 Mo.
21, 1708.

[1] Robert Cuppage, born in Cumberland, England, in 1619, married
Elizabeth, daughter of Joshua and Sarah Warren, of Colchester, England.
He had been a major in the army, but became convinced of the Quaker
principles, and in 1662, at Wexford, for refusing to take the oath of
"Grand-Juryman," he "was committed to Prison" (*Besse*, II., 472).
In 1672, for tithes, he had taken from him hay, wheat, barley, oats, and
lambs, to the value of over £1 (*Stockdale*, 23). He died at Lambstown, 7 Mo. 15, 1683 (*Leadbeater*, 92; *Rutty*, 149). At a meeting of
the Board of Property at Philadelphia, 2 Mo. 7, 1712, there was a recital
of a deed, dated Oct. 6 and 7, 1708, in which Thomas Cuppage, of
Lambstown, Parish, of Whitechurch, County Wexford, Ireland, gentleman, since deceased, appears as one of the grantees. (*Penna. Archives*,
2nd Series, XIX., 506.)

[2] *Penna. Archives*, 2d Series, XIX., 521.

and John Burnyeat published a small book called "The INNOCENCY of the Christian QUAKERS Manifested," etc.[1]

About 1716, Robert Strettell went to London and engaged in trade, but losing a large amount of money in the South Sea Bubble, he decided to remove to Pennsylvania. A certificate of removal, dated 11 Mo. 26, 1736, for himself and family, from Friends' Meeting at Horslydowne, Southwark, was received by Philadelphia Monthly Meeting, 4 Mo. 24, 1737. He made his residence in Philadelphia and opened a shop; in a newspaper of 1738 is this advertisement: "late imported and to be sold by Robert Strettell at his store in Water Street facing Fishbourne's Wharf," muslin, cambrics, "flowered damask," India velvet, blue and white China plates, Japanese tea kettles, Scotch snuff, "fine London Pigtail tobacco," etc. His business prospered, and by 1744, when William Black visited the city, he had attained such affluence that he was able to keep up a country house at Germantown. Black writes in his *Journal*,[2] June 1, 1744:

> Mr. Strettell carried us to Germantown about a mile further where he had a little County House to which he used to come and spend some part of the Summer Months, his Wife was then there: . . . We staid till near Sun-down at Mr. Strettell's Villa, where we were very kindly Received by Mrs. Strettell, she appeared to be a very Agreeable Woman, and Consider-

[1] Joseph Smith, *Catalogue of Friends' Books*, II., 640.
[2] *Penna. Mag.*, I., 408.

ing she was in years was Admirably well Shap'd : Mr. Strettell had not
been long in Philadelphia ; he came over from London with a Cargoe of
Goods about 9 years Since, and had very Good Success in Trade ; he was
one of the Friends . . . he, I really do believe, appear'd what he really
was, a very Honest Dealer, and Sincere in everything he Acted ; he was a
very Modest Man in Company, Spoke little, but what he said was always
worth the Noticing, as he gave everything Consideration before he Deliver'd
it ; he was . . . very Moderate in Drinking and kept Good horses . . .
he had only one son [Amos] who Liv'd with him, about 19, and was in
Partnership with him in Trade, he appear'd to be a very Promising Sober
and well Inclin'd young Man, and much attach'd to Business, even uncommon for his years.

Strettell began his public career in 1741. In
that year he was elected a member of the Common Council of the City and also appointed to the
Provincial Council. In 1748, he was elected
Alderman, and in 1751, Mayor of Philadelphia.
He was a Friend, but like James Logan, was a
believer in defensive war.[1]

He was married, 5 Mo. 18, 1716, at Reigate,
Surrey, to Philotesia Owen.[2]   He died in June,
1761, and in his will mentions his "Proprie-

[1] In 1741, he was appointed on a committee to determine whether or not
a letter on defensive war, written by James Logan to the Yearly Meeting,
should be read before that body.   Strettell was in favor of having the
letter read, but the other members of the committee overruled and a nega-
tive report was made to the Meeting.   Thereupon, Strettell arose in his
seat and began to express himself as adverse to the decision, but one of the
committee caught him by the coat, saying sharply, " Sit thee down, Robert,
thou art single in that opinion."—Letter of Richard Peters to John Penn,
October 20, 1741. (*Penna. Mag.*, VI., 403.)

[2] Philotesia Owen was born at Coulsdon, England, 5 Mo. 17, 1697, and
died June 28, 1782.   She was the daughter of Nathaniel Owen (died 11
Mo. 7, 1724), formerly of Seven Oaks, Kent, afterward of Coulsdon, in
Surrey, and subsequently of Reigate, in the same county, by Francis Ridge
(born 1662, died 2 Mo. 6, 1724), his second wife.

tary Rights in West Jersey" and his "Greek, Latin, and French authors." His children were: Frances, born Sept. 17, 1717, married, Feb. 13, 1742–3, to Isaac Jones, sometime Mayor of Philadelphia; Amos Strettel, born 1720, married, Nov. 2, 1752, Hannah, daughter of Samuel Hansell, Provincial Councillor, and served as Alderman of Philadelphia in 1766, and as Assemblyman in 1780; John Strettell,[1] born 8 Mo. 29, 1721, in Cheapside, London, married, 1776, Mary Hayling; Ann, died unmarried, 4 Mo. 26, 1771; Robert, resided in Dublin after his father's removal to America, but came to Philadelphia about 1745, where he died 2 Mo. 28, 1747.[2]

William Stockdale, Provincial Councillor of Pennsylvania, and minister of the Society of Friends, first appears in the annals of Friends in 1657, as of Lanarkshire, Scotland. On February 26th of that year he wrote a short statement of some of the sufferings of Friends in Scotland, which is given in the second[3] edition of a Quaker pamphlet called, "The DOCTRINES and PRINCIPLES: the Persecutions, Imprisonment, Banish-

[1] John Strettell remained in England and was brought up to business by his uncle, John Owen. He became an opulent merchant in Lime Street, London, for some time residing at Croyden in Surrey. He died in 1786, leaving an estate of over £45,000.

[2] For an extended account of the descendants see Keith's *Provincial Councillors*.

[3] Probably it is also in the first edition of 1657, but I have not been able to see that edition.

ment, Excomunicating of the Saints of God, by the Priests and Magistrates of Scotland, contrary to the Doctrine of CHRIST and the APOSTLES,"[1] issued by him[2] and several others in 1659.

In this little work is the following account of Stockdale's persecutions:

> William Stockdale, and John Boweram, being moved of the Lord to go to Strahaven [Strathaven] in Evandale [Avondale, Lanarkshire], and declaring the word of truth there one a Market-day to the people, was oftentimes knockt down with stones, and stoned out of the town with violence by the wicked people (p. 3).
>
> William Stockdale, was knockt down in the Steeple-house yard of Damanoy, and the people set their feet upon him, and pulled much hair off his head; insomuch that some of them cried he is kild, for he could not speak nor rise off the ground for along time (p. 4).
>
> William Stockdall, was put in prison four days in a hole where he could scarce get room to lye down for speaking to James Nesmith, Priest of Hambleton (p. 6).[3]

In 1670, we find William Stockdale living in County Tyrone. Ireland, probably in the Parish of Benburb, for 'in this year he had a "pair of Pothooks" valued at 5 d. seized for refusing to contribute 2 d. towards the repairs of the "Seats and Glass windows of Benburb Parish Worship house."[4] He was a member of Grange Meeting near Charlemont, and with the exception of two years spent

---

[1] London, Printed for Robert Wilson at the Signe of the Black-spread Eagle and Winde-Mill in Martin's-lane near Aldersgate, 1659.

[2] Joseph Smith's *Catalogue* (II., 655, 686) does not mention Stockdale as one of the authors of the first edition.

[3] On page 80 it is stated that Stockdale held a discussion with a "Priest" in the "Steeple-house of Lesmahagow," Lanarkshire.

[4] *A Brief Relation of Some of the Sufferings of . . . Quakers in Ireland*, etc., by Thomas Holme and Abraham Fuller, 37 ; Besse II., 479.

in missionary effort at Londonderry,[1] he seems
to have resided in that neighborhood until his removal to Pennsylvania. John Whiting in his
Memoirs, published in 1715, says that he "travelled much in the Service of Truth in England
and Scotland and was very serviceable; especially
in Scotland as aforesaid, and also in Ireland, where
he dwelt."[2]

In 1683, he published a book entitled, "The
Great Cry of Oppression: or A Brief Relation of
some part of the Sufferings of the People of God,
in scorn called *Quakers* in *Ireland*, for these 11
years—for Tithes, &c.—with a Testimony against
taking and paying Tythes."[3]

He sailed from Ireland for Pennsylvania with
his family, probably in the ship *Friendship*, of Liverpool, in 1684–5,[4] as he witnessed a will made
on board that vessel, January (11 Mo.) 16, 1684

[1] Says *Rutty* (footnote, 343), "about the year 1673, William Stockdale
a Friend of the ministry, and Thomas Francis another Friend, removed
their Dwelling from Charlemont to Londonderry and kept a meeting there
for two years," but met with so little success in their missionary work that
they returned to their former abode.

[2] *Persecutions Expos'd in some Memoirs Relating to the Sufferings of
John Whiting*, etc. (London, 1715), 231–2.

[3] He states that in 1680 he had seven "carloads of Hey" taken for
tithes (p. 150). In 1682, "William Stockdale, after his Tryal at the Assizes in Londonderry, for being at a Religious Meeting, to worship God,
in the County of Tyrone, was closely imprisoned for ten Months, upon Pretence of Fees, by Procurement of John Rooke, Clerk to Richard Reeves,
who was then Judge there."—*A Compendious View* (Dublin, 1731), 58.

[4] Whiting (*Memoirs*, 131–2) says he came over in 1687, but this is
doubtless an error.

(probated at Philadelphia, 11 Mo. 8, 1685).[1]   He lived for a number of years in the northeast part of New Castle County, of which he was chosen a Justice of the Peace in 1685 (July 29), 1689, and 1690.[2]   He was a member of Newark Meeting, the Newark Monthly Meeting registers recording the deaths of his daughter Ruth, 6 Mo. 30, 1687, and his wife Jane, 7 Mo. 8, 1688.   In 1689, he was again married, under the care of the Monthly Meeting, to Hannah Druett.

On 2 Mo. 1, 1689, he was admitted to the Provincial Council as a representative from New Castle County,[3] and took an active part in its deliberations.   His name does not appear in the minutes after 7 Mo., 1690.   In the doctrinal controversy between George Keith and the Friends he was an ardent defender of the principles of the Society.

At Philadelphia Monthly Meeting, 3 Mo. 26, 1692, he "appeared before the meeting and Signified his mind to leave this Province and desired a Certificate," but 8 Mo. 28th, "his inclination for removal of his family at present is ceased." He had now become much reduced in circumstances, so that at the above meeting a committee was directed "to look into his necessity and

[1] *Publications of the Genealogical Society of Pennsylvania*, I., No. 4 208.

[2] *Penna. Archives*, 2d Series, IX., 648.

[3] *Col. Rec. of Penna.*, I., 268.

relieve him out of the public Stock." He[1] died 7 Mo., 1693, and was buried at Philadelphia on the 23d.[2]

Nicholas Newlin, who represented Chester County in the Provincial Council from 1685 to

1687, inclusive,[3] had resided for many years prior to his emigration within the limits of Mountmellick Meeting, Queen's County, Ireland. From Stockdale's[4] account of his sufferings for tithes, and from other sources, it is evident that he was a prosperous farmer with large flocks and herds and several servants.

In 1680, there were taken from him for tithes, seventeen "truckle-loads of Hey, and nineteen sheaves of Beans, and thirty-three sheaves of small Barly, all worth one pound one shilling";[5] seventeen "fleeces of Wooll" and five lambs, valued at £1. 7 s. The church-wardens took from him, 4

---

[1] Whiting (*Memoirs*, 131–2) says: "William Stockdale an ancient Publick Friend formerly belonging to Charlemount Meeting in the North of Ireland . . . removed to Pennsylvania in the year 1687 (?) and was concerned in the Controversie with G. Keith and there died . . . 1693."

[2] *Registers Philadelphia Mo. Mtg.*

[3] *Penna. Archives*, 2d Series, IX., 625.

[4] *The Great Cry of Oppression*, 155, 156.

[5] *Ibid.*, 155.

Mo. 13, 6 lambs worth 15 s.; 4 Mo. 23, three fleeces of "Wooll," eight "Lambs fleeces" and some coarse wool, worth 5 s.   4 Mo. 25, church officers "brought a pair of Sheep-shears and took a Sheep and shore it, then the said Nicholas caused the Pen to be broken, and the Sheep to be drove out, as he had done before, to hinder their intent; the said persons struck many blows with a stick on the Backs, Arms and Hands of those that drove out his Sheep; afterwards the said persons penned up the Sheep again, and shore and carried away with them five fleeces of Wooll," in all valued at £2. 15s.[1]

With the hope of ending these persecutions he made ready to remove with his family to Pennsylvania.   Mountmellick Meeting signed a certificate for him and his family, 12 Mo. 25, 1682, stating, as we have seen on page 58, that he had "walked honestly," but that Friends were "generally dissatisfied with his so removing, he being so well settled with his family, and having sufficient substance for food and raiment . . .; but our Godly jealousy is that his chief ground [for removal] is fearfulness of sufferings here."   He sailed the early part of 1683, in the *Levee* of Liverpool, James Kilner, Master,[2] and settled on a large tract of land in Concord, now Delaware County.

[1] *The Great Cry of Oppression*, 156.
[2] Colonial Records, I., 79-80.

Here he built a mill and became an important man in the affairs of the meeting and neighborhood. Meetings were held at his house as early as 1687, and after his death were continued for a number of years at his widow's. For a time he served as Judge of the Chester County Courts. He died in Concord, May, 1699.[1]

We have already mentioned his son Nathaniel Newlin, the owner of Newlin Township. He was born about 1660, and came from Ireland with his father. He resided in Concord, and was also a prominent character. In 1698, he was elected to the Provincial Assembly from Chester County, and was re-elected several times. In 1700, he was one of the committee to consider and draw up a new Frame of Government and to revise the laws. He was subsequently appointed one of the Commissioners of Property and a Judge of the County Courts. In 1722, he became one of the Trustees of the General Loan-Office of the Province. He died in May, 1729.[2]

Lydia Darragh,[3] of Philadelphia, the well-known heroine of the Revolution, who risked the safety of herself and family to give General Washington

Nathaniel Newlin

Lydia Darragh

---

[1] Futhey and Cope, *History Chester County*, 669.

[2] *Ibid.*, 669.

[3] See *Lydia Darragh, of the Revolution*, by Henry Darrach, in *Penna. Mag.*, XXIII., 86–91 ; Hazard's *Register*, I., 48 ; Appleton's *Cyclopædia of American Biography*, II., 79, etc.

18

warning of the intended attack of the British on his army at White Marsh, in 1777, was an Irish Quaker. She was born about 1729, the daughter of John Barrington, a Friend, of Dublin, and was married 11 Mo. 2, 1753, at Friends' Meeting, in Sycamore Alley, Dublin, to William Darragh (born about 1719) of the same city. They came to Philadelphia about 1765 and lived, it is thought, on Second Street, below Spruce.

William Darragh died 6 Mo. 8, 1783, and his widow, on April 22, 1786, purchased a house on the west side of Second Street, between Market and Chestnut Streets, where she resided and kept a shop. She died 12 Mo. 28, 1789, and, although she had been disowned from the Society for neglecting to attend meetings, she was buried in Friends' burial ground at Fourth and Arch Streets. The inventory of her estate amounted to £1628 17 s. 9 d. In her will she mentions her son Charles Darragh, who served in the American Army, as "Ensign in Second Penna Feby 1777 and 1st Lieut retired 1 July 1778."[1] For this breach of discipline he was disowned by Philadelphia Monthly Meeting, in 1781.[1]

We have now noticed a group of Irish Quakers who were most conspicuous and influential in the governmental affairs of Pennsylvania during the

---

[1] For record of descendants of Lydia Darragh, see *Penna. Mag.*, XXIII., 90-91.

Quaker regime, 1682–1756. Many others of prominence have been referred to in the chapter on "Places of Settlement," and still others receive attention in the Appendix.

While outnumbered by the English and Welsh Quakers, these Irish Quakers compare favorably in the performance of public services; for they gave to the Province eight Provincial Councillors, three acting Governors, one Proprietary Secretary, two Receivers-General, one Register-General, one Surveyor-General, one Provincial Treasurer, one Chief Justice, three Judges, one Master of Chancery, two Keepers of the Seal, twenty-two Justices of the Peace, eighteen Assemblymen, two Sheriffs, one County Treasurer and three Mayors of Philadelphia.[1] Serving in these important capacities in a province, which, it is significant to remember, was founded and controlled by Quakers down to 1756, and which has ever been of foremost rank in the union of States, the Irish Quakers have had a strong formative influence upon our State and national institutions, and thus have been important factors in stamping upon these institutions imperishably the doctrines of civil and religious liberty.

Nor did the Irish Quakers play a less important part in the social order. Here also they were a distinct element of strength. Like most of the

Contribution of the Irish Quakers

---

[1] *Penna. Archives*, 2d Series, IX., 621–800.

Quaker settlers they were plain yeomen and tradesmen, springing from that great middle class of society which has ever been the stay and strength of Britain, not only upon the field of battle but also in the pursuits of peace. They had escaped from a land of contest, imprisonment, disaster, and suffering, and found within the Quaker commonwealth religious freedom and economic opportunity. Their thrift and energy made them a substantial and stable part of the population ; and their principles as exemplified in their lives have entered into the bone and sinew of our Republic.

APPENDIX

List of Certificates of Removal from Ireland Received at the Monthly Meetings of Friends in Pennsylvania, 1682–1750; With Genealogical Notes from Friends' Records of Ireland and Pennsylvania, Genealogies, County Histories, and Other Books and Manuscripts. (See Bibliography.)

PHILADELPHIA MONTHLY MEETING

Established in 1682.

Thomas Holme, from Meeting at Waterford City, Ireland, dated 11 Mo. 29, 1681. See notice of him, pages 247–256.

John and Joseph Low, from Men's Meeting at Ballyhagen, Parish of Kilmore, County Armagh, Ireland; dated 5 Mo. 31, 1682.

In 1679, John Loe, of Parish of Terteryan, County Armagh, suffered persecution for tithes.—Stockdale, *A Great Cry of Oppression*, 125.

Archibald Michael [Mickle], from Men's Meeting at Richard Boyes' house, near Lisburn, County Antrim, Ireland, dated 6 Mo. 2, 1682.

Archibald Mickle, cooper, was married at Philadelphia, in 1686, to Sarah Watts. Four years later he purchased from Robert Turner a tract of 250 acres in Newton, and removed thither from Philadelphia. He died there in 1706, his wife Sarah surviving him. His children were: John, m. Hannah, daughter of William Cooper, in 1704; Samuel, m. Elizabeth, daughter of Joseph Cooper, in 1708; Daniel, m. Hannah Dennis, in 1711; Archibald, m. Mary Wright, in 1719; Joseph, m. Elizabeth Eastlack, in 1723; James. m. Sarah Eastlack, in 1732; Sarah, m. Ezekiel Siddon; Mary, m. Arthur Powell; and Rachel, m. Benjamin Cooper, in 1718.[1]

[1] See Judge Clement's *First Settlers in Newton*, 139-148. (His own corrected copy at Hist. Soc. of Pa.).

JAMES ATKINSON.—" 1682, 9 $\frac{10}{\text{mo}}$ The Antelope of Bellfast arrived here [Philadelphia] from Ireland.   James Attkinson arrived here and Jn° Ashbrooke his servant.'' (*Penna. Mag.*, VIII., 329).

He produced a certificate, dated 8 Mo. 23, 1681, from Friends at Drogheda [Ireland] to Philadelphia Mo. Mtg.   At Phila. Mo. Mtg., 1 Mo. 6, 1683,   "Several Certificates were brought into the meeting & Produced, amongst which there was a certain Certificate, dated from Clanbrazill [probably Lurgan Meeting] in the County of Armagh in Ireland, touching one James Atkinson (who now resides at Griffith Jones's) his coming into this province contrary to the Consent of friends of the meeting whereunto he belonged, whom friends by the aforesaid Certificate signifyed to be very much in Debt, and C·.''

At the Mo. Mtg., 5 Mo. 3, 1683,   '' Agreed that Thomas Holme, Thomas Wynne and Griffith Jones do satisfy by a few lines, the friends of the meeting at Canbrazill concerning James Atkinson, as touching his departure out of England and Ireland into Pennsylvania ''   In 1684, he married Hannah, widow of Mark Newbie, of Newton Meeting, N. J.   James Atkinson, of Philadelphia, shopkeeper, being aged, made his will 2 Mo. 16, 1711 (probated Sept. 6, 1711) and mentions son Thomas.

In 1655, William Edmundson (*Journal*, 20) says, '' We came to a Widow Woman's House, one Margery Atkinson, a tender, honest Woman, whose House [near Killmore, County Armagh] I had been at before :   She was convinced of the Truth and received us lovingly.   So we had a Meeting there ; the tender People thereabouts generally came to Meeting, most of them received the Truth . . .   We settled a Meeting there, which became large.''   In 1660, for a demand of 8s. 4d. tithes, Margery Atkinson had taken from her two cows worth £3, 10s. (*Besse* II., 467).

DENNIS ROCHFORD, son of William Rochford, was born in Emstorfey [Enniscorthy] Co. Wexford, Ireland, about 1647.

He became a Friend about 1662.   According to Besse's *Sufferings* (II., 476) he and other Friends being ''assembled in their usual Meeting-place in Bride-street [Dublin, in 1669,] were taken thence'' and committed to prison for five weeks, and also imprisoned in Wicklow ''Gaol,'' in 1670, for attending a meeting at the house of Thomas Trafford, in Wicklow (*Ibid.*, 479).

He '' went into England and landed in Whitehaven in Cumberland the 30th of the 3d month, 1675 ; dwelt in Brighthelmston in

Sussex 3 years and kept a grocer's shop, and came into the province of Pennsilvania with Mary his wife, Daughter of John Heriott,
of the parish of hostper poynt [Hurstpierrepoint] in Sussex in
Old England (she was Born on the 14th of the 3d month [16]52)
in the ship called the *Welcom*, Robert Greenaway comander,
with two servants, Tho: Jones & Jeane Mathews: the said
Dennis' two daughters, Grace and Mary Rochford, dyed upon the
seas in the said ship; Grace being above 3 years old and
Mary being 6 months old: the said Dennis Rochford Landed
with his family in Pennsilvania about the 24th day of the 8th
month 1682 [not so early by a few days]. Mary Rochford the
second daughter of Dennis & Mary Rochford was born in the
Province of Pennsilvania at Egely poynt, in the county of Philadelphia, the 22th of the 8th mo. 1683, between 10 & 11 at night,
she being the second daughter of that name" (*Hist. of Chester Co.*,
23 ; *Penna Mag.*, VIII., 334).

Dennis Rochford settled in Concord Township, Chester (now
Delaware) County, where he had located a large tract of land.
In 1683, he represented Chester County in the Provincial Assembly (Dr. Smith's Hist. of Delaware Co., 497). Later, apparently, he removed to Philadelphia, where his name appears
on the minutes of the Monthly Meeting, 5 Mo. 1, 1684.

ROBERT TURNER and family, from Men's Meeting in the City
of Dublin ; dated 5 Mo. 3, 1683. He being "an Antient
ffriend of this meeting" and "a Widdow man." See
notice of him, pages 257–262.

PHILIP ENGLAND, certificate dated 3 Mo. 21, 1683, from
Men's Meeting, Dublin, Ireland.

BENJAMIN CHANDLEE, unmarried, son of William Chandlee,
of Kilmore, County Kildare, Ireland, from Edenderry
Mtg., King's County, Ireland, dated 11 Mo. 18 [year
omitted, but probably about 1701 or 1702]. Signed by
William, Jr., and Nath. Chandlee.

Benjamin Chandlee, son of William, of Kilmore, County Kildare, Ireland, came to Philadelphia and learned the trade of a
clock and watchmaker with Abel Cottey, whose daughter Sarah
he married, 3 Mo. 25, 1710, and about 1715 settled on a tract of
land in Nottingham, Chester County, which had belonged to his
father. There he built a smithy and made brass cow bells, then
much needed. In 1741, they removed to Wilmington, Delaware,
where he died about 1745. (See further account in *Hist. Chester
Co.*, p. 496.)

In 1676, in County Meath, one William Chanley, of Killncross, Parish of Trim, had his goods seized for tithes.—*Stockdale*, 68.

CHRISTOPHER PENNOCK was married prior to 1675 to Mary, daughter of George Collett, of Clonmell, County Tipperary, Ireland.   After residing there and in Cornwall, England, for some time, he emigrated to Philadelphia about 1685, and died in that city in 1701.   A son, Joseph, born at Killhouse, near Clonmell, Ireland, 11 Mo. 18, 1677, was a merchant in Philadelphia until about 1714, when he removed to West Marlborough Twp., Chester Co., and settled on a large tract of land, of which he became proprietor by virtue of a grant from William Penn to George Collett, his grandfather.   In 1738 he erected a large mansion, "Primitive Hall," in which he died, 3 Mo. 27, 1771.   (See pages 144–6.) By his wife, Mary Levis, he had twelve children, an account of whom may be seen in *History of Chester County*, p. 680.

According to Besse's *Sufferings of the Quakers*, in 1660 (II., 467), 1666 (II., 475) Christopher Pennock, of Cork, Ireland, was imprisoned for attendance at Friends' meetings, and in 1670, for the same reason, he had 49 yards of "stuff" worth £2, 9s., taken from him (II., 478).   In William Stockdale's *Sufferings* (p. 12), printed in 1683, he is mentioned as having 6s. taken from him for maintenance of a "Priest."   In 1675, in Cork the "Priest" took seven shillings out of his "shop-box." —*Stockdale*, 60.   In Cork, in 1676, Mary Pennock for keeping shop open on Christmas day was imprisoned for one night.— Stockdale, *A Great Cry of Oppression*, 231.   In the summer of 1900, the writer saw the original MS. of Dr. John Rutty's *Rise and Progress of the Quakers in Ireland* (in possession of John Pim, J.P., a Friend, of Bonaven, Antrim Road, Belfast), bound in a piece of old parchment, which on a hasty inspection seemed to be a seventeenth century deed, containing the names of Christopher Pennock and George Collett, both of Cork.   In 1680, George Collett, of Clonmell, had seized for tithes six "Pewter Dishes and a Pewter Candlestick," valued at £1.—*Stockdale*, 165.

The following extract from a letter, dated 2 Mo. 7, 1685, addressed to Christopher Pennock, doubtless refers to George Collett : " Dear Brother Pennock, Myne and my wife's affectionate love is to thee, and we are heartily glad it is in thy wife's hart to be with thee, and that the way is made for her ffather's condescension and willingness thereto." (*Pennock Papers*, belonging to Mrs. William H. Miller, of Media, Pa.)

JOHN MCCOMB, from Ireland, was at Philadelphia, in 1688.

"To friends of the Monthly Meeting at Philledelphy these are to Satisfie yu conserning John McComb who I doe understand is intended to take a wife Amongst yu that Soe fare as I know he came a cleer man from all wiming out of Ireland Save only my daughter which the lord was pleased to take out of the bodey to whom he should have ben maried if She had lived & about three nights before I came from my being in Ierland his father was with me and as to his maridge left him to his owne liberty & choise this I Satisfie under my [hand] this 19th of the 6th month, 1688.—Wm. Stockdall."

"JOHN FULLER, of the towne & Countie of Philadelphia," merchant, made his will 3 Mo. (May) 25, 1690, and it was proved 10 Mo. 5, 1692, by Robert Turner, executor. Samuel Carpenter and Patrick Robinson were assistant executors.

He leaves "To Elizabeth Cuppage,[1] of Lemsone [Lambstown, County Wexford], in the Kingdome of Ireland, my mother the sum of" £130 "to be paid to her in Ireland," in "case the ship *Tryall* in which I goe for England shall goe well home, then I doe give unto my s^d mother further the sum of twenty pounds money aforesd—to Robert Turner younger—the sum of five pounds, and to Mary Turner, Daughter to the s^d Robt Turner S^r the sum of five pounds—to my friend George Keith of Philadelphia, the sum of twenty Pounds—to Benjn Acton of Salem in West New Jersey—the sum of five Pounds—to my friend Sam^ll Carpenter—the sum of five Pounds—to John MacCombe—the sum of thirty Pounds—to my friend Patrick Robinson of Philadelphia —the sum of five Pounds, to the Poore of the People called Quakers in the towne of Philadelphia the sum of Tenn Pounds." Residue "of Estate, reall & Person, Lands, Letts, goods & chat tells to Robert Turner Elder of Philadelphia Mrcht."

Witnesses: Andrew Robeson, John Vest, Samuell Buckley.[2]

GUIAN STEPHENS, unmarried, of Loughgall, Co. Armagh, Ireland, "hath from his Childhood been brought up amongst us." From Mtg. at Ballyhagen, Ireland, dated 7 Mo. 5, 1700. Received 2 Mo. 25, 1701.

WILLIAM ABBOTT and daughter from Bandon Meeting, Ireland, received 2 Mo. 25, 1701.

[1] Elizabeth, daughter of Joshua and Sarah Warren, of Colchester, England, b. 1 Mo., 1627, m. first, 5 Mo., 1645, Robert Valentine, who d. 5 Mo., 1651; m. second, Henry Fuller, who d. 4 Mo., 1665; m. third, 5 Mo., 1667, Robert Cuppage, of Lambstown, Ireland. She d. at Ballinacarrick, 2 Mo., 1695. Her son John Fuller was b. 1657. Her daughter Mary Fuller, b. 1653. m. Henry Hillary, and d. 8 Mo., 1697.

[2] *Publications of the Genealogical Society of Pennsylvania*, Vol. I., 81–82.

JAMES LOGAN, single man, "now of Pensilvania, Late of this Citty have Desired a Certificate from this meeting." From Mtg. at Bristol, England, dated 12 Mo. 9, 1701. Original on file.   See notice of him, pages 237–247.

ELIZABETH GREEN, unmarried, from Dublin, Ireland, dated 4 Mo. 26, 1702 ; received 4 Mo. 25, 1703.   "Lived here in this City [Dublin] several years."

ELIZABETH AND ELINOR ARNOLD, unmarried, were "brought up by William Browne, an honest friend and at his Death he Left them Sumthing to live on and his Will Recomended them to ye care of us undernamed, they having no parents." From Wexford, Ireland, dated 12 Mo. 5, 1704.   Received 4 Mo. 29, 1705.

MARY WILSON, unmarried, daughter of John Wilson, of Greenridge, in Coldbeck, Cumberland, England, "who for some years past hath Lived as a Servant in this Citty," intends "to Return into her native Contry again and from thence (if nothing Lett) to Transport herselfe into pensilvania."   From Mtg. in Dublin, Ireland, dated 10 Mo. 19, 1704.   Also, another certificate from Coldbeck Mtg. Cumberland, dated 11 Mo. 7, 1704, states that she "hath lived for some years last past in the Citty of Dublin and now Returned to her father's house."   Thomas and John Wilson signed certificate.   Received 11 Mo. 25, 1705.

PAUL WOOLLFE, from Mo. Mtg. at Dublin, dated 12 Mo. 24, 1706–7.   Received 12 Mo. 28, 1706–7.

EDWARD SKULL, unmarried ("now Supposed in or about Pensilvania"), from Mtg. in Cork, Ireland, dated 1 Mo. 9, 1706.   He served his apprenticeship with John Dennis, a Friend of Cork.   Said Skull wrote to John Dennis for a certificate of removal.   Original on file.   Received 3 Mo. 30, 1707.

JOHN TANNER, a letter concerning him from Lurgan Mtg., Ireland, dated 12 Mo. 26, 1706.   He is now in Phila., and has married Mary Rea.   Letter brought before the Mo. Mtg., 5 Mo. 25, 1707.   Not recorded.

MARY CAMM. She "hath had her Residence in this Citty from Childehood, has also been a member of our womans meeting for Several years." Her husband intends to go with her. From Mtg. at Cork, Ireland, dated 6 Mo. 23, 1708. Received 10 Mo. 31, 1708.

JOHN CAMM, "by occupation something of yᵉ combing trade & some other branch of that manufactory." His wife, two children, and servants; dated 6 Mo. 23, 1708, from Mtg. at Cork. Received 9 Mo. 26, 1708. A letter concerning him from Cork, dated 5 Mo. 4, 1709. Not recorded.

John Camm probably settled in Philadelphia for a time, but subsequently removed to what is now Delaware County, where his name appears in a list of taxables in 1715. On August 29, 1716, then residing in Upper Providence Township, and styled stocking weaver, he purchased from Elizabeth, widow of Charles Booth, a messuage and one hundred acres of land in the said township, for a consideration of £75. Mr. Ashmead in his *Delaware County* (670) is authority for saying that John Camm was the first stocking weaver in America. In 1732, Camm inserted the following advertisement in the *American Weekly Mercury*, issued December 10th.
"*Whereas*, Matthew Burne, of Chester County, served John Camm two years (that is, ten or twelve months at stocking weaving and other work), during which time John Camm's stockings bore many reflections, and now the said Matthew Burne goes about selling stockings in John Camm's name as though they were his own make, which is false and not true.
"John Camm." [1]
Camm's will, dated September 7, 1736, mentions his wife, Mary, and son, Henry.

ELIZABETH JACOB, wife of Caleb Jacob, "has Lived in this Citty for aboute 7 years and have been a member of our womens meeting for a year or more." From Cork, Ireland, dated 6 Mo. 23, 1708. Received 9 Mo. 26, 1708.

JOHN PEELL, young, son of Luke Peell, of Loughgall, Ireland. From Mtg. at Ballyhagan, dated 8 Mo. 17, 1708. Received 11 Mo. 28, 1708.

In 1681, Luke Peel, of Parish of Loughgall, County Armagh, had goods taken from him for tithes.—*Stockdale*, 176.

[1] *Ashmead*, 669–670.

WILLIAM GREEN, unmarried, a young servant. From Mtg. at Ballycane, County Wicklow, Ireland, dated 6 Mo. 8, 1708. Has lived some years with a Friend as a servant. Endorsed by Dublin Mtg. 6 Mo. 15, 1708.

SAMUEL COMBE, "Late of ye Citty Corke, Cooper, having transported himselfe and family to Pensilvania at Such time as severall friends of this place were Removing to that Country and not knowing he Should goe with them, they Layd their Intentions of going before our meeting time nor Season afterwards did not offer for his getting a Certificate to Cary with him wherefore Since his arrivall there he having writ unto a friend here to procure one for him." Said Samuel being a Bristol man, "came over into this Country with his wife Some time after ye Wars ended to settle in Corke and follow ye Cooping trade and although he was observed to be a Laborious painfull man, ye world favoured him not with Success we hope and desire it may be better in that country where we suppose workmen of that Calling are not so plenty as in this nor materials to worke on Soe hard to be obtained as here." Clear in relation to marriage. Received 2 Mo. 28, 1710.

SARAH MASSEY, wife of Samuel Massey, and daughter of Thomas Wight, of Cork, intending to go to America with "her husband and tender babes." From Cork, Ireland, dated 7 Mo. 18, 1710. In *To the Parliament of England* (p. 1), issued by the Irish Friends, in 1659, Daniel Massey "a Souldier" for speaking a few words to "a Priest in the Steeple-house at King-sail," was imprisoned. Also at the same time and place Sarah Massey for discussing with the "Priest" in her own shop was put in prison. In 1670, Daniel Massey "opening his shop in Bandon-bridge on Holy day was stoned and beaten."—(Holme and Fuller, *A Brief Relation*, 47.) In 1671, Sarah Massey, of Bandon, was imprisoned for keeping her shop open on Christmas day.—*Stockdale*, 209.

SAMUEL MASSEY, tallow chandler and soap boiler, "having had Inclinations for severall years past (as he Informs us) to settle in" Pennsylvania. "The cheife motive Represented to us for his Remove is ye want of trade to answer ye great Rents here and charges of his family wch he hopes will be easier to him in that Country he is Industrious and Carefull, and his Conversation orderly having a wife and five children besides servants." From Cork, dated 5 Mo. 17, 1710.

" At our 3 weeks meeting in Corke 28 $\frac{mo}{3}$ 1711 upon ye Sorrowfull news of ye above Samuel Massey and family being taken by ye french whereby as he writes from Antegue he was deprived of his Certificate and Desiring the Coppy thereof to be sent him ; we ye under named doe Certifie that ye above is a Coppy of what we finde to be Coppy of ye originall Delivered the sayd Samuel Massey ye 18th 7th mo : past." Received 8 Mo. 25, 1711. See page 93.

SAMUEL HILLARY, unmarried, son of Henry Hillary, of Wexford, County Wexford, Ireland, was brought up a Friend.

" When he was grown up his Desire was to go to Sea to wch his parents Consented, and put him apprentice to a friend, and he served him honestly to ye best knowledge and since he hath been out of his time he hath Continued at Sea, but some time agoe his uncle Thomas Cuppage a friend of good account with us Dyed, and left him part of his Reall Estate to ye value of a hundred pounds per annum, and he ye sayd Samuel hath further acquainted that he hath Intentions of mariage with one Jane Waterman in ye province of pensilvania to wch his parents have given there consent." From Mtg. in Wexford, dated 4 Mo. 10, 1711. Received 9 Mo. 30, 1711.

In 1678, Henry Hillery, of Wexford, for 4s. " Poundage " had " one Iron pot," valued at 8s. 6d., taken from him.—*Stockdale*, 114.

One Nathaniel Hillary, of Lurgan, and Grizell Miller, of Dunclady, were married at the house of Katherine Henderson, in the town of Dunclady, 8 Mo. 23, 1706.—*Minutes of Ulster Prov. Mtg.*

In 1670, one Christopher Hillary, " a Soldier in the Militia under Captain Draper, . . . being convinced of the Unlawfulness of Wars and Fightings under the Gospel for that Reason refused to continue any longer in bearing Arms ; For this he was set on a Wooden Horse with three Muskets at each of his Legs, and after that Punishment, was committed to Goal."—Besse's *Sufferings of the Quakers*, 479.

In 1670 " Christopher Hillary, of Shankill Parish [County Armagh] being one of the Militia, under Captain Draper ; and afterwards convinced of Truth, . . . and so for Conscience sake could no longer bear Carnal Weapons ; for which he was put on a thing called a Wooden-Horse, in Charliamount, with three Musquets at each Legg, and ordered so to sit till four inches of Match was burned, and afterwards committed to Goal," where he yet remains.—Holme and Fuller, *A Brief Relation*, 46.

In 1680 in County Antrim, Francis and Marmaduke Hillery had their goods seized for tithes.—*Stockdale*, 142.

JOHN KNIGHT, unmarried, son of Thomas Knight, of Bandon, County Cork, Ireland, dated 8 Mo. 22, 1711, from meeting in Cork. He now resides in Philadelphia and has written to his father in regard to his certificate. Received 1 Mo. 28, 1712. Original on file.

In 1678, in the City of Cork, Margery Knight had taken for tithes, "a Brass pot" (7s.), "a Brass Pestle and Mortar, with a small Platter," total value, 16s. 4½d.—Stockdale, *A Great Cry of Oppression*, 114.

MARK CARLETON and family, dated 4 Mo. 3, 1711, from Mo. Mtg. at Mountmellick, Ireland. He is "ye Son of an early Labourer (after ye breaking forth of ye Gospel day) in ye word and Testimony of our Lord Jesus, and his wife ye Daughter of honest friends of this meeting." Original on file. Received 8 Mo. 25, 1711. He died in 1711. See page 96.

Thomas Carleton, born in 1636, in Little Salkeld, Cumberland, England, like his father spent much of his life as a farmer. He was one of the early converts to Quakerism and became an eminent minister of the Society. In 1663, for the non payment of tithes he was put in prison and kept there for several years. In 1669, he married Isabel Mark, of Mosedale, Cumberland. About 1674, he removed to Ireland and settled at Ballinacarrick, County Wicklow. In 1681, according to William Stockdale (*A Great Cry of Oppression*, 252), Thomas Carleton, of Bellynacarge, County Wicklow, had taken (2 Mo. 19) by the church wardens "one Brass pan and one Pewter dish," valued at 6s. 3d. for "repairing the Parish Worship-house at Rathdrum." The titles of several of his works, the first of which was *The Captive's Complaint*, etc., printed in 1668, are given in Joseph Smith's *Catalogue* (I.). He died at his house at Ballinacarrick, 9 Mo. 16, 1684, leaving a wife, at least three children, and several servants.[1]

Mark Carleton, of Ballylickbo, son of Thomas and Isabella Carleton, formerly of Mosedale, Cumberland, was married, 11 Mo. 25, 1698, to Susanna Watson, of Ballymeane, at Edenderry.[2] They removed to Pennsylvania in 1711, producing a certificate of removal, dated 4 Mo. 3, to Philadelphia Monthly Meeting, 8 Mo. 25, 1711. Mark Carleton apparently soon died, and in 1713, his widow married Richard Parks, a settler in Goshen, Chester County.

Thomas Carleton, son of Mark and Susanna Carleton, was born 9 Mo. 19, 1699, at Ballyhaken, near Edenderry, Ireland,

[1] *Leadbeater*, 92.
[2] Records of Mountmellick Meeting.

and in 1720 settled in Kennett Township, Chester County, where he married, 3 Mo. 20, 1730, Hannah Roberts, widow of Robert Roberts, and daughter of William Howell, of Haverford. She was born 5 Mo. 17, 1689, and died 5 Mo. 6, 1758. Thomas died 9 Mo. 30, 1792.[1] He and his wife were active members of Kennett Meeting, and both eminent ministers. Their children were Susanna, who married Michael Harlan, and Thomas, born 8 Mo. 21, 1732, died 6 Mo. 26, 1803, who married, 10 Mo. 26, 1757, Lydia Gregg, daughter of Thomas and Dinah. Thomas had children—Hannah (m. William Passmore,) Dinah, Martha, Mark, Sarah, Samuel, Thomas, Lydia (m. Abner Mendenhall) Thomas, and Caleb.[2]

BENJAMIN MAYNE. At the Mo. Mtg. 9 Mo. 30, 1711. "A paper of Condemnation against one Benjamin Mayne from the Monthly Meeting of Cork in Ireland was read."

JAMES MORRIS, unmarried, dated 1 Mo. 7, 1711–12, from Mtg. in Dublin, Ireland. Original on file. Received 5 Mo. 25, 1712.

JOSHUA BAKER " (who for Som years past hath dwelt in this Citty)," dated 2 Mo. 13, 1712, from Mtg. in Waterford, Ireland. Original on file. Received 1 Mo. 27, 1713.

Joshua Baker, b. Feb. 16, 1678; m. Margery Knight, of Bandon Bridge, in Ireland. She was born July 15, 1690. They probably lived a few years in Philadelphia; then some time prior to 1728, settled in Christiana Hundred, New Castle Co. now Delaware. For account of descendants, see *Hist. Chester, Co.*, p. 470. In 1677, one Thomas Baker, "of Clanfekiel Parish" had his goods seized for tithe by " by Andrew Clerke, for John Speer Farmer of Tithe from the said Dean of Ardmagh."—*Stockdale*, 82.

WILLIAM MOORE, unmarried, "who had his Education in this Citty." "A great Reson of his Removeall is for want of a good Imploy his trade being bad here." From Waterford, Ireland, 2 Mo. 13, 1712. Received 1 Mo. 27, 1713. Original on file. James Moore signed certificate.

[1] Jacob Pierce, of Longwood, East Marlborough Township, Chester County, notes in his MS. Diary, under date of 10 Mo. 2, 1792: "Went to burial of our Antient friend Thomas Carlton who departed this life the 30th of last month in morning & this morning the ground was Cover'd half inch deep with Snow."

[2] *Futhey and Cope*, 493.

ABIGAIL HETHERINGTON. Her master is a Friend of this city with whom she has lived some years. From Dublin, 1 Mo. 17, 1712–13.

JOHN LANCASTER, unmarried, " Came about ten years agoe out of Cumberland into this nation (his parents being deceased) and was Convinced of Truth amongst us about three after since wch time he hath had his conversation here." Dated 4 Mo. 3, 1711, from Mo. Mtg. of Mount-mellick, Ireland. Received 1 Mo. 26, 1714.

ISAAC BARTON, of Clonmell, cutler, and family, dated 3 Mo. 16, 1714, from Six Weeks Mtg., at Killcomonbegg, Ireland. Received 8 Mo. 29, 1714.

FRANCIS EROTT, unmarried, a Friend by birthright, from Ballycaine, Co. Wicklow, Ireland. Dated 4 Mo. 9, 1714 ; received 11 Mo. 8, 1714. His father consents to his removal. His mother is deceased. William Erott signed certificate.

In 1676, in County Wexford, Francis Errot had goods (maslin, sheaves of white peas, hay, "one Barrel of Potatoes and a Lamb"), valued at £1. 19 s. 6 d., seized for tithes.—Holme and Fuller, *A Brief Relation*, 72.

THOMAS GRIFFITTS, unmarried. His father George Griffitts, of the city of Cork, requested a certificate for him. Certificate from Mtg. at Cork, dated 8 Mo. 16, 1716. Also from a Mtg. in Kingston, Jamaica, dated 11 Mo. 21, 1716. Another letter, dated " Corke ye 17th of 8 mo : 1716," signed by George and Frances Griffitts :

" Esteemed friends Isaac Norris and Jonathan Dickinson these serves to advise you ; my son Thomas Griffitts wrote to me from ye bay of donna Maria that he was bound to philadelphia and desired me to make application to our meeting for a Certificate of his Clearness in Relation to marriage." He appeared at Philadelphia, 12 Mo. 22, 1716. Certificate received 1 Mo. 29, 1717.

MARTHA GRIFFITTS, " whose Husband of Late being settled at kingstown in Jaimaca and hath wrote for his wife to come over to him and she being willing to goe by an opertunity of Shiping that put into this Harbour by Contrary winds bound to Jaimaca." She was born of believing parents. From Cork, Ireland, 6 Mo., 6, 1709. Frances Griffitts signed certificate. Original on file.

ROBERT PENROSE, of Ballykenny, County Wicklow, wife Mary, two daughters, Margaret and Ann Penrose, and a single son, Christopher Penrose, who was brought up a Friend and bound an apprentice to a Friend in Dublin. (Christopher's certificate is dated 3 Mo. 21, 1717, from Two Weeks Meeting at Dublin. Original on file.) Received 8 Mo. 25, 1717.

Rutty (page 128) says the Penroses of County Wicklow, Ireland, became Friends in 1669.

In 1673, in County Wicklow, Robert Penrose "because for Conscience sake he could not take an Oath to be a Constable, was committed to Prison" and detained ten weeks.—William Stockdale, *A Great Cry of Oppression*, 218.

In the same year, Richard Penrose, for having questioned a "Priest" in regard to an address made at a burial was committed to Wicklow jail for above a year.—*Ibid.*, 218.

In 1677, John Penrose, County Wicklow had his goods taken for tithes.—*Ibid.*, 91.

Rebecca Penrose, daughter of William and Margaret Penrose, of Waterford, b. in 1703, married Isaac Jacob, of Waterford, Ireland, and died 2 Mo. 3, 1728.—*Piety Promoted* (Phila., 1854) II., 300. In 1716, Thomas Story (*Journal*, 544) notes a visit to John Penrose, living near Ballycane Meeting, County Wicklow.

Robert Penrose, son of Robert and Jane Penrose, born in Yorkshire, England, removed to Ireland, and in 1669 was married to Anna Russell.

A son Robert, born in 1670, probably in Back Lane, Dublin, was married in 1695 to Mary Clayton, by whom he had thirteen children. With a part of their family they came to Pennsylvania about 1717. They resided for a time in Philadelphia; then in Marple Township, now Delaware County; and in 1734 took a certificate of removal from Chester to Gwynedd Monthly Meeting.

Christopher, son of Robert and Mary Penrose, m. 3 Mo. 1719, at Middletown Meeting, now Delaware County, to Ann, daughter of Peter and Jane Hunter, of Middletown. Another son, Robert,[1] m., Sept. 13, 1733, Mary Heacock, at Springfield Meeting, now Delaware County.

One William Penrose, who was probably a son of Robert and Mary Penrose, was married about 1738, under care of Exeter Monthly Meeting, Berks County, to Ann Wiley. About 1762, they removed to Warrington, York County, bringing a certificate,

[1] For a record of his descendants see Ellwood Roberts, *Old Richland Families*, 205.

dated 6 Mo. 24, 1762, from Exeter to Warrington Monthly Meeting, 9 Mo. 11, 1762, where both William and Ann served as overseers.   Late in life they removed to Huntington Township, now Adams County, where he died in the autumn of 1785 leaving his wife to survive him.   She died 2 Mo. 26, 1804.

Children: Mary, m. 10 Mo. 21, 1762, at Warrington Meeting, Thomas Edmundson, son of Caleb and Mary ; Jane, m. 5 Mo. 3, 1764, at Warrington, Jediah, son of John Hussey ; Phebe, m. 5 Mo. 13, 1766, at Warrington, to Thomas, son of Thomas and Sarah Leech ; Hannah, m. 4 Mo. 23, 1772, at Warrington, Samuel, son of Samuel John, late of Newberry ; Thomas, m. 5 Mo. 11, 1775, at Warrington, Abigail, daughter of David Cadwallader, late of Loudon Co., Va. (children of Thomas and Abigail : Amos, b. 3 Mo. 13, 1776 ; Hannah, b. 4 Mo. 29, 1779 ; Ann, b. 6 Mo. 22, 1781 ; William, b. 5 Mo. 9, 1784) ; William ; John ; Susanna, m. 5 Mo. 17, 1781, at Warrington, David Cadwallader.

THOMAS BARGER, wife and family, from Meeting held in Clonmell, County Tipperary, dated 1 Mo. 24, 1716–17. Original on file.

JOSEPH WOOD, wife and family.   Daughters Ellen and Sarah unmarried.   He " was queried of concerning his Reasons for Removing and the weightiness of the undertaking (considering his age) was Layd before him and then it was Left to Montrath Meeting (to wch he did belong) for what further might be needful and his wife was queried of by friends of Montrath perticular meeting Concerning the Reasons of there going and he gave account that they had Relations there and that he understood that his trade (wch is making parchment and glue) is far better there than here."   From Mountmellick Mtg., dated 2 Mo. 8, 1717.   Received 4 Mo. 27, 1718.

WILLIAM TAYLER, unmarried, saddletree maker, who now dwells in Philadelphia.   Charles Howell, of this meeting, was written to by Friends in Pennsylvania asking for a certificate for him.   From Clonmell, County Tipperary, Ireland, dated 1 Mo. 24, 1716.   Received 5 Mo. 25, 1718.

MILES STRICKLAND, from Dublin Mtg., received 6 Mo. 29, 1718.

THOMAS LINSLEY (Lindley in Minutes), unmarried, a smith, lately wrote from Philadelphia for a certificate. He was put an apprentice in Dublin. After "he was out of his aprentiship he set up trade for himself at Ringsend near this citty." From Dublin, 11 Mo. 27, 1718. Received 7 Mo. 24, 1719.

RICHARD HOY, unmarried, "an Irish man having lived three years and a halfe with a friend of our meeting." Dated 12 Mo. 7, 1724, from Richmond Mo. Mtg., held at Chantrey, County York, England. Received 12 Mo. 25, 1725.

SAMUEL VERNER.—At a meeting of the Board of Property at Philadelphia, 8 b'r, 29th, 1725, "Sam'l Verner (from Ireland) requests the Grant of a parcell of Land for a Settlement on Pecque [Pequea Creek, Lancaster County], he has set down for some time. He produces good Credentials, both from our Friends in Ireland and others. Sam'l Verner being dead, his Son David requests the Grant, 200 A's."—*Penn'a Archives*, 2nd Series, XIX., 734.

GEORGE and ELIZABETH DEEBLE, children of Richard Deeble, of Cork, deceased. The father died "about three years and a halfe [ago] and Left nine small children behinde him, over whom ye care of friends of this Citty for theire good has not been wanting and Some of theire near Relations in Pensilvania having Lately given Some Encouragement to Receive Some of them if they were Sent thither, the above named George and Elizabeth ye two Eldest were very Desirous to go with a younger Sister." Dated 2 Mo. 23, 1722, from Mtg. at Cork, Ireland. Received 6 Mo. 31, 1722. Original on file.

In 1681, George Deeble, of Cork, was imprisoned for refusing to buy firearms for the militia.—*Stockdale* 252.

In 1677, at Cork, Jerom Deeble had taken "a pair of Andirons" (12s.) and Richard Jacobs, two "Sledges" and a hammer (10s.) in all valued at £1.2s.—Stockdale, *A Great Cry of Oppression*, 92.

Letters of administration on estate of Jerome Deeble, of Chester County, were granted 10 Mo. 13, 1716, to Henry Miller and Isaac Bellarby. Henry Miller,[1] of Upper Providence, now Delaware County, in his will, dated 12 Mo. 14, 1731-2, mentions his cousins George, Elizabeth, and Jane Deeble.

[1] Henry Miller, of Bradninch, Devonshire, England, m. 6 Mo. 27, 1702, at Mynehead, Somersetshire, to Sarah Deeble, of Alcombe, Somersetshire, daughter of George Deeble (who m., 4 Mo. 17, 1669, Dorothy Thorne).

ANN CLIFTON " who was Lately in your parts and came over to see her Relations here sum time agoe Is now Intending soon to Return in order to Dwell amongst you." From Dublin, dated 2 Mo. 13 and 14, 1724. Received 7 Mo. 25, 1724.

ROBERT WOODCOCK, of Lambstown, Co. Wexford, Ireland, and wife, who is a daughter of Jacob and Ruth Barcroft. Dated 1 Mo. 12, 1727, from Cooledine Mtg., Ireland. Not recorded.

JOHN WALBY and wife Susanna, dated 2 Mo. 10, 1728, from Mtg. at Moat, Ireland. " He was born in England, & came unto this Nation [Ireland] in the Nature of a Scool Master. And first Settled with our ffrd Samuel Wattson in the County of Catherlough, where he removed for Som years, till he maried Susannah Russell Daughter to our ffrd. John Russell, of this Meeting. And lived amongst us more than a year, during which time his behaveiour has been orderly, he allso brought us good Certificates both from England and Carlow Men's Meeting " Signed by Mary Russell and two John Russells. Received 7 Mo. 27, 1728.

MARY BOYES, daughter of Jacob and Lucy Turner, was married 6 Mo. 17, 1720, in the Meeting House at Lurgan, to John Boyes. Dated 5 Mo. 30, 1729, from Lurgan Mtg., Ireland. Jane, Ann, Elizabeth, Sarah, John, Jacob, Thomas, and Samuel Turner signed certificate. Original on file. Received 11 Mo. 30, 1729-30. Not recorded.

In 1681, Richard Boys, Anne Richardson, and Robert Oliver, of Parish of Magheramisk had their goods taken for tithes.—Stockdale, *A Great Cry of Oppression*, 170.

ANN GOODBODY, unmarried; dated 5 Mo. 29, 1729, from Dublin. Received 10 Mo. 29, 1729.

WILLIAM HENDERSON. At Phila. Mo. Mtg., 6 Mo. 29, 1729, a letter, dated 2 Mo. 22, 1729, was received from Mtg. in Dublin, Ireland, enclosing a testimony of disownment, dated 11 Mo. 21, 1717, against William Henderson, formerly a minister.

GEORGE HOWELL and wife, from Mtg. at Cork, dated 2 Mo. 28, 1729.

SARAH MARSHALL, daughter of Richard and Deborah Marshall, dated 4 Mo. 1, 1729, from Mo. Mtg. at Edenderry, Ireland. Received 6 Mo. 29, 1729. Original on file.

LETTICE HATTON, unmarried, of this city, "was not educated in our Profession by her Parents they not being of us but she lived about seven years a Servant to sundry friends in this City who give a good report of her she having been five years & half in the frd^s service in wch she is now likely to remove and for about four years past has frequented our Religious meetings." From Dublin, dated 5 Mo. 29, 1729. Received 2 Mo. 24, 1730. Original on file.

JOHN LOW, unmarried, "hath lived severall years servant to Robert Greer & his Son John till of late he removed himself to Lurgan." Dated 2 Mo. 11, 1722, from Mtg. at Grange, near Charlemont, County Armagh, Ireland. Also a certificate, dated 3 Mo. 7, 1729, from Mtg. at Lurgan, Ireland.

ANN CUNNINGHAM, and niece, Ann, unmarried ; dated 5 Mo. 29, 1729, from Dublin, Ireland. The niece, Ann Cunningham, about sixteen years of age, "Goes over as Apprentice or Servant to and along with our Friend Thomas Millhouse and his wife. Also Elizabeth and Mary Cunningham, the small sisters of the niece Ann go with her." Original on file. Received 10 Mo. 26, 1729. Not recorded.

In 1672, one Elinor Cunningham, widow, of County Armagh, had her goods seized for tithes.—*Stockdale*, 14.

WILLIAM SANDWITH, unmarried, "who resided for some time in this City and is lately removed into your Parts." Dated 1 Mo. 24, 1729-30, from Dublin, Ireland ; signed by Samuel Sandwith. Also a certificate from Wexford Mo. Mtg. held at Coledine, dated 1 Mo. 8, 1729, stating that he is "a young man who was Educated amongst frds from his youth & served an apprenticeship here honestly, and for some time past hath betaken himself to a seafareing Employ who wrote for a Certificate to our parts." Was at Philadelphia as early as 8 Mo. 27, 1727. Original on file.

His grandson, William Drinker, writing about 1795, says that William Sandwith was a native of County Wexford, and descended from a family formerly seated at Sandwith, near Whitehaven, England. "He was between seventy and eighty years ago a merchant and ship owner of this city (Philadelphia), and sometimes commander of his own vessels." (See *Extracts from the Journal of Elizabeth Drinker*, 3.) William Sandwith married Sarah, daughter of Martin Jarvis, an Irish Friend, of Philadelphia. Their daughter Elizabeth, born in the house of her grandfather Jarvis, married Henry Drinker, and kept a diary (1759-1807), interesting extracts from which were printed in 1889.

DINAH BUSHBY, from Mo. Mtg. held at Dublin, dated 3 Mo. 6, 1729. Received 4 Mo. 26, 1730.

EUNICE CONOLLY, unmarried, about to remove along with her mother and relatives and friends into Pennsylvania. She was brought up a Friend, "but hath lived as a Servant to Severall Friends of this city." Dated 6 Mo. 12, 1729, from Mtg. at Dublin, Ireland. Original on file. Received 1 Mo. 27, 1730.

JOHN ALMENT and wife, and MARK EVES.—At Philadelphia Monthly Meeting, 10 Mo. 30, 1730, "A Certificate for John Alment & Wife [Elizabeth] to Friends at Ballycaine in Ireland was read & by order of the Meeting signed by the Clerk and sent to the Women Friends to Sign, being Indorst on the back of the Certificate they brought with them. Also a few lines were Indorst on the back of Mark Eves jun[r] Certificate, which he brought from the same place & is returned thither again."

HANNAH HUDSON, unmarried, dated 4 Mo. 2, 1730, from Mtg. in Dublin. Went to Pennsylvania about a year ago. Original on file. Received 9 Mo. 27, 1730.

ELIZABETH HAWKINS, dated 2 Mo. 6, 1731, from Dublin, Ireland. Received 5 Mo. 30, 1731.

WILLIAM NICHOLSON, unmarried, "of this City did some time ago remove himself from hence into your parts and hath since desired a Certificate . . . He was Educated in the profession of Truth from his Childhood by his unckle Joseph Nicholson a frd of this City unto whom also he was bound an apprentice but before his time was out his unckle died and being inclinable to go to America his aunt, who was his Mistress, consented thereto and Paid his Passage." Certificate from Dublin. Original on file. Received 7 Mo. 29, 1732.

In 1680, one William Nicholson, of Parish of Terterian, County Armagh, had his goods seized for tithes.—*Stockdale*, 149.

ISAIAH McNICE, widower, with a large family, who hath lived "within the compass of our meeting these Twenty years." From Mtg. at Cootehill, County Cavan, Ireland, dated 2 Mo. 21, 1736. Received 2 Mo. 24, 1736. Original on file.

SARAH SMITH, unmarried, dated 11 Mo. 25, 1731, from Dublin, Ireland. Received 4 Mo. 30, 1732. Not recorded.

RUTH STEER, JR., unmarried, "descended from an honest Parentage." Dated 3 Mo. 23, 1734, from Six Weeks Mtg. at Lisburn, in the north of Ireland. Certificate signed by Ruth Steere, Sr., Isaac, Catherine, Mary, and Richard Steere. Received 2 Mo. 26, 1735. Not recorded.

ELIZABETH DEANE, dated 2 Mo. 10, 1736, from Ballinacree, County Antrim, Ireland. Received 6 Mo. 28, 1736.

JOHN PATERSON, "who went from hence severall years ago & Since has resided in your parts is now about to marry a young woman amongst you and requesting a few lines from us by way of Certificate." He served his apprenticeship with a Friend of Dublin. Dated 3 Mo. 25, 1736, from Mtg. in Dublin, Ireland. Original on file. Received 8 Mo. 29, 1736.

RUTH WEBB, dated 1 Mo. 31, 1736, from Mtg. in Lurgan, Ireland. She and Moses Shaw went "away from this place." Original on file. Received at Philadelphia 10 Mo. 29, 1736.

Roger Webb, son of Edward Webb, then of Dunmurry, Co. Antrim, and wife Margaret, was born at Dunmurry, about 1622. He was by trade a wheelwright or turner. He was maried, 12 Mo. 3, 1649, to Ann, daughter of Adam Snowcroft, "of hartfoord green now Charlo," in Lancashire, England and Margery, his wife. Children : Edward, James, John, Edward (2), Deborah, Jonathan, Ruth, Mary, Roger.—*Lurgan Records.*

SARAH WILCOCKS, wife of Issachar, "some ago remov'd with her 2ᵈ Husband into the Compass of your meeting." She was "marry'd by a priest to her present Husband." Dated 1 Mo. 27, 1737, from Mo. Mtg. at Mountrath, Ireland. Received 11 Mo. 27, 1737. Not recorded.

JAMES HILL and "wife Margaret Hill alias Oliver." Dated 5 Mo. 21, 1738, from Preparative Mtg. held near Ballinderry, Ireland. Original on file. Received 10 Mo. 29, 1738 ["they being lately removed to settle at Willingstown in New Castle County."]

MARY SHARP "to Live with her Husband James Sharp, who Some time past left this City, and as we are Informed is Settled amongst you." Dated 1 Mo. 28, 1738, from Dublin, Ireland.

MARY ERWIN (lately married) with husband John Erwin; dated 4 Mo. 19, 1739, from Dublin.

THOMAS ROOK, unmarried, "Granson to our Ancient and Esteemed Friend George Rook of this City." Dated 1 Mo. 12, 1739–40, from Mtg. in Dublin, Ireland.

George Rooke, an eminent Quaker minister of Ireland, son of Thomas, was born at Boltonwood [parish of Boulton] in Cumberland, England, in 1652. He lost his father when he was eleven years old, and his mother was left with several small children to support. At sixteen he was apprenticed to Thomas Drewry, a carpenter and joiner, one of the Society of Friends, and became a member of the Society. At about the age of twenty-five he appeared in the ministry and travelled much in that service. In 1686, he removed to Limerick, Ireland, and married Joan the daughter of John Cooke. In 1693, he settled in Dublin. His wife died there, 7 Mo. 17, 1737 and was buried in Friends' burial ground on Cork Street, aged eighty-four. He spent his declining years with his widowed daughter Rachel Carlton, and her children, and died 12 Mo. 7, 1742.—*Rutty* 334–7 ; *Leadbeater*, 212–226.

HUGH CANADY, unmarried, and family. The "Said Hugh frequainted our Religious meeting for worship from his Childhood, & Since his Wife's Decease (they being maried orderly amongst us) has been Endusterous in Labouring for a livelihood for his Children, & some of them being Grown up has behaved prity orderly Considering their yeares." Dated 2 Mo. 3, 1741, from Men's Meeting held near Charlemont, Ireland. Original on file. Not recorded. See page 98.

Hugh Kenedy and Elizabeth Parker, both of Grange Mtg. near Charlemont, were m. there, 9 Mo. 6, 1723.—*Minutes of Ulster Province Mtg.*

ABEL CHAMBERLAIN, unmarried, served his apprenticeship in this city, dated 11 Mo. 26, 1740, from Three Weeks Mtg. in Cork, Ireland. Original on file. Received 3 Mo. 22, 1741.

JAMES MOORE, widower, dated 1 Mo. 6, 1740-1, from Mtg. at Waterford, Ireland. Original on file. Received 4 Mo. 26, 1741.

JOSEPH DEANE, unmarried, son of Alexander Deane, "who formerly resided within the Compass of this Meeting & has lately left this in order to Transport himself to Your Province he having been in sd Province before." Dated 5 Mo. 14, 1740, from Mtg. in Antrim, Ireland. Received 7 Mo. 25, 1741.

JOSEPH GARNETT, unmarried, of Dublin, dated 5 Mo. 27, 1742, from Dublin Mtg. Original on file. At the Mo. Mtg. of Phila., 10 Mo. 31, 1742, he is reported as having returned to his home in Dublin.

DAVID DEAN, "a young man who was born and hitherto Educated within the bounds of this Meeting." Unmarried. Dated 2 Mo. 25, 1747, from Mtg. in Antrim, Ireland. Received 10. 25, 1747.

JOHN NEVITT accompanies his brother "into your parts." Dated 2 Mo. 28, 1751, from Moate, Ireland. Received 8 Mo., 25, 1751.

PATIENCE RICHARDSON, unmarried, dated 6 Mo. 28, 1750, from Dublin. Received 12 Mo. 27, 1751.

ELIZABETH LITTLE sometime ago returned from this city to settle in Pennsylvania as a servant. From Dublin, dated 1 Mo. 12, 1750-1.

JOHN TAGART and wife Mary, dated 5 Mo. 11, 1750, from Lurgan, Ireland.

JOHN BRITTEN and three children, Jacob, John and Susanna, all unmarried. From Cooledine Mtg., County Wexford, Ireland. Received 6 Mo. 31, 1750.

WILLIAM JOHNSON. "He served an apprenticeship to a merchant within the bounds of Lisburn Meeting." Dated 6 Mo. 11, 1752, from Ballyhagen Mtg., Ireland. Received 1 Mo. 26, 1753.

JAMES EDDY and wife, dated 5 Mo. 1, 1753, from Dublin. Received 9 Mo. 28, 1753.

MARY ANDERSON, wife of Samuel, late of this city, having some years since removed to Philadelphia. Dated 5 Mo. 3, 1751, from Waterford, Ireland. Received 11 Mo. 30, 1753.

LYDIA DARRAGH, from Dublin, Ireland, dated 9 Mo. 17, 1765, she having removed thither with her husband and family. See pages 273–4.

FALLS MONTHLY MEETING

In Bucks County.   Established in 1683.

JAMES DOWNEY, received 6 Mo. 1, 1711, "from friends in Ireland." Married Hannah Ellott in 1712. His certificate is recorded in Certificate Book of Middletown Mo. Mtg.   (See Middletown Monthly Meeting.)

BUCKINGHAM MONTHLY MEETING

In Bucks County.   Established in 1720, from Falls.

RICHARD CHURCH, received 9 Mo. 4, 1729, from Ireland, dated 3 Mo. 4, 1729.

JOHN STEPHENSON, received 1 Mo. 7, 1742–3, from Edenderry [King's Co.], Ireland. Also credentials from Friends in Chester County, where he has for some considerable time resided.

One James Stephenson, of Ballyhagen Mtg., and Mary Milikin of Monallan Mtg., were married, 12 Mo. 17, 1708, at Monallan Mtg.—*Minutes of Ulster Prov. Mtg.*

WRIGHTSTOWN MONTHLY MEETING

In Bucks County. Established in 1734, from Buckingham.

A certificate for James Dean and most of his family to Ireland was signed 7 Mo. 5, 1738.

ALEXANDER DEAN,[1] unmarried, received 11 Mo. 5, 1741-2, from Friends at the Grange in the north of Ireland. A certificate for him to Ireland was signed 3 Mo. 2, 1741-2. A certificate for Alexander Dean[2] and

JAMES DEAN, Jr., from the Six Weeks Meeting at Antrim in Ireland, was received 9 Mo. 2, 1742-3.

SAMUEL DEAN from same meeting, received 11 Mo. 4, 1742-3.

JOHN DEAN, received 11 Mo. 6, 1746-7, from Six Weeks Meeting at Grange, Ireland. A certificate for him to Ireland, signed 9 Mo. 7, 1749.

[1] At Grange Meeting, County Antrim, 2 Mo. 7, 1740, "James Deane Recomending his son Alexander to this meeting for a certyfycate, he having a mind to Transport himself to America, a certifycate was this day signed, setting forth that the said Alexander Deane was in unity with Friends and free from Ingagements in Relation to marriage" etc.

At Antrim Meeting, 5 Mo. 14, 1740, "Ruth the wife of Alexander Deane came into this meeting and requested a certyfycate for her son Joseph who has lately left this in order to Transport himself to America, on which a certyfycate was drawn and signed setting forth his honest behaveour, free of scandall &c, and altho wee could not say he was in close unity wth us wth respect to discipline yet he lived pretty much in love with friends, frequented our meetings for worship and was free of engagements in relation to marriage, wee recommend him to the care of Friends in America."

Alexander Dean and Ruth Wilkison, both of Antrim Mtg., were married in the town of Antrim, 3 Mo. 13, 1713.—*Minutes of Ulster Province Mtg.*

[2] A certificate for Alexander Deane to Antrim, Ireland, was signed at Wrightstown, 7 Mo. 3, 1745. At Antrim Meeting, Ireland, a certificate to America for Alexander Deane was signed 10 Mo. 27, 1760.

MIDDLETOWN MONTHLY MEETING

In Bucks County.   Established in 1683.

ANN MILLCUM [Malcum or Milcomb], certificate, dated 1
Mo. 31, 1682, from Ballyhagan Meeting, Parish of Killmore, County Armagh, with her daughter, Jane Greer, of
Loughall, Parish of Loughall, County Armagh, Ireland,
laid intentions of removal before our meeting, 4 Mo. 9th
last, "Where the said meeting inquired of them the reason why they had a mind to such a great journey, having
no man in their family except they might get a servant or
servants, and having no want of things necessary for a
livelihood ; the said Ann Millcum replied that her daughter Jane had a great desire to go and being not willing to
part with her, after such a manner, was rather willing to
take her adventure with her other daughter, and so go all
together, being accompanied with another daughter of hers,
and her husband and children, with several neighbors also,
and seeing it was her resolution to go as aforesaid."
In 1680, in County Armagh, Ann Malcum, widow, had six
" car-loads of Hey" seized for tithes.—*Stockdale*, 149.   In 1673,
in County Down, one John Malcum had his goods seized for
tithes.—*Ibid.*, 26.

JAMES DOMEY (dated 7 Mo. 25, 1709), of Parish of Ballinderry, County Antrim, Ireland, "hath frequented our
meetings several years and hath lived with an honest
friend, one John Haldon nine or ten years."   Unmarried.
From Meeting held at Richard Boyes' (Ballinderry Mtg.).

JANE HEARLAM, dated 1 Mo. 11, 1713, from Mountmellick
Meeting, Queen's County, Ireland, "having dwelt among
us about fifteen years, was educated by her uncle William
Huddleston."

ABINGTON MONTHLY MEETING

In Montgomery County.   Established in 1683.

THOMAS STRICKLAND, received 5 Mo. 28, 1718, from Dublin, Ireland.

JOHN FIRTH, received 9 Mo. 25, 1728, two certificates, one from London to Dublin and one from Dublin to Pennsylvania.

WILLIAM LANDER, received 4 Mo. 29, 1730, from Ireland.

JOHN, THOMAS, and JAMES ROSE, received 5 Mo. 27, 1740, from Ireland.

John Rose received a certificate to Buckingham in 1734. Later he was living in Germantown. James Rose received a certificate to Buckingham in 1735. Thomas Rose m. Margaret Lucken, in 1738, and resided in Germantown. For many years he served as overseer and elder of Germantown Meeting and as clerk of Abington Monthly Meeting. He died 9 Mo. 17, 1785, aged 84 years and 3 months.

ISAAC DAVENPORT, received 10 Mo. 30, 1734, from Ireland.

PATRICK HOLLAND and wife from Ireland, received 7 Mo. 28, 1741.

PATRICK HENDERSON,[1] received 11 Mo. 3, 1708, two certificates, one from Ballyhagan, Ireland, and the other from Long Island. See page 97.

GWYNEDD MONTHLY MEETING

In Montgomery County. Established in 1714, from Radnor.

PETER CLOAK and wife, received 3 Mo. 28, 1723, one certificate from Britain and the other from Ireland.

MARGARET COLLINS, received 6 Mo. 29, 1732, from Dublin, Ireland.

JAMES WOOD, received 8 Mo. 28, 1735, from Dublin.

REBECCA BYRN, received 3 Mo. 31, 1737, from Ireland.

At Newark Monthly Meeting, 3 Mo. 4, 1745, Rebecca "Burn" produced a certificate from Gwynedd ; but 4 Mo. 1, 1745, the said

[1] Jonathan Burnyeat (*Diary*, 41, London, 1857) states that on 10 Mo. 26, 1705, he "came to Dunglody, to Katherine Henderson's house (Patrick's mother), where we had a meeting." In 1716, Thomas Story (*Journal*, 537) notes that he came to the widow Henderson's at Dunclaudy, County Antrim.

Rebecca "being removed back again" her certificate was returned to Gwynedd.

One Joshua Bryne (b. in 1718, d. 7 Mo. 29, 1777), of Wilmington, Delaware, son of Daniel and Rebecca Bryne, was married, 1 Mo. 15, 1750, to Ruth Woodcock, at Wilmington.—*Kennett Records.*

RADNOR (HAVERFORD) MONTHLY MEETING

In Delaware County.   Established in 1684.

MOSES COATES and wife [Susanna], dated 3 Mo. 8, 1717, from Carlow Meeting, County Carlow, Ireland.   He was brought up at Carlow from a child, and took his wife from among Friends in the Province of Munster.

Moses Coates,[1] who has already been noticed on pages 154-155, settled at the site of Phœnixville.   He and his wife Susanna had the following children : Thomas, m. 3 Mo. 21, 1741, Sarah, daughter of Henry Miller, of Providence, now Delaware County (children : Henry, Susanna, Jonathan and Samuel); Samuel, m. in 1743, Elizabeth Mendenhall (children : Aaron, Moses, and Isaac); Moses, m. Priscilla Hutchinson (children : Sarah, Susanna, Phebe, Moses, Mary, John, Thomas, Mahlon, Priscilla, and Aquila); Benjamin, m. in 1756, Ann Longstreth (children : Jane, Susanna, Benjamin, and Tacy); Jonathan, m. Jane Longstreth (children : Ann, James, Hannah, Jonathan, Susanna, Phebe, Keziah, Grace, Isaac, Jane, and Elizabeth); Aaron ; and Elizabeth, m. John Mendenhall.

Moses Coates, son of Samuel, and grandson of the emigrant, married in 1770, Hannah Musgrave, and after her death married Mary Vickers, by whom he had a son Dr. Jesse Coates, founder of Coatesville, Chester County.

THOMAS COURTNEY, received 9 Mo. 12, 1742, dated 2 Mo. 22, 1741, from the monthly meeting [Grange] held near Charlemont, Co. Armagh, Ireland.

One Thomas Courtney, of Grange Mtg., and Ruth Trueman, of Lurgan Mtg., were married 1 Mo. 25, 1702, in the town of Lurgan.—*Minutes of Ulster Prov. Mtg.*

In 1681, Toby Courtney, of Parish of Maherlin, County Down, had his goods seized for tithes.—*Stockdale,* 170.

---

[1] One William Coats, of Ballenbagert, Parish Kilmore, County Armagh, made his will, 8 Mo. 11, 1697, and mentions his children Joseph and Sarah. John Coats was a witness. (*Recorded in Friends Records.*)

CHESTER MONTHLY MEETING

In Delaware County. Established in 1681.

THOMAS JACOB, received 6 Mo. 28, 1710, from Cork, Ireland, endorsed by Darby Mo. Mtg., Pa.

EDWARD THOMPSON, received 4 Mo. 30, 1712, from Lurgan Meeting, County Armagh, Ireland.

JOHN SAUL, unmarried, received 3 Mo. 31, 1714, dated 10 Mo. 1, 1713, from Two Weeks Meeting, Dublin, Ireland, "from Cumberland in England Some years ago."

SAMUEL WORTHINGTON, son of Robert, received 9 Mo. 24, 1712, dated 5 Mo. 25, 1711, from meeting at Moate of Greenage, County West Meath, Ireland.

FRANCIS JONES, and family, received 6 Mo. 31, 1713, dated 6 Mo. 17 1711 ; "about three years ago they came over here to Pembrocksheire [Wales] from Ireland and ever since did belong to our monthly meeting at Redstone."

THOMAS COEBOURN, wife and children, received 10 Mo. 27, 1714, dated 2 Mo. 11, 1714, from Monthly Meeting at Ca-shell, County Tipperary, Ireland.

Thomas Coebourn (father of above Thomas), with his wife Eliza-beth, came from Berkshire, England, accompanied by sons William and Joseph. They arrived at Chester in 1682, a short time before the first visit of William Penn, and settled on a large tract of land in Chester Township, which after the death of his wife in 1688, Thomas conveyed to his two sons. William was married to Mary, daughter of Joseph Baker, in 1686, and Joseph to Susanna Churchman, in 1690. Thomas was a carpenter. For some time after his arrival he took an active part in the affairs of Chester Monthly Meeting. About the year 1687, he built a mill—the second on Chester Creek—which gave offence to Caleb Pusey and the other proprietors of the Chester Mills.—Smith's *History of Delaware County*, 454 ; Gilbert Cope.

Joseph Coebourn, of Aston Township, now Delaware County, made his will 3 Mo. 28, 1723, and it was probated 4 Mo. 5, 1723. Mentions wife Sarah and children—Sarah, Dinah, Lydia, Susanna, Joseph, Thomas, and Elizabeth (Pedrick).

Israel Acrelius in his *History of New Sweden* (printed at Stock-holm, 1759), printed in translation in 1876 (*Memoirs of Hist. Soc. of Penna.*, XI., 156), writes : "Joseph Cobern, in Chester, twenty years ago, had the blessing to have his wife have twins, his cow two calves, and his ewe two lambs, all on one night in the month of March. All continued to live.''

BENJAMIN HEAD and family, received 11 Mo. 28, 1716, a certificate from Cork, dated 1 Mo. 17, 1715, and also one from Charlwell, Ireland, dated 4 Mo. 10, 1715.

SARAH HARRIS, {widow of Roger, and children, received 4 Mo. 27, 1715, from New Garden Meeting, County Carlow, Ireland.

ALEXANDER ROSS, a Friend, migrated from Ireland, and settled within the bounds of Chester Monthly Meeting, early in the 18th century.

In 1706, he married Catharine Chambers, of Chichester, now Delaware County, and in 1713 removed to Haverford, in the same county. In 1715, he returned to Chester Meeting, and from thence removed to New Garden Meeting, Chester County, where it seems he remained till about the year 1732, when he and a number of other Friends obtained a grant for 100,000 acres of land near the Opequan Creek, in what is now Frederick County, Virginia. To this place Ross and his assoiates removed, formed a settlement, and established Hopewell Monthly Meeting. Ross's children were Mary, Lydia, Rebecca, John, George, and Albeinah. —Dr. Smith's *History of Delaware County*, 497.

JAMES HIND, wife Ruth, and daughter, received 12 Mo. 25, 1716, from Moat Monthly Meeting, County West Meath, Ireland.

RACHEL COEBOURN, received 4 Mo. 25, 1717, from Killcommon Monthly Meeting, County Wicklow, Ireland.

PETER HUNTER, of Ballenecarick, County Wicklow, Ireland, wife and daughter Ann (unm.), received 6 Mo. 26, 1717, dated 11 Mo. 13, 1716, from Ballycane Meeting, County Wicklow, Ireland.

ANN WELDIN, received 9 Mo. 25, 1717, from Killcommon Monthly Meeting, County Wicklow, Ireland.

REBECCA STARR, received 1 Mo. 31, 1718, from Carlow Meeting, County Carlow, Ireland.

ROBERT PENROSE, Jr., tanner, unmarried, received 3 Mo. 25, 1724, dated 3 Mo. 10, 1721, from Dublin, Ireland.

WILLIAM ROBISON, unmarried, received 3 Mo. 25, 1724, dated 7 Mo. 16, 1722, from Ballycane Meeting, County Wicklow, Ireland.

One John Robinson, of Killageonahan, Co. West Meath, was married to Jane Lecky, of Kilmeany, daughter of Robert and Mary, at Carlow, 7 Mo. 19, 1733. She was born 2 Mo. 12, 1687, at Staplestown.—*Records of Carlow Mo. Mtg.*

THOMAS Parke, who "lived Since his Convincement which is Nigh 40 years amongst us" and family. Two sons, Thomas and Jonathan are unmarried. Received 11 Mo. 25, 1724-5, dated 2 Mo. 15, 1724, from Carlow Meeting, County Carlow, Ireland. See pages 69–79.

Thomas Parke,[1] of Ballean contra Ballylean, County Cavan, born about 1660, was married, 10 Mo. 21, 1692, at New Garden Meeting, County Carlow, to Rebecca Warr or Ward, of Ballyredmond. She was born about 1672. Thomas Parke[2] was a farmer in Ireland, and in 1720 owned some land in Ballilean, Ballaghmore and Coolisnacktah. In May, 1723, he sold his stock of cattle and prepared to leave Ireland. On May 21, 1724, with all his family except Mary and Susanna, he took passage at Dublin on the ship *Sizargh*, of Whitehaven, Jeremiah Cowman, master, and after a rough voyage, as his son Robert notes in his journal, they arrived within Delaware Bay on August 21st.[3] Thomas leased from Mary Head (an Irish Friend) a property near Chester, as a temporary home, but on December 2d purchased from Thomas Lindley 500 acres of land in the Great Valley on the west side of what is now Downingtown, Chester County. He was an elder of

[1] Children of Robert and Margery Park : Eleanor, b. 1 Mo. 2, 1684, at Ballyredman, Co. Carlow ; Martha, b. 12 Mo. 3, 1686, at same place ; Robert b. 8 Mo. 13, 1688, at same place ; William b. 10 Mo. 11, 1690, at same place ; Thomas, b. 11 Mo. 20, 1694, at same place.—*Records Carlow Meeting.*

[2] *Records of Carlow Meeting, Ireland; History of Chester County*, 673 ; *Smedley Genealogy*, 166–7 ; *The Parke Family* (by James Pemberton Parke, printed in *Chester County Journal*, Downingtown, Feb. 8, 1868); copy of J. P. Parke's MS. history of Parke family.

[3] There were ninety-four passengers aboard the vessel.

20

Caln Meeting and well esteemed by Friends. He died 1 Mo. 31, 1738, and his widow, 6 Mo. 21, 1749. Children were:

I. Mary Parke, b. 7 Mo. 18, 1693, at Ballintrain.

II. Robert Parke, b. 1 Mo. 23, 1694, at Ballintrain, had been a storekeeper in Dublin, in 1720–1, but on his arrival in Pennsylvania he became a clerk and conveyancer in Chester. For some years he served as Recorder of Deeds in Chester County. In 1727, he made a voyage to Bristol, England, and to Dublin, a ship companion on the voyage being Elizabeth Whartenby, a minister of the Society. In 1728, he made the return voyage bringing over six indented servants. He died Feb. 9, 1736–7, unmarried.

III. Susanna Parke, b. 10 Mo. 22, 1696, at Ballintrain; remained in Ireland, unmarried.

IV. Rebecca Parke, b. 11 Mo. 27, 1698, at Ballintrain; m. Hugh Stalker. Came over on the *Sizargh* with Thomas Parke.

V. Rachel Parke, b. Dec. 26, 1700; m. Aug. 17, 1727, William Robinson, who came from County Wicklow to Chester Monthly Meeting about 1722.

VI. Jean Parke, b. April 6, 1703; died Apr. 12, 1705; buried at Ballikelly.

VII. Thomas Parke, b. March 13, 1704–5; d. Oct. 17, 1758; m. 2 Mo. 26, 1739, Jane, daughter of Jacob and Sarah Edge. He became the owner and landlord of the "Ship" tavern in East Caln. Children were Robert, m. Ann Edge; Sarah, m. Owen Biddle, of Philadelphia, and had a son Clement Biddle, who m. Mary Canby; Rebecca, m. William Webb; Hannah, m. Benjamin Poultney; Thomas, b. Aug. 6, 1749, m. in 1775, Rachel, daughter of James Pemberton, and became a distinguished physician of Philadelphia; Jane; Jacob.

VIII. Abel Parke, b. Feb. 22, 1706–7; d. July 21, 1757; m. Deborah ———. In 1735, he built the "Ship" tavern on the main road from Philadelphia to Lancaster.

IX. Jonathan Parke, b. April 18, 1709; d. April 5, 1767; m. 2 Mo. 29, 1731, Deborah, daughter of Abiah and Deborah Taylor, and settled on 200 acres of land in East Bradford, Chester County, conveyed to him by his father-in-law. Children: Joseph; Deborah, m. Samuel Cope; Abiah; Rebecca, m. James Webb; Alice, m. Col. John Hannum; Jonathan; Mary.

X. Elizabeth Parke, b. Oct. 5, 1711; d. April 16, 1746; m. John Jackson.

JANE HUNTER, dated 3 Mo. 8, 1724, from Ballycane, County Wicklow, Ireland.

GEORGE DEEBLE, " A Youth who Came over hear about two years ago and brought with him a Certificate from ffriends of Cork in Ireland Concerning him and his Sisters giving Some account of the Occasion of their Coming over to Some near Relations of theirs in Province . . . who after Some Short Stay here went to Some of his Relations and lives within the Verge of your Monthly Meeting." Received 1 Mo. 29, 1729, dated 1 Mo. 26, 1725, from Philadelphia.

MARY RICHARDSON, dated 2 Mo. 13, 1727, late from Ireland, certificate from Bridgetown Monthly Meeting, Barbadoes Island, West Indies.

ISABELL BELL, received 7 Mo. 29, 1729, from Ballinderry, County Antrim, Ireland.

ABIGAIL BELL, sometime "from native country of Ireland," received 7 Mo. 25, 1732, dated 2 Mo. 11, 1732, from Cecil Monthly Meeting, Kent County, Md.

MARY ASHTON, wife of Peter, received 8 Mo. 30, 1732, dated 2 Mo. 30, 1732, from Mountrath Monthly Meeting, Queen's County, Ireland ; " was Convinced about two years ago and hath ever since Lived within the Compass of our Monthly Meeting, but now with her husband " is going to Pennsylvania.

JOSEPH SLEIGH, received 6 Mo. 26, 1734, from Monthly Meeting at Cork, Ireland.

One Joseph Sleight, tanner, of Dublin, joined with Robert Turner and other Irish Friends, in the purchase of one share of West Jersey, April 12, 1677.—Book D, p. 240, *Clement Papers*, Hist. Soc. of Penna.

THOMAS FAWCETT, wife Lydia, and three sons, Thomas, John, and Richard, received 9 Mo. 29, 1736, from Ballinderry, County Antrim, Ireland.

One John ffawsett and Judith Thwayts, both of Parish of Shankill, County Armagh, were married 5 Mo. 19, 1682, at the house of Mark Wright.—*Lurgan Records*.

Thomas ffawsett of Grange Mtg. and Lydia Boyes, of Ballinderry Mtg., were married at the house of Richard Boyes, 4 Mo. 2, 1708.—*Minutes of Ulster Prov. Mtg.*

JOHN PARVIN, received 6 Mo. 28, 1732, from Moat, County West Meath, Ireland. He not "intending to reside here long it [his certificate] was returned to him and agreed he should have a few lines on the back of the said Certificate when he returns if he request it."

NICHOLAS NEWLIN, wife, and sons, Nathaniel and John, dated 12 Mo. 25, 1682, from Mountmellick Mtg., Ireland.—*Jackson Genealogy*, p. 118. See biographical notice, pages 57-9, 271-3.

JANE HINKSON, wife of John Hinkson, dated 5 Mo. 30, 1764, from Men's Meeting at Cootehill, County Cavan, Ireland; received 1 Mo. 27, 1766. Certificate states that she was a "a Woman of an Easey, mild, modest behavior, Held in Esteem by friends and others; Walked Orderly During her Residing here; was in unity with friends when she Left this."

John Hinkson and wife Jane came from Ireland as early as 1764. By deed of March 20, 1764, in which he is styled "of the city of Philadelphia, yeoman," he purchased from Charles Morris and wife two adjoining farms in Nether Providence Township, now Delaware County, for £860. Towards the close of that year he was assessed with 200 acres of land and buildings, worth £16 per annum, 3 horses, 4 cattle, 10 sheep, and 2 servants. He died about 1785, being survived by his wife and eight children: Jane, m. Thomas Dell Weaver; John, d. 2 Mo. 17, 1819, m. about 1784, Abigail Engle; James, m. Betty Crosley; Thomas, m. 5 Mo. 11, 1797, Mary Worrilow; George, m. Catharine Fairlamb and went to Ohio; Mary, d. unmarried; Sarah, m. William Hawkins; Ann, m. Joseph Dickinson.—See Cope's *Smedley Genealogy*, 209-10.

CONCORD MONTHLY MEETING

In Delaware County. Established in 1684.

JOHN FRED and family, "late of Ireland," received 5 Mo. 13, 1713, dated 12 Mo. 25, 1712-13, from Carlow Meeting, County Carlow, Ireland. Children Nicholas and Rachel, are clear in a relation to marriage.

BENJAMIN FRED, son of John, late of Ireland, unmarried, received 5 Mo. 1713, dated 10 Mo. 21, 1712. He returned to Ireland on business in 1713, and remained perhaps a year.—*Hist. Chester Co.*, p. 553.

John Fred, of Parish of Drumlane, County Cavan, was married 11 Mo. 6, 1685, at Belturbet to Catherine Starkey, of County Cavan. Children of John and Catharine Fred, of Drumlaine, County Cavan: Benjamin, b. 9 Mo. 5, 1687 ; Mary, b. 8 Mo. 2, 1691, d. 11 Mo. 27, 1704, buried at New Garden ; Nicholas, b. 1 Mo. 2, 1694 ; Abigail, b. 2 Mo. 4, 1696, buried 6 Mo. 28, 1697 ; Rachel, b. 5 Mo. 29, 1698 ; Sarah, b. 7 Mo. 15, 1700, at Coolattin [Cooladine] ; John, b. 12 Mo. 20, 1703, at Coolattin. (*Records of Carlow Monthly Meeting.*)

In 1671, in County Armagh, John Fred had his goods seized by the "priest" of Loughall for tithes (*Stockdale*, 4). William Edmundson (*Journal*, 280) states that in 1706 he came "to Enniscorphy [Enniscorthy] and the next Day went to John Fred's and had a large Meeting in a Barn, it being on first Day of the Week."

John Fred and his family settled in Birmingham, Chester County, where John died March, 1719–1720, and his widow in 1723.

Catharine Fred, the widow, whose will was made 8 Mo. 23, 1723 (probated 9 Mo. 12, 1723), mentions her cousins Mary Hutton and Deborah Starr and her brother-in-law, Thomas Jackson.

Benjamin Fred, son of John, was m. 4 Mo. 20, 1721, to Deborah, daughter of Simon Hadly, of New Castle County, and removed to New Garden, where he died in 1752, leaving no children. His sister Rachel married 4 Mo. 20, 1721, James Miller, son of Gayen, of Kennett, and after his death married James Miller, son of James and Catharine.

Nicholas Fred, son of John, married about 1720, Ann, daughter of Joseph Need, of Darby. He lived in Birmingham and was interested in a mill there. Had children : Mary, John, Joseph, Catharine.

Joseph Fred was married 10 Mo. 18, 1753, to Sarah, daughter of Joshua Hadly, then of Virginia. He removed to the neighborhood of New Garden, and had children : Mary, Ann, Benjamin, Joseph, Joshua, Thomas, and Nicholas.—Futhey and Cope, *Hist. Chester County*, 553–4.

JOHN VASTON, "late of Ireland," received 8 Mo. 10, 1715, dated 2 Mo. 27, 1714, from Dublin, Ireland.

ABRAHAM WIDDOS, received 2 Mo. 7, 1718, from Mountmellick Meeting, Queen's County, Ireland. He married Elizabeth Pyle, in 1720, and in the same year was recommended as a minister.

DANIEL MOORE and wife, late of Ireland, received 11 Mo. 7, 1722, from a "Select meeting held at Balynacree," County Antrim, Ireland.

JOHN NEVIETS, late of Ireland, received 3 Mo. 3, 1725, dated 3 Mo. 1, 1724, from Dublin, Ireland.

JOSEPH GAWIN, received 2 Mo. 1, 1731, dated 3 Mo. 10, 1730, from Monthly Meeting at Edenderry, King's County, Ireland.

JOHN JACKSON, received 1 Mo. 5, 1732–3, dated 3 Mo. 10, 1730, late of Ireland, from Edenderry Meeting, King's County.

AMOS BOAKS, unmarried, received 1 Mo. 5, 1732–3, dated 2 Mo. 30, 1732, from Monthly Meeting at Mountrath, Queen's County, Ireland.

Amos Boake, of East Caln Township, Chester County, made his will Oct. 9, 1750, and it was probated Nov. 2, 1751. He mentions his wife Sarah, his brother Abel Boake and his daughter Anne Boake.

THOMAS MARSHALL, received 1 Mo. 7, 1736–7. "friends in Ireland Sent a few Lines of Recomendation to friends here [Concord] Concerning a Servant boy that Came here and is in the Servis of William Trimble his name is Thomas Marshall he came with the Consent of his Mother & relations which was Signed by the Consent of friends of Dublin Meeting."

GEORGE WILSON, received 1 Mo. 1, 1741–2, dated 3 Mo. 14, 1740, wife [Ruth] and children, from [Grange] Meeting, near Charlemont, County Armagh, Ireland.

George Wilson,[1] b. about 1715, and Ruth Douglas, widow, b. about 1709, were complained of, 11 Mo. 3, 1738, by the meeting at Grange near Charlemont, for marriage by a "priest," "Yᵉ Sᵈ Ruth Duglass being formerly married orderly amongst us." They produced an acknowledgment, 3 Mo. 14, 1740, and there-

---

[1] In 1681, John Wilson, a Friend, of Antrim, had his goods seized for tithes.

upon a certificate of removal to Pennsylvania was signed for them. This certificate was received by Concord Monthly Meeting, now Delaware County, 1 Mo. 1, 1741–2. About 1747, they removed to what is now Adams County, bringing a certificate, dated 3 Mo. 4, 1747, from Concord to Warrington Monthly Meeting, 2 Mo. 16, 1748, and settled on a farm in Menallen Township, near the site of Bendersville (formerly called Wilsonville), where he died 9 Mo. 15, 1785, and his wife Ruth, 7 Mo. 12, 1784. Children : Alice, b. 7 Mo. 10, 1741 ; Benjamin, b. 7 Mo. 20, 1743 ; Sarah, b. 1 Mo. 15, 1745 ; Lydia, b. 2 Mo. 30, 1747.

Of these, Benjamin Wilson m. 12 Mo. 14, 1774, at Menallen Meeting, Sarah, daughter of Thomas and Jane (Edwards) Bowen. Children were : (1) Ruth, b. 11 Mo. 1, 1785, d. 5 Mo. 7, 1848, m. James Mather ; (2) Mary, b, 9 Mo. 13, 1780, unmarried ; (3) Alice, b. 12 Mo. 6, 1782, d. 8 Mo. 12, 1834, m. John Wright ; (4) Sarah, b. 1 Mo. 29, 1785, d. 2 Mo. 1, 1855, m. William Garretson (removed to Bedford County); (5) George, b. 3 Mo. 10, 1778, m. 5 Mo. 30, 1798, m. Sarah Wright, daughter of John and Elizabeth.

John Wilson, of Grange Mtg. near Charlemont and Mary Wilson, of Lurgan Mtg. were married at Lurgan, 9 Mo. 6, 1700.

John Wilson and Alice Whitefield, both of Grange Mtg. near Charlemount, were married 11 Mo. 16, 1705, at Grange.—*Minutes of Ulster Province Mtg.*

At Ulster Province Meeting, 9 Mo. 1, 1701, it is reported that John Wilson has offered a convenient place to build a meeting house in the town of Antrim.

"Att a Province mens meeting held at Richard Boyes [Parish of Ballindery, Co. Antrim] ye 24th 11 Mo. 1701, Thomas Wilkinson advises this meeting yt ye Lord Masserdden is willing that friends have yt part of John Willsons houlding in Antrim to build a meeting house upon."

NEWARK OR KENNETT MONTHLY MEETING

Of Chester County, Pa., and New Castle County, Delaware.

Established in 1686.

VALENTINE HOLLINGSWORTH, wife Ann, and children came over to Pennsylvania in 1682, from Balleniskçrannell, Parish of Sego, County Armagh, Ireland, and settled in New Castle County on Delaware.

HENRY HOLLINGSWORTH, son of Valentine, came over from
Ireland in 1683, in the Ship *Lion,* as an indented servant
to Robert Turner.—*Penn'a Mag.* VIII., 334.

VALENTINE HOLLINGSWORTH,[1] son of Henry Hollingsworth, of
Belleniskcrannell, Parish of Segoe, County Armagh, Ireland, and
Catharine, his wife, was born at Belleniskcrannel, ''about the sixth
month in the yeare 1632''; was married 4 Mo. 7, 1655, to Ann
Ree, daughter of Nicholas Ree,[2] of Tanderagee, County Armagh.
She was born about 1628, at Tanderagee, and died 2 Mo. 1, 1671.
He then was married a second time, 4 Mo. 12, 1672, to Ann Cal-
vert, daughter of Thomas Calvert, of Dromgora, Parish of Segoe,
County Armagh, and Jane his wife.   The following is a copy
of the marriage certificate :

"**This is to certifie** the truth to all people that Valentine Hollen-
worth[3] in yᵉ psh of Sego in yᵉ county of Armagh, and Anne Calvert of the same psh having intentions of marriage according to
the ordinance of God, and Gods joining, Did lay it before mens
meeting before whom theire marriage being propounded, then yᵉ
meeting desired them to wait some time, wᶜʰ they did, so the
meeting makeing inquiry between the times whether yᶜ man be
free from all other women, and the woman free from all other men,
and so the second time they comeing before the mens meeting,
all things being found clear, so they being left to theire freedome.
A meeting of the people of god being appointed and assembled
together at the house of Marke Wright, in the psh of Shankell the
twelfth day of the fourth month in yᵉ yeare 1672 whene they tooke
one another in marriage in the presence of god and of his people

---

[1] The records of this family in Ireland are from the registers of Lurgan
Meeting, County Armagh.   There is, of course, no foundation for the tradition that Valentine Hollingsworth married Catharine, daughter of Henry
Cornish, High Sheriff of London, who was executed in 1685.   It is prob-
able that the Hollingsworths went over from England to Ireland with other
planters early in the seventeenth century, but there is no proof to show
that they came from Cheshire, as stated by some historians of the family.
For an extended record of descendants of Valentine Hollingsworth see
Hollingsworth Genealogical Memoranda, by William B. Hollingsworth
(Baltimore, 1884); also see *McFarlan-Stern Genealogy,* 6–11, 56–60,
History of Chester County, 605.

[2] In 1681, one John Rea, of Parish of Maherlin, County Down, had his
goods seized for tithes.—*Stockdale,* 170.

[3] Page 85, *Marriage Book of Lurgan Monthly Meeting.*

according to y⁰ law of god, & we are witnesses of the same
whose names are hereunto subscribed y⁰ day and yeare aforesaid

VAL: HOLENGWORTH
ANNE HOLENGWORTH
1672.

ffrancis Robson	William Williams	Jo: Calvert	Chris: Hillery
Hugh Stamper	George Hodgshon	Jam: Harison	dorothy Hillery
Roger Webb	Will pearson	Nic: Harison	Elis: Gnus
Robert Hoope	Marke Wright	John Wright	Alice Williams
Michael Staise	Timo : kirk	James Bradshaw	An. Bradshaw
Tho. Wederall	Rob Chambers	Tho: Calvert	debora Kirk
Will dixon	Antho. Dixon	fergus Softly	Alice Wright
		dina Kirke	Mary Walker"

William Stockdale[1] gives the following account of Hollingsworth's persecutions for tithes :

1671, County Armagh, "Valentine Hollingsworth had taken
from him for Tithe, by Thomas Ashbrook Tithmonger twenty
nine stooks of Barly, and three stooks and a half of Oats, all
worth one pound one shilling ;'' 1672, "Valentine Hollingsworth
for Tithe by Edward O'Maghan, 26 stooks wheat. 3 car-loads
Hey, 26 stooks of Oats, 26 stooks of Barley, Value £2, 18s ;"
1673, corn and hay, valued at £2 ; 1674, wheat, hay, oats, barley,
valued at £3 4s.

In 1682, Valentine Hollingsworth and his family, accompanied
by his son-in-law, Thomas Connaway, and by John Musgrave,
an indented servant, sailed from Belfast for the Delaware,[2] and,
as we have already stated,[3] settled on a large plantation of nearly
a thousand acres on Shelpot Creek in Brandywine Hundred, New
Castle County, about five miles northeast of the present city of
Wilmington. He was prominently identified with the affairs of
Friends, the early meetings being held at his house. In 1687, he
gave "unto ffriends for a burying place half an Acre of land for
yᵗ purpose." A meeting-house was afterward built on this plot
and the meeting known as Newark, from the name of the plantation, which in the original survey was called "New Worke."
Valentine Hollingsworth was appointed a Justice of the Peace for
New Castle County, in 1685, and represented the county in the
Assembly in 1682-3, 1687, 1688, 1689, 1695, and 1700.[4] He died
subsequent to 1710, and his wife Ann died 8 Mo. 17, 1697. They
were interred in Friends' ground at Newark.

[1] *A Great Cry of Oppression*, 3, 15, 27, 37.

[2] Deposition of Samuel, son of Valentine Hollingsworth, made before
the Mayor of Philadelphia, June 4, 1735 (printed in *McFarlan-Stern
Geneology*, 58-59).

[3] See page 120.

[4] *Penna. Archives*, 2nd Series, IX., 648, 651, 652, 653.

The children of Valentine Hollingsworth by his first wife, Ann Ree, were as follows :

1. Mary Hollingsworth, born 1 Mo. 25, 1656, at Belleniskcrannell, married, first, 4 Mo. 28, 1682, at the house of Francis Robson, Parish of Segoe, County Armagh, to Thomas Conway or Connaway, of Parish of Lisburn, County Antrim. They came to the Delaware with her father in 1682, and settled near him in New Castle County. Thomas Connaway died 11 Mo. 30, 1688–9, and his widow, in 1693, married, secondly, Randal Malin, widower, of Upper Providence, now Delaware County (originally of Great Barrum, Cheshire, England). Randal Malin became a Quaker minister and in 1727 removed with his wife and family within the limits of Goshen Monthly Meeting.

By her first husband, Thomas Connaway, she had three children : (1) Elizabeth, b. 7 Mo. 9, 1687, m. 1st Charles Booth, 1705, and 2d, Thomas Babb, in 1720 ; Ann, born about 1688, m. Philip Taylor, 6 Mo. 10, 1705 ; Sarah b. about 1689, m. 3 Mo., 1710, to John Yearsley, b. in England about 1685, son of John and Elizabeth. By her second, Randal Malin, she had three children : Hannah, b. 1 Mo. 7, 1695–6, m. Daniel Williamson, Jr., about 1716 ; Rachel, b. 5 Mo. 24, 1702, m. John Cain or Cane, 9 Mo. 7, 1722 ; and Katharine, who married —— Tate, in 1721.

2. Henry Hollingsworth,[1] b. 9 Mo. 7, 1658, at Belleniskcrannell, is thought to have come over to Pennsylvania as a redemptioner to Robert Turner, in 1683. Subsequently he lived for a time with his father in New Castle County. In 1688, he returned to Ireland for a wife and on 6 Mo. 22d of that year was married to Lydia Atkinson, of Parish of Segoe, County Armagh, whom he shortly after brought to Pennsylvania.[2] For a number of years he was Deputy Surveyor of Chester County. In 1695, he resided in Chester, and was Sheriff of the County. He also represented New Castle County in the Provincial Assembly. In 1700, and for some time after he was Clerk of the Courts, and Coroner of Chester County. He removed to Elkton, Md., about 1712, in which year he was appointed (3 Mo. 9 by Lord Baltimore) Surveyor of Cecil County. His manuscript commonplace book, which is a medley of receipts, poetry, astrology, alchemy, chemistry, some of which is in Latin, is in the collection of the Hon. Samuel W. Pennypacker, of Philadelphia. He died 2 Mo. or 3 Mo. 1721. His children were : Ruth, m. George Simpson, 12

---

[1] See Smith, *History of Delaware County*, 469.

[2] The original marriage certificate is in possession of Miss Margaret Gilpin, of Cecil Co., Md.

Mo. 24, 1706 ; Stephen, who m. Ann ——, was a Magistrate in Cecil County, Md., in 1730, removing subsequently to Virginia, where, in 1734, he obtained a grant of 472 acres of land on the west side of the Shenandoah River, in Orange County ; Zebulon, b. 1696, d. Cecil County, 8 Mo. 8, 1763, m. 4 Mo. 18, 1727, Ann, daughter of Col. Francis Mauldin ; Catharine m. —— Dawson, of Kent County, Md.; Abigail, m. Richard Dobson, in 1720 ; and Mary.

3. Thomas Hollingsworth, b. 3 Mo., 1661, at Belleniskcrannell, d. 1732-3, in Winchester, Va. He resided for a time in Rockland Manor, New Castle County but later removed to Winchester, Va. His first wife Margaret (by whom he had one son Abram, born 1 Mo. 19, 1686), died in 8 Mo. 1687. He then married 1 Mo. 31, 1692, Grace Cook, of Concord. Children by second wife : Elizabeth, b. 11 Mo. 8, 1694, m. —— Stroud, in 1718 ; Hannah, b. 1 Mo. 17, 1697, m. William Dixon, in 1718 ; Thomas, b. 12 Mo. 23, 1698, m. Judith Lampley in 1723 ; Jacob, b. 1 Mo, 4, 1704, m. Rachel Chandler, 1729 ; Sarah, b. 8 Mo. 7, 1706, m. John Dixon, in 1724 ; Joseph, b. 3 Mo. 11, 1709, m. Martha Houghton, in 1730, and removed to Virginia ; Grace, b. 3 Mo, 9, 1712.

4. Catharine Hollingsworth, b. 5 Mo., 1663, at Belleniskcrannell ; d. 6 Mo. 29, 1746 ; m. 11 Mo. 2, 1688, George Robinson,[1] who was born in the north of Ireland, about 1666, came to the Delaware in 1687, and died 9 Mo. 8, 1738. Their children were : Mary, m. Thomas Jacobs, 8 Mo, 13, 1710 ; Ann, m. Jonathan Ogden, in 1720 ; Valentine, m. Elizabeth Booth, in 1740.

At Newark Monthly Meeting (women's branch), 12 Mo. 4, 1698, "Wee have ordered that Katherine Robinson bee purser to this meeting Given in Collection £5.10s."

The children of Valentine Hollingsworth by his second wife, Ann Calvert, were :

5. Samuel Hollingsworth, b. 1 Mo. 27, 1673, at Belleniskcrannell ; d. 1748 ; m. in 1701, Hannah Harlan, daughter of George and Elizabeth Harlan. He lived in Birmingham Township and held several important public offices. In 1729 and 1738, he was appointed Justice of the Peace for Chester County. From 1725 to 1728 he represented the county in the Provincial Assembly. Children : Enoch, m. 1st Joanna Crowley, 10 Mo. 23, 1725, 2d

---

[1] See Philadelphia *Friend*, XXIX., 404. About 1735, George Robinson, of Brandywine, New Castle County, aged about 69 years, deposed in the Penna.-Md. boundary dispute that he " has dwelt in the said County about 49 years."—*No. 175, Miscellaneous Papers (1655-1805), Three Lower Counties, Hist. Soc. of Penna.*

Elizabeth Chads, widow of William Pyle ; John, m. Mary Reed, in 1732 ; Samuel, m. Barbara Shewin, in 1738, and died in 1751 ; George ; Elizabeth, m. Henry Green, in 1734.

6. Enoch Hollingsworth, b. 6 Mo. 7, 1675, at Belleniskcrannel ; died in New Castle County, 8 Mo. 24, 1687.

7. Valentine Hollingsworth, b. 11 Mo. 12, 1677, at Belleniskcrannell ; d. 1757 ; m. in 1713, Elizabeth Heald.

8. Ann Hollingsworth, b. 10 Mo. 28, 1680, at Belleniskcrannell ; m. James Thompson in 1700.

9. John Hollingsworth, b. 2 Mo. 19, 1684, in New Castle County ; d. in 1722 ; m. Catherine Tyler, in 1706.

10. Joseph Hollingsworth, b. 5 M. 10, 1686, in New Castle County.

11. Enoch Hollingsworth, buried 9 Mo. 26, 1690.

THOMAS CALVERT,[1] son of John Calvert,[2] "of Moore Some[3] (neere Gisbrough)," Yorkshire, and wife Grace, was born in 1617

[1] *Registers Lurgan Meeting, County Armagh.*

[2] It is possible that John Calvert was of the same kin as the Calverts, Lords Baltimore and Proprietors of Maryland ; for he came into Ireland prior to 1617, from Moorsham, Yorkshire, only about twenty-five miles from Kilpin, in the same county, where about 1580 was born George Calvert, the first Lord Baltimore (son of Leonard Calvert, a well-to-do country gentlemen, by Alice Crosland, his wife, and grandson of John Calvert).— See " George Calvert " in *Dictionary of National Biography* and pp. 1–4, *George and Cecilius Calvert* (" Makers of America " Series, by William Hand Browne, N. Y., 1890).

In the latter part of the seventeenth century there was a presumption that such a relationship existed ; for on June 4, 1735, Samuel Hollingsworth, of Chester County, made a deposition before the Mayor of Philadelphia, in connection with the boundary dispute between the Penns and Lord Baltimore, that in 1683 one Colonel Talbot and a party of Lord Baltimore's surveyors were the guests one night at the home of his father, Valentine Hollingsworth, in New Castle County ; and that in the course of conversation during the evening "the said Talbot enquiring into the Place from whence this affirmat's ffather and Mother came and the maiden name of his mother, which was Calvert, the said Collonel Talbot invited this affirmant's ffather to come down and live in Maryland, assuring him his Lordship would be very kind to him on account of his wife's having been a Calvert."—*McFarlan-Stern Genealogy,* 58. Mary Calvert and William Whitesite, were married 3 Mo. 27, 1696, by Friends' ceremony at the house of Thomas Calvert near Carrickfergus.

[3] " *Great Moorsham,* a township in the parish of Skelton, East Division of the liberty of Langbaurgh, of the county of York, 6 miles (E. by S.) from Guilsbrough, containing 338 inhabitants."—Lewis's *Topographical Dictionary of England.*

at Lygasory, near Lurgan, County Armagh, and about 9 Mo. 11, 1647, married Jane Glasford, daughter of Hugh Glasford and wife Margaret, of "Stranmillis (nere Belfast)," County Antrim. At Ulster Province Meeting, 4 Mo. 7, 1680, £1. 13. 9d. was paid to Thomas Calvert for the apothecary at Carrickfergus, evidently for attendance on Friends confined in Carrickfergus jail ; for on 6 Mo. 6, 1681, L. Alyson and T. Calvert were directed to supply the wants of prisoners there, £2. 10s being appropriated for the purpose. In 1681, Thomas Calvert, of Parish of Carrickfergus, County Antrim, had some hay and oats, valued at 11s., taken for tithes.[1]

Children of Thomas and Jane Calvert :

1. John, born 8 Mo. 6, 1648, near Belfast.

2. Ann, born about 9 Mo. 1650, in Killwarlin, near Hills-brough, County Down.

3. Margaret, born about 4 Mo. 24, 1661, at Killurigan, Parish of Sego, County Armagh.

4. Elizabeth, born 4 Mo. 26, 1664, in County Armagh ; m. 10 Mo. 25, 1701, at Ballyhagen Meeting, Thomas Toppen, of Bally-hagen, County Armagh.

John Calvert,[2] son of Thomas Calvert, of Drumgor, Parish of Segoe, County Armagh, Ireland, and Jane, his wife, was born 8 Mo. 6, 1648, in Stranmillis, near Belfast ; was married 3 Mo. (May), 29, 1673, at the house of Roger Webb, to Judith Stamper, daughter of Hugh Stamper and Bridget, his wife, of Lurgan, County Armagh. Judith Stamper was born 3 Mo. 12, 1652, at " bowlton wood," [3] County Cumberland, England.

John Calvert removed with his family about 1683 to Pennsyl-vania, and settled in Upper Providence Township, now Delaware County, where he owned 300 acres of land, granted to him by William Penn, 1 Mo. 13, 1683. An adjoining tract of 300 acres was also granted at the same time for Thomas Calvert, the father, who probably did not come to this country. Still another tract of 100 acres, contiguous to the above, was granted on the same date to Margaret Calvert, probably the daughter of Thomas. On 2

---

[1] William Stockdale, *A Great Cry of Oppression*, 167.

[2] *Records of Lurgan Meeting ;* Gilbert Cope, *Smedley Genealogy*, 122.

[3] " *Bolton* (All Saints), a parish in Allerdale ward below Derwent, county of Cumberland, 1½ (N. by W.) from Ireby, containing, with the township of Bolton High-side, and Bolton Low-Side 1245 inhabitants, of which number 352 are in Bolton High-Side and 893 in Bolton Low-Side, . . . A copper battle-axe was lately found in the moss at Bolton Wood, four feet below the surface."—Lewis, *Topographical Dictionary of Eng-land.*

Mo. 11, 1691, it was ordered that a patent for the whole tract should be made to John Calvert, to whom it was made appear to belong.[1]   At Chester Monthly Meeting, 4 Mo. 6, 1687, mention is made of a difference between John Calvert and Thomas Hollingsworth (stepson of John Calvert's sister Ann, who married Valentine Hollingsworth) about dividing their lands in Upper Providence.

Children of John and Judith (Stamper) Calvert :

I. Ruth, b. 6 Mo. 2, 1674, at Lurgan, Ireland ; m. about 1697, Edward Paviour, of Upper Providence.

II. Isaac, b. 9 Mo. 2, 1676, at Lurgan.

III. Thomas, b. 9 Mo. 27, 1678, at Lurgan, bought a lot in Chester, in 1700, and sold it in 1702.

IV. Joshua, b. 8 Mo. 18, 1680, at Lurgan.   At a Chester County court, held 6 Mo. 25, 1702, the sheriff made a return of an execution on the estate of John Calvert, which was sold to Thomas, Joshua, and Thomas Calvert for £243.   Joshua was constable of Upper Providence in 1704.   In 1724, he had 370 acres of the Calvert land in Upper Providence.   The remainder seems to have been in possession of Daniel Calvert.   Joshua Calvert m., in 1709, Deborah, daughter of George and Elizabeth Harlan, and is thought by Gilbert Cope to have been the parents of Thomas Calvert, who married Sarah Williamson, about 1739, lived in Edgmont, now Delaware County, and probably in East Marlborough, Chester County.

V. Daniel, b. 5 Mo. 6, 1685, in Pa.; m. about 1709, Elizabeth Pritchett.

VI. Mary, b. 12 Mo. 19, 1687, in Pa.

VII. Judith, m. 10 Mo. 8, 1725, Daniel Broom, of Marple, now Delaware County.

JOHN MUSGRAVE, born about 1669, came over from Belfast, with his master, Valentine Hollingsworth, in 1682, and served his time for four years in New Castle County.

Later he removed to Sadsbury, Lancaster County, and on June 4, 1735, then aged about sixty-six, made a deposition in connection with boundary dispute between Pennsylvania and Maryland.[2]

John Musgrave, of Lancaster County, made his will in 1745. Mentions children : John, James, Thomas, Abraham, Esther, wife of John Griffith, Martha, wife of Benjamin Miller, Sarah, wife of Theophilus Owen, and two other daughters who married John Ferree and Thomas Powell.

[1] *Penna. Archives*, 2d Series, XIX., 66.
[2] *McFarlan and Stern Genealogy*, 58–59.

THOMAS CONWAY, or CONNAWAY, of Lisburn, County Antrim, was married 4 Mo. 28, 1682, at the house of Francis Robson, Parish of Segoe, County Armagh, to Mary Hollingsworth, daughter of Valentine (*Records of Lurgan Meeting*), and in the same year came over and settled near his father-in-law, in Brandywine Hundred, New Castle County. The records of Newark Monthly Meeting give the date of birth of a daughter, Mary Conaway, as 7 Mo. 9, 1687, and the date of Thomas Connaway's death as 7 Mo. 17, 1689. In 1693, the widow, Mary Connaway, married Randal Malin, of Upper Providence, and in 1727 removed and settled with her husband within the limits of Goshen Monthly Meeting.

WILLIAM DIXSON and Isabelle Rea, both of Parish of Sego, County Armagh, Ireland, were married at the house of Roger Webb, Parish of Sego, 5 Mo. 4, 1683. Among those who signed the marriage certificate were Henry Dixson, Rose Dixson, Thomas Harlan, and Isabelle Logan.—*Marriage Book of Lurgan Mo. Mtg.*, Ireland.

This, no doubt, is the same family that came over to New Castle Co., prior to 1690. Henry Dixson, it is said, kept an inn at New Castle and had three children: (I.) *William* was married about 1690 to Ann Gregg, daughter of William Gregg,[1] who, it is believed, also came from the north of Ireland. William was a weaver by trade and settled on Red Clay Creek, in Christiana Hundred, New Castle County. He made his will 1 Mo. 31, 1708, and it was probated Sept. 20, 1708. He mentions his wife Ann, and appoints his brothers, Michael Harlan and John Gregg,

[1] William Gregg settled on a tract of 400 acres of land in Christiana Hundred, New Castle County, surveyed to him 3 Mo. 11, 1685. He died "ye 1st of ye 7th month and was buried on his own plantation 1687." Children: Richard; Ann; John, b. *circa* 1668, d. 1738, m. 11 Mo. 1694, to Elizabeth Cooke [John Gregg, of Christiana Hundred, New Castle County, yeoman, aged about 67 years, made a deposition about 1735, "that he has dwelt in the s^d County about" 51 years (No. 175, *Miscellaneous Papers, 1655–1805, Three Lower Counties*, Hist. Soc. of Penna.)]; George. It is presumed by the writer that William Gregg came from the north of Ireland with the Hollingsworths, Dixsons, Sharplys; but no doubt the point could be fully proven if a diligent investigation were made in Ireland.

One William Gregg, of Toberhead Mtg., and Ann Wilkinson, of Antrim Mtg., County Antrim, were married at Antrim, 11 Mo. 5, 1702; and George Gregg, of Toberhead Mtg. and Alice Richardson, of Ballyhagen Mtg., were married 8 Mo. 12, 1714, at Ballyhagen.—*Minutes of Ulster Province Mtg.*

William Edmundson attended a meeting, in 1700, at the house of Thomas Gregg, at Toberhead, Co. Antrim.—*Journal*, 223.

as advisors. The widow, Ann Dixson, then married John Hough-
ton, of New Castle County. (II.) *Dinah* married Michael Harlan,
1 Mo., 1690, at Newark Mtg. (III.) *Rose* married in 1690,
Thomas Pierson, widower, Deputy Surveyor of New Castle
County. (See account of Thomas Pierson by the writer in *Penna.
Mag.*, XXI., 506–7.)[1]

GEORGE AND MICHAEL HARLAN.—

"George Harlan yᵉ Sone of James Harlan of Monkwearmouth
was baptized at Monkwearmouth [Co. Durham] in old England
yᵉ 11th day of 1 Mo. 1650." "Michael Harlan came from the
north of Ireland with his Brother George, about the year 1687–
and ye beginning of the year 1690 he married Dinah ye Daughter
of Henry Dixon and Settled first Near ye Center Meeting house
in Christiana Hundred & County of New Castle on Delaware and
afterwards removed into Kennett in Chester County, where they
lived Many years."—*Records of Kennett or Newark Mo. Mtg.*

George Harland, of Parish of Donnahlong, Co. Down, Ireland,
and Elizabeth Duck, of Lurgan, Parish of Shankill, Co. Armagh,
were married "at the house of Marke Wright in ye Parish of
Shankell," 9 Mo. 17, 1678. Signers to marriage certificate :

Henry Hollingsworth	Wm Porter	George Harland
John Calvert	Timothy Kirk	Elizabeth Harland
Roger Kirk	Alphonsus Kirk	
	deborah Kirk	
	Elinor Hoope	
	Robert Hoope	
	Thomas Harland	

—*Marriage Book of Lurgan Mo. Mtg.*, p. 91.

Thomas Harland, of Donnahlong Parish, Co. Down, Ireland,
son of James Harland, was born "nigh Durham In Bishoprick,"
England, and was married 2 Mo. 7, 1680, at the house of Francis
Robson, Parish of Sego, Co. Armagh, Ireland, to Katharine,
daughter of George Bullock, of Lurgan. Among signers to marriage certificate were : Isabella Harland, Elizabeth Kirk, deborah
Kirk, Roger Kirk, George Harland, Timothy, Alphonsus and
and Robert Kirk.

The wife Katherine Harland died 3 Mo., 1690, and Thomas was
married again, 11 Mo. 8, 1702–3, to Alice Foster, of Lisnegarvy.
Children by first wife, Catherine : Ananias, b. 4 Mo. 19, 1682,
at Donochlong ; Rebecca, b. 9 Mo. 24, 1683 at Donochlong;
Patience, b. 6 Mo. 18, 1685, at Donochlong ; Christian, b. 12

[1] See "Gregg–Dixon–Houghton, of New Castle County, Delaware" in
Historical and Genealogical Department of the *Literary Era* (A. D. 1898)
Vol. V., p. 331. (Library of Hist. Soc. of Penna., Phila.)

Mo. 16, 1687, at Donochlong; Catherine, b. 9 Mo. 12, 1689, at Donochlong. Children by second wife, Alice: James, b. 9 Mo. 3, 1703, at Corking, Co. Down; Thomas, b. 5 Mo. 4, 1705, at Corking; Abigail, b. 2 Mo. 24, 1708, at Corking. Patience Harland and James Alderdice, both of Lurgan, Co. Armagh, were married at Lurgan Meeting, Jan. 6, 1707. Marriage certificate signed by: Thomas, Christian, and Catharine Harlan. (*Records of Lurgan Mo. Mtg.*) I have seen no evidence to show that any of the family of Thomas Harlan came over to Pennsylvania.

George Harlan settled at first about where the village of Centreville, New Castle Co., Delaware, now is, and the early meetings were held at his home. Later he removed farther up Brandywine Creek, and purchased 474 acres of land in Kennett, now Pennsbury, Township, Chester County. While living here he had for his neighbors over the creek, in a great bend, a settlement of Indians. After they had gone away he obtained, in 1701, a warrant for 200 acres of land in the bend of the creek, granted "in regard of the great trouble and charge he has bore in fencing and maintaining the same for the said Indians while living thereon." He died in 1714, and was buried by the side of his wife at Centre Meeting House.

In his will, dated 2 Mo. 21, 1714, probated 8 Mo. 2, 1714, George Harlan mentions his brother Michael Harlan, his servant Mary Mathews, and directs that his body be interred in the new burying ground on Alphonsus Kirk's land.—*Hist. Chester Co.*, p. 587; *Chester County Wills*.

"George Harland [County Down, in 1680] had taken from him for Tithe, by Daniel Mac Connell . . . twelve stooks and a half of Oats, three stooks and a half of Barly, and five loads of Hey, all worth ten shillings ten pence."—William Stockdale's *A Great Cry of Oppression.*

Children of George[1] and Elizabeth Harlan: Ezekiel, b. 7 Mo. 16, 1679, m. (1) Mary Bezer and (2) Ruth Ruffington; Hannah, b. 2 Mo. 4, 1681, m. Samuel Hollingsworth, in 1701; Moses, b. 12 Mo. 20, 1683–4, m. 1712, Margaret Ray, a native of Lurgan, Ireland, and made a final settlement in Menallen Township, now Adams County; Aaron, b. 10 Mo. 24, 1685, m. Sarah Heald, in 1713–14; Rebecca, b. 8 Mo. 17, 1688, d. 8 Mo. 17, 1775, m. William Webb, 1 Mo. 22, 1709–10, Deborah, b. 8 Mo. 28, 1690, m. Joshua Calvert, in 1710; James, b. 8 Mo. 19, 1692, m. Elizabeth ——, in 1716; Elizabeth, b. 8 Mo. 9, 1694, m. Joseph Robinson, in 1713; Joshua, b. 11 Mo. 15, 1696–7, m. Mary Heald, in 1719.

[1] Mrs. Ida Saxton McKinley, widow of the late William McKinley, President of the United States, is a descendant of George Harlan.

21

Children of Michael and Dinah (Dixson) Harlan : George, b. 10 Mo. 4, 1690, m. Mary, widow of Alexander Stewart, and daughter of Joel and Ann Baily ; Abigail, b. 9 Mo. 23, 1692, m. Richard Flower, 12 Mo. 17, 1724-5 ; Thomas, b. 4 Mo. 24, 1694, m. Mary Carter, in 1720 ; Stephen, b. 2 Mo., 1697, m. Hannah Carter, 7 Mo. 26, 1723 ; Michael, b. 2 Mo. 7, 1699, m. Hannah Maris ; Solomon, b. 10 Mo. 7, 1701 ; James, b. 1703, m. Susanna Oborn, 10 Mo. 19, 1733 ; Dinah b. 8 Mo. 23, 1707, m. Thomas Gregg, 2 Mo. 20, 1729.—See *Hist. Chester County*, 587.[1]

THOMAS CHILD, from the neighborhood of Lurgan, Ireland, died 10 Mo. 8, 1694, at the house of Valentine Hollingsworth, in New Castle County. See George Harlan's letter on pages 62–3.

LYDIA HOLLINGSWORTH, wife of Henry. In 1687, Henry Hollingsworth returned to Ireland, and, 8 Mo. 22, 1688, married Lydia Atkinson, of the Parish of Segoe, County Armagh, who shortly afterward came over to New Castle County with her husband.

ALPHONSUS KIRK, son of Roger and Elizabeth Kirk, of Lurgan, Ireland, settled in New Castle County, in 1689.
The following account of the Kirk family is found in the records of Lurgan Meeting :

" Roger Kirk and Elizabeth his wife dwelt in Neshag in ye prsh of Skelton and in ye County of York [England]. Came to ireland with his wife and five children in ye yeare 1658 (being a Couper by traide) since wᶜʰ time he hath dwelt at Tolly gally nere Lurgan in ye County of Ardmagh and had by his wife Children as followeth " :
Christian (daughter) b. 10 Mo. 21, 1645 ; Deborah b. 3 Mo. 27, 1650 ; Timothy, b. 3 Mo. 27, 1652 ; Roger, b. 2 Mo. 20, 1654 ; Dinah, b. 10 Mo. 14, 1656 ; Alphonsus, b. 5 Mo. 14, 1659 ; Robert, b. 1 Mo. 28, 1662, at Tollegally, Parish of Shankill, County Armagh ; Elizabeth, b. 4 Mo. 12, 1664, at same place.
Timothy Kirk, of Parish of Shankill and Catharine Robson of Parish of Sego, County Armagh, were married 3 Mo. 17, 1676, at house of Mark Wright, Parish of Shankill, County Armagh. Among signers to certificate were : Val. and Ann Hollingsworth, Judith, John, and Thomas Calvert, and Robert Hoope.
In 1680, Timothy and Roger Kirk, of County Armagh, had their goods taken for tithes. (*Stockdale*, 144.)

[1] A. H. Harlan, of New Burlington, Ohio, is about to issue an elaborate genealogy of the Harlan family.

The following is a list of the children of Timothy Kirk : Deborah, b. 7 Mo. 5, 1677 ; Samuel, b. 10 Mo. 15, 1678 ; Jacob, b. 10 Mo. 30, 1680 ; Sarah, b. 8 Mo. 9, 1682 ; Joseph, b. 1 Mo. 23, 1685 ; Roger, b. 2 Mo. 31, 1686 ; John, b. 10 Mo. 31, 1687 ; Ruth, b. 7 Mo. 29, 1690 ; Jane, b. 7 Mo. 18, 1692.

Roger Kirk, son of Timothy, came to Pennsylvania from Ireland, as early as 1712, and about 1714 married Elizabeth Rich· ards, of New Garden, Chester Co. He settled in Nottingham, that county, and died 3 Mo. 28, 1761. His children were: Mary, Timothy, William, Elizabeth, Deborah, Rebecca, and Samuel. (For details of this branch of the family see a *Historic Genealogy of the Kirk Family*, by Dr. Charles H. Stubbs, printed in 1872 ; also Potts, *Our Family Ancestors*, 262, and *Hist. Chester County*, 624.)

Deborah Kirk, of Parish of Shankill, County Armagh, and Francis Hillary, of Parish of Donnahlong, County Down, were married, 7 Mo. 8, 1682, at the house of Roger Webb, in Parish of Segoe, County Armagh. (*Records of Lurgan Meeting*.)

Robert Kirk and Ann Halliday declared their intentions of marriage, 2 Mo. 25, 1696.

Samuel Kirk and Mary Johnson, both of Lurgan Meeting, were married at Lurgan, 4 Mo. 24, 1702. (*Minutes of Ulster Province Meeting*.)

Alphonsus Kirk, son of Roger and Elizabeth, and uncle of the Roger Kirk (son of Timothy) who came to Pennsylvania about 1712, took passage from Belfast, 11 Mo. 11, 1688, and landed at Jamestown, Va., 1 Mo. (Mar) 12, 1689. He arrived in New Castle County 3 Mo. 29, 1689, bringing with him a certificate of removal, dated 10 Mo. 9, 1688, from the meeting at John Robson's [Lurgan Meeting] stating "that he hath lived with his father from his infancy until now . . . and since his convincement he hath belonged to our Meeting." This document was signed by the following members of the Meeting : Robert Hoopes, Jno. Robson, William Porter, Timothy Kirk, Jno. Hoop, Robt. Kirk, Mark Wright, William Crook, Thos. Wainwright, Jno. Webb, James Webb, William Williams, Jacob Robson, and Thomas Walker.

The father and mother, Roger and Elizabeth Kirk, added a postscript certifying "that we are willing our son above named should take this journey herein mentioned . . . and if it be his portion to marry we do give our consent, provided it be to a Friend, and in unity with Friends, according to the order of truth." (Certificate is printed in full in *Friends' Intelligencer*, of Philadelphia, 3 Mo. 30, 1872, Vol. XXIX., p. 71.)

He was married 12 Mo. (Feb.) 23, 1692–3, to Abigail, daughter of Adam and Mary Sharpy, of Shelpot Creek, New Castle

County on Delaware. He settled in Christiana Hundred, near what is now Centreville, in that County. Centre Meeting House was built on his land. He died 7 Mo. 7, 1745, and his wife in 1748. Their children were: Roger, b. 1 Mo. 21, 1694, d. 1 Mo. 19, 1762; Elizabeth, b. 4 Mo. 23, 1695, m. Daniel Brown; Jonathan[1] b. 11 Mo. 15, 1697, d. 9 Mo. 1, 1735; Mary, b. 8 Mo. 31, 1689, d. 9 Mo. 1, 1699; Deborah, b. 11 Mo. 1699, d. 7 Mo. 23, 1704; Abigail, b. 7 Mo. 1701, d. 7 Mo. 29, 1704; Timothy b. 3 Mo. 6, 1704, d. 8 Mo. 19, 1704; Alphonsus, b. 8 Mo. 2, 1705, d. 1 Mo. 1, 1730–1; Adam, b. 3 Mo, 1, 1707, d. 10 Mo. 8, 1774; William, b. 1 Mo. 4, 1708, d. 3 Mo. 2, 1787; Timothy, b. 5 Mo. 1, 1711; d. 5 Mo, 2, 1786.

Of these children Roger removed to Nottingham, and William and Timothy settled in East Caln or Pikeland. William was twice married, and had nineteen children, of whom one was Rachel Price, a minister of the Society. (*Hist. Chester County*, 624.) See pages 207–8.

Jacob Kirk, son of Timothy, and grandson of Roger Kirk, was born 10 Mo. 30, 1680, and according to the minutes of Ulster Province Meeting, was married 7 Mo. 20, 1716, at Hillsborough Meeting, to Rebecca Robison, of Lisburn Meeting, County Antrim. He produced a certificate of removal from Ballinderry Meeting, County Antrim, to New Garden Monthly Meeting, Chester County, 11 Mo. 31, 1729, and settled on Conestoga Creek, in Lampeter Township, Lancaster County. He died prior to 1744, leaving at least three children:

1. Jane Kirk, m. (1) Joseph Miller, 2 Mo. 18, 1738, (2) William Richards, 5 Mo. 10, 1759.

2. John Kirk, d. 1798–9, m. Ann Wollaston, of Wilmington, Delaware, 3 Mo. 7, 1744, and had children: Jacob, John, Jeremiah, Sarah, m. John Owen, Rebecca, m. Evan Griffith, Catharine, m. Joshua Wollaston, Jane, m. William Steady. John Kirk was a resident of Lampeter Township, Lancaster County. He was a slave-owner, but manumitted his slaves about 1779.

3. Rebecca Kirk, who is mentioned in the meeting records as " Rebecca Kirk ye younger," m. (1) James Miller, 1 Mo. 6, 1749,

---

[1] The Records of Old Swedes Church, Wilmington Del. (Printed by Hist. Soc. of Pa., 1890), page 260, state that in 1720 " The Quakers', Alphonsi Kirk and wife Abigail's son Jonathan, 21 years old, [was] baptised in St. James' Church, July 10th." Jonathan Kirk and Mary Anderson were married by license, Aug. 16, 1720 (*Ibid.*, 258). Nov. 19, 1721, James Kirk, three weeks old, son of Jonathan and Mary (p. 266), and on Jan. 26, 1723, Elizabeth Kirk, born Jan. 11, 1723, daughter of above, were baptized (p. 279).

and had children (Rachel, Sarah, Hannah, Jane) ; m. (2) Isaac Richards, 11 Mo. 10, 1763.—(See Potts, *Our Family Ancestors*, 263.)

NATHANIEL CARTMILL and wife Dorothy came from Ireland to Pennsylvania, in 1685 and settled within the limits of Newark Monthly Meeting. They had at least two children : Martin, b. 1 Mo. 19, 1685, at sea on the voyage from Ireland ; and Thomas, b. 2 Mo. 29, 1689, disowned 12 Mo. 4, 1715, for marriage out of Society (*Records of Newark Mo. Mtg.*). In 1689–90, Nathaniel Cartmill and Timothy Atkinson were each granted 200 acres of land in the Manor of Rockland, New Castle County, at a rent of one penny per acre, "being unwilling such good Husbandman should leave the Government" (Minutes of the Board of Property, *Penn'a Archives*, 2d Series, XIX., 25). At Newark Monthly Meeting, 7 Mo. 3, 1715, Nathaniel Cartmill was dealt with for consenting to his son's marriage out of the Society ; for this breach of order he produced a satisfactory acknowledgment. In 1669, Godfrey and John Cantrell, of Queen's County, Ireland, had goods taken from them for refusing to contribute money for the church at Rosenallis (Besse's *Sufferings of the Quakers*, II., 477).

GAYEN MILLER, who first appears in Chester County in 1702, is

thought to have been a near relative of John Miller, of New Garden. As stated on page 128, he purchased 200 acres at the site of Kennett Square, and in 1712 acquired 700 acres in New Garden. He also secured several other tracts. He took his seat in the Provincial Assembly in 1714. He died in 1742, leaving a will, dated 3 Mo. 31, 1742 (proved Aug. 31, 1742), in which he mentions "my cousin James Miller," probably a son of John Miller of New Garden. Children of Gayen Miller by his wife Margaret :

1. James Miller, b. 11 Mo. 5, 1696 ; d. 1732 ; m. Rachel, daughter of John and Katharine Fred, 4 Mo. 20, 1721, and had children : Sarah, b. 1723, m. John Jackson ; Deborah, b. 1725, m. Joseph Sharp ; James, b. 1728, m. (1) Sarah Way and (2)

Phebe Jones ; Jesse, b. 1730, m. Lydia Baily.   Rachel, the widow, m. 2d, James Miller, son of James and Katharine, and died 12 Mo. 3, 1748–9.

2. William Miller, b. 8 Mo. 30, 1698 ; d. 1767 ; m. Ruth Rowland, 7 Mo. 30, 1724, and had children : Mary, m. James Miller, 1744 ; Hannah, m. William Whiteside ; Margaret, m. Jonathan Hanson, April 23, 1766.

3. Robert Miller, b. 3 Mo. 3, 1703 ; m. Ruth Haines ; and had children : Margaret, b. 1726, m. William Bentley ; Solomon, b. 1727, m. Sarah Matthews ; Dorothy, b. 1729, m. George Matthews ; Patience, b. 1730–1, m. (1) ——— Bishop and (2) James Davis ; Hannah, b. 1734, m. Curtis Lewis ; Warwick, b. 1735, d. 1777, m. Elizabeth Price ; Isaac, b. 1737–8, d. 1752 ; Jacob, b. 1739 ; Rebecca, b. 1742, m. Jas. Allen ; Joseph, b. 1744 ; Rachel, b. 1746, m. Joseph Johnson ; Sarah, b. 1748, m. John Boyd (2); Benjamin, b. 1752 ; James, b. 1754, m. Hannah Pim.

4. Sarah Miller, b. 9 Mo. 1, 1704 ; m. Joshua Johnson, son of Robert, and had children (James, Lydia, Margaret, William, Sarah, Joshua, Hannah, Robert, Dinah, Rebecca, and David).

5. Mary Miller, b. 3 Mo. 7, 1707 ; m. William, son of Samuel Beverly, 2 Mo. 22, 1730, and had children (Samuel, James, Mary).

6. Patrick Miller, b. 12 Mo. 28, 1708 ; m. (1) Patience Haines, 9 Mo. 5, 1735, and had children (Joseph, Ruth, Mary, Patience) ; m. (2) Anne ———, in 1745, and had other children (Susanna Anne).

7. Samuel Miller, b. 4 Mo. 14. 1711 ; d. Nov, 1764 ; m. Margaret Halliday, 4 Mo. 29, 1732.   No issue.

8. Elizabeth Miller, b. 5 Mo. 7, 1713 ; m. Joseph Dickinson, 8 Mo. 25, 1732, and had children (Margaret, Sarah, Gayen, Elizabeth, Mary, Hannah, Deborah, Joseph, Daniel, James).

9. Joseph Miller, b. 7 Mo. 14, 1715 ; d. 1741 ; Jane Kirk, 4 Mo. 18, 1738.

10. Benjamin Miller, b. 6 Mo. 4, 1717 ; m. 10 Mo. 7, 1738, Martha (Musgrove) Walter, widow of John Walter, and daughter of John Musgrave.   He settled in Lancaster County.

11. John Miller, b. 11 Mo. 6, 1720–1, m. Margaret Smith, 8 Mo. 28, 1741.   Settled in Lancaster County.

12. George Miller, b. 5 Mo. 19, 1723.   He married "out of meeting" about 1744.[1]

John Miller, wife Mary (received 4 Mo. 4, 1709), and children from Grange near Charlemont, in 1709.

[1] Potts, *Our Family Ancestors*, 250–253.

John Miller,[1] son of John Miller, born at "Breckenbrough, in
y⁰ Parish of Kerbywilk in Yorkshire," in 1633, went over into
Ireland as a planter, in 1657, and married Ann, daughter of William Clibborn, who was born in 1630, at Cowley, in the County
of Durham, England. Their children were: William, b. 1659,
at Moate, Margaret, b. 1662, Shurrch? d. 1668; John, b. 1665,
at Moate; Thomas, b. 1667, at Ballynalinch; Abraham, b. 1670,
at Glin, County West Meath; and Isaac, b. 1672, at Glin,
County West Meath. (Potts, *Our Family Ancestors*, 245–6.)

One John Miller, possibly a son of the above John Miller, married Mary, sister of Andrew Ignew and as early as 1693 was living within the limits of Grange Meeting near Charlemont, County
Armagh, Ireland. He and his family arrived in Chester County,
Pa., in 1709, and, as we have seen on page 135, settled on a large
tract of land in New Garden Township. He was a prominent
member of New Garden Meeting and was elected to the Provincial Assembly in 1714, but died that same year.

Mary Miller, his widow, died in 1730. In her will, dated 5
Mo. 12, 1730, probated August 10, 1730, she mentions her
"Kinsman John Too" and leaves £30 "to pay y⁰ passage of or
Charges of three of my brother Andrew Ignews [2] Children in Com-
ing to this Country, provided they Come in y⁰ Space of two years
after my decease."

Children of John and Mary (Ignew) Miller:

1. James Miller, b. 1 Mo., 1693, near Charlemont, County
Armagh; m. 3 Mo. 24, 1722, Ann Cain (daughter of John and
Ann) who was born in County Armagh. They had issue: Mary,
b. 1724; Ann, b. 1726; Sarah, b. 1727; John, b. 1730; Joseph,
b. 1732; Susanna, b. 1734–5; Hannah, b. 1737; William, b.
1739; James, b. 1745.

2. Mary Miller, who died in 1736, m. Joseph Hutton, in 1714,
and had issue: John, Thomas, Joseph, Susanna, Samuel, William,
Benjamin, Nehemiah, Ephraim.

3. William Miller, b. 2 Mo., 1698, "within the virge of Grange
Monthly Meeting, County Tyrone, Ireland"; d. 1768; m. Ann
Emlen, 4 Mo. 15, 1732, and had issue: John, b. 1733; Hannah,
b. 1734; William, b. 1737; Mary, b. 1741; Ann, b. 1743;
Joshua, b. 1746.

[1] In 1677, one Robert Miller, of County Antrim, had goods seized for
tithes.—*Stockdale*, 76.
In 1681, Robert Miller, of Parish of Denniskean, County Antrim, had
his goods taken for tithes.—*Ibid.*, 166.
[2] In 1672, Andrew Ignew, of County Antrim, had his goods seized for
tithes, and in 1673 was imprisoned at Carrickfergus. In 1681, Andrew
Ignew, of Ballinderry Parish, County Antrim, had his goods taken for
tithes.—Stockdale, *A Great Cry of Oppression*, 13, 36, 169.

4. Joseph Miller, d. 7 Mo. 30, 1727 ; m. Ann, daughter ot Joseph Gilpin, 10 Mo. 31, 1724, and had children : John, b. 1725 ; Isaac, b. ·1727.

5. Sarah Miller, m. Nehemiah Hutton, 1723.

6. Elizabeth Miller, b. 1 Mo., 1704, in Ireland ; d. 2 Mo. 8, 1783 ; m. William Chambers, 8 Mo. 22, 1729, and had ten children.

7. Martha Miller, m. (1) John Jordan and (2) Nathaniel Houlton.

8. Elinor Miller, m. Richard Chambers, 4 Mo. 19, 1729, and had eight children.

9. Susanna Miller, m. Joseph Jackson, 2 Mo. 18, 1734.

JAMES STARR, from Catterlaugh [Carlow] Meeting, Ireland, received 4 Mo. 7, 1712.

John Starr, whose father is said to have served in the Parliament Army as a captain of infantry, and to have removed to Ireland, resided at Old Castle, County Meath. By Mary, his wife, he had children : John, b. 7 Mo., 1674 ; James, b. 10 Mo. 28, 1676 ; George, b. 2 Mo. 16, 1679 ; Mary, b. 7 Mo. 15, 1682 ; Elizabeth, b. 9 Mo. 12, 1684 ; Susanna, b. 9 Mo. 23, 1686 ; Jeremiah, b. 8 Mo. 17, 1690 ; Moses, b. 8 Mo. 27, 1692 ; Isaac, b. 9 Mo. 23, 1697.

Of these, James Starr, of Coothill, was married 6 Mo. 22, 1705, to Rachel Laybourne, daughter of Joseph Laybourne, of Black Hadleigh, County Durham, England, deceased, and of Rachel, his wife, now of Ardnahue, County Carlow, Ireland. She was born 8 Mo. 7, 1686, at Ramestown. James was a farmer in County Cavan, whence he came to Pennsylvania in 1712, and settled in New Garden, Chester County. In 1714 he was chosen clerk of Newark Monthly Meeting and overseer of New Garden Meeting. Upon the establishment of New Garden Monthly Meeting, in 1718, he became the clerk and served until 1726. In 1731, he removed with his family to Charlestown Township, Chester County, and located at the present site of Phœnixville. His children were Mary, Joseph, John, James, Rachel, Moses, Samuel, and Susanna.

Jeremiah Starr, son of John, m. 11 Mo. 10, 1716, Rebecca, daughter of Isaac and Ann Jackson, and toward the close of 1717 came to Chester County and settled in London Grove Township, a little northwest of the Borough of Avondale.

Moses Starr, son of John, m. 6 Mo. 2, 1715, at Old Castle Meeting, Deborah, daughter of Merrick King, of that place. They came over with Jeremiah and his family, and after a time settled at Maiden Creek, Berks County. He was the first and for many years the old representative of Berks County in the Provincial Assembly.

Isaac Starr, the youngest brother, also came to Pennsylvania, and was married 12 Mo. 20, 1723, to Margaret, daughter of Thomas Lightfoot, by whom he had several children.   For further details see *Hist. of Chester County*, 729, *Record of the Jackson Family*, 72-73, and Cope's *Smedley Genealogy*, 146.

Merrick King, of Old Castle Meeting, and Mary Starr, of Bally-haes Meeting, were married 3 Mo. 2, 1699, at John Starr's.

John Starr, "ye younger," and Sarah Martin, both of the meeting near Ballyhaes, were married 6 Mo. 11, 1706, at John Bell's.

Richard King, of Old Castle Meeting, and Elizabeth Starr, of Ballyhaes Meeting, were married 12 Mo. 24, 1702, at Killagh Meeting.

Thomas Martin and Susanna Starr, both of Ballyhaes Meeting, were married 7 Mo. 10, 1710, at John Bell's near Ballyhaes.— *Records of Carlow Meeting.*

In 1679, John Starr and William Haddock, of Parish of Ma-gheragall, County Antrim, suffered persecution for tithes.—Stock-dale, *A Great Cry of Oppression*, 120.

MARGARET RAY, unmarried, from Lurgan Meeting, County Armagh, Ireland, received 1 Mo. 7, 1713.   Married Moses Harlan.

EDWARD THOMPSON, received 3 Mo. 5, 1711, from Ireland.

THOMAS GARNETT, wife Sarah, and brother Joseph Garnett, received 3 Mo. 5, 1711, from County Tyrone, Ireland.

Thomas Garnett and Sarah Baker, both of Grange Meeting, near Charlemont, County Armagh, were married 4 Mo. 16, 1708, at Grange Meeting.   (*Minutes of Ulster Province Meeting.*) Thomas Garnett resided in New Garden, Chester County, until about 1717, when he removed to Kent County, Maryland.   A son George was born 2 Mo. 29, 1710.

Joseph Garnet m. in 1716 Margaret, widow of John Lowden.

JOSEPH SHARP, received 6 Mo. 4, 1711, from Ireland.

ELIZABETH HOBSON, dated 9 Mo. 22, 1710, from Friends in Ireland ; received 2 Mo. 5, 1712.

In 9 Mo., 1712, she married John Hope, of Kennett.

FRANCIS HOBSON, received 2 Mo. 5, 1712, from Grange near Charlemont, Ireland.

Francis and Lawrence Hobson were among those convinced by the preaching of William Clayton and William Edmundson in the neighborhood of Grange near Charlemont, in 1655.   (*Rutty,*

91.) In 1666, Francis Hobson, of County Armagh, had taken for tithes, goods valued at £7. 10s. (*Besse*, II., 475), and in 1670, goods valued at £3. 5s., for refusing to contribute to the repair of the "Parish Worship-house at Kilmore," County Armagh. (*Ibid.*, II., 479.) In 1671, he had taken for tithes, wheat, barley and oats, valued at £3. 14. (*Stockdale*, 4.)

In 1673, in County Armagh, "Francis Hobson was sued in the Bishop's Court at Ardmagh for £2 Tyths of Milch-Money, by George Walker, Priest, and by Warrant from two Justices of the Peace, upon a definitive Sentence, was taken by David Mulligan, Constable, the 2d Day of the sixth Month, and committed to the Goal of Ardmagh, and was Prisoner two Years and four Months, and about the 13th of the tenth Month, 1675, died in the said Goal." (*A Compendious View*, 79–80.)

One Francis Hobson, of Drumilly, Parish of Loughgall, County Armagh, and Mary Harding, of Lissacurran, Parish of Shankill, said county, were married 11 Mo. 29, 1694. (*Lurgan Meeting Records.*)

Francis Hobson, the emigrant, of 1712, born about 1686, purchased 200 acres of land in New Garden, Chester County, by deed of May 1, 1713, in which he is styled weaver, for the sum of £40. This land is still held by descendants of the name. In 3 Mo. (May), 1716, he was married to Martha Wainhouse, from Dublin. He died 9 Mo. 29, 1766, in his eightieth year, and his widow 11 Mo. 25, 1775, aged eighty-three. Their children were: Francis, b. 9 Mo. 12, 1720, removed to what is now Montgomery County, and died 9 Mo. 29, 1792, in Limerick Township, m. 8 Mo. 17, 1744, to Martha Shaw ; Mary, b. 12 Mo. 19, 1724, m. 4 Mo. 18, 1747, to Robert Boyce, of New Garden ; John, b. 7 Mo. 7, 1726 ; Joseph, b. 10 Mo. 23, 1731, d. 12 Mo. 11, 1797, m. 4 Mo. 15, 1767, at London Grove Meeting, to Elizabeth Foster ; Martha, b. 2 Mo. 19, 1738, d. 6 Mo. 30, 1811, m. to Samuel Miller, Jr. (See *History of Chester County*, 605.)

JOSEPH HUTTON, received 4 Mo. 7, 1712 from Catterlaugh [Carlow] Meeting, Ireland.

Thomas Hutton[1] of Killeagh, County Cavan, Ireland [wid-

[1] In 1658, John Hutton and other Quakers were taken from a meeting at Cavan and imprisoned eleven days.—(*Besse* II., 464.)

In 1677, John Hutton, County Meath, had seized for tithes two out of sixteen lambs, two "clamps of Turfe," four "Fleeces of Wool," three loads of hay, one load of barley, nine loads of oats, eleven "sheaves of Beare," four "car loads of Beare," etc., valued at £3. 11s.—*Stockdale*, 84.

In 1680, Joseph Leybourn, County Carlow, had seized for tithes, nine "sheaves of Beans," eight "sheaves of Beare," fourteen "Kishes of Turfe," etc., valued at 12s.—(*Stockdale*, 158.)

ower] was married, 3 Mo. 23, 1703, at New Garden Meeting, County Carlow, to Rachel Laybourne, of Ardnahue, County Cavan, widow of Joseph Laybourne (*Records of Carlow Meeting*). See Thomas Hutton's letters, pages 64–7.

Joseph Hutton, son of Thomas, settled in New Garden, Chester County, and in 1714 married Mary, daughter of John and Mary Miller. He died in the autumn of 1735, and his widow in the following winter. They had children: John, Thomas, Joseph, Susanna, Samuel, William, Benjamin, Nehemiah, and Ephraim. John, b. 6 Mo. 31, 1715, m. 3 Mo. 6, 1741, at London Grove, Chester County, Ann Harry, and removed to Warrington, York County, about 1753; Thomas, b. 12 Mo. 20, 1715, m. 3 Mo. 9, 1739, at London Grove, Elizabeth Harry; Joseph, b. 5 Mo. 28, 1720, m. 9 Mo. 5, 1747, at New Garden, Chester County, Betty, daughter of Henry Willis, and about 1753 removed to Newberry Township, York County; Samuel, b. 2 Mo. 15, 1724, removed to Menallen Township, now Adams County, about 1753, and m. 5 Mo. 9, 1753, at Menallen Meeting, Mary, daughter of John Wright; William, b. 12 Mo. 14, 1725, m. 9 Mo. 15, 1750, Deborah, daughter of John Todd, of London Grove, and removed to Warrington Monthly Meeting, York County, about 1751; Benjamin, b. 12 Mo. 1, 1728–9; Nehemiah b. 6 Mo. 27, 1731, m. 11 Mo. 8, 1753, Ann Hiett.

Children of Joseph and Betty (Willis) Hutton: Joshua, b. 7 Mo. 25, 1748, m. 5 Mo. 13, 1772, at Newberry Meeting, York County, Rachel, daughter of Timothy Kirk, of Newberry; Rachel, b. 8 Mo. 21, 1750; Joseph, b. 10 Mo. 30, 1755; Susanna, b. 6 Mo. 18, 1758, d. 4 Mo. 27, 1762; Betty, b. 2 Mo. 20, 1761; Simon, b. 2 Mo. 17, 1765.

In 1681, in County Carlow, Gregory Russell and Joseph Leybourne had taken from them for tithes 28 " fleeces of Wooll," 9 lambs, also hay and corn, wheat, " Beare," beans, white peas, " Turfe," " potatoes," " a Goose," all valued at £7.

" The said Gregory and Joseph carrying home their Hay James Nowlan struck Gregory with a Pitchfork, and Joseph Leybourn holding up his arm to save the blow, the other run the Pitchfork in his Arm, and Joseph reproving them for their rude and uncivil carriage, one of them struck him three blows with a Spade, and the said Nowlan said, if any did oppose them he would kill them, and Joseph telling them he could not pay Tithes for Conscience sake, one of them said, there was no Conscience used in these times, with many other uncivil reproachful words not fit to be mentioned." —*.bid.*, 191–2.

In 1678, in County Carlow, John and Gregory Russell had their goods taken for tithes. The officers "pulled John Russell off a Corn Stack, and tore his Coat, and swung his Wife about by the Arm until they tore her Wastcoat and her Shift, and threw her into the Weeds, she being great with Child."—*Ibid.*, 110.

Children of William and Deborah (Todd) Hutton : Levi, b. 6
Mo. 5, 1752, d. 10 Mo. 3, 1753; Tamer, b. 2 Mo. 3, 1754;
Susanna, b. 12 Mo. 17, 1755 ; Levi, b. 1 Mo. 31, 1758, d. 2 Mo.
22, 1844, m. Martha.

NEHEMIAH HUTTON, unmarried, from Coothill, County Cavan,
Ireland, received 11 Mo. 5, 1716.

Nehemiah Hutton, another son of Thomas Hutton, also came
to Pennsylvania, and, 5 Mo. 25, 1723, m. Sarah, daughter of
John and Mary Miller. They made their final settlement within
the limits of Exeter Monthly Meeting, Berks County. Their children were : Susanna, b. 11 Mo. 20, 1724 ; John, b. 2 Mo. 7, 1727 ;
James ; Mary ; Sarah ; Abigail ; Deborah ; Martha ; and Tamar.

John Hutton, brother of Joseph and Nehemiah, married in
1724, Sarah, daughter of Michael Lightfoot, and had a son
Thomas and other children. (*History of Chester County*, 609 ;
records of New Garden and Warrington Mo. Mtgs.)

MICHAEL LIGHTFOOT, received 4 Mo. 7, 1712, from Catterlaugh [Carlow] Monthly Meeting, Ireland.

JOHN WILEY, received 4 Mo. 7, 1712, from County West
Meath. Unmarried. Married Martha Newby in 1713.

One John Wyly, of Hillsborough Mtg., and Sarah Walker, of
Grange Mtg., near Charlemont, declared their intentions of marriage at Grange Preparative Mtg., 3 Mo. 24, 1727.

At Ulster Province Meeting, 6 Mo. 29, 1696, Thomas Wyly,
of Coleraine, was mentioned as having been to London Yearly
Meeting.

Samuel Miller and Jane Wyly, both of Lisnegarvy Mtg., were
married 9 Mo. 21, 1698, at the house of Richard Boys. William
Wyly, of Coleraine Mtg., and Ruth Courtney, of Lisnegarvy Mtg.,
were married at the house of Richard Boys, 5 Mo. 12, 1704.—
Minutes of Ulster Province Mtg.

In 1677 and 1679, John Wyly, of Parish of Ahalee, suffered persecution for tithes.—Stockdale, *A Great Cry of Oppression*, 76,
120.

In 1681, Robert Willy, of Parish of Ballinderry, County Antrim,
had taken barley, oats, hay, wheat, and maslin ; value £3.—
Ibid., 168.

In 1681, John Wyly, of Parish of Killoan, County Antrim, had
his goods taken for tithes.—*Ibid.*, 166.

Allen Wyly and Sarah Adams were married in 1694.—*Minutes
of Ulster Province Meeting.*

Thomas Wily, son of Allen Wily, of New Garden, Chester

County, Pa., and Rachel, daughter of Thomas Rowland, were married 9 Mo. 13, 1729, at New Garden Meeting.

At Lisburn Meeting, County Antrim, 10 Mo. 28, 1676, "John Wily layd before us his intentions of mariadg with An Boyes & their proceeding hath been Soe orderly that we can not but lett them proceed to the Six weeks mg."

At Lisburn Meeting, 4 Mo. 16, 1684, Robert Mickle and John Wiley "layd before Frds. their going to Pensillvania."

Christopher Willson

CHRISTOPHER WILSON, received 4 Mo. 7, 1712, from County West Meath, Ireland.   Unmarried.

He was born about 1690, in Yorkshire, England, of parents who were members of the Church of England.   When he reached manhood he became a Friend and removed to Ireland. In 1712, he came over as a servant and settled in New Castle Co., Delaware, where he married Esther Woodward, 8 Mo. 22, 1719, and left numerous descendants.   About 1728 he became a minister of the Society of Friends.   He died 7 Mo. 11, 1740, in the 50th year of his age (See *A Collection of Memorials*, Phila., 1787, p. 102-3).   "About a Month agoe I agreed with Christopher Wilson a Weaver who dwells at John Griggs for a parcel of Land on ye lower Side of Brandywine," 200 acres next below Valentine Hollingsworth.—James Steel to John Taylor in a letter, dated Philadelphia, 11 Mo. 7, 1718, among the *Taylor Papers, Correspondence, 1683-1723*, Historical Society of Pennsylvania.

JOHN SHARP, received 7 Mo. 6, 1712, from Ireland.

John Sharp and Joseph Sharp, probably brothers, were no doubt nearly related to Anthony Sharp, a native of Gloucestershire, England, who became a Friend and removed to Dublin in 1669.

John Sharp m. 2 Mo. 16, 1726, at New Garden Meeting, Ann Bryan, of New Garden.   He died about 1748.   His widow then married, 3 Mo. 30, 1751, at New Garden Meeting, John Nichols, of Kennett, and died about 1782, her will being proved that year.

Children of John and Ann (Bryan) Sharp were:

I. John, b. 5 Mo. 19, 1730.

II. Elizabeth, b. 4 Mo. 23, 1732, m. 5 Mo. 2, 1754, at New Garden Meeting, James, son of John Nichols, of Kennett.

III. George, b. 2 Mo. 27, 1735, d. Dec. 9, 1761, m. (1st) about 1763, at Old Swede's Church, Wilmington, Delaware, Abigail, daughter of Thomas and Dinah Gregg, of Kennett (children by 1st wife—Thomas, Samuel), and (2d) Sarah (Chambers) Gregg, widow of Benjamin Gregg (children by 2d wife—Abiah, Eli, Jesse).

IV. Benjamin, b. 7 Mo. 25, 1738, m. 2 Mo. 3, 1762, Hannah, daughter of William and Hannah Wiley, of Kennett.

V. Mary, b. 8 Mo. 26, 1740, m. about 1758, John Woodward, Jr.

VI. Thomas, b. 11 Mo. 12, 1747, d. March, 1768, m. Rachel.

Joseph Sharp, of Newark or Kennett Monthly Meeting, tanner, came from Ireland about 1711, and settled in London Grove, Chester County ; m. 9 Mo. 4, 1713, at Concord Meeting, Mary, daughter of Nicholas and Abigail Pyle. By deed of March 25, 1714, he purchased two tracts of land of 200 acres each in New Garden. He died in 1746.

Children of Joseph and Mary (Pyle) Sharp :

I. Abigail, b. 5 mo. 26, 1714, d. 9 Mo. 27, 1726.

II. Elizabeth, b. 5 Mo. 25, 1717, d. 10 Mo., 1719.

III. Mary, b. 7 Mo. 17, 1710, d. 10 Mo., 1719.

IV. Elizabeth, b. 12 Mo. 19, 1720, m. Jeremiah Douglass. (Children, Joseph, Mary, Elizabeth.)

V. Sarah, b. 6 Mo. 5, 1723, d. 10 Mo. 22, 1723.

VI. Joseph, b. 8 Mo. 19, 1724, m. Deborah Miller, and removed to Iredell County, S. C.

VII. George, b. 9 Mo. 4, 1726, d. young.

VIII. Abigail, b. 2 Mo. 1729, m. (1st) William Sharpless, (2d) Moses Palmer.

IX. Mary, b. 6 Mo. 21, 1731, d. 6 Mo. 30, 1731.

X. Samuel, b. 8 Mo. 30, 1734, d. about 1819, m. Mary, widow of Isaac Starr, and daughter of Richard and Abigail (Harlan) Flower. See Cope's *Sharpless Family*, 182.

ELIZABETH SHARP, received 5 Mo. 4, 1713.

JOHN LOWDEN and wife Margaret, from Ireland, received 4 Mo. 6, 1713.

John Lowden, of Antrim Meeting, and Margaret Tanner, of Carricksfergus Meeting, were married at the house of John Wardell, "neere Carrickfergus," 4 Mo. 20, 1699. (*Minutes of Ulster Province Meeting*.) Sometime after 1703 he removed to New Garden, County Carlow, whence in 1711 (Samuel Smith in *Hazard's Register*, VII., 3), he came to Chester County, Pennsylvania, and settled in the township of New Garden, which it is believed he was instrumental in naming for his old home in Ireland. He was an eminent minister of the Society and made religious visits to New York and New England. He died 1 Mo. 19, 1714, at Abington (near Jenkintown, Pa.). His widow, Margaret, was married to Joseph Garnett, in 1716. A son William Lowden was born 9 Mo. 10, 1703, in County Antrim (see page 230). Richard Lowden, another son, was married 4 Mo. 5, 1728, at Samuel Blunston's house, in Hempfield (now Columbia, Lancaster County) to Patience Wright, daughter of John, of Hempfield. A daughter Mary married ――― Updegraff.

By deed of 1734, William Lowden, yeoman, Richard Lowden, cordwainer, and Mary Updegraff, children of John Lowden, deceased, sold a part of the Lowden tract in New Garden.

THOMAS JACKSON, received 4 Mo. 6, 1713, from Mountmelmellick Monthly Meeting, Queen's County, Ireland.

Thomas Jackson, son of Nicholas Jackson, of Kilbank, in Seathwaite, Lancashire, England, was born at that place. He removed thence to Ireland, and married Ann, daughter of Francis and Judith Man, born at Mountmellick, Queen's County. He leased some land at Dreighet, Parish of Arkhill, Barony of Carberry, County Kildare, about 1709, which he sold to William Knott. They came to Pennsylvania in 1713, sailing from Dublin on the 25th of 1 Mo., and settled in New Garden Township, Chester County, where by deed of Jan. 1, 1713, he purchased 200 acres of land. About 1711 he removed to Marlborough, Chester County, where he died in 1756.

Children of Thomas and Ann Jackson : John, b. 9 Mo. 14, 1703, at Ballinolarbin, King's County (children—George, Sarah and David) ; Judith, b. 12 Mo. 27, 1705, m. Daniel Every ; Mary, b. 12 Mo. 8, 1708, at Timahoe, County Kildare, m. Jacob Wright, of East Marlborough (son of Jacob), 2 Mo. 8, 1741, at London Grove Meeting (no issue) ; Thomas, b. 6 Mo. 10, 1710, at Drechet, King's County, m. Lydia, daughter of John Smith, of Marlborough, 3 Mo. 17, 1738 (children—Ann, Caleb, Mary, and Joshua) ; Ann, b. 7 Mo. 5, 1714, at New Garden, d. 7 Mo. 28, 1757 ; Jonathan, b. 12 Mo. 16, 1717, at New Garden, m. Mary Hayes, 10 Mo. 3, 1743 (children—Mary, Thomas, Sarah, Ann, Elizabeth and Ruth); Elizabeth, b. 10 Mo. 8, 1720, m. Henry Chalfant, son of John, of West Marlborough, 8 Mo. 15, 740, at London Grove (children—Jonathan, Thomas, Henry, Ann, Elizabeth, Jacob, Mary, Abner, and Caleb). For further account see *Jackson Genealogy*, 285–88.

JAMES LINDLEY, and wife Eleanor, from Carlow Meeting, Ireland, received 8 Mo. 3, 1713.

Eleanor Lindley was a sister of Thomas Parke. James Lindley purchased 200 acres of land in New Garden, in 1713, and 400 in London Grove, in 1722, in the deed for which he is styled blacksmith. Thomas Lindley, a brother, perhaps, was a blacksmith in Philadelphia, but owned land in Caln Township, Chester County.

The children of James and Eleanor Lindley were Thomas, b. 2 Mo. 25, 1706; Rachel, b. 5 Mo. 11, 1707; James, b. 4 Mo. 30, 1709; Margery; Robert, b. 4 Mo. 32, 1712; William, b. 12 Mo. 20, 1714, d. 10 Mo. 26, 1726; Alice, b. 2 Mo. 25, 1716; Mary, b. 9 Mo. 4, 1717; Jonathan, b. 3 Mo. 11, 1719, m. Deborah Halliday, 2 Mo. 15, 1741; Elizabeth, b. 8 Mo. 4, 1720; Hannah, b. 1 Mo. 11, 1723; Eleanor, b. 1 Mo. 11, 1727–28.

James Lindley died 10 Mo. 13, 1726, and his widow married Henry Jones. Thomas, the eldest son, married Ruth Hadley, and went to Orange County, North Carolina. The children of Jonathan and Deborah Lindley were Jacob (who became an eminent minister of the Society of Friends), b. 9 Mo. 18, 1744, m. 11 Mo. 14, 1782, to Hannah, widow of William Miller; James, b. 10 Mo. 18, 1746; Jonathan, b. 9 Mo. 18, 1750; Deborah, b. b. 12 Mo. 26, 1753; Ruth, m. 11 Mo. 6, 1800, to David Wilson. —*History of Chester County*, 637.

JOHN CANE, and wife Ann, from Ballyhagen Meeting, County Armagh, Ireland, received 10 Mo. 5, 1713. ✦

They settled in London Grove, Chester County, where he died shortly after. His widow is supposed to have married ——— Todd. Children of John and Ann Cane: John, m. 9 Mo. 7, 1722, Rachel, d. of Randal and Mary Malin; Ann, m. in 1722, James Miller; Margaret (?), m. in 1720, John Todd; Robert (?), m. in 1730, Ann Dixon.—*History of Chester County*, 492.

WILLIAM HALLIDAY, and wife Deborah (from Dublin, received 12 Mo. 7, 1713) from Moate Meeting, County West Meath, Ireland, received 12 Mo. 6, 1713.

One James Halliday and Hannah Leaze, both of Lurgan, were married at Lurgan Meeting, 8 Mo. 27, 1703 (*Minutes of Ulster Province Meeting.*)

William and Deborah Halliday had six children: Robert, b. 7 Mo. 16, 1702, in Ireland; Rachel, b. 10 Mo. 25, 1704, m. Andrew Moore, of Sadsbury, 4 Mo. 24, 1725; Jacob b. 8 Mo. 18, 1706, d. 5 Mo. 24, 1721; Margaret, b. 11 Mo. 13, 1709, m.

Samuel Miller, son of Gayen, 4 Mo. 29, 1732; Sarah, b. 1 Mo. 14, 1713; Deborah, b. 2 Mo. 28, 1716, m. Jonathan, son of James Lindley, 2 Mo. 15, 1743, and had four children (Jacob, b. 9 Mo. 18, 1744, m. Hannah Miller, and was an eminent Quaker minister; James b. 10 Mo. 18, 1746; Jonathan, b. 9 Mo. 18, 1750; Deborah, b. 12 Mo. 26, 1753).

Robert Halliday, son of William and Deborah, m. 1st Miriam Haines, daughter of Joseph, of Nottingham, 4 Mo. 3, 1730; m. 2d, in 1739 or 1740, Mabel Anderson, a Friend from Ireland. They had two children: (1) Jacob, m. 1st to Patience, daughter of Thomas and Hannah Painter, of Concord, 4 Mo. 13, 1768, and 2d to Ann ———. He died 3 Mo. 22, 1822; she died about 1836 or 1837. (2) Phebe m. 10 Mo. 24, 1765, Isaac Jackson, son of John and Sarah (Miller) Jackson.—*Jackson Genealogy*, 221–2.

At a meeting of the Board of Property, 12 Mo. 2, 1726, "Alex' Mongumry requests (By his Brother-in-Law Wm. Halliday) the Grant of a piece of Land near Octoraro Creek, for a Settlement."—*Penna. Archives*, 2d Series, XIX., 745.

JOHN ALLEN, from Ireland, received, 2 Mo. 3, 1713.

John Allen

John Allen, b. 8 Mo. 3, 1694; d. 9 Mo. 16, 1771; m. in 1719, Amy Cox, and settled in London Grove Township, Chester County. Children: (1) John, b. 2 Mo. 8, 1720; d. 10 Mo. 1, 1754; m. 9 Mo. 12, 1740, Phebe Scarlett, and lived in London Grove (2) Rebecca, b. 8 Mo. 8, 1722; m. (1st) Alexander Mode and (2d) William Chandler. (3) Emey (Amy), b. 6 Mo. 8, 1725; m. Philip Ward. (4) Elizabeth, b. 2 Mo. 29, 1728; m. Simon Dixson. (5) William, b. 8 Mo. 3, 1730; m. 5 Mo. 24, 1758, Sarah Greave. (6) Joseph, b. 5 Mo. 12, 1733; m. 11 Mo. 13, 1755, Deborah Hill. (7) Mary, b. 11 Mo. 1, 1738; m. Moses Fraizer. (8) Phebe, b. 2 Mo. 9, 1739; d. 10 Mo. 19, 1787. (9) Benjamin, b. 8 Mo. 4, 1742; m. 12 Mo. 20, 1764, Hannah Greenfield.—*History of Chester County*, 463.

One William Allen and Martha Mackie, both of Ballyhagen Meeting, County Armagh, were married, 1 Mo. 6, 1700, at Ballyhagen Meeting.—*Minutes of Ulster Province Meeting*.

WILLIAM TAYLOR, from Ballytore, County Kildare, Ireland, received 10 Mo. 4, 1714.

22

ROBERT JOHNSON, and wife Margaret, from Carlow Meeting, Ireland, received 12 Mo. 5, 1714.

Robert Johnson and wife Margaret, *née* Berthwaite, settled on a tract of 200 acres of land in New Garden, where he died in 1732, leaving children : Benjamin, James, Joshua, Robert, Abigail, 'and Ann. Of these Joshua, b. 7 Mo. 29, 1696, at Coleboy, County Wicklow, m. Sarah, daughter of Gayen and Margaret Miller. (Children : James, Lydia, Margaret, William, Sarah, Joshua, Hannah, Robert, Dinah, Rebecca, and David.)   Robert Johnson, Jr., m. Katharine, daughter of Simon and Ruth Hadly, and had children : Hannah, Simon, Caleb, Lydia, Stephen, Jonathan, and Isaac.—*History of Chester County,* 615.

MARTHA WAINHOUS, from Dublin, dated 1 Mo. 17, 1714; received 12 Mo. 4, 1715.

THOMAS LIGHTFOOT, from Moate Meeting, County West Meath, Ireland, received 6 Mo. 4, 1716.

Thomas Lightfoot,[1] a highly esteemed minister of the Society of Friends, was born about 1645, perhaps in Cambridgeshire, and may have been the son of another Thomas Lightfoot who suffered persecution for his Quaker belief at Cambridge, in 1653,[2] and was a companion of George Whitehead in his religious journeys.   In 1692, the younger Thomas was living in the neighborhood of Lisburn Meeting, County Antrim, Ireland ; for on 8 Mo. 27 of that year he was appointed on a committee to buy the Friends graveyard at Lisburn from Robert Richardson. In 1694, he removed from the north of the Island to Moate Meeting in County West Meath.[3]   Thence in 1716[4] he came to New Garden, Pennsylvania.   Early in 1724 he paid a religious visit to New England.   He died at Darby, now Delaware County, 9 Mo. 4, 1725, "greatly beloved" says his intimate friend Thomas Chalkley,[5]

---

[1] Gilbert Cope, *Genealogy of the Smedley Family,* 194–6, *History of Chester County,* 637 ; *A Collection of Memorials,* 63–4 (Phila. 1787); *Bowden,* II., 260–1.

[2] *Besse,* I., 85.

[3] At Ulster Province Meeting, 5 Mo. 31, 1697, Thomas Lightfoot is mentioned as having the custody of £15 of meeting funds.

[4] *Proud,* II., 188.

[5] *Journal,* 163.

"for his Piety and Virtue, his sweet disposition and lively Ministry."

The name of his first wife is thought to have been Mary, after whose death he married Sarah Wiley, a widow, about the time of his removal to West Meath. Toward the close of 1724 he was married to Margaret, widow of John Blunston, of Darby, to which place he removed. He had at least nine children :

. 1. Catharine, m. 1700, James Miller, and arrived in Philadelphia in 1729, where she died a few days later.

2. Michael Lightfoot,[1] b. about 1683, m. in Ireland, Mary Newby, daughter of John Newby, of Dublin, and came to New Garden, Chester County, in 1712. He was appointed an elder in 1725, and recommended as a minister in 1728. He travelled extensively in religious service in America, Great Britain, and Ireland. In 1743, he removed to Philadelphia to take the post of Provincial Treasurer, an office he held until his death, 12 Mo. 3, 1754. His children were: Sarah, b. 4 Mo. 30, 1707, m. John Hutton ; Elinor, b. 10 Mo. 16, 1708, m. 3 Mo. 2, 1734, at New Garden, Francis Parvin ; Mary, b. 1 Mo. 20, 1710–11, m. Samuel Clarke ; Katharine, b. 6 Mo. 12, 1714 ; Thomas, b. 5 Mo. 16, 1716 ; William, b. 3 Mo. 22, 1720, m. Jane George.

3. William Lightfoot, m. 2 Mo. 24, 1706, Isabel Holmes, of Lahinchey, King's County, Ireland. He made a visit to his relatives in Pennsylvania, in 1725.

4. Abigail, m. Joseph Wiley, in Ireland, in 1715, and came to Pennsylvania with her father. Children : Sarah, b. 11 Mo. 6, 1716 ; Ann, b. 9 Mo. 6, 1718 ; John, b. 11 Mo. 19, 1721.

5. Elizabeth, b. 1 Mo. 11, 1695–6, at Bally Kieran, County West Meath, m. 2 Mo. 1717, Arthur Jones, of Merion Meeting, Penna.

6. Sarah, b. 5 Mo. 29, 1698 ; d. 1702.

7. Samuel Lightfoot, b. 2 Mo. 5, 1701, m. 7 Mo. 30, 1725, at New Garden Meeting, Chester County, to Mary, daughter of Benjamin and Sarah (Abbott) Head, and afterwards settled in Pikeland Township, Chester County. He was a prominent surveyor and Justice of the Peace ; d. near Chester, 2 Mo. 26, 1777. Children : Benjamin, b. 6 Mo. 28, 1726, also a surveyor ; Thomas, b. 2 Mo. 7, 1728, d. 10 Mo. 5, 1793 ; Samuel Abbott, b. 1 Mo. 7, 1729–30, d. 7 Mo. 30, 1759, at Pittsburgh ; William, b. 1 Mo. 20, 1732, d. 11 Mo. 25, 1797.

8. Margaret, b. 12 Mo. 18, 1702 ; m. 12 Mo. 20, 1723, Isaac Starr, of New Garden.

[1] Cope, *Genealogy of Smedley Family,* 195 ; *Proud,* II., 232 ; *Bowden,* II., 387.

9. Jacob Lightfoot, b. 10 Mo. 16, 1706, at Bally Kieran, near Athlone, Ireland; m. 3 Mo. 21, 1735, at Darby Meeting, Mary, daughter of Obadiah and Sarah (Bethel) Bonsall, of that place. He took a certificate from New Garden to Chester, in 1733, and removed thence, about 1735, to Maiden Creek, Berks County, where he died 6 Mo. 17, 1781. His wife, who was a minister among Friends, died at Maiden Creek, 8 Mo. 10, 1777. Children: Joseph, b. 6 Mo. 30, 1736, d. 9 Mo. 27, 1784, m. Deborah, daughter of Nehemiah Hutton; Sarah, b. 10 Mo. 28, 1738, d. 7 Mo., 1775, m. Francis Parvin, 5 Mo. 16, 1759; Thomas, b. 7 Mo. 21, 1742, d. 12 Mo. 24, 1821, m. Hannah Wright, 5 Mo. 11, 1774; Ann, b. 1 Mo. 3, 1745, d. 4 Mo. 17, 1807; Grace, b. 7 Mo. 17, 1748, d. 9 Mo. 11, 1784, m. William Tomlinson, 5 Mo. 12, 1773.

JOSEPH WILEY, son-in-law of Thomas Lightfoot, Moate Meeting, County West Meath, received 6 Mo. 4, 1716.

SIMON HADLEY, and wife Ruth from Moate Meeting, County West Meath, received 6 Mo. 4, 1716.

They came from Ireland about 1712, and settled in New Castle County, near the New Garden line. A house which he erected in 1717 was still standing in 1881. Children: Joseph, b. 8 Mo. 25, 1698; Deborah, b. 2 Mo. 25, 1701; Joshua, b. 3 Mo. 6, 1703; Simon, b. 12 Mo. 23, 1704-5; d. 11 Mo. 4, 1730-1; Hannah, b. 11 Mo. 16, 1709-10; Ruth, b. 12 Mo. 6, 1711-2; Katharine, b. 2 Mo. 25, 1715; Ann, b. 12 Mo. 7, 1717-18. The mother died 12 Mo. 18, 1750-1, and was buried at New Garden, after which Simon married Phebe, widow of Richard Buffington, of Bradford, Chester County. (*Hist. Chester County*, 576.)

JOHN STARR, received 8 Mo. 5, 1717, from Old Castle Monthly Meeting, County Meath, Ireland.

THOMAS JACKSON, received 10 Mo. 7, 1717, from Old Castle Monthly Meeting, County Meath, Ireland.

Thomas Jackson, of Old Castle, County East Meath, linen-draper, by deed of Jan. 19, 1715, purchased from Ebenezer Pike, of Cork, merchant, land in Pennsylvania (Phila. Deeds, F. 7, p. 326). By first wife he had four children : Ruth, who married Joseph Martin, Isaac, Samuel, and Benjamin. He came to Pennsylvania about 1717, and was married a second time, 10 Mo. 25, 1718, at New Garden Meeting, to Mary Wiley, of New Garden, probably a step-daughter of Thomas Lightfoot. He died in East Marlborough, in 1727.

At New Garden Monthly Meeting, 7 Mo. 28, 1728, "Mary Jackson acquainted this Meeting that she intended to go to Ireland to Visit her Relations and Requested to have a Certificate." Her certificate was signed 8 Mo. 26, 1728.

Mary, widow of Thomas Jackson, of East Marlborough, made her will 8 Mo. 28, 1729, and it was probated Dec. 20, 1729. She states that she is now "at Sea aboard the *Sizargh*, of Whitehaven, Jeremiah Cowman, Master, Bound for Philadelphia, I now being Indisposed in Body." She mentions her sons-in-law, Samuel, Isaac, and Benjamin Jackson ; her brother, John Wiley, in Pennsylvania (to whom she leaves £40) ; and her daughter-in-law, Ruth Martin, in County Cavan, Ireland (to whom she bequeaths £20). Witnesses to the will were : James Miller, Lambert Emerson and Robert White. In the accounts of her estate is a record of "Cash Pd Nathan Cowman," £3.4.4.

JOSEPH MARTIN, and wife Ruth, received 10 Mo. 7, 1717, from Old Castle, County Meath, Ireland. At New Garden Montly Meeting, 8 Mo. 11, 1718, a certificate to Philadelphia was signed for them.

MOSES STARR, and wife Deborah, received 10 Mo. 7, 1717, from Old Castle, County Meath, Ireland.

JEREMIAH STARR, received 3 Mo. 3, 1718, from Carlow Meeting, Ireland.

SAMUEL KIRK, unmarried, received 12 Mo. 6, 1719, from Lurgan Meeting, County Armagh, Ireland.

WILLIAM WHITAKER, received 10 Mo. 2, 1721, from Dublin, Ireland.

EDWARD THORNBURY, received 9 Mo. 6, 1725, from Lurgan Meeting, County Armagh, Ireland.

THOMAS WILSON and family received 7 Mo. 3, 1726, from Ballynacree Meeting, County Antrim, Ireland.

GEORGE MARSH, son of Joshua, unmarried, received 7 Mo. 6, 1727, dated 5 Mo. 22, 1728, from Grange Monthly Meeting, near Charlemont, County Armagh, Ireland.

MIRIAM ANDREWS "produced a Certificate from Iurgan [Meeting, County Armagh] in the north of ierland," to the woman's branch of Newark Mo. Mtg., 7 Mo. 6, 1729.

As her husband, William Andrews, did not produce a certificate, it is presumed he was not a Friend. In his will,[1] dated 11 Mo. 23, 1747–48, probated March 25, 1748, he is mentioned as yeoman of Christiana Hundred, New Castle County, upon Delaware. He speaks of his "servant, James Nash, a man bought of George Robinson," and bequeaths his property to his wife Miriam and children, Ruth, Ezekiel, Hannah, and John. The Andrews were related in some way to the Hollingsworths ; for "At a meeting of the Commissioners of Property 8 b' 2 d 1731 * * * Samuel Hollingsworth (on behalf of his Kinsman Wm. Andrees) request the Grant of about 100 Acres of vac⁺ Land in Kennet, between the Land late Ezekiel Harlan's and James Wallis."

Miriam Andrews, of the Borough of Wilmington, widow of William Andrews, in her will, dated 6 Mo. 20, 1750, probated Sept. 5, 1750 (G. 1, p. 419), mentions her "cosin Jane Hartley wife of Thomas Heartly," her sons Ezekiel and John Andrews and daughters, Hannah West and Ruth Andrews, the latter to be placed as an apprentice with Elinor Robinson.

The children of William and Miriam, as shown by meeting records, were as follows :

1. Ezekiel, b. 11 Mo. 21, 1729 ; d. 3 Mo. 4, 1772 ; m. 5 Mo. 8, 1761, Rebecca Robinson. Their son, James Andrews, removed to Darby, now Delaware County, Pa., married Martha Bunting, and had a son James, who married Hannah Lloyd.

2. Hannah, b. 5 Mo. 14, 1732, m. 8 Mo. 19, 1749, Joseph West.

3. Ruth, b. 7 Mo. 23, 1734.

4. John, b. 6 Mo. 2, 1736, m. Sarah Ferris.

In 1671, Christian Anderson for tithe had taken by the "Priest of the Parish of Kilmore," County Armagh, wheat, barley, oats, maslin, and hay to the value of £4. 15s. 6d.—Stockdale, *A Great Cry of Oppression*, 4.

WILLIAM MACCOOL, received 7 Mo. 6, 1729, from Ballynacree, Antrim County, Ireland.

[1] Book G. 1, page 109, Register's Office, Wilmington, Del.

JOHN CLARK, son of Walter, received 7 Mo. 6, 1729, dated 3 Mo. 27, 1729, from Grange, County Antrim, Ireland.

SAMUEL CLARK, unmarried, son of Walter Clark, received 8 Mo. 4, 1729, dated 3 Mo. 27, 1729, from Grange, County Antrim, Ireland, where he was "born and bred." Original in possession of Gilbert Cope, West Chester Pa. Samuel Clark, of Marlborough, Chester County, Pa., son of Walter Clark, of Grange, County Antrim, Ireland, was married, 8 Mo. 6, 1727, at New Garden, to Mary, daughter of Michael Lightfoot.

JOHN CLARK, son of Walter Clark, received 4 Mo. 5, 1731, from Grange, County Antrim, Ireland, dated 3 Mo. 27, 1729. Original in possession of Gilbert Cope, of West Chester, Pa.

THOMAS CHRISTY, received 9 Mo. 4, 1735, from Ballyhagan Monthly Meeting, County Armagh, Ireland.

In 1675, in County Antrim, Alexander Christy, for tithe by "John Charlton, Tithmonger (being his Landlord) at the payment of his Rent, eight shillings, and would not receive the rest, unless he would give eight shillings more ; and because Alexander would not, for one pound of Rent due he took a Cow from him worth one pound ten shillings."—*Stockdale*, 49.

SAMUEL CLARK, unmarried, dated 4 Mo. 26, 1735, from Lisburn Meeting, County Antrim, Ireland, formerly of Grange, County Antrim, "having for some time past dwelt at Hillsborough which is a branch of our Meeting." Original in possession of Gilbert Cope, West Chester, Pa.

MARY VARMAN (a young woman), daughter of Hattill Varman, dated 1 Mo. 8, 1729–30, from Monthly Meeting at Cooladine, probably in County of Wexford, Ireland.

OLIVIA McCOOL, "ye Bearer Widow & Relict, to John McCool Deceased," dated 2 Mo. 7, 1729, from Ballynacree Meeting, County Antrim, Ireland. Original in possession of Gilbert Cope, West Chester, Pa. The McCools apparently removed to Kent County, Maryland.

ELIZABETH CLARK, unmarried, daughter of Walter Clark, received 1 Mo. 6, 1735–36, dated 3 Mo. 10, 1735, from

Antrim Meeting, Ireland, endorsed, 4 Mo. 26, 1735, by Six Week's Meeting in Lisburn, County Antrim, Ireland. She "was born and Educated at Grange within the Limmits of this Mens Meeting, and her parents were friends in Unity with us, (whose memory is dear unto many of us)." Her father died a "Good Many Years agoe, & Some more than three Years Since her Mother also Dyed, on which account she found it Nessasery to Remove from Grange to some of her Relations at Dublin and Hillsborough after her mother's death." "She dwelt for Some Years past at Hillsborough as within mentioned." Original MS. in possession of Gilbert Cope, of West Chester, Pa. She married Benjamin Jackson, in 1736.

About 1655, "a Meeting was settled at the Grange, below Antrim (Co. Antrim), at the house of Gabriel Clark, an honest, religious, antient man, who received Truth as also his Wife and Family."—*Rutty*, p. 91. Gilbert Cope, of West Chester, Pa., has a very full and interesting manuscript account of Gabriel Clark and family.

At Ulster Province Meeting, 2 Mo. 14, 1705, it was stated that "Walter Clark hath built a meeting house at Grange for y⁰ Service of truth and use of friends." In his will, dated 5 Mo. 7, 1705, James Greenwood mentions his brother-in-law, Walter Clark. Nathaniel Clark and Elizabeth Greenwood, both of Grange Mtg., Co. Antrim, were married there, 10 Mo. 22, 1701.—*Minutes of Ulster Province Meeting*.

At Ulster Province Meeting, 2 Mo. 14, 1705, report was made that "Walter Clark hath built a meeting house at Grange for y⁰ Service of truth & use of friends." In 1716, Thomas Story (*Journal*, 537) mentions that he came to "Grange to Walter Clark's."

MABEL ANDERSON, unmarried, received 1 Mo. 4, 1737–8; dated 3 Mo. 12, 1737, from Ballyhagan, County Armagh, Ireland; "with ye Consent of her Mother and Relations Consent." She goes "in company with her uncle William." Original certificate in possession of Gilbert Cope, West Chester, Pa. She was married, about 1740, by a "priest" to Robert Halliday, of New Garden, who was not a Friend.

MARY VARMAN, unmarried, from Ireland, received 4 Mo. 24, 1732.

SARAH PRINGLE, from Ballyhagen Meeting, Ireland, received
11 Mo. 4, 1734–5.

ROBERT WHINERY, unmarried, from Grange, Ireland, received 5 Mo. 1, 1738.

Robert Whinery,[1] weaver, came from Grange, near Charlemont, about 1738. and seems to have settled at Wilmington, Delaware, his certificate from Grange being received at Newark or Kennett Monthly Meeting, 5 Mo. 1, 1738. About the latter part of 1740, he was married by a Presbyterian minister to Isabel ———, who was not a Friend. Wilmington Preparative Meeting made report of this infraction of the Society's rules to Newark Monthly Meeting, 1 Mo. 7, 1740–1. After some delay Whinery was induced to make the following acceptable acknowledgment, which was read in a First-day Meeting at Wilmington :

"To the Monthly Meeting of Newark held at Kennett y⁹ 4th: of y⁹ 5th: Mo. 1741. Dear friends : These May inform you that Contrary to y⁹ principle of truth in my own heart as well as the Repeated & Continued Caution & Advice of my friends, I have accomplished my marriage out of y⁹ good order Established amongst them by a Presbyterian Minister which hath been cause of Sorrow to me ; Which act I hereby Condemn & take y⁹ blame to my self with desires of your Prayers for my future preservation in the way of Peace ; from your friend

"ROBERT WHINERY."

In 1749, Robert Whinery was assessed in Kennett Township, Chester, but about 1750, he removed with his family to York County, settling within the limits of Newberry Meeting, his certificate of removal from Newark, dated 7 Mo. 1, 1750, being received at Warrington Monthly Meeting, 10 Mo. 21, 1752. Robert Whinery's membership in the Society of Friends was discontinued in 1754.

[1] John and Elinor Whinery were present at a marriage at Ballyhagen Meeting, in 1702, and Matthew Whinery was at a marriage at the same place, in 1703.

Thomas Whinnery and Katharine Smith, both of Parish of Kilmore, County Armaugh, members of Ballyhagen Meeting, were married at Ballyhagen Meeting House, 11 Mo. 23, 1706. Among the signers were THOMAS WHINNERY, KATHARINE WHINNERY, Mary Smith, Sr., Mary Smith, Rose Smith, Francis Hobson, John Smith, James Smith.

In 1749 and 1750, one Patrick Whinnery was licensed as a peddlar in Chester County, Pa. In his petition to the court he stated that he had been a weaver, but having broken a thigh had "fallen into a consumption." —*Hist. Chester County*, 432. He was assessed as a single freeman in Kennett Township in 1747 and 1749, and in East Marlborough Township, in 1750, 1753, and 1754.

By deed of May 19, 1771, Robert Whinery, of Newberry Township, York County, weaver, and Isabel, his wife, conveyed to their son Thomas a tract of 290 acres of land which had been granted to Robert by warrant of April 4, 1768 (*Recorder's Office, York, Pa*). In his will, dated Jan. 7, 1785, probated Sept. 23, 1791, Robert Whinery mentions his children, Hannah McCreary, Thomas, William, and Catharine Whinery, and grandchild Sarah McCreary.

I. Hannah Whinery, m. ———— McCreary. Child, Sarah.

II. Thomas Whinery, of Newberry Township, m. 12 Mo. 18, 1771, at Newberry Meeting, Phebe, daughter of Robert Mills, of same place. Among those who signed the marriage certificate were Robert, Isabel, Ann, and William Whinery, Robert and Mary Mills. Children were: Thomas, b. 10 Mo. 5, 1779, m., about 1807, Ruth Miller, who was not a Friend. (She and her daughter Phebe, b. 1808, were received as members of Warrington Monthly Meeting, in 1808. This family removed to Warren County, Ohio, in 1809, taking a certificate of removal to Centre Monthly Meeting.)

III. William Whinery, of Newberry Township, York County, m. about 1776, Abigail McMillan, daughter of John and Jane (Boyd) McMillan. In 1791, William Whinery and his six children—Robert, John, Thomas, William, James, and Jane—were received as members of Warrington Monthly Meeting. About 1806, this family removed to Columbiana County, Ohio, and made a location in Butler Township, near the present town of Winona, a certificate of removal to Salem Monthly Meeting, Ohio, being signed by Warrington Monthly Meeting, 1 Mo. 11, 1806. Children were: Robert, m. 10 Mo. 14, 1801, at Newberry Meeting, Phebe, daughter of Thomas and Phebe (Penrose) Leech (they removed westward about 1803 and settled near Winona); John received a certificate to Middleton Monthly Meeting, Ohio, in 1804, and settled near Salem, Columbiana County; Thomas, m. 9 Mo. 12, 1805, Lydia, daughter of Jediah and Jane (Penrose) Hussey (removed to near Salem, Ohio, about 1806); William, m. Margery Carroll; James, b. 3 Mo. 10, 1787, m. Sarah Carroll in Ohio (children, b. near Salem, Ohio, were Elizabeth, William, Joseph, Zimri, Dr. John C., Thomas, James, Edward, Eliza, Abigail, Ellwood, Newton, Sarah, and Isabel); George; Jane, m. David Burson; Zimri, m. Judith Wright; Sarah, m. David Comley; Abigail. m. Benjamin Pettit.

IV. Catharine Whinery.

NEW GARDEN MONTHLY MEETING

In Chester County.   Established in 1718, from Newark or Kennett.

SAMUEL BEVERLY and wife Jennet, received 12 Mo. 9, 1722–3, from Ballynacree Monthly Meeting, Ireland.

"Samuel Beverly and Jannett Hunter, both of Ballymony meeting," were married "at James Moors, ye 19th $\frac{11}{mo.}$ 1703/4 as by certificate may appear." (*Minutes Ulster Province Meeting.*) They settled in East Marlborough, Chester County, and were accompanied by two children, William and Mary.   William married Mary Miller in 1730, and dying before his father, left a son Samuel, who in 1753 married Ruth Jackson, daughter of Samuel Jackson, East Marlborough Twp., Chester Co.   Mary Beverly, daughter of Samuel and Ruth, became the wife of William Gause and the mother of Jonathan Gause, principal of the celebrated Unionville (Chester Co.) Academy, which was attended by Bayard Taylor, the distinguished author and traveller.—*Hist. Chester Co.*, p. 481.

JOHN HUTTON, received 9 Mo. 9, 1723, from Dublin, Ireland.   See Joseph Hutton, pp. 330–2.

SAMUEL MILLER and wife Margaret (b. 1683), received 10 Mo. 14, 1723, from Ballynacree Monthly Meeting, County Antrim, Ireland.

They settled at Sadsbury, and were among the organizers of Sadsbury Meeting.   He died in 1774.   Children : Mary, m. William Cooper, 8 Mo. 18, 1730, and had children (Robert, Calvin, and William) ; Elizabeth m. William Reed, 8 Mo. 19, 1738 ; Robert, m. Sarah McClung, 1 Mo. 7, 1741–2, and had children (Margaret, b. 1742 ; Samuel, b. 1744 ; Mary, b. 1747 ; Sarah, b. 1749 ; Robert, b. 1755).—Potts, *Our Family Ancestors*, 247–8.

One Samuel Miller and Jane Wyly, both of Lisnegarvy Meeting, were married at the home of Richard Boys (Ballinderry, County Antrim) 9 Mo. 21, 1698.

ELI CROCKET, unmarried, received 12 Mo. 8, 1723–4, from Ballynacree Meeting, County Antrim, Ireland.   He and John Crocket had arrived as early as 1722.   On 6 Mo. 8, 1724, Eli was made overseer of Bush River Meeting, in Maryland.

One Eli Crocket and Elizabeth Wilkison, both of Ballymoney Meeting, were married 11 Mo. 4, 1715, at the house of James Moore.—Minutes of Ulster Prov. Mtg.

In 1676, Gilbert Crockett, of Bellirushane Parish, County Antrim, suffered persecution for tithes.—*Stockdale*, 75.

In 1681, Gilbert and Eli Crockett, of Parish of Bellyrashean, County Antrim, had goods seized for tithes.—*Ibid.*, 166.

Eli Crockett, of Ballymoney, was on a committee of Ulster Province Meeting, in 1695.

ANDREW MOORE, received 6 Mo. 8, 1724, from Ballynacree Meeting, County Antrim, Ireland.

"Andrew Moore[1] and Margaret Wilson, both of Dunclady Meeting," were married "att yᵉ house of Kathrine Henderson in Dunclady [County Antrim] yᵉ 27ᵗʰ day of yᵉ $\frac{2}{Mo.}$ 1715 as by yᵉ certificate may appear." (*Minutes of Ulster Province Meeting, Ireland.*)

Andrew Moore, according to his biographer and descendant, Dr. Passmore, was born 6 Mo., 1688, in County Antrim, and was a son of James Moore, of Ballynacree, County Antrim. His wife Margaret died probably about 1722 or 1723, shortly before his emigration. He and his family arrived at New Castle on Delaware, 8 Mo. 3, 1723, and settled on a tract of land lying in Sadsbury Township, Chester and Lancaster Counties. Here he engaged in milling and farming and was an active and influential member of Sadsbury Meeting. He was married a second time, 4 Mo. 24, 1725, to Rachel, daughter of William Halliday, another Irish Friend. He died 7 Mo. 5, 1753, and was interred in Friends' burial ground, at Sadsbury Meeting House. Children were as follows :

1. James, b. 3 Mo. 6, 1716, came to Pennsylvania with his father in 1723 ; m., 1st, 2 Mo. 16, 1741, at New Garden Meeting, Ann, daughter of Jeremiah and Rebecca (Jackson) Starr ; m. 2d Mary, daughter of Joseph Wildman, of Bucks County ; m. 3d Ann, daughter of Caleb Jackson ; m. 4th Ann, daughter of John Minshal. He died 8 Mo. 1, 1809.

2. Mary, b. in 1718, m. 1st in 1742, William Carson, and resided for a time in Menallen Township, now Adams County ; m. 2d James Hamel, of Tyrone Township, now Adams County.

[1] In 1897, Dr. John A. M. Passmore, of Philadelphia, issued an elaborate and carefully prepared genealogy of *Andrew Moore and his Descendants*, in two large octavo volumes of 1600 pages. In the light of the above marriage record it would seem that he had come to a wrong conclusion in stating, on page 7, that Andrew Moore had married Margaret, daughter of Gayen and Margaret (Henderson) Miller.

3. Margaret, b. in 1719, m. Alexander Love. After living some years in York County they removed to near the present town of Yorkville, South Carolina, where Alexander became a prominent citizen, serving as a member of the Provincial Congress of S. C.

4. Thomas, b. 1722, d. 8 Mo. 12, 1728.

5. William, b. 10 Mo. 27, 1726; m. 5 Mo. 20, 1749, at Sadsbury, Rachel, daughter of William Marsh.

6. Robert, b. 9 Mo. 1, 1728; d. 3 Mo. 25, 1732.

7. David, b. in 1731; d. 5 Mo. 20, 1744.

8. Andrew, b. 12 Mo. 1, 1733; m. 9 Mo. 26, 1754, at Sadsbury, Rebecca, daughter of Jeremiah and Rebecca (Starr) Jackson. He died 5 Mo., 1801.

9. Joseph, b. 7 Mo. 13, 1736; m. 1 Mo. 22, 1756, at Sadsbury Meeting, Jane, daughter of Henry Marsh. He died 7 Mo. 13, 1805.

10. Robert, b. 10 Mo. 22, 1739, m. 11 Mo. 10, 1768, at Sadsbury, Mary, daughter of Moses Brinton; d. 2 Mo. 9, 1826.

11. John, b. 10 Mo. 3, 1742; m. 5 Mo. 1, 1765, to Sarah, daughter of William Downing, d. 6 Mo. 28, 1821.

12. David, b. 10 Mo. 13, 1745; m. 10 Mo. 5, 1768, at Sadsbury, Martha, daughter of Joseph Williams; d. 1 Mo. 16, 1829.

13. Rachel, b. 3 Mo. 12, 1742; m. 11 Mo. 12, 1761, at Sadsbury, John, son of Thomas Truman; d. 7 Mo. 1, 1828.

14. Sarah, m. 11 Mo. 1, 1769, at Sadsbury, William Truman, son of Thomas. (*Moore Genealogy.*)

WILLIAM LIGHTFOOT, received 8 Mo. 9, 1725, from Moate Monthly Meeting, County West Meath, Ireland, to "visit his father & relations." A certificate for him to return to Ireland was signed 10 Mo. 11, 1725.

ISAAC JACKSON and wife, received 9 Mo. 10, 1725, dated 1 Mo. 28, 1725, from Carlow Monthly Meeting, County Carlow, Ireland.

Anthony Jackson, born at Eccleston, Parish of St. Michael, Lancashire, England, removed, in 1649, with his elder brother, Richard Jackson, sometime soldier in the Parliamentary Army, and settled at Lurgan, County Armagh, Ireland. Here they were among the first converts to Quakerism in Ireland. In 1655 they removed to Cavan, where Anthony probably resided the remainder of his life. In 1670, and as late as 1681, he is mentioned in Besse as suffering persecution and imprisonment for non-payment of tithes.

Isaac Jackson (1665–1750), son of Anthony, was married 2

Mo. 29, 1696, at Oldcastle Mtg., Co. Meath, to Ann Evans, daughter of Rowland Evans, of Balliloing, Co. Wicklow. After residing for some years at Oldcastle and Clonerany, Co. Wexford, they removed, about 1706–07, to Ballytore, Co. Kildare. From here they removed to Pennsylvania, taking passage at Dublin on the *Sizargh*, and reached New Castle, on Delaware, 9 Mo. 11, 1725. They proceeded at once from New Castle to the home of a son-in-law, Jeremiah Starr, who had married a daughter, Rebecca Jackson, at Ballytore, 11 Mo. 10, 1716, and had settled in London Grove Twp., Chester Co. An extended record of the descendants of Isaac Jackson's ten children will be found in Halliday Jackson's *Jackson Family* and in *History of Chester County*, p. 610.

Sismore Wright and wife, received 9 Mo. 10, 1725, from Ballycane Monthly Meeting, County Wicklow, Ireland.

Children of Sismore and Margaret Wright, born in Ireland, as follows : Isaac, 12 Mo. 4, 1718 ; Thomas, 5 Mo. 11, 1719 (d. 3 Mo. 29, 1802, in Berks County) ; Margaret, 10 Mo. 18, 1720 ; Ann, 4 Mo. 21, 1723. New Garden Monthly Meeting, 2 Mo. 26, 1735, signed a certificate for this family to North Wales (Gwynedd) Monthly Meeting, and they settled within the limits of Exeter Meeting, in Berks County.

One Mark Wright, son of Rowland Wright, of "Sheep Pastor, (nere) Gisborough," Yorkshire, England, and wife, "Ayles," was born 2 Mo. 25, 1619, at "Sheep Pastor." About 1647, "he married Ann, daughter of Thomas Carlyle, "of Newton (nere Whittby)," England. Came to Ireland 6 Mo., 1654. Children : Jane, b. 9 Mo. 1651, at Numebeck, Yorkshire ; Ayles, b. 4 Mo. 1653, at same place ; John, b. 3 Mo. 1656, at Lygatory, Parish of Shankill, Co. Armagh ; Ann, b. there 8 Mo., 1658 ; Mark, b. there 4 Mo., 1660 ; Jane, b. there 1662.—*Lurgan Records.*

Jonathan Garnett and wife Mary, received 10 Mo. 30, 1727, from Grange Monthly Meeting, near Charlemont, County Armagh, Ireland.

Thomas Valentine, received 2 Mo. 27, 1728, from Carlow Monthly Meeting, Ireland.

Thomas Valentine, of Ballybrumhill, County Carlow, Ireland, son of George Valentine,[1] of same place, was married, 9 Mo. 22, 1715, at Kilconner, to Mary Parke, of Ballylean, daughter of

[1] In 1677, in County Wexford, George Valentine had his goods seized for tithes.—*Stockdale*, 89.

Thomas and Rebecca Parke, of same place (*Records of Carlow Monthly Meeting*). They made their first settlement after their arrival in this country in New Garden Township, Chester County, where in 1729 and 1730 Thomas was assessed. A little later they removed to New Providence now Montgomery County, where he died about 1747, leaving children, Robert, John, Thomas, Jonathan, and perhaps others.

Robert Valentine,[1] son of Thomas, b. 7 Mo. 21, 1717, at Ballybrumhill; d. East Caln, 7 Mo. 21, 1786; m. 4 Mo. 4, 1747, at Caln Meeting, Rachel, daughter of John and Mary Edge. She was b. 6 Mo. 29, 1725; d. 1 Mo. 31, 1779. They were both buried in Friends' ground at Uwchlan, Chester County. Children were: Thomas, Mary, Robert [2] (m. Ann Bond), Rachel (m. Joseph Malin), Jane, Sarah, Phebe (m. Abraham Sharpless), George (m. Phebe Ashbridge), John, Susanna (m. George Massey). Robert Valentine became an eminent minister of Friends and travelled extensively in that service, including a visit to Great Britain at the close of the Revolution.

Thomas Valentine, son of Thomas, m. Nov. 23, 1750, his cousin Rebecca Robinson and d. 1762, in Charlestown Township, Chester County, leaving children, Thomas, William, Mary, Rachel, and John.

Jonathan Valentine, son of Thomas, b. about 1730; m. in 1755 or 1756, Lydia, daughter of John and Lydia (Pusey) Baldwin. They settled in East Caln, where Jonathan died about 1811. Children: Absalom, Jehu, John, Jonathan, Elizabeth, Mary, Lydia (m. Jesse Evans) and Thomas.[3]

FRANCIS PARVIN, received 6 Mo. 31, 1728, from Moate Monthly Meeting, County West Meath.

Francis Parvin[4] (whose ancestors according to tradition removed from Yorkshire to Ireland) of Ballykilroe, County West Meath, was married, 12 Mo. (Feb.) 16, 1723-4, at Edenderry Meeting, King's County, to Deborah Pearson, of Drighen, County Kildare.[5] About 1728 they came to Pennsylvania, the wife dying shortly after the arrival. He settled for a short time in New Garden, and then about 1732 removed to Chester. On 3 Mo. 2,

[1] Some of this branch of the family removed to Bellefonte, Centre Co., Pa., and were largely interested in iron manufacture.
[2] For a full record see *Smedley Genealogy*.
[3] *History of Chester County*, 750-51.
[4] Francis Parvin was a Justice of the Peace and also represented Berks County in the Provincial Assembly.
[5] Marriage certificate in possession of a descendant, Jeremiah Starr Parvin, Leesport, Berks County, Pa.

1734, he was married at New Garden, to Eleanor, daughter of Michael Lightfoot, of New Garden, and removed about this time to Maiden Creek, Berks County, where he died 7 Mo. 6, 1767, and his wife Eleanor, 12 Mo. 17, 1775.

In his will dated 6 Mo. 20, 1767 (probated Sept. 3, 1767), he provides for his wife Eleanor ; leaves to his son Francis a tract of 120 acres of land, including "my dwelling house with Tanyard"; to son Thomas Parvin, 143 acres in Maiden Creek ; to sons Benjamin and John 143 acres each, in Maiden Creek ; to son William "My Grist & saw mill" and about 136 acres in same township ; remainder to be equally divided among son Pearson Parvin and daughters Mary Pearson, Ann Wright, and Eleanor Parvin.

Children of Francis Parvin : [1]

I. Thomas Parvin, m. 4 Mo. 17, 1754, at Goshen Meeting, Chester County, Mary, daughter of Isaac Starr, of Goshen.

II. Francis Parvin, Jr., son of Francis, by his first wife Deborah, m. 5 Mo. 16, 1759, at Maiden Creek Meeting, Berks County, Sarah, daughter of Jacob and Mary Lightfoot, of Maiden Creek. She died 7 Mo. 1775, and he m. secondly, Susanna ——— (d. 10 Mo. 23, 1808). He made a visit to Ireland, 1752–1754. Children by first wife : Deborah, b. 4 Mo. 23, 1760 ; Mary, b. 7 Mo. 11, 1762 ; Hannah, b. 9 Mo. 10, 1764, d. 3 Mo. 1, 1769 ; Sarah, b. 10 Mo. 4, 1766 ; Francis, b. 2 Mo. 27, 1769 ; Hannah, b. 10 Mo. 21, 1771, d. 8 Mo. 18, 1790 ; Jacob, b. 7 Mo. 10, 1775, d. 12 Mo. 14, 1813. Children by second wife : Thomas, b. 10 Mo. 10, 1782, d. 6 Mo. 30, 1799 ; Susanna, b. 1 Mo. 29, 1785 ; d. 3 Mo. 1, 1870 ; Elizabeth, b. 10 Mo. 9, 1786 ; d. 12 Mo. 26, 1787 ; Elizabeth, b. 12 Mo. 8, 1788 ; d. 10 Mo. 3, 1861.

III. Pearson Parvin, b. 12 Mo. 3, 1734–5.

IV. Mary Parvin, b. 3 Mo. 19, 1736 ; m. Benjamin Pearson, 1752.

V. John Parvin, b. 2 Mo. 8, 1738 ; m. Mary, daughter of Lawrence and Edith Pearson, 5 Mo. 4, 1768, at Maiden Creek Meeting.

VI. William Parvin, of Maiden Creek, m. 7 Mo. 17, 1765, at Maiden Creek Meeting, Mary, daughter of Merrick and Phebe Starr.

VII. Ann Parvin, b. 9 Mo. 3, 1742 ; m. Benjamin Wright, 1766.

VIII. Eleanor Parvin, b. 8 Mo. 2, 1746 ; m. Isaac Wright, 1768.
—Records of Exeter Monthly Meeting.

THOMAS PARVIN, unmarried, received 6 Mo. 13, 1728, from Moate Monthly Meeting, County West Meath, Ireland.

[1] In 1680, in County West Meath, one "Francis Pervin of Bellykilroe in the Barony of Clonlonnon," had four lambs, valued at 8 s., seized for tithes. *—Stockdale*, 153.

LAWRENCE RICHARDSON, unmarried, received 6 Mo. 31, 1728, from Grange Meeting, Ireland.

HATTILL VARMAN and wife Abigail, from Cooladine Meeting, County Wexford, dated 2 Mo. 28, 1728, received 3 Mo. 31, 1729.

In 1672, one "Henry Vernam, for 20 s. demanded of him for Tithes, was prosecuted in the Ecclesiastical Court, and committed to Wexford Goal, at the Suit of Miles Swinney, Priest of Encyscorf, was kept prisoner there about a year and nine months, till the 6th of October 1673, and then released by the Bishop of Loughlin and Fernes, but before his discharge the Priest had sent his Servants with Cart and Horses, who took away more than half the Man's Corn to the Value of 5 l."—Besse's *Suffering of the Quakers*, II., 480 ; Stockdale, *A Great Cry of Oppression*, 10.

In 1685, Henry and Edward Varman, of Parish of Castle Ellis, County Wexford, by their attorney, John Fuller, of West Jersey. conveyed to John Hugg, of West Jersey, a tract of land in the Irish Tenth of West Jersey, that had been granted to Henry Varman, April 9, 1682, by Joseph Sleight, of Dublin.[1]

Hattill Varman,[2] b. 1670, in County Wexford, Ireland ; d. 12 Mo. 27, 1747 ; buried at Leacock ; came to Pennsylvania in 1728, and settled in Leacock Township, Lancaster County. His wife, Abigail, d. 3 Mo. 14, 1760. Children : Mary, m. 10 Mo. 7, 1733, at Leacock, John Beeson, of Leacock, son of Richard ; William ; Grace, m. 1st 11 Mo. 5, 1742, at Leacock, to Joseph Edgerton, of Newton, Gloucester Co., N. J. (child Abigail) ; 2d Joseph Steer ; Eleanor, m. 3 Mo. 5, 1747, at Leacock, Moses Brinton, son of Joseph ; Sarah, m. 1st John Low, and 2d 7 Mo. 11, 1751, at Lampeter, John Parks, son of Richard, of Goshen.

THOMAS McCLUN, and wife Elizabeth, from Moate Monthly Meeting, County West Meath, dated 3 Mo. 11, 1729, received 6 Mo. 30, 1729.

Thomas Clung and Elizabeth Hainan, both of Rathfryland Meeting, were married, 6 Mo. 19, 1714, at the house of Robert Wilson. (*Minutes of Ulster Province Meeting.*)

At New Garden Monthly Meeting, 5 Mo. 29, 1729, Thomas McClun and family is reported as being settled within the limits of Concord Monthly Meeting, to which a certificate was signed 1 Mo. 28, 1730.

---

[1] D, p. 246, *Clement Papers*, Hist. Soc. of Penna.
[2] *Friends' Miscellany*, IV., 25.

23

JOHN STEER, received 6 Mo. 30, 1729, dated 2 Mo. 11, 1728, from Ballinderry Meeting, County Antrim, Ireland.

SAMUEL MORTON, received 6 Mo. 30, 1729, dated 7 Mo. 1, 1728, from Ballyhagen Meeting, County Armagh, Ireland.

Samuel Morton (d. 3 Mo. 20, 1766), son of William and Elinor, was born in Parish of Kilmore, County Armagh, Ireland; m. 2 Mo. 6, 1728, at Ballyhagen Meeting, Eliza (d. 6 Mo. 12, 1763), daughter of John and Mary Blackburn, a native of County Armagh. Children: Margaret, b. 10 Mo. 1, 1728, at sea; m. John Hadley; John, b. 4 Mo. 28, 1729, d. 9 Mo., 1741, buried at London̄ Grove; Samuel, b. 7 Mo. 27, 1732; William b. 1 Mo. 9, 1734-35; Mary, b. 9 Mo. 9, 1737; Thomas, b. 7 Mo. 6, 1740.— *Records of New Garden Monthly Meeting.*

WILLIAM MCNABB, wife Dorothy and daughters, Elizabeth and Jane, received 6 Mo. 30, 1729, dated 1 Mo. 5, 1729, from Old Castle Monthly Meeting, County Meath, Ireland.

William McNabb settled in East Lampeter Township, Lancaster County, where he owned a farm of 200 acres. His son, John McNabb, in 1749, gave two acres of land to Friends' Meeting at Bird-in-Hand.

JOSEPH EVANS, wife Mary, and son Joseph, received 8 Mo. 25, 1729, from Moate Monthly Meeting, County West Meath, Ireland.

NEAL O'MONEY, wife Ann, received 8 Mo. 23, 1729, from Ballynacree Meeting, County Antrim, Ireland.

Neal Mooney, of East Marlborough, Chester County, made his will 9 Mo. 9, 1751, and it was probated Nov. 26, 1751. Mentions wife Ann, children Samuel, Joseph, James, and son-in-law, Henry Neal.

SAMUEL SHAW, received 8 Mo. 25, 1729, from Lisburn Meeting, County Antrim, Ireland.

In 1679, Martha Shaw, widow, and James Shaw, both of the Parish of Loughgall, County Armagh, had some of their effects taken for tithes.—Stockdale, *A Great Cry of Oppression,* 125.

JAMES TAYLOR, and wife, received 10 Mo. 27, 1729, from Ballynacree Monthly Meeting, County Antrim, Ireland.

JAMES O'MONEY, received 8 Mo. 25, 1729, from Ballynacree Meeting, County Antrim, Ireland.

SAMUEL EVANS and wife, from Moate Meeting, County West Meath, Ireland, received 10 Mo. 27, 1729.

JACOB KIRK, from meeting near Ballinderry, County Antrim, Ireland, received 11 Mo. 31, 1729.

THOMAS MILHOUS, and wife Sarah, from Dublin, Ireland, dated 5 Mo. 29, 1729, received 12 Mo. 28, 1729.

Thomas Milhous[1] m. Sarah, daughter James and Catharine (Lightfoot) Miller, in Ireland, and came to Pennsylvania in 1729, settling first within the limits of New Garden Monthly Meeting, and about the year 1744 removing to Pikeland Township, Chester County. Their children were: John, b. 1 Mo. 8, 1722–3, at Timahoe, Ireland; James, b. 7 Mo. 21, 1727; Thomas, b. 2 Mo. 27, 1731; Robert, b. 11 Mo. 26, 1733; Sarah, b. 4 Mo. 3, 1736, m. Thompson Parker; William, b. 6 Mo. 12, 1738 (*Hist. of Chester County*, 658).

At Ulster Province Meeting, 12 Mo. 1, 1695, one John Millhouse and Sarah Miller declared their intentions of marriage. 3 Mo. 25, 1695, Richard Millhouse and Sarah Clark declared their intentions of marriage.

JOHN GRIFFITH,[2] and son Christopher (unmarried), from Grange near Charlemont, received 12 Mo. 28, 1729, dated 2 Mo. 18, 1729. Christopher Griffith, of Sadsbury Meeting, produced an acknowledgement, 9 Mo. 30, 1734, for marriage out of the Society.

Thomas Griffith, who may have been a son of John Griffith, was married out of the Society about 1742, to Eve ———. He removed to Menallen Twp., now Adams County, and died in the spring of 1769; was buried in Friends' burial ground at Old Menallen, where his gravestone bearing the inscription "T. G. 1769" may still be seen. Children: Mary, b. about 1751, Rebecca, b. about 1755; Eve; Thomas; Ann; Jesse; Wm., eldest son; Elizabeth m. Thomas Blackburn; John, Susanna. (Records of Orphans' Court of York County, Docket B, 223, 224.)

ANN MARSHALL, widow of New Garden, "late from Ireland," made her will 9 Mo. 30, 1729, and it was probated Feb. 10, 1729–30.

[1] Thomas Milhouse and Mary Hoope, of Lurgan, were married at Lurgan Meeting, Nov. 2, 1720.

[2] Thomas Griffith and Elizabeth Ford, both of Grange Meeting near Charlemont, were married at Grange, 9 Mo. 16, 1715 (*Minutes Ulster Province Meeting*).

She mentions her sons John and William Marshall, her friends William Halliday and Benjamin Fred, of New Garden, and desires to be buried in the Friends' ground at New Garden. Witnesses were John Griffith, Sismore Wright, and William Read. The names of her father, John Griffith, and her brother, Christopher Griffith, appear in the accounts of the estate.

Jacob Marshall and Ann Griffith, both of Grange near Charlemont, were married at Grange Meeting, 9 Mo. 19, 1718.—*Minutes of Ulster Province Meeting.*

Margaret Marshall, wife of Jacob, of Grange near Charlemont, d. 1 Mo. 23, 1739. Jacob d. 5 Mo. 1, 1743.

JOHN MARSHILL, son of Jacob Marshill, Jr., deceased, from Grange Meeting, near Charlemont, Ireland. He settled in New Garden and was married 8 Mo. 14, 1742, at New Garden, to Ruth Hadly, daughter of Joshua Hadly, of Mill Creek Hundred, New Castle County on Delaware. Among signers to marriage certificate were John and Christopher Griffith, Jacob and Rebecca Hinshaw, and William Marshill. A certificate for him and his wife to Concord Monthly Meeting, signed by New Garden, 3 Mo. 28, 1743.

SAMUEL STANFIELD, and wife Jane, from Lurgan, County Armagh, received 1 Mo. 28, 1730, dated 3 Mo. 7, 1729.

Samuel Stanfield and Jane Andrew, both of Lurgan Meeting, were married at Lurgan, 9 Mo. 14, 1711.—*Minutes of Ulster Province Meeting.*

JAMES MILLER, dated 5 Mo. 20, 1729, from Dublin, Ireland, received 2 Mo. 25, 1730.

James Miller, possibly a brother of Gayen and John Miller, married Catharine, daughter of Thomas Lightfoot, in Ireland, and lived for some time at Timahoe Meeting, County Kildare. They arrived at Philadelphia, in the *Sizargh*, of Whitehaven, 9 Mo. 10, 1729. Here the wife, who was a minister in the Society, died, 10 Mo. 17, 1729. James Miller then settled with his children in New Garden. He was married a second time to Ruth Seaton, of London Grove, 2 Mo. 10, 1734, and removed to Leacock Township, Lancaster County, where he died in the early part of 1749.

Children of James and Catharine Miller : 1. Sarah, m. Thomas Milhouse, in Ireland, and came to New Garden in 1729. 2. Elizabeth, m. Thomas Hiett, in Ireland, and came to New Garden in 1733. 3. James, b. about 1708, d. 1758 ; m. 1st Rachel

(Fred) Miller, widow of James (son of Gayen), 1733, and had children (Thomas, Benjamin, Katharine). He m. 2d Rebecca, daughter of Jacob Kirk, 1 Mo. 6, 1749, and had children (Rachel, Sarah, Hannah). 4. Mary, m. Isaac Jackson (son of Thomas), 4 Mo. 11, 1730, and had seven children ; they removed to Eno, North Carolina, in 1751. 5. Katharine, b. 1 Mo. 30, 1713, at Timahoe County, Kildare, Ireland ; d. 4 Mo. 2, 1781 ; m. William Jackson, 9 Mo. 9, 1733. 6. Ann, m. William Farquhar, 2 Mo. 19, 1733. 7. Hannah, m. James Jackson, 8 Mo. 31, 1745. No issue.—Potts, *Our Family Ancestors*, 248–9.

WILLIAM EVANS, wife Hannah, and daughter Rachel, from Ballycane, County Wicklow, Ireland, received 7 Mo. 26, 1730, dated 1 Mo. 22, 1730.

William Evans, was a son of Rowland Evans, of Balliloing County Wicklow. William Evans, of Coaladang, County Wicklow, weaver, and Hannah Eves, of Ballemurin, same county, were married 1 Mo. 22, 1709. Among signers to marriage certificate[1] were Mark, Elizabeth, Joseph, and John Eves, Robert, John, and Dorothy Penrose, and Rowland, James, Thomas, Ann, Margaret, and Elizabeth Evans. They settled on a tract of 1,000 acres at Lampeter, about five miles from Lancaster, Lancaster County. Children were : John, died unmarried, in 1782 or 1783 ; William, m. Catharine ——— ; Hannah, m. James Webb, 10 Mo., 15, 1742, and died 1762, leaving children ; and Isaac, m. 1st, Alice Pennock, daughter of Joseph and Mary, of West Marlborough, 5 Mo. 5, 1756, by whom he had one child that died in infancy, and m. 2d, 2 Mo., 1760, to Anne, daughter of Francis and Mary (Jackson) Windle.—*Jackson Genealogy*, 69, 187.

ALICE GIBSON, from Ireland, received 6 Mo. 30, 1729.

KATHARINE WHITAKER, from Dublin, Ireland, received 2 Mo. 25, 1730.

ROBERT AND JOHN MICKLE [brothers], from Dublin, Ireland, dated 4 Mo. 2, 1730, received 7 Mo. 26, 1730.

Robert Mickle, m. 10 Mo. 19, 1733, at London Grove Meeting, Chester County, Mary, daughter of Samuel and Jane Beverly, of Marlborough. Children : Ann, b 8. Mo. 7, 1734, m. ——— McFarlan ; John, b. 8 Mo. 12, 1736 ; Sarah, b. 3 Mo. 12, 1739 ; Jane, b. 9 Mo. 9, 1741.

John Mickle, brother of Robert, m., "by a priest," about 1736, to Jane ———. They removed to Menallen Township, Adams County, about 1747. Children : Sarah, b. 10 Mo. 29, 1737, m.

---

[1] In 1894 the original certificate was in possession of Hannah W. Lovell, of Philadelphia.

about 1760, to John Mickle, her first cousin, for which she was disowned; Elijah, b. 2 Mo. 8, 1740 (at Warrington Mo. Mtg., 11 Mo. 18, 1758, Menallen Meeting reported that Elijah Mickle and John Shepperd "hath both left the parts unknown to their parents"); Mary, b. 10 Mo. 4, 1741, m. "out," about 1761, to —— Sheppard; Hannah, b. 10 Mo. 14, 1745, m. "out," about 1765, to —— Rail; Jane, b. 1 Mo. 16, 1747–48; John, b. 12 Mo. 4, 1753, m., 6 Mo. 17, 1772, at Menallen Meeting, Rebecca, daughter of Thomas Griffith; Samuel, b. 2 Mo. 26, 1756, m. about 1778, Eve, d. of Thomas Griffiith, and d. March 26, 1819.

At Warrington Mo. Meeting, 4 Mo. 10, 1762, John Mickle, of Menallen Meeting, it is apprehended, has connived at his daughter's keeping company in order for marriage with one not of our Society. 6 Mo. 12, 1762, Jane Mickle charged with the same offence. 10 Mo. 9, 1762, she acknowledges that "she Carelessly went away from my own house untill my daughter Mary took the opportunity to go away with a man not in unity with friends, in order to accomplish her marriage by a priest; I being warned to the Contrary I do now look upon my self to have been remiss in my duty."

2 Mo. 12, 1763, John Mikle reported somewhat condescending. 6 Mo. 11, 1763, he acknowledges that "I inadvertently went abroad at the time my Daughter Mary ran away to be married, notwithstanding I was Cautioned to take Care of her, & that she was to run away that night; for which I am heartily sorry."

3 Mo. 11, 1769, John Mickle, Sr., was complained of by Menallen, "for joining with others in dancing so far as to be present & se it & imitate it himself & also that he has for a considerable time neglected attending our Religious meetings," disowned 7 Mo. 8, 1769 — *Warrington Mo. Mtg. Records.*

In 1678, Robert Mickle, of the Parish of Magherlin, County Down, for tithes, had hay, barley, wheat and oats taken to the value of £1. 6s. 6d.—Stockdale, *A Great Cry of Oppression*, 97.

JOHN MURRAY, and wife Ann, from Lurgan, County Armagh, Ireland, dated 2 Mo. 16, 1729, received 8 Mo. 31, 1730.

JOSEPH DIXON, unmarried, from Lurgan, County Armagh, received 8 Mo. 31, 1730.

Joseph Dixson, of London Grove Township, Chester County, and Sarah, daughter of Evan Powell, of New Garden Township, were married, 10 Mo. 13, 1733, at New Garden.

SOLOMON SHEPHERD,[1] unmarried, from Grange Meeting near Charlemont, Ireland, dated 8 mo. 1, 1729, received 11 Mo. 30, 1730-1.

[1] In 1681, one John Sheppard, of Parish Killaman, County Tyrone, had his goods seized for tithes (*Stockdale*, 178).

"Att a mens meeting held [at Grange] y⁰ 22 aforesaid [5 Mo. 1729] Solomon Shepard y⁰ younger having transported himself to America as an Aprentice with Jacob Marshill & Desired of us a Certificate," etc. He settled for a time in New Garden and was married, 9 Mo. 15, 1733, at New Garden Meeting, to Jane Wilson, of New Garden.

They removed to Menallen Township, now Adams County, and in 1748, Solomon became a recommended minister of Warrington Monthly Meeting. He died about 1749, his will being dated July, 1748, and probated March 29, 1749. He mentions his wife Jane and children, John, Sarah, Solomon, and Elizabeth. Jane Shepherd served for several years as overseer of Menallen Meeting. In 1767 she and her daughter Elizabeth received a certificate to remove within the limits of New Garden Monthly Meeting, North Carolina.

Solomon Shepherd, Jr., of Menallen Township, son of Solomon and Jane, m. 10 Mo. 19, 1763, at Menallen Meeting, to Margaret, daughter of John and Rebecca Blackburn.

Sarah, daughter of Solomon and Jane Shepherd, m. 12 Mo. 20, 1758, at Menallen Meeting, William, son of John Braselton, of Frederick County, Md.

JONAS CHAMBERLIN, unmarried, from Edenderry Meeting, King's County, Ireland, dated 11 Mo. 5, 1731, received 1 Mo. 31, 1733.

In 1660, Anne, wife of Jonas Chamberlin, was imprisoned in Wexford for two weeks.—Holme and Fuller, *A Brief Relation,* 17.

In 1671, in County Wexford, Jonas Chamberlain, was taken a prisoner "upon a definite Sentence" for 7s. small tithes, and kept in prison for nine months. In the meantime the "Priest" went with four men and abused his servants, and took away two lambs worth 5s.—Stockdale, *A Great Cry of Oppression,* 9.

Jonas Chamberlain, the emigrant, settled in Sadsbury, Lancaster County. He m. 8 Mo. 9, 1734, Jane, daughter of Alexander Bane, of Goshen. He died 9 Mo. 8, 1771, and his widow, 3 Mo. 4, 1777. Children: Joshua, Hannah, Jane, Mary, Hannah, Jonas, Joseph, William, and Jane. Of these, Joshua m. 11 Mo.

John McRannell and Elizabeth Sheppherd both of Grange Meeting, near Charlemont, were married 6 Mo. 18, 1714, at Grange.

Elizabeth, daughter of Solomon Sheppard, "of Bellis," Parish of Donagh, County Monaghan, was married, 10 Mo. (Dec.) 14, 1733, in Meeting House at Castleshane, County Monaghan, to William Whitten, of Drummon, Parish of Mullabrack, County Armagh, Irèland.—*Friends' Records of Ulster Province.*

24, 1756, Mary Powel and Jonas married, 12 Mo. 3, 1766, Elizabeth Powel, both daughters of Joseph Powel, of Sadsbury, Chester County.—*History of Chester County*, 496.

THOMAS HIETT, and wife Elizabeth, received 8 Mo. 27, 1733, dated 4 Mo. 10, 1733, from Moate Meeting, County West Meath, Ireland. Children born in Ireland as follows: Katharine, b. 2 Mo. 26, 1728, married 2 Mo. 13, 1749, at New Garden Meeting, to Thomas Hutton, of New Garden, son of Joseph, deceased; Ann, b. 1 Mo. 1, 1729, married 11 Mo. 8, 1753, at New Garden, Joseph Hutton, of New Garden, brother of Thomas. Thomas Hiett died in 1751, and 7 Mo. 1, 1756, his widow, Elizabeth Hiett, married Jeremiah Starr, Jr., son of Jeremiah, of London Grove.

ALICE GIBSON, received 11 Mo. 26, 1733, from Dublin, Ireland.

ANN EVINS, received 9 Mo. 24, 1733, from Moate Monthly Meeting, County West Meath, Ireland.

RUTH SEATON, received 9 Mo. 24, 1733, from Ballinderry Meeting, Ireland.

Alexander Seaton, an eminent minister of Friends in Ireland, son of John Seaton, of the Seatons of Meldrum, was born about 1652, at Cuttle-Craggs, near Lethinty, Parish of Daviot, Aberdeenshire, Scotland, and brought up a scholar, studying for some time in the college in the old town of Aberdeen. Here in 1675, he became convinced of the Quaker principles. From Glasgow, in 1699, he removed to Ireland, making his residence at Hillsborough, County Down. He died 1 Mo. 1723.—*Rutty, Leadbeater, Piety Promoted.*

JAMES SMITH, and wife Jane, received 9 Mo. 24, 1733, dated 4 Mo. 8, 1732, from Ballyhagen, Armagh County, Ireland.

SAMUEL HILL, and wife Ann, received 8 Mo. 25, 1735, dated 2 Mo. 29, 1735, from Limerick Meeting, Ireland.

JOHN WILSON, received 8 Mo. 25, 1735, dated 3 Mo. 25, 1735, from Limerick, Ireland.

ROBERT SMITH, and wife Jane, received 6 Mo. 28, 1736, dated 4 Mo. 18, 1732, from Ballyhagen, County Armagh.

JOHN BLACKBURN, wife and children, received 8 Mo. 30, 1736, dated 4 Mo. 2, 1736, from Ballyhagen Meeting, County Armagh, Ireland.

John Blackburn[1] and family settled within the limits of Warrington Monthly Meeting, York County. He was appointed overseer of Warrington Meeting, 4 Mo. 18, 1748, and was released 1 Mo. 17, 1756. He died prior to 7 Mo. 5, 1758. Children were Joseph, Rachel, and probably John, Anthony, and Thomas.

John Blackburn, Jr., m. Rebecca ———. They resided in Menallen Township, now Adams County, where he died 8 Mo. 24, 1767, and she, 3 Mo. 30, 1766. Their children : Margaret, b. 10 Mo. 16, 1740, m. Solomon Shepherd in 1763 ; Rachel, b. 9 Mo. 1, 1742, m. 11 Mo. 11, 1767, Nathan McGrew, son James and Mary ; Thomas, b. 8 Mo. 19, 1744, m. 10 Mo. 11, 1768, Elizabeth, daughter of Thomas and Eve Griffith ; Moses, b. 9 Mo. 16, 1746, m. 11 Mo. 18, 1767, at Menallen Meeting, Mary, daughter of James and Mary McGrew ; Anthony, b. 6 Mo. 17, 1749, m. 5 Mo. 16, 1770, Mary, daughter of Thomas and Eve Griffith ; Mary, b. 6 Mo. 19, 1751 ; John, b. 6 Mo. 21, 1753 ; Elizabeth, b. 10 Mo. 2, 1755 ; Joseph, b. 11 Mo. 7, 1757 ; Rebecca, b. 12 Mo. 12, 1760 ; Samuel, b. 5 Mo. 17, 1762, Abigail b. 5 Mo. 9, 1764 ; Eleanor, b. 3 Mo. 30, 1766.

Anthony Blackburn, of Menallen Meeting, supposed to be a son of John, was complained of 5 Mo. 16, 1752, at Warrington Mo. Mtg., for marriage by a "priest."

Joseph Blackburn, of Menallen, son of John, deceased, m. 7 Mo. 5, 1758, at Menallen Meeting, Deborah McGrew, of Menallen. Their children were : Mary, b. 4 Mo. 30, 1759 ; John, b. 1 Mo. 8, 1762 ; James, b. 10 Mo. 16, 1763 ; Thomas, b. 11 Mo. 10, 1765 ; Anthony, b. 6 Mo. 12, 1767 ; Joseph, b. 2 Mo. 11, 1769.

Rachel Blackburn, of Menallen, daughter of John, m. 8 Mo. 29, 1759, at Menallen, Andrew Dennen.

WALTER HAYDOCK, unmarried, received 12 Mo. 25, 1737–8, dated 2 Mo. 21, 1737, from meeting at Lisburn, County Antrim, Ireland.

He resided for a time within the limits of London Grove Meeting ; then on 7 Mo. 29, 1739, he received a certificate to North Wales (Gwynedd) Monthly Meeting, and settled in Richland Township, Bucks County.

Walter Haddock, of Richland, Bucks County, yeoman, made his will Jan. 17, 1787 (proved March 13, 1787). Appoints Wil-

[1] One John Blackburn and Mary Winter, both of Ballyhagen Mtg., were married 8 Mo. 2, 1701, at Ballyhagen. In County Armagh, in 1667, "John Blackburn, being sued for Tythe to the value of 2s. 1d. 2q. in the Mannor Court of *Loughall* by *Humphrey Pettard*, Priest, the said John produced the Statute against all proceedings in Temporal Courts for Tithe; notwithstanding the Jury said" etc., Blackburn's horse, worth £2, taken for tithe of 2s. 1d. 2q.—Holme and Fuller, *A Brief Relation*, 26.

liam Penrose executor. Mentions brother John and sisters Sarah
and Mary Haddock, of County Antrim, Ireland ; also mentions
Richard Fossett, of Fairfax County, Va., and Jonathan, William
and John Penrose, of Richland.—*Bucks County Wills.*

Henry Haydock, of Stengmore,[1] Parish Clonfeakle, County
Tyrone, and Mary Bullogh, of Allneoanoge (?), said Parish, were
married 3 Mo. 3, 1734, at Meeting House near Charlemont.
Among signers were : John Haydock, James Henderson, John
Whitsite, John King, John Hinshaw, Jacob Hinshaw, Mary Hay-
dock, Elizabeth Bullogh, Sarah Greer, Alice Hinshaw, Mary
Gilpin, Margaret Hinshaw.

In 1673, John and William Haddock, of County Antrim, and
in 1681, John Haddock, Sr., and John Haddock, Jr,. of Ballinderry Parish, County Antrim, had their goods taken for tithes.—
Stockdale, *A Great Cry of Oppression*, 25–26, 169.

JOHN BOYD, wife Jane, and children, from Ballynacree Meeting, County Antrim, Ireland, dated 2 Mo. 10, 1736, received 12 Mo. 26, 1736–7.

John Boyd and Jane Bell, both of Lurgan Meeting, were mar-
ried "in ye town of Lurgan ye 20th $\frac{11}{mo.}$ 1707 as by ye certificate
may appear."—*Minutes Ulster Prov. Mtg.*

They became members of Sadsbury Meeting, Lancaster
County, and resided within the limits thereof until about 1765 ;
then removed to York County. At Warrington Mo. Mtg., York
County, 11 Mo. 9, 1765, a certificate, dated 8 Mo. 21, 1765, from
Sadsbury Mo. Mtg., was received for John Boyd and wife. He

---

[1] Mrs. Sarah Barcroft, of Stangmore Lodge, near Dungannon, County
Tyrone, has some ancient deeds for her property in which the name Hay-
dock appears.
    Jacob Haydock, of Cabragh, County Tyrone, son of John Haydock, of
Stangmore, same county, descended from the Haydocks of Lancashire, was
married, 7 Mo. 29, 1742, to Mary Hinshaw. They had seven children :
John, Rebecca, Mary, Margaret, Jacob, Joseph, and Henry. Of these
children, Henry, born in 1764, m. in 1796 at Moyallon Meeting, Frances
Bell, and lived at Corcraney, near Lurgan. Of Henry's eight children
John, b. 1802, d. 1859, m. Ann Crosley. Descendants of this branch have
come to America in recent years.
    [2]In 1681, one John Boyd, of Parish of Killead, County Antrim, had
goods seized for tithes.—*Stockdale*, 166.
    In 1673, in County Londonderry, William Boyd had his goods seized
for tithes.—*Ibid.*, 25.
    Robert Henry, of Colerain, and Mary Boyd, of Antrim, were married in
the town of Antrim 6 Mo. 10, 1709 (*Minutes Ulster Prov. Mtg.*)
    Benjamin Boyd and Jane Clark, both of Grange Meeting, m. 5 Mo. 4,
1710, at Grange (*Ibid.*)

made his will (Q 313, Wills at York, Pa.), Aug. 8, 1770, and it was probated Oct. 31, 1777. Mentions seven children as follows: I. William ; II. Samuel ; III. George ; IV. Sarah Leech ; V. Ann Bready ; VI. Elizabeth Stedham ; VII. Jane McMillan ; and a grandchild, Jane Marsh.

I. William Boyd became a member of Sadsbury Mo. Mtg., Lancaster County, and was married 9 Mo. or 10 Mo, 1737, to Hannah Minshall, widow. At Sadsbury Mo. Mtg., 6 Mo. 7, 1749, he was complained of "for marriage out by a priest," and 11 Mo. 6, 1752, produced an acknowledgment for this breach of discipline. At the same Mo. Mtg., 3 Mo. 4, 1754, a certificate of removal was signed for him and his daughter to Warrington Mo. Mtg., York County. The certificate was received at Warrington 4 Mo. 20, 1754. At Warrington, 1 Mo. 8, 1763, a certificate to Hopewell Mo. Mtg., Virginia, was signed for him and his three children.

II. Samuel Boyd was reported to Sadsbury Mo. Mtg., 5 Mo. 4, 1743, as having married out by a "priest," and was disowned 8 Mo. 3, 1743.

III. George Boyd produced a certificate, dated 10 Mo. 22, 1760, from Sadsbury to Warrington Mo. Mtg. and seems to have been a member of Newberry Meeting York County. He made his will Sept. 17, 1796, then of Warrington Township, and it was probated. Oct. 22, 1796. His executors were Thomas Leech and John McMillan. He mentions his wife Catharine and children, James, Ann, Jane, and Rachel. Of these children, Ann was received into membership by Warrington Mo. Mtg, 1, Mo. 7, 1792. She was complained of 5 Mo. 12, 1798, for marriage out to one Jones and sent an acknowledgment. According to her cousin James McMillan's Bible record, Ann Jones, daughter of George and Catherine Boyd, died Sept. 9, 1830.

IV. Sarah Boyd, was married 2 Mo. 17, 1739, at Sadsbury Mtg. to Thomas Leech, son of Richard and Sarah (Cox) Leach. They removed to Warrington, York County.

V. Jane Boyd was born, as her son James states in his Bible, in 1728, died 5 Mo. 12, 1782, and was buried in the burial ground at Warrington Meeting House. She was complained of 7 Mo. 5, 1748, by Sadsbury Mo. Mtg. for marriage out to Joseph Green and produced an acknowledgment, 12 Mo. 3, 1753. Jane Green, widow of Joseph Green, of Sadsbury, was married 5 Mo. 4, 1756, at Sadsbury Meeting, to John McMillan, of Warrington Township, York County, son of Thomas and Deborah (Marsh) McMillan. He was born in 1728, in County Antrim, Ireland, died 9 Mo. 17, 1791, and was buried beside his first wife, Jane.

By her first husband, Joseph Green, Jane Boyd had two children: (1) Joseph and (2) John. These two children were received into membership by Warrington Mo. Mtg., 8 Mo. 11, 1764. (1) Joseph Green, of Warrington, son of Joseph, deceased, was married 12 Mo. 16, 1773, at Warrington Mtg., to Lydia Holland, daughter of Henry and Lydia (Fell) Holland, of same place. A certificate for Joseph and his wife Lydia to Westland Mo. Mtg., Washington County, was signed by Warrington, 3 Mo. 7, 1795. They settled near Brownsville where they owned a farm and grist mill. Lydia Green, daughter of Joseph, married Joseph Richardson, a tanner of Columbiana Co., Ohio, and became the mother of the eminent physician, Dr. Richardson. (2) John Green was disowned by Warrington Mo. Mtg., (1) Mo. 14, 1775, probably for marriage out. Possibly he married the daughter of one John Abbot, of Berwick Twp., York County, who made his will Jan. 27, 1786 (probated March 8, 1786) and mention his wife, Alice, and daughter Margaret, wife of John Green. By her second husband, John McMillan, Jane Boyd had five children : Sarah, Thomas, John, Abigail, and James.—See McMillan family.

ROBERT BOYES, from Ballyhagen, County Armagh, dated 2 Mo. 21, 1736, received 1 Mo. 26, 1737.

One John Boyes, of Lackey, Parish of Maagharagall, County Antrim, and Mary Turner, of Lurgan, County Armagh, were married 6 Mo. 17, 1720, at Lurgan.—*Lurgan Meeting Records.*

In 1680, Richard Boyes, County Antrim, had his goods to the value of 18s. seized for tithes. (*Stockdale*, 139.) In 1716, Thomas Story (*Journal*, 538) notes that he came to the widow Mary Boyes' at Ballinderry.

ISAAC PIGON, unmarried, from Meeting at Grange near Charlemont, dated 6 Mo. 27, 1736, received 2 Mo. 30, 1737.

At New Garden Monthly Meeting, 9 Mo. 25, 1738, "Isaac Pigen having rec'd a Letter from his father y^t lives in Ireland, since our Last mo^{ly} meeting which requests him to return thither as soon as possible & ye season not permitting him to stay untill next meeting, a certificate is to be prepared and signed for him."

ISAAC STEER, wife Ruth and daughter Katharine, the latter unmarried, dated 5 Mo. 7, 1736, received 6 Mo. 27, 1737, from Ballinderry Meeting, County Antrim.

William Steer, a Friend, of County Armagh, Ireland, in the period 1665–1669, for refusing to contribute to the repair of the parish church of Kilmore, "had Money taken out of his Shop-

3ox, also a Hat, and other things worth 7s. 2d, and 2s. 2d more
demanded had Cloth and Pewter taken from him worth 11s."—
Holme and Fuller, *A Brief Relation*, etc., 735.

William Steer, of Leggatory, Parish of Kilmore, County Armagh, made his will May 10, 1685, and mentions his daughter
Hannah, to whom he bequeaths £90, and his only son, Isaac
Steer, to whom he leaves £400 and the house and lands that "I
have by lease from my landlord Edward Richardson."—*Recorded
in Friends' Records of Ulster.*

Isaac Steer, son of William, was married by Friends' ceremony
in 1696 to Ruth Mercer. (*Minutes of Ulster Province Meeting.*)
Isaac Steer, with his wife and daughter, followed their sons to
Pennsylvania about 1737, bringing a certificate to New Garden
Monthly Meeting, but settling within the limits of Sadsbury
meeting. Children were :

I. Nicholas Steer, b. 2 Mo. 15, 1702 ; settled at Sadsbury, m.
Ann Lewis. Children were : Benjamin, b. 10 Mo. 17, 1745, m.
Ann Everett, 9 Mo. 7, 1774 ; William, b. 9 Mo. 24, 1748 ;
Hannah, b. 6 Mo. 15, 1751, m. John Gregg, 9 Mo. 7, 1775 ;
Ann, b. 2 Mo. 10, 1754 ; Ruth, b. 4 Mo. 17, 1758.

II. John Steer, m. 2 Mo. 21, 1732, at Leacock Meeting (since
called Lampeter), Rachel Evans, and in 1749, removed with his
family to Fairfax County, Virginia. Children : Mark ; James, m.
Abigail, daughter of Joseph and Grace (Varman) Edgerton, 5 Mo.
21, 1761 ; Isaac, b. 10 Mo. 10, 1749, d. in Loudon County, Va.,
12 Mo. 17, 1819, m. Elizabeth George, 6 Mo. 13, 1775 ; John,
m. Mary George and removed with his family to Kentucky ; Joseph,
m. Ellen George.

III. Joseph Steer, b. 1709 ; d. 1795 ; m. 3 Mo., 1746, Grace
Edgerton, widow of Joseph Edgerton, and daughter of Hattill and
Abigail Varman. Children : Ruth, Hannah, Sarah, Mary, Joseph,
and Isaac. For detailed record see *Steer Genealogy*, by Isaac S.
Russel (New Market, Md., 1891).

IV. Catharine Steer, m. in 1743 Thomas Nevitt, son of Joseph
and Mary Nevitt, of Mountrath, Queen's County, Ireland.

FAITHFUL RICHARDSON, from Ballyhagen, County Armagh,
Ireland, received 12 Mo. 26, 1736.

WILLIAM BOYD, unmarried, son of John, dated 6 Mo. 18,
1733, from Meeting in Antrim, Ireland, received 6 Mo.
27, 1737.

JOSEPH WHITSITT, young and unmarried, from Grange near
Charlemont, dated 4 Mo. 7, 1738, received 11 Mo. 27,
1738-9. A certificate for him to return was signed 7 Mo.
29, 1739.

One John Whitsitte, of Grange near Charlemont, and Ruth Robson, of Lurgan Meeting, were married 6 Mo. 11, 1703, at the house of Ann Webb (*Minutes of Ulster Province Meeting*).

Abstract of the will of William Whitsitt, of Dreemore, manor of Dungannon, Ireland, dated 1 Mo. 9, 1732.

To daughter Catherine Richardson, farm in Monaghan, parish of Clowish, interest in Soloran in estate of Lord Charlemont, and one fourth of Bernagh in said manor.

To son-in-law, William Richardson, Esq., £300.

To the Quakers of the meeting near Charlemont, £25.

Mentions relatives Thomas Greeves and James Pillar.

To relative Joseph Calvert £10.

To wife Mary Whitsitt, alias Calvert, and "my only child," Catherine, wife of William Richardson, other bequests.—*Recorded in Friends' Records.*

One George Whitsitt, of Birmingham, Chester County, made his will Aug. 7, 1736, and it was probated Oct. 5, 1736. He left to his brother Thomas Bullock "my ivory head cane." Wife Rebecca Whitsitt to be one of the executors.

HENRY NEAL, son of Robert Neal, of Ireland, was married 10 Mo. 19, 1739, at Sadsbury Meeting, to Sarah, daughter of Neal O'Mooney, of Sadsbury, and resided in East Marlborough, Chester County.

Children : Ann, m. 5 Mo. 22, 1766, at London Grove Meeting, Benjamin Hutton ; William, m. 9 Mo. 24, 1766, at Sadsbury Meeting, Rachel Leonard ; Hannah, m. 3 Mo. 22, 1775, at London Grove Meeting, James Pyle.

THOMAS NEVETT, received 3 Mo. 26, 1739, dated 2 Mo. 28, 1738, from Moat Meeting, County West Meath, Ireland.

Thomas Nevitt, of Sadsbury, m. in 1743, Catharine, daughter of Isaac Steer, of Leacock, Lancaster County, and died prior to 1760. His widow Catharine was disowned by Warrington Monthly Meeting, in 1761, for marriage to —— Harry, who was not a Friend. Children of Thomas Nevitt : Isaac who removed from Warrington to Fairfax, Loudon Co., Va., about 1765 ; Mary, m. 11 Mo. 27, 1766, William Wickersham ; Ruth, took a certificate to Hopewell, Va., in 1766 ; Elizabeth, received a certificate to Hopewell, Va., 1768.

JACOB HINSHAW, and wife Rebecca, received 11 Mo. 30, 1741–2, dated 2 Mo. 3, 1741, from [Grange] Meeting, near Charlemont, County Armagh, Ireland. See page 98.

"Thomas Hinshaw & Mary Marshall, both of [Grange Meeting near] Charliamount" were "married att y⁸ grange meeting near Charliamount y⁸ 21st of $\frac{5}{mo.}$ 1708" (*Minutes of Ulster Province Meeting*). In 1726, Thomas Hinshaw was appointed a representative from Grange to the Province Meeting.

Jacob Hinshaw,[1] of Grange, in Parish of Clanfekill, County Tyrone [born about 1710, son of Thomas and Mary Hinshaw[2]] and Rebecca Mackie, of Kincon, Parish of Kilmore, County Armagh [born about 1716, daughter of Joseph and Ann Mackie[2]], were married 9 Mo. (Nov.) 6, 1735, in Friends' Meeting House, in Ballyhagen, County Armagh. Signers were :

David Keel	Mary Hinshaw	JACOB HINSHAW
Benjamin Mackie	Mary Greer	REBECCA HINSHAW
Michel Hampton	Ann Mackie	Joseph Mackie
David M'Cann	Jane Bell	Ann Mackie
Willᵐ. Bedwell	Margaret Hinshaw	John Mackie
Patrick McCrannall	Rebecca Smith	Benjamin Mackie
William Delap	Abigail Gray	Benjamin Marshall
Jacob Sinton	Mary Richardson	William Hinshaw
ffrancis Hobson		Robert Maddon
William Gray		John Nicholson
		Jonas McKitrick
		William Allen
		David Kell

In 1741, Jacob Hinshaw removed with his family to Pennsylvania, bringing a certificate, dated 2 Mo. 3, 1741, from Meeting at Grange near Charlemont, to New Garden Monthly Meeting, Chester County, 11 Mo. 30, 1741. They lived for a time within the limits of New Garden and then settled at Menallen Meeting, in York, now Adams, County, taking their certificates to Warrington Monthly Meeting about 1748. From Menallen they removed to Monaghan Township, York County, where they were living in 1758. About 1765 they removed to North Carolina and settled within the limits of Cane Creek Monthly Meeting, Orange County, producing a certificate, dated 10 Mo. 12, 1765, to Cane Creek, 1 Mo. 4, 1766. According to the Cane Creek records, Jacob Hinshaw, son of Thomas and Mary, died 3 Mo. 31, 1796, aged about 86 years, and Rebecca his wife, daughter of Joseph and Ann Mackey, died 6 Mo. 16, 1796, aged about 80 years. Their children were Ann (m. George McMillan, in 1758, and remained at Warrington), and probably Benjamin, Thomas, and William.

[1] *Marriage Book Ulster Quarterly Meeting*, 33.
[2] *Records of Cane Creek Monthly Meeting, North Carolina.*

Several other families of Hinshaws, who also came to America, were doubtless nearly related to Thomas and Jacob Hinshaw.

Jesse Hinshaw, a son of John and Elizabeth Hinshaw, was born in County Tyrone, Ireland.[1] He was married (mentioned as of Dunsdead, Parish of Clanfeakill, County Tyrone), 11 Mo. (Jan.) 1, 1745, at Friends' Meeting House, at Grange near Charlemont, to Abigail Marshall, of Grange, daughter of Benjamin and Ruth Marshall (Marriage Book of Ulster Quarterly Meeting). According to Grange Meeting records "It Appears that Jesse Hindshaw, Absolem Hindshaw & Willm Hindshaw[2] with their respective families and also Alice Hindshaw[3] removed to America in the year 1768." They settled in North Carolina, bringing certificates to Cane Creek Monthly Meeting, Orange County, as follows: Jesse Hinshaw and family, received 2 Mo. 4, 1769, Absolem Hinshaw and family, 5 Mo. 6, 1769, and William Hinshaw and family, 11 Mo. 4, 1769.

Children of Jesse and Abigail Hinshaw: John, b. 8 Mo. 11, 1747; Benjamin, b. 10 Mo. 2, 1749; Joseph, b. 6 Mo. 7, 1752; William, b. 10 Mo. 30, 1757;[4] Ruth, b. 6 Mo. 11, 1763; Abigail, b. 7 Mo. 1, 1766; Jesse, b. 9 Mo. 8, 1770, m. (1) Mary (b. 6 Mo. 29, 1773, in Orange Co., N. C.) daughter of Jacob and Margaret Marshill, and (2) Elizabeth, b. 9 M. 29, 1780, daughter of Benjamin and Elizabeth Hinshaw.

Absolem Hinshaw and Rebecca Haddock, of Parish of Killiman, County Tyrone, Ireland, were married 4 Mo. 15, 1748, at Friends' Meeting at Grange, near Charlemont. Among the signers to the certificate were John Haddock, Jesse, William and Abigail Hinshaw, and Joseph Marshill. (*Marriage Book of Ulster Quarterly Meeting.*) Children: Elizabeth, b. 10 Mo. 27, 1750, Absolem, b. 8 Mo. 31, 1752; Jacob, b. 8 Mo. 31, 1762; Rebecca, b. 1 Mo. 29, 1764. (*Records of Grange Meeting.*) They removed to Cane Creek, North Carolina, in 1768.

John Hinshaw, of Grange, Parish of Clanfeakel, County Tyrone, and Alice Greer, of Mulloughlocher, Parish of Ann, County Cavan, were married 10 Mo. (Dec.) 10, 1733, in the Meeting House at Bellyhays, County Cavan. Among signers were: JOHN HINSHAW, ALICE HINSHAW, Robert Greer, Mary Greer, Jacob Hinshaw, Deborah Greer, Susanna Greer, Thomas Greer, Benjamin Marshall.

[1] *Records of Cane Creek Monthly Meeting, North Carolina.*
[2] At the Meeting at Grange near Charlemont, 1 Mo. 25, 1758, one William Hinshaw produced an acknowledgment for marriage by a "priest." Jacob Hinshaw, son of William and Mary, died 6 Mo. 10, 1779. (*Cane Creek Records.*)
[3] One Alice Hinshaw died 9 Mo. 25, 1786. (*Cane Creek Records*).
[4] *Records of Grange Meeting, Ireland.*

William Hinshaw, of Grange, Parish of Clanfekil, County Tyrone, and Mary Courtney, of Ballymaconn, Parish Mackerallin, County Down, were married 2 Mo. (Apr.) 1, 1742, at Meeting House, near Ballinderry, County Antrim. One Margaret Hinshaw signed certificate.

John Hinshaw, of Grange, Parish of Clanfekil, County Tyrone, and Rebecca Wethereld, of Mulladry, Parish Kilmore, County Armagh, were married, 1 Mo. 21, 1744, at Ballyhagen. William and Margaret Hinshaw and others signed certificate.

Margaret Hinshaw, of Grange, County Tyrone, and Joseph Haddock, of Strangmore, Parish of Clanfekil, said Parish, were married 5 Mo. (July) 1, 1747, at Grange, near Charlemont. Signed by Jesse, William, and Abigail Hinshaw.

David Glan and Dorothy Henshaw declared their intentions of marriage at the meeting at Grange, near Charlemont, 11 Mo. 13, and 11 Mo. 27, 1748. At the meeting, 2 Mo. 13, 1750, William Hinshaw, the younger, was disowned for marrying a young woman of Ballinderry Meeting by a "priest."

THOMAS WILSON, and family, received 1 Mo. 27, 1742, dated 12 Mo. 25, 1740, from [Grange] Meeting, near Charlemont, County Armagh, Ireland.

MARY SIDGWICK, received 9 Mo. 26, 1743, dated 9 Mo. 7, 1741, from Meeting near Ballinderry, County Antrim, Ireland.

SAMUEL MORTON, received 7 Mo. 29, 1750, dated 2 Mo. 13, 1750, from Grange Meeting, near Charlemont.

One John Morton, of Minalan Mtg. and Sarah Fletcher of Lisburn Mtg., were married at Lisburn Mtg., 3 Mo. 1, 1712.—*Minutes of Ulster Prov. Mtg.*

JEREMIAH STARR and ROBERT GREER, unmarried, "two young men Lately arrivd from Ireland, produc'd Certificates [New Garden Mo. Mtg., 7 Mo. 30, 1749] from ye Moly meeting of Coat Hill in ye North of Ireland Bearing date ye 23d of ye 2d Mo. 1749." At New Garden Mo. Mtg. 11 Mo. 24, 1753, Robert Greer requested a certificate to return to Ireland, but at the meeting 12 Mo. 29, 1753, report is made that "ye Vessel being Ready to sail we understand he is gone without it."

JOHN RUSSELL, dated 12 Mo. 10, 1754, from Men's Meeting, Dublin, Ireland, received 12 Mo. 27, 1755. At New

24

Garden Monthly Meeting, 10 Mo. 8, 1763, "John Russell being about to transport himself into Ireland Requests our Certificate Directed to the Men's Meeting of Dublin." Granted 11 Mo. 4, 1763. At New Garden, 10 Mo. 6, 1764, "John Russel being returned from Ireland Produced a Certificate from the Men's Meeting in Dublin, bearing date ye 29th of ye 5th mo. last."

John Russel, b. 1 Mo. 6, 1735, son of Thomas and Sarah Russel, of Ireland, probably of Dublin, was married 11 Mo. 11, 1767, to Hannah, daughter of John and Jane (McNab) Fincher. They resided in Chester County until 1779, when they removed their certificates of membership from Kennett to Pipe Creek Monthly Meeting, Frederick County, Md., and lived for a time near Union Bridge. Their final settlement was near New Market, Frederick County, where he died 11 Mo. 14, 1815. Children were: Thomas, b. 9 Mo. 16, 1768, m. Sarah Roberts; Sarah, b. 4 Mo. 10, 1770, m. John Roberts; Jesse b. 3 Mo. 17, 1772, m. Content Garretson; Mary, b. 2 Mo. 11, 1774, m. Joseph L. Scholfield; Rachel b. 6 Mo. 30, 1776, d. aged 7 years; James, b. 4 Mo. 3, 1779, m. Susan Janney; Abel, b. 5 Mo. 23, 1781, m. Elizabeth Roberts; John, b. 5 Mo. 7, 1783, m. Ann Hughes; Hannah, b. 12 Mo. 29, 1785, d. 9 Mo. 2, 1807.—See *Russell Genealogy*, 1-2 (by Isaac S. Russel, New Market, Md., 1887).

BRADFORD MONTHLY MEETING

In Chester County.   Established in 1737, from Newark, or Kennett and Concord.

Evan Wilkinson, unmarried, from Ballinacree Meeting, County Antrim, Ireland, dated 10 Mo. 2, 1736, received 5 Mo. 21, 1737. "Hath Lived within the bounds of this Meeting from his Childhood, his parents were Creditable friends among us." Original on file.

Ann Wilkinson, from Ballinacree Meeting, County Antrim, received 4 Mo. 15, 1738.

She was disowned by Bradford Monthly Meeting, 11 Mo. 15, 1740, for marriage by a "priest" to Ferguson Graham.

Joseph Wilkinson, unmarried, from Ballinacree Meeting, County Antrim, dated 2 Mo. 23, 1737, received 12 Mo. 16, 1737. A "Son to Francis Wilkinson Deced." Has lived within "the Compass of this Meet⁸ from his Child-hood."

Francis Wilkinson[1] seems to have resided near Ballinacree, or Ballymoney, County Antrim, and besides his son Joseph, probably had other children: Evan, Ann, and Samuel, all of whom came to Pennsylvania about the same time as Joseph. At Ulster Province Meeting, 5 Mo. 2, 1698, Francis Wilkinson was appointed to inquire into the "clearness" of John Hunter, of Ballymoney, who desired to marry Jane Sterling, of Coleraine, County Antrim.

Joseph Wilkinson came over to Pennsylvania in 1737 and was married 10 Mo. 31, 1740, to Elizabeth, daughter of Thomas and Elizabeth Fisher, of Kennett, Chester County. They resided in East Caln, in the latter county, but afterwards resided at other places. He died 9 Mo. 10, 1760, having had the following children: Frances, b. 12 Mo. 15, 1741; Susanna, b. 12 Mo. 29, 1743; Thomas, b. 12 Mo. 5, 1745; Elizabeth, b. 6 Mo. 30, 1748; Joseph, b. 7 Mo. 17, 1750; Mary, b. 3 Mo. 20, 1752; Ruth, b. 7 Mo. 27, 1754; Alice, b. 12 Mo. 10, 1755.

The widow, Elizabeth Wilkinson, and her family removed within the limits of Warrington Monthly Meeting, York County, not long after the death of her husband, and she was married a second time to Joseph, son of Peter and Sarah (Gilpin) Cook, of Warrington. She died at York early in the nineteenth century and was buried in Friends' graveyard at York.

Francis Wilkinson, son of Joseph and Elizabeth, m. 4 Mo. 11, 1770, Hannah Mode, daughter of Alexander and Rebecca, and settled in London Grove Township, Chester County. Children: Rebecca, m. William Hoopes; Elizabeth, m. James Trimble; Joseph; Hannah, m. Joseph Pennock; Francis, m. Phebe Pusey; Susanna, m. Moses Way; Mode; Amy, m. Thomas Hicks; William; Ruth, m. John Edge.—*Hist. Chester County*, 763-4.

[1] James Moore, of Ballynacreemore, in his will dated Dec. 29, 1727, mentions his daughter Frances Wilkinson and her son William Wilkinson.
In 1678 and 1681, William Wilkinson, of Antrim, had his goods taken for tithes.—Stockdale, *A Great Cry of Oppression*, 97, 166.
In 1681 Thomas Wilkinson, of Antrim, had his goods seized for tithes.—*Ibid.*, 166.
Samuel Wilkinson, of Antrim Meeting, and Mary Sedgwick, of Ballinderry Mtg., m. 4 Mo. 24, 1713, at the house of Widow Boyes.
Elizabeth Wilkinson and Eli Crocket, both of Ballymoney Meeting, m. 11 Mo. 4, 1715, at house of James Moore.
At a meeting in County Antrim, 10 Mo. 2, 1708, one Joseph Wilkinson received a certificate to take with him to England, "whither he goes to improve himself in the world."

WILLIAM PURDY, unmarried, from Ballynacree Meeting, County Antrim, dated 2 Mo. 23, 1737, received 4 Mo. 15, 1738.

In 1671, in County Tyrone, one William Purdy, for tithes had taken 14 loads of "Turf," some "Hey," and barley, valued at 2s. 6d.—*Stockdale*, 6.

In 1674 William Purdy, of County Tyrone, had taken for "Clerks Wages" "a Pick-ax," valued at 2s. 6d.—*Ibid.*, 220.

One Thomas Purdy and Ann Coots, "Als Ridge," were married at the meeting at Grange, near Charlemont, 2 Mo. 16, 1701. —*Minutes of Ulster Province Meeting.*

WILLIAM SHEPPARD, unmarried, from Grange, near Charlemont, Ireland, dated 4 Mo. 20, 1739, received 8 Mo. 18, 1739. He is a birthright member. His parents removed "from this neighborhood (when he ye S^d William was but young) to a small meeting Some miles Distant from us, Yet under our Care, being in ye Compas our mens meeting. Among signers were Benjamin and John Shepherd, Jacob, Joseph, and Benjamin Marshill, and Lawrence and Benjamin Hobson. Original on file.

William Shepherd, of Menallen Meeting, now Adams County, son of Solomon Shepherd, deceased, of Ireland, was married 3 Mo. 31, 1749, at London Grove Meeting, to Richmunday Wood, of London Grove, Chester County. Among his children were Mary, Solomon, Thomas, and William Shepherd.

THOMAS PAINE, unmarried, from Mountmellick Meeting, Queen's County, Ireland, dated 2 Mo. 26, 1738, received 9 Mo. 17, 1743. He "for Some-time hath made profession with us and Served an Aprentiseship within ye Compass of our Monthly Meeting." Original on file.

WILLIAM PIM.

Richard Pim, of Leicestershire, England, in his old age, about 1655, removed to Ireland. His son William m. Dorothy (d. 9 Mo. 1, 1685; buried at Tineal, near Rosenallis), daughter of William Neal, and went with his family also to settle in Ireland, in the same year. John Pim, son of William, b. in Leicestershire; d. 5 Mo. 29, 1718, at Mountrath, Ireland; m. in 1663, Mary (d. 2 Mo. 5, 1726), daughter of William Pleadwell, and lived at Mountrath, Ireland. He had eleven children, of whom the eldest was Moses, b. 7 Mo. 19, 1664, d. 1 Mo. 5, 1716 (killed by machinery of his rope mill), m. Ann, daughter of Christopher and Phillipa Raper. Ann Raper, b. 1 Mo. 9, 1664, at Ivan Mills, near Ballinakill, Queen's County, d. 3 Mo. 18, 1743 ; buried at Mountrath.

William Pim, son of Moses, was born at Lackah, Queen's County, 11 Mo. 15, 1692 ; m. 11 Mo. 2, 1715, at Mountrath, Dorothy, daughter of Thomas and Dorothy Jackson. She was born 8 Mo. 22, 1694, at Killenare. William Pim and family came to Pennsylvania in 1730, and settled in the Great Valley, near East Caln Meeting, Chester County. Here Dorothy died 1 Mo. 15, 1732. He married, secondly, 1 Mo. 13, 1733, at Concord Meeting, Ann, widow of James Gibbons, of Westtown Township, Chester County.

For many years he served as clerk of Bradford Monthly Meeting, as elder in East Caln Meeting, and as Justice of the Peace. He died 10 Mo. 11, 1751, in East Caln Township. In his will, dated 1751, he mentions his sister, Susanna Purdy.

Children of William and Dorothy (Jackson) Pim : Moses, b. at Killenare, Queen's Co., 10 Mo. 27, 1716, d. unmarried ; Sarah, b. 4 Mo. 23, 1719, at Durrow, Kilkenny, m. at Caln Meeting, 9 Mo. 2, 1737, George, son of Aaron and Rose Mendenhall ; Thomas, b. at Durrow, 3 Mo. 1, 1721, d. East Caln, 10 Mo. 3, 1786, m. at East Caln Meeting, Frances, daughter of James Wilkinson, late of Wilmington, Delaware (children : Moses ; Ann, m. John Edge ; William ; Thomas ; Hannah, m. James Miller ; Sarah, m. Amos Lee ; John ; Rachel, m. Nathan Spencer) ; Hannah, b. Durrow, 4, Mo. 18, 1723, d. 10 Mo. 1756, m. Thomas Paine ; Richard, b. Arkhill, Co. Kildare, 10 Mo. 10, 1728, d. East Caln, 4 Mo. 12, 1760, m. Hannah Lewis ; Mary, b. East Caln, 6 Mo. 6, 1731, d. 1 Mo. 30, 1732.—See Cope, *Smedley Genealogy*, 161–4, *History of Chester County*, 685.

William Pim wrote a long letter,[1] dated 6th of 2d Mo., 1732, to his uncles, Thomas and Joshua Pim, of Montrath, Queen's Co., Ireland, in which he tells of loss of his wife and youngest child by the small-pox, then prevalent in the colony. He speaks of it as the third visitation of the disease since the settlement of the country by the English. He had lost a servant, Jo : Gavin, by it, making three out of his family of 12 persons. "I am in expectation of Ja : Nicholson in a little time, ⅌ whom I expect an acc᛭ from Ireland & if he dont bring me a servant or servants I shall be in great want, for I am soe now. I hired an Indifferent hand lately at Husbandry & it cost me 36ˢ for 4 weeks (& diet)."

" This Country I find most agreeable to my Health (else it is wᵗʰ working harder) : this country also is governed by more agreeable Laws than that."

[1] A full copy of this letter is in the collection of Gilbert Cope, of West Chester, Pa.

The following letter[1] was written by an uncle of the emigrant, William Pim, to his grand-nephew, Joshua Pim, of Usher's Island, Dublin :

"TULLYLAST, CO. KILDARE,
11th of 11 mo. 1768.

" JOSHUA PIM,
Loving Cousin,

In answer to thy request mentioned in thine of the 9th instant I send thee this : I can go no further back than to my great grandfather Richard Pim, who before his marriage lived a considerable time, a cook, with (I think he was called) Sir John Stanhope, ancestor to the Earl of Chesterfield. I heard of but one brother that he had, called Robert Pim, who he said came into Ireland when young, of whom he heard no more. We suppose he was that Robert Pim that Sir John Temple mentions to have been murdered by the Rebels at Graigue-ne-manch, in the County of Kilkenny. Richard Pim, before his marriage, had acquired what they call three livings : I suppose that to be three small pieces of land with each a dwelling on it.

He took a liking to a neighbor's daughter, a comely young girl of thirteen years of age, and as he and his fellow servants rode out on a merry-making, one of his fellow-servants took a pillow behind him and found her playing ball with other girls and asked her to go with them, which she did (it is probable that this was by conceit) and the said Richard married her and sent her to a boarding school for two years and then took her home at fifteen years of age. By her he had my grandfather, William Pim, and several daughters ; one married Godfrey Cantrell and one married to William Neale.

My grandfather, William Pim, married Dorothy, the sister of William Neal, and dwelt if I remember right, at his grandfather Neales house in Castledunnington, in Leistershire, in the year 1641 ; and in the year 1655 Godfrey Cantrell and family came into Ireland and Richard Pim, then very old, came with him and some time after died at Godfrey Cantrell's house, near Rosenallis (in the Queen's County), and was buried in the Church at Rosenallis. The same year my grandfather William Pim, and William Neal and families came over and settled in the County of Cavan, where after some years my grandfather died and was buried in his orchard at his own request, tho of the profession of the church of England ; about which time William Edmundson and Richard Jackson and some other Friends removed to the Queen's Co. William Edmundson settled near Rosenallis, Richard Jackson and my father near Mount Melick. My father had his mother to take care of, and one sister, Ellen, afterwards the wife of Thomas Nevitt. My father joined partnership with Richard Jackson in

[1] Cope, *Smedley Genealogy*, 162–64.

the Butchering trade, and at Mount Melick became acquainted with my mother, Mary, the daughter of William Pleadwell, who was born at Normanton upon Scre, in Nothinghamshire. My grandfather, William Pleadwell and his wife came into Ireland in 1655, they being Baptists, and settled near Killaloe. He had by his first wife Tobias Pleadwell, and by a second wife John Pleadwell, and by a third wife Thomas Pleadwell and my mother and two other daughters, one of whom was married to William Neale ; and some time after my grandfather settled near Killaloe he was convinced by the ministry of Edward Burroughs and died not after ; and as his son Tobias Pleadwell was convinced some time before his father and settled at Mount Melick, my grandmother and her children came to dwell at Mountmelick, and in the year 1663 my father & mother married and settled at Mountmelick ; but in the year 1665 my father and several other friends were sent to prisoners for Tythe to Maryborough Gaol, where they continued prisoners for several years, though he had nothing titheable but a garden ; so he got a house in Maryborough for my mother to dwell in and by favour of the Gaoler or Gaolers followed some business in his trade at Maryborough, and after they were discharged from the prison he took a farm at Coalnecart, part of the lands thy father now holds, and in 1678 or 1679 he went to live at Mountrath. As to the time and place of the births and burials of my brothers and sisters I refer thee to the abstract of the monthly meeting records of births and burials of Mount Melick Monthly Meeting, which abstract, so far as relates to Mountrath meeting is mostly in my handwriting. I suppose it is in the hands of John Clendenon.

THOMAS PIM.

P. S. Richard Jackson, before mentioned, had three sons, John, Thomas and Robert, and one daughter, Sarah, the wife of Nicholas Gribble. John I had no acquaintance with : Thomas, thy grandfather, lived at Killenare, and Robert at Mountmelick : thy grandmother, Sarah Pim, was born at Killenare. Thou may get all their genealogies out of the records of births and burials of Mountmelick monthly meeting.'' [1]

[1] Thomas Pim, the writer of the above letter, was the sixth son of John and Mary Pim. He resided at Mountrath until about 1735, when he went to live with his son's family at Tullylast, County Kildare. He died a few months after he wrote the letter, in his 86th year. He had two sons who had large families. My mother was his son Robert's eldest child. She was 16 years old when he died, and often spoke of him with great respect. His last grandchild, John Pim, died last summer in his 89th year. His sister, Hannah, died in her 91st year in 1849. There are now not any of his descendants of the name of Pim among Friends.—*Robert Goodbody writing in 1852.*

GOSHEN MONTHLY MEETING

In Chester County.   Established in 1722, from Chester.

JOSHUA MARSH, wife Elizabeth, children, Jonathan, Peter, and Abigail, received 9 Mo. 15, 1736, dated 4 Mo. 2, 1736, from Grange Meeting, near Charlemont.   See Marsh family.

JOHN MARSH and wife Elizabeth, received 8 Mo. 18, 1736, dated 4 Mo. 2, 1736, from Grange Meeting, near Charlemont.

THOMAS McMOLLIN [McMillan] and wife Deborah, received 8 Mo. 15, 1739, dated 3 Mo. 6, 1738, from Ballinacree County Antrim, Ireland.   See McMillan family.

WILLIAM VANCE, wife Elizabeth, dated 2 Mo. 3, 1741, from [Grange] Meeting, near Charlemont, Ireland.

THOMAS PARVIN, received 7 Mo. 10, 1750, dated 2 Mo. 24, 1750, from Dublin, Ireland.

NOTTINGHAM MONTHLY MEETING

In Cecil County, Maryland.   Established from New Garden in 1730.

MARY NORTON, daughter of Edward Norton, "of y⁰ County of Armagh," Ireland, was married 9 Mo. 24, 1733, under auspices of Nottingham Mo. Mtg., to Richard Brown, son of William Brown, of West Nottingham.

EDWARD NORTON, of West Nottingham, Chester County, son of Edward Norton of "ye City and Parish of Armagh," Ireland, deceased, was married 8 Mo. 16, 1739, at Nottingham, Mo. Mtg., to Elizabeth Brown, daughter of William Brown.

JOSEPH McRANNELLS, received 11 Mo. 27, 1737, dated 2 Mo. 27, 1737, from Grange Meeting, Ireland.

SAMUEL RUTTER, received 11 Mo. 17, 1753; dated 3 Mo. 30, 1753, from Dublin, Ireland.

ELIZABETH CRAINER, unmarried, dated 7 Mo. 7, 1754, from Ballyhagen Meeting, Ireland. Original certificate in Friends' Historical Library of Swarthmore College.

JOSEPH TREMBLE [TRIMBLE], son of William and Mary Tremble, of Ireland, was married 11 Mo. 31, 1744, at Nottingham Meeting to Sarah, daughter of John and Hannah Churchman, of East Nottingham.

Joseph Trimble, or Tremble, as the name was generally written, emigrated from Ireland when some fifteen years of age, probably about 1730, and served a time of farming and wagoning with William Brown, a miller, of Nottingham. In 1741 he settled on a farm near by, which remained in the family until 1856. His wife was born 2 Mo. 17, 1716, and died 8 Mo. 2, 1750, leaving three children. Joseph was married, secondly, 2 Mo. 22, 1753, to Ann Chandler, daughter of William and Ann, of London Grove. She died 12 Mo. 31, 1793. Children : William, b. 10 Mo. 1, 1745, d. 5 Mo. 30, 1819; John, b. 12 Mo. 16, 1746, d. about 1809, near Chillicothe, Ohio ; Mary, b. 7 Mo. 11, 1748 ; Joseph, b. 10 Mo. 29, 1754, d. 12 Mo. 5, 1831 ; Thomas, b. 5 Mo. 4, 1756 ; Jacob, b. 2 Mo. 27, 1758 ; Sarah, b. 5 Mo. 23, 1760, m. Job Sidwell ; James, b. 4 Mo. 20, 1762, d. 12 Mo. 5, 1831 ; Elisha, b. 3 Mo. 18, 1765, d. 8 Mo. 28, 1848.

One William Trimble, born 1705, in County Antrim, Ireland, and James Trimble, probably a brother, came over from Ireland, and in 1734–35 joined Friends at Concord Monthly Meeting. William was married 9 Mo. 13, 1734, to Ann, daughter of John and Martha Palmer, of Concord, and died 8 Mo. 5, 1795, in Concord Township, now Delaware County. James Trimble, b. in Ire-Ireland, June 24, 1707, arrived in Pennsylvania about 6 Mo., 1719, and died 11 Mo. 21, 1792, in West Bradford, Chester County. He married 10 Mo. 3, 1735, Mary Palmer, another daughter of John and Martha. For a more extended account of the Trimbles see Futhey and Cope's *History of Chester County*, 748–750.

BARNABAS MCNAMEE, of Ireland, and Mary Pearson, daughter of John and Margaret, of Middletown, now Delaware County, were married 4 Mo. 8, 1756, at Nottingham.

SADSBURY MONTHLY MEETING

In Lancaster County. Established in 1737, from New Garden.

SAMUEL WILKISON, received 12 Mo. 6, 1737–8, dated 2 Mo. 23, 1737, from Ballinacree Meeting, County Antrim, Ireland.

JAMES HUNTER, recieved 1 Mo. 6, 1738, dated 3 Mo. 10.
1736, from Ballinacree Meeting, County Antrim, Ireland,

John Hunter of Lisburn Mtg. and Elizabeth Matthews, of Lurgan, were married at Lurgan, 10 Mo. 24, 1701.—*Minutes of Ulster Prov. Mtg.*

William Hunter, County Londonderry, in 1671, had taken 6
" stooks of Barley, 20 stooks of Oats and one load of Hey," valued at 11s. 2d.—Stockdale, *A Great Cry of Oppression*, 1.

In 1674, one John Hunter, County Antrim, had his goods seized for tithes.—*Ibid.*, 35.

In 1678, John Hunter, of Ballinderry Parish, County Antrim, had his goods taken for tithes.—*Ibid.*, 95.

In 1681, John and James Hunter, of Ballinderry Parish, County Antrim, had goods taken for tithes.—*Ibid.*, 169.

One John Hunter, of Ballymoney Meeting, and Jane Sterling, of Coleraine Meeting were married 5 Mo. 12, 1698, at the house of Sarah Melvin in Coleraine, County Antrim.

NICHOLAS STEER, received 1 Mo. 6, 1737–8, dated 3 Mo. 23, 1734, from Lisburn, County Antrim, Ireland.

THOMAS BOLOUGH, or Bulla, received 4 Mo. 4, 1739, dated 3 Mo. 19, 1738, from Grange, Ireland.

One Richard Bullough and Rachel Morton, both of Minnallan Mtg., were married 8 Mo. 20, 1715, at Minnallan, Ireland.—*Minutes of Ulster Prov. Mtg.*

Thomas Bollo, of Sadsbury Township, Lancaster County, Pa., yeoman, was married, 12 Mo. 10, 1742–43, at Sadsbury Friends' Meeting House, to Anne Williams, of East Sadsbury Twp., Chester Co., Pa., widow of Zacharias Williams.

JAMES LOVE, received 9 Mo. 12, 1741, dated 2 Mo. 17, 1739, from Ballyhays Meeting, County Cavan, Ireland; also a certificate from New Garden [Ireland], dated 8 Mo. 28, 1738. Married Faithful Richardson, at Leacock Meeting, 12 Mo. 13, 1745.

SAMUEL BOYD, received 10 Mo. 6, 1742, dated 5 Mo. 8, 1741, from Grange, Ireland.

WILLIAM COURTNEY, dated 5 Mo. 1, 1763, from Ballinacree Meeting, County Antrim.

WARRINGTON MONTHLY MEETING

In York County.   Established in 1747, from Sadsbury.

WILLIAM DELAP and wife Ruth, received 11 Mo. 16, 1747–8, dated 5 Mo. 6, 1747, from Ballyhagen Meeting, County Armagh, Ireland.

They settled in Menallen Township, now Adams County. Children: George, b. 11 Mo. 1, 1743–4 ; Sarah, b. 1 Mo. 2, 1748-9 ; Robert, b. 8 Mo. 15, 1750 ; John, b. 9 Mo. 15, 1752 ; William, b. 2 Mo. 26, 1755 ; Abigail, b. 9 Mo. 8, 1757, d. 8 Mo. 23, 1758 ; Mary, b. 10 Mo 8, 1759.

DANIEL WINTER, received 3 Mo. 21, 1748, dated 4 Mo. 5, 1737, from Ballyhagen, County Armagh, Ireland. He resided in Menallen Township, now Adams County.

THOMAS WILSON, received, 4 Mo. 17, 1748, dated 4 Mo. 2, 1736, from [Grange] Meeting, near Charlemont, County Armagh, Ireland. A certificate for him and his wife to Fairfax Mo. Mtg., Va., was signed by Warrington, 4 Mo. 17, 1749.

THOMAS BLACKBURN and wife, received 3 Mo. 19, 1750, dated 4 Mo. 18, 1749, from Ballyhagan, County Armagh, Ireland.

Thomas Blackburn, of Ballyhagen, Parish of Killmore, Co. Armagh, was married 4 Mo. 17, 1742, at Ballyhagen Meeting to Alice Hewit, daughter of Benjamin Hewit, of Clandroet, said parish and county. Marriage certificate signed by Benjamin, Robert, John, Mark, and Alice Hewitt and Antho. Blackburn.— *Marriage Books of Ulster Quarterly Meeting*, p. 64.

He settled in Menallen Township, now Adams County, where he died about 1794, his will dated Jan. 6, 1784, being probated Nov. 1, 1794. He mentions his wife Alice and children, Thomas and John.

WILLIAM NEVET, received 8 Mo. 19, 1751, dated 1 Mo. 10, 1750–1, from Moat, County West Meath, Ireland.

William Nevitt, son of Joseph and Mary Nevitt, was born 9 Mo. 3, 1718, at Mountrath, Queen's County, Ireland. About 1750 he came to Pennsylvania, and settled at Warrington, York County. He m. 5 Mo. 10, 1753, at Warrington Meeting, Hannah, daughter of Peter and Sarah (Gilpin) Cook, of Warrington. In 1770, he made a visit to his relatives in Ireland, taking

a certificate to Moat Meeting; he returned in the summer of
1771. In 1788, he was "recommended" a minister of the Society and in that service frequently visited meetings in Pennsylvania, Maryland, and Virginia. He died without issue, 8 Mo.
15, 1800, in his 82d year. In his will[1] he mentions Isaac, Ruth,
and Elizabeth Nevitt, children of his brother, Thomas Nevitt,
deceased.[2]

WILLIAM PILLAR, dated 6 Mo. 16, 1765, from Grange near
  Charlemont, received 6 Mo. 13, 1767. He returned to
  Ireland in 1769.

FINLEY McGREW, a Scotch-Irishman, who was assessed in
  London Grove Township, Chester County, as early as
  1729, and as late as 1735, became a member of Sadsbury
  Monthly Meeting, Lancaster County, in 1746. He settled
  at an early date in Tyrone Township, now Adams County,
  where he died about 1766. By his wife Elizabeth he had
  the following children: James b. 12 Mo. 27, 1744–5, m.
  Jane ———— ; Nathan, b. 9 Mo. 26, 1746, m. Martha
  Hendricks; William b. 1 Mo. 24, 1748–9; Finley, b. 2
  Mo. 23, 1751, m. Mary Hendricks; Isabelle, b. 3 Mo. 4,
  1752, d. 8 Mo. 1, 1752; Peter, b. 5 Mo. 19, 1755, m.
  Patience Hendricks; Archibald, b. 4 Mo. 14, 1757.

JAMES McGREW, kinsman, doubtless a brother of Finley Mc-
  Grew, brought a certificate for himself and wife from
  Hopewell, Va., to Warrington Monthly Meeting, in 1750.
  A James Magrew, probably the same, was assessed in London Grove, Chester County in 1729 and 1734. Children
  of James and Mary McGrew: Finley, b. 1 Mo. 13,
  1735–6, m. Dinah Cox, and removed about 1787 to the
  Redstone region of Pennsylvania; Deborah, b. 7 Mo. 14,
  1739, m. Joseph Blackburn, in 1758; Ann, b. 4 Mo. 29,
  1741, m. ———— Newlin; Nathan, b. 3 Mo. 10, 1743, d.
  1769, m. Rachel Blackburn, in 1767; Simon, b. 11 Mo.
  5, 1745; Mary, b. 11 Mo. 5, 1748, m. Moses Blackburn,
  in 1767; James, b. 6 Mo. 25, 1751, m. Elizabeth McFerran,

[1] Recorder's Office, York, Pa.

[2] William, son of William and Elizabeth Nevitt, was born 1 Mo. 25, 1714,
at Mountmellick. William Nevitt, son of William and Ann Nevitt, b. 2 Mo.
22, 1726, at Mountmellick Queen's County, Ireland. William Nevitt and
Ann Hancock, both of Lisburn, County Antrim, m. 6 Mo. 7, 1753, at
Hillsborough, County Down.

about 1774, and removed to the Redstone region, about 1794. Children of James and Elizabeth (McFerran) McGrew: Mary, b. 3 Mo. 10, 1774, m. Joel Hutton; Nathan, m. Elizabeth Winder; Jane; James B.; Deborah, m. Samuel McGrew; Joseph; Simon; Finley; Thomas; John B.; Jacob; Archibald, m. Susanna Gilbert.

FRANCIS HOBSON, and wife Ann, from Ballyhagen Meeting, County Armagh, Ireland, dated 7 Mo. 4, 1764, received 1 Mo. 12, 1765.

Francis Hobson, of Drumilly, Parish of Loughgall, County Armagh, m. 9 Mo. 25, 1741, at Ballyhagen Meeting, Ann, daughter of Joseph Mackey, of Kincon, Parish of Kilmore, County Armagh. He died 12 Mo. 17, 1777, aged 72 years, and was buried at Menallen. Children : Mary, m. —— Blackney, about 1768; Elizabeth, m. 7 Mo. 17, 1777, at Warrington, Richard Blatchford; Ann, m. 3 Mo. 22, 1770, at Warrington, Henry Atherton; Francis, m. 12 Mo. 12, 1770, at Menallen, Susanna Jones (he made a trip to Ireland about 1772); Phebe, m. 5 Mo. 18, 1775, at Warrington, Richard Atherton; Joseph, b. 1746, m. Ann ——, about 1778, and removed to near Richmond, Jefferson County, Ohio, about 1800; Robert, being in ill health in 1776, was placed in care of Dr. David Jemmison, of York, York County.

ELIZABETH WRIGHT, from meeting of Grange near Charlemont, Ireland, dated 12 Mo. 25, 1774, received 10 Mo. 14, 1775.

JOSEPH HEWIT and family, dated 4 Mo. 22, 1772, from Ballyhagen Meeting, Ireland, received 9 Mo. 12, 1772.[1]

A son Geoge, b. 12 Mo. 25, 1750; d. 2 Mo. 15, 1841; m. 11 Mo. 16, 1774, at Menallen Meeting, Deborah, daughter of John and Mary Morton, of Menallen.

---

[1] Children of Jonathan and Ann Hewitt, of Menallen : Abel, b. 3 Mo. 5, 1779; Sarah, b. 11 Mo. 24, 1780; Joseph, b. 9 Mo. 25, 1782.

One John Hewet, of Ballyhagen Meeting and Isabelle Hoope, of Lurgan Meeting were married, 2 Mo. 16, 1701, at Lurgan, Ireland.

One Mark Hewit, of Clandrule, Parish Kilmore. County Armagh, and Mary McKetrick, of Derryerue, Parish Loughgall, County Armagh, were married 1 Mo. 25, 1742, at Ballyhagen. Among signers were: Hannah and Jonas McKetrick, John, Robert, and Benjamin Hewit, John Allen.

SOME IRISH CERTIFICATES RECEIVED AT MEET-
INGS IN NEW JERSEY AND DELAWARE

HADDONFIELD (FORMERLY GLOUCESTER) MO.
MTG., N. J.

Established in 1695.

MARK NEWBY and WILL: BATTES, dated 6 Mo. 21, 1681, from
Bellicare Mtg., County Wicklow, Ireland.

، THOMAS DENNIS. "Dwelt Amongst us about nine years."
From Moat Mtg., County West Meath, near Athlone, Ireland, dated 1 Mo. 26, 1682.

JONATHAN WOOD, wife and children, "he Being A Weaver
by trade hath followed that Imployment untill It did soo fale
that he & his famely Could not Live Comfortably of itt
& being his Stock but smale And farme Lytle." Two
daughters and one son, dated 5 Mo. 8, 1683, from Ballyhagen, County Armagh, Ireland.

THOMAS THACKARA, wife Esther, and children, from Dublin, dated 6 Mo. 16, 1681.

SALEM MONTHLY MEETING, N. J.

Established in 1676.

JOSEPH WHITE, son of Samuel and ———? White, born 1
Mo. 20, 1651–2, in a town called Sulyrane, in North
Hampshire, England. He went from England to Ireland
in 1672, taking ship 7 Mo. 25. Afterwards he married
"Elizabeth Church, who came from Dolbay of the Woulds
in Lestershire in England to Ireland." They belong to New
Garden Mtg., "their dwelling place and took Ship at
Dublin in Ireland for West Jersey in Amerika who After
eight weeks, two days Arrived to Elsinburgh," West Jersey,
9 Mo. 17, 1681, together with servants as followeth.

"Hugh Middleton whoose father was of Lestershire and his
mother of Glocestershire.

"Allsoo Mathias bellore (?), his father and mother weere
English people.

" 3ly Hannah Asbury her father an Englishman her mother borne in Ireland."

THE IRISH QUAKER SETTLERS OF NEWTON, NOW IN CAMDEN COUNTY, NEW JERSEY

THOMAS SHARP, "woolstead comber," of Dublin, nephew of of Anthony Sharp, a wealthy Quaker merchant of that city, was one of the leaders of the Irish Quaker settlement of Newton, N. J. He has left the following interesting account of his immigration and settlement, written in 1718 : [1]

"Let it be remembered y* upon y* nineteenth day of September, in y* year of our Lord one thousand six hundred and eighty-one, Mark Newby, William Bates, Thomas Thackara, George Goldsmith and Thomas Sharp, set saile from y* Harbor belonging to y* city of Dublin in y* Kingdom of Ireland, in a pink called _Y* owner's adventure_, whereof Thomas Lurtin, of London, was commander, and being taken sick in y* city, his mate John Dagger, officiated in his place ; in order to transport us, and y* we might settle ourselves in West Jersey, in America. And by y* good providence of God we arrived in y* Capes of Delaware y* eighteenth day of November following, and so up y* bay until we came to Elsenburg, and were landed with our goods and families at Salem, where we abode y* winter. But it being very favourable weather and purchasing a boat amongst us, we had an opportunity to make search up and down in y* which was called y* Third tenth, which had been reserved for y* proprietors dwelling in Ireland, where we might find a place suitable for so many of us to settle down together, being in these early times somewhat doubtful of y* Indians, and at last pitched down by y* which is now called Newton creek, as y* most invitingist place to settle down by, and then we went to Burlington, and made application to y* commissioners y* we might have warrants directed to Daniel Leeds, y* Surveyor General, to survey unto every of us, so much land as by y* constitution at y* time was alloted for a settlement being five hundred acres, or y* we had a right to, for a taking up it under, which accordingly we obtained.

"At which time also Robert Zane, who came from ye city of

[1] Liber A, of Gloucester County deeds, page 98, in the Office of the Secretary of State, Trenton, N. J. (See Judge Clement's _First Settlers in Newton_, 24-26.)

Dublin, and had been settled in Salem, four years before, joined in with us who had a right to a tenth, Mark Newby to a twentieth, William Bates to a twentieth, Thomas Thackara to a twentieth, Thomas Sharp (out of his uncle Anthony Sharp's right) a twentieth, and George Goldsmith (under ye notion of Thomas Starkey's right) a tenth ; all which of us excepting William Bates who took his on ye southerly side of Newton creek, we took our land in one tract together for one thousand seven hundred and fifty acres, bounding in ye forks of Newton creek and so over to Cooper's creek and by a line of marked trees to a small branch of ye fork creek and so down ye same as by ye certficate of it standing upon record in ye Secretary's office it doth appear. And after some time finding some incoveniency in having our land in common together being at ye time settled at ye place now called Newton in ye manner of a town for fear as aforesaid at which being removed we came to an agreement to divide. George Goldsmith he chose the head of the creek, Thomas Sharp the forks or lower end of the land next towards the river by which means the rest kept to their settlements without any disadvantage to themselves.

And so ye land was divided according to every man's right.

* * *

Given under my hand the 3rd month, 3rd, 1718.

THOMAS SHARP.''

Thomas Sharp was Recorder and Clerk of the Courts of Gloucester County for many years. He was also a surveyor and made several important maps of the early settlements which are reproduced in facsimile in Judge Clement's *First Settlers of Newton*. He acted as agent for his uncle, Anthony Sharp, of Dublin, who had large holdings in New Jersey. In 1684, he was made Commissioner of Highways, and in the following year was returned as a member of the Legislature. In 1700, he became Judge of the Gloucester County Courts.

Thomas Sharp was married in 1684, to Sarah Fearn, of Darby. A daughter Elizabeth, m. 8 Mo. 3, 1709, at Darby, John, son of John and Mary Hallowell, and resided at Darby and Newton. Children of John and Elizabeth Hallowell : Sarah, b. 11 Mo. 16, 1710, d. 7 Mo. 17, 1747, m. John Hurst ; Samuel, b. 3 Mo. 10, 1713 ; John, b. 7 Mo. 10, 1715, d. 7 Mo. 26, 1778, m. Hannah Lewis ; Thomas, b. 11 Mo. 13, 1717, d. 8 Mo. 29, 1788, m. Ann. Thomson ; Joseph, b. 12 Mo. 28, 1721, d. 5 Mo. 8, 1792, m. Elizabeth Holcomb ; Mary, b. 2 Mo. 1, 1729, d. 12 Mo. 16, 1791, m. John Elmslie.

ISAAC SHARP, son of Anthony Sharp, of Dublin, came to New Jersey about 1702–3, and settled at Blessington, now Sharptown.

He was Judge of Salem Court and served as a member of the Assembly from 1709 to 1725. About 1726 he returned to Ireland and resided on his estate called "Roundwood," in Queen's County, where he died in 1735. He married in 1704, Margaret Braithwaite, of Salem, and had children : Anthony, Isaac (of Blessington, Salem County, N. J., died in 1770. He was also Judge of Salem Court), Joseph, Sarah, Rachel (m. Daniel Delaney, of Queen's County, Ireland, by whom she had children : Sharp, William, Martin).—*American Genealogist*, 146.

ROBERT ZANE, of Dublin, "Serge Maker," pioneer settler of Newton, or the Irish Tenth, in Gloucester County, N. J., probably came out with John Fenwick and his party, in 1675, for he was one of the members of the Friends' Meeting established at Salem that year.

By deed of April 12, 1677, he became one of the Proprietors of West New Jersey. In 1679 he was married, at Burlington Meeting, to Alice Alday, who is thought to have been an Indian. In 1681 he became a settler at Newton. He was elected to the first Legislature in 1682, and was returned in 1685. He died in 1694, leaving his second wife, Elizabeth (daughter of Henry Willis, of Hempstead, Long Island), and several children to survive him.

Children were : Nathaniel, b. about 1673, m. Grace Rake straw, of Philadelphia, in 1697 ; Robert, m. Jane ——— ; Elnathan ; Simon ; Mary ; Esther; and Sarah. (For further details see Clement's *First Settlers of Newton*, 11–22, and *Penna. Mag.*, XII., 123–25.)

WILLIAM BATES, carpenter, of County Wicklow, who was imprisoned in 1670, for attending Friends' Meeting at Thomas Trafford's house in Wicklow (*Besse*, II., 470), was one of a company of Friends who purchased a share of West New Jersey, by deed of April 12, 1677.

He sailed from Dublin in September, in 1681, in *Ye Owners Adventure*, and settled with the other Irish Friends at Newton, where he owned 250 acres of land. In 1683 he was one of the representatives from the Irish Tenth in the Legislature of the Province of West New Jersey, and was the same year appointed constable. The next year he was again returned as a member of the Legislature, and was appointed one of the commissioners for laying out highways. He died in 1700. His children, all born

25

in Ireland, were : Jeremiah, m. Mary, daughter of Samuel Spicer ; Joseph, m. Mercy Clement, in 1701 ; Abigail, m. Joshua Fearne, in 1687 ; William, said to have married an Indian girl ; Sarah, m. Simon Ellis, in 1692.[1]

GEORGE GOLDSMITH, a Friend, came over from Dublin, in *Ye Owners Adventure,* in 1681–2, and settled at Gloucester, N. J.[2]

His grandson, James Parrock, a Friend, of Philadelphia, shipwright, aged seventy-six years, in a deposition made at Philadelphia, Jan. 2, 1751, states that his grandfather had formerly lived at Ballinakill, Queen's County, Ireland, and had served in Ireland as Lieutenant in Cromwell's Army.[3]

JOHN HUGG, from the Parish of Castle Ellis, County Wexford, was an early settler on Little Timber Creek, in the Newton settlement, where in 1683 he purchased 500 acres of land from Robert Zane.

He served as a member of the Jersey Legislature in 1685. He died in 1706. His children were : John, Judge of Gloucester County courts, 1695–1706, Provincial Councillor of West New Jersey, etc., m. Priscilla, daughter of Francis Collins ; Elias, m. Margaret, sister of Priscilla Collins ; Joseph, m. Sarah ———— ; and Charles.[4]

MARK NEWBIE, says Judge Clement, "was a resident of the city of London, and a tallow chandler." He was a member of a Friends' Meeting, whose house of worship was in a street of that city, called "Barbican," and removed to Dublin, in 1681.

Unfortunately the Judge does not give his authority for this statement or it might be confirmed ; but this date of removal to London is at least ten years too late, for Stockdale mentions Newbie as a persecuted Quaker shopkeeper residing in Thomas Street, Dublin, in 1671. Says Stockdale :[5]

In 1671, Mark Newby, of Thomas Street, Dublin, "because for Conscience sake he could not be an observer of Holidays (so-called) he opened his Shop on the 25th of the 10th month, called Christmas day." For this he "had his house assaulted by a

---

[1] Clement's *First Settlers of Newton,* 47–56.
[2] Judge Clement's *First Settlers in Newton,* 67–70.
[3] *Ibid.,* the author's corrected copy. (Hist. Soc. of Penn'a.) Typewritten note inserted at page 70.
[4] See Judge Clement's *First Settlers of Newton,* 283–291.
[5] *A Great Cry of Oppression,* 205

rude multitude," who with great violence threw dirt and stones into "his Shop, endangering his Life and his Families ; spoyled Shop-goods, broke Glass-windows and Pewter vessels, abused their Neighbours for reproving them ; the said Mark was damnified" 16 s. 6 d.

Mark Newby set out for New Jersey, in the latter part of 1681, in *Ye Owners Adventure* and settled at Newton, the first Friends' meetings being held at his house. In the political affairs of New Jersey he took a prominent part and filled several positions of trust and responsibility. At the May term of the Legislature, in 1682, he appeared as a member, and was selected by the Governor as one of his Council. He was made one of the Land Commissioners and one of the Committee of Ways and Means to raise money for the use of the government. He died probably early in 1683, for at the May term of the Legislature in 1683 he is mentioned as deceased.

As far as ascertained, he had two sons and two daughters : Rachel, m. Isaac Decou, in 1695 ; Stephen, m. Elizabeth Wood, in 1703 ; Edward, in Hannah Chew, in 1706 ; and Elizabeth, m. John Hogg, in 1714.

Hannah, the widow of Mark Newbie, married James Atkinson, in 1685.[1]

THOMAS THACKARA, "stuff maker," of Dublin, by deed of April 12, 1677, in conjunction with other Friends, purchased one whole share of West New Jersey.

He sailed with his family from Dublin, in September, 1681, in *Ye Owners Adventure*, and settled on 250 acres at Newton. He became one of the leading men of the settlement, serving as a member of the first Legislature that sat at Burlington to frame and adopt laws for the Province. In 1682, he was appointed one of the Judges of the Court for the Irish Tenth and served until 1685, inclusive. He was also one of the land commissioners. The first Friends' meeting house built at Newton stood upon lands conveyed by him to the trustees of the Society. He died about 1702, letters of administration on his estate being granted in that year. His first wife probably died after his settlement here, as in 1689 he married Hepzibah, daughter of Francis Eastlake.

Children were : Benjamin, m. Mary, daughter of William Cooper ; Thomas, m. (1) Ann Parker and (2) Abigail Bates ; Hannah, m. John Whitall ; Sarah, m. John Eastlack ; and Hepzibah.[2]

[1] For a further account see Judge Clement's *First Settlers of Newton*, 37–46.
[2] For further details see Judge Clement's *First Settlers of Newton*, 57–66.

JOHN JARVIS, or Jervis,[1] a Friend, of Roscore, King's County,
Ireland, with his son Martin, as stated in the deposition of
James Parrock, made at Philadelphia, in 1751, was "obliged
to fly from Ireland [in 1688] with as much haste and pri-
vacy as he could for fear of being massacred by the Papists."
He came to New Jersey by way of Boston and took up his
residence with his old friend George Goldsmith, of Gloucester, N. J., where he remained until 1691, when he settled on a large tract of land which he had purchased at
Cape May.   He was appointed Justice of the Peace for Cape
May County in 1695, 1696, and 1697.   In 1701, he returned to Ireland.   He had five[2] sons: I. Charles Jarvis[3]
(b. about 1675 in Ireland, d. in London, in 1739) studied
in London under Sir Godfrey Kneller, court painter, and
became a celebrated artist.   (He was a friend of Pope, the
poet, and translated *Don Quixote*.—See *National Dictionary of Biography*, XXIX., p. 354.)   II. John Jarvis, whoin
1753,[4] was living in King's County, Ireland.   III. Mathew,
died young.   IV. Trevor, died young.   V. Martin Jarvis,
shoemaker, b. about 1675, d. 1742, says Parrock, settled for
a time in Newton, then Gloucester County, N. J., and married in 1698, Mary Champion (whose father John Champion
came afterwards from Long Island and settled near Gloucester).   In 1705, Martin Jarvis purchased a house and lot on 2d
Street, between Market and Chestnut Streets, Philadelphia,
and made his residence there the remainder of his life.
His daughter Sarah married William Sandwith, an Irish
Friend, of Philadelphia, and became the mother of Elizabeth (Sandwith) Drinker (wife of Henry Drinker, of Philadelphia, one of the Quaker exiles to Virginia, in the war of
the Revolution), whose diary,[5] covering the period 1759–
1807, is a valuable record of the social life of the time.

[1] MS. note by Judge Clement in his own copy of his *First Settlers o
Newton* (Hist. Soc. of Penna.), 148.

[2] Parrock says one of the sons was bound an apprentice in Boston.

[3] Parrock states that he was bound an apprentice to a "Limner" (artist)
of London.

[4] William Drinker's sketch of the Jarvis family written in 1795 (Elizabeth Drinker's *Journal*, 3-4).

[5] *Extracts from the Journal of Elizabeth Drinker*, 1759–1807, edited
by Henry D. Biddle, Philadelphia, 1889.

DUCK CREEK (CAMDEN) MONTHLY MEETING, DELAWARE, ETC.

Established in 1705.

MARY MACKEE, from Cork, Ireland, received 12 Mo. 21, 1708–9.

SARAH HILL, from Friends in County Antrim, Ireland, received 3 Mo. 21, 1711.

GEORGE PLUM, received 9 Mo. 17, 1712.

"A Friend lately from Ireland and now settled at Georges Creek appeared at this meeting and Signifyed that he had a Certificate with him from Friends in Ireland and since he came into Pennsylvania He swimming in a Creek with his Horse his said Certificate was destroyed by the water and riding with it in his Pocket afterwards sinch which Accident he has produced a paper under the Hands of two Friends from Bristol in Pennsylvania who declare they saw the said Certificate which this Meeting Receives."

" GABRIEL McCOOL produced a Certificate for himself and his Brother James MaCool fr the meeting at Dunglane in the County of London Derry in Ireland signed by Ten friends in behalf of the said Meeting." Received 9 Mo. 22, 1725.

In 1717 John McCool, from George's Creek and Mary Howie were married. Olivia McCool married John Hall, in 1763.

In 1731, Thomas Chalkley (*Journal,* 25), on a voyage from the Barbadoes was wrecked at Reedy Island in the Delaware, and while recovering from injuries received was cared for at the " House of John M'Cool, who with his Wife, were tender in their Care and Love towards me."

ELIZABETH ROBINSON, with husband, Francis Robinson, dated 7 Mo. 12, 1752, from Ballycane Meeting, County Wicklow, Ireland, to Wilmington Monthly Meeting, Delaware; they had removed some years before (see p. 93).

In 1668, in County Armagh Patrick Robinson for tythes had taken from him "a Tub, a Pot, a Frying-Pan, and a Parcel of Yarn, being most of what was in the House worth £1. 6s."—*A Compendious View,* 78.

In 1672, Francis Robinson, County Armagh, had his goods seized for tithes (*Stockdale*, 14). In 1676, in County Down, Francis Robinson, of Segoe Parish, suffered persecution for non-payment of tithes.—*Ibid.*, 64.

THOMAS BRIAN, son of William, of Waterford. m. Ann, daughter of David Kells, of Armagh, Ireland. Children : Mary (b. 8 Mo. 3, 1781), Rebecca, Thomas, David, Ann.—*Records of Wilmington* (Del.) *Monthly Meeting.*

At Richland Monthly Meeting, Bucks County, 10 Mo. 18, 1759, THOMAS STALFORD produced a certificate from Ireland.

SOME EXTRACTS FROM RECORDS OF LURGAN MONTHLY MEETING, IRELAND, ETC.

ARCHIBALD BELL, tailor, son of Archibald Bell, "of Arkinhoome in parish Stablegarden, shire of Jadforrest," Scotland, and wife Ann, was born about 8 Mo., 1620, at Arkinhoome, and was married about 1648, to Ann, daughter of Alexander Yuruns, of Arkinhoome. Came to Ireland in 1655. Children : Jare (daughter), b. Arkinhoome, 7 Mo. 1649 ; Archibald, b. same place 9 Mo. 1651 ; John, b. *circa* 1 Mo. 1653, at "Branton of gillslard," Co. Cumberland, England ; Mary, b. *circa* 1 Mo., 1655, at "dirlet near Markate hill, County Armagh," Ireland ; Richard, b. *circa* 9 Mo. 1657, in Parish Ballyards, Co. Armagh ; Alexander, b. 9 Mo. 1659, Parish Lishley, Co. Armagh ; George, b. 4 Mo. 1662, at Drumtullan, Parish Benbarb, Co. Armagh ; Elizabeth, b. 4 Mo., 1665, at Ballytullan, Parish Benbarb ; Sarah, b. 3 Mo. 1669, at Tarrahmoore, Parish Shankill, Co. Armagh.

In 1681, Archibald Bell, of Parish of Magheramisk, County Antrim, had his goods taken for tithes.—Stockdale, *A Great Cry of Oppression*, 169.

In 1707, after attending meeting at Monallen [Moyallon?] William Edmundson says in his *Journal*, 288, "After this Meeting we went to see Archibald Bell, he being very old and feeble, and having walked in the Truth many Years ; we lodged at his House one Night, and the next Day went to the Meeting at Richard Boyes', and so to Lisburn."

One Simon Bell, son of William Bell, of Parish of Shankill, County Armagh, married Ann, daughter of Richard Crooks, of Kilmore, said Parish, and had a daughter Jane, b. 7 Mo. 20, 1693.

ALEXANDER MATHES, blacksmith, son of Hugh Mathes (of Donmurry, Co. Antrim) and wife Jane, was born *circa* 7 Mo. 1648, at Donmurry. Removed to Lurgan 12 Mo. 9, 1668. He was married 8 Mo. 7, 1671, to Elizabeth, daughter of John and Dorothy Harding, of near Makeralin, Co. Down. Children : John, b. 1 Mo. 24, 1672, at Lurgan ; Jane, b. 1 Mo. 10, 1674, at Lurgan.

ROBERT CHAMBERS, son of Thomas Chambers, of Mooresome, near Gisbrough, Yorkshire, England, and wife Jane, was born in Moorsome, 9 Mo., 1646. Came to Ireland in 1661, and was married 5 Mo. 9, 1673, to Jane, daughter of Mark Wright and Ann, his wife, of Lygatory, Parish of Shankill, Co. Armagh. Children : John, b. 6 Mo, 5, 1674, at Dromgora ; James, b. 7 Mo. 14, 1676, at Tanniferglasson.

JAMES GREER, son of Henry Greer, of Newton, Parish of "Sheelbiller," Northumberland, England, and Mary, his wife, was born at Newton *circa* 4 Mo. 1653. Was brought to Ireland "ye same year." He was married 6 Mo. 20, 1678, to Elinor, daughter of John Rea and Elinor his wife, of Lissacurran, Parish of Shankill, Co. Armagh. She was born about 2 Mo. 25, 165–, at Lissacurran. Children : Henry, b. 1 Mo. 5, 1681, at Lissa-curran ; Mary, b. 12 Mo. 7, 1685 ; John, b. 7 Mo. 9, 1688 ; Thomas, b. 12 Mo. 1, 1690 ; James, b. 6 Mo. 18, 1693.
Henry Greer, of Lurgan, and Sarah Henderson, of Dunclady, were married at the house of Katharine Henderson, widow, in Dunclady, 5 Mo. 6, 1704.—*Minutes of Ulster Province Mtg.*
In 1673, in County Tyrone, "Henry Greer had taken from him for Tithe by the said Edward ['Conrey Tithmonger for the Dean of Ardmagh'] and William Dickson, one stook of Wheat, three stooks of Rye, seventeen stooks of Oats, fifteen stooks of Barly, and cut one yard of Hey out of his Stack, being but eight yards in all worth one pound.
"Afterwards the said Edward forceably entered the said Henry's Stackyard, threw down a Stack, and took away what Corn he pleased ; a Son of Henrys taking one of their Horses by the Bridle, said, he could find in his heart to take him to the Pound, the said Edward came behind him and knock'd him down with his Sword in the sheath, and the same day afterwards took out of his Barn what Corn he pleased."—William Stockdale, *A Great Cry of Oppression*, 30.

JAMES BRADSHAW, son of William Bradshaw, of Prestwaith Parish, near Manchester, Lancashire, England, and Elizabeth, his wife, was born there *circa* 4 Mo., 1619. Came to Ireland as a soldier in 1649. Was married 10 Mo. 24, 1657, to Ann, daughter of Robert Patterson, of Carrickfergus, and Katherine, his wife. Had ten children, as recorded in Lurgan records.

ROBERT HOOPES [Hoope] "Son of John Hoopes of Moorsom (neer Gisbrough) in Yorkshire in England, and of Isabell his wife, was born in Moorsom aforesd" 8 Mo. 18, 1639. "He came to Ireland Anno dom : 1660 being a tailor by trade. About the beginning of the eight moneth Anno dom : 1663 he took to wife Ellener ye daughter of John Hodgkinson and of An his wife of Preston in Anderness in Lancashire in England aforesd who was borne in the Sd towne about the Anno dom 1638 : and had by her Children borne as followth " : Ann, b. 10 Mo. 22, 1664, at Lurgan ; John, b. 10 Mo. 4, 1666, at Lurgan ; Abraham, b. 11 Mo. 14, 1668, at Lurgan.—*Lurgan Records.*

Robert Hoop, of County Armagh, in 1671, had taken from him for tithes, barley, flour, oats, and hay.—Besse's *Sufferings of the Quakers*, Vol. II.

Robert Hoope and Ann Harding, both of Lurgan, were married at Lurgan, County Armagh, 9 Mo. 17, 1702.—*Minutes of Ulster Province Mtg.*

In 1680, "Robert Hoop and George Hodgen having a shop in Lurgin, the aforesaid John Weatherby ["Priest" of Parish of Shankill] bought some Broad cloth and other things of the said Robert and when he had bargained, pulled Mony out of his Pocket, and laid his hand on the Counter with Mony in it, and said, 'Cast up what it comes to, and I will pay you very well in your hand,' and while Robert was casting it up, he sent away the Taylor with the Goods, which come to sixteen shillings and a penny, and kept all for small Tithe, and other things, which he called Church-rights, due (as he said) from the said Robert and George, and although Robert told him of his treacherous dealing yet he went away and paid him nothing."—*Stockdale*, 145.

FRANCIS ROBSON, son of John Robson, of Farebee, Yorkshire, England, and wife Elizabeth, was born at Farebee, about 1607. When but young he was brought into Ireland. About 1634 he was married to Isabelle, daughter of John Anderson, of Tanniferarbat, Parish of Sego, Co. Armagh, Ireland. Children : John, b. 1650, at Hillsborough, Co. Down ; Catherine, b. 1651, at Killwarlin, Co. Down ; Joseph, b. 1656, at Tanniferarbat ; Joan, b. 1653, at same place ; Jacob, b. 1 Mo. 1, 1663, at same place.—*Lurgan Records.*

WILLIAM EDMUNDSON,[1] the founder of Quakerism in Ireland, m. in 1652, Margaret, daughter of Thomas Stanford, of Bramley, Derbyshire, England. She died in 1691 and he m. 2d, 10 Mo. 1, 1697, at Mountmelick Meeting, Ireland, Mary Strangman, who died in 1732. Children: Mary, b. 1654, at Antrim, m. William Fayle; William, b. 1655, at Lurgan, left Friends; Samuel, b. 1659, at Tineal, near Rosenallis; Hindrance, b. 1662, at Tineal, m. ——— Seale; Susanna, b. 1666, at Tineal, m. Eleazer Sheldon; Anna, b. 1669, at Tineal, m. Lawrence Moore; Trial, b. 1671, d. 1722, m. in 1699, Abigail, daughter of Richard and Elizabeth Johnson.

Children of Trial and Abigail Edmundson, all born at Tineal: William, b. 1700, d. 1705; John, b. 1701, d. 1705; Margaret, b. 1703, d. 1705; Caleb, b. 1705; Joshua, b. 1705, m. in 1744 Susanna, daughter of Tobias and Elizabeth Pim; Elizabeth, b. 1707; Abigail, b. 1709; William, b. 1712, m. 6 Mo. 6, 1750, Jane, daughter of Robert and Sarah Roberts; Samuel, b. 1714, m. Elizabeth Russell, of Dublin.

Children of Samuel and Elizabeth Edmundson: Elizabeth, William, Thomas, Abigail, Hannah (m. Thomas Harvey), Samuel (m. Elizabeth), Joshua (m. in 1801, Charlotte Goff).—*Data from Joshua William Edmundson, a Friend, of Dublin, grandson of Joshua and Charlotte Edmundson.*

AT ULSTER PROVINCE MEETING, 7 Mo. 27, 1695, the following friends were appointed to visit families:

Old Castle.—Nicholas Starky, Thomas Langbree.

Charlemont.—William Whitesitt, Robert Greer.

Ballyhagen.—Francis Hobson, John Nicholson.

Lurgan.—Thomas Wainwright, Timothy Kirk, Richardson Mayson, Alexander Christy.

Ballenderry.—John Holding.

Lisburn.—Thomas Squire, John Combe.

Antrim.—Thomas Wilkinson, John Boyd.

Grange.—James Greenwood, Edward Hudson.

Ballymoney ⎫ Andrew Melvin
Toberhead ⎬ Andrew Knox
Coleraine ⎭ ffrancis Sarson
Thomas Gregg

---

[1] It has been said that William Edmundson's brother John was the same John Edmundson, a wealthy Quaker planter who resided in Talbot County, Maryland, as early as 1660; but this cannot be correct for as late as 1679 John Edmundson suffered persecution in Queen's County, Ireland, to which he had removed with his brother William.—Stockdale, *A Great Cry of Oppression*, 245; Rutty, 345; Besse, II., 466, 468.

10 Mo. 30, 1699. Friends appointed to get subscribers for Barclay's Apology: *Old Castle, Ballyhaes, and Coothill,* John Freeman, Merrick King, Thomas Hutton, and John Bell ; *Carrikfergus,* Mathias Calvert; *Ballymoney,* James Mooreand Eli Crockett.

AT ULSTER PROVINCE MEETING, 8 Mo. 3, 1702, "Whereas there is one George Mento who professes truth lives now att Bryans ford,and being about to undertake Some work for y⁰ Lady Dungannon and he having no certificate from friends concerning faithful behaviour in truths way, and friends nott being assured of his honesty & punctuallity this meeting therefore thinks it convenient to avoid any reproach y⁰ may happen to come upon truth by him do appoint Richard Mercer & Thomas Courtney to acquaint y⁰ Said woman y⁰ if She deal with trust, or putt any confidence in him it may be upon his own account, and not upon account, of his being called a Quaker."

AT ULSTER PROVINCE MEETING, 3 Mo. 1, 1703, Barclay's Apology to be delivered to : James Starr for Old Castle, John Combs for Lisburn, Samˡ. Wilkinson for Antrim, Eli Crocket for Ballymoney, Robert Miller for Dunlady, George Fox for Monallen, Eli Crocket for Coleraine, Edward Hudson for Grange, William Whitsitt for Charlemont, William Gray for Ballyhagen, Richard Boys for Ballinderry, John Walker for Lurgan, Mathias Calvert for Carrickfergus.

At Ulster Providence Meeting, 3 Mo. 30, 1702, "That friends be reminded to give account to y⁰ next meeting how many of y⁰ book called y⁰ rise and progress they will take each friend to pay for what he takes, which being returned are as follows : Old Castle—3, Thomas Hutton ; Charlemount—10, Wm. Whitsitt ; Ballyhagen—19, William Gray ; Lurgan—26, John Robson ; Lisburn—33, Richᵈ Boyes ; Antrim—7, Thomas Wilkesson ; Grange—4, Walter Clark ; Ballymoney—7, Eli Crockett ; Coleraine—5, William Wyly ; Dunlady and Toberhead—6, Patrick Henderson and Robᵗ Miller.   Total, 115."

THE WRIGHT FAMILY

JOHN WRIGHT[1] and wife Elizabeth, from Castleshane, County

[1] Sources of information : Meeting Records ; MS. Chart of Wright Family, made about 1840, by General William Wierman Wright, etc. At Warrington Mo. Mtg., 10 Mo. 14, 1775, one Elizabeth Wright produced a certificate of removal from Grange, near Charlemont, Ireland.

Monaghan, Ireland, had settled in Menallen Twp., York, now Adams County, Pa., as early 1748, and were members of Warrington Monthly Meeting. A certificate for John Wright and children, directed to Sadsbury, was granted at New Garden Monthly Meeting, Chester County, 4 Mo. 28, 1746. Their daughter daughter Rachel, as stated in her memorial [1] ''was born at Castleshane,[2] in Ireland, in the year 1737, and removed to Pennsylvania with her parents, John and Elizabeth Wright, who, after some years, settled in York County, within the compass of Warrington monthly-meeting.'' They had nine children: I. Mary; II. Samuel; III. Rachel; IV. Joseph; V. Alice; VI. Benjamin; VII. John; VIII. Joel; IX. Jonathan.

I. MARY, m. 5 Mo. 9, 1753, at Menallen Friends' Mtg., to Samuel Hutton, of Menallen, son of Joseph Hutton, deceased.

II. SAMUEL WRIGHT, m. 9 Mo. 4, 1754, at Huntington Friends' Meeting, now Adams County, Gertrude Wierman, daughter of William and Gertrude (Sietman) Wierman. He died probably about or prior to 1781, and she married secondly, William Ferguson, widower, of Menallen. She died in 1802, having had eight children by her first husband, Samuel Wright, as follows:

1. *John Wright*, m. 12 Mo. 12, 1781, at Menallen Friends' Meeting, to Ann Griffith, daughter of Thomas and Eve Griffith, of Menallen, and had seven children: Samuel, Thomas, Mary, William, Ann, John, and Rachel.

(1.) Samuel Wright, b. 9 Mo. 27, 1783, m. 3 Mo. 28, 1804, at Menallen Mtg., Rebecca Harris, daughter of Benjamin and Rebecca Harris. Children: Jacob, Thomas, Rebecca, Barbara, Mary Ann, Nathan, Melinda, Ann, and Ruth Anna.

(2.) Thomas Wright, b. 8 Mo. 6, 1784, m. Anna Harris. Children: Israel, Leah, Lydia, Lucy, Harris, Hanson, Anna, Julia, and Isaac.

(3.) Mary Wright, b. 6 Mo. 5, 1786, m. 5 Mo. 27, 1807, at Menallen Mo. Mtg., Jacob Harris, son of Benjamin and Mary Harris. Children: John, b. 10 Mo. 9, 1808; Samuel, b. 11 Mo. 25, 1810; Mary Ann, b. 12 Mo. 31, 1812; Silas, b. 2 Mo. 19, 1815; Rachel, b. Mo. 12, 1817; Rebecca, b. 9 Mo. 5, 1819; Ellen, b. 10 Mo. 28, 1821; William; Benjamin.

(4.) William Wright, b. 12 Mo. 21, 1788, d. 10 Mo. 25, 1865, m. Phebe Wierman, daughter of William and Hannah (Griest) Wierman, at Huntington Mtg., 11 Mo. 7, 1817. She was born

---

[1] A Testimony from Pipe Creek Mo. Mtg., Md., concerning Rachel, wife of William Farquhar, Jr.—*A Collection of Quaker Memorials*, printed at Phila., in 1787, page 388.

[2] A Friends' meeting was established at Castleshane, 1723.—*Rutty*, 343.

2 Mo. 8, 1790, and d. 1 Mo. 30, 1873. They were both buried near their ancestors, in the graveyard at Huntington Friends' Meeting House, near York Springs, Adams Co., Pa. William Wright and his wife were probably the most active and prominent agents of the Underground Railroad in Adams County, and hundreds of slaves fleeing from southern masters found rest and shelter in their hospitable home until forwarded over the Underground Railroad to the promised land of Canada. Two interesting oil paintings of William and Phebe, his wife, are (1902) in possession of the only surviving child, Mrs. Annie Phillips, of Lancaster, Pa. Children : General William Wierman Wright, b. 7 Mo. 27, 1824, d. 3 Mo. 9, 1882, unmarried, buried beside his parents ; Mrs. Rachel W. Day, d. 1901 ; Mrs. Hannah Mifflin, d. 1901 ; Mrs. Annie Phillips.

(5.) Ann, b. 3 Mo. 4, 1791.

(6.) John, b. 4 Mo. 8, 1793.

(7.) Rachel, m. John Farquhar. Children : Augustus, Sarah, Ann, Angeline, and Caroline.

2. *Hannah*, d. unmarried.

3. *Rachel*, m. 6 Mo. 13, 1781, at Menallen Meeting, James Hodgson, son of John and Martha Hodgson, of Berkley Co., Va. Child : James.

4. *William Wright*, m. Agnes Tanger. Children : Agnes and Margaret.

5. *Jesse*, m. first, Alice Hammond, and had one child, Samuel ; m., secondly, Catharine Davis, and had one child, Jesse (m. Elizabeth Mantz. Children : Eliza and Jane).

6. *Benjamin Wright*, m. first, Hannah Hendricks. Went to Kentucky and married a second time.

7. *Samuel Wright*, m. Eve Latchew. Children : Hannah, m. Nathan Harris, and removed to Salem, Ohio ; Jane, m. Daniel Minnich ; William ; Jesse, m, Susanna Pittendorff.

8. *Phebe*, m. William Ferguson.

III. RACHEL, born in 1737, at Castleshane, Ireland; died 4 Mo. 19, 1777 ; m. 10 Mo. 31, 1759, at Menallen Mtg., William Farquhar, Jr. (b. 10 Mo. 11, 1735), of Pipe Creek, Frederick, now Carroll Co., Md., son of William and Ann (Miller) Farquhar. She became a minister of the Society of Friends. Children : Joel and James.

IV. JOSEPH WRIGHT, m. in 1761, Mary Farquhar, daughter of William and Ann. Children : William, Samuel, Moses, Elizabeth, Mary, Rachel, and Susanna.

V. Alice, m. 1 Mo. 29, 1766, at Menallen Meeting, Samuel Hendricks, of Menallen. Children : Stephen, Elizabeth, and Hannah.

VI. BENJAMIN WRIGHT, m. 5 Mo. 20, 1766, at York Mtg., York Co., Pa., Jane Falkner, daughter of Jesse Falkner, of Hellam Township, York Co. Children :
1. *Martha*, b. 8 Mo. 10, 1767, m. Levi Hutton. Children : Benjamin, m. Beulah Harris ; Jane, m. Benjamin Harris. (Children : Samuel, Martha, etc.); Samuel ; Jesse.
2. *John Wright*, b. 9 Mo. 16, 1769, m. Susanna Griest. Children : Daniel, Benjamin, Jesse, Ann.
3. *Alice*, b. 11 Mo. 7, 1771, d. 7 Mo. 1777.
4. *Jesse*, b. 3 Mo. 30, 1774, m. in Virginia.
5. *Elizabeth*, b. 7 Mo. 12, 1776, d. unmarried.
6. *Alice*, b. 2 Mo. 16, 1779, m. David McCreary. Children : Benjamin, Thomas, David, Jesse.
7. *Samuel B. Wright*, m. Elizabeth Harvey. Children : William H., m. Jane Cook, dau. of Henry and Mary (Way) ; Martha ; Ann, m. Moses Price ; Rebecca.
8. *Benjamin Wright*, m. —— Harvey.
9. *Thomas Wright*, m. a sister of Jesse's wife.

VII. JOHN WRIGHT, b. 1739 or 1740, probably at Castleshane, Ireland ; d. 6 Mo. 29, 1820 ; m. 9 Mo. 30, 1767, at Menallen Mtg., Elizabeth Hammond, daughter of John and Deborah Hammond. She was born in 1749 or 1750 ; d. 7 Mo. 23, 1824. Children :
1. *Deborah*, b. 6 Mo. 23, 1768 ; m. Jonathan Potts. Children: John, etc.
2. *Elizabeth*, b. 4 Mo. 15, 1770 ; d. 12 Mo. 24, 1846 ; m. Jacob Koch. Children : John, Jacob, Ruth (m. John Blake).
3. *Ruth*, b. 2 Mo. 2, 1772 ; m. Thomas Hammond. Child, Elizabeth m. Eli Thomas, and lived in Salem, Ohio.
4. *Sarah*, b. 5 Mo. 4, 1774 ; m. George Wilson. Children : William ; Mary Wierman ; Benjamin m. Susan Wierman ; Ruth m. James Wills and had two children (the late Judge David Wills, of Gettysburg, and Ruth, m. Walhay) ; John.
5. *Rachel*, b. 8 Mo. 6, 1777.
6. *William Wright*, b. 9 Mo. 29, 1778, d. 3 Mo. 8, 1853, m. Rachel Thomas. Children : Abel ; Ellen, m. George Hewitt ; Thomas, m. Charlotte Stewart ; Isaac, m. Sarah Garretson ; Elizabeth ; Susanna.
7. *Samuel*, b. 4 Mo. 7, 1781.
8. *John Wright*, b. 4 Mo. 28, 1782 ; d. 12 Mo. 20, 1860 ; m. 10 Mo. 24, 1804, Alice Wilson. Children : Sarah, m. Enos McMillan, son of Jacob and Ruth (Griffith) ; George, m. Lucy Wright ; Joel ; Eliza, m. Jacob B. Hewitt ; Ruth ; Jane ; Charles S., m. 9 Mo. 30, 1846, Hannah G. Penrose.
9. *Nathan Wright*, b. 9 Mo. 28, 1784, d. 10 Mo. 4, 1853, m. Elizabeth Harris, 10 Mo. 24, 1810. Children : Elijah, m. Mary

————; Maria; Hiram S., m. Alice Garretson; Ruthanna; Lydia; John, m. Mary Nebinger.

10. *Mary*, b. 8 Mo. 2, 1790, d. 10 Mo. 1, 1844, m. Daniel Davis. Children : Uriah and Franklin.

VIII. JOEL WRIGHT m. Elizabeth Farquhar, daughter of William and Ann. Children :

1. *Allen Wright*, m. ———— Ellicott.

2. *Ann*, m. Joseph Elgar. Two daughters : Elizabeth and Margaret.

3. *Jonathan Wright*, m. Mary Bateman. Children : Mahlon, Aaron, Josiah, Hannah (m. Dr. Plummer).

4. *Rachel*, m. Joseph Hibberd.

5. *Israel Wright*, m. Leah Ferree, of Lancaster County. Children : Oscar and Isaac.

6. *Elizabeth*, m. Jarrett Cowman.

IX. JONATHAN WRIGHT, m. 5 Mo. 16, 1770, Susanna Griffith, daughter of Thomas Griffith, deceased, and Eve, his wife. Removed to Ohio in 1801, and finally settled at Poplar Ridge, Fayette Co., Ind. Children : Thomas, agent to the Cherokee Indians in Mississippi; Rachel, m. Benjamin Farquhar; Elizabeth, m. John Shaw; Mary; Jonathan, m. Susan Jones; Joel; Phebe, m. Oliver Mathews; Susanna; Rebecca.—See *Friends' Intelligencer* for 2 Mo. 29, 1896, Vol. LIII., pp.; *Literary Era*, Vol. VII., 125.

THE FARQUHAR FAMILY

ALLEN FARQUHAR, who was not a Friend, came from Ireland, and in 1725 and 1726 was a resident taxable in Chester County, Pa., as of New Garden Township. After this he removed to Pipe Creek, now Carrol County, Md. His son William, b. in Ireland 7 Mo. 29, 1705, d. at Pipe Creek 9 Mo. 21, 1778, remained in Chester County for some time, and became a member of New Garden Mo. Mtg., where he married, 2 Mo. 19, 1733, Ann Miller, daughter of James and Katharine (Lightfoot) Miller, also from Ireland (see pages 356–7). In 1735 they removed to Pipe Creek, taking a certificate of removal to Hopewell Mo. Mtg., in Virginia, and settled near where the town of Union Bridge, Carrol County, Md., now stands, on land conveyed to him by his father, with the provision that he was to move from " ye province of Pennsylvania to ye province of Maryland," and occupy the same.

William Farquhar was influential in establishing the Friends' Meeting at Pipe Creek, the meetings for the first few years being held at his house. Children of William and Ann Farquhar : James, b. 1733; William, b. 10 Mo. 11, 1735, m. (1) Rachel Wright and (2) Mary Baily; Allen, b. 10 Mo. 16, 1737, m. Phebe Hibberd; Mary, b. 11 Mo. 22, 1739, m. Joseph Wright; George,

b. 6 Mo. 9, 1742 ; Samuel, b. 5 Mo. 8, 1745, m. Phebe Yarnall ;
Elizabeth, b. 6 Mo. 13, 1748, m. Joel Wright ; Moses, b. 11 Mo.
3, 1750; Susanna, b. 9 Mo. 1753, m. Solomon Shepherd.

Allen Farquhar, another son of Allen the emigrant, died 12
Mo. 12, 1800 in his 81st year, and Sarah his wife 7 Mo. 4, 1829,
in her 97th year. They had seven children : Thomas, b. 11
Mo. 16, 1751, m. Hannah Edundson ; Sarah b. 11 Mo. 13,
1753 ; William, b. 12 Mo. 24, 1755 ; Rachel, b. 2 Mo. 7, 1764 ;
Robert, b. 7, Mo. 13, 1766 ; Mary, b. 11 Mo.'6, 1769 ; Samuel,
b. 9 Mo. 21, 1772.—Cope, *Genealogy of the Sharpless Family*,
202-3.

THE McMILLAN FAMILY

"Thomas McMullen of Grange meeting in County of Antrim
& Deborah Marsh" [daughter of Joshua and Elizabeth (Rogers)
Marsh] of [Grange] meeting [near Charlemont, County Ar-
magh, Ireland] "were married near Charlemount on ye 10th day
of ye $\frac{5}{mo.}$ 1727 as by certificate may appear."—*Minutes of Ulster
Province Meeting, Ireland*.

Thomas McMillan seems to have lived for some years within
the limits of Ballinacree Meeting, near Ballymoney, County
Antrim ; then in 1738 or 1739 he removed with his wife Deborah
and children to Pennsylvania, and settled near his father-in-law,
Joshua Marsh, in East Nantmeal Township, Chester County. On
his arrival he produced the following certificate of removal to
Goshen Monthly Meeting (8 Mo. 15, 1739):

"From our men's meeting held in Ballanacree the 6th of ye 3
mo. 1738 To friends in Pro: Pennsylvania or elsewhere in them
parts Lo friends we hereby acquaint & Certify you that Thomas
McMollin his Wife and Family lived within the Compass of our
Meeting for several Years and always Behaved themselves pretty
orderly for anything known to us & leaveth this in unity with us
& free of Debts a man & woman of a Good Report and Pretty
well beloved both by friends and others and so Concludes with
desires that you will be pleased to afford them Such Councel &
advice in the further Conduct of their Life as the Lord may
Enable you with all ; Signed in and on behalf of said Meeting by

James Moore	John Sterling
Thomas Ervin	Willm Moore
Benj. Boyd	George Gregg
William Gregg	Sams^n Courthey
John Hunter	Willm Moore " [1]
Willm McMollin	

[1] Recorded in Goshen Mo. Mtg. Book of Removals, p.'56, Goshen Mo.
Mtg. Records, at Friends' Library, 142 North Sixteenth Street, Philadelphia.

About 1749 or 1750 he went with his family to York County, and settled on a tract of 193½ acres of land called Adington, in Warrington, now Washington, Township, granted by the Penn Proprietors by warrant dated May 29, 1749.[1] He died in 9 Mo., 1753, and was buried in the burial ground at Warrington Friends' Meeting House, near the present village of Wellsville. Letters of administration on his estate were granted Aug. 8, 1754, to his widow, Deborah McMillan. She died 9 Mo. 22, 1764, and was buried beside her husband. Their graves lie in the McMillan row at Warrington, and although it was contrary to the rules of discipline obtaining in the Society of Friends at that time, the graves were carefully marked by thin, neatly-cut sandstones, scarcely a foot in height, which still remain in a good state of preservation, and if one kneels and scrapes away the moss and lichens which have grown over the stones he may read the inscriptions:

9 M   9 M
1753   1764
T ✕ M   D ✕ M

Thomas and Deborah (Marsh) McMillan had five children: I. John, II. George, III. William, IV. Mary, V. Elizabeth.

I. JOHN MCMILLAN, as his son James states in his Bible, was born in 1728, in Co. Antrim, Ireland; died 9 Mo. 17, 1791, and was buried in Friends' burial ground at Warrington Meeting House; was married 5 Mo. 4, 1756, at Sadsbury Meeting, Lancaster County, Pa., to Jane, widow of Joseph Green, of Sadsbury, and daughter of John and Jane (Bell) Boyd. She was born in 1728 in Co. Antrim, Ireland, died 5 Mo. 12, 1782, and lies buried beside her second husband at Warrington. After the death of his first wife John McMillan was married, 7 Mo. 15, 1784, at Warrington Friends' Meeting, to Joanna, widow of William Griffith, of Warrington, and daughter of William and Mary Craig. Joanna died 4 Mo. 21, 1794, and was buried at Warrington. Children of John McMillan, all by his first wife Jane:

1. Abigail McMillan, b. 4 Mo. 18, 1757, in Warrington, York County Pa., m. in 1776, William Whinery, son of Robert and Isabel. Removed to near Salem, Columbiana County, Ohio. Children: Robert, John, Thomas, William, James, George, Jane, Zimri, Sarah, and Abigail.

2. Sarah, b. 3 mo. 3, 1760, d. 1 Mo. 25, 1790.

---

[1] See Patent Deed, granted to his son George McMillan, Dec. 5. 1771, by Thomas and John Penn. Patent Book AA, Vol. 13, Dept. of Internal Affairs, Harrisburg, Pa.

3. Thomas McMillan, b. 5 Mo. 14, 1762, d. 4 Mo. 12, 1831; buried at Warrington; m. 10 Mo. 11, 1791, at West Grove Friends' Meeting, Chester County, Pa., Ruth Moore, daughter of Joseph and Jane (Marsh) Moore (see *Andrew Moore and his Decendants*). She was born 1 Mo. 33, 1763; d. 4 Mo. 11, 1846, and was buried in Friends' burial ground, Short Creek, Jefferson County, Ohio. Children : Joseph, Jacob, Maria, and Mahlon.

4. John McMillan, b. 1766; d. 3 Mo. 16, 1838; buried at West Grove, Harrison County, Ohio; m. first, 1787, to Esther Griffith, daughter of William and Joanna (Craig) Griffith. She was born 1 Mo. 13, 1766, in Warrington Twp., York County, Pa.; d. 6 Mo. 7, 1818; buried at West Grove, Harrison County, Ohio. They removed from Warrington, York County, Pa., to Short Creek Meeting, Ohio, in 1804. John, m. secondly to Alice Barnard. Children, all by first wife : Jane, Ruth, Joanna, Sarah, Amos, John, James, Griffith, Elisha, Jesse, and Maria.

5. James McMillan, b. 9 Mo. 4, 1768, in Warrington Twp., York County, Pa.; d. 1. Mo. 7. 1856, buried in Friends' graveyard, Harrisville, Harrison County, Ohio.; m. 3 Mo. 21, 1798, in York County, Pa, to Mary Griffith, daughter of William and Joanna (Craig) Griffith. She was born 3 Mo. 16, 1771, in Warrington Twp. ; d. 1 Mo. 8, 1856; buried in same ground as her husband.

James McMillan, as he records in his diary, learned the hatting trade in youth and followed that occupation for thirty years. For three years he kept a tavern and store in York County; then, about 1803, he removed with his wife and settled in Harrison Co., Ohio, where he followed various callings : milling, farming, surveying, and conveyancing. For two years he served as Senator in the State Legislature of Ohio. Children : Uriah ; Edith, m. John Gwynn, in 1819 ; Asa, m. Mary Kelly, in 1827 ; Gulielma Maria, m. her brother-in-law, John Gwynn, in 1830 ; Ira James, m. Ann Christy, in 1847 ; Myra, m. Joseph Crawford, in 1831 ; Joanna ; Sarah, m. Joshua P. Watson.

II. "GEORGE McMILLAN Son of Thomas and Deborah McMillan born in the year of our Lord 1732 The 2d day of the 4th Month About [record torn] Noone and 18th of the Moons age," [1] probably in County Antrim, Ireland. He died 7 Mo. 11, 1795, in Warrington, now Washington Township, York County, and is buried in Friends' burial ground at Warrington, York County, where his and his wife's inscribed gravestones are still to be seen. Ac-

[1] According to the record in his family Bible, " Printed by Alexander Kincaid His Majesty's Printer MDCCLXII," now (1902) in possession of a descendant, Elmira J. Cook, Flora Dale, Adams Co., Pa.

26

cording to his marriage certificate[1] "George McMillan of Warrington in the County of York and Province of Pencilvania Son of
Thomas McMillan Deceased and Ann Hinshaw of Manahon in
the County and Province aforesd Daughter of Jacob Hinshaw"
[and wife Rebecca Mackey] were married 10 Mo. 5, 1758, in a
Friends' Meeting at Warrington Meeting House, York Co., Pa.
The following are the names of the signers to the certificate :

Anne Hussey	William Ward	Alexander Underwood	GEORGE McMILLAN
Sarah Underwood	Abraham Griffith	William Garretson	ANN McMULLAN
Ruth Underwood	Eneas Foulk	Petter Cook	
hannah nevitt	Jesse Cook	William Underwood	Jacob Hinshaw
Susannah Ward	John mcadams	William Griffith	Deborah mcmillan
eliseth Sloss	John Collins	William Nevitt	John mcmillan
Ann Collins		Robert Vale	William mcmillan
mary Collins		John Sharp	Peter Marsh
ann Cook		peter cook	Jonathan Marsh
		John hill	Margaret Marsh
		Chas Horseman	John Marsh
		Eli Horseman	Jean mcmillan
		Richard Ross	Thomas Hinshaw

Ann, wife of George McMillan, was born 3 Mo. 18, 1739, in
Co. Armagh, Ireland ; died 1 Mo. 29, 1815.

After the death of his mother, George McMillan took the farm,
" His Brothers & Sisters " releasing their shares by deed of Oct.
28, 1765. Although the land was granted by warrant to his father
in 1749, George McMillan did not receive a patent until Dec. 5,
1771, when the tract is described as 193½ acres, called Adington,
in the Manor of Maske, Warrington Township, York County, the
several courses being as follows : beginning at a black oak, corner of Peter Cleaver's land, thence by the same and Baltzer
Smith's land, S. 42°, W. 179 P. to a white oak ; then by William
Garretson's and John Underwood's land S. 23°, E. 218 P. to a
marked white oak ; then by Samuel Morthland's land, N. 27°, E.
165 P. to a white oak ; thence by Jonathan Marsh's land N. 82°,
W. 20 P. to a white oak ; N. 35°, E. 22 P. to a stone ; N. E.
118 P. to a white oak ; thence by Mine Bank N. 46°, W. 28 P.
to a stone ; thence by Jacob Brindley's land, S. 43°, W. 55 P. to
stones for a corner ; N. 30°, W. 119 P. to place of beginning.

ABSTRACT WILL OF GEORGE McMILLAN, of Warrington Township, York County, Penn'a, "being Sick and weak in body but
of sound disposing Mind and Memory." Dated 7 Mo. 6, 1795 ;
probated Aug. 7, 1795.

Imprmis.—Just debts and funeral expenses to be paid.

[1] Recorded in Warrington Marriage Book, page 29. The original MS.
is in the possession of a descendant, Mrs. Emma Wickersham Pyle, 720
N. Fair Oaks Ave., Pasadena, Cal.

Item.—To "my Son George McMillan my Plantation and Tract of Land on Beaver Creek in Warrington Township aforesaid (Excepting a Grist Mill and Saw Mill and Mill Seat with a Lot of Ground including the Same)."

Item.—To son Thomas McMillan said grist mill and saw mills on land adjoining William How and Abraham Griffith [at the foot of Round Top].

Item.—"I give and devise my present dwelling plantation to my two Sons Jacob McMillan and Joseph McMillan," etc.

Item.—"My tract of Land in Monaghan Township to my four daughters, Rebekah, Ann, Deborah and Mary."

Item.—"I give and Bequeath unto my beloved Wife Ann McMillan two Beds, & bedding her choice and a case of drawers and as much of my household and Kitchen goods and furniture as She Shall Choose," ten bushels of wheat and £20 yearly, "the Western end of my Dwelling house including a room and Kitchen for her use during her Natural life, and also a pipe Stove for Said room and also a Sufficient quantity firewood drawed to her door & made ready for immediate use by my said Sons Jacob and Joseph . . . it is my Will that the Stove in the mill at Beaver Creek be brought to my present Dwelling house and put in place of the one given to my Said Wife."

Item.—Son Joseph to be sent to school and to "unite with my Son Jacob in labouring and farming my present dwelling plantation." Wife to receive the "profits of my Said plantation until my Son Jacob arives to the Age of twenty one Years and that then my Said Wife do receive one half of said profits, and my Said Son Jacob the other half until my Said Son Joseph arives to the Age of Twenty one Years."

Item.—To sons Jacob and Joseph "my Bay and Gray horses, and my two Year old Yearling Colts to enable them to farm my Said plantation"; also "my Waggon, plows, harrow and horse Geers."

Item.—To daughter Ann "my young Gray mare, Saddle & bridle."

Item.—To son Thomas "my Spring Colt and one Cow which is at Beaver Creek."

Item.—After daughters have received in all £150 remainder of estate to be divided equally "among my Eight children."

Item.—To "my Said Wife my old gray mare, One Cow and her Saddle."

Executors: Wife Ann, son-in-law Joseph Garretson, and son George.

Witnesses: Elihu Underwood, Jesse Underwood, William Hinshaw.

Children of George and Ann (Hinshaw) McMillan, born in Warrington, now Washington, Township, York County :

i. Rebecca McMillan, b. 7 Mo. 7, 1759, d. 12 Mo. 14, 1814, m. 10 Mo. 12, 1779, at Warrington Meeting, to Joseph Garretson, of Newberry, York County, son of John and Jane (Carson). He was born 7 Mo. 28, 1759. Children : Ann, John I. (m. Ann Pierce), George (m. (1) Lydia Wickersham and (2) Ann Griffith), Joseph (m. Maria McMillan), Sarah (m. John Thomas), Rebecca (m. John Wickersham), Jane, and Elijah (m. (1) Ann Nichol and (2) Ann Prowell).

2. George McMillan, b. 5 Mo. 26, 1763, d. 5 Mo. 24, 1846, buried in Friends' ground at Warrington, m. (1) 11 Mo. 6, 1792, at West Grove Friends' Meeting, Chester County, to Rebecca, daughter of Benjamin and Susanna (Dunn) Cutler. She died 4 Mo. 14, 1816, and he m. (2) 2 Mo., 1826, to Jane, daughter of Jacob and ———— (McClellan) Laird. She was born 7 Mo. 22, 1792, and died 9 Mo. 1, 1862. Children by first wife were : George, Eli, Susanna (m. Edward J. Wickersham), Amos, Jesse, Elisha, and Anna. Children by second wife were : Joseph, John, William (living in Marshall, Mo., in 1902.)

3. Ann McMillan, b. 8 Mo. 21, 1766, d. 2 Mo. 23, 1850, m. 6 Mo. 25, 1795, at Warrington Meeting, to Willing Griest, son of Willing and Ann (Garretson) Griest. Resided at Warrington, York County. Children : Anne (m. Abner Wickersham), Amos (m. Margaret Garretson), Edith, Cyrus (m. Mary Ann Cook, daughter of Samuel. Children were: Hiram, George M., Jane C., Ann M., Cyrus S., Jesse W., Maria E., Elizabeth M., and Amos W.), Mary (m. Josiah Cook, son of Henry), Ruth (m. William W. Cook, son of Isaac), Josiah (m. Mary Ann Squibb).

4. Deborah McMillan, b. 12 Mo. 6, 1768, m. (1), 10 Mo. 19, 1763, William Griffith, son of William. He died 4 Mo. 21, 1799, and she m. (2) 2 Mo. 13, 1806, John Vale, son of Robert and Sarah. Removed from Warrington, York County, to Columbiana County, Ohio, 1814. Children by William Griffith : George, Anne, William, Oliver, and Julia. Children by John Vale : Deborah, John, Jacob, and Caroline.

5. Mary McMillan, b. 2 Mo. 16, 1771 ; d. 8 Mo. 8, 1827 ; m. 1 Mo. 29, 1818, William Vale, son of Robert and Sarah. No issue.

6. Thomas McMillan, b. 10 Mo. 16, 1773, d. 3 Mo. 28, 1843, m. 11 Mo. 15, 1798, at Warrington Meeting, Jane Taylor, daughter of Joseph and Jane. Removed from York County to Washington County, Pa., in 1808, and two years later settled in Columbiana County, Ohio, where he practiced the Thomsonian system of medicine. Children : Taylor, b. 10 Mo. 10, 1803, d. 11 Mo. 8, 1893, m. 1834, Sarah Bell (who was b. 6 Mo. 15, 1806, d. 5 Mo. 25, 1901, and was buried besides her husband in Carmel Friends' ground) and had children of whom one is Smith Bell McMillan, of Signal, Ohio ; Jane, m. 1st Abel Lee Crawford and 2nd John Clay ; Ann ; Maria, m. Joseph Bell (had a son Mark) ;

Ann, m. William Longshore ; Joseph, m. Hannah Burt ; Eliza, m. Adam Siddall.

7. Jacob McMillan,[1] b. 6 Mo. 28, 1777, d. 1 Mo. 1833, buried in Friends' ground at Warrington, where the gravestones of him and his wife may yet be seen ; m. 12 Mo. 13, 1798, at Warrington Meeting, Ruth, daughter of William and Joanna (Craig) Griffith. She was born 1 Mo. 22, 1770 and died 3 Mo. 2, 1829. He succeeded to his father's homestead and died there. Children : Enos (m. Sarah Wright and died at Marshalltown, Iowa, in 1890), Ann (m. Joseph Leech, and died in Clermont County, Ohio, in 1888), Cyrus (m. Sarah Raney), Edith (d. young), Ruth (b. 3 Mo. 3, 1808, d. 3 Mo. 23, 1887, m. 9 Mo. 20, 1831, at Warrington Meeting, Jesse Cook, son of Henry and Mary (Way) Cook ; a daughter, Sarah A., married John T. Myers), George (removed to Baltimore and m. Sarah Dickinson ; a daughter, Emma C., married Edward Duffy, sometime Judge of the Superior Court of Baltimore), and Rebecca (d. young).

8. Jane McMillan, b. 9 Mo. 29, 1780, d. 11 Mo, 28, 1782.

9. Joseph McMillan, b. 10 Mo. 10, 1782, d. 3 Mo. 26, 1826, m. 5 Mo. 24, 1809, at Newberry Meeting, York County, to Rebecca Garretson, daughter of Samuel and Alice. No issue.

III. WILLIAM McMILLAN, son of Thomas and Deborah, m. 2 Mo. 20, 1760, at Nantmeal Meeting, Chester County, Deborah, daughter of Henry and Lydia (Fell) Holland, of East Nantmeal Township. Resided in Warrington Township, York County. Children were :

1. Mary McMillan, b. 4 Mo. 20, 1761, m. (1) 12 Mo. 17, 1789, at Warrington Meeting, James Miller, of Newberry Township, York County, son of Robert and Sarah (McClung) Miller ; m. (2) Joseph Baxter, in 1806. Removed to Miami, Ohio, in 1806.

2. Thomas McMillan, b. 4 Mo. 22, 1763, m. 2 Mo. 12, 1794, at Newberry Meeting, Jane Jones, daughter of Edward and Content (Garretson) Jones. Children : Edith and Deborah.

3. Deborah McMillan, b. 9 Mo. 13, 1764, d. 11 Mo. 24, 1766.

4. Lydia McMillan, b. 9 Mo. 21, 1766. Removed to Miami Mo. Mtg., Ohio, about 1806, and married William Jay.

5. William McMillan, b. 10 Mo. 13, 1767. Removed to Miami, Ohio, about 1806.

6. Samuel McMillan, b. 2 Mo. 26, 1770, d. 4 Mo. 10, 1777.

7. Jonathan McMillan, b. 3 Mo. 2, 1772, m. 11 Mo. 16, 1797, at Warrington Meeting, Ann Hussey, daughter of Jediah and Jane. They removed to Miami Monthly Meeting, Ohio, about 1806.

---

[1] Three of his letters, written in 1814, 1815, and 1826, are in possession of a great-grandson, the writer.

8. David McMillan, b. 3 Mo. 2, 1772, m. 4 Mo. 13, 1797, at Warrington Meeting, Hannah Hussey, sister of the wife of his twin brother Jonathan. They removed to Miami, Ohio, about 1805. Children : Josiah, Eli, Deborah, Mary, David.

9. Henry McMillan, b. 11 Mo. 20, 1774.

10. Deborah McMillan, b. 8 Mo. 10, 1778, d. probably 12 12 Mo., 1782.

11. John McMillan, b. 7 Mo. 18, 1785.

IV. MARY McMILLAN, daughter of Thomas and Deborah, m. 6 Mo. 25, 1767, at Warrington Meeting, Nathan Phillips, son of Edmund, of Warrington

Children were :

1. Thomas Phillips, m. Margaret Foster. Children : William, John, Thomas Monroe.

2. Jesse Phillips, m. 1st Elizabeth Borum and 2d Ann (Frazier) Morris. Children by 1st wife : Elizabeth, Mary Ann (m. John McConnell), Jane, Deborah, Rebecca.

3. Deborah Phillips, m. Alexander Underwood and resided in Middleton Township, Columbiana County, Ohio. Children : Jesse (m. ——— Borum), Alexander.

4. Jane Phillips, b. 8 Mo. 1776, d. 9 Mo. 17, 1856, m. about 1825, Jared Marlnee and resided in Middleton Township, Columbiana County, Ohio. No issue.

5. Elizabeth Phillips received a certificate from Warrington Mo. Mtg., 12 Mo. 19, 1827, to remove to Carmel, Columbiana County, Ohio.

V. ELIZABETH McMILLAN, daughter of Thomas and Deborah, married Jacob Smith ; removed to Middleton Township, Columbiana County, Ohio, where she died in the spring of 1820. She was interred in Friends' ground at Carmel Meeting House. Children as far as ascertained : Jacob, Rebecca, Eve Catharine (m. Ellis Brown, in 1831), Casper (m. Sarah Burt), Elizabeth, (m. Samuel Smith), Thomas (m. Elizabeth Burt).

THE MARSH FAMILY

JOHN MARSH, a Friend, of Armagh, County Armagh, Ireland, was residing in that town as early as 1664, for in his will, dated 1688, he mentions "the half tenement and Garden plott Situate lying and being in the Scotch Street in Ardmagh which I have by lease from the primate of Ireland bearing date the twentyeth day of October 1664." He was staunch and true to his Quaker principles and on account of them had to endure severe persecutions. From the record of these sufferings it was evident that he was a thrifty yeoman or farmer, having servants and cattle and sheep, and raising wheat, oats, barley, etc. In 1660, "*John Marsh* [County Armagh] being sued for Milch-money and Offerings, to the value of about 3l. at the Mannor Court of *Loughall* (by *Humphrey Pettard* Priest) had taken from him so many of his Cattel as were worth 18l."

"The said John Marsh being sued again, in the said Court, for five years' Tythe of sixty-two Sheep (by the said Priest) had the very whole number of sixty-two Sheep taken from him (being all he had) worth 12l." [1]

In 1666, for refusing to pay tithes he had taken from him "Cattle and Sheep worth £30," [2] and in 1669 "*John Marsh* being sued for *Priests* and *Clarks* Dues (so-called) and such like things, to the value of 8s. 3d. in a Temporal Court at *Ardmagh*, by *Thomas Blevin* Clark, had taken from him by the Bailiffs, a Brass Pot, and four Pewter Dishes, worth £1. 17s. [3] In 1673, he was one "Of those who suffered Distress for Tithes of Corn, Hay, &c." [4] "In this and some preceding Years, several had suffered Distress for refusing to contribute to the repairing of the Parish Worship-house at Kilmore, in the County of Armagh." Among these, from John Marsh were taken "two Heifers, three Sheep, and two Calves, worth £3. 7s." [5] In 1673 "John Marsh had taken from him for Tithe, for the Dean of Ardmagh, forty three stooks of Barly and fifteen car-loads of Hey, all worth one pound sixteen shillings." [6]

"ANNO 1674. Isabel Lancaster, Servant to John Marsh, of the County of Armagh, was sued in the Primate's Temporal Court for carrying Home her Master's Corn, under Pretence of its being Tithe, though it was neither markt nor set forth as such. An Execution was obtained against her, on which she was imprisoned in the Bayliff's House, and after two Weeks removed thence to another Bayliff's, where she was detained six months." [7]

In 1674 "John Marsh had taken from him for Tithe, by the Servants of James Downham, Dean of Ardmagh, thirty stooks of Barly out of two hundred thirty eight, and nine stooks of Oats out of three score and ten, worth one pound four shillings six pence." [8] He also suffered similar persecutions in 1675 and in 1676.

[1] Holme and Fuller, *A Brief Relation*, 25.
[2] Besse's *Sufferings of the Quakers*, II., 475.
[3] Holme and Fuller, *A Brief Relation*, 27.
[4] Besse's *Sufferings of the Quakers*, II., 278.
[5] *Ibid.*, II., 479.
[6] William Stockdale, *A Great Cry of Oppression*, 29.
[7] *Besse*, II., 480.
[8] *Stockdale*, 40.

At the time of the making of his will John Marsh was "Sick in body" and probably died about that time, in 1688, leaving Dorothy, his wife, to survive him.   Children, probably by Dorothy, his wife, were : Joseph, Rebecca, Sarah, Hester, and perhaps others. The following is a copy of the will :

"The last Will[1] and Testyment of John Marsh of Ardmagh in the Prsh and County of the Said Ardmagh being Sick in body but perfect in Memory in Which Will And testyment and for the due pformance thereof I doe Constytute apoynt and ordeaine My beloved Wife Dorothy My onely and Soale Executorex

imps—I doe desire that my body may buryed in the burying place in the Towne land of the Munney near Killmore where many of my deare friends have been formerly buryed and as to my Worldly goods I dispossose of them as followeth

first—I give to my eldest daughter Namely Hester five Shillings to be paid to her att the end or within one yeare from the date hereof

2dly—I give to my daughter Sara five Shilling to be paid her att the end or within one yeare as aforesaid

3dly—I give unto my daughter Rebecca one Pound to be given her att the end or within one yeare from the date hereof

4th—I give unto Jonathan fletcher my grandson two pounds ten Shillings to be payd unto whom I Shall nomynate in trust for his use att the end or within two yeares from the date hereof

5thly—I give unto Joshua Marsh and Margery Marsh Son and daughter of my Son Joseph Marsh deceased the half tenement and Garden plott Situate lying and being in the Scotch Street in Ardmagh which I have by lease from the primate of Ireland bearing date the twentyeth day of October 1664 with alsoe the Said lease of the Same with all the apurtenants thereunto belonging paying and performing for the Same all rents and other dutyes due to the bond Conteined in the Said lease from the time they Shall renewe the Said halfe tenement

6th—I give unto my grandaughter Hanna Shaw four pounds to be payd unto those whom I shall hereafter in trust [appoint] to receive itt for her use within or att the end of two years from the date hereof

7th—I doe by these present Nominate ordeane and apoynt William Lawder of the Said Armagh Robert Robinson of bellyhagan and ffergus Saftlaw of Bellylamy both in the psh of Killmore and County of Ardmagh aforesaid (to demand and receive from my Said executorex the aforesaid two pounds ten Shill given to Jonathan above Said and the Said four pounds given to my grandaghter Hanna aforesaid) to dispose of the fund for the use of the

[1] Public Record Office, Dublin.

said Jonathan and Hanna for their best advantage and to be
accountable [for ?] the same when the said Jonathan and Hanna
Shall Come to age Con [torn 1 inch] to desire futh account

8thly—And lastly I draw and bequeath all the rest of my
worldly goods and Chattells of all kindes and sorts what soeve¹
for the payment of my debts and for the use and maintenance or
my Said beloved wife my onely and Soale executorex as witness my
hand and Seale this 7th day of the 11th month Called January
1688.

Signed Sealed and	John Marsh [Seal]
delivered to my	his M Marke
Said exeratorex in	
the presents of	
Alexander heron	
Tho : King	Robert Robinson
William Williamson	ffergus Saftlow
William Landar	Sam¹ : Unthanke.''

JOSEPH MARSH, son of John Marsh, for some breach of discipline, was disowned from membership in the Society of Friends,
10 Mo. 5, 1674, at Lurgan Meeting, held at Roger Webb's
house near Lurgan, County Armagh. In the testimony issued
against him he is mentioned as late of Lisneny near Loughgall,
County Armagh, widower, '' who for several years past frequented
our meetings.'' According to his father's will Joseph died prior to
11 Mo. (Jan.) 7, 1688, leaving at least two children, Joshua and
Margery.

JOSHUA MARSH, of Drumanicannon, Parish of Sego, County
Armagh, son of Joseph Marsh, was married, 6 Mo. (Aug.), 28,
1695, at Friends' Meeting place at Alexander Christy's, County
Armagh, to Elizabeth Rogers, of Drumanicannon, possibly a
daughter of John Rogers, whose name appears at the head of the
list of men signers to the marriage certificate. Christy Rogers,
who heads the list of the women signers, may have been the
mother. The following interesting records of the marriage have
been found :

'' At our [Ulster] Province Meeting held at Richard Boyes'
house [near Ballinderry, County, Antrim] yᵉ 6th of yᵉ 5th Mo.
1695 . . . Joshua Marsh and Elizabeth Rogers haveing apeared
and Declared their Intentions of Marrage with each other before
This Meeting and at present nothing appearing to Obstruct them,
yᵉ Meeting have taken Their Intentions into Consideration and
have apointed Alexʳ Mathews Lawrence Allyson Margrit Christy &
Aylce Williams To make Enquiry Concerning Their Clearness
and Consent of Parents and return their answer to The next Pro-

vince Meeting, a Certificate from ye Sd Eliz : father of his Consent To ye Sd Intended Marage."

"At our Province Meeting held at Ballyhagen [County Armagh] ye 17th day of ye 6th month 1695 ffriends of Ballyhagen Meeting and friends of The Meeting beyond Charlemont [Upper Grange Meeting], have agreed that once in two mens Meetings Some friends from Ballyhagen Meeting goe to ye mens Meeting beyond Charlemont And also That Some friends from beyond Charlemont goe to The mens Meeting at Ballyhagen once in two mens Meetings. . . .

Joshuah Marsh and Elizabeth Rogers haveing appeared ye Second time and Declared their Intentions of Marrage before this Meeting as formerly and the partyes appointed to make enquiry Concerning their Clearness and Consent of Parents have returned Their answers That they find nothing To Obstruct Them but That they may lawfully marry, So its The apointmt of this Meeting That ye Said Joshua Marsh do publish (or Cause to be Published) Their Said Intentions in two Severall Meetings at (or neer) Lurgan, and in two Severall Meetings at Monnallon, and if no Thing Then apear against Them They may at a Convenient Season Take each other in Marrage, Alexr Mathes, John Hoope, and William Porter are desired To See ye Said Marrage be perfected in good Order."

The marriage was accordingly accomplished on the 28th of 6 Mo. (Aug.), 1695. The names of the signers to the marriage certificate appear in the following order in the old Marriage Record Book of Lurgan Meeting (page 121) :

{ Joshua Marsh
Elizabeth Marsh

John Rogers	George Blacker	Christy Rogers
Roger Kirk	John Willson	Ellin Wollsy
Peter Rogers	Alexr Christy	Margrit Blacker
George Whaly	John Moorton	Mary Horner
Richard Hollin	ffrancis Hillary	Deborah Kirk
James Hallyday	Robart Kirk	Ann Whaly
Alexander Mathew	John Christy	Eliz : Atkinson
Lancelot Pearson	Timothy Kirk	Joan Mathew
John Williams	James Moorton	Joan Adams
Samuell Kirk	Tho : Wainwright	
Jacob Kirk	Tho : Bullough	
John Thirkeld	George Black	
	Tho : Bradshaw	

In addition to his share in the leased property in the town of Armagh, bequeathed to him by his grandfather John Marsh, Joshua Marsh owned a small farm in Ireland ; for in his will, made in Pennsylvania in 1747, he mentions " my farm in Bele-

nacar in Clambrasel in the County of Armagh in the Kingdom of
Ireland Containing Thirty three Acres of Land with the Rights
members and Appurtnances thereof.''

Early in the spring of 1736, Joshua and his son John began to
make ready to remove with their families to Pennsylvania. "Att
a mens [Preparative] meeting [at Grange, near Charlemont,
County Armagh] held ye 2d of ye 4th month [1736] Joshua March
having an Intention to transport himself & family to America &
desires from us a certificate therefore Jacob Marshill & James
Pillar is desired to draw Suitable ones for him & his Son John
. . . yt they may be Signed next meeting.''

In accordance with the request of the meeting certificates [1] were
drawn up as follows :

"From our Monthly Meeting of men & women friends, held at
Grange Near Charlimount in the North of Ireland ye 2 of 4 Mo.
1736. To friends and Brethren of pensylvania or elsewhere in
America Greeting.

"Dear Friends whereas our friend Joshua March [Marsh] &
his Wife Did Acquaint us Some Time Ago that they had a mind
to transport themselves & family to pensylvania or Some place in
America and Desires of us a Certificate we therefore Do Certify
that He the Sd Joshua & his wife was of an orderly Life & good
Conversation Both amongst us their Brethren as amongst their
Neighbours where they Dwelt & now Leaveth us in Unity they
had also the privilege of Sitting in our Meeting of Disapline likewise their three children Viz Jonathan peter and Abigail were of
Orderly Lives & Conversation whilst here & is free from marriage
or any Entanglement that way & all the Above friends have left
this place free from Debts or Defraud to any man & we have Cause
to hope & believe that they will So behave themselves for ye future
yt they may Deserve ye Religious notice & Care of friends for
their good.

"Signed by order & on behalf of our Sd Meeting by

Mary Greer	Thos. Nichalson	William Gray
Eliz. Greer	Joseph Kerr	Jacob Marshall
Abigail King	Benj[a] Marshill	Jno. Whitsitt
Mary Pow	James pillar	Thomas Greer
Ann Sloan	James Dawson	Tho. Griffith
Mary Pillar	francis Robson	Israel Thompson
Eliz. Dawson	Saml Gray	Wm. Vance ''
Abigail Gray	Jona[t] Richardson	
Ruth Delapp.		

[1] Pages 39, 52, *Book of Certificates of Removal Received of Goshen
Monthly Meeting*, Penn'a, in the vault, Friends' Library, 142 N. 16th
Street, Phila.

"From our Men & Womens Meeting held at Grange Near Charles Mount in Ireland ye 2 of ye 4th mo 1736 to friends of pensylvania or Elsewhere In America Greeting   Whereas our friends John March [Marsh] & his wife Did sometime ago Acquaint us that they had to transport themselves to pensylvania or Some place In America & Desires of a Certificate we therefore do Certifie yt the Said John March & his wife hath behaved themselves Orderly amongst us their Brethren & Sisters   Also was of a peaceable Life & Conversation amongst their Neighbours hav- ing Left us & our Neighbours Clear of Debt   They had Also privilege to Set in our Meetings for Decipline & we hope they will So behave as will deserve the Religious Notice & Care of our friends & Brethren whose it may Please Divine providence So to order their Lot to Settle & Remain.

" Signed by order & on behalf our Said Meeting by

Ann Sloan	Mary Greer	Benjᵃ Marshil	Jacob Marshill
Mary pillar	Eliz. Greer	James Dawson	John Whitsitt
Eliz. Dawson	Abigail King	James Pillar	Thos. Greer
			Thos. Griffith
			Israel Thompson
			Wm. Vance
			Thos. Nichalson
			Joseph Ker "

In the spring of 1736, shortly after the signing of the above certificates, the Marsh family started on the long and wearisome voyage to Pennsylvania, where they arrived, it is believed, some time in August, for in John Marsh's land warrant, dated Nov. 24, 1736, he is mentioned as having been settled on the land "about three months." The two families of the father and son settled near each other on two tracts of land in East Nant- meal Township, Chester County, adjoining other Irish Friends, William and Timothy Kirk, of the Kirks of Lurgan Meeting, County Armagh. Soon after their settlement the Marshes were received as acceptable members of Goshen Monthly Meeting, Chester County, as appears from the following extracts from the minutes of that meeting :

Minute of Men's Meeting, 8 Mo. 18,1736.—" John Marsh Pro- duced a Certificate to this Monthly Meeting from the Monthly Meeting of friends held at Grange near Charlemount in ye North of Ireland dated ye 2d of ye 4 Mo : 1736 in behalf of himself & wife [Elizabeth] which [is] to friends Satisfaction and ordered to be recorded."

Minutes of Women's Meeting.—" At our Monthly Meeting held at Goshen the Eighteen Day of Eighth Month [1736] Eliz- abeth Marsh Produced to this Meeting a Certificate from Friends in Ireland jointly with her Husband which we accept on her behalf.''

Minutes Men's Meeting.—''At our Monthly Meeting held at Goshen ye 15th day of ye 9th Mo. 1736 Joshua March [Marsh] Produced a Certificate to this Monthly Meeting from the Monthly Meeting of friends at Grange in Charlemount in the North of Ireland dated ye 2d of ye 4th month last in behalf of himself & wife [Elizabeth] & 3 of his children, viz : Jonathan, Peter & Abigail which is to the Satisfaction of friends here & ordered to be Recorded.''

Minutes of Women's Meeting.—'' At our Monthly Meetnig held at Goshen the Fifteenth Day of the Ninth Month [1736] . . . Elizabeth Marsh Produced to this Meeting a Certificate from the Monthly Meeting of Grange in Ireland which this Meeting Accepts on her behalf.''

Joshua Marsh settled on a tract of two hundred acres of land which he purchased from the Penn Proprietors. The following abstract of his land title is from the records preserved in the Department of Internal Affairs, at the capital, Harrisburg, Pa.:

No. 55. *Joshua Marsh*, of Chester Co., Pa., warrant for 200 acres of land ''Adjoyning the Lands of John Griffith and John Rees in the Township of Nantmill,'' granted October, 26, 1737 ; patented Oct. 12, 1742, 195 acres returned (A. 10, p. 505).[1]

Patent Deed : (Survey, May 10, 1738.)

John, Thomas, and Richard Penn, Proprietors of Penn'a., on Oct. 12, 1742, patented to Joshua Marsh, of Chester Co., in consideration of £30, 4s., 195 acres of land in Nantmeal Twp., Chester Co., described as follows,—

Beginning at a corner marked hickory, in a line of William Kirk's land, and from thence extending by John Griffith's land, W. by N. 210 P. to a marked chestnut ; thence by William Branson's land, N. 81 P. to a post, thence by John Ree's land, E. N. E., 113 P. to a black oak marked, and N. N. W., 48 P. to a marked black oak ; thence by the lands of the said William Branson, N. E. by E., 44 P. to a post ; thence by Daniel Brown's land, S. S. E. 76 P. to a marked chestnut, N. E. by E. 60 P. to a marked black oak and S. S. E. 30 P. to a marked hickory ; thence by vacant land, S. 60° E. 80 P. to a marked hickory ; thence by the said William Kirk's land S. W. by W. 135 P. to a marked black oak and S. E. by S. 60 P. to place of beginning, containing 195 acres and allowance.

Joshua attended Uwchlan Friends' Meeting until the establishment of Nantmeal Meeting in 1740, and was appointed a representative from Uwchlan Preparative to Goshen Monthly Meeting,

[1] See Survey, No. 446, *Taylor Papers*, Hist. Soc. of Penn'a.

to which Uwchlan was subordinate. The minutes of the Monthly Meeting show that he was appointed on committees to inquire into requests for certificates of removal, to oversee marriages, etc. His name appears for the last time in the meeting records, 9 Mo. 1, 1745, when he signed a marriage certificate. He was taxed in East Nantmeal Township, in 1737–8, 1s.; in 1739, 1s. 3d ; in 1740–1, 1s. 6d.[1]

He died probably in the spring of 1748, for his will was made August 18, 1747, and probated May 17, 1748. As his wife is not mentioned in the will, he must have survived her. The following is a copy of the will :

"I JOSHUA MARSH[2] of East Nantmell, in the County of Chester in the province of Pennsylvania yeoman Being in Health of body and of Sound disposing Mind and memory in thankfullness of heart to almighty God for his mercies and favors and in Consideration of the uncertainty of our Time here do make and ordain this my last will and Testament in Manner following.

Imprimis its my Will that after my Decease my body be buried in a Decent manner at the Discretion of my Executor hereafter Named and as for what temporal Estate it hath Pleased God to Bestowe Upon me in this Life, I Give Devise and Dispose of the Same in manner Following.

In the first place its my Will that my just Debts and Funeral Charges be paid and Discharged

Item I Give to my Son John Marsh the sum of Five Shillings Lawful Money of this Province

Item I Give to my son George Marsh Five Shillings Money Aforesaid

Item, I Give to my son Peter Marsh Five Shillings Money aforesaid

Item I Give to my Daughter Deborah McMullen Five Shillings Money Aforesaid

Item I Give to my Daughter Abigail Atherton Five Shillings Money aforesaid

Item, I Give and Bequeath all my Personal Estate & Goods and Chattels after my Debts Funerall Charges and Legacies Aforesaid are Paid and Discharged unto my Son Jonathan his Executors and Administrators

Item I Give and Devise all and Singular my Messuage Plantation and Tract of Land whereon I now Live in East Nantmell aforesaid with the rights members and Appurtances thereof unto my s[d] Son Jonathan Marsh his heirs and Assigns for Ever

[1] Tax Lists in County Commissioners' Office, West Chester, Chester Co., Pa.

[2] Papers No. 1144, Book 3, p. 15, Register's Office, West Chester, Pa.

Item I Give and Devise that my farm in Belenacar in Clambrasel in the County of Armagh in the Kingdom of Ireland Containing Thirty three Acres of Land with the Rights members and Appurtances thereof Unto my Said Son Jonathan Marsh his heirs and Assigns Forever.

Item I Nominate and Appoint my son Jonathan Marsh to be sole Executor of this my Last will and Testament and Lastly I do Revoke and Declare to be null and void all Former and other wills and Testaments by me Made in word or writing and do Declare this only to be my Last Will & Testament In Witness whereof I have hereunto Set my hand and Seal Dated the Eighteenth Day of the Sixth Month Called August Anno Dom 1747

Joshua Marsh [SEAL]"

Witnesses :
David Davies
Richd Davies
Ellis Davies

The following inventory of the estate of Joshua Marsh was filed at Chester, then the county seat of Chester County, May 2, 1748 :
"the 26th Day of ye 3^d : mo^th : in ye year 1848 A true Inventory of the goods and efects of Joshua Marsh deceased

	£	S	d
"To a bed and beding	4	3	o
To a chest	o	2	6
To a table cloth and napkin	o	2	6
To a pair of leather Briches and Sundries	o	18	o
To a horse Saddle and bridle	4	o	o
To a mare	3	10	o
To Books	2	15	o
To a bedstead Barrels and Sundries	o	12	6
To pots and Sundries	1	3	6
To carpenters Tools	o	14	o
To tongs and pothangers & Sundries	o	14	o
To chair haccles & Sundries	o	9	o
To flax seed and Sundries	o	16	6
To leather & Sundries	2	9	10
To yaarn	3	5	o
To three bags		10	o
To a cart and tacklings	8	o	o
To a Dough trough & Sundries	o	11	6
To a harrow	o	18	o

	£	s	d
To a grinding Stone	0	5	0
To bees	1	4	0
To a plow & axes and mattock	1	3	0
To Sheep.	1	17	6
To hoggs.	2	18	0
To chains and Sundries	0	5	0
To a loom & wool & Sundries	2	2	6
To Some wareing apparel	1	1	0
To Credit for wool	0	5	6
To two Smoothing iron	0	4	0
To unbroke flax	0	5	0
To a plantation	200	0	0

Appraised by us the Day &
year above written
  Wm Kirk
  John Griffiths ''

Joshua and Elizabeth (Rogers) Marsh had children as follows :
I. Deborah ; II. Joseph (?) ; III. John ; IV. George ; V. Abigail ; VI. Peter ; VII. Jonathan.

I. DEBORAH MARSH, from whom the writer descends, was married 5 Mo. 10, 1727, at Grange Meeting, near Charlemont, County Armagh, Ireland, to Thomas McMullen [McMillan], of Grange Meeting, County Antrim. See ''McMillan Family,'' page 399.

II. JOSEPH MARSH, ''of Crenah in the parish of Tillenesky & Countie of Tyrone'' (who is thought to have been a son of Joshua Marsh, since Joshua's name appears on the marriage certificate next to that of the bride's father, Francis Hobson, who heads the list of signers in the column reserved for relatives under the bride and groom's names), probably named for his grandfather, Joseph Marsh, was married 5 Mo. (July) 27, 1732, in the Friends' Meeting House at Ballyhagen, County Armagh, Ireland, to Ruth Hobson, ''Daughter of ffrancis Hobson of Drummilly in the parish of Loughgall & Countie of Ardmagh.'' Some of the signers to the marriage certificate [1] were : :

ffrancis Hobson	Sarah Hobson	JOSEPH MARSH
Joseph Hobson	(and others)	RUTH MARSH
John Hobson	Deborah M'Moollon	
(and others)	Abigail Marsh	Peter Marsh
	Hannah Hobson	ffrancis Hobson
	(and others)	Joshua Marsh
	Mabel Anderson	George Rodgers
		William Vance
		William Hobson
		(and others)

[1] Page 7, Marriage Book, 1731–1786, Ulster Quarterly Meeting.

Joseph Marsh is not mentioned in Joshua Marsh's will and nothing further has been learned of him.

III. JOHN MARSH, son of Joshua, married Elizabeth ———, prior to or about 1724, as has been stated above, came over from Ireland, in 1736, and settled in East Nantmeal Township, Chester County. The following abstract of his land title is from the records of the Department of Internal Affairs at Harrisburg:

No. 52. *John Marsh*, of Chester County, 200 acres "of Land scituate in Nantmil Township, whereon He has been about three months settled & adjoining to William and Timothy Kirk," granted Nov. 24, 1736; patented Mar. 14, 1790. Acres returned 11.76. Patentees, John Marsh (Vol. A 14, p. 268), James Pugh (Vol. P 18, p. 251). Survey.[1]

Patent Deed: Thomas and Richard Penn, Proprietors of Penn'a, on June 9, 1747, patent to John Marsh, of Chester County, Pa., in consideration of £33. 3d., 213 acres of land and allowance, in East Nantmeal Twp., Chester County, decribed as follows:

Beginning at a marked hickory by Timothy Kirk's land, S. 25° E. 100 P. to a marked hickory; S. 65° W. 30 P. to a marked chestnut at a corner of Robert Wetherall's land, by same, S. 25° E. 44 P. to marked black oak; E. 20 P. to marked hickory; S. 25° 149 P. to marked black oak, by Henry Phillip's land S.E. 40 P. to post by Callowhill Manor, corner of Vincent Township; N. 42° E. 150 P. to corner post, by John Well's land; N. 48° W. 80 P. to marked black oak standing at a corner of John Price's land, thence by same N. 18° W. 26 P. to a marked white oak; N. W. by W. 16 P. to a marked chestnut; W. N. W. 126 P. to a corner post, thence by Simon Woodrow's land; W. S. W. 40 P. to a corner marked white oak; thence, by the Meeting Land, N. 85° W. 80 P. to place of beginning, containing 213 acres.

John Marsh and his son Joshua, on complaint of Uwchlan Preparative Meeting, for breach of discipline were disowned by Goshen Mo. Mtg., 3 Mo. 17, 1742. About 1750 John Marsh removed with his family from Chester County and settled on a tract of land adjoining his brother-in-law, Thomas McMillan, in Warrington Township, York County, Pa. The records at Harrisburg show the following purchases of land:

Warrant No. 41, John Marsh, 25 acres, "adjoining Thomas McMillan & Peter Cook on Doe Run in Warrington Township," York County, granted Sept. 10, 1751: patented May 25, 1855.— (Patent Book G. 489).

Warrant No. 233, John Marsh, Sr., 24 acres, "joining his

[1] Also see *Taylor Papers*, Warrants, No. 405, Historical Society of Penn'a.

27

other Land & Elihu Underwood & Isaac Kole in Warrington"
Twp., York County, granted Oct. 21, 1769; patented Dec. 14,
1822. (Survey.)

Warrant No. 236, John Marsh, Sr., 26 acres, "joining his
other Land granted by warrant of the 21st of October Instant in
Warrington" Twp., York County, granted Oct. 30, 1769; pat-
tented Dec. 14, 1822. (Survey.)

John Marsh was living in 1769, but the date of his death has
not been learned. His wife, Elizabeth died in or prior to 1761.
As far as can be learned they had the following children : 1.
John ; 2. Margaret ; 3. Joshua ; 4. Jonathan ; William (?) :
Ruth (?)

1. *John Marsh*, born in Ireland, in 1724, died 3 Mo. 10, 1804,
and was buried in Friends' graveyard at Warrington Meeting
House, York Co., where his gravestone, with inscription, may
still be seen. He probably removed from Chester to York Co.,
with his father, about 1750, but his certificate of removal from
Goshen Mo. Mtg., dated 8 Mo. 17, 1752, was not received at Warrington Mo. Mtg., until 11 Mo. 18, of that year. At Warrington
Mo. Mtg., 5 Mo. 20, 1758, he produced an acknowledgment for
marrying "by a Justice with a young woman not Joined amongst
friends." His wife Margaret was received into membership, 7
Mo. 12, 1760.

By warrant, No. 125, dated June 4, 1762, John Marsh, Jr.,
was granted 125 acres " adjoining Peter Cook in Warrington"
Twp., York Co.; patented July 11, 1795 (Z, 281). Survey.

In his will, dated, Washington Twp., York Co., 4 Mo. 30,
1802, probated Apr. 2, 1804, he mentions his wife Margaret, his
eleven children, and a lot of ground within fourteen rods of
" Baltimore Town." Children by his wife Margaret were : (1)
Jonathan, b. 6 Mo., 1, 1760, d. 3 Mo. 20, 1850, removed to
Baltimore, Md., about 1798, and finally to Middleton Mo. Mtg.,
Ohio, in 1808 ; (2) Elizabeth, b. 7 Mo. 27, 1762, removed to
Baltimore 1 about 1797 ; (3) Margaret, b. 11 Mo. 28, 1764, removed to Baltimore about 1797 ; (4) Mary, b. 1 Mo. 16, 1767,
took a certificate to Baltimore in 1801 ; (5) Rebecca, b. 3 Mo.
16, 1769, d. 11 Mo. 13, 1770 ; (6) Susanna, b. 3 Mo. 7, 1771,
m. 9 Mo. 12, 1793, John Everitt, son of Isaac and Martha ; (7)
John, b. 3 Mo. 7, 1771, d. 1806, m. in 1802, Catharine ———— ;
(8) William, b. 7 Mo. 28, 1775, took a certificate to Baltimore in
1797 ; (9) Rebecca, b. 8 Mo. 2, 1777, d. 4 Mo. 14, 1858,
buried at Warrington ; (10) Lydia, b. 10 Mo. 20, 1779, m. John
Walker, son of Benjamin, of Warrington[1] ; (11) Hugh, disowned by Warrington Mo. Mtg., 3 Mo. 22, 1809, for marriage

[1] See *Lewis Walker and Descendants*, by Priscilla Walker Streets.

out; (12) Hannah produced an acknowledgment for marriage
out, in 1808.

2. *Margaret Marsh* was married 12 Mo. 30, 1756, at Warrington Mtg., York Co., to Elihu Underwood, schoolmaster, of Warrington, son of Alexander. Signers to marriage certificate were:

Jane McMillan	Mary Morthland	ELIHU UNDERWOOD
Rebecca Fincher	John McMillan	MARGRET UNDERWOOD
Elizabeth Hussey	John Harry	
Richard Wickersham	Ruth Cook	Alexander Underwood
James Peckett	Rebeca Morthland	Sarah Underwood
Charles Morthland	Ann Hussey	John Marsh
James Jones	Elizabeth Wickersham	William Marsh
Samuel Morthland	William Morthland	Ruth Marsh
Jonathan Marsh	George McMillan	Ruth Morthland
Susanah Ward	Armel Fincher	Petter Marsh
	Christopher Hussey	Deborah McMillan
	Joseph Garretson	Mary McMillan
	Aaron Frazer	

3. *Joshua Marsh* seems to have disappeared from the records
after his disownment.

4. *Jonathan Marsh*, of Warrington, was married, 1st, 6 Mo.
18, 1761, at Warrington Mtg., to Rebecca, daughter of Hugh
Morthland, deceased, and Rebecca, his wife; m. 2d 12 Mo. 16,
1768, at Merion Meeting, Chester Co., to Ann Packer, of Haverford, daughter of Philip and Ann. He served a number of years
as overseer of Warrington Meeting. He died in 1795, leaving at least four children: (1) James, by first wife, m. 9 Mo. 14,
1797, at Warrington, Edith Hussey, daughter of Record and
Miriam, of Warrington, took a certificate to Baltimore, in 1810,
with wife—children, Zilla and Amos—, and finally removed to
Ohio; (2) Ann, by first wife, m. 1797, to John Edmonson, of
Warrington; (3) John, by second wife, m. 5 Mo. 14, 1789, to
Hannah Hussey, daughter of Record and Miriam, removed to
Gunpowder Mtg., Md., in 1790; (4) Elizabeth, m. 1 Mo. 12,
1792, at Warrington Mtg., to Joseph Edmondson.

5. *William Marsh*, supposed to have been the son of John,
was disowned by Warrington Mo. Mtg., in 1763, for marriage
out.

6. *Ruth Marsh*, supposed to have been the daughter of John.

IV. GEORGE MARSH, the first of the family to come to Pennsylvania, produced the following certificate of removal to Kennett
Mo. Mtg., Chester Co., 7 Mo. 6, 1729. He is mentioned in his
father's will, but no further record of him has been found: [1]

[1] Original MS. in possession of Gilbert Cope, of West Chester. See
facsimile, page 84.

" from our Meeting at the Grange
Near Charlemont the 22ᵈ of the
5th month *1728*
" Whereas George Marsh Son to Joshua Marsh hath a Minde
to Transporte himselfe to pensilvania in A Merica and desires our
Sertificate These are therefore to Sertifie to all whome may be
Concerned that the Said George Marsh is the son of honest parents
whoe were Concerned to b[r]ing him up in the way of truth and
in as much as he is now groone into years Capable to worke for
his Liveing and having an inclination to goe to Amergea to Leave
his Sᵈ parants hath Consented thereunto and he being of apretty
orderly Conversation therefore we doe recommend him to the
Care of friends where he may Come for his preservation in the
truth   Signed in be[half] of our [torn] Meet[ing]
" Post Script we doe further Sertifie that we doe believe that
the Said George Marsh is free from any engagement of marriage
with any woman here   " Robert Green
                                        Bartho : Garnett
                                        Wm. Whitesite
                                        Jacob Marshill
                                        James Pillar
                                        John Griffin
                                        Thoˢ Greer
                                        Joshua Marsh
                                        Joseph Marsh "

V. ABIGAIL MARSH was married 9 Mo. 4, 1741, at Nantmeal
Friends' Meeting House, Chester Co., to Thomas Atherton, son
of Henry and Jennet (Thelwall) Atherton.   The following persons signed the marriage certificate :

Hester Hockley	William Williams	THOMAS ATHERTON
Ruth Roberts	Cadʳ Jones	ABIGAIL ATHERTON
Ann James	Awbrey Roberts	
Jane Rees	Henry Hockley	Joshua Marsh
Percy Hinton	John Griffith	Jonathan Marsh
Mary Evans	Samuel John	Peter Marsh
Ruth Evans	John Rees	Henry Atherton
Ann Hockley	Arnold Baset	Thomas Evans
Margaret Evans	Noble Butler	Eliza Evans
Rachel Butler	Jacob Jenkin	Thomas McMollin
Mary Griffith	William Kirk	Deborah McMollin
	Timothy Kirk	Richᵈ Thomas Jun
		Hannah Thomas
		Elizabeth Thomas
		Ester Evans
		William Taylor
		Henry Taylor
		Robert Thompson

Thomas Atherton was taxed 2s. in East Nantmeal Twp., Chester County, in 1740–1. At Goshen Mo. Mtg., 6 Mo. 18, 1740, " Thomas Atherton with the approbation of Uwchlan Preparative Meeting Proposes to joyn himself to our Religious Society who is Received by us as his Conduct Proves Agreeable to our Our Principles." He was appointed an overseer of Nantmeal Meeting, in 1754. In 1763 he received a certificate to remove with his wife Abigail and three children, Richard, Henry, and Elizabeth, to Warrington Mo. Mtg., York County. The certificate was received at Warrington, 1 Mo. 14, 1764. He died, probably in 1782, for his will[1] was dated Feb 2, 1774, and probated Sept. 23, 1782. His wife and three children survived him. Children : (1) Henry ; (2) Richard ; (3) Elizabeth.

  1. *Henry Atherton*, m. 3 Mo. 22, 1780, at Warrington Mtg., to Ann Hobson, of the same place daughter of Francis and Ann Hobson, Friends from Ireland. In 1784, Henry was disowned by Warrington Mo. Mtg. for attending musters. About 1790 they removed to Western Pennsylvania, and in 1794 were reported as living in the Glades of Stony Creek, probably in Bedford County. Children : Mary, Thomas, Francis, and Ann.

  2. *Richard Atherton*, m. 5 Mo. 18, 1775, to Phebe Hobson, sister of Henry's wife. The committee appointed to oversee the marriage reported that the occasion had been orderly, " Except having assistants to pull off the glove and hat." In 1784 he produced an acknowledgment for marriage by a " hireling Teacher." He removed within the limits of Westland Mo. Mtg., about 1790.

  3. *Elizabeth Atherton*, m. 1 Mo. 16, 1777, to Alexander Elliot, of Newberry Twp., York County, son of Isaac, deceased. At Warrington Mo. Mtg., 6 Mo. 13, 1778 ; they were complained of by Newberry Mtg. for having differed and parted ; disowned 8 Mo. 8, 1778. In his Diary (1780–1786) Benjamin Walker, of Warrington, under date of 5 Mo. 22, 1781, 3d-day, notes that he was " Diging a Grave for Elizabeth Ellet formerly Atherton," at Warrington Friends' burial ground.

  VI. PETER MARSH, with the concurrence of Uwchlan Preparative Mtg., requested of Goshen Mo. Mtg., 4 Mo. 21, 1740, a certificate of removal to Oley (Exeter) Mo. Mtg., Berks County. The certificate was received at Exeter 6 Mo. 28, 1740. A certificate for him to return to Goshen was signed by Exeter, 8 Mo. 29, 1741. At Goshen Mo. Mtg., 6 Mo. 15, 1743, " The Representatives of Uwchlan Preparative Meeting Acquaints this Meeting that Peter Marsh Persists in keeping Company in Order for marriage with a young woman not of our Religious Society." At the

[1] Will in Register's Office, York, Pa.

meeting 7 Mo. 12, 1743, he was reported married out of the Society.   He was then disowned, 9 Mo. 21, 1743, the testimony against him to be read at Nantmeal Meeting House.   He was taxed in Nantmeal Township, in 1739.   In the tax list for 1740–1 his named has been crossed off.

He removed to Warrington Township, York County, about 1750, about the same time as his brother John and his brother-in-law Thomas McMillan, and settled on a tract of land at the foot of Round Top.   A warrant (No. 36) for 25 acres of land ''on a Branch of Beaver creek adjoining Robert Veale [Vale] in Warrington Township,'' was granted to him May 7, 1751 ; patented Dec. 7, 1762 (G. 489).   In his will,[1] dated 4 Mo. 21, 1788, probated April 4, 1789, he speaks of his ''meadow next Roundtop.'' He leaves 88 acres of land, which was surveyed May 3, 1753, to his son Jonathan, and mentions his other children, John, Mary Jones, Deborah Frazer, Jane Phillips, Lydia Brunton, Rachel Howe, Rebecca, and Esther.

Deborah, daughter of Peter Marsh, born 4 Mo. 5, 1746 ; m. 1 Mo. 22, 1772, to Joshua Frazer, son of James and Rebecca (Cox) Frazer.   A daughter, Elizabeth Frazer, married William Brinkerhoff, who when living in Ohio, in 1876, at the age of ninety-two years, gave the following interesting reminiscences[2] of the Marshes and Frazers :

Peter Marsh's wife Margaret was a Welsh Quakeress of gigantic size.   Deborah, the daughter, was buried beside her husband and parents at Warrington Meeting House.   Joshua Frazer was first engaged to a younger sister of Deborah's of about his own age, and they were to have been married in the spring of 1771 ; but in the fall of 1770, with an eye to securing some ready money to help him set up housekeeping, Joshua kissed his sweetheart good bye and went down into North Carolina to chop wood during the winter.   Here he met with such success that he concluded to stay a little longer than had been arranged for, and wrote to his intended to that effect.   But, unfortunately for him, she never received his letter, and when he failed to appear at the proper time ''the girl was mad and up and married another fellar to wonst.''

Soon after, the young Joshua returned with his pockets weighted with hard earned money and his mind filled with pleasant anticipations of the coming event.   But, alas, for all his high hopes, the girl had gone with another man.

At length, Deborah, an older sister, came to the rescue.   It was true she was somewhat too old, but what better could be

[1] Register's Office, York, Pa.
[2] Notes taken at the time by Smith Bell McMillan, now of Signal, Ohio.

done? So, in 1772, she became my future mother-in-law. When Joshua asked Peter Marsh for Debby, Peter replied:

"Joshua, I gave thee one girl, and I'm not going to give thee another.—But, if thee will come with two horses and a side-saddle, and the girl wants to go with thee, take her right along."

The test was soon made and with a happy result for Joshua, for "the girl she climbed into the saddle, she did."

VII. JONATHAN MARSH was married, in 1748, by authority of Exeter Mo. Mtg., Berks Co., to Mary Long, of that meeting, probably a daughter of Robert and Rachel Long. The marriage was authorized 9 Mo. 24, and reported accomplished 10 Mo. 29, 1748, so that the ceremony must have occurred between the two dates. He died shortly afterward, letters of administration on his estate being granted to his widow Jan. 19, 1749–50. The following inventory[1] of his estate was filed March 1, 1748-9:

"Inventory of the Goods and Chattels &c of Jonathan March Dececed apprised this 23 Day of January Anno Dom, 1748/9 by us the subscribers.

	£	s	d
to wering apparil Riding Creator Saddle and Briddle	15	0	0
to Horce & Meare	5	10	0
to 4 Cows a Steear and 2 yond haffars	13	0	0
to 6 Hogs	1	15	0
to 6 Sheeps	2	5	0
to a plow harrow and Tacklens	1	15	0
to a Steel of a Colling Box and Sum old Cart Iron	0	4	0
to a Cart	8	0	0
to all the wheat and Ry in the Ground	12	0	0
to 5 Stocks of Beeas a heay fork 22 Skikls a Grindstone 2 Sithes	1	12	0
to Lome and tacklens & horse Gears and Cart Sadle	2	10	0
to hog meat and a podring tube and Cealor	1	6	0
to flax and hampe brocken and one broken	0	17	6
to a womans Sadel	1	10	0
to Long wheal a pettecot Sum will and other Lumber	0	6	0
to Sum malt Barly flaxseed a tube a basket and peal	0	10	6
to flax yearn Toney earn and Sum Salt	3	3	0
to a Bag of fatthers	1	10	0
to a Bed and Bed Cloath	1	10	0
to a Grubing howe Sum axes and old iron	0	18	0
to 3 pots a Crock and hangers a frian pan Sum other things	0	18	0
to 5 Bells and Bell Collars and Breack iron	0	15	0
to Chair 2 peals 2 Bags and Ridel	0	8	0
to 2 wheals	0	12	0
to putter Earthen pans trunchers and Nogans	1	6	6
to two glace ——(?) 2 Knifes and Sum other things	0	3	0
to Sum Candels and tallow	0	5	6

[1] Papers No. 1217, Register's Office, West Chester, Pa.

	£	S	d
to Kneding trogh 2 Barals a Chist and the pekin	0	11	0
to a table Cloth and a towel Sum tow Cloath	1	3	0
to Bed and Bed Cloas	4	10	0
to 2 Books and Sum drest Cloth	2	15	9
to a Stack of hay	1	0	0
	103	0	9

The above was apprised by us the Subscribers the day year above written

his
Enin **E**. Williams
mark
Thomas Slycer
Griffith Griffith"

Elizabeth Marsh, the only child of Jonathan Marsh, was born 7 Mo. 29, 1749, after her father's death. At an Orphans' Court, held at Chester, March 20, 1749,[1] "Mary Marsh petitioned the Court on behalf of Elizabeth Marsh ye daughter of Jonathan Marsh dece^d for the Court to appoint Proper persons to be her Guardians wch was allow'd of and the Court appoints Thomas Downing and Samuel James to be her Guardians &c."

Mary Marsh, the widow, spoken of as a "young woman," was married, by authority of Exeter Mo. Meeting, between the dates 2 Mo. 26, and 3 Mo. 31, 1750, to John Williams, of Nantmeal Meeting, Chester Co., the Mo. Meeting having seen that "Guardians [were] chosen to take Care of her Child." John Williams removed with his wife Mary, children Henry and William, and step-daughter, Elizabeth Marsh, to Exeter Mo. Mtg., in 1757, the certificate of removal from Goshen being presented 10 Mo. 27th of that year. In 1765 they returned again to Chester Co., with children, Henry, William, Jonathan, and Miriam, presenting certificates to Uwchlan Mo. Mtg. Elizabeth Marsh, "now Ellis," was complained of in Uwchlan Mo. Mtg., 6 Mo. 8, 1769, for marrying a Friend before a Justice, and was disowned 7 Mo. 6, 1769.

THE MACKEY FAMILY.

JOHN MACKEY,[2] or Mackie, of Kincon, Parish of Kilmore, County Armagh, "being weak in body, but perfect in memory," made his will 4 Mo. 11, 1699. *First.* He leaves to his wife the

[1] Records of Orphans' Court, Vol. V., **51**, in office of Clerk of the Courts, West Chester, Pa.

[2] In 1681, " John Macky [County Down] had taken from him for Tithe, by Hugh Powell and Edmond MacElcoshker, two Stooks of wheat, eleven Stooks of Oats and two Stooks of Barly, all worth seventeen shillings."— *Stockdale,* 175.

third part of "all my goods & Chattells quick and dead within and without and alsoo my house & Land duering her Life and after her decease to fall to my Sons Joseph and Benjamin" to be equally divided between them.

Item. "After my wifes third parte is taken off I doe give the one half of what remains to my Son William and my Son Joseph and my daughter Rebecca," to be divided equally.

Item. "I leave the other halfe to my Son Benjamin and my daughter Martha" to be equally divided.

Item. Wife to be executrix.

Item. William Brownlee, Jr., and William Gray to be overseers and guardians to see that "my wife doe fully execute this my will."

Lastly. Directs that his "body be buried in the buering Place in the mueny belonging to the meeting of balley hagen."

Witness : Charles Brown   John Mackey [Seal]
Kellren Brown

7 Mo. 6, 1699, William Macky, David Kell, Joseph Mackey certify that they have "Received full Satisfaction of our mother concerning our fathers Last will." (*Recordsof Ballyhagen Meeting.*)

Children of John Mackey : I. Joseph, II. William, III. Benjamin, IV. Rebecca, and V. Martha.

I. JOSEPH MACKEY,[1] of Kincon, and Ann Sweethen[2] ["Sweeton" in minutes of Province Meeting], of Cloughan, both in Parish of Kilmore, County Armagh, were married, 4 Mo. 24, 1703, at Ballyhagen Meeting. The signers were :

JOSEPH MACKY

Mongow McKenell	Sarah Sweethen	ANN MACKY
William Morton	Mary Garner	Richard Mathewes
John Blackburn	Martha Allen	Alexr : Sweethen
William Nickalson	Hannah Sweethen	John Lennox
Robert Barns	Elizabeth Brownloe	Thos. Toulerton
John Williamson	Mary McKenell	William Sweethen
William Gray	Elinor Garner	William Hampton
James Tough	Margery keel	George Garner
Matthew Whinery	Mary keel	William Alen
James Stevenson	Abigail Gray	david kell
Patrick Hogg		
John Winter		
William Hobson		
John Scott		
Benj: Macky		

[1] Marriage Book Ballyhagen (Richhill) Meeting.

[2] Mary Sweethen, of Cloughan, Parish Kilmore, County Armagh, was married, 8 Mo. 22, 1702, to John Lenox of Drycroency, Parish Clanfekill, at Ballyhagen Meeting ; among signers were Alexander Sweethen, John

Joseph Mackie,[1] of Kincon, County Armagh, "being advanced in years," made his will April 7, 1760 and it was probated April 17, 1760. Directs that he be buried in graveyard at "Munny Hill." To son Benjamin, "My Cheese Press and no more having already Provided for him." To grandson, John Mackie, son of William, deceased, £6 when he is twenty-one. To Hannah Wicklow one cow or £2 in case there is no cow. To Jane Frizle, 5s. To Sarah Allen, 5s. To Martha Jackson, 5s. To Ann Hobson, 5s. To Margaret Fox, 4s. and check reel. To John Keller "my clothes." Mentions sons Samuel and William Mackie. David Bell and Nicholas Raye to be executors.

his
John J Mackie
mark

Witnesses : hew wat
David Kell
John Kell

Children of Joseph and Ann (Sweethen) Mackey :

1. William Mackey died prior to his father. Had a son John.

2. John Mackie, of Kincon, Parish of Kilmore, County Armagh, Ireland, and Elizabeth Hinshaw, of Grange, Parish of "Clanfeakill," County Tyrone, were married, 10 Mo. (Dec.) 12, 1733, in Meeting House near Charlemont, County Tyrone. Among the signers were: JOHN MACKIE, ELIZABETH MACKIE, Jacob Marshal, Thomas Greer, Benjamin Marshel, William Poell, Thomas Griffith, William Mackie, Sarah Mackie, Joseph Marshel, Joseph Mackie, William Allan, John Allan, Jacob Hinshaw, William Vance, James Morton.

3. Rebecca Mackey, born about 1716, married Jacob Hinshaw and removed to Pennsylvania in 1741.

4. Margaret (?) m. ——— Fox (?).

5. Benjamin Mackee, of Kincon, Parish of Kilmore, County Armagh, son of Joseph Mackey, and Mary, daughter of William Williamson, of Ballyhagen, said Parish, were married 2 Mo. 1, 1742, at Ballyhagen. Some of those who signed certificate were : Joseph, William, John, Ann, John, Samuel, William and Benjamin Mackie.

6. Samuel Mackey, living in 1760.

7. Ann Mackie, daughter of Joseph Mackie, of Kincon, Parish of Kilmore, County Armagh, and Frances Hobson, of Drumolley, Parish of Loughgall, County Armagh, were married 9 Mo. 25, 1741, in Meeting House at Ballyhagen. Among signers were :

Hinshaw, Dorothy Hinshaw, Elinor Whinery, Robert Lennox, Thomas Hinshaw, John Whinery.

[1] *Bay 4, R Tray, No. 8, Public Record Office, Dublin.*

Francis Hobson, Ann Hobson, Joseph, Benjamin, William, John, Samuel, Benjamin and John Mackie, and Ruth Marsh.

8. Hannah (?), m. ——— Wicklow (?).

9. Jane Mackie, daughter of Joseph and Ann, b. 2 Mo. 20, 1704 ; m. ——— Frizle (?)

10. Sarah (?), m. ——— Allen (?).

11. Martha (?), m. ——— Jackson (?).

II. William Mackie (son of John), of Rockmacreany, Parish of Kilmore, County Armagh, made his will 10 Mo. 20, 1735. To be buried in the Money. £6 to poor of Ballyhagen Meeting. Mentions son-in-law, Jacob Sinton ; grandson, William Sinton ; son, Samuel Mackie ; brother Benjamin's three sons, John, William, and Joseph ; Benjamin Mackie's daughters, Mary and Jean ; sister, Rebecca Smith ; John Kell ; William, son of Joseph Mackie ; Jane Mackie, daughter of Samuel ; daughter Sarah Sinton ; grandsons, Thomas and Jacob Sinton. (*Records of Ballyhagen Meeting.*)

III. Benjamin Mackey (son of John), of Rockmackany, Parish of Kilmore, County Armagh, and Sarah, daughter of John Williamson, of Ballyhagen, were married at Ballyhagen Meeting, 3 Mo. 24, 1716. Among those who signed the marriage certificate were John Williamson and Jane, William, Joseph, and Ann Mackey. They resided at Drumore, Parish Mullobrack, County Armagh. Children were :

1. John Mackie (son of Benjamin ?), of Parish Loughall, County Armagh, and Katharine Meredith, of Parish of Blaris, County Down, were married 2 Mo. (Apr.) 22, 1737, in Meeting House in Lisburn, County Antrim. Among signers were : John Mackie, Katharine Mackie, John Meredith, Jacob Hinshaw, Benjamin Mackie, John Hinshaw.

2. William Mackie.

3. Mary Mackie, daughter of Benjamin Mackie, of Drumore, Parish Mullobrack, County Armagh, and Robert Smith of Corabeak, Parish Kile, County Armagh, were married 9 Mo. 21, 1739, at Ballyhagen. Among signers were : Robert Smith, Mary Smith, James Smith, and Benjamin, John, William, John, Samuel, Joseph, Ann, Samuel, Jane, and Benjamin Mackie.

4. Jane Mackie, daughter of Benjamin Mackie, of Drumore, Parish of Mullaghbrack, County Armagh, and Joseph Meredith, of Ahentriske, Parish Blaris, County Down, were married 9 Mo. 30, 1740.

5. Joseph Mackie.

IV. Rebecca Mackey, m. ——— Smith.

V. Martha Mackey and William Allen, both of Ballyhagen Meeting, were married at that meeting, 1 Mo. 6, 1700.

THE MOORES OF BALLINACREE, COUNTY ANTRIM

JAMES MOORE,[1] Quaker, was residing on an extended estate in the Townland of Ballinacree,[2] Parish of Ballymoney, County Antrim, Ireland, as early as 1675. In that year he had "taken from him for Tithe, by James Cunningham, Tithemonger under John Dunbar Priest of Bellimunny Parish, twelve Stooks of Barley, forty nine Stooks of Oats, and seven car-loads of Hey, all worth three pounds four shillings six pence." (Stockdale, *A Great Cry of Oppression*, 48, printed in 1683.) The following year the same "Priest" took his oats, barley, wheat, and hay to the value of £2. 13s.; and thus each year down to 1682 he suffered a similar loss. In 1682, the birth of a son is thus recorded in the Friends' Registers: John Moore, son of James and Elizabeth Moore, of Ballyacree, County Antrim, was born 6 Mo. 9, 1682.

A Friends' Meeting (*Rutty*, 343) was established at Ballinacree,[3]

[1] According to the tradition in the family, the Moores came to Ireland from Cumberland, England, during the plantations of James I.

[2] About three miles to the northwest of Ballymoney.

[3] Ballinacree Meeting.—At Ulster Province Meeting, 2 Mo. 27, 1702, "The former desire from this meeting concerning building a meeting house for ye meeting near Ballymony being renewed & discoursed att this meeting butt for want of Some friends from yt & Colerain meetings this meeting cannot have So Satisfactory account as they could desire what methods may be taken to answer friends desire in yt matter: therefore its ye desire of this meeting yt one or more friends from those meetings do allways hereafter attend ye pro: meeting & yt if no progress be made towards building a meeting house nor James Moore ye younger willing to accept or receive ye meeting or allow ground to build a meeting house upon, then ye mens Meet. of yt quarter is desired to endeavour to gett a convenient place about ye center of friends to build a meeting house & conveniency for friends horses. And if ye friends of those meetings are nott willing to be at ye charge, to propose ye Same to this meeting who is willing to help & advise ym therein, concerning, which this meeting desires answer to ye next province meeting."
At the Province Meeting 4 Mo. 21, 1707, "Friends of Ballymony meeting give account yt [they] are making preparation towards building a meeting house, tho they have not yett gott ye place made Sure So they are Still desire to continue their care."
Whether or not the plans for building a meeting-house were carried out at this time I have been unable to determine. In 1796, Thomas Scattergood (*Memoirs*, 190) records in his journal that he "Rode to Ballynacree, and on the 22d (1 Mo.) held the preparative Meeting. This meeting-house joins a dwelling, and on sitting down, it seemed like sitting in a cellar: two men, two women and three children composed it." On a visit in 1809, Thomas Shillitoe (*Life of Friends' Library*, 120-1) says that Ballinacree Meeting consisted of parts of two families and that the Meet-

near Ballymoney, in 1673, and doubtless was held at James Moore's house, as later meetings were regularly held there. John Gratton, a Quaker minister, notes in his *Journal* (183) under date of 6 Mo. 14, 1696, that he lodged at "J Moor's" at Ballinacree. James Moore's daughter Alice was married in a Friends' Meeting at his own house, 10 Mo. 17, 1697, to Thomas Irwin, of Lisnegarvy (*Minutes of Ulster Province Meeting*). 6 Mo. 13, 1698 at the Province Meeting there is mention of "ye men and womens meeting held at James Moors ye 30ᵗʰ of yᵉ $\frac{2}{\text{mo.}}$ 1698." From this time on there are constant references to this meeting. In 1698, James Moore, of Ballymoney, was appointed on a committee of the Province Meeting to obtain subscribers for Barclay's *Apology*.

Thomas Story, a Quaker minister, gives the following account (*Journal*, 537) of his visit to the Moores, in 1716:

"On the 18th [7 Mo.], the great Rains having raised the Waters, we had but a small Meeting at Dunclaudy; but a very broken tender Time it was, and we were generally comforted. That Evening I went forward about ten Miles to James Moor's at Ballimuny; but his Wife being ill he directed us to his Son James about a mile farther; where we staid that night.

"On the 19th I had a Meeting near James Moor's, the elder; which was small, being Harvest, and wet weather, and not so open as the last; and yet a good Meeting. That Evening I went over the River again to Ely Crocket's."

The following is an abstract of the will[1] of James Moore, made in 1727, and probated by his three sons who are styled "Quakers":

Abstract of the will of James Moore, of Ballynacreemore, Parish of Ballymoney, County Antrim, Ireland, dated Dec. 29, 1727.

My son Wm. Moore out of the £500 he oweth me by bonds to pay the following legacies: to his son John Moore £100; to his son Clotworthy Moore £50; to his son James Moore £50; to his daughter Jean Whittsitt £50. The remaining £250 I leave and bequeath to himself. I also bequeath to him the Quarter Land of Lischeighan during his natural life, then to his son John Moore and his heirs male forever, and failing male heirs in him to the next of male kindred; also to him my silver Tankard.

My son James Moore out of the £500 he oweth me by bond to pay the following legacies: to the five children of my son George Moore,—

ing-house was under the same roof as a dwelling. On my visit in 1900 I found that the Society at this place was extinct and was unable to locate the site of the meeting-house; but I saw the old Friends' burial ground called the Lamb's Fold, at Enogh, near O'Hara Brook, about two miles west of Ballymoney.

[1] Public Record Office in Dublin.

William, James, George, Sarah, and Elizabeth Moore, £20 each when they come of age, with interest at six per cent; to my daughter Alice Erwin's children £100 and six small silver spoons—the £100 to be put at interest and the interest to be paid to my daughter Alice Erwin during her life and at her death to be given to her children as she is pleased to appoint; to my grandson William Moore, son of John Moore, £50. Then, I bequeath the remaining £250 to himself. Also, I leave to my son James Moore my tenant right of Ballinacreemore and my part of Unckunagh, Claughy, Enogh, and Cabragh, he or his executors paying to my daughter Alice Erwin during the present lease £20 per year out of said profit rent. I bequeath to my said son James Moore the Quarterland of Beltyton "and my bigg Bible and silver drinking dram coops" during his natural life and then to his son William Moore and his heirs male forever.

To my son John Moore the bonds due me by him and the interest due on them.

To my son George Moore 5s. and the debt he is due me by bonds and otherwise.

Joseph Moore out of the £550 he oweth me by bonds to pay the following legacies : to daughter Elizabeth Whitsitt £100 and four silver spoons ; to the children of my daughter Sarah Henderson alias Courteny £100 at the death of their mother it being put to interest at six per cent to be paid to her during her life yearly and at her death to be divided among her children of the name of Courteny ; to my granddaughter Elizabeth Erwin £50, with four silver spoons, and the best bed and bed "close that I now possess" ; to my granddaughter Elizabeth Crockett £20 ; to my said grandson, John Moore, the son of my son John Moore, £30. Then I leave the remaining £250 to my son Joseph Moore, as also my tenant right to the Quarterland of Broadmillan and the Quarterland of Rosnashane and 29 acres of Diserderrin as now in his possession during his natural life ; then to his son William Moore and his heirs male forever.

To my daughter Frances Wilkinson the right of a lease I let to her son William Wilkinson and the right of the lease let to William Moore of Drumrahegle in trust for her and husband, her husband paying the rent.

Sons William, James, and Joseph Moore appointed executors.

JAMES MOORE.

The following are the children of James Moore,[1] probably all by his wife Elizabeth : [2]

[1] See Burke's *Landed Gentry*, II., 1422-3 (London, 1894).

[2] Robert Moore, of Ballmoney Meeting, and Jennet Miller, of Dunclady Meeting, County Antrim, were m. 6 Mo. 6, 1703, at the house of the Widow Henderson, in Dunclady.

James Moore, of Ballymoney Meeting, and Susanna Forster, of Antrim Meeting, were m. 5 Mo. 7, 1714, in the town of Antrim.

"David Moore and Mary Wilkisson both of Ballymony Meeting" were married "att y⁰ house of James Moore near Ballymony y⁰ 7th day of y⁰ $\frac{4}{mo}$ 1715."

Joseph Moore, of Ballymoney and Mary Henderson, of Dunclady, were m. 3 Mo. 3, 1721, at the house of Katharine Henderson, in Dunclady.

William Moore, son of James Moore, of Parish of Ballymoney, County

I. ALICE MOORE was married 10 Mo. 17, 1697, at a Friends' meeting at her father's house, to Thomas Erwin, of Lisnegarvey. Had a daughter Elizabeth and other children.

II. A DAUGHTER, who married ——— Crockett and had a daughter, Elizabeth Crockett.

III. WILLIAM MOORE, by his father's will, received the Quarterland of Lischeighan. In 1702 he settled at Killead, County Antrim, and became High Sheriff of Antrim in 1718. He married ——— Clotworthy, and had issue: (1) John Moore, of Moore's Grove, County Antrim, High Sheriff of Antrim in 1733, grandfather of Captain Roger Moore, of Killead, who was High Sheriff of Antrim in 1750, and who, in conjunction with Captain Thomas Thompson, in 1760, marched a contingent of 173 volunteers from Killead and vicinity to oppose the landing of the French at Carrickfergus ; (2) Clotworthy ; (3) James ; (4) Jean, married ——— Whitsitt.

IV. JAMES MOORE, JR., of Ballymoney Meeting, and Susanna Whitsite, of Grange Meeting, near Charlemont, were married by Friends' ceremony at the latter meeting, 10 Mo. 24, 1701. From his father he inherited the estate of Ballinacreemore, Unckunagh, Claughy, Enogh, Cabragh, and the Quarterland of Beltyton. James Moore, Jr., continued in membership with Friends, the meetings being held at his house. His son, William Moore, inherited the Ballinacree estate. The latter died, leaving an only daughter Susanna, who married ——— Strettle. At her death Ballinacree passed to her cousin, Samson Moore, a descendant of X. Joseph Moore.

V. JOHN MOORE, of Lurgan, County Armagh, was married 4 Mo. 24, 1702, at the Friends' Meeting at Lurgan, to Ruth Hoope, of Lurgan. Children, born at Lurgan : William, b. 8 Mo. 21, 1704 ; Francis, b. 2 Mo. 1, 1705 ; Eleanor, b. 2 Mo. 24, 1707 ; James, b. 5 Mo. 9, 1708 ; Robert, b. 4 Mo. 9, 1709.

VI. GEORGE MOORE, married, 7 Mo. 2, 1702, at Lurgan Meeting, Mary Hoope, of Lurgan. Had five children : William, James, George, Sarah, and Elizabeth.

Antrim, " Linnen Draper," and Mary Gregg, daughter of George Gregg, of Parish of Termoneny, County Londonderry, farmer, were married 2 Mo. (Apr.) 14, 1737, at Toberhead. Signers to certificate were :

William Holems	Samson Brady	William Gregg	WILLIAM MOORE
William Moore	Lewes Raford	Samson Moore	MARY MOORE
Andrew Spotswod	John Evens	Mary Hancock	George Gregg
William Reeves	John Downing	Mary Richardson	Thomas Gregg
	Jackson Clark	Elizabeth Moore	William Whitsitt
	Robert Clark	Elizabeth Moore	William Whitsitt
			James Moore
			John Moore
			Joseph Moore

—Marriage Book of Ulster Quarterly Meeting, 40.

VII. ELIZABETH MOORE, was married, 11 Mo. 2, 1705, at the
meeting at her father's house, to Joseph Whitsite, of Grange
near Charlemont.

VIII. SARAH MOORE, married, 1st, ——— Henderson, and
2d, 12 Mo. 9, 1708, at a meeting at her father's house, Joseph
Courtney, of Grange Meeting. She had children by second
marriage.

IX. FRANCES MOORE, married ——— Wilkinson, and had at
least one son, William Wilkinson.

X. JOSEPH MOORE, of Ballymoney Meeting, and Susanna
Brady, of Grange Meeting, County Antrim, were married 12 Mo.
6, 1706–7, at Grange Meeting. (*Minutes of Ulster Province
Meeting*).   Joseph Moore, by his father's will of 1727, received
the Quarterlands of Broadmillan and Rosnashane, and 29 acres
of Desertderrin (now called Moore Lodge), County Antrim.
Issue: (1) William, eldest son; (2) James, of Desertderrin, ancestor of the Moores, of Moore Fort, County Antrim ; (3) John,
b. 1712, ancestor, of the Moores of Lischeihan ; (4) Joseph, b.
1716, of Ahoghill, line extinct ; (5) Samson, of Moore Lodge, High
Sheriff of Antrim, 1767, died 1775 ; (6) George.

(1.) William Moore, the eldest son, of Rosnashane, b. Aug. 4,
1708, m. Elizabeth Courtney, of Glenburn, and had three
daughters and two sons (1. Joseph, Barrister at-Law, and 2. William).

Of these two sons, 2. William Moore of Killagan, County Antrim, High Sheriff, in 1778, m. the daughter of Rev. J. Warren,
Rector of Kilrea, County Londonderry, and had two sons : (*a*)
Samson, of Moore Lodge, who subsequently came into the Ballinacree estate on the death of his cousin Susanna Strettle. He
was Captain in the Antrim Regiment ; married Sarah, daughter of
William Warren, and died without issue in 1843, when Ballinacree[1] was sold out of the Moore family. (*b*) William, officer
in the 3d Dragoons, afterwards Captain in the Antrim Regiment, and High Sheriff of Antrim, 1808. He succeeded his
brother Samson in the Moore Lodge estates on the accession of
the latter to the Ballinacree estates. He m. Elizabeth, daughter
of Richard Rothe, Esq., of Mount Rothe, County Kilkenny, and
was succeeded by his son, George, on whose death, unmarried,
Moore Lodge was inherited by his cousin

WILLIAM MOORE, son of Samson (d. 1832), grandson of Alexander[2] (d. 1840), and great-grandson of (1) Joseph, Barrister.

[1] Ballinacree House, eventually passed into the hands of Marcus Gage,
now deceased, who pulled down the old mansion and built a new one.
When I visited the place in 1900 it was owned by Dr. Hamilton Ross.
[2] Alexander's estate of Rosnashane was sold about 1844.

William Moore, the above, of Moore Lodge, J.P., M.D., was born
on Nov. 13, 1826, and died 1901. Was High Sheriff, County
Antrim, 1890; President of the King and Queen's College of
Physicians, Ireland, 1883–1884; King's Professor of Medicine,
Trinity College, Dublin; was appointed Physician-in-Ordinary to
the Queen in Ireland, in 1885. He m. Sept. 3, 1863, Sydney
Blanche, daughter of Captain Abraham Fuller, of Woodfield.
Children: William; John; Alexander; George; Sydney; and
Roger Clotworthy.

Of these, WILLIAM MOORE,[1] JR., b. Nov. 22, 1864; K. C.,
1899; M. P. (conservative) for North Antrim, since 1899; succeeded to the family estate of Moore Lodge.[2] He was graduated
from Trinity College, Dublin, with the degree of B.A., in 1888;
was called to the Irish Bar in 1887 and the English Bar in 1899.
Married Helen Gertrude, daughter of Joseph Wilson, D.L., of
County Armagh, in 1888. Children: William Samson, b. April
17, 1891, etc.

[1] See *Who's Who*, 1902, page 920.
[2] The estate of Moore Lodge, formerly called Desertderrin, is pleasantly
situated on the River Bann, about six miles south of Ballinacree.

BIBLIOGRAPHY

I. Printed Sources

A Collection of Memorials Concerning Deceased Ministers . . . of the Quakers, Philadelphia, 1787.

A Compendious View of Some Extraordinary Sufferings of the People called Quakers both in Person and Substance in the Kingdom of Ireland, from the Year 1655 to the End of the Reign of King George the First. In Three Parts. 1. Contains the true Grounds and Reasons of their Consciencious Dissent from other Religious Denominations in Sundry Particulars,—By A. Fuller and T. Holms, Anno 1671. 2. Contains manifold Examples of their grievous Sufferings under *Oliver Cromwell* and the Reign of King *Charles* the IId for the aforesaid Reasons. III, Is a Brief Synopsis of the Numbers of Prisoners, &c. Dublin Printed by and for Samuel Fuller, at the Globe in Meathstreet, 1731. A copy in the Library of Haverford College.

Acrelius, Israel, *History of New Sweden*, Memoirs of the Historical Soc. of Penn'a, XI., Philadelphia, 1874.

Adams County, *History of,* Chicago, 1886.

American Weekly Mercury, Philadelphia, 1731. Also facsimile of issue for 1721, published by the Colonial Society of Pennsylvania, 1900.

American Friend, Philadelphia.

Armistead, Wilson, *Memoirs of James Logan*, London, 1851.

Ashmead, Henry Graham, *History of Delaware County*, Philadelphia, 1884.

Backhouse, James, *Memoirs of Francis Howgill*, York, England, 1828.

Barclay, Abram R., *Letters, etc., of Early Friends*, London, 1841.

Beck, William, *The Friends: Who They Are—What They Have Done*, London, 1893.

Bedford County, *History of,* Chicago, 1884.

Besse, Joseph, *A Collection of the Sufferings of the People Called Quakers,* 2 vols., London, Luke Hinde, George Yard, Lombard Street, 1753.

Biddle Henry D., *A Sketch of Owen Biddle,* Phila., 1892.

Black, William, *Journal of,* in 1744, Penn'a Mag., I.

Bolles, Albert S., Ph.D., LL.D., *Pennsylvania : Province and State,* 2 vols., Phila., 1899.

Book of Meetings of the Society of Friends in Great Britain and Ireland for 1900, London.

Bowden, James, *The Society of Friends in America,* 2 vols., London, 1850.

Brown, Levi K., *Account of the Meeting of the Society of Friends within the limits of Baltimore Yearly Meeting,* Phila., 1875.

Burnyeat, Jonathan (died 1709), *Diary,* London, 1857.

Canby, Margaret Tatnall, *A Sketch of the Early History of Wilmington,* in the *Literary Era,* VIII., Phila., 1901.

Chalkely, Thomas, *Journal,* London. Printed and sold by Luke Hinde at the Bible in George-Yard, Lombard Street, 1751.

Clement, John, *Sketches of the First Emigrant Settlers in Newton Township Old Gloucester County, West New Jersey,* Camden, N. J., 1877.

Church, Samuel H., *Oliver Cromwell,* New York and London, 1895.

Cook, Margaret, *Journal* (1778–1801), in *Friends' Intelligencer,* LIV., Phila., 1897.

Cope, Gilbert (see **Futhey**), *Genealogy of the Sharpless Family,* Phila., 1887 ; *Genealogy of the Smedley Family,* Lancaster, Pa., 1901.

Dankers, Jasper, and **Peter Sluyter,** *Journal of a Voyage to New York and a Tour in Several of the American Colonies,* in 1679–80, Memoirs of the Long Island Historical Society, Vol. I., Brooklyn, N. Y., 1867.

Drinker, Elizabeth, *Extracts from the Journal of* (1759–1807), Phila., 1889,

Earle, Alice Morse, *Home Life in Colonial Days,* New York, 1898.

Edmundson, William, *Journal,* 2d edition, London, Mary Hinde, in George-Yard, Lombard Street, 1774.

Egle, William H., M.D., *Notes and Queries, Historical, Biographical, and Genealogical,* annual volume for 1900, Harrisburg, Pa., 1901.

Elfreth, Jacob R., *Philadelphia Meeting Houses*, in *American Friend*, VII., Phila., 1900.

Ellis, Franklin, *History of Fayette County*, Pa., Phila., 1882.

Ellis, Franklin, and **Samuel Evans**, *History of Lancaster County*, Pa., Phila., 1883.

Evans, Samuel, see **Franklin Ellis**.

Fiske, John, *The Dutch and Quaker Colonies in America*, 2 vols., Boston and New York, 1899.

Fothergill, John, *An Account of the Life and Travels of*, London. Printed and sold by Luke Hinde, at the Bible in George-yard, Lombard-street, 1753.

Fox, George, *Journal*, 3d edition, London, 1765.

Frame, Thompson, *Historical Sketch of the Friends' Meeting-house at London Grove*, Chester County, Pa., in *The Friend*, LXXVII., Phila., 1901.

Friend, The, Philadelphia.

Friends' Intelligencer, Philadelphia, Vols. LIII. and LIV.

Froude, James A., *The English in Ireland*, 3 vols., London, 1882.

Fuller, Abraham, see **Thomas Holme**.

Futhey, J. Smith, and **Gilbert Cope**, *History of Chester County*, Pa., Phila., 1881.

Gardiner, Samuel R., *A Students' History of England*, London and New York, 1892.

Gibson, John, *History of York County*, Pa., Chicago, 1886.

Glenn, Thomas Allen, *The American Genealogist*, Ardmore, Pa., 1899–1900.

Gough, John, *History of the Quakers*, 4 vols., Dublin, Ireland, Robert Jackson, Meath Street, 1790.

Green, John Richard, *A Short History of the English People*, new edition, New York, 1896.

Hallowell, Richard P., *The Quaker Invasion of Massachusetts*, 4th edition, Boston, 1887.

Hart, Albert Bushnell, *American History told by Contemporaries*, Vol. I., New York, 1898.

Hazard, Samuel, *Annals of Pennsylvania*, 1609–1782, Phila., 1850.

Hodgkin, Thomas, *George Fox*, Boston and New York, 1886.

Hollingsworth, William B., *Hollingsworth Genealogical Memoranda*, Baltimore, Md., 1884.

Holme, Thomas, and **Abraham Fuller.** A Brief Relation of some of the Sufferings of the True *Christians,* The People of God (in Scorn called *Quakers*), in IRELAND, for these last 11 years, viz., from 1650 until 1671. With an *Occasional Treatise* of their Principles and Practices, briefly stated, whereby the Innocency of their course for which they so suffer, is not only plainly Demonstrated ; but also, from all false Aspersions and causeless Pretences sufficiently Vindicated. Collected by T. H. and A. F. Printed in the year, 1672.

Copies in Friends' Historical Library of Swarthmore College and in Friends' Library, 142 N. 16th Street, Philadelphia.

Hough, Oliver, *Captain Thomas Holme, Surveyor-General of Pennsylvania and Provincial Councellor,* Penn'a Mag., XIX., XX.

Jackson, Halliday, *Genealogy of the Jackson Family,* Phila., 1878.

Janney, Samuel M., *History of Friends.* 4 vols., Phila., 1861 ; *Life of William Penn,* 6th edition, revised. Phila., 1882.

Jenkins, Howard M., *Historical Collections Relating to Gwynedd,* Phila., 1884 ; *Memorial History of Philadelphia* (one of a series edited by John Russell Young), New York, 1895 ; *The Family of William Penn, Founder of Pennsylvania : Ancestry and Descendants,* Phila., 1899.

Kalm, Peter, *Travels into America* in 1748, London, 1772.

Keith, Charles P., *Provincial Councillors of Pennsylvania,* Phila., 1883.

Lawless, Emily, *The Story of Ireland* (Story of Nations Series), New York, 1895.

Leadbeater, Mary, *Biographical Notices of Friends in Ireland,* London, 1823.

Lewis, Samuel, *A Topographical Dictionary of Ireland,* 2 vols., London, 1837 (Hist. Soc. of Pa.).

Literary Era, Philadelphia (bound volumes at Hist. Soc. of Penna.).

Lodge, Henry Cabot, *A Short History of the English Colonies in America,* New York, 1886.

Logan, Dr. George, *Memoir of,* Hist. Soc. of Penn'a, Phila., 1899.

McFarlan-Stern Genealogy. See **Cyrus Stern.**

Map Showing the Location of Meetings Within the Limits of Philadelphia Yearly Meeting. Prepared by Young Friends' Association and published by Friends' Book Association, Philadelphia, 1897.

Memoirs of the Historical Society of Pennsylvania, 4 vols. Phila., 1826–1850.

Michener, Ellwood, *History of New Garden,* Chester County Pa., in weekly issues of the *Kennett Square* (Pa.) *Advance* 1898–9 ; also portions of MS. not yet printed. (See foot note, pages 131, 132.)

Michener, Ezra, M.D., *A Retrospect of Early Quakerism,* Phila. 1860.

Miscellaneous Genealogica et Heraldica. III. Second Series London, 1890.

Myers, Albert Cook, *Quaker Arrivals at Philadelphia, 1682- 1750,* Philadelphia, 1902.

Oldmixon, John, *British Empire in America* (London, 1707), re printed in *Hazard's Register,* V., Philadelphia, 1830.

Parrish, John, *Journal of,* Penna. Mag., XVI.

Passmore, John, A.M., *Andrew Moore and His Descendants,* vols., Phila., 1897.

Penn and Logan Correspondence, *Memoirs of the Historical So ciety of Pennsylvania,* IX. and X., Philadelphia, 1870, 1872

Pennsylvania Magazine of History and Biography, Vols. I.- XXVI., published by the Hist. Soc. of Penna., Phila., 1877- 1902.

Pennsylvania Colonial Records and Archives (1st, 2d, 3d, 4t] series). Published by the State, 1837–1902.

Pennypacker, Samuel W., *Annals of Phœnixville,* Pa., Phila. 1872.

Piety Promoted, 4 vols., Phila., 1854. (First printed in London 1701.)

Pike, Joseph, *Autobiography, Friends' Library,* II., 351–414 Phila., 1838.

Potts, Thomas Maxwell, *Our Family Ancestors,* Canonsburg Pa., 1895.

Prendergast, John P., *The Cromwellian Settlement of Ireland* 2d edition, London, 1870.

Proud, Robert, *History of Pennsylvania,* 2 vols., Phila., 1797–98

Publications of the Genealogical Society of Pennsylvania, I. Phila., 1898.

Records of Old Swedes Church, Wilmington, Del., published b the Hist. Soc. of Penna. in 1890.

Richardson, Jane M., *Six Generations of Friends in Irelan* (1655–1890), 2d edition, London, 1894 ; 3d edition, London, 1895.

Russell, Isaac S., *Russell Genealogy*, New Market, Md., 1889 ; *Steer Genealogy,* New Market, Md., 1891.

Rutty, John, *History of the Rise and Progress of the Quakers in Ireland,* revised and enlarged from Thomas Wight's MS. (see footnote, page 22), Dublin, J. Jackson, in Meath Street, 1751.

Robert, Ellwood, Old Richland Families.

Salkeld Family, printed in Delaware County, 1867.

Scattergood, Thomas, *Memoirs,* Philadelphia, 1845.

Scharfe, J. Thomas, *History of Delaware,* 2 vols., Phila., 1888.

Scharfe, J. Thomas, and **Thompson Westcott,** *A History of Philadelphia,* 3 vols., Phila., 1884.

Sharpless, Isaac, *A Quaker Experiment in Government,* Phila., 1898 ; *The Quakers in the Revolution,* Phila., 1899 ; *Two Centuries of Pennsylvania History,* Phila., 1900.

Shepperd, William R., *A History of Proprietary Government in Pennsylvania,* New York, 1896.

Shillitoe, Thomas, *Journal, Friends' Library,* Philadelphia, 1839.

Smith, George, M.D., *History of Delaware County,* Pa., Phila., 1862.

Smith, Joseph, *Catalogue of Friends' Books,* 2 vols., London, 1867 ; *Supplement,* London, 1893.

Smith, R. Morris, *The Smiths of Burlington* (N. J.), *A Family History,* Phila., 1877.

Smith, Samuel, *History of Pennsylvania,* Hazard's Weekly Register, VI., Phila., 1850 ; also original MS., Hist. Soc. of Pa. (see *Winsor,* III.).

Stern, Cyrus, *McFarlan and Stern Genealogy,* Wilmington, Del., 1885.

Stockdale, William, and five others, *The Doctrines and Principles : The Persecutions, Imprisonment, Banishment, . . . By the Priests and Magistrates of Scotland,* etc. London 1659.

Copies are in Friends' Historical Library of Swarthmore College and in Friends' Library, 142 N. 16th Street, Philadelphia.

Stockdale, William, *The Great Cry of Oppression; or, a Brief Relation of some Part of the Sufferings of the People of God in Scorn called Quakers. In Ireland,* 1671–1681. Small 4to. Printed in 1683.

Rare. Copies are in the British Museum ; in the Friends' Library at Devonshire House, Bishopsgate Street, London ; and in the private library of the late Charles Roberts, Philadelphia.

Stone, Frederick D., See *Winsor*, Vol. III.

Story, Thomas, *Journal*, New Castle-upon-Tyne, England, 1747.

Streets, Priscilla Walker, *Lewis Walker of Chester Valley and his Descendants*, Philadelphia, 1896.

Stubbs, Dr. Charles H., *Historic Genealogy of the Kirk Family*, printed in 1872.

Tanner, William, *Three Lectures on the Early History of Friends in Bristol and Somersetshire*, London, 1858.

Thomas, Allen C., and **Richard H.**, *A History of the Society of Friends in America*, Philadelphia, 1895.

Thwaites, Reuben Gold, *The Colonies*, New York and London, 1894.

To the Parliament of England, *who are in place to do Justice, and to break the Bonds of the Oppressed.* A NARRATIVE *of the Cruel and Unjust Sufferings of the People of God of the Nation of Ireland, called Quakers.* London, Printed for Thomas Simmons at the Bull and Mouth near Aldersgate, 1659. 4to.

Copies in Friends' Library, 142 N. 16th Street, Philadelphia, and in Ridgeway Branch of Philadelphia Library Company.

Traill, H. D., editor, *Social England*, 6 vols., New York and London, 1895.

Tylor, Moses Coit, *A History of American Literature* (1607–1765), New York, 1881.

Veech, James, *The Monongahela of Old*, Pittsburgh, Pa., 1858–1892.

Watson, John F., *Annals of Philadelphia*, Phila., 1830.

Weeks, Stephen B., *Southern Quakers and Slavery*, Baltimore, 1896.

Weld, Isaac, *Travels through the States of North America*, 1795–97, London, 1799.

Wescott, Thompson (See **Scharfe**), *Historic Mansions of Philadelphia*, Phila., 1895.

Whiting, John, *Persecutious Exposed in some Memoirs Relating to the Sufferings of John Whiting*, London, 1715.

Winsor, Justin, editor, *Narrative and Critical History of America* (III.), 8 vols, Boston and New York, 1886–9.

Yarnall, Peter, *Journal, Comly's Friends' Miscellany*, II., Phila., 1832.

II. MANUSCRIPT SOURCES

1. *Friends' Monthly Meeting Records of Pennsylvania* [1] *:*

Falls (1683–1750), in fireproof vault, National Bank, Newtown, Bucks Co., Pa. An order to see them may be had from Mark Palmer, Yardley, Pa.

Buckingham (1720–1759), at same place as above. An order to see them may be obtained from Anna Jane Williams, Holicong, Bucks Co., Pa.

Wrightstown (1734–1750), at same place. An order to see them may be obtained from Horace T. Smith, Buckmanville, Pa.

Middletown (1683–1750), in a safe at residence of Mary Bunting, Langhorne, Pa. An order to see them may be obtained from Susanna Rich, Woodbourne, Pa.

Richland (1742–1750), in fireproof safe in Friends' Meeting House, Quakertown, Pa. An order to see them may be obtained from Edward Shaw, Quakertown.

Abington (1683–1750), in safe at Abington Meeting House, near Jenkintown, Pa. Accurate typewritten copies, made by Gilbert Cope, in Library of the Historical Society of Pennsylvania, 1300 Locust St., Philadelphia. Benjamin F. Penrose, Ogontz, Pa., custodian of original records.

Gwynedd (1714–1750), in fireproof vault, Friends' Library, 142 N. 16th St., Philadelphia.

Radnor (1684–1750), in fireproof vault, Friends' Meeting House, 15th and Race Sts., Philadelphia; in charge of Benjamin Walton.

Chester (1681–1750), in fireproof vault, Friends' Meeting House, Media, Delaware Co., Pa. Custodian, Henry Mendenhall, of Media. Women's Minutes (1695–1750), in charge of Charles Palmer, Attorney-at-law, Chester, Pa.; kept in safe in his office.

Concord (1684–1750), in fireproof safe, Concord Friends' Meeting House, Concordville, Delaware Co., Pa. Custodian, Lewis Palmer, Concordville.

Philadelphia (1682–1750), in fire-proof vault, Friends' Meeting House, 4th and Arch Streets, Philadelphia. Custodian, George J. Scattergood, 119 S. 4th St., Philadelphia. An accurate copy of the Book of Certificates of Removal, made by Gilbert Cope, is in the Library of the Historical Society of Pennsylvania.

[1] Abstracts of nearly all registers of births, deaths, and marriages of these meetings are at the Historical Society of Pennsylvania.

Newark or Kennett (1686–1750), in charge of Ruthanna Michener, widow of Ellwood Michener, and kept in a fire-proof safe at her house, one mile south of Toughkenamon P. O. and Station, Chester Co., Pa. Women's Minutes (1696–1750) in charge of Susanna F. Savery and kept in a safe at her house, two miles southwest of West Chester, Chester Co., Pa.

New Garden (1718–1750), in a safe at Friends' Meeting House, West Grove, Chester Co., Pa. Custodian, Truman C. Moore, West Grove.

Bradford (1737–1750), in fire-proof vault, Friends' Library, 142 N. 16th St., Philadelphia.

Goshen (1721–1750), at same place.

Nottingham (1730–1750) in vault, Friends' Meeting House, Park Avenue and Laurens Street, Baltimore. Custodian, Kirk Brown, 1813 N. Caroline Street.

Sadsbury (1737–1750) Friends' Library, 142 N. 16th St., Philadelphia. Another copy at Friends' Meeting House, 15th and Race Sts., Philadelphia.

Warrington (1742–1750), in a wooden book-case, Menallen Friends' Meeting House, near Flora Dale P. O., Adams Co., Pa. Custodian, Hannah G. Wright, Flora Dale Pa. Accurate abstracts, made and indexed by Gilbert Cope, are in the Library of the Historical Society of Pennsylvania.

Menallen (1780 to date), at same place. An abstract at Hist. Soc. of Penn'a.

Exeter (1737–1750), in fire-proof vault, Friends' Meeting House, Fifteenth and Race Sts., Philadelphia.

Darby (1684–1750), in fire-proof safe, Friends' Meeting House, Darby, Delaware Co., Pa. Custodian, Morgan Bunting, of Darby.

2. *Other Monthly Meeting Records :*

Duck Creek, Delaware, Friends' Meeting House, 15th and Race Streets, Philadelphia. Copies of Minutes at Hist. Soc. of Pa.

Gloucester, or Haddonfield, New Jersey, Friends' Library, 142 N. 16th Street, Philadelphia.

Salem, New Jersey.

Cane Creek, North Carolina, in charge of Hugh M. Dixon, Snow Camp, N. C.

3. *Friends' Meeting Records of Ireland:*

Minutes of Ulster Province Meeting, 1694–1717.
Marriage Book of Ulster Quarterly Meeting, 1731–1786.
Minutes of Preparative Meeting of Grange near Charlemont, 1726–1770.
Carlow Records.
Moate Records.
Mountmellick Records.
Lurgan Records.
Ballyhagen Records.

4. *Other Manuscripts:*

Diary of Richard Barnard, of East Marlborough, Chester County, Pa. (1774–1792), in possession of a descendant, Milton Barnard, North Brook, Chester County.

Journals of Joshua Brown, Friends' Library, 142 N. 16th St., Phila.

Clement Papers, Hist. Soc. of Pa.

Commonplace Book of Henry Hollingsworth (b. 1658, d. 1721), of Chester County, Pa., and Cecil County, Md. In collection of Judge Samuel W. Pennypacker, of Philadelphia.

Hutton Letters (1726–1734), Gilbert Cope, West Chester, Pa.,

Miscellaneous Papers (1655-1805), Three Lower Counties, Hist. Soc. Penna.

Account Book of George McMillan, of Warrington, York County, Pa. (1769–1795). In collection of the writer.

Original Certificates of Removal brought to Newark or Kennett Monthly Meeting, in collection of Gilbert Cope, West Chester, Pa.

Pemberton Papers (70 vols.), Vol. III., Hist. Soc. of Penna.

Diary of Jacob Pierce, of Longwood, East Marlborough Township, Chester County, Pa. (1791–1800), in possession of a descendant, Mrs. Lucy Polk, of Kennett Square, Pa.

Diary of John Smith, of Burlington, N. J., and Philadelphia (1736–1752), Ridgeway Branch, Philadelphia' Library Company.

Smith MSS., I. (1678–1743), at same place.

Taylor Papers, *Miscellaneous* (1672–1775), *Correspondence* (1683–1723), Hist. Soc. of Penna.

Diary of Benjamin Walker, of Warrington, York Co., Pa., (1780–1786), in possession of a descendant, Mrs. Phebe A. Smith, York, Pa.; a copy in collection of the writer.

Wills in Public Record Office, Dublin, Dublin, Ireland.

Early Land Warrants, Surveys, Patents, of Pennsylvania, Department of Internal Affairs, Harrisburg, Pa.

Wills, Deeds, Assessment Lists, Inventories, Court Records, etc., at Philadelphia, West Chester, York, Reading, and Lancaster, Pa.

Private Collections, etc.

INDEX

ABBOTT, Alice, 364
   John, 364
   Sarah, 339
   William, 281
Act of Toleration for Protestant Dis-
   senters, 27
Acton, Benjamin, 101, 281
Acts of Uniformity, cause of emigra-
   tion, 42
Adams County, 172–176
Adams, Joan, 410
   Sarah, 332
Addy, James, 298
Ails, Stephen, 168, 169
Alday, Alice, 385
Alford, George, 168
Alison, (See Allyson) James, 165
   James, Jr., 165
Alderdice, James, 321
Allen family, 337
   Amy, 337
   James, 326
   John, 141, 142, 337, 381, 426
   Sarah, 426, 427
   William, 367, 426
Allyson, Lawrence, 317, 409
Alment, John, 294
Anderson, Isabelle, 392
   John, 392
   Mabel, 337, 344, 416
   Mary, 298, 324
   Samuel, 298
Andrew, Jane, 356
Andrews family, 342
   Miriam, 342
   William, 342
Anglo-Irish Friends, 36–37
Antrim, Edmundsons settle at, 15
Arnold, Elinor, 282
   Elizabeth, 282
Arrival of Irish Quakers, 188
Asbury, Hannah, 383
Ask, Samuel, 94

Ashbridge, Phebe, 351
Ashbrook, John, 278
   Thomas, 313
Ashton, Mary, 306
   Peter, 307
   Robert, 130
Atherton family, 420–421
   Abigail, 414
   Henry, 381
   Richard, 212, 381
   Thomas, 420
Atkinson, Elizabeth, 410
   Grace, 113
   James, 278, 387
   Lydia, 314, 322
   Margery, 278
   Timothy, 325
Aubrey, Letitia, 128, 132
   William, 128

BABB, Thomas, 314
   Baily, Ann, 322
   James, 165
   Joel, 126, 149, 150, 322
   Kesia, 150
   Lydia, 326
   Mary, 398
   William, 149, 150, 165
Baker, Joshua, 287
   Joseph, 303
   Mary, 303
   Sarah, 329
   Thomas, 287
Baldwin, John, 121, 351
   Lydia, 351
Ballinacree, 428, 432
Baltimore, Lord, see Calvert family,
   316
Bane, Alexander, 359
   Jane, 359
Bank Meeting House, 107–108
Barber, Robert, 162
Barclay, John, 97

445

Barcroft, Jacob, 292
Ruth, 292
Sarah, 362
Barger, Thomas, 290
Barnard, Alice, 401
Milton, 143
Richard, diarist, 143, 197
Barnes, Robert, 425
Barrington, John, 274
Barton, Isaac, 288
Baset, Arnold, 420
Bateman, Mary, 398
Miles, minister, visits Ireland, 16
Bates family, 385–386
Abigail, 387
William, 382, 383, 384, 385–386
Baxter, Joseph, 405
Beale, Elizabeth, 151
John Bewley, custodian of Friend's records, Dublin, 34, 35
Joshua, 151, 152
Joseph, 152
Rachel, 152
Samuel, 152
Sarah, 152
Thomas, 151
Beals, Caleb, 172
Jacob, 172
John, 172
Rachel, 172
William, 173, 236
Bears, 207–8
Bedwell, William, 367
Beeson, Henry, 181
John, 353
Richard, 353
Belhaven, Lord, 237
Bell family, 390
Abigail, 307
Archibald, a Scotch-Irish Friend, 36, 390
David, 426
Frances, 362
Isabell, 307
Jane, 362, 367, 400
John, 329, 394
Joseph, 404
Mark, 404
Sarah, 404
Bellarby, Isaac, 291

Belley [Baily?], Caisia, 165
Bellore, Mathias, 382
Bennett, John, 117
Joseph, 164, 165, 168
Rebecca, 163, 165, 168
Bentley, William, 326
Berks County, 109
Berthwaite, Margaret, 338
Bethel, Sarah, 340
Beverly family, 347
James, 326
Jane, 357
Jennett, 347
Mary, 225, 326, 357
Samuel, 147, 326, 357
William, 326
Bewley, Mungo, of Dublin, 48, 100
Bezer, Mary, 321
Biddle, Clement, 306
Owen, 306
Bishon, Nicholas, 174
Birmingham, 117
Bishop, Patience, 326
Black, George, 410
William, diarist, 245, 265
Blackburn family, 360–361
Alice, 379
Anthony, 174, 183, 232, 379
Elizabeth, 223
Eliza, 354
John, 174, 175, 231, 232, 354, 359, 360, 361, 379, 425
Joseph, 183, 232, 380
Margaret, 359, 380
Mary, 354
Moses, 176, 380
Rebecca, 174, 359
Thomas, 171, 174, 176, 181, 232, 355, 379
Blacker, George, 410
Blackney, Mary, 381
Blake, Edward, 120
John, 397
Blatchford, Richard, 381
Blaugden, Barbara, minister, visits Ireland, 24–25
Blevin, Thomas, 407
Blunston, Samuel, 162, 335
John, 339
Margaret, 339

Boaks or Boake, Amos, 60, 310
    Abel, 310
    Anne, 310
    Sarah, 310
Bond, Anne, 351
Bonsall, Mary, 340
    Obadiah, 340
    Sarah, 340
Books, 235-6
Boone, Daniel, Kentucky pioneer, 109
    George, 109
Booth, Charles, 283, 314
    Elizabeth, 283, 315
Borum, Elizabeth, 406
Bowen, Jane, 311
    Sarah, 311
    Thomas, 311
Boweram, John, 268
Boyd family, 362-364
    Benjamin, 230, 399
    George, 167
    Jane, 362, 400
    John, 160, 171, 362, 365, 393, 400
    Patrick, 102
    Samuel, 160, 378
    William, 160, 171, 365
Boyes, Ann, 333
    John, 292, 326, 364
    Lydia, 307
    Mary, 292, 364
    Richard, 277, 292, 300, 307, 311, 332, 347, 364, 394
    Robert, 330, 364
Boyne, After Battle of the; 30
Bradford Monthly Meeting, 152
Bradshaw, Ann, 313
    James, 313, 391-392
    Lemuel, 101
    Thomas, 410
    William, 391
Brady, Samson, 431
    Susanna, 432
Braithwaite, Joseph, 385
    Margaret, 385
    Rachel, 385
    Sarah, 385
Branson, William, 413
Braselton, John, 359
Bready, Ann, 363
Brian, *see* Bryan

"Brick Meeting," 158
Brientnall, Joseph, 219
Brindley, Jacob, 402
Brinkerhoff, William, 422
Brinton, Joseph, 353
    Mary, 349
    Moses, 349, 353
    William, 198
Britten, Jacob, 298
    John, 298
    John, 298
    Susanna, 298
Broom, Daniel, 318
Brown, Charles, 425
    Daniel, 324, 413
    Elizabeth, 172, 376
    Ellis, 406
    James, 116, 158
    Jeremiah, 236
    Joshua, traveling minister, 184
    Kellren, 425
    Richard, 376
    William, 158, 236, 376, 377
Brownlee, Elizabeth, 425
    William, 425
Brunton, Lydia, 422
Bryan family, 390
    Ann, 333
    Thomas, 390
    William, 390
Bryn, Rebecca, 301
Bryne, Daniel, 302
    Joshua, 302
    Rebecca, 302
Buckley, Samuel, 281
Bucks County, 109
Buffington, Phebe, 340
    Richard, 340
    Ruth, 321
Bulla, or Bullough, Elizabeth, 362
    George, 320
    Katharine, 320
    Mary, 362
    Richard, 378
    Thomas, 161, 164, 366, 378, 410
Bullock, *see* Bulla
Bullough, *see* Bulla
Bunting, Martha, 342
Burne, Matthew, 283
Burrough, Edward, minister, visits Ireland, 20-24, 375

Burson, David, 346
Bushby, Dinah, 294
Butler, Noble, 420
  Rachel, 420
Burt, Elizabeth, 406
  Hannah, 405
  Sarah, 406
Business Meetings, 220–222

CADWALADER, Abigail, 290
  David, 290
  Susanna, 290
Caldwell, Vincent, 126
Cales, Aiolce, 101
Caln Meeting, 152–153
Calvert family, 316–318
  Ann, 312
  George, Lord Baltimore, 316
  Grace, 316
  Jane, 312, 317
  John, 313, 316, 320, 322
  Joshua, 321
  Joseph, 366
  Judith, 322
  Leonard, 316
  Mathias, 394
  Mary, 366
  Thomas, 312, 313, 316, 322
Camm, Henry, 283
  John, 283
  Mary, 283
Canady, Elizabeth, 297
  Hugh, 296, 297
Canby, Mary, 306
Cane, Ann, 141, 327, 336
  John, 141, 143, 227, 234, 314, 327, 336
  Margaret, 336
  Robert 143, 336
Cannassetego, Chief of the Onondagas, 242
Cantrell, Godfrey, 325, 374
  John, 325
Card-playing, 222
Carleton, Caleb, 287
  Dinah, 287
  Hannah, 287
  Isabel, 286
  Lydia, 287
  Mark, 96, 286, 287
  Martha, 287

Carleton, Rachel, 296
  Sarah, 287
  Samuel, 287
  Susanna, 286, 287
  Thomas, 126, 286, 287
Carlyle, Ann, 350
  Thomas, 350
Carolinas, Irish Friends in, 42
Carpenter, John, letter of, 67–68
  Samuel, 128, 141, 281
Carroll, Margery, 346
  Sarah, 346
Carson, Agnes, 174
  Ellen, 174
  Jane, 404
  Margaret, 165
  Mary, 348
  Patrick, 165
  Richard, 212
  Walter, 174
  William, 348
Carter, Hannah, 322
  Mary, 322
Cartmill, Dorothy, 325
  Martin, 325
  Nathaniel, 325
  Thomas, 325
Castleshane Meeting, 395
Causes of emigration, religious and economic, 42–49
Cavan Meeting established, 19
Celtic-Irish, 32–35
Center Meeting, New Castle County, 122–124
Center Square Meeting House, 108
Certificates of removal, 56, 57
Certificate of removal, The, 84–85
Chads, Elizabeth, 316
Chalfant family, 335
  Henry, 335
  John, 335
  Jonathan, 335
Chalkley, Thomas, 218, 389
Chamberlin family, 359
  Abel, 297
  Jonas, 160, 164, 359
Chambers family, 391
  Catharine, 304
  Deborah, 211
  John, a Scotch-Irish Friend, of Dublin, 36, 211

Chambers, Richard, 328
   Robert, 313, 391
   William, 328
Chandlee, Benjamin, 157, 279
   Nath., 279
   William, 172, 279, 280
Champion, John, 388
   Mary, 388
Chandler, Ann, 377
   Rachel, 315
   William, 337, 377
Charlemont, Lord, 366
Charles II., Restoration of, 25
Charlton, John, 343
Checochinican, Indian chief, 147, 148
Chesnon, Richard, 174
Chester County, 124–159
Chester Meeting House, built in 1693, 113, 114
Chester Mills, 115
Chester Monthly Meeting, 110, 113
Chew, Hannah, 387
Chichester Meeting, 116, 117
Child, Mary, 62
   Thomas, 62, 322
Church, Elizabeth, 382
   Richard, 298
Churchman, Hannah, 377
   John, 158, 236, 377
   Sarah, 377
   Susanna, 303
Christy, Alexander, 343, 393, 409, 410
   Ann, 401
   John, 410
   Margaret, 409
   Thomas, 343
Clapboard house, The, 190–192
Clark family, 343–344
   Elizabeth, 343
   Jackson, 431
   Jane, 362
   John, 343
   Robert, 431
   Samuel, 339, 343
   Sarah, 355
   Walter, 343, 394
Clarridge, Samuel, 54
Clay, John, 404

Claypoole, James, letter-book of, 55
   James, 252
   John, 252
Clayton, Mary, 150, 289
   Richard, minister, visits Ireland, 17–18, 149, 150
Clearing the Land, 190
Cleaver, Peter, 169, 402
Cleck, Moses, Presbyterian minister, becomes a Quaker, 36
Clement, Judge John, 42
   Joseph, 386
   Mercy, 386
Clemson, James, 165
Clendenon, John, 375
Clibborn, Ann, 327
   William, 327
Clifton, Ann, 292
Cloak, Peter, 301
Cloud, Mordecai, 149, 150
Clung, Sarah, 405
Coates family, 179, 302
   Aaron, 171
   Ann, 372
   Dr. Jesse, 154
   Moses, 77, 154, 155, 302
   Susanna, 302
   Thomas, 154
Coatesville named for an Irish Quaker, 154
Cocks, *see* Cox
Coeburn family, 303
   Elizabeth, 303
   Joseph, 199, 201, 303
   Rebecca, 304
   Thomas, 303
   William, 303
Collett, George, 144, 280
   Mary, 280
   Tobias, 139
Collins, Ann, 402
   Francis, 386
   John, 177, 402
   Joseph, 177
   Margaret, 301, 386
   Mary, 402
   Priscilla, 386
Combe, John, 393
   Samuel, 47, 284
Combs, John, 394
Comley, David, 346

29

Concord Meeting, 116
Concord Monthly Meeting, 116, 117
Conway or Connaway family, 314, 319
    Thomas, 119, 313, 314
Conolly, Eunice, 294
Conrey, Edward, 391
Contribution of the Irish Quakers, 275–276
Cook, Ann, 402
    Edward, becomes a Quaker, 21–22; 24
    Elmira, J., 401
    Elizabeth, 319
    Grace, 315
    Hannah, 379
    Henry, 397, 404, 405
    Jane, 397
    Jesse, 402, 405
    Joan, 296
    John, 296
    Joseph, 371
    Josiah, 404
    Margaret, travelling minister, 182
    Mary, 397, 405
    Mary Ann, 404
    Peter, 168, 371, 379, 402, 417, 418
    Ruth, 405, 419
    Sarah, 172, 371, 379
    Thomas, 168
    William W., 404
Cooper family, 277, 347
    Calvin, 164
    Mary, 387
    William, 347, 387
Cope, Gilbert, historian, 113, 119, 124
    Samuel, 306
Coppock, Bartholomew, 115
    William, 160
Cornish, Henry, 312
Cottey, Abel, 279
    Sarah, 279
Courtney, Elizabeth, 432
    Joseph, 432
    Mary, 369
    Ruth, 332
    Samson, 399
    Sarah, 430, 432
    Toby, 302

Courtney, Thomas, 302, 394
    William, 378
Courtship, 215–216
Cowman, Jarrett, 398
    Jeremiah, sea-captain, 69, 71, 76–77, 305, 341
    Nathan, sea-captain, 95, 341
Cox, (see Cocks) family, 172
    Amy or Emey, 174, 337
    Ann, 168
    Dinah, 176, 380
    Isaac, 168
    Jacob, 176
    John, 168, 172, 174
    Mary, 165, 168, 176
    Rebecca, 165, 168, 422
    Samuel, 165
    Sarah, 363
    Thomas, 165, 168
    William, 121, 165
Cradle for cutting grain introduced into Chester County, 197
Craig, Joanna, 400, 401, 405
    Mary, 168, 400
    William, 400
Crainer, Elizabeth, 377
Crawford, Abel Lee, 404
    Joseph, 401
Cresap War, 144
Crispin, Silas, 256
    Captain William, 256
Crockett, Eli, 157, 347–348, 371, 394, 429
    Elizabeth, 430, 431
    Gilbert, 348
    John, 347
Crook, Grace, 115
    William, 323
Crooks, Ann, 390
    Richard, 390
Crops, failure of, a cause of emigration, 48
Crosland, Alice, 316
Crosley, Ann, 362
    Betty, 308
Crowley, Joanna, 315
Cromwell, Henry, Lord Lieutenant of Ireland, 11, 25
    Oliver, in Ireland, 9–10
Cromwellian soldiers in Ireland become Quakers, 12, 20, 21, 37

Cromwellian Settlement, 10–12
Crumpton, John, shipmaster, 101
Cunningham, Ann, 293
    Elinor, 293
    Elizabeth, 293
    James, 428
    Mary, 293
Cuppage, Elizabeth, 281
    Experience, 264
    Major Robert, 264
    Robert, 281
    Thomas, 264, 285
Curlis, Richard, 101
Curry, Dr., 217
Cutler, Benjamin, 404
    Rebecca, 404
    Susanna, 404

DAGGER, John, 383
    Dancing, 222–223
Darragh, Charles, 274
    Lydia, 273–274, 298
    William, 274
Davenport, Isaac, 301
Davis, Catharine, 396
    Daniel, 398
    David, 415
    Ellis, 415
    Esther, 165, 168
    Franklin, 398
    James, 326
    Richard, 415
    Uriah, 398
Darlington, Margaret, 93
Dawson, Catharine, 315
    Elizabeth, 86, 87, 411, 412
    James, 86, 87, 411, 412
Day, Ann, 163, 165
    John, 163, 164, 165, 166
    Mrs. Rachel W., 396
Dean, Alexander, 230, 297, 299
    David, 297
    Elizabeth, 295
    James, 230, 299
    John, 299
    Joseph, 297, 299
    Ruth, 299
    Samuel, 299
    William, 149, 150
Decou, Isaac, 387
    Rachel, 387

Deeble, Dorothy, 291
    Elizabeth, 291
    George, 291, 307
    Jane, 291
    Jerome, 291
    Sarah, 291
Delaney, Daniel, 385
    Martin, 385
    Rachel, 385
    Sharp, 385
    William, 385
Delap family, 379
    John, 214
    Ruth, 86, 379, 411
    Sarah, 213
    William, 98, 174, 175, 367, 379
Dennen, Andrew, 361
Dennis, Hannah, 277
    John, 282
    Thomas, 382
Delaware County, 110
Dellwood, Dr., 217
Descriptive pamphlets of Pennsylvania induces immigration, 54
Desertderrin, 430, 432, 433
Dickinson, Jonathan, 203, 262, 288
    Joseph, 308, 326
    Sarah, 405
Dicks, Elizabeth, 174
Disorderly conduct, 227–228
Distribution of Irish Friends, 106
"Divine Light," 5
Dixon or Dixson family, 179, 319, 320
    Ann, 336
    Anthony, 313
    Henry, 121, 184, 319, 320
    John, 121, 184, 315
    Joseph, 358
    Rose, 319
    Simon, 337
    William, 122, 129, 313, 315, 319, 391
Dobson, Abigail, 315
    Richard, 315
Domey, James, 300
Douglas, Jeremiah, 334
    Ruth, 310
    Samuel, 85
Downey, Hannah, 298
    James, 298

Downham, James, 407
Downing, John, 431
    Sarah, 349
    Thomas, 424
    William, 349
Drayton-in-the-Clay, 3
Dress, 202–205
Drewett, Morgan, 119
Drewry, Thomas, 296
Drinker, Elizabeth, 294, 388
    Henry, 294, 388
    William, 294
Drinking, 223–226
Driskle, Elizabeth, 199
Drogheda, Taking of by Cromwell,
    10
Druett, Hannah, 270
Dublin, First meeting held at, 20
Duck, Elizabeth, 320
Duffy, Emma, 6, 405
    Judge Edward, 405
Dunbar, John, 428
Dundas, Bethia, 238
    James, 238
    Laird of, 238
Dungannon, Lady, 394
Dunn, Susanna, 404
Dwelling, The, 190–193

EARL of Chesterfield, 374
    Earle, John, 168
Early, Daniel, 168
East Caln Township, 153–154
Eastlack, Elizabeth, 277
    Francis, 387
    Hepzibah, 387
    John, 387
    Sarah, 277
East Nantmeal Township, 155–156
East Nottingham, 159
Eavenson, Richard, 149, 150
    Jemima, 150
Economic causes of emigration, 46–
    49
Edge, Ann, 306
    Jacob, 306
    Jane, 306
    John, 115, 356, 371, 373
    Mary, 351
    Rachel, 351
    Sarah, 306

Edgerton, Abigail, 365
    Grace, 365
    Joseph, 353, 365
Edmunds, Thomas, 132, 133
Edmundson family, 393
    Caleb, 290
    Grace, 13
    Hannah, 399
    John, 13, 14, 15, 419
    Joseph, 419
    Joshua William, 14
    Mary, 290
    Margaret, 14
    Thomas, 15, 290
    William, sketch of, 13–16 ; re-
    turns to England to confer with
    George Fox, 17 ; travels in
    the ministry and is imprisoned,
    18–19 ; removes to County
    Cavan and becomes a farmer,
    19 ; is instrumental in releas-
    ing Friends from prison, 26 ;
    assists in organizing Irish
    Quakerism, 27 ; champions
    cause of Friends during
    troubles between William and
    James, 29 ; his sufferings after
    Battle of the Boyne, 30 ; his
    death, 31 ; mentioned, 58 ;
    100, 110, 218, 374, 393
Edward, Jane, 311
Elgar, Elizabeth, 398
    Joseph, 398
    Margaret, 398
Elliott, Allen, 398
Elliott, Alexander, 421
    Elizabeth, 421
    Hannah, 298
Ellis, Elizabeth, 424
    Simon, 386
Elmslie, John, 384
Ely, George, 235
Emerson, Lambert, 341
Emigration, obstructions to, 189
Emlen, Ann, 327
    Hannah, 247
Empson, Cornelius, 120
England in the middle of the Seven-
    teenth Century, 3
England, Philip, 279
Engle, Abigail, 308

English, Joseph, 149, 150
Enniskillen, Siege of, 28
Enogh, 429
Equipment of House and Farm, 193–202
Errott, Francis, 288
William, 288
Erwin, Alice, 430
Elizabeth, 430, 431
John, 296
Mary, 296
Thomas, 230, 399, 429, 430, 431
Essex House, 111, 113
Estaugh, John, 141
Eustace, Sir Morris, 26
Evans, family, 357
Ann, 350
Evan, 132, 133, 142
Esther, 420
Eliza, 420
Jesse, 351
John, 132, 133, 431
Joseph, 354
Mary, 354, 420
Margaret, 420
Rachel, 365
Rowland, 350
Ruth, 420
Samuel, 355
Thomas, 420
William, 160
Everitt, Isaac, 418
John, 418
Martha, 418
Every, Daniel, 335
Eves, Elizabeth, 357
Hannah, 357
John, 357
Joseph, 357
Mark, 294, 357
Exeter Meeting, 109
Expansion of Pennsylvania Quakerism southward and westward, 177–185

FADE, James, 45
Fagg's Manor, 144–145
Fairlamb, Catharine, 308
Fairman, Thomas, mansion of, 107 ; 141, 253

Fairs, 75, 206–207
Falkner, Jane, 397
Jesse, 177, 397
False reports go to Ireland, 71
Famine year of 1729 in Ireland, 48
Farquhar family, 396, 398–399
Allen, 398
Ann, 398
Benjamin, 398
Elizabeth, 398
John, 396
Mary, 396
Rachel, 395
William, 357, 398
William, 395
Faucett family, 115, 307
Grace, 113
Richard, 362
Thomas, 60
Walter, Sketch of, 113, 114
Fayle, Joshua, 100
Samuel, 100
William 14, 393
Fearne, Rebecca, 115
Sarah, 384
Fegan, James, 235
Joshua, 386
Fell, Lydia, 364, 405
Margaret, 22
Fenny Drayton, 3
Fenwick, John, 385
Ferguson, William, 395, 396
Ferree, John, 318
Leah, 398
Ferris, Sarah, 342
Fifth Monarchy men, Rising of, 25
Fincher, John, 168, 370
Francis, 165, 168
Hannah, 165
Jane, 168, 370
Rebecca, 419
Fire-place, 193–195
Fioland, Thomas, 165
First Friends' Meeting in Penna., 110
Firth, John, 301
Fisher, Elizabeth, 371
Martha, 261
Thomas, 371
Fitzwater, Sarah, 263

Fletcher, Elizabeth, minister, visits Ireland, 19–20
  Jonathan, 408
  Sarah, 369
Flower, Abigail, 334
  Mary, 334
  Richard, 322
Food, 224
Ford, Elizabeth, 355
Forster, Susanna, 430
Foster, Alice, 320
  Elizabeth, 330
  Margaret, 406
Fothergill, John, 219
Foukes, Richard, first meeting in Dublin held at his house, 20
Foulk, Eneas, 402
Fox, Christopher, 4
  George, sketch of, 3–6; mentioned, 15; organizes Irish Quakerism, 27; suggests a Quaker Colony in America, 50; 394
  Mary, 4
Francis, Thomas, 269
Frazier, or Frazer, Aaron, 419
  Alexander, 168
  Ann, 406
  Deborah, 422
  Elizabeth, 422
  James, 168, 422
  Joshua, 422
  Moses, 337
  Rebecca, 422
Fred or Fredd family, 308–309
  Benjamin, 60, 130, 132, 133, 134, 139, 210, 211, 223, 225, 229
  John, 117, 198–200, 211, 308, 325
  Katharine, 325
  Nicholas, 117, 308
  Rachel, 211, 325
Free Society of Traders induces immigration, 54; 147
Freeman, John, 394
Frizle, Jane, 426, 427
Fuller, Abraham, 218, 250, 281
  Capt. Abraham, 433
  Henry, 281
  Mary, 281
  Sydney Blanche, 433

Funerals, 216–217
Furnace family, 101
  John, 101

GAGE, Marcus, 432

Garner, Elinor, 425
  George, 425
  Mary, 425
Garnett, Bartholomew, 420
  Jonathan, 350
  Joseph, 136, 143, 297, 329, 335
  Mary, 350
  Thomas, 131, 132, 133, 134, 136, 142, 196, 329
Garretson, Alice, 167, 405
  Ann, 163, 165, 168, 404
  Christopher, 163
  Content, 163, 165, 168, 370, 404, 405,
  George, 167
  Jane, 404
  John, 163, 165, 168, 404
  Joseph, 165, 168, 172, 177, 214, 403, 419
  Martha, 165, 172
  Margaret, 404
  Mary, 172
  Naomi, 172
  Rebecca, 405
  Samuel, 167, 405
  Sarah, 311, 397
  William, 165, 166, 168, 169, 172, 311, 402
Gause, Jonathan, 347
  William, 347
Gavin, Jo., 100, 373
Gawin, Joseph, 310
George, Elizabeth, 365
  Ellen, 365
  Jane, 339
  Mary, 365
Gibbons, Ann, 373
  James, 373
  John, 116
Gibson, Alice, 357, 360
Gilbert, Susanna, 381
Gilpin, Ann, 328
  Joseph, 328
  Mary, 362

Gilpin, Sarah, 371, 379
Glan, David, 369
Glasford, Hugh, 317
  Jane, 317
  Margaret, 317
Gnus, Elizabe h, 313
Groff, Charles, 393
Goldney, Henry, 139
Goldsmith, George, 383, 384, 386, 388
Goodbody, Ann, 292, 375
Gould, Anne, minister, visits Ireland, 18
Graffitt, Margaret, 263
Graham, Ferguson, 370
Graves, *see* Greeves, Samuel, 123
Gray, Abigail, 86, 411, 367, 425
  James, 234
  Samuel, 86, 411
  William, 86, 394, 411, 425
Great Meeting House, Phila., 108
Great Rebellion of 1641, 8-9
Great Valley of Chester County, 151, 152-154
Greave, Sarah, 337
Greaves, *see* Graves, Thomas, 366
Green, Elizabeth, 282, 316
  Henry, 316
  Jane, 363, 400
  Joseph, 363, 364, 400
  John, 364
  Lydia, 364
  Margaret, 364
  William, 384
Greenway, Robert, captain of ship *Welcome*, 111, 279
Greenfield, Hannah, 337
Greenwood, James, 344, 393
Greer family, 368, 391
  Elizabeth, 86, 87, 411, 412
  Jane, 300
  John, 293
  Mary, 86, 87, 367, 411, 412,
  Robert, 293, 369, 393, 420
  Sarah, 362
  Thomas, 86, 87, 98, 411, 412, 420, 426
Gregg family, 178, 179, 319, 334
  Dinah, 287
  George, 399, 431
  John, 130, 365

Gregg, Lydia, 287
  Mary, 431
  Michael, 67-68
  Thomas, 184, 287, 322, 393, 431
  William, 122, 399, 431
Gribble, Nicholas, 375
  Sarah, 375
Griest family, 404
  Ann, 404
  Hannah, 395
  Susanna, 397
  Willing, 404
Griffin, John, 420
Griffith family, 355-6, 404
  Abraham, 402, 403
  Ann, 395, 404
  Christopher, 160
  Elizabeth, 361
  Esther, 318, 401
  Evan, 324
  Eve, 361, 395, 398
  Griffith, 424
  Joanna, 400, 401, 405
  John, 160, 318, 413, 416, 420
  Mary, 401, 420
  Ruth, 397, 405
  Susanna, 398
  Thomas, 86, 87, 358, 361, 395, 398, 411, 412, 426
  William, 165, 168, 400, 401, 402, 404, 405
Griffitts, Frances, 262, 288
  George, 262, 288
  Hannah, 263
  Isaac, 263
  Martha, 89, 288
  Mary, 263
  Thomas, sketch of, 262-263; 288
Griggs, John, 333
Gwynn, John, 401
Hackel, Ed., 240
Haddock (*see* Haydock),
  John, 368
  Margaret, 369
  Rebecca, 368
  William, 329
Hadly or Hadley family, 179, 340
  Deborah, 309, 338, 340, 356
  Joseph, 223

Hadly, John, 354
  Joshua, 309
  Katharine, 216, 338
  Ruth, 336
  Sarah, 309, 356
  Simon, 132, 133, 134-5, 137, 196, 211, 216, 229, 236, 309, 338, 340
Hainan, Elizabeth, 353
Haines, Joseph, 236
  Joseph, 337
  Miriam, 337
  Patience, 326
  Ruth, 326
Haldon, John, 300
Halhead, Miles, minister, visits Ireland, 16
Hall, John, 389
Halliday family, 336
  Ann, 323
  Deborah, 211, 336, 337
  Jacob, 337
  James, 410
  Margaret, 326
  Phebe, 337
  Rachel, 348
  Robert, 337, 344
  William, 131, 132, 133, 135, 136, 193, 211, 223, 336, 337, 348
Hambridge, Row:, 101
Hamel, James, 348
Hamilton, Thomas, 174
Hammond, Alice, 396
  Deborah, 397
  Elizabeth, 397
  John, 397
Hampton, Michael, 367
  William, 425
Hancock, Ann, 380
  Mary, 431
Hannum, Col. John, 306
Hansell, Samuel, 267
Hanson. Jonathan, 326
Harding, Elizabeth, 391
  Ann, 392
  Dorothy, 391
  John, 391
  Mary, 330
Harlan family, 179, 320-332
  Aaron, 129, 193

Harlan, Abigail, 334
  A. H., 322
  Deborah, 318
  Dinah, 320
  Elizabeth, 315, 318, 320
  George, letter of, 62-63; 122, 123, 126, 128, 129, 149, 150, 176, 193, 195, 217, 315, 318, 320
  Ezekiel, 128, 129, 146, 147, 342
  Hannah, 315
  Isabella, 320
  James, 129, 320
  Joshua, 129
  Margaret, 176
  Michael, 122, 129, 143, 226, 287, 319, 320
  Moses, 129, 143, 176,
  Stephen, 149
  Susanna, 287
  Thomas, 319, 320
  William, 146
Harris family, 395, 397
  Elizabeth, 397
  Nathan, 396
  Roger, 304
  Sarah, 304
Harrison, James, 313
  Nicholas, 313
Harry, Ann, 331
Hartley, Jane, 342
  Thomas, 342
Harvey, Elizabeth, 397
  Thomas, 393
Harvests, 226
Harwood, John, 239
Hatton, Lettice, 293
Hawkins, Elizabeth, 294
  William, 308
Hawley, Benjamin, 117
Haydock family, 361-362
  (*see* Haddock) Walter, 361
Hayes, Stephen, 214
  Mary, 335
Hayling, Mary, 267
Heacock, Mary, 289
Head, Benjamin, 304, 339
  Mary, 69, 211, 305, 339
  Sarah, 305
Heald, Elizabeth, 316

Ieald, Mary, 321
Sarah, 321
Iearlam, Jane, 300
Iearth, 193-195
Iempfield Meeting, 162
Ietherington, Abigail, 288
Iewitt family, 379, 381
George. 176, 397
Jacob B., 397
Joseph, 176, 381
Ienderson, James, 362
Katharine, 286, 301, 348, 391
Margaret, 348
Mary, 430
Patrick, 97, 301, 394
S., 234
Sarah, 391, 430, 432
the Widow, 430
Thomas, 97
William, 292
Iendrick, Jacob, Swede, of N. J.,
192
Iendricks, family, 396
Hannah, 396
Martha, 380
Mary, 380
Patience, 380
Ienry, Robert, 362
Ieron, Alexander, 409
Ierriott, John, 279
Ieston, Zebulon, 181
Iibberd, Joseph, 398
Phebe, 398
Iicks, Thomas, 371
Iiett, family, 178, 179, 360
Elizabeth, 360
Thomas, 356, 360
Iill, Ann, 360
Deborah, 337
James, 296
John, 402
Margaret, 296
Richard, 96
Samuel, 360
Sarah, 389
illary, Christopher, 285, 313
Dorothy, 313
Francis, 285, 323, 410
Henry, 285
Marmaduke, 285
Mary, 281

Hillary, Nathaniel, 285
Samuel, 285
Hind, James, 304
Ruth, 304
Hinkson, Jane, 308
John, 308
Hinton, Percy, 420
Hinshaw family, 179, 366-9
Ann, 402
Dorothy, 426
Elizabeth, 426
Jacob, 98, 174, 176, 356, 362,
366, 402, 426, 427
John, 362, 426, 427
Margaret, 362
Mary, 362
Rebecca, 356, 366, 402
Thomas, 402, 426
William, 402
Hoaker or Hooper, Hugh, 75
Hoare, Samuel, 152
Hobson family, 167, 179, 184, 329-
330, 381
Ann, 421, 426, 427
Benjamin, 372
Elizabeth, 329
Francis, 132, 133, 136, 171,
176, 199, 329, 345, 367, 381,
393, 416, 421, 426
Hannah, 416
John, 416
Joseph, 416
Lawrence, 372
Martha, 78
Phebe, 212, 421
Richmond P., 171
Ruth, 416
Sarah, 416
William, 416, 425
Hockley, Ann, 420
Henry, 420
Hester, 420
Hockessin Meeting, 121
Hodgen, George, 392
Hodgin, Robert, 164, 165
Theodate, 168
Hodgkinson, Ann, 392
Eleanor, 392
John, 392
Hodgson family, 396
George, 313

Hodgson, James, 396
Hogg, John, 387
   Patrick, 425
Holcomb, Elizabeth, 384
   Richard, 256
Holding, John, 393
Holems, William, 431
Holland, Henry, 405
   Henry, 364
   Lydia, 364, 405
   Patrick, 301
Hollin, Richard, 410
Hollingsworth family, 178, 179, 311–316
   Ann, 311, 322
   Catharine, 215
   Henry, 60, 101, 127, 130, 312, 320, 322
   Lydia, 322
   Mary, 319
   Samuel, 117, 321, 342
   Thomas, 122, 123, 318
   Valentine, 62, 117, 118, 120, 122, 123, 126, 129, 159, 311, 318, 322
Holm, Patrick, 98
Holme, Benjamin, letter of, 67 ; 211
   Eleanor, 256
   Esther, 256
   Michael, 256
   Sarah, 256
   Thomas, sketch of, 247–256 ; 44, 277, 278
   Tryall, 256
Holmes, Isabel, 339
Hoope or Hoopes family, 392
   Eleanor, 63, 320
   Isabella, 381
   John, 323
   Mary, 355, 431
   Robert, 63, 313, 320, 322, 323, 392, 410
   Ruth, 431
Hooper, Nicholas, 73, 78
Hoopes, William, 235, 371
Hope, Thomas, 126
Hopewell Meeting, Va., 178
Horne, William, 198
Horner, Mary, 410
Horseman, Charles, 402
   Eli, 402

Hospitality of Old Settlers, 188
House Building, 190–193
Houston, Anthony, 132, 133
Houghton, John, 320
   Martha, 315
Houlton, Nathaniel, 328
How, Abraham, 403
Howe, Rachel, 422
Howell, Charles, 79, 290
   George, 292
   William, 287
Howgill, Francis, minister, visits Ireland, 20–24
Hoy, Ralph, 291
Hudson, Edward, 393, 394
   Hannah, 294
Hugg family, 386
   John, 353, 386
Hughes, Amy, 370
   Samuel, 199
Huse, William, 132, 133
Hunt, Samuel, diarist, 197
Hunter, James, 160, 289, 378
   Jane, 306
   John, 371, 378, 399
   Peter, 289, 304
   William, 378
Huntington Meeting, 172–173
Hume, Isabel, 238
   James, 238
Hurst, John, 384
Hussey, Ann, 163, 165, 172, 402, 405
   Christopher, 165, 168, 419
   Edith, 177, 419
   Elizabeth, 419
   Hannah, 406, 419
   Jane, 290, 405
   Jediah, 290, 405
   John, 120, 290
   Lydia, 346
   Margaret, 165
   Miriam, 419
   Nathan, 163, 165, 168, 177
   Record, 419
Hutchinson, Priscilla, 302
Hutton family, 184, 327, 330–332
   Benjamin, 366
   Deborah, 340
   John, 64, 66, 167, 339, 347

Hutton, Joseph, 64, 66, 131, 132, 133, 136, 166, 167, 199, 211, 225, 360, 395
Joel, 381
Levi, 397
Mary, 211, 309
Nehemiah, 65, 66, 110, 211, 212, 223, 225, 328, 340
Samuel, 171, 395
Thomas, letters of, 61, 64–67; 110, 360, 394, 395
William, 171

IGNEW, Andrew, 327
Mary, 327
Immigrants, assisted by meetings, in Penna., 95–98; in Ireland, 98
Immigration to Pennsylvania, inducements for (*see* William Penn), 50–80
Indented servants, *see* Redemptioners
Indians, Newlin's difficulty with, 147–149
Ingrum, Leathe, 197
"Inner Light," 4
Intemperance, 223–226
Inventories, 195–201
Ireton succeeds Cromwell in Ireland, 10
Irish Quakers on *Welcome*, 111
Irish Quakers well adapted for pioneer life, 189–187; mostly of English stock, 187
Irish Tenth of West Jersey, 42
Irish Friends return to Ireland on business trips, 60
Irish landholders dispossessed and driven into Province of Connaught, in 1652, 11
Isickers, Valentine, 172
Istariot, James, 230

JACKSON family, 179, 335, 341, 349–350
Ann, 211, 328, 348, 349
Anthony, 349
Caleb, 348
Dorothy, 373
Elizabeth (*see* Pike),
Isaac, 71, 328, 337, 349, 357
James, 357
Joseph, 328

Jackson, John, 306, 310, 325, 337
Jeremiah, 349
Mary, 211
Martha, 426, 427
Richard, 349, 374
Ruth, 347
Sarah, 337
Samuel, 159, 161, 211, 347
Richard, 349, 374
Rebecca, 328, 348, 349
Thomas, 131, 132, 133, 135, 136, 137, 146, 199, 201, 209–212, 214, 217, 225, 229, 236, 309, 340, 357, 373
William, 357
Jacob, Caleb, 283
Elizabeth, 283
Isaac, 289
Rebecca, 289,
Thomas, 303
Jacobs, Richard, 291
Thomas, 315
James II., Accession of, 28; Invades Ireland, 29
James, Ann, 420
Samuel, 424
Janney, Susan, 370
Jarvis or Jervis family, 388
Charles, 388
John, 388
Martin, 294, 388
Sarah, 294
Jay, William, 405
Jemmison, Dr. David, of York, Pa., 381
Jenkin, Jacob, 420
Jervis, *see* Jarvis
Job, Andrew, 158, 236
John, Hannah, 290
Samuel, 290, 420
Johnson family, 179, 326, 338
Abigail, 393
Elizabeth, 393
James, 211
Joseph, 326
Joshua, 326
Margaret, 210, 211
Mary, 323
Richard, 393
Robert, 132, 133, 136, 210, 211, 216, 326

Johnson, William, 217, 298
Jones, Ann, 363
  Arthur, 211, 339
  Cadwallader, 420
  Content, 405
  Edward, 405
  Francis, 303
  Griffith, 278
  Henry, 336
  Isaac, 267
  James, 419
  Jane, 405
  John, 97
  Mary, 422
  Phebe, 326
  Susan, 398
  Susanna, 381
  Thomas, 279
Jordan, John, 328
Journey to new home, 189

KEAN, William, 199
  Keimer, Samuel, 219
Keith, George, 239, 281
Kell, Ann, 390
  David, 367, 390, 425, 426, 427
  John, 426, 427
  Margery, 425
  Mary, 425
Kelly, Joseph, 199
  Mary, 401
Kenedy (*see* Canady), Hugh, 98
Kennett Monthly Meeting, 125–130
Kennett, origin of name, 128
Kennett Square, 129
Kennett Township, 128–130
Kenworthy, Joshua, 168, 172
  Rebecca, 172
Kerr, Joseph, 86, 87, 411, 412
Kilmore, Friends convinced at, 18
King, Abigail, 86, 87, 411, 412
  Deborah, 328
  John, 362
  Merrick, 328, 329, 394
  Richard, 329
  Thomas, 409
Kirk family, 177, 178, 184, 322–325
  Alphonsus, 119, 122, 157, 207–208, 227, 320, 321
  Abigail, 208
  Deborah, 313, 320, 410

Kirk, Dinah, 313
  Elizabeth, 320
  Jacob, 167, 355, 357, 410
  Jane, 326
  Rachel, 331
  Rebecca, 357
  Robert, 320, 410
  Roger, 157, 227, 320, 410
  Samuel, 311, 410
  Thomas, 201
  Timothy, 152, 156, 157, 167, 208, 223, 313, 320, 331, 393, 410, 412, 417, 420
  William, 156, 208, 412, 413, 416, 417, 420
Kitchien, John, 199
Koch, Jacob, 397
Kole, Isaac, 418
Kneller, Sir Godfrey, 388
Knight, John, 286
  Margery, 286, 287
  Thomas, 286
Knox, Andrew, 393

LACY, John, 181
  Lago, Mary, *see* Mary Fox
Laird, Jacob, 404
  Jane, 404
Lamb's Fold, 429
Lampley, Judith, 315
Lancaster, James, minister, visits Ireland, 16
  Isabel, 407
  John, 288
Lancaster County, 159–162
Lander, William, 301
Langbree, Thomas, 393
Lashly, George, 149, 150
Lawder, or Lander, William, 408, 409
Lawlessness of the Irish Catholics a cause of emigration, 45
Latchew, Eve, 396
Laybourn, Joseph, 328, 330, 331
  Rachel, 328, 331
  Samuel, 64
Leacock Meeting, 161
Leaze, Hannah, 336
Lecky, Jane, 305
  Mary, 305
  Robert, 305
Lee, Amos, 373

Leech, Joseph, 405
  Phebe, 290, 346
  Richard, 363
  Sarah, 290, 363
  Thomas, 290, 346, 363
Leeds, Daniel, 383
Lennox, John, 425
  Robert, 426
Leonard, Richard, 366
Letitia's Manor, 127–128, 130, 132
Letters to and from Ireland 62–79,
  89–92, 230, 374–375
Lewis, Ann, 365
  Curtis, 326
  Ellis, 149, 150
  Elizabeth, 150
  Hannah, 373, 384
  Henry, 233
Lightfoot family, 338–340
  Benjamin, 110
  Catharine, 356, 398
  Eleanor, 352
  Jacob, 211
  Margaret, 329
  Mary, 343
  Michael, 131, 132, 133, 135,
    137, 152, 195, 196, 211, 229,
    236, 332, 339, 343, 352
  Samuel, 152, 211
  Sarah, 332
  Thomas, 60, 70, 139, 152, 211,
    218–219, 236, 329, 338, 356
  William, 60, 61, 349
Lindley family, 179, 336
  Deborah, 193, 337
  Eleanor, 211, 336
  Jacob, 336, 337, 352
  James, 75, 78, 131, 132, 133,
    134, 136, 142, 143, 161, 210,
    211, 216, 229, 236, 336, 337;
    inventory of, 200
  Jonathan, 337
  Mabel, 194
  Mary, 352
  Sarah, 211, 352
  Thomas, 69, 161, 227, 291,
    305, 336
Little, Elizabeth, 297
Littler, Samuel, 236
Lloyd, David, leader of Popular
  Party, 242

Lloyd, Hannah, 342
  Robert, 101
  Thomas, 256
Loe, Thomas, minister, visits Ire-
  and converts William Penn,
  27, 250
Logan, Hannah, 237
  Isabelle, 237–240, 319
  James, 36, 127, 130, 145, 148;
    sketch of, 237–247; autobi-
    ography, 238–240; Gov. of
    Pa., 241; leader of Proprie-
    tory Party, 241–242; relations
    with Indians, 242; literary
    pursuits, 243; personal ap-
    pearance, 245; unsuccessful
    courtship, 245–247; marriage
    and death, 247; his runaway
    servant, 102; 266, 282
  Patrick, 36, 237, 238, 239, 240
  Sarah, 247
  William, 238, 247
Log house, The, 192–193
London Grove Meeting House, 143
  Township, 132, 136–143
  Meeting, 143
  Monthly Meeting, 139
  Land Company, 132, 139–141
Londonderry, Friends convinced at,
  18
  Siege of, 28
Long, Mary, 423
  Rachel, 423
  Robert, 423
Longshore, William, 405
Longstreth, Ann, 302
  Jane, 302
Louge, William, 101
Love, Alexander, 349
  Faithful, 378
  James, 160, 171, 177, 378
Low, John, 277, 293, 353
  Joseph, 277
  Joshua, 167
Lowden family, 334–335
  John, 130, 131, 132, 133, 134,
    195–196, 217, 229, 329, 334
  Margaret, 136, 329, 334
  William, 226, 228–231, 335
  Richard, 335
Lowden vs. Smith, case of, 228–231

Lucken, Margaret, 301
Ludlow, 10
Luffe, Edward, 96
Lurgan, Edmundsons settle at, 15; meeting established at, in 1654, 16
Lurting, Thomas, Quaker sea captain, 42, 383
MACCONNELL, Daniel, 321
MacElcoshker, Edmund, 424
Mackey family, 424–428
    Ann, 367, 381
    Benjamin, 367
    John, 367
    Joseph, 367, 381
    Martha, 337
    Mary, 389
    Rebecca, 367, 402
MacWard, Miles, 102
Maddon, Robert, 367
Malcum (see Millcum), John, 300
Malin family, 314
    Joseph, 351
    Randal, 314, 336
    Mary, 336
    Rachel, 336
Malone, William, 64
    " Little Tom," 64
Man, Ann, 335
    Francis, 335
    Judith, 335
Manchester Meeting, *see* Newberry
Manor of Steyning, 127–128, 130, 132
Mantz, Elizabeth, 396
Map of Newlin Township, 149
Mark, Isabel, 286
Markets, 206–207
Maris, George, 115
    Hannah, 322
Marlborough Township, Chester County, 143–147
Marlnee, Jared, 406
Marriage Certificate, The, 210–211
Marriages, 209–215
Marsh family, 406–424
    Abigail, 85, 88
    Elizabeth, 88, 89, 376, 399
    George, 342
    Henry, 349
    Jane, 349, 363, 401

Marsh, John, 85–88, 155, 171, 376, 402
    Jonathan, 85, 88, 171, 402
    Joshua, 84–88, 155, 171, 376, 399
    Peter, 85, 88, 161, 402
    Rachel, 349
    Ruth, 427
    William, 171, 349
Marshall (also Marshill), Abigail, 368
    Abram, 131, 132, 133, 211
    Abraham, 149, 150
    Ann, 199, 217, 224, 356
    Benjamin, 85, 86, 87, 98, 367, 372, 411, 412, 426
    Deborah, 293
    Jacob, 84, 85, 86, 87, 356, 359, 368, 372, 411, 412, 420, 426
    John, 356
    Joseph, 368, 372, 426
    Mary, 367
    Richard, 393
    Ruth, 368
    Margaret 356, 368
    Sarah, 293
    Thomas, 310
    William, 356
Martin, Joseph, 341
    Ruth, 211, 341
    Sarah, 329
    Thomas, 329
Maryland, Irish Friends in, 42
Massey, Daniel, 284
    George, 351
    Samuel, 48, 93, 285
    Sarah, 93, 284
Matthews, Mathew, or Mathes family, 391
    Alexander, 409, 410
    Elizabeth, 378
    George, 326
    Jean, 279
    Joan, 410
    Margaret, 199
    Mary, 321
    Oliver, 398
    Richard, 425
    Sarah, 326
    William, 177

Mauldin, Col. Francis, 315
  Ann, 315
Maule, Bethia, 238
  William, 238
May, John, 234, 235
Mayne, Benjamin, 287
Mayson, Richardson, 393
McAdams, John, 402
McAnabley, Sarah, 165
McAnele, Charles, 165
McCann, David, 367
McClun or McClung, 34
  Elizabeth, 353
  Sarah, 347
  Thomas, 160, 353
McCollum, Thomas, 213
McComb, John, 280, 281
McCool family, 33, 179
  Gabriel, 389
  James, 389
  John, 389
  Olivia, 343, 389
  William, 342
McConnell, John, 406
McCrannall, Patrick, 367
McCreary family, 397
  David, 397
  Hannah, 346
  Sarah, 346
McCurdy, D., 234
  Daniel, 235
McFerran, Elizabeth, 380
McGrew family, 380-381
  Alexander, 184
  Deborah, 361
  Elizabeth, 174
  Finley, 174, 184, 380
  James, 183, 227, 361, 380
  Mary, 361
  Nathan, 361
  Simon, 183
McKenell, Mary, 425
  Mongow, 425
McKetrick or McKitrick, Hannah, 381
  Jonas, 367, 381
  Mary, 381
McKinley, Mrs. Ida Saxton, 321
  William, late Pres. of U. S., 321
McKoy, Mary, 215
  Robert, 215

McMillan, McMollin, or McMullen family, 34, 184, 399-406
  Abigail, 346
  Deborah, 363, 376, 399, 414, 416, 419, 420
  Enos, 397
  George, 169, 171, 201-202, 233-235, 367, 419
  Jacob, 397
  James, 363
  Jane, 346, 363, 419
  John, 171, 346, 363, 419
  Mary, 419
  Rebecca, 214
  Ruth, 397
  Smith Bell, 202
  Sarah, 397
  Thomas, 156, 169, 363, 376, 399, 416, 417, 420, 422
  William, 170, 171, 399
McNabb, 34
  Dorothy, 354
  Elizabeth, 354
  Jane, 354, 370
  John, 354
  William, 160, 354
McNamee, Barnabas, 184, 377
McNiece or McNice, 34
  Isaiah, 97, 295
McQuillan, 35
McRannell or McRannells, John, 230, 359
  Joseph, 376
Meetings for Worship, 217-220
Meetings for Business, 217-222
Meeting Discipline, 222-233
Melvin, Andrew, 393
  Sarah, 378
Men, work of on farm, 205
Menallen Meeting, 173-176
Mendenhall, Aaron, 373
  Abner, 287
  Elizabeth, 302
  George, 373
  John, 153, 302
  Rose, 373
Mento, George, 394
Meredith, John, 427
  Joseph, 427
  Katharine, 427
  Reece, 132, 133

Mercer, Richard, 394
  Ruth, 365
Method of Purchasing Land, 189
Michener, Dr. Ezra, 133
  Ellwood, 131, 133
Mickle family, 277, 357–358,
  Archibald, 277
  John, 174, 213, 277, 357
  Robert, 176, 333, 357
  William, 235
Middleton, Hugh, 382
Midkiff, Esther, 207
Mifflin, Mrs. Hannah, 396
Milhous family, 179, 535
  Peter, 172
  Sarah, 355
  Thomas, 132, 133, 134, 152,
    293, 355, 356
Miliken, Mary, 298
Millcum, (Malcum or Milcomb),
  Ann, certificate of, 56–57, 300
Miller family, 325–328, 347, 356–
  357
  Ann, 396, 398
  Benjamin, 318
  Catharine, 309, 355, 398
  Deborah, 334
  Gayen, 126, 128, 129, 131, 132,
    136, 211, 309, 325, 338, 348
  Grizel, 285
  Hannah, 336
  Henry, 291, 302
  James, 137, 199, 236, 309, 325,
    336, 339, 341, 355, 356, 373,
    398, 405
  Jennett, 430
  John, 131, 132, 133, 135, 136,
    137, 196, 198, 325, 331, 332
  Joseph, 324
  Margaret, 211, 325, 338, 347,
    348
  Martha, 211, 318
  Mary, 136, 211, 331, 332, 347
  Robert, 153, 167, 394, 405
  Richard, 355
  Ruth, 346
  Samuel, 167, 228, 330, 332,
    347
  Sarah, 211, 302, 332, 338, 355,
    405
  William, 336

Military Service, 231–233
Mills, Mary, 346
  Phebe, 346
  Robert, 346
Minnich, Daniel, 396
Minshall, Ann, 348
  Hannah, 363
  John, 348
Mires, Eleazer, 168
Mode, Alexander, 337, 371
  Hannah, 371
  Rebecca, 371
Monocacy Meeting, Md., 178
Montgomery, Alexander, 337
Montgomery County, 109
Monthly Meeting, 221–222
Moody, John, 234, 235
  Samuel, 235
Moone, Paul, 238
Moony (see O'Mooney), Neal, 199
Moore family, 348–349, 428–433
  Andrew, 159, 161, 164, 336
  Daniel, 310
  James, 165, 230, 297, 347, 348,
    371, 394, 399
  Jane, 401
  Joseph, 401
  Lawrence, 393
  Mary, 213
  Robert, 174
  Ruth, 401
  William, 287, 399
Moore Lodge, 432, 433
Morris, Ann, 406
  Anthony, 96
  James, 287
Morthland, Charles, 419
  Hugh, 419
  Mary, 419
  Rebecca, 419
  Ruth, 419
  Samuel, 402,
Morton family, 354
  Deborah, 381
  Elinor, 354
  James, 410, 426
  John, 176, 369, 381, 410
  Mary, 381
  Richard, 378
  Samuel, 354, 369
  William, 354, 425

Moss, Joseph, 256
Mountrath, Earl of, 26
Mulleanoux, Edward, 168
Mulligan, David, 330
Murray, Earl of, 238
  Ann, 358
  John, 358
Musgrove family, 179, 318
  Hannah, 154, 302
  James, 228
  John, 119, 159, 213, 228, 313, 318, 326
  Joseph, 129
  Martha, 326
  Thomas, 63, 154
Myers, John T., 405
  Sarah A. (Cook), 405

NANTMEAL Meeting, 156
  Nash, James, 342
Naylor, James, 15
Neal family, 366
  Dorothy, 372
  Henry, 354, 366
  Robert, 366
  William, 372, 374
Nebinger, Mary, 398
Need, Ann, 309
  Joseph, 309
Nelson, Samuel, 235
Nevitt or Nevet family, 366
  Ann, 380
  Elizabeth, 380
  Ellen, 374
  Hannah, 379, 402
  Isaac, 380
  John, 297, 310
  Joseph, 365, 379
  Mary, 365, 379
  Ruth, 380
  Thomas, 160, 176, 365, 366, 374, 380
  William, 171, 379-380, 402
Newark Meeting, 118-120
Newark Monthly Meeting, 125-130
Newberry Meeting, 163-167
Newberry, Nathaniel, 152
Newby or Newbie family, 386-387
  John, 339
  Mark, 42, 278, 382, 383, 384, 386-387

30

Newby, Martha, 332
  Mary, 339
New Castle County on Delaware, 118, 132
New Castle Meeting, 120
New Garden Meeting, County Carlow, Ireland, 130
New Garden Meeting, Pa., 136-138
New Garden Monthly Meeting, Pa., 138-139; records of, 139
New Garden Township, Chester County, 130-136
New Garden Dinner Table, A, in 1714, 197
New Jersey, Irish Friends in, 42, 383
Newlin family, 179, 184
  Ann, 380
  John, 58, 149, 150, 308
  Nathaniel, 58, 116, 147-150, 207, 273, 308
  Nicholas, 57-59, 116, 271-273, 308
  William, 176
Newlin Township, Chester County, 147-150; map of, 149
Nichol, Ann, 404
Nichols, James, 334
  John, 333, 334
Nicholson, James, 100, 373
  John, 367, 393
  Joseph, 294
  Thomas, 86, 87, 411, 412
  William, 294, 295, 425
Noblet, Ann, 165, 168
  John, 165, 168
Norris, Isaac, 247, 262, 288
  Mary, 262
Norton, Edward, 376
  Mary, 376
Nottingham Meeting, 156-159
Nowlan, James, 331

OATHS, testimony against, a cause of emigration, 44
Oborn, Susanna, 322
Ogden, Jonathan, 315
O'Hara Brook, 429
O'Heil, 35
Old Court House, 108
Oldest House in Penna., 115
Oley Meeting, *see* Exeter

Oliver, Margaret, 296
  Robert, 292
O'Maghan, Edward, 313
O'Mooney (*see* Moony) family, 34, 354
  Ann, 354
  James, 354
  Neal, 160, 354, 366
  Sarah, 366
Opequan Meeting, *see* Hopewell
Organization of Quakerism in Ireland, 27
Origin of Irish Friends, 32–37
Orrery, Earl of, 26
Outfit of Farm, 198
Owen, Griffith, 130
  John, 324
  Nathaniel, 266, 267
  Philotesia, 266
  Sarah, 318
  Theophilus, 318

PACKER, Ann, 419
  Philip, 419
Pack horses, 189
Palmer, Ann, 377
  John, 377
  Martha, 377
  Mary, 377
  Moses, 334
Pain or Paine, Hannah, 373
  Thomas, 154, 372
Painter, Ann, 337
  Hannah, 337
  Patience, 337
  Thomas, 337
Panmure, Earl of, 238
Parke family, 69, 70, 305–306
  Abel, 72
  James Pemberton, 70
  Jonathan, 72, 305
  Mary, 305, 350
  Rebecca, 351
  Robert, letter of, 69–79; 93, 101, 305
  Susanna, 305
  Thomas, 69, 153, 305, 336, 351
Parker, Ann, 387
  Elizabeth, 297
  Thompson, 355
Parks, John, 353
  Richard, 286, 353

Parks, Susanna, 286
Parrish, John, 181
Parrock, James, 386
Parvin family, 351–352
  Francis, 110, 339, 340, 351
  John, 60, 308
  Thomas, 376
Passage, Cost of, 98–99
Passmore, John A. M., 348
  Mary, 212
  William, 287
Paterson, Ann, 392
  John, 295
  Katharine, 392
  Robert, 392
Pearce, Richard, of Limerick, becomes a Quaker, 24
Pearson (*see* Pierson), Benjamin, 352
  Deborah, 351
  Edith, 352
  John, 377
  Lancelot, 410
  Lawrence, 352
  Margaret, 377
  Mary, 352, 377
  William, 313
Peckett, James, 419
Peckover, Edmund, travelling minister, 160
Pedrick, Elizabeth, 303
Peel, John, 283,
  Luke, 283
Pemberton, Israel, 48, 67, 97
  James, 306
Penn, Letitia, 127, 128; *see* Aubrey
  Sir William, 50
  Thomas, 144, 240
  William, converted to Quakerism, 27; founder of Pennsylvania, 50–53; his charter, 50–51; his scheme of colonization, 51; constitution and laws, 51–52; growth of Pennsylvania, 52; his invitation to emigrants, 52; his personal influence in Ireland, 53; arrival in Pennsylvania in 1682, 111; 139, 240
  William, Jr., 127, 130
Pennington, Edward, 127
Pennock family, 184

'ennock, Alice, 357
  Christopher, 280
  Joseph, 144–145 ; his letter,
    145–146 ; 225, 280, 357, 371
  Mary, 280
  Mary, 357
  Nathaniel, 146
Pennsylvania (*see* William Penn),
  inducements for immigration
  to, 50–80
Penrose family, 289
  Abigail, 290
  Amos, 290
  Dorothy, 357
  Hannah, 290, 397
  Jane, 290, 346
  John, 290, 359, 362
  Jonathan, 362
  Mary, 290
  Phebe, 290, 346
  Robert, 350, 357
  Susanna, 290
  Thomas, 290
  William, 169, 362
Perkinson, James, 233, 234, 235
Persecutions, 25–27
Pettard, Humphrey, 361, 407
Pettitt, Benjamin, 346
Phayre, Colonel, Governor of Cork,
  22
Philadelphia Meeting, 107–109
Phillips family, 406
  Charles, 168
  Henry, 417
  Jane, 422
  Mrs. Annie, 396
Phoenixville, founded by Irish
  Quakers, 154
Physicians' charges, 217
Pidgen or Pidgeon, Charles, 174
  Isaac, 364
  Joseph, 262
  Mary, 262
  William, 85
Pierce, Ann, 404
  Caleb, 228
  Henry, 128
  Jacob, 287
Pierson, Rose, 320
  Thomas, 119, 320
Piercy, Richard, 250

Pikeland Township, 150–152
Pike family, 150
  Anne, 151
  Benjamin, 151
  Ebenezer, 151–341
  Elizabeth, 150–151, 152
  Joseph, of Cork, owner of New-
    lin Township, 150 ; life of,
    150–151
  Mary, 151, *see* Beale
  Rachel, 151
  Richard, 150–151, 152, 153
  Samuel, 151
  Sarah, 151
Pillar, James, 84, 85, 86, 87, 98,
  366, 411, 412, 420
  Mary, 86, 87, 411, 412
  William, 171, 380
Pim family, 372–375
  Elizabeth, 393
  Hannah, 326
  John, of Belfast, J. P., 35, 280
  Richard, 153
  Susanna, 393
  Thomas, 153
  Tobias, 393
  William, 100, 153, 199, 201
Pittendorff, Susanna, 396
Places in Ireland whence Friends
  came, 81–82
Places of embarking and landing, 89
Places of settlement, 105–106
Plantations of Queen Mary, 7 ; of
  James I., 7 ; of Charles I., 8 ;
  of Oliver Cromwell, 10–12
Pleadwell, John, 375
  Mary, 372, 374
  Thomas, 375
  Tobias, 58–59, 375
  William, 372, 374
Plum, George, 389
Plummer, Dr., 398
Poell, William, 426
Polk, William W., 67
Pope, Elizabeth, 174
  John, 172, 174, 231
  Samuel, 174
Porter, William, 62, 63, 320, 323,
  410
Potter, William, 234
Potts, Jonathan, 397

Poultney, Benjamin, 306
Pow, Mary, 86, 87, 411
Powell, Arthur, 277
  Elizabeth, 172, 360
  Evan, 358
  Hugh, 424
  John, 172
  Joseph, 360
  Mary, 360
  Sarah, 358
  Thomas, 172, 318
Power, Mary, 211
Price, Elizabeth, 165, 326
  John, 417
  Rachel, 207-208, 324
Pringle, Sarah, 345
Pritchett, Elizabeth, 318
Proctor, Richard, 174
  Sarah, 172
Protestant workmen leave Ireland, 46
Prowell, Ann, 404
Pugh, James, 417
Purdy, Susanna, 373
  Thomas, 372
  William, 372
Pusey, Caleb, 115, 139, 143, 211, 236, 303
  Lydia, 351
  Phebe, 371
Pyle, Abigail, 334
  Elizabeth, 309, 316
  Mrs. Emma Wickersham, 402
  Hannah, 366
  James, 366
  Mary, 334
  Nicholas, 334
  William, 316

Quakerism, Beginnings of, 3-6
  Quare, Daniel, 139
Quarry, Robert, leader of Church Party, 242
Quarterly Meeting, 220-221

RACIAL origin of Friends of Ireland, 32-37
Radley, Joseph, formerly Headmaster of Ulster Provincial School, 34
Raford, Lewis, 431

Rail, Hannah, 358
Rake, Grace, 385
Randall, Samuel, 258
Raney, Sarah, 405
Rankin, John, 226
Raper or Roper, Ann, 372-373
  Christopher, 58, 372-373
"Rapparees," 11, 30
Rawle, Francis, 262
Rea, Ree, or Ray family, 391
  Ann, 312
  Elinor, 391
  Isabelle, 319
  John, 312, 391
  Margaret, 321, 329
  Mary, 282
  Nicholas, 312, 426
Read, Charles, 247
  John, 224
  Sarah, 247
  William, 356
Redemptioners, 74-75, 77, 99-102, 228-231
Reed, Elizabeth, 347
  Mary, 316
Rees, Jane, 420
  John, 413, 420
Reeves, John, 101
  William, 431
Reford (*see* Raford), Lewis, 230
Religious causes of emigration, 42-46
Removal, the certificate of, 84-85
Rents, high, a cause of emigration, 47
Reports favorable to Penn'a returned to Ireland, by ministers and others, 55-60; by letters, 60-80
Restrictions on manufacture and commerce, a cause of emigration, 46
Revolution of 1689, 29
Revolutionary War, attitude of Friends in, 231-235
Revolutionary taxes and fines, 233-235
Reynolds, Henry, 158, 236
Richards, Elizabeth, 323
  Thompson, 131
  William, 324

Richardson, Anne, 292
  Alice, 319
  Catharine, 366
  Dr.,'364
  Edward, 365
  Faithful, 365, 378
  Jane M., of Moyallon House,
    Gilford, Ireland, 35
  Jonathan, 86, 411
  John, 120
  John Grubb, 33
  Lawrence, 161, 353
  Mary, 307, 367, 431
  Patience, 297
  Robert, 338
  William, 366
Ridge, Alice, 372
  Francis, 266
Riley, Thomas, 165
Robinson family, 315
  Catharine, 215
  Eleanor, 342
  Elizabeth, 93, 389
  Francis, 93, 389, 390
  George, 315, 342
  John, 305
  Joseph, 321
  Patrick, 281, 389
  Rebecca, 324, 342
  Robert, 408, 409
  William, 230, 305, 306
Robeson, Andrew, 281
Robson family, 392
  Catharine, 322
  Francis, 86, 313, 319, 320, 392,
    411
  Jacob, 323
  John, 323, 394
  Ruth, 366
Roberts, Anne, 264
  Aubrey, 420
  Elizabeth, 370
  Hannah, 278
  Jane, 393
  John, 370
  Mary, 264
  Robert, 287, 393
  Roger, 264
  Ruth, 420
  Sarah, 370, 393
Rochford, Dennis, 54, 111, 278–279

Rochford, Grace, 279
  Mary, 279
  William, 278
Rogers, Andrew, 168
  Christy, 409, 410
  Elizabeth, 151, 399, 409
  Francis, 151
  George, 416
  John, 409, 410
  Rebecca, 168
  Peter, 410
Rooke, George, 79, 296
  Thomas, 296
Rose, James, 301
  John, 301
  Thomas, 301
Ross family, 304
  Alexander, 178, 304
  Andrew, 235
  Dr. Hamilton, 432
  Richard, 402
Rothe, Elizabeth, 432
  Richard, 432
Rowan, William, 224
Rowland, Mary, 131, 132, 133,
    134
  Rachel, 333
  Ruth, 326
  Thomas, 333
Ruddock, Elizabeth, 261
  Sarah, 174
Russell family, 64, 370
  Anna, 289
  Elizabeth, 393
  Gregory, 331
  John, 292, 331, 369, 370
  Mary, 292
  Michael, 139
  Susanna, 292
Rutledge, William, 132, 133
Rutty, Dr. John, 22; his MS. of
    Rise and Progress of the
    Quakers in Ireland, 280
Rutter, Samuel, 376

SADSBURY Meeting, 161
  Sadsbury Monthly Meeting, 162
Sadler, Richard, 174
Salkeld, John, minister, 219
Sandham, Lieutenant Robert, be-
  comes a Quaker, 20

Sandwith, Elizabeth, 294
  ' Samuel, 293
  Sarah, 294
  William, 293, 294, 388
Sarson, Francis, 393
Saul, John, 303
Scarlett, Phebe, 337
Schofield, Joseph L., 370
Schools, 235
Scotch country of Ireland, 34
Scotch-Irish Friends, 35–36
Scotch-Irish squatters in Faggs Manor, Chester County, 145
Scott, John, 425
Seal, Joseph, 164
  Theodate, 164, 165
Seale, Hindrance, 393
Seaton, Alexander, a Scotch-Irish Friend, 36, 360
  Ruth, 356, 360
Sedgwick, Mary, 371
Selection of land affected by ties of kin and friendship, 189
Selford, Robert, 101
Servants, Indented, *see* Redemptioners
Settlement, Cromwellian, 10–12
Settlement, Places of, 105–116
Shackamaxon Meeting, 107
Shanks, Thomas, 234
Shank, ——, 235
Sharmon, Robert, 66
Sharp family, 179, 333–335
  Anthony, 383, 384, 385
  Isaac, 385
  James, 296
  John, 132, 133, 134, 136, 333, 402
  Joseph, 131, 132, 133, 124, 142, 229, 325, 329
  Mary, 296
  Samuel, 142
  Thomas, 383–384
Sharpless, Abraham, 351
  William, 334
Sharply, Abigail, 119
  Adam, 119
  Benjamin, 119
  Charity, 119
  Rachel, 119
  Ralph, 119

Sharply, William, 119
Shaw, Hannah, 408
  James, 354
  John, 398
  Martha, 330, 354
  Moses, 295
  Samuel, 354
Sheldon, Eleazer, 393
Shepherd or Sheppard family, 358–359
  Benjamin, 372
  Jane, 174
  John, 174, 183–184, 358, 372
  Mary, 372
  Richmunday, 172, 174
  Solomon, 176, 183, 358, 359, 361, 372, 399
  Thomas, 372
  William, 174, 372
Shewin, Barbara, 316
Shipley, William, 121
Shippen, Ann, 245–247
  Edward, 245–247
Sicklemore, Captain James, becomes a Quaker, 20; 24
Siddall, Adam, 405
Siddon, Ezekiel, 277
Sidgwick, Mary, 369
Sidwell, Job, 377
Sietman, Gertrude, 395
Simcock, 145
  John, 115
Simpson, George, 314
Sinton, Jacob, 367, 427
  Sarah, 427
  William, 427
Sizargh, ship, 69, 94, 95
Skull, Edward, 282
Sleigh, Joseph, 307
Sleight, Joseph, 353
Sloan, Ann, 86, 87, 411, 412
Sloss, Elizabeth, 402
Slycer, Thomas, 424
Small Capital of Immigrants, 188
Smallwood, Joseph, 256
  Sarah, 256
Smedley, Samuel L., 64
Smith family, 406
  Baltzer, 402
  Elizabeth, minister, visits Ireland, 19–20

Smith, Francis, 128
James, 161, 345, 360, 427
Jane, 360
John, of Burlington, N. J., 143, 247
John Jay, 247
John, of Chester County, 211
John, 228–237, 335, 345
Katharine, 345
Lydia, 335
Margaret, 326
Mary, 345, 429
Rebecca, 367, 427
Robert, 360, 421
Rose, 345
Samuel, the historian, 126
Sarah, 295
Snowcroft, Adam, 295
Ann, 295
Social Intercourse, 208
Social Life of the Irish Quakers, 186–236
Softly, Fergus, 313, 408, 409
Southward movement of Quakerism from Pennsylvania, 177–179
Spangler, Rudolph or Rudy, silversmith, of York, 202
Spencer, Nathan, 373
Spicer, Mary, 386
Samuel, 386
Spotswood, Andrew, 431
Squire, Thomas, 393
Squibb, Mary Ann, 404
Staise, Michael, 313
Stalford, Thomas, 390
Stalker, Hugh, 306
Stamper, Bridget, 317
Hugh, 313, 317
Judith, 317
Stanfield family, 179
Jane, 356
Samuel, 356
Stanford, Margaret, 14, 393
Thomas, 14, 393
Stanhope, Sir John, 374
Starky, Catharine, 309
Nicholas, 393
Thomas, 384
Starr family, 179, 328–329
Ann, 348
Deborah, 211, 309, 341

Starr, Isaac, 334, 339, 352
James, 64, 65, 131, 132, 133, 136, 137, 139, 142, 154, 155, 195, 196, 211, 236, 394
Jeremiah, 142, 211, 236, 341, 348, 350, 360, 369
John, 340
Mary, 334, 352
Merrick, 352
Moses, 65, 109–110, 155, 341
Phebe, 352
Rebecca, 211, 304, 348, 349
Statistics of migration, 81–82
of settlement, 106
Steady, William, 324
Stedman, Joseph, 115
Stedham, Elizabeth, 363
Steel, James, of land office, 145
Steer family, 178, 179, 364–365
Catharine, 295, 366
Isaac, 160, 228, 295, 364
Joseph, 353
John, 160, 228, 354
Mary, 295
Nicholas, 160–161, 171, 378
Richard, 295
Ruth, 295, 364
"Stenton," home of James Logan, 243
Stephens, Guian, 281
Stephenson, James, 298
John, 298
Sterling, Jane, 371, 378
John, 399
Stevenson, Elizabeth, 174
James, 425
Stewart, Alexander, 322
Charlotte, 397
John, sea captain, 92
Mary, 322
Steyning or Stenning, Manor of, 127–130, 132
Stockdale, Jane, 270
Ruth, 270
William, 119, 281; sketch of, 267–271
Stoding, Major, Governor of Kinsale, 22
Story, Thomas, visits Ireland in 1716, 36, 246–247
Strangman, Mary, 393

Strettell family, 263-264.
  Amos, 218, 263, 264, 266, 267
  Ann, 267
  Experience, 263
  Frances, 267
  Hugh, 263
  John, 267
  Mary, 263
  Robert, sketch of, 263-267
  Susanna, 431, 432
  Thomas, 263
Strickland, Miles, 290
  Thomas, 300
Stroud, Elizabeth, 315
Suffering of Friends in Ireland, statistics of, 44
Swarthmore Hall, 22-23
Swayne, Francis, 211
Sweethen family, 425
Swett, Benjamin, 120
Swinney, Miles, 353

TAGART, John, 297
  Mary, 297
Talbot, Colonel, 316
Tanger, Agnes, 396
Tanner, John, 282
  Margaret, 334
  William, 134
Tarbut, Allen, 170
Tate, Katharine, 314
Taylor, Abiah, 306
  Bayard, 347
  Deborah, 306
  Dr., 217
  Frances, 96
  Henry, 420
  Isaac, deputy surveyor of Chester County, 141, 217
  James, 354
  Jane, 404
  John, surveyor, 131, 145
  Joseph, 404
  William, 290, 337, 420
  Philip, 314
Temple, Sir John, 374
Temporary Home near Landing Place, 188
Thackara family, 387
  Esther, 382
  Thomas, 382, 383, 384, 387

Thelwall, Jennet, 420
Thirkeld, John, 410
Thomas, Eli, 397
  Elizabeth, 420
  Hannah, 420
  John, 132, 133, 170, 404
  Jonah, 170
  Rachel, 397
  Richard, 420
Thompson, Ann, 384
  Capt. Thomas, 431
  Edward, 303
  Edward, 329
  Israel, 86, 87, 411, 412
  James, 316
  Ralph, 149, 150
  Robert, 420
Thornbury, Edward, 341
Thorne, Dorothy, 291
Thorton, Joseph, 77
  Samuel, 77
Threwecks, Robert, 101
Thwayts, Judith, 307
Tiffin, John, minister, visits Ireland, 17
Tithes and other ecclesiastical dues, causes of emigration, 43
Todd, Ann, 336
  Deborah, 331
  John, 331, 336
Tomlinson, William, 340
Too, John, 327
Toppen, Thomaz, 317
Tough, James, 425
Toughkenamon Hill line, 132-133
Toughkenamon, origin of name, 134
Toulerton, Thomas 425
Townsend, Richard, 112
Trafford, Thomas, 278, 385
Trimble or Tremble family, 377
  James, 371
  Joseph, 377
  William, 310
Trotter, Peg, 94
Truman, John, 349
  Ruth, 302
  Thomas, 349
  William, 349
Turner, Abraham, 261
  Ann, 292
  Elizabeth, 261, 292

Turner, Jacob, 292
Jane, 292
John, 292
Lucy, 292
Martha, 101, 260, 261
Mary, 257, 261, 281, 364
Robert, 53, 54, 55, 60; his redemptioners, 101 ; wardrobe of, 204 ; sketch of, 257–262; 277, 279, 281, 307, 312
Samuel, 292
Sarah, 292
Thomas, 292
Tyler, Catherine, 316
Tyrconnel, Earl of, becomes Lord Lieutenant of Ireland, 28

UNDERWOOD, Alexander, 168, 172, 174, 402, 406, 419
Elihu, 418, 419
Jane, 172
John, 402
Olive, 172
Richard, 172
Ruth, 172, 402
Samuel, 168
Sarah, 174, 402, 419
William, 168, 169, 172, 402
Unthank, Samuel, 409
Updegraff, Harman, 177
Joseph, 177
Mary, 335

VALE, John, 404
Robert, 402, 404, 422
Sarah, 404
William, 404
Valentine family, 350–351
John, 72
Mary, 69, 70, 79
Robert, 154, 155, 281
Thomas, 67, 70, 98, 79, 154, 350
Vance, Elizabeth, 376
William, 86, 87, 376, 411, 416, 426
Varman family, 353
Abigail, 353, 365
Grace, 365
Hattiel, 160, 161, 343, 353, 365
Henry, 353
Mary, 343, 344

Vaston, John, 309
Vendues, 224
Verner, David, 291
Samuel, 291
Vernon, Randall, 115
Robert, 115
Thomas, 115
Vessel, A favorite, 94
Vest, John, 281
Vickers, Mary, 302
Virginia, Irish Friends in, 42
Voyage, Dangers of, 92–93

WAANKIN Anne, 168
Wade, Robert, 110, 111, 113
Wainhouse, Martha, 75, 330, 338
Wainwright, Thomas, 393, 410
Walby, John, 292
Susanna, 292
Walhay, Ruth, 397
Walker, Benjamin, 170, 418, 421
John, 394, 418
Mary, 313
Sarah, 332
Thomas, 323
Wallis, James, 342
Walter, John, 326
Martha, 326
War, 231–235
Ward, Susanna, 402, 419
Philip, 337
William, 402
Warr or Ward, Rebecca, 305
Wardell, John, 334
Warming-pan, 199
Warren, Elizabeth, 264, 281
Joshua, 264, 281
Rev. J., 432
Sarah, 264, 281, 432
William, 432
Warrington Meeting, 168–172
Monthly Meeting, 162
Watson, Joshua P., 401
Samuel, 64, 292
Susanna, 286
Wastwood, Julianna, minister, visits Ireland, 18
Watts, Sarah, 277
Waves of Migration, 83
Way, Mary, 397, 405
Moses, 371

Way, Sarah, 325
Ways and Means of Migration, 84–102
Welsh, Susanna, 261
  the widow, 125
  William, 261
Welcome, ship, 111
Weldin, Ann, 304
Wells, John, 417
Wethereld (*see* Wederall) Rebecca, 369
  Robert, 417
West, Joseph, 342
West Nottingham, 159
Westward movement of Quakerism, 177, 180–185
Whaly, Ann, 410
  George, 410
Whartenby, Elizabeth, 306
Wexford, battle of, 10
Weaver, Thomas Dell, 308
Weatherby, John, 392
Webb family, 295
  Ann, 366
  Ezekiel, 45, 117
  James, 306
  James, 357
  Richard, 117
  Roger, 313, 317, 319, 323, 409
  Ruth, 295
  William, 306, 321
Wederall, Thomas, 313
Weddings, 209–215
Wheddon, Elizabeth, 151
  Henry, 151
Whinery family, 184, 345, 346, 400
  Elinor, 426
  John, 426
  Matthew, 425
  Robert, 167, 226, 345
  William, 400
Whitaker, Katharine, 357
  William, 341
Whitall, John, 387
White, John, 54
  Joseph, 382
  Robert, 341
  Samuel, 64, 382
Whitefield, Alice, 311
Whitehead, Edward, 174

Whitsite, Whitsitt, or Whitside, Elizabeth, 430
  George, 366
  Jean, 429
  John, 86, 87, 98, 362, 366, 411, 412
  Joseph, 365, 432
  Mary, 366
  Susanna, 431
  William, 316, 326, 393, 394, 420, 431
Whitten, William, 329
Wicklow, Hannah, 426
Wickersham, Abner, 404
  Alice, 211
  Edward, J., 404
  Jesse, 167
  John, 404
  Lydia, 404
  Richard, 168, 419
  Susanna, 404
  Thomas, 126, 211
  William, 366
Widdos, Abraham, 309
Wierman, Gertrude, 172, 395
  Hannah, 172, 395
  Henry, 172
  John, 172
  Mary, 397
  Nicholas, 172
  Phebe, 395
  Priscilla, 172, 174
  Sarah, 172, 174
  Susan, 397
  William, 172, 395
Wigs, 203–204
Wight, Rice, 22
  Thomas, first historian of the Irish Quakers, 93, 284
Wilcocks, Issachar, 296
  Sarah, 296
Wild Animals, 207
Wildman, Joseph, 348
  Mary, 348
Wilkinson family, 370–371, 373
  Ann, 319, 370
  Elizabeth, 171, 348, 371
  Evan, 154, 370
  Francis, 154, 171, 230, 370, 373, 430, 432
  James, 373

Wilkinson, Joseph, 154, 371
  Mary, 430
  Ruth, 299
  William, 230, 394, 430, 432
  Thomas, 171, 311, 393
  Samuel, 97, 160, 230, 377, 394
Wily or Wiley, Abigail, 211, 339
  Ann, 289, 339
  Allen, 332
  Hannah, 334
  Jane, 332, 347
  John, 132, 133, 135, 136, 211,
    332, 333, 341
  Joseph, 211, 340
  Martha, 211
  Mary, 209, 212, 341
  Robert, 332
  Sarah, 339
  Thomas, 332
  William, 332, 334, 339, 394
Williams family, 424
  Alice, 313
  Anne, 378
  Daniel, 235, 314
  Enion, 424
  Jacob, 169
  John, 410, 424
  Joseph, 349
  Martha, 349
  William, 313, 420
  Zacharias, 378
Williamson, Alice, 409
  John, 425, 427
  Sarah, 318, 427
  William, 409, 426
Willis, Betty, 331
  Elizabeth, 385
  Henry, 331, 385
  William, 177
Wills, James, 397
  Judge David, 397
  Ruth (see Walhay), 397
Wilmington Meeting, and Monthly
    Meeting, 121-122
Wilson family, 178, 310-311, 397
  Alice, 397
  Christopher, 124, 333
  Esther, 333
  George, 176, 310
  Helen Gertrude, 433
  John, 174, 282, 310, 360, 410

Wilson, Joseph, 433
  Mary, 282
  Margaret, 348
  Michael, 174
  Robert, 353
  Ruth, 310
  William, 167
  Thomas, 85, 171, 341, 369, 379
Winder, Elizabeth, 381
Windle, Anne, 357
  Francis, 357
  Mary, 357
Winter, Daniel, 174, 176, 379
  John, 425
  Mary, 361
Witherow, John, 233
Wolf, Paul, 282
Wollaston, Ann, 324
  Joshua, 324
Wollsy, Ellen, 410
Women, Work of, on Farm, 206
Wood, Elizabeth, 387
  Ellen, 290
  James, 301
  Jonathan, 382
  Joseph, 290
  Mary, 174
  Richmunday, 372
  Sarah, 290
Woodcock, Robert, 292
  Ruth, 302
Woodrow, Simon, 417
Woodward, John, 334
  Esther, 333
Work on Farm, 205-206
Worrall, Peter, 165
Worrilow, Mary, 308
Worsley, Daniel, 236
  Sarah, 210, 211
Worthington, Robert, 303
  Samuel, 303
Wright family of Adams Co., Pa.,
    350, 394-398
  Alice, 311, 313
  Ann, 352, 391
  Benjamin, 352
  Elizabeth, 174, 311, 381
  Hannah, 340
  Isaac, 352
  Jacob, 335
  James, 210

Wright, Jane, 391
    Joel, 399
    John, 162, 174, 176, 227, 311,
        313, 331, 335, 394
    Judith, 346
    Mark, 307, 312, 313, 320, 323,
        350, 391
    Mary, 277, 331
    Nathan, 174
    Patience, 335
    Rowland, 350
    Sarah, 311, 405
    Sismore, 350, 356
    William, 174
Wynne, Thomas, 278

Yarnall, Peter, travelling minister,
    184
    Phebe, 399
    Rachel, 212
Yearly Meeting, 221
Yearsley, Elizabeth, 314
    John, 314
York County, 162–177
    Meeting, 176–177
Young, Jane, 174
    William, 174
Youngblod, Jacob, 165
Yuruns, Alexander, 390
Zane family, 385
    Robert, 383, 385, 386

Errata and Addenda 477

ERRATA AND ADDENDA

Pages 32–33. John Fothergill, a Quaker minister of Yorkshire, notes in his *Journal* that in 1724 he "went to Coothill . . . and lodged with Terrence Cayle, who with his Wife are of the native Irish, yet had received the Knowledge of the Truth [of Quakerism] in the love of it, and I hope will continue to grow therein."—Page 211, *Journal of John Fothergill*, London, 1753.

Page 89. Line 19, *1736*, not *1763*.

Page 110. Line 2, *in*, not *into*.

Page 164. Footnote 2, line 2, *Robert*, not *Rodbert*.

Page 171. Footnote, for *ancestor* read *probably an ancestor*.

Page 173. Footnote 4. Menallen was doubtless so named by the early Irish Quaker settlers at that place in memory of Monallen (Edmundson, *Journal*, 288; Story, *Journal*, 538), now called Moyallon Meeting, in County Down, Ireland.

Page 176. Line 1, after *Assembly*, a comma, not a period.

Page 211. Second column of signers, fifth name, *Ruth*, not *Rnth*.

Page 219. Line 3, *Fothergill*, not *Fothervill*.

Page 240. Side-note, *1699*, not *1690*.

Page 250. Last line, *Fuller*, not *Duller*.

Page 266. Footnote 2, next last line, *Frances*, not *Francis*.

Page 314. Footnote 2, Miss Margaret Gilpin, of *Elkton*, Cecil Co., Md.

Page 323. Last line, *Sharpley*, not *Sharpy*.

Page 327. Line 11, John Miller and Mary Agnew were married in 1691.—*Ulster Friends' Records*.

Page 330. Last line, Thomas Hutton and Sarah Sterky were married in 1684.—*Ulster Friends' Records*.

Page 333. Line 8, William Willy and Sarah Hunter were married in 1685.—*Ulster Friends' Records*.

John Wyly and Margaret Courtney were married in 1690.—*Ibid*.

Page 343. Line 2, Walter Clark and Elizabeth Haddock were married in 1690.—*Ulster Friends' Records*.

Page 348. Line 9, Eli Crockett and Agnes Knox were married in 1683.—*Ulster Friends' Records*.

Page 355. Line 7, Thomas Milhouse and Sarah Perry were married in 1691.—*Ulster Friends' Records*.

Page 371. In 1691, Francis Wilkinson and Frances Moore [daughter of James Moore, of Ballinacree] were married by Friends' ceremony.—*Ulster Friends' Records*.

Page 420. First signer to George Marsh's certificate, Robert *Greer*, not *Green*.

Page 432. Line 7, Frances Moore married Francis Wilkinson. (See page 371.)

www.ingramcontent.com/pod-product-compliance
Lightning Source LLC
Chambersburg PA
CBHW071823270326
41929CB00013B/1889